WORLD PREHISTORY AND ARCHAEOLOGY

An Integrated Picture of Prehistory as an Active Process of Discovery

World Prehistory and Archaeology: Pathways through Time, fourth edition, provides an integrated discussion of world prehistory and archaeological methods. This text emphasizes the relevance of how we know and what we know about our human prehistory. A cornerstone of *World Prehistory and Archaeology* is the discussion of prehistory as an active process of discovery. Methodological issues are addressed throughout the text to engage readers.

Archaeological methods are introduced in the first two chapters. Succeeding chapters then address the question of how we know the past to provide an integrated presentation of prehistory. The fourth edition involves readers in the current state of archaeological research, revealing how archaeologists work and interpret what they find. Through the coverage of various new research, author Michael Chazan shows how archaeology is truly a global discipline.

Learning Goals

Upon completing this book, readers will be able to:

- Gain new perspectives and insights into who we are and how our world came into being.
- Think about humanity from the perspective of archaeology.
- Appreciate the importance of the archaeological record for contemporary society.

Michael Chazan is a professor in the Department of Anthropology and the director of the Archaeology Centre at the University of Toronto, Canada. He earned his PhD in anthropology at Yale University, USA. Before coming to Toronto, Professor Chazan was a postdoctoral fellow with the Centre National de la Recherche Scientifique in Paris, France, and at the Hebrew University in Jerusalem, Israel. His field experience includes excavations in New Jersey, France, Israel, Jordan, Egypt, and South Africa. Professor Chazan's previous publications include a monograph on the Lower Paleolithic site of Holon, Israel, coauthored with Liora Kolska-Horwitz.

WORLD PREHISTORY
AND
ARCHAEOLOGY

PATHWAYS THROUGH TIME

FOURTH EDITION

MICHAEL CHAZAN

Routledge
Taylor & Francis Group

NEW YORK AND LONDON

Fourth edition published 2018
by Routledge
711 Third Avenue, New York, NY 10017

and by Routledge
2 Park Square, Milton Park, Abingdon, Oxon, OX14 4RN

Routledge is an imprint of the Taylor & Francis Group, an informa business

© 2018 Taylor & Francis

First edition published by Pearson Education, Inc. 2008
Third edition published by Pearson Education, Inc. 2014, and Routledge 2016

Library of Congress Cataloging-in-Publication Data
Names: Chazan, Michael, author.
Title: World prehistory and archaeology : pathways through time / Michael Chazan.
Description: Fourth edition. | Milton Park, Abingdon, Oxon; New York, NY :
    Routledge, 2017. | Includes bibliographical references.
Identifiers: LCCN 2017007940 | ISBN 9781138632554 (hardback: alkaline paper) |
    ISBN 9781315208183 (ebook)
Subjects: LCSH: Prehistoric peoples. | Human evolution. | Anthropology, Prehistoric. |
    Social archaeology. | Archaeology.
Classification: LCC GN740. C43 2017 | DDC 930.1—dc23
LC record available at https://lccn.loc.gov/2017007940

ISBN: 978-1-138-63255-4 (hbk)
ISBN: 978-1-138-08946-4 (pbk)
ISBN: 978-1-315-20818-3 (ebk)

Typeset in Bembo
by Apex CoVantage, LLC

Visit the companion website: www.routledge.com/cw/chazan

FOR **MICHELLE**

BRIEF CONTENTS

CONTENTS

List of Boxed Features xvi   Preface xvii   Acknowledgements xxii

PART ONE

THE PAST IS A FOREIGN COUNTRY: GETTING FROM HERE TO THERE 2

Introduction: Questions of Time and Ethics 3

CHAPTER 1
GETTING STARTED IN ARCHAEOLOGY 6

CHAPTER 2
PUTTING THE PICTURE TOGETHER 34

PART TWO

Human Evolution 56

Introduction: Our Place in Nature 57

PART TWO

PART THREE

PART FOUR

The Development of Social Complexity 258

Introduction: Defining Social Complexity 259

PART FOUR

PART FOUR

LIST OF BOXED FEATURES

TOOLBOX

○ FROM THE field

○ ARCHAEOLOGY in the world

PREFACE

New for the Fourth Edition

These are exciting times to be an archaeologist. Major social movements are leading us to take a new look at our past. Fears of the impact of global warming have stimulated interest of how prehistoric societies reacted to climate change and have led to the proposal that we recognize our contemporary world as part of the Anthropocene, a distinctive geological epoch shaped by human activity. Occupy Wall Street and the Bernie Sanders presidential campaign have raised awareness of growing social inequality. As a result, there is a new relevance to the question of how inequality became an established element of human society. An increasing awareness of and sensitivity to the rights of transgender people raise new questions about how we think about the origins of gender roles. Sadly, we are also confronted by the massive destruction of archaeological heritage as a casualty of war. These atrocities, along with the less visible destruction wrought by development, challenge us to come up with mechanisms to protect our fragile and irreplaceable cultural heritage.

At the same time that archaeology is increasingly relevant to global and local social issues, we are in the process of fundamental changes in the practice of archaeology. The digital revolution is having reverberations across the discipline in the way we collect data in the field, image artifacts in the lab, and make the results of our research publicly available. The rapid advances in molecular biology are providing a new perspective on the past, as geneticists excavate the genomes of living humans and extinct hominins, as well as domesticated plants and animals, to uncover a buried past. Archaeology increasingly works at the microscopic and molecular scale, a far cry from the heroic days of massive excavations.

This book is built around a view of archaeology as a dynamic study of the past. Archaeology is both socially engaged and at the cutting edge of science. In this new edition the emphasis on the social engagement is found throughout the text in the *Archaeology in the World* features and in the reports from archaeologists on their experiences of working in the field. New material includes discussion of the origin of the 1%, and the impact of the conflict in Syria. The first chapter introduces the methods of archaeology and in this edition includes a new section on biomolecular archaeology and isotopic analysis as well as digital imaging techniques, including 3D scanning, photogrammetry, and LIDAR.

Archaeology is not just a collection of methods for recovering data but also ways of thinking about the past. In this edition there is new discussion of the archaeology of gender, the Anthropocene, and niche construction theory. The shift to digital technology raises new ethical issues of access to information that are discussed in the context of the role of open-source publishing in archaeology.

The preparation of a new edition also provides an opportunity to incorporate new discoveries. In the archaeology of human origins these include the discovery of *Homo naledi*, new data on Neanderthal diet, the role of fire in early hominin societies and adaptation, the origins of stone-tipped spears, and the ecological context of hominin occupation at Olduvai Gorge. There is also expanded discussion of the advances made by genetic studies in understanding the relationship between modern humans, Neanderthals, and the enigmatic Denisovans. No area has seen more significant activity than the study of early human occupation in the Americas, with major new discoveries in Mexico, Brazil, Peru, Chile, Florida, and Alaska.

In the study of the origins of agriculture, genetic research has begun to have an impact on our understanding of animal and plant domestication. This edition includes discussion of new field discoveries in Europe, the Middle East, the Amazon, and China. There are also new insights into poorly understood domesticates, including turkeys, chili, bottle gourds, and cacao.

In the study of the origin of social complexity we have added new discussion of spatial analysis of Angkor, the bioarchaeology of the Ur burials, the development of the ceremonial center at the Maya site of Ceibal, and evidence for pre-Nasca lines in Peru.

The epilogue looks at the archaeology of the modern world. The topics covered include the archaeological perspectives on capitalism and slavery.

Archaeology has never been more exciting. It is a field of exploration. In approaching the material presented here, bring your questions, critical thinking, and ideas. These are the tools that advance our understanding of the archaeological past.

Organization

Part One of this book, "The Past Is a Foreign Country: Getting from Here to There," presents an introduction to archaeological method and theory. The first chapter, "Getting Started in Archaeology," begins in the field and discusses how archaeologists locate and excavate sites. From the field, we move into the laboratory to look at how the remains recovered in an excavation are analyzed. Archaeology involves not only conducting field and laboratory work, but also developing a framework for thinking about the past. In Chapter 2, "Putting the Picture Together," we consider how well we know the past and how much we can learn about it. This chapter presents a brief history of the ways archaeologists have thought about the past.

From here, we turn to what we currently know about prehistory. The next three parts of the text examine human evolution, agricultural beginnings, and the development of political complexity, respectively. Part Two, "Human Evolution," covers the period from the first evidence of tool manufacture to the spread of modern humans (*Homo sapiens*) throughout the globe. Human evolution involves the interaction between changes in human anatomy and changes in the way humans lived and in the tools they used. The four chapters in this part follow the process of biological evolution while tracking the geographic spread of human populations and developments in the way they lived.

Part Three, "Perspectives on Agriculture," examines the shift to an agricultural way of life. The development of agricultural societies demanded a profound reorientation of the way humans related to plants and animals, along with equally significant changes in society and technology. Because the transition to agriculture took place independently in several distinct regions, it is possible to take a comparative approach to the origins of this new way of life to gain a broad understanding of the process. Chapter 7, "Towers, Villages, and Longhouses," presents the archaeological record pointing to the beginnings of agriculture in the Middle East and the spread of agriculture into Europe. Chapter 8, "Mounds and Maize," focuses on the origin of maize (corn) agriculture in Mesoamerica and its spread into North America. The adoption of maize agriculture in eastern North America is particularly interesting and complex, as maize was integrated into an existing indigenous agricultural system. Chapter 9, "A Feast of Diversity," broadens the comparative perspective by briefly considering a number of other civilizations in Africa, China, New Guinea, and Peru. It becomes clear that the development of agriculture often spanned a period of several thousands of years and that the process differed significantly among regions.

Following the adoption of agriculture, societies in many parts of the world expanded in scale and increased in population, which in turn led to increased social inequality. Power and access to resources came to be controlled by a smaller segment of people, resulting in the emergence of state societies. The final part, Part Four, "The Development of Social Complexity," covers many of the world's most spectacular and enigmatic archaeological sites, including Stonehenge, the pyramids at Giza, and the cities of the Maya. As with agriculture, social complexity developed independently in a number of regions. Thus, it is again possible to use a comparative approach to gain a broad understanding of this process.

The first chapter of Part Four—Chapter 10, "Complexity without the State"—considers the monumental sites of Stonehenge, Pueblo Bonito, Cahokia, and Great Zimbabwe, constructed by societies that were characterized by emerging social inequality. The remaining chapters present case studies of early states and empires and are organized geographically. Coverage has been expanded to include Japan and Angkor. Coverage of early states in China, Mesoamerica, and the Andes has also been expanded. The text concludes with an epilogue entitled "Bringing It Back Home," in which we look at the traces of the past in our familiar world.

Pedagogy

Every chapter contains a number of pedagogical elements to guide students through the text. Each chapter opener includes satellite location maps and timelines to orient students in time and place to the sites discussed. Learning objectives help students focus their reading of each chapter. Key terms, concepts, and place names are defined or described when they first appear within the text; they are also defined in the margin of the page. Subsequently, they are all listed together in a section at the end of each chapter called *Key Terms*, along with a *Chapter Summary* and a list of *Review Questions*. Each chapter contains dozens of stunning illustrations and photographs to engage students in the subject matter, demonstrate key concepts, and visually convey the spectacular nature of our stops along the pathways through time.

Distinctive Features

The main purpose of this book is to present an integrated picture of prehistory as an active process of discovery. From this perspective, we cannot relegate methodological issues to the opening chapters alone. After students are introduced to archaeological method in the first two chapters, the question of *how* we know the past comes up on numerous occasions throughout the remaining text. A number of features have been developed to draw together an integrated presentation of prehistory.

■ Toolbox Sections

Toolboxes introduce aspects of archaeological methods that are particularly relevant to the material covered. There are two *Toolboxes* per chapter. *Toolboxes* are critical for achieving the aim of this book: to integrate prehistory with an introduction to archaeological methods. Examples of *Toolboxes* include "Archaeoacoustics" (Chapter 2), "Faunal Analysis and Taphonomy" (Chapter 2), "Isotope Analysis" (Chapter 4), "Experimental Archaeology" (Chapter 6), "Archaeology and Genetics" (Chapter 11), "Underwater Archaeology" (Chapter 12), "Space Syntax" (Chapter 12), and "Human Osteoarchaeology" (Chapter 13).

■ From the Field

A primary goal of this text is to draw students into the process of archaeological research. Rather than sitting on the sidelines observing the game, students should be on the playing field. This does not mean that this book is suitable only for future archaeologists; rather, it is meant to provide the tools to give any student a lifelong engagement with archaeology, whether through traveling, visiting museums, reading, or joining in a research project. Toward that end, we have also included in each chapter a feature called *From the Field*, in which people—including students—who are actively involved in archaeological research write an informal report about a project relevant to the chapter subject. A new *From the Field* segment in this edition is "Gender and Sexuality in the Field" (Chapter 13). Additional *From the Field* segments include "Following the Footsteps of Our Ancestors" by Andrew Du, a student at Rutgers University (Chapter 3); "A Paleoepiphany," by Lynne A. Schepartz (Chapter 4); "'Towns They Have None': In Search of New England's Mobile Farmers," by Elizabeth S. Chilton (Chapter 8); and "Chavín de Huántar: The Beginnings of Social Complexity in the Andes," by John W. Rick (Chapter 14). I have also contributed features on my own fieldwork experiences in South Africa, Jordan, and Egypt. I hope that these sections will inspire some readers to consider volunteering on an excavation or enrolling in a field school. No words can replace the experience of uncovering the buried remains of the human past.

■ Archaeology in the World

Despite the stereotype of the archaeologist as a cloistered academic, archaeology is very much a discipline that takes place in the real world. Issues such as control over human burial remains, the antiquities trade, and the preservation of threatened cultural resources are every bit as important to the field as trowels and levels. Archaeology is not only the study of what happened in the past, but also the examination of the role of the past in today's world.

To emphasize the significance of the role of the past in the present, every chapter includes a boxed feature called *Archaeology in the World*. These boxes pinpoint ethical issues relevant to the archaeology of the periods discussed in the chapter. Through reading these features, students will see that archaeology plays a role in the present. *Archaeology in the World* topics include "Religion and Evolution" (Chapter 4), "Repatriation of Indigenous Burial Remains" (Chapter 6), "The Trade in African Antiquities" (Chapter 10), and "The Catastrophe of Warfare: Iraq and Syria" (Chapter 11). This edition includes features on "Community Archaeology" (Chapter 1), "Political Borders and Archaeology" (Chapter 7), "Who Owns the Past?" (Chapter 8), "Archaeology and the Environment" (Chapter 9), "Archaeology and Development" (Chapter 12), "Archaeology and Tourism" (Chapter 13), and "Ancient Agriculture and Modern Development" (Chapter 14).

The Cover Image

The cover shows a spectacular 1.5-meter-tall stucco mask depicting the storm god Chahk found on the top of the El Diablo Pyramid at the Maya city of El Zotz, Guatemala (A.D. 350–400). The image on the cover was created using photogrammetry rather than traditional photography, which allowed archaeologists to capture the detail of this complex monumental structure in 3D. The use of photogrammetry at El Zotz by the Proyecto Arqueológico El Zotz, Brown University, is an example of how digital technology is transforming archaeological practice. You can read more about El Zotz in S. Houston, S. Newman, E. Roman, and T. Garrison's 2015 *Temple of the Night Sun: A Royal Tomb at El Diablo, Guatemala*, Mesoweb Books, San Francisco.

A Final Note

Australian aboriginal societies speak of the *dreamtime* as the time when their ancestors walked the land. The actions of ancestors are inscribed in the land and experienced in the landscape. Archaeology explores the "scientific dreamtime"—the time of our ancestors that we discover through archaeological research. This book is an introduction to the current state of archaeology. It is not a simple catalogue of finds, but rather an attempt to give coherence to the vast expanses of human experience studied by archaeologists. Our hope is that readers will keep in mind the uncertainty that characterizes the study of prehistory. What is meant by "uncertainty"? Archaeology is a constant process of questioning and improving our understanding of the past. As in any science, all claims can and should be questioned. Archaeology is a report on the current state of the human endeavor to understand our own past. We invite you to join this endeavor, in which we reveal the present state of archaeological knowledge and introduce you to the methods used to gain that knowledge. We hope that these tools will enable you to actively engage in thinking about humanity from the perspective of archaeology, to think about processes that stretch over millennia and are global in scale, and to walk the pathways of our own "scientific dreamtime."

ACKNOWLEDGMENTS

In writing this book, I have drawn on practically every experience I have had as an archaeologist. First, I would like to thank some of my teachers. The late James Sauer taught me much of what I know about pottery and showed me that archaeology has the potential to build bridges across the chasms produced by conflict. Andrew Moore and Frank Hole supported me as I stepped out of the classroom and into research and provided me with the freedom that I now try to give my own students. Learning to be an archaeologist takes place in the field as much as in the classroom. I have had the opportunity to work with project directors who somehow had the patience to put up with a novice. I am very grateful to Avi Gopher, Nigel Goring-Morris, and François Valla for teaching me how to excavate a Neolithic site; to Ofer Bar-Yosef, Liliane Meignen, and Bernard Vandermeersch for showing me why the Paleolithic is fascinating; and to Mark Lehner for the incredible experience of working at the Giza pyramids. I would also like to thank my friend Zahi Hawass for making it possible for me to work in Egypt.

My views of archaeology have been greatly enriched by my association with research groups in France and Israel. Catherine Pèrles warmly welcomed me into the Prehistory and Technology Research Group of the Centre Nationale de la Recherche Scientifique in Meudon, outside of Paris. During my year at Meudon, I learned from researchers Eric Boëda, Anne Delagnes, Jacques Pelegrin, and Valentine Roux, among others, how to look at technology as an aspect of human behavior. In Jerusalem, I have long enjoyed a connection with faculty at the Hebrew University, where I have been welcomed by Na'ama Goren-Inbar, Anna Belfer-Cohen, Erella Hovers, and Nigel Goring-Morris. Most recently, I have developed a number of collaborative projects with colleagues, including Francesco Berna, James Brink, Joel Janetski, Paul Goldberg, Liora Kolska-Horwitz, Ari Matmon, Hervé Monchot, David Morris, and Naomi Porat, among others. I thank them for their patience, as I sometimes have had to balance my responsibilities to these projects with the excitement of writing this book.

I have been lucky to find an ideal home in the city of Toronto and wonderful colleagues and students at the University of Toronto. Much of this book stems from the courses that I teach at the university, as well as from courses I taught at Tufts and Brandeis before coming to this city. The dynamism of the University of Toronto is built on an appreciation of diversity that I hope is reflected in the book. I am particularly grateful to the graduate students who have worked with me, including Carla Parslow, Alexandra Sumner, Sarah Stewart, Jayne Wilkins, and Danielle Macdonald.

The actual process of developing the first edition was facilitated by the people at Allyn & Bacon, who believed that we could pull off the project. I never imagined the amount of effort that goes into such a book. I want to thank Jennifer Jacobson, who shepherded me through the first edition with a skill that combined patience and enthusiasm.

Beginning with the second edition, I have been guided by a team led by Nancy Roberts, Publisher for Anthropology at Pearson. The editorial development was skillfully handled by Monica Ohlinger. For the third edition, Anne Ricigliano managed the production process—coordinating all of the moving pieces was no easy feat. Tom Scalzo oversaw the accompanying media, and Kelly May conceived the creative marketing plan.

Without the input from the following generous and insightful reviewers, whom I wholeheartedly thank, we would not have been able to achieve the high level of quality of this book:

Fourth Edition Reviewers—Joseph Gingerich, Ohio University; Lisa Maher, University of California–Berkeley; Christopher Milan, Yale University; Nancy H. Olsen, De Anza College.

Third Edition Reviewers—Jules Angel, The Ohio State University; Brad Biglow, Florida State College at Jacksonville; Michael Danti, Boston University; Brett Houk, Texas Tech University; Robert Tykot, University of South Florida; LuAnn Wandsnider, University of Nebraska–Lincoln; and Andrew Wyatt, University of Illinois at Chicago. Gina Barnes kindly agreed to read the new material on Japan. I am in her debt, and, of course, all shortcomings are my own.

Second Edition Reviewers—Timothy E. Baumann, Missouri Valley College; Richard Blanton, Purdue University; Georgia L. Fox, California State University, Chico; Lisa Frink, University of Nevada, Las Vegas; Paul Mullins, Indiana University–Purdue University Indianapolis; Lauren W. Ritterbush, Kansas State University; Kevin Vaughn, Purdue University; and Renee B. Walker, SUNY College at Oneonta. Carl Knappett, Dimitri Nakassis, Edward Swenson, Gina Barnes, and David Cohen kindly agreed to read the new material on the Aegean, Mesoamerica, the Andes, and China. I am in their debt, and, of course, all shortcomings are my own. I would also like to thank Julie R. Angel from The Ohio State University for her work on the supplements and MyAnthroLab.

First Edition Reviewers—Lisa Marie Anselmi, Buffalo State College; Mary C. Beaudry, Boston University; Charles A. Bollong, University of Arizona; Thomas H. Charlton, University of Iowa; Elizabeth S. Chilton, University of Massachusetts, Amherst; Lisa Cole, Maricopa Community College; Charles O. Ellenbaum, College of DuPage; James Fitzsimmons, University of Vermont; Charles L. Hall, University of Maryland; Bryan K. Hanks, University of Pittsburgh; Michael Heckenberger, University of Florida; Audrey Horning, College of William and Mary; Sibel Kusimba, Northern Arizona University; Randy McGuire, SUNY, Binghamton; Barbara Mills, University of Arizona; Karen Muir, Columbus State Community College; Paul Mullins, Indiana University; Mark Muniz, University of Colorado; Timothy R. Pauketat, University of Illinois; Bonnie Lynn Pitblado, Utah State University; Thomas J. Pluckhahn, University of Oklahoma; Mary Pohl, Florida State University; Corey Pressman, Pressman Productions; Mark A. Rees, University of Louisiana, Lafayette; Barbara Roth, University of Nevada, Las Vegas; Scott Simmons, University of North Carolina, Wilmington; Steven R. Simms, Utah State University; Alisa Strauss, University of Cincinnati; and LuAnn Wandsnider, University of Nebraska.

Since *World Prehistory and Archaeology: Pathways through Time* is used as a course text, I hope that instructors and students may wish to contact me. I would appreciate receiving questions, comments, and criticisms at mchazan@chass.utoronto.ca.

I would like to take the opportunity to thank my parents, who have been a constant source of inspiration and support. I am delighted to have shared this project with my wife, Michelle Fost, and our children, Gabriel and Nathan. This has been in every sense a team effort.

Michael Chazan
mchazan@chass.utoronto.ca

WORLD PREHISTORY AND ARCHAEOLOGY

PATHWAYS THROUGH TIME

PART ONE

THE PAST IS A FOREIGN COUNTRY: GETTING FROM HERE TO THERE

Archaeology is the study of the human past through the traces of the past that exist in the present. After reading this introduction, you should understand:

- The structure of the discipline of archaeology.
- The fundamental elements of archaeological ethics.

Introduction: Questions of Time and Ethics

The thing the Time Traveller held in his hand was a glittering metallic framework, scarcely larger than a small clock, and very delicately made. There was ivory in it, and some transparent crystalline substance. "This little affair," said the Time Traveller, resting his elbows on the table and pressing his hands together above the apparatus, "is only a model. It is my plan for a machine to travel through time."
(Wells [1895] 1984, 39)

Time travel, as imagined by H.G. Wells in his visionary novel *The Time Machine* and by others in countless subsequent films and books, remains a tantalizing impossibility. We cannot climb into the saddle of an apparatus, or for that matter the seat of a DeLorean, that will whisk us back in time. We are rooted firmly in the present.

Archaeologists have developed a solution to the problem of time travel that is every bit as intricate as the mechanism built by Wells's hero. Archaeological excavation and analysis is a highly developed scientific discipline that allows us a means of access to the human past. Archaeology does not take us into the past, but enables us to read the traces of the past that exist with us in the present.

A simple "thought experiment" can give a sense of how archaeology works. Imagine a building that you are familiar with, perhaps your family home or a school you have attended. Picture how this structure looks today, and then attempt to remove any elements that were added in the past 20 years. If the building is old, try pushing back 40, 60, or even 100 years. Now extend your view to encompass a larger landscape, perhaps a neighborhood or a town. Although we cannot reenter the past, we are surrounded by its material traces. Uncovering and understanding these traces is the archaeologist's task (Figure I.1).

Because archaeological remains can take many forms—objects made or modified by people, organic material, geological features—the discipline of archaeology is diverse. As a result, archaeology is often found spread across academic disciplines. In the United States, archaeology is considered a subfield of anthropology, and departments of archaeology are rare. Anthropologists study the diversity of human experience, and archaeology provides an important bridge between biological anthropologists and anthropologists studying modern society and culture. Archaeology also provides time depth and gives a clear material focus to anthropology. Archaeologists working on the ancient civilizations of Mesopotamia, Egypt, and the biblical world are often found in departments of Near or Middle Eastern studies, while archaeologists of classical Greece and Rome are usually in departments of classics or art history. Archaeologists are also employed as curators in museums.

Archaeologists today tend to work outside of the university or museum setting. In the United States, most professional archaeologists are employed by private companies, dedicated to excavating and surveying areas in advance of impending construction. This type of archaeology, usually referred to as cultural resource management, or CRM, is critical to preserving our heritage in the face of development.

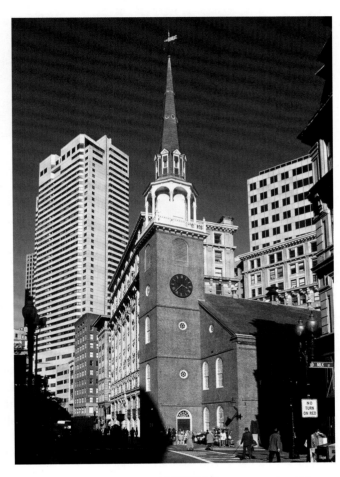

FIGURE I.1 In Boston, the Old South Meeting House stands in stark contrast to the surrounding modern city

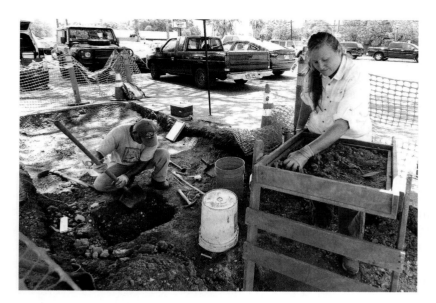

FIGURE I.2 Archaeologists from Cultural Surveys Hawaii sift through sediment at a site in a parking lot in Lahaina, Hawaii

CRM is increasingly a global enterprise and includes firms that operate internationally. Other archaeologists work in various branches of the government, particularly the National Park Service. Archaeologists working in the public sector play a critical role in both the preservation and the presentation of cultural heritage (Figure I.2). Archaeologists have also begun to find employment in law enforcement, interdicting illegally traded artifacts and halting illegal excavation. Finally, archaeologists contribute to the development of methods of forensic science and remain active in projects documenting crime scenes, both on the local level and internationally in conjunction with investigations of war crimes.

Training in archaeology is based on a combination of university course work and practical experience. Most professional archaeologists have advanced training, at least at the master's level. Archaeological research is expensive, supporting both the process of excavation and the scientific analysis of the recovered materials. For CRM firms, the costs of excavation are paid by the landowner, as required by law. In most cases, the firm has to bid for a contract, the terms of which bind and limit the firm. Academic and museum-based archaeologists have the luxury of pursuing projects that develop from a program of research rather than from the imperatives of development. However, to pursue research, it is necessary to raise funds from government and private agencies. In the United States, the National Science Foundation and the National Endowment for the Humanities provide critical funding for archaeological research.

Archaeology is a varied field of study, and archaeologists follow a range of career paths. However, the discipline is bound both by shared methods and interests and by a shared ethic. Archaeologists have recently begun to recognize the importance of exploring and codifying archaeological ethics (Figure I.3). The Register of Professional Archaeologists (RPA) was founded in 1998 as a listing of archaeologists with both graduate training and practical experience who agree to abide by an explicit code of conduct and standards of research performance (www.rpanet.org). The Society for American Archaeology has set out the following eight principles of archaeological ethics (www.saa.org/public/resources/ethics.html):

FIGURE I.3 In Jerusalem, the close juxtaposition of the sacred remains of the past and the modern city creates a landscape fraught with tension, highlighting the ethical dimension of archaeology

- Stewardship. The archaeological record is irreplaceable, and archaeologists are responsible for acting as stewards, working for long-term conservation and protection of the archaeological record. Stewards are caretakers and advocates who work for the benefit of all people. The archaeological record includes archaeological materials, sites, collections, records, and reports.

- Accountability. Archaeologists are accountable to the public and must make an effort to consult actively with all groups affected by their research.

- Commercialization. Archaeologists should discourage and avoid the enhancement of the commercial value of archaeological objects, particularly those not curated in public institutions or those inaccessible to the public.

- Public Education and Outreach. Archaeologists should reach out to and cooperate with interested members of the public.
- Intellectual Property. Original materials and documents from archaeological research should not be treated as personal possessions. After a limited and reasonable time, these materials should be made available to others.
- Public Reporting and Publication. Knowledge gained from archaeological research should be published within a reasonable length of time to a wide range of interested publics. If necessary for the preservation of a site, its location and nature may be obscured in publications.
- Records and Preservation. Archaeologists should actively work for the preservation of archaeological records and reports.
- Training and Resources. Archaeologists must have adequate training, facilities, and support before carrying out research.

Archaeologists study the past, but they work for the present and the future. Although we are motivated by the excitement of discovery, we are also compelled by the importance of conservation. The practical decision of how much of a site to excavate offers an example of maintaining a balance between exploration and conservation. While archaeologists might like to clean out every nook and cranny of a site as they search for critical pieces of data, such an approach is acceptable only in situations where the site faces imminent destruction. In all other cases, the desire to explore is tempered by the imperative of leaving material for future generations of archaeologists who may arrive with new methods capable of unlocking aspects of the archaeological record that are inaccessible today.

From Indiana Jones to Lara Croft, archaeologists have become popular movie heroes. The irony is that the reality of archaeology is much closer to moviemaking than to the exploits of a movie hero. Like making a film, archaeology involves the logistics of working with a team on location, for long hours, and with an eye toward pragmatic compromise. Like filmmakers, archaeologists do a great deal of unglamorous pre- and postproduction work. Archaeology calls less for bravery in battle than it does for the courage to take creative leaps based on intuition. The result of archaeological research is not triumphantly grasping a trophy, but rather reaching conclusions that open an entirely new vista of questions.

SUMMARY

- Because archaeological remains can take many forms, including objects made or modified by people, organic material, and even geological features, the discipline of archaeology is highly varied.
- In the United States and Canada, the academic discipline of archaeology is usually found in departments of

anthropology, as well as in departments of Near or Middle Eastern studies, classics, and fine arts.
- Most archaeologists today work outside of academia, in either cultural resource management firms or government agencies.
- Archaeological ethics are based on the idea that archaeologists should act as stewards of the archaeological record.

REVIEW QUESTIONS

1. Can you think of a place you are familiar with where the physical remains of the past are apparent?
2. How does stewardship of the archaeological record differ from ownership?

3. In what ways do archaeologists work for the future?

GETTING STARTED IN ARCHAEOLOGY

This chapter introduces you to how archaeologists find and excavate sites, as well as to the basics of archaeological laboratory research. After reading the chapter, you should understand:

- The goals of archaeological survey.
- The methods of horizontal and vertical excavation.
- The use of quantification in artifact and ecofact analysis.
- The methods used to construct an archaeological chronology.

1

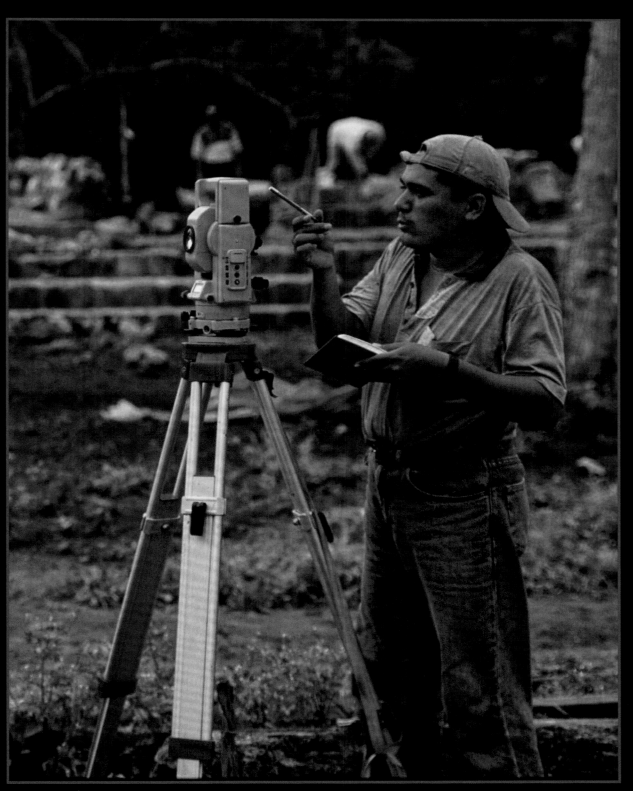

A surveyor works at the Chac restoration site in Mexico.

We experience the past at almost every instant. Think of how you hear a piece of music. You do not simply hear a succession of notes as they unfold in time. Rather, your hearing of each note is shaped by your memory of the preceding notes and your anticipation of what is to come. The human present is created through a fusion of past, present, and future.

As humans, we live in a present shaped by our consciousness of the past. Our sense of the past exists in our memories—in our visual, auditory, and olfactory images and sensations. Athletes also speak of a "body memory" that allows them to carry out elaborate, fine-tuned sequences of action. But memory goes far beyond our minds and our bodies. Writing systems and, more recently, computer technologies store memory externally. Anthropologists speak of collective memories—particularly memories of traumas, such as the events of September 11—that are held by a group rather than being the property of an individual. Objects and places can also embody memory; most families have heirlooms that carry a memory and a direct connection to previous generations (Lillios 1999).

Archaeology is a science that probes the depths of the human past. But archaeology is not time travel: Archaeologists and the objects they study remain firmly anchored in the present. The essential trick of archaeology is how to use static objects that exist in the present to infer the dynamics of past societies (Binford 1983). Put more simply, the goal of archaeological method is to be able to use the objects we dig up to understand the lives of people who lived in the past.

The goal of this chapter is to introduce you to archaeological method—to show you how archaeologists look at the world. We begin with fieldwork, first the way that archaeologists locate sites and then how sites are excavated. Archaeological excavation draws heavily on tools used in geology, so we also take time to consider aspects of geological stratigraphy. We then move to the laboratory to see how the objects recovered in excavations and surveys are analyzed. We pay particular attention to the quantitative methods archaeologists use to glean information from the totality of the recovered material.

1.1 Reading the Landscape

The first challenge facing archaeologists is finding the traces of human action. The purpose of an archaeological **survey** is to map the physical remains of human activity. The scale of surveys can range from an entire region to the surface of a single site. The evidence recorded can be as fine-grained as individual stone tools and potsherds or as massive as large standing structures.

■ Survey Design

The most obvious reason for carrying out an archaeological survey is to discover sites, be they sunken ships, buried cities, or hunter-gatherer camps. But archaeologists also use surveys to understand the distribution of sites within a region, how sites are distributed across the landscape, or where different activities took place within a site. In some cases, the goal is to determine whether sites will be destroyed by construction projects. Often, there is pressure to gain as complete a picture as possible at the lowest possible cost.

Archaeological surveys must be designed with the goals of the project in mind (Banning 2002). Simply recording everything is rarely possible, or even necessary, so archaeologists usually determine a strategy to sample the survey area. Statistical

survey An archaeological survey maps the physical remains of human activity.

sampling in archaeological survey works on the same basis as in a public-opinion poll. In both cases, a carefully selected sample is used to represent a larger population. The goals of survey research can range widely. In an important survey project carried out in southern Iraq, Robert McCormick Adams and his colleagues were able to trace the hierarchy of settlements surrounding the large urban centers of early Mesopotamia (Adams and Nissen 1972). Archaeologists working across the western United States have used similar survey methods to track the mobility of small-scale societies of hunter-gatherers (Kelly 1988).

in situ Archaeological material is considered to be in situ when it is found in the place where it was originally deposited.

■ Geological Factors

It would be naïve to expect that we can simply walk across the landscape and find traces of all past human activity. Archaeological survey must take into consideration geological factors that affect the preservation and visibility of sites. Often, sites are so deeply buried that no artifacts are visible on the surface. Early prehistoric sites in East Africa, such as Olduvai Gorge, are examples of this kind of deeply buried context. At Olduvai Gorge, sites can be discovered only where natural erosion has cut through the accumulation of sediments, exposing fossil- and artifact-bearing levels.

Although erosion is often the archaeologists' indispensable ally, erosion can also complicate the interpretation of survey results. In many cases, stream channels have cut through archaeological sites and redeposited material far downstream. Archaeologists must take care to determine whether archaeological material picked up on a survey is actually in the place where it was originally deposited or whether it has been redeposited by erosion. Archaeologists refer to material that is in the place where it was originally deposited as **in situ**. It is often possible to identify archaeological material that has been transported by water on the basis of characteristic wear patterns and the absence of very small fragments.

■ Recovery Methods and GIS

Most surveys involve little more than a team of archaeologists walking slowly, with heads bent, across the landscape. The problems faced in surface collection vary tremendously according to the context of the research. On the one hand, in locations where there is heavy brush coverage, actually seeing artifacts can be extremely challenging (see Figure 1.1). On the other hand, there are areas where one is walking on a "carpet of artifacts"—a situation that is problematic because one has to decide what to pick up and record.

In a depositional environment, where there is a constant buildup of sediments, artifacts may not always be found on the surface. In such a context, many archaeologists rely on a strategy of digging small test pits to find buried artifacts. The type of survey and the extent of available resources together determine the placement of the test pits.

FIGURE 1.1 Ground-penetrating radar survey at the Bestwood site, South Africa. In this case geophysical survey provides a map of the prehistoric landscape now covered by a thick layer of sand.

Archaeologists draw on a wide range of technologies to increase their ability to detect archaeological deposits and to collect and organize spatial information:

- Methods of remote sensing, including aerial photography and satellite imagery, play a critical role both in discovering sites and in orienting exploration (see the Remote Sensing Toolbox in Chapter 10, p. 279). **Airborne LIDAR**, a technique that uses lasers to map physical features, has shown tremendous potential to map landscapes and features that are obscured by vegetation (Opitz and Limp 2015).

- Geophysical techniques are used to gain an idea of what lies below the surface of a site without having to excavate, allowing archaeologists to detect invisible features. The two main geophysical methods used in archaeological survey are magnetometry and ground-penetrating radar (see the Geophysical Methods Toolbox in Chapter 13, p. 367).

- The precise location of archaeological sites can be determined with handheld Global Positioning System (GPS) receivers.

  - Drones mounted with cameras have become increasingly inexpensive and easy to operate, providing a tool for collecting aerial views of sites and landscapes. When multiple images are taken from a drone it is possible to use photogrammetry software (see discussion on p. 21). Figure 1.2 shows a drone flying above the site of Cerro Chepen in Peru.

Archaeologists have access to a wide range of geographical information. Satellite images, aerial photographs, topographic maps, and the coordinates of locations of sites already found make up a rich body of data. **Geographical Information Systems (GIS)** are suites of software applications that allow spatial data to be brought together and consolidated. GIS software works as a series of layers or overlays that the software sets to the same scale (see Figure 1.3). Imagine that you have a series of "documents," including an aerial photograph of a site, a topographic map of the region in which the site is located, a soil map of the same region, and, from a survey, the coordinates of archaeological finds at the site (Wheatley and Gillings 2002). For any one of these documents to be used in a GIS environment, the exact

FIGURE 1.2 Drone flying above the site of Cerro Chepen, Peru. Drones are used by archaeologists to create aerial views of excavations and to create 3D models of sites using photogrammetry.

longitude and latitude of two or three points in the area covered by the map must be known, allowing the document to be georeferenced. Once the image is georeferenced, it must be digitized as either a digital or a raster image. A digital image is one in which all points are digitized; a raster image is simply a scanned picture. Once each of the documents is digitized and georeferenced, all of them are ready to be treated as layers by a GIS program. The program will overlay the images at a uniform scale and location. One can then see how a particular site lies relative to the find spots identified in a survey, the distribution of soils, the hydrology, and the topography of the area. GIS programs come with tools to both visualize and analyze these data. To help archaeologists visualize a region, topographic maps can be used to create three-dimensional models of the terrain and to statistically test the association of find spots with elevation, slope, and soils. One popular application is to analyze the "viewshed"—what would have been visible to a person from a given spot in the landscape.

When GIS was first introduced, it was used largely within an ecological framework, looking at relationships between site locations and the availability of natural resources. Other applications were developed to model migration routes and to predict where sites would likely be found. In recent years, a number of archaeologists have begun to use GIS software as a means of exploring the way people in the past would have experienced the environment.

FIGURE 1.3 Screenshot of a Geographical Information System (GIS) analysis of Caffarella Park in Rome, Italy. The GIS software allows for the integration of the topography, landscape, and archaeological features.

1.2 Excavation

The archaeological "time machine" consists of simple tools such as trowels, screens, and levels. The fundamental characteristic of archaeological excavation is the careful attention paid to recording the context in which artifacts are discovered. Intensive documentation is what distinguishes archaeological excavation from vandalism and looting.

FIGURE 1.4 A moment frozen in time. Excavation of casts of bodies trapped in volcanic ash at Pompeii.

■ Horizontal Excavation

In A.D. 79, the Roman city of Pompeii was rapidly buried by volcanic material from the eruption of Mount Vesuvius. The archaeological site at Pompeii preserves the last moments of the city in often gruesome detail (see Figure 1.4). Pompeii provides a unique snapshot of life in a Roman city at a single moment in time. The effort to reconstruct such a moment is one of the major goals of archaeological excavation. At most sites, time is not frozen quite as spectacularly as at Pompeii, and archaeologists must work with fragmentary remains that have been significantly altered both by subsequent occupants of the site and by natural processes.

When archaeologists work to reconstruct a particular moment in time, it is necessary to excavate broad areas of a site. Such an approach is referred to as horizontal excavation. This is contrasted with vertical excavation, which focuses on the sequence of occupations of the site. Figures 1.5 and 1.6 show examples of horizontal and vertical excavations.

FIGURE 1.5 Example of a horizontal excavation: an Iroquoian longhouse at Crawford Lake, Ontario. Remains of this structure are postholes (marked by sticks), pits, and a large sweat lodge.

FIGURE 1.6 Excavations at the site of Megiddo, Israel, include massive trenches that have exposed over 2,000 years of occupation. Note how the trenches cut into the mound that is built up of successive occupation levels.

Horizontal excavations can be carried out on any type of site, from simple hunter-gatherer camps to large urban centers. The French prehistorian André Leroi-Gourhan was among the pioneers of horizontal excavation (Leroi-Gourhan 1984). At the site of Pincevent in the Paris Basin, Leroi-Gourhan excavated a prehistoric hunter-gatherer encampment from the Magadalenian period. These people left behind no traces of architecture, yet by carefully mapping every stone tool and every animal bone found on the site, Leroi-Gourhan was able to reconstruct the locations of tents and estimate the number of family groups using the site. Pincevent was a perfect site for this undertaking because it had only one major layer of occupation, which had been rapidly buried by river silts.

Another ideal setting for horizontal excavation, on a much grander scale, is offered by the city of Amarna in Egypt. A new capital city, Amarna was constructed by Akhenaton as part of his program of religious reformation (1350 B.C.). Following Akhenaton's death, his reforms were repudiated and his city abandoned, never to be reoccupied. Excavations at Amarna have exposed large parts of the city plan, giving us an invaluable perspective on New Kingdom Egyptian town planning (Kemp 2006).

■ Vertical Excavation

Most archaeological sites include more than a single period of occupation. Many archaeologists are drawn to sites with a lengthy history of occupation because their interest is in long-term processes of culture change. Several archaeologists have emphasized that sites such as Pincevent and Amarna are in fact quite rare and also more complex than they at first seem. Thus, for all archaeologists, an understanding of how sites develop over time is critical. **Vertical excavations** focus on exposing the record of a sequence of occupation. Emphasis is placed more on excavating the entire depth of deposits than on opening large horizontal areas. In vertical excavation, archaeologists analyze the sequence of deposits, or stratigraphy, of the site. The basic concepts of stratigraphy are drawn from geology; applied to archaeology, they

horizontal excavation An excavation for which the goal is to excavate a broad area in order to expose the remains of a single point in time.

vertical excavation An excavation for which the goal is to excavate a significant depth of deposits in order to expose the record of a sequence of occupations.

have led to the development of methods of archaeological stratigraphy that take into account the particular characteristics of archaeological sites.

GEOLOGICAL STRATIGRAPHY. When sediments are deposited in an undisturbed environment, a stratigraphic sequence will develop over time. The buildup of sediments is said to be stratigraphic in that it follows the **law of superposition**, which states that, in any undisturbed depositional sequence, each layer is younger than the layer beneath it. A stratigraphic sequence can be either continuous or discontinuous. In a continuous sequence, the sediments or rocks are uniform throughout, with no clear breaks. In a discontinuous sequence, there are clear breaks in either the types of rocks or the types of sediments. In a discontinuous sequence, it is possible to identify discrete layers, or, as they are often called in archaeology and geology, strata. Geological **strata** can be characterized either by the type of rock or sediment they consist of or by the fossils they contain.

The surface of the earth is not an undisturbed depositional environment. The movements of the plates of the earth's crust cause mountain chains and rift valleys to form. Volcanic activity brings igneous rocks from the earth's mantle to the surface. Erosion by wind, water, and glaciers breaks down and transports rocks and sediments. As a result of all of this activity, the law of superposition applies only in localized contexts where deposition has taken place. The geological science of stratigraphy has as its goal the correlation of strata across wide areas.

In many cases, geologists drill deep into the earth to gather samples for stratigraphic analyses. Such exploratory work is essential in prospecting for minerals and oil. In other cases, such as road cuts that slice through part of a hill, it is possible to see stratigraphy directly. The exposure left by a road cut, or by natural erosion as shown in Figure 1.7, is called a stratigraphic *section* or *profile*. If the rocks in the profile are sedimentary rocks—rocks that have formed from sediments in a depositional environment—we can apply the law of superposition to deduce that the rocks lower down in the sequence are older than those higher up. Often, in road cuts, the folding of the rocks from the processes associated with mountain building is apparent, and we can follow strata along their folds. Of course, one does need to make sure that what one is looking at is actually sedimentary rock. In many cases, what one sees in a road cut consists of either metamorphic rocks, which have formed deep in the earth's crust at high temperature and pressure, only to be thrust out onto the surface as the result of uplift, or igneous rocks, which have squeezed through the crust from the earth's mantle. The law of superposition does not necessarily apply to these kinds of rocks.

HOW ARCHAEOLOGICAL SITES FORM. Most environments on the surface of the earth can be classified as either erosional or depositional—locations where sediment is being either carried away or deposited, respectively. Buried archaeological sites form in depositional environments. In some cases, artifacts are deposited on a surface and then, over time, become incorporated into the geological strata. Most early prehistoric sites were formed in this way. In discussing the stratigraphy of such sites, one is usually referring to the position of the archaeological deposits in geological strata.

law of superposition In any undisturbed depositional sequence, each layer of sediments is younger than the layer beneath it.

strata Discrete layers in a stratigraphic sequence.

FIGURE 1.7 Erosion in a riverbed in upstate New York exposes strata of sedimentary rock

anthropogenic deposits Deposits that result from human activity. Human activities range from building fires on ephemeral hunter-gatherer camp sites to erecting the palaces and fortifications of great cities.

depositional unit The material deposited at a site at a particular point in time.

On most archaeological sites, *stratigraphy* refers to the accumulation of strata that result from a combination of geological and anthropogenic deposits. **Anthropogenic deposits** are produced by human activities ranging from building fires on ephemeral hunter-gatherer camp sites to erecting the palaces and fortifications of great cities. For village and city sites, it is necessary to understand the methods and materials used in their construction, and it is also important to understand how structures decay and collapse. In many areas, the main construction material used until recently has been unbaked mud brick. As mud-brick structures fall out of use, they are usually eroded along the base, which causes them to collapse. The resulting collapsed house forms a mound of earth that was simply leveled out before new structures were built. As layers of collapsed mud-brick houses accumulate, large artificial mounds, known in the Middle East as tels, often develop. In areas where wood or stone was the main building material, such mounds will not form because wood will decay and stones are liable to be reused.

ARCHAEOLOGICAL STRATIGRAPHY. Archaeological sites are rarely, if ever, a simple "layer cake" of strata. Archaeological layers or strata emerge only through the process of stratigraphic analysis (see Figure 1.8). The basic units of archaeological sites are **depositional units**—material that was deposited at a particular point in time. In practice, depositional units go by many names, including *locus* and *stratigraphic feature*.

Any process that has led to the accumulation of material on an archaeological site is considered to be a depositional event. Because deposition is not continuous on archaeological sites, archaeologists are able to define depositional units. What makes the concept of depositional units confusing is that they can be of many types, including walls, floors, and the infill of pits.

In practice, interpreting an archaeological sequence often hinges on paying attention to the relationships among depositional units. One example of the types of problems faced in the field is determining the date of a burial pit (see Figure 1.9). The burial is not part of the depositional unit it cuts into. Rather, it is in superposition to the depositional unit, even though they are at exactly the same height. It is critical to find the surface of origin of the pit—the surface from which the pit was excavated.

FIGURE 1.8 At the site of Hammath Tiberius in northern Israel, a crude stone wall and pillars are cut into an earlier mosaic floor. In most archaeological contexts, it is more difficult to identify construction phases.

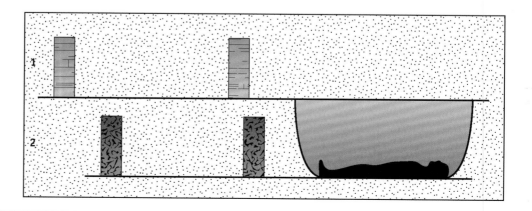

FIGURE 1.9 In this diagram of a stratigraphic profile, the surface of origin for the burial pit is in the upper level (1). Which building was contemporary with the burial?

Archaeologists use a range of methods to assist in a stratigraphic analysis:

- Soil micromorphology is used to characterize the accumulation of sediments at a microscopic scale (see the Geoarchaeology and Micromorphology Toolbox in Chapter 5, p. 114).
- The Harris matrix is a method for placing depositional units in stratigraphic order (see the Harris Matrix Toolbox in Chapter 7, p. 199).
- Taphonomic analysis examines the natural and cultural processes that have affected the formation of archaeological sites (see the Faunal Analysis and Taphonomy Toolbox in Chapter 2, p. 47).

provenience The precise context in which an object is recovered in an excavation.

datum point The linchpin for the control of excavation. It serves as a reference point for all depth measurements on the site.

■ Controlling Horizontal and Vertical Space

The critical task for archaeologists is to record the precise context, or **provenience**, of objects recovered during excavation. Control of horizontal and vertical space is essential to modern archaeological excavation. The first job on an archaeological site is to create a grid that covers the intended excavation area (see Figure 1.10). The size of the squares forming the grid varies from 1 square meter on early prehistoric sites to 25 square meters (5 meters × 5 meters) on large excavations (see Figure 1.11). In some contexts, linear trenches are used rather than squares. The size of the squares and their spacing will depend on the goals of the excavation. If the goal is to get a sample representing an entire settlement, small squares might be distributed randomly across the site. If the goal is to get a broad exposure, excavation squares will cover a single continuous area. The grid is usually laid out with pegs and string. However, in cave sites, the grid can be suspended from high-tension wires anchored into the walls of the cave.

Control of vertical space requires the establishment of a fixed **datum point**, or simply datum, that serves as a reference for all depth measurements on the site (see Figure 1.10). Ideally, this datum is at a known elevation above or below sea level. It is essential, though not always easy, for the datum to be marked on an object or a location that will not be moved or damaged in the future. The datum point is the linchpin for the control of the excavation; loss of the datum point would make it difficult to return to the site and continue the excavation.

A wide range of tools is used for laying out grid squares and measuring depths relevant to the datum. Most excavations make use of a theodolite, which is able to

FIGURE 1.10 A datum point provides a point of reference for measuring depth, while a grid provides a means of controlling horizontal space

FIGURE 1.11 Excavation of Tel Knedig, Syria. The excavation consists of a series of square excavation units. Most of the baulks have been removed at this stage of excavation to provide a continuous view of the architecture.

measure both distance and elevation relative to a given point. Increasingly, archaeologists use digital surveying equipment during excavation, allowing for the precise recording and automatic storage of spatial data.

Excavating in square units makes it easier to draw plans of the layout of architectural remains and artifacts because one can measure the locations of objects and features with reference to the sides of the excavation square. The other advantage of excavating in square units is that the sides of the holes provide a record of the stratigraphic sequence. The sides of excavation units, known as stratigraphic profiles, show the stratigraphy of the site much in the way that a road cut gives a view of the geological stratigraphy (see Figure 1.12). Often, a half-meter area called a baulk is left standing around each excavation square to provide profiles. Baulks also facilitate movement around the excavation without trampling on newly exposed deposits. Drawings of the profiles left in baulks are critical records of a site's stratigraphy. Great care is taken during the excavation to ensure that these profiles are protected and that they are as straight as possible.

During excavation, it is necessary to keep moving between a horizontal and a vertical perspective. In excavating an urban site, it is critical to think in terms of the architecture being excavated. However, if, at the same time, one does not keep in mind the site's stratigraphy, there is the danger of erroneously combining walls from different phases of occupation.

■ Recovery Methods

The digging tools used in an archaeological excavation vary with the scale and goals of the project. Backhoes and bulldozers are often employed to dig exploratory trenches or to clear overlying deposits. Hand tools range from shovels and hoes to trowels and dental picks. Most excavations involve screening the excavated sediments to make sure that all artifacts are recovered. The size of the screen mesh is important in determining what sizes of objects will be recovered. If one of the goals of the excavation is the recovery of small artifacts and bones, then it is necessary to use a very fine mesh, together with water, to break up the sediments and move

Trench E   Section Q-B

FIGURE 1.12 Stratigraphic profile from the site of Abu Hureyra, Syria. The numbers in circles indicate discrete depositional units. These units include walls, floors, and fill. The scale on the left shows elevation above mean sea level. How does this archaeological stratigraphy differ from the geological stratigraphy shown in Figure 1.7 on page 13?

them through the screen. This process, called **wet screening**, is usually carried out by spraying water onto the sieve.

The recovery of botanical material (wood and seeds) requires special methods. In many locations, the most effective method is **flotation**, which involves vigorously mixing sediments in water. In the process, charred remains of seeds and wood float to the surface, while the mineral sediments settle to the bottom. The charred botanical material can then be skimmed off and dried for analysis. On sites where recovering botanical material is a high priority, it is possible to set up a system that will process sediments rapidly.

At every step of recovery, whether collecting objects from excavation, from the sieve, or from flotation, it is essential that the context from which the objects were recovered be carefully tracked. Every bucket of earth that goes to the sieve must be clearly labeled so that its precise context is known. After the earth is sieved, the label must be transferred to the bag of recovered objects. Ultimately, each object should be labeled in ink, with the label stating the exact provenience of the find.

■ Recording Methods

Archaeological excavation is essentially a destructive act. One cannot go back and excavate an area a second time. What is destroyed in excavation is not, one hopes, archaeological objects. Rather, it is the context within which these objects are found—the matrix of depositional units—that is destroyed. The goal of recording methods is to allow archaeologists to go back and reconstruct that context on paper after excavation. Also, it is essential that all recovered objects be linked with as precise a provenience as possible.

There are almost as many recording systems as there are archaeologists. The basic unit is usually the depositional unit, also called a locus or stratigraphic feature. Each depositional unit has its own recording sheet, which includes plan maps at various stages of excavation, stratigraphic sections showing the relation among different

wet screening The process of spraying water onto a sieve to break up sediments and move them through the mesh to make sure that all artifacts are recovered during an excavation.

flotation The process used to recover botanical material (wood and seeds) that involves mixing sediments vigorously in water. In the process, charred remains of seeds and wood float to the surface, while the mineral sediments settle to the bottom. The charred botanical material can then be skimmed off and dried for analysis.

depositional units, and a description of the contents of the depositional unit. A careful description of soil color and texture is often also included.

Architectural features can be treated as depositional units. In practice, many archaeologists prefer to treat walls and buildings separately from other depositional units. On excavations of urban sites, the excavation team often includes an architect whose job is to draw plans of architectural remains. Increasingly, digital media are being integrated into the process of excavation. Digital photography allows excavators to annotate photographs during the excavation and to point out significant details. Digital video allows for an ongoing recording of the excavation process.

1.3 Cultural Resource Management

Most archaeological research in the United States takes place in the framework of **cultural resource management (CRM)**, archaeology carried out with the aim of mitigating the effects of development. Archaeologists working in CRM must comply with legislation that is often complex and must also operate within a business environment. Negotiation with various stakeholders, including local communities, is increasingly an essential aspect of the work of a CRM archaeologist.

The legislation guiding CRM archaeology puts a heavy emphasis on the process to be followed in carrying out a project. There are three phases in the CRM process: identification, evaluation, and treatment (Barker 2009; Neumann, Sanford, and Harry 2010). In Phase 1, the identification stage, archaeologists combine survey with archival research to locate archaeological sites in the path of development. The scope of Phase 1 research can be quite massive, as is the case, for example, for surveys in advance of pipeline construction. In Phase 2, the evaluation stage, the significance of sites is determined. Because not listing a site as significant often leads to the site being destroyed without documentation, archaeologists tend to err on the side of caution in identifying sites as significant (Chandler 2009). Phase 2 often involves excavation of test pits across sites identified in Phase 1. Once a site has been evaluated as significant, it is necessary to determine a course of treatment. Often, it is possible to protect a site simply by altering the design of a project—for example, changing the course of a pipeline or highway to avoid a site. In other cases, an ephemeral site, such as a surface scatter of artifacts, can be collected as part of Phase 2 research. Phase 3, the mitigation stage, takes place when a site evaluated as significant will be damaged or destroyed. Mitigation involves intensive data recovery, usually by excavation. Once a CRM project is completed, a report must be compiled in compliance with legislation. The clients for CRM research may be government agencies or private contractors.

The scale of CRM is increasing to include "mega-projects" such as the massive excavations in advance of construction of the new terminal at London Heathrow Airport (www.framearch.co.uk/t5/). The Heathrow excavation employed 80 archaeologists over a period of 15 months. This scale of operation opens new opportunities to look at human activity across a landscape but also raises new challenges for archaeological methods of data recovery and management.

1.4 Artifacts and Ecofacts

The objects recovered in excavations can be divided into artifacts and ecofacts. **Artifacts** are objects that show traces of human manufacture. Artifacts include tools

cultural resource management (CRM) Public archaeology carried out with the goal of mitigating the effects of development on archaeological resources.

artifacts Objects that show traces of human manufacture.

The Author on His Fieldwork at Wonderwerk Cave, South Africa

Wonderwerk Cave is a spectacular site located in the Northern Cape Province of South Africa, on the edge of the Kalahari. Although this is a remote area, our living conditions are quite good. We stay in small brick chalets built near the site, and most of the roads are tarred. The view from the cave is of an immense open space, a flat grassland that reaches to the horizon. A nice part of working at the site is that not only do we lack Internet access, but we have to walk out to the main road to even get cell phone reception—a welcome break from my heavily connected life in Canada. However, this remote place is also the nexus of an international research team, as well as a diverse range of community interests. My role at Wonderwerk seems more like that of a ringmaster in a circus than that of an archaeologist.

It might be best to begin by explaining how I ended up working at this site. In the late 1990s, I was completing a project in Israel with my colleagues Liora Horwitz and Naomi Porat. Liora is a faunal analyst, Naomi is a geologist, and I am an archaeologist who specializes in stone tools, so we make a good team. We began looking for a new project that would allow us to continue to study the shift from the Lower Paleolithic to the Middle Paleolithic, or, as they are known in Africa, the Earlier to the Middle Stone Age. By chance, Liora was off to South Africa to visit family, which included a visit to her uncle's farm in the Free State. En route, she stopped off in Kimberley, a diamond-mining city that is home to Peter Beaumont. Peter is famous for excavating sites of the time range we were interested in, and before I knew it, I was off to South Africa for an unforgettable tour with Peter. The wealth of sites he showed us and the extent of the excavations he

had carried out were simply staggering. We resolved to develop a project to analyze the collections from Peter's excavations at Wonderwerk Cave housed at the McGregor Museum, carry out small-scale field projects to document the stratigraphy on the site, and collect samples for geological and botanical analysis.

Seven years later we are still hard at work. Our research team has swelled to over 15 members from South Africa, England, Israel, Canada, and the United States. Our most exciting result is the dating of the base of the deposit at Wonderwerk to 2 million years ago. The stone tools from this stratum provide the earliest evidence for hominin cave occupation in the world. My job as the codirector of this project is not simply to analyze stone tools, but also to coordinate the activities of all the scientists working at the site. This is a fascinating undertaking, since each

member of the team comes to the project with his or her own perspective, and meshing these perspectives is a tremendous challenge. We have also found ourselves involved in ongoing discussions with the local community. Wonderwerk Cave is a candidate for World Heritage status and a critical element of the tourism development in this area. Wonderwerk is also integrated into the local school curriculum, and all children from the area schools visit the site during their primary years. Combining the educational, tourism, and scientific potentials of this site is every bit as complex as the analysis of Earlier Stone Age stone tools. Days at Wonderwerk tend to be a bit unpredictable and are almost always interesting. A day that begins with conversations with local Tswana chiefs might also involve careful excavation and complex discussions of stratigraphy and geophysics. One couldn't ask for much more. ▲

FIGURE 1.13 Taking samples for paleomagnetic dating of the early hominin occupation at Wonderwerk Cave, South Africa

ecofacts Objects recovered from an archaeological context that are either the remains of biological organisms or the results of geological processes.

and vessels, as well as the waste resulting from a manufacturing process. An example of a waste artifact is slag, a by-product of smelting ores. These are some of the major areas of archaeological artifact analysis:

- Lithic analysis is the study of stone tools (see the Stone Tools Toolbox in Chapter 3, p. 75).
- Ceramic analysis is the study of pottery and other objects made of fired clay (see the Hand-Built Pottery Toolbox in Chapter 8, p. 222).
- Metallurgy is the study of metal artifacts and the by-products of smelting (see the Metallurgy Toolbox in Chapter 14, p. 396).

Ecofacts are objects recovered from an archaeological context that are either the remains of biological organisms or the results of geological processes. The major areas of biological analysis include the following:

- Faunal analysis is the study of animal bones recovered on archaeological sites (see the Faunal Analysis and Taphonomy Toolbox in Chapter 2, p. 47).
- Paleoethnobotany is the study of archaeological plant remains, such as charred seeds and pollen (see the Paleoethnobotany Toolbox in Chapter 7, p. 204).
- Human osteoarchaeology is the study of the biological characteristics of human skeletal material recovered on archaeological excavations (see the Human Osteoarchaeology Toolbox in Chapter 13, p. 362).

Ecofacts are studied with an eye toward reconstructing the ecological setting of the site or looking for evidence of human activity on the site. Often, these two goals are closely linked. For example, in studying the animal bones from a hunter-gatherer site, one needs to reconstruct the ecological setting in order to understand the occupants' hunting strategies.

Archaeologists have developed conventions for representing objects in drawings. One example is the illustration of ceramic vessels, shown in Figure 1.14. The convention is to show a view of the outside of the vessel, including any surface

FIGURE 1.14 This archaeological illustration of a ceramic vessel shows the exterior of the vessel on the left side and a section through the vessel wall on the right

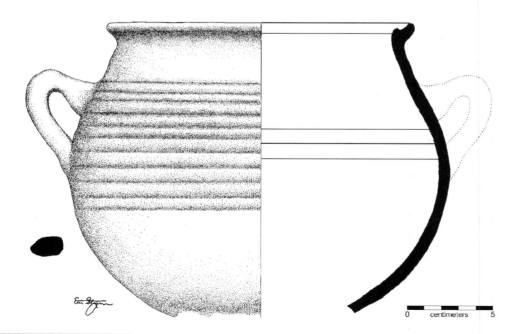

0   centimeters   5

treatment and decoration, on one side of the drawing. The other side of the drawing reveals a section through the vessel wall, which gives a sense of the thickness of the vessel and the shape of the rim and base. This convention can be used both with complete vessels and with fragments from the rim of the vessel—what archaeologists refer to as rim sherds. In drawing a rim sherd, the original diameter of the vessel is calculated on the basis of the arc of the fragment of the rim. Digital imaging is providing new ways for archaeologists to approach documentation and analysis. Laser scanning and photogrammetry are both methods that create a digital 3D model of an object. A laser scanner uses laser beams to create a matrix of points that correspond to the outer surface of an object. This 3D array of points can then be converted into a polygon mesh and overlain with an image of the object to create a model that is easily manipulated and can even be printed out with a 3D printer. **Photogrammetry** is software that creates a similar 3D model using multiple

Photogrammetry is software that creates a similar 3D model using multiple images taken with a digital camera.

FIGURE 1.15 Photogrammetric model of a Moai sculpture (height 2.42 meters) from Easter Island. Photogrammetric software creates a 3D model (shown in three different views in the bottom of the figure) by combining multiple images. The upper part of the figure is a screenshot showing the camera positions used to create the model.

images taken with a digital camera. To create a 3D model using photogrammetry it is critical to have multiple overlapping images taken from different angles while the camera's focal length remains constant. Digital 3D models are now used routinely in artifact illustration and analysis. The great potential of 3D imagery is that it allows us to think about artifacts in new ways. As shown in Figure 1.15, archaeologists working at the British Museum have used photogrammetry to create a 3D model of one of the statues from Easter Island (Miles et al. 2014). This model makes it possible to explore in detail how the ancient sculptors created this monumental figure.

Advanced methods of radiography such as CT scans and tomography are also beginning to show promise for archaeological analysis. These methods produce a 3D model not only of the surface of an object, but also of the interior structure. At the Roman site of Herculaneum a burnt library was uncovered, but any attempt to manipulate this trove of scrolls reduces the object to dust. Initial studies have shown that the distinctive chemical properties of the ink in comparison to the background papyri makes it possible to detect letters while the document is still rolled up (Mocella et al. 2015). The tantalizing possibility now exists that 3D technology will make it possible to read an entire new library of classical literature.

1.5 Biases in Preservation

Look around the room you are sitting in, and imagine what would be preserved thousands of years from now. Most organic materials, such as paper and leather, would be preserved only under remarkable conditions, such as rapid burial in an environment with no oxygen (e.g., a bog; see Figure 1.16). Valuable metals are likely to have been reused unless they are left behind when a site is abruptly abandoned or they are placed in a ritual context such as a tomb. Differences in preservation create a bias in what is found on archaeological sites. Archaeologists must take into consideration **postdepositional processes**—those events that take place after the site was occupied. Postdepositional processes can be caused by climate (such as frost heave) and biological agents (including termites, earthworms, and rodents), both of which can move material around the site and distort its stratigraphy. A number of archaeologists have pointed out that cultural practices, such as where garbage is disposed of, will also shape the archaeological record (Schiffer 1987).

Taphonomy is the study of the processes that affect organic remains after death. An important line of evidence for all taphonomic studies is traces found on the surface of bones recovered on archaeological sites. The overall condition of the surface of the bone can indicate whether it has been transported by water or has suffered significant chemical weathering. Chewing by animals ranging from rodents to bears often leaves characteristic marks on the surface of the bone. If a bone has passed through the digestive tract of an animal such as a hyena or a dog, the surface of the bone will show characteristic etching. Human action can often be detected through the identification of cut marks left when meat was sliced off the bone or the carcass was disarticulated with a stone tool. Human action can also be detected on the basis of percussion marks left when the bone is smashed open to access marrow.

FIGURE 1.16 The soft tissue of the 2,500-year-old burial from Denmark known as the Tollund Man has been preserved because it was buried in a bog, resulting in a process of natural mummification

1.6 Microarchaeology

Much of the most exciting research in archaeology today takes place under the microscope (Weiner 2010). A range of techniques are expanding the scope of research into the archaeological past and pushing a wide range of collaborations between archaeologists and specialists in fields such as mineralogy, genetics, and biochemistry. Microarchaeology includes the following:

- Micromorphology is a method that allows archaeologists to look at the details of the processes of site formation. Visual identification of depositional structures under the microscope can be augmented by techniques such as Fourier Transmitted Infrared Spectroscopy, which allows for the quantitative identification of minerals and organic materials (see Toolbox on Geoarchaeology and Micromorphology in Chapter 4, p. 114).

- Microbotanical remains such as pollen and phytoliths can provide insight into climate, diet, and the fuels used for fire (see Toolbox on Pollen, Phytoliths, and Starch Grains in Chapter 9, p. 243).

- Use-wear analysis examines edge damage on stone tools to determine how they were used (see Toolbox on Use-Wear Analysis in Chapter 5, p. 138).

- Residue analysis uses methods from biochemistry to identify food residues left on artifacts such as ceramic vessels (See Toolbox on Residue Analysis in Chapter 9, p. 252).

- **Isotope analysis** looks at the proportion of isotopes in bone to determine aspects of the diet of humans or animals, shedding light on diet and the environment. Isotope analysis can also be used to identify the movement of populations or individuals (See Toolbox on Isotope Analysis in Chapter 4, p. 111).

- aDNA, or ancient DNA, provides access to information about the relationship between different species of human ancestors. In more recent time periods aDNA can also be used to study the social structure of ancient populations and to track migrations. The rapid development of techniques for recovering and sequencing aDNA has led to a string of important discoveries that have expanded our understanding of the archaeological past (see Toolbox on Archaeology and Genetics in Chapter 11, p. 318).

1.7 Quantification and Sampling

In early excavations, representing what had been found was a simple process. One just took all the complete vessels and tools, placed them in a row, and snapped a photograph or made a sketch of the collection. Figure 2.8, shown on page 42, provides an excellent example of this. But this approach works only so long as one recovers complete artifacts and discards everything else. Today, archaeologists recover all artifacts, including broken pieces and waste, as well as a wide range of ecofacts. Only in rare cases is it possible to present each object individually. Certainly, unique pieces and artifacts of particular historical or artistic merit receive individual attention. However, the vast bulk of the material can be represented only by quantitative methods. The methods of **quantification** used by archaeologists range from simple databases, which provide counts of various types of objects, to sophisticated statistical techniques.

In analyses of large bodies of data, it is often possible to use a sampling strategy such that only a portion of the material is analyzed. In studying artifacts and ecofacts,

isotope analysis The study of diet through the chemical signature of bones.

quantification Methods used by archaeologists to represent the large quantities of material recovered in excavations and surveys.

archaeologists often rely on statistical sampling strategies to allow a true representation of the site to emerge without having to measure or describe every single object recovered. On many sites, the number of artifacts and ecofacts recovered is in the hundreds of thousands, making sampling an essential tool.

■ Counting Bones

Using quantitative methods requires that one understand the way these methods work. Problems that at first glance seem quite simple often turn out to be far more complex. For example, counting animal bones would seem to be quite a straightforward undertaking (Davis 1987). If one is able to identify the bones by species, then one should be able to make a chart illustrating the relative frequency of bones of different animals found on the site. This method of counting is known as number of identifiable specimens (NISP). Some archaeologists have argued that NISP does not provide an accurate quantitative picture of the relative frequency of different animals that make up an assemblage. To illustrate this point, imagine a site that produced the complete skeleton of a rabbit and 10 left tibias from cows. According to NISP, there would be more rabbits represented on the site than cows. But in fact, there are the remains of 1 rabbit and 10 cows. To get around this problem, some archaeologists prefer to use a method known as minimum number of individuals (MNI). According to this method, each skeletal element (i.e., left tibia or first upper premolar) is counted individually. The number of examples of a given element is then divided by the number of bones of that type that occur in an individual skeleton. For example, there are 2 first upper premolars in any individual skeleton, so the number of upper premolars found would be divided by 2. It is quite likely that not all skeletal elements will indicate the same number of animals, so the largest number is used to determine the MNI for animals at the site. In the case just described, the MNI for rabbits would be 1, and the MNI for cows would be 10 (see Figure 1.17). Of course, if the goal of analysis is to make inferences about diet, we still have the problem that the meat yield of a rabbit is quite a bit smaller than the meat yield of a cow. One way to overcome this challenge is to multiply the number of individuals by the average weight of a carcass of the species. What this example highlights is the fact that the way objects are counted will shape the picture that emerges.

FIGURE 1.17 The method used to quantify the animal bones found on an archaeological site will have a major impact on the picture that emerges. In this case, the use of NISP and MNI leads to very different conclusions about the proportion of rabbits and cows.

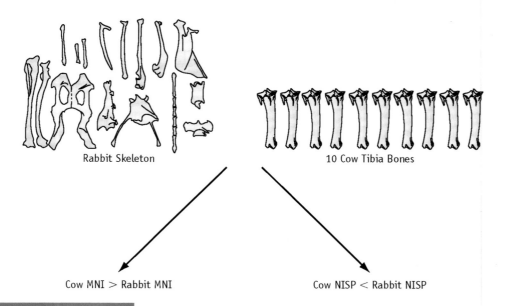

Rabbit Skeleton

10 Cow Tibia Bones

Cow MNI > Rabbit MNI

Cow NISP < Rabbit NISP

■ Counting Artifacts

If you were asked to go through your kitchen and inventory its contents, you would create a list of appliances, utensils, and vessels. You would be unlikely to have much difficulty coming up with names for these various objects. Archaeologists working on colonial and historical periods in the United States have access to inventories, known as probate records, drawn up by assessors who went carefully through a person's home after his or her death (Orser 2004). However, archaeologists working on prehistoric sites do not have access to lists of artifacts drawn up by the people who lived there at the time. One of the first steps of artifact analysis is to create a classification of the objects.

Most artifact classifications begin by defining major categories of objects. In your kitchen, you would be likely to separate appliances from vessels and utensils. You might then define vessels as objects used to hold food and utensils as tools used to process food by hand. It would then be rather simple to divide vessels into pots, pans, plates, and bowls and to divide utensils into forks, knives, and spoons. Archaeologists follow such a process, often sorting artifacts on the basis of their material of manufacture (e.g., bone tools, stone tools, pottery, metal).

Archaeologists usually want to go beyond simply reporting how many bowls and plates were found on a site. It is often critical to describe the detailed characteristics of the artifacts. Including this type of information, even in the inventory of your own kitchen, might be challenging. How do you describe a plate, a fork, or a knife? Archaeologists often develop detailed systems of classification based on types of artifacts. A **typology** is a list of artifact types for a particular archaeological context. Archaeologists use typologies to draw up an inventory of the artifacts they have found.

A good example of a typology is the list of types of ceramic vessels used in classical Greece (see Figure 1.18). These vessel types are known by the names the ancient Greeks gave them. Most archaeological typologies, however, are far more refined than a simple description of vessel types. The purpose of detailed archaeological typologies is to register nuances of style that reflect when and where an artifact was manufactured. A modern artifact that has undergone regular changes in form is the ubiquitous Coca-Cola bottle. Ever since a standard bottle was adopted for Coca-Cola in 1916, the shape and decoration of the bottle have changed regularly. These

typology A list used to draw up an inventory of types of artifacts found by archaeologists in a particular archaeological context.

FIGURE 1.18 Greek pottery vessels with their Greek names. Do we have a similar system for the vessels we use?

TOOLBOX

Ethnoarchaeology

Ethnoarchaeology refers to research carried out by archaeologists living with and observing communities in order to make a contribution to archaeology. Archaeologists bring to the study of modern cultures an intense interest in the material aspects of human lives. Ethnoarchaeological research covers a wide range of domains, including subsistence, technology, ideology, and site formation.

Much of our understanding of stone tool manufacture comes from ethnoarchaeological studies of societies that still use stone tools or have used them recently. Among the stone tool techniques studied by ethnoarchaeologists are ground stone axe manufacture in Papua New Guinea, flint knapping in Australia, obsidian tool manufacture and use in Ethiopia, and stone bead manufacture in India. All of these studies provide insight into the process of tool manufacture and the way tools are used. Ethnoarchaeological studies have also provided insight into how people think about the tools they are making. For example, on the basis of ethnoarchaeological research in Australia, Brian Hayden has questioned whether people making stone tools ever think about making a specific type of tool. Interestingly, in the group Hayden worked with, the focus of attention was on the type of edge produced, and the actual form of the tool was of little importance.

Ethnoarchaeological research also can provide a reminder of the limitations of the archaeological record. In 1974 and 1975, Robert and Priscilla Janes lived for 22 weeks with the Slavey Dene people in the Northwest Territory of Canada (Janes 1983). The Slavey Dene spend most of the year in Fort Norman, but move to seasonal camps during the late winter or early spring. The Janeses' research examined the structure of one of these camps. According to David and Kramer (2001), the Janeses' experience living with the Slavey Dene led them to recognize the "potential immensity of the gap . . . between the results of field archaeology and the richness of a living culture" (288). This gap is particularly wide in the case of hunter-gatherer societies, which made most artifacts out of perishable material.

In some cases, ethnoarchaeologists do not simply make observations, but rather collaborate with members of local communities to carry out experiments. During the 1970s, Peter Schmidt and his colleagues collaborated with members of a Haya community from northeastern Tanzania to smelt iron by traditional methods (Schmidt 1997). Because the Haya had not practiced traditional smelting for over 50 years, this project was guided by Haya elders who remembered participating in smelting operations as children. The resulting smelt was only partially successful, but it did provide an opportunity to carefully document the functioning of the iron furnace, as well as the processes involved in producing charcoal and in mining the clay used to build the furnace. The furnace produced in the experiment served as an important point of reference for the interpretation of archaeologically excavated furnaces.

Despite the obvious value of ethnoarchaeological research, some archaeologists have reservations about the use of ethnographic analogies in archaeology. Martin Wobst (1978) has written of the "tyranny of the ethnographic record," which leads archaeologists to assume that the cultures they are investigating were similar to ethnographically known cultures. A slavish adherence to analogy can dull our awareness of those aspects of past societies that are unique and different from characteristics of societies living in the present. The use of ethnographic analogy is also not helpful in studying long-term processes of cultural change that last hundreds, thousands, or even tens of thousands of years and that are of particular interest to archaeologists. ●

ADDITIONAL READING: Nicholas David and Carole Kramer. 2001. *Ethnoarchaeology in Action.* Cambridge: Cambridge University Press.

FIGURE 1.19 Richard Lee conducting fieldwork with San hunter-gatherers in Botswana

changes can be used as chronological indicators. For example, if you find a bottle with the logo "Coca-Cola" painted on it, the bottle must date to after 1958, the date when painted bottles first appeared (Orser 2004).

Archaeological typologies are often highly detailed, with dozens of types for each category of artifact. Once a typology has been developed, the number of objects belonging to each type can be counted to create a quantitative inventory of artifacts found in a particular context. Typologies are built from combinations of artifact attributes that the archaeologist intuitively selects to define the various types. An **attribute** is a particular characteristic of an artifact. For a simple ceramic bowl, one can observe a surprising number of attributes. Some of these attributes describe the clay out of which the bowl was made and the decoration applied to the bowl. Other attributes describe the shape of the bowl, including the form of the base, the curvature of the walls, and the shape of the rim. Still other attributes measure the size of the bowl. Some archaeologists see the value of typologies as limited, arguing that types can be defined only on the basis of a statistical analysis of the attributes of all of the vessels found in a context. Other archaeologists argue that the idea of vessel types should be discarded completely in favor of the analysis of attributes. From this perspective, artifact types are an unjustified abstraction that distort our picture of the archaeological record.

1.8 Creating a Chronology

Depositional units are dated on the basis of material recovered within the unit during excavation. This is one of the reasons it is so important to know the exact provenience of every recovered object. Objects can be dated by a variety of methods. Some artifacts are of a known date of manufacture. Coins are a good example of such artifacts. Artifacts with a known date of manufacture allow archaeologists to create an **absolute chronology** stated in terms of calendar years. Other artifacts can be placed within a regional chronology on the basis of style. Often, pottery is used to date archaeological sites because of frequent, identifiable changes in the shape and decoration of vessels. Frequently, chronologies based on artifact typology are **relative chronologies** that place assemblages in a temporal sequence not directly linked to calendar dates.

In most regional chronologies, artifacts are used to correlate the stratigraphic sequence of a site with the chronological framework for a region. In the absence of artifacts with a known date of manufacture, the relative frequency of different artifacts is used to fit a particular context into a regional chronology. The method of comparing the relative frequency of artifact types between contexts is known as **seriation**. The assumption behind seriation is that the frequency of an artifact form will increase gradually over time and then decline gradually after reaching a peak.

An important illustration of the principle that the frequency of an artifact form will increase gradually over time and then decline gradually after reaching a peak is found in shifting preferences for design motifs on gravestones in colonial America, like the one shown in Figure 1.20 (Deetz 1996). From 1720 to 1750, the main motif used on gravestones was the death's head. Between 1760 and 1780, the frequency of death's heads declined as cherub motifs increased. The number of cherub motifs reached a peak between 1780 and 1789. After 1780, the frequency of cherub motifs gradually declined as urn and willow motifs increased.

A number of scientific methods have been developed for determining absolute dates of material recovered from archaeological sites:

- Radiocarbon dating measures the decay of carbon isotopes. Charcoal, bone, and other organic material can be dated with this method. Radiocarbon

attribute A particular characteristic of an artifact.

absolute chronology A chronology stated in terms of calendar years.

relative chronology A chronology that places assemblages in a temporal sequence not directly linked to calendar dates.

seriation The method of comparing the relative frequency of artifact types between contexts.

dating can be used for sites younger than 40,000 years. Accelerator Mass Spectrometry (AMS) radiocarbon dating is an advanced method that can date extremely small samples. Radiocarbon dates need to be calibrated to arrive at calendrical ages (see the Radiocarbon Dating Toolbox on p. 29, the Calibration Toolbox in Chapter 6, p. 162, and the AMS Toolbox in Chapter 8, p. 218).

- Argon dating identifies the time of a volcanic eruption. Argon dating can be used on early hominin sites in contexts where there are layers of volcanic ash (see the Dating Early Hominin Sites Toolbox in Chapter 3, p. 80).

- Paleomagnetism measures reversals in the earth's magnetic field. Paleomagnetism is most useful for dating early hominin sites (see the Dating Early Hominin Sites Toolbox in Chapter 3, p. 80).

- Luminescence dating methods are used to measure the uptake of radioactive material. Luminescence methods can be used to date soils (optically stimulated luminescence), animal teeth (electron spin resonance), and burnt flint (thermoluminescence) from early hominin sites. Particularly useful for the period between 300,000 and 30,000 years ago, luminescence can also be used for more recent periods to learn when pottery vessels were fired (see the Luminescence Dating Toolbox in Chapter 5, p. 129).

- Dendrochronology uses sequences of tree rings to date wood found on archaeological sites. In some areas of the world, the dendrochronological sequence has been established for a period of thousands of years (see the Dendrochronology Toolbox in Chapter 10, p. 281).

- Obsidian hydration measures the decay of the surface of obsidian artifacts. Obsidian hydration is often used on sites several thousand years old or younger.

Absolute dates can be expressed on a number of time scales. In this text, we employ a time scale that uses the birth of Christ as the point of reference. Dates after the birth of Christ can be expressed as years A.D. or years C.E. In this book, we use

FIGURE 1.20 Two illustrations of seriation. Shifts occurred over time in the designs carved on New England headstones, such as the winged skull carved on the top of this headstone from 1747. The changing frequency of death's head, cherub, and willow and urn motifs provides an excellent illustration of the principles underlying seriation. In a more contemporary context, the shifts in technologies used by the recorded music industry demonstrate the same principles.

TOOLBOX

Radiocarbon Dating

The story of radiocarbon dating begins in the upper atmosphere, where neutrons from cosmic rays bombard atoms of nitrogen to produce carbon-14 atoms. Carbon-14 is an isotope of carbon, which means that it is chemically identical to other forms of carbon, including carbon-12 and carbon-13. However, because of its extra neutron, carbon-14 is unstable, or radioactive. The half-life of carbon-14 is 5,730 years. Thus, in a sample of carbon-14, half of the atoms will decay to a more stable carbon isotope over a period of exactly 5,730 years. In other words, 1% of the sample will decay every 83 years.

Once carbon-14 atoms form in the atmosphere, they rapidly combine with oxygen to form molecules of carbon dioxide (CO_2). These molecules then spread through the atmosphere, the oceans, and the biosphere, entering plants through photosynthesis. Remarkably, the ratio between carbon-14 and nonradioactive molecules of carbon is the same throughout the atmosphere, the oceans, and the biosphere, known collectively as the carbon exchange reservoir.

Carbon-14 decays at a constant rate and is found in the same concentration throughout the carbon exchange reservoir. How do these facts allow us to use carbon-14 to date archaeological remains? Animals, trees, and plants are all part of the carbon exchange reservoir. While they live, these organisms maintain the same concentration of carbon-14 found throughout the reservoir. This is as true for you as it is for a tree. The tree exchanges carbon through photosynthesis, and you participate in the exchange reservoir by eating plants, or animals that eat plants. However, when a plant or animal dies, it ceases

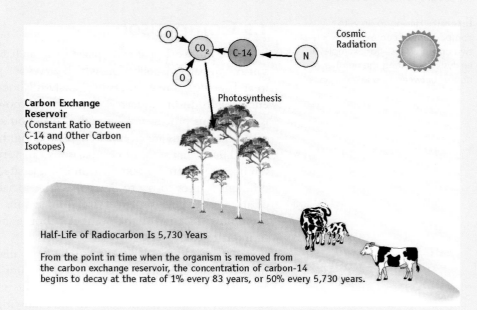

Carbon Exchange Reservoir (Constant Ratio Between C-14 and Other Carbon Isotopes)

Cosmic Radiation

Photosynthesis

Half-Life of Radiocarbon Is 5,730 Years

From the point in time when the organism is removed from the carbon exchange reservoir, the concentration of carbon-14 begins to decay at the rate of 1% every 83 years, or 50% every 5,730 years.

FIGURE 1.21 Radiocarbon dating is based on the participation of all living organisms in the carbon exchange reservoir

to exchange carbon. From that point in time, when the organism is removed from the carbon exchange reservoir, the concentration of carbon-14 begins to decay at the rate of 1% every 83 years, or 50% every 5,730 years.

Radiocarbon dating calculates the time since an organism was removed from the carbon exchange reservoir by measuring the concentration of carbon-14 relative to stable isotopes of carbon (carbon-13 and carbon-12). By calculating the amount of carbon-14 that has decayed, it is possible to determine when the organism stopped exchanging carbon. This event usually marks the death of the organism; however, in trees, it marks the end of an annual growth cycle (see the Dendrochronology Toolbox in Chapter 10, p. 281).

The impact of radiocarbon dating on archaeology has been nothing short of revolutionary. Carbon-14 provided the first means of finding an absolute

age for archaeological discoveries, an achievement that earned W. F. Libby the Nobel Prize. In later chapters, we will look at two further developments of this method: calibration (see the Radiocarbon Calibration Toolbox in Chapter 6, p. 162) and Accelerator Mass Spectrometry, or AMS (see the AMS Radiocarbon Dating Toolbox in Chapter 8, p. 218).

Radiocarbon dating works for samples less than 40,000 years old, although some researchers are attempting to transcend this frontier. Almost all organic materials, including bone and wood, can be dated. All radiocarbon dates are reported with an error range that reflects statistical limits of the method, as well as limits in the precision of laboratory equipment. (To simplify the presentation, the error range is not given with dates in this book.) ●

ADDITIONAL READING: R. E. Taylor and Martin J. Aitken, eds. 1997. *Chronometric Dating in Archaeology*. New York: Plenum.

intrasite Having to do with comparisons of contexts within a single site—for example, an analysis comparing the sizes and contents of different houses to try to determine the social structure of a society.

intersite Having to do with comparisons of contexts between two or more sites—for example, an analysis comparing the number of houses between sites in a region.

years A.D. Years before the birth of Christ can be expressed as years B.C. or years B.C.E. In this book, we use years B.C. When archaeologists work on early prehistoric sites, they tend to count years back from the present rather than using years B.C. In this book, such dates are expressed as years before present, or years B.P.

1.9 Comparison

Much of the work that takes place in an archaeological laboratory involves comparison. A comparative collection, which serves as a point of reference, is an important tool in archaeological research. Faunal analysis laboratories usually have an extensive reference collection of modern skeletons from known species. Preparing these collections is a laborious process involving the collection and defleshing of carcasses. Faunal reference collections are essential for identifying the bones found on archaeological sites.

The spatial scale of comparisons can vary. **Intrasite** comparisons look at differences between contexts within a single site. Comparing the size and contents of different houses to try to determine the social structure of a society is an example of an intrasite analysis. **Intersite** comparisons examine differences between two or more sites. Comparing the number of houses between sites in a region is an example of intersite analysis.

Archaeologists have often relied on analogies to descriptions of living cultures to help interpret archaeological remains. Some archaeologists practice "living archaeology," using observations made in the present to help interpret archaeological remains. Two such techniques are the following:

- Ethnoarchaeology is research carried out by archaeologists living with and observing communities in order to make a contribution to archaeology (see the Ethnoarchaeology Toolbox on p. 26).

- Experimental archaeology involves attempts to replicate archaeological features or objects (see the Experimental Archaeology Toolbox in Chapter 6, p. 158).

1.10 Conservation, Display, and Publication

The process of excavation also includes the conservation of excavated areas and, in some cases, the consolidation of remains for display (Figure 1.22). At the most basic level, it is essential that excavated areas be filled back in after excavation unless there is a clear plan for exhibition in place. When exhibition of the site is involved, the exposed remains need to be consolidated.

Recent excavations at the Neolithic site of Çatalhöyük, Turkey, directed by Ian Hodder, are unusual in that a consideration of the use of the site for exhibition is fundamental to the project as a whole (www.catalhoyuk.com). Çatalhöyük is well known for spectacular frescoes discovered in earlier excavations. Hodder and his team have worked to develop methods of preserving these frescoes and allowing them to be viewed by the public. They are also working to integrate the archaeological process into the exhibit. In

FIGURE 1.22 Visitors view the skeletal remains of a settler from Jamestown, Virginia. How would you describe the visitors' reaction to the exhibit? Why do you think the reconstructed head of the settler (visible to the right of the actual skull in this photograph) was included in the exhibit?

Community Archaeology

There is a general trend in archaeology toward including local communities in the process and the benefits of archaeological research (McGuire 2008). In recent years, some archaeologists have taken this idea a step further and worked to develop a truly community-based archaeology, in which the archaeologists relinquish to the local community at least partial control over their program of research (Marshall 2002). In many cases, archaeologists are trying to react with sensitivity to painful histories of colonialism and disenfranchisement. In a project at the site of Quseir in Egypt, Stephanie Moser and her colleagues (2002) have developed some guidelines for the practice of Community Archaeology. They identify the following components for Community Archaeology projects:

1. Communication and collaboration
2. Employment and training
3. Public presentation
4. Interviews and oral history
5. Development of educational resources
6. Creation of a photographic and video archive
7. Community-controlled merchandising

Moser and her colleagues make it clear that not all circumstances will fit this template and that Community Archaeology must be sensitive to local conditions. However, the range of topics included gives a good sense of the complexity of adopting a community-driven approach. The project at Quseir addresses elements of economic development, including employment and training, as well as merchandising; aspects of local identity through the development of archives and oral history; and initiatives related to education. Some archaeologists, while appreciating the importance of a community-based approach, stress the complexities involved in such an undertaking. One of the most difficult problems is the definition of the community that is at the very root of Community Archaeology (Chirikure and Pwiti 2008). In many areas of the world, the definitions of communities are deeply contested. However, this issue can feed into the process of Community Archaeology as archaeologists are drawn into discussions of the construction of local identities.

FIGURE 1.23 An archaeologist at the George Mason plantation in Virginia talks with a group of elementary school students. How would you describe the interaction between the archaeologist and these members of the community?

a similar vein, excavations in historical Annapolis, Maryland, aim at providing the public the opportunity to engage in the reinterpretation of the history of that city (Leone, Potter, and Shackel 1987).

Archaeological publication can take the form of monographs on particular sites, site reports, or articles on particular research question. The process of publication is very demanding and many excavations never reach the stage of a final publication. In the context of CRM archaeology many of the results of fieldwork remain trapped in what is known as the "grey literature," which consists of reports that are submitted to government agencies or contractors but never published. Eric Kansa raises a series of troubling questions about how archaeologists treat their data, asking: "Why should the public continue to finance research that largely languishes on aresearcher's hard drive, only to go see very limited and highly selective exposure in obscure journals locked behind cost-prohibitive paywalls? If archaeologists themselves routinely neglect and withhold irreplaceable contextual data, how can they condemn others for their mistreatment of such information?" (Kansa 2012 , 9). One solution to this problem is the creation of open access repositories for archaeological data and open access publications. Examples of such initiatives include the *Journal of Open Archaeological Data* (http://openarchaeologydata.metajnl.com/) and the Digital Archaeological Record (http://core.tdar.org/).

SUMMARY

- Archaeological surveys involve mapping sites of the physical remains of human activity.
- Horizontal excavations have as their goal the reconstruction of a single occupation. Vertical excavations focus on exposing the record of a long sequence of occupations.
- A stratigraphic sequence develops where sediments are deposited over time. Strata can be identified when the deposition is discontinuous. The law of superposition states that, in an undisturbed depositional sequence, each layer is younger than the layer beneath it.
- Archaeological sites are made up of depositional units.
- Grids are used to control horizontal space at the site of an excavation, while measurement from a datum point is used to control the vertical dimension. Recovery methods used on excavations include sieving, wet sieving, and flotation.
- Artifacts are objects that show traces of human manufacture. Ecofacts are objects recovered from an archaeological context that are either the remains of biological organisms or the results of geological processes.
- Quantification is used to represent the large samples of artifacts and ecofacts recovered from archaeological

excavations. Often, a sampling strategy is used to select a representative group of artifacts for study.
- Minimum number of individuals (MNI) and number of identifiable specimens (NISP) are two methods for quantifying animal bones.
- Quantitative studies of artifacts often rely on the use of typologies, in which the artifacts are classified according to a list of discrete types.
- In some cases, archaeologists analyze artifacts on the basis of a statistical analysis of their attributes. Attributes are particular characteristics of an artifact.
- A range of scientific methods is used to date archaeological contexts. Artifact typology and seriation can also be used to date archaeological contexts.
- Intrasite comparisons are made within a site, while intersite comparisons are made between sites.
- The goal of cultural resource management (CRM) archaeology is to mitigate the effects of development. CRM archaeologists must comply with legislation that emphasizes the process that must be followed when carrying out a project.

KEY TERMS

absolute chronology, 27
aDNA, 23
airborne LIDAR, 10
anthropogenic deposits, 14
artifacts, 18
attribute, 27
cultural resource management (CRM), 18
datum point, 15
depositional unit, 14
ecofacts, 20
flotation, 17
Geographical Information System (GIS), 10
horizontal excavation, 12
in situ, 9
intersite, 30

intrasite, 30
isotope analysis, 23
law of superposition, 13
photogrammetry, 21
postdepositional processes, 22
provenience, 15
quantification, 23
relative chronology, 27
seriation, 27
strata, 13
survey, 8
taphonomy, 22
typology, 25
vertical excavation, 12
wet screening, 17

1. What is the difference between horizontal and vertical excavations? How would you decide which type of approach to choose in a given archaeological situation?

2. Are there limits to the kind of information archaeologists can recover?

3. Why do archaeologists use sampling?

4. Why is quantification important for archaeological analysis? What methods of quantification are used in the analysis of animal bones?

5. What is the difference between an analysis based on typology and an analysis based on attributes?

PUTTING THE PICTURE TOGETHER

The history of archaeology has been a process of developing ideas about how we can use material remains to learn about the past. After reading this chapter, you should understand:

- The process by which the depth of human antiquity was recognized.
- The development of an explicitly scientific approach to archaeology by the New Archaeologists, also known as processual archaeologists.
- The questions raised about a scientific approach by postprocessual archaeology.

Unsealing the tomb of Tutankhamun

FIGURE 2.1 A page from Diderot and D'Alambert's *Encyclopedia* showing a pottery factory. Notice that the authors try to show both the manufacturing process in the upper part of the plate and the products on the bottom.

I n the mid–1700s, two philosophers of the French Enlightenment began one of the most audacious schemes in the history of publishing. Diderot and D'Alembert planned to write an encyclopedia that would collect all human knowledge into a series of massive tomes (see Figure 2.1). The resulting lavishly illustrated volumes fell far short of this goal. Today, however, the Enlightenment dream embodied in Diderot and D'Alembert's *Encyclopedia* is alive and well, particularly on the Internet, where attempts to collect massive quantities of information have reached a level unimaginable even a decade ago. Still, regardless of technological advances, the Internet is likely to fail, just as the two French philosophers failed 250 years ago.

The basic flaw in Diderot and D'Alembert's plan was that they failed to realize that knowledge does not emerge from a collection of facts. If nothing else, data in the absence of ideas simply overwhelms our capacity to assimilate information; nobody could actually read the entire *Encyclopedia*. This is a critical insight for archaeologists. The archaeological record includes the totality of traces left by human activity over a period of more than 2 million years, across almost the entire surface of the globe. If archaeology were simply the collection of data, then we would be engaged in a futile task, one in which we would rapidly drown in masses of information. Methods of recovery, recording, and analysis are not enough for archaeology to function. Archaeologists cannot simply be technicians (Taylor 1948); archaeologists must also develop the ideas that guide and give meaning to their search through the human past.

The previous chapter discussed the methods archaeologists use in the field and in the laboratory. These methods are tightly linked to ways of thinking about the past and about what we can learn about it from the material remains found on archaeological sites. This chapter presents a brief history of the development of **archaeological theory** and method. Archaeological theory consists of the ideas archaeologists have developed about the past and about the ways we come to know it. We begin the chapter with an examination of the origins of archaeology and the recognition of the depth of human antiquity. We then consider the growing awareness that archaeologists must develop a body of self-reflexive theory—theory that addresses the question of how we use the archaeological record to gain access to the past. We look at the powerful set of ideas advanced by the New Archaeologists of the 1960s and the sharp reaction to their ideas developed by the postprocessual archaeologists beginning in the 1980s. We finish by briefly surveying some of the emerging new directions in archaeological theory.

2.1 Origins of Archaeology

Relics of human activity have been present in the landscape for millions of years. However, the earliest evidence of a conscious recognition of ancient objects comes from the early state societies of Mesopotamia, Egypt, and China. For example, Nabonidus, who ascended to the throne of Babylon in 556 B.C., wrote about the city of Ur: "At that time Egipar, the holy precinct, wherein the rites of the high priestess used to be carried out, was an abandoned place, and had become a heap of ruin. . . . I cut down the trees, removed the rubble of its ruins, I set eyes on the temple and its foundation terrace

archaeological theory Ideas that archaeologists have developed about the past and about the ways we come to know the past.

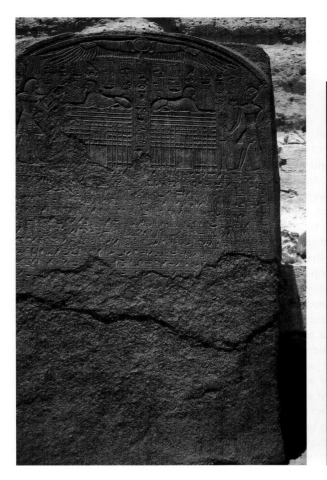

FIGURE 2.2 The stela in front of the sphinx records a dream in which Thutmose IV was told to free the sphinx from the sands that buried it

FIGURE 2.3 Until the nineteenth century, polished stone axes like these examples from the Neolithic of France were thought to be thunderstones that formed where lightning struck the earth

became visible" (Schnapp 1996, 41). In Egypt, King Thutmose IV (1412–1402 B.C.) set up a monumental inscribed stone, or stela, between the paws of the Great Sphinx at Giza (see Figure 2.2). The inscription relates a dream Thutmose had as a young man in which the sun god promises him kingship in return for freeing the sphinx from the sands that bury it (Hallo and Simpson 1971, 265). When Nabonidus and Thutmose IV excavated antiquities, they both did so out of reverence. There is no evidence in either case for the use of the physical remains they found to explore the past.

The first clear evidence for the use of excavation to recover and explore the past was in Renaissance Europe. An emblem book written by Johannes Sambucus in 1564 provides the earliest depiction of excavation for antiquities. The interest of Renaissance antiquarians (as the early archaeologists are known) was drawn to Greek and Roman antiquities and to questions about the origins of the Celts. By the eighteenth century, there was increasing sophistication among European antiquarians in the way they drew monuments and documented and collected artifacts.

Until the nineteenth century, antiquarians struggled with a number of interrelated problems. The most striking problem was the difficulty in distinguishing objects of human manufacture from objects created by natural processes. For example, ground stone axes were believed to be "**thunderstones**"—objects that formed in spots where lightning struck the earth (see Figure 2.3). Arrowheads were identified as fossilized serpent tongues.

thunderstones Objects such as ground stone axes that people in medieval Europe believed were formed in spots where lightning struck the earth.

Thomas Jefferson, the Archaeologist

The life and career of Thomas Jefferson shaped many facets of American life. One of Jefferson's lesser-known achievements was carrying out one of the first archaeological excavations in America. In 1781, he decided to excavate a prehistoric burial mound on his property. The following passage from Jefferson's *Notes on the State of Virginia* gives a sense of the goals and methods of his research, including attention to stratigraphy, as well as of the attitudes of one of the founding fathers toward native people:

I know of no such thing existing as an Indian monument: for I would not honour with that name arrow points, stone hatchets, stone pipes, and half-shapen images. Of labour on the large scale, I think there is no remain as respectable as would be a common ditch for the draining of lands: unless indeed it be the barrows, of which many are to be found all over this country. . . . That these were repositories of the dead, has been obvious to all: but on what particular occasion constructed was a matter of doubt. . . . There being one of these in my neighbourhood, I wished to satisfy myself whether any, and which of these opinions were just. For this purpose I determined to open and examine it thoroughly. It was situated on the low grounds of the Rivanna, about two miles above its principal fork, and opposite to some hills, on which had been an Indian town. It was of a spheroidical form, of about forty feet diameter at the base, and had been of about twelve feet altitude. . . . I first dug superficially in several parts of it, and came to collections of human bones, at different depths, from six inches to three feet below the surface. These were lying in the utmost confusion, some vertical, some oblique, some horizontal, and directed to every point of the compass, entangled, and held together in clusters by the earth. Bones of the most distant parts were found together, as, for instance, the small bones of the foot in the hollow of a scull, many sculls would sometimes be in contact, lying on the face, on the side, on the back, top or bottom, so as, on the whole to give the idea of bones emptied promiscuously from a bag or basket, and covered over with earth, without any attention to the order. . . . There were some teeth which were judged to be smaller than those of an adult; a scull, which on a slight view, appeared to be that of an infant, but it fell to pieces on being taken out, so as to prevent satisfactory examination; a rib, and a fragment of the under-jaw of a person about half grown; another rib of an infant; and part of the jaw of a child, which had not yet cut its teeth. . . . I proceeded then to make a perpendicular cut through the body of the barrow, that I might examine its internal structure. This passed about three feet from its center, was opened to the former surface of the earth, and was wide enough for a man to walk through and examine its sides. At the bottom, that is, on the level of the circumjacent plain I found bones; above these a few stones, brought from a cliff a quarter of a mile off, and from the river one-eighth of a mile off; then a large interval of earth, then a stratum of bones, and so on. At one end of the section were four strata of bones plainly distinguishable; at the other, three; the strata in one part not ranging with those in another. ●

FIGURE 2.4 Along with his many other achievements, Thomas Jefferson carried out one of the first archaeological excavations in the Americas

Against this background of traditional beliefs, methods for recognizing objects of human manufacture emerged. Experience with societies that still used stone tools certainly had an effect on that recognition. Michele Mercati, a Vatican doctor who lived from 1541 to 1593, wrote of the thunderstones: "Those who study history judge that before the use of iron they were struck from very hard flint for the folly of war" (Schnapp 1996, 347). In 1732, the French naturalist Antoine de Jussieu compared the thunderstones with stone tools from the American Islands and Canada. On the basis of this comparison, he wrote that "the savages of these countries have different ways of using nearly similar stones which they have fashioned by almost infinite care by rubbing them against other stones, lacking any tool of iron or steel" (Heizer 1962, 68).

However, there was still no method for determining the age of artifacts. In the absence of such a method, all prehistoric relics were assumed to have come from a fairly brief period of time. In 1797, John Frere reported on the discovery of elephant remains together with stone tools (what he called "weapons of war") at the site of Hoxne, England. His conclusion was that "the situation in which these weapons were found may tempt us to refer them to a very remote period indeed; even beyond that of the present world" (Heizer 1962, 71). This report was ignored for over 50 years.

2.2 The Emergence of Archaeology

The development of Darwin's theory of evolution was one of the most far-reaching achievements of nineteenth-century science. That century also saw a tremendous growth in the scope of scientific research in almost every domain. The nineteenth century was the period when archaeology emerged as a clearly defined discipline. Two of the major achievements of nineteenth-century archaeologists were the creation of the **Three-Age system** and the determination of the depth of human antiquity. It is important to realize that the growth of archaeological research was closely linked to the expansion of European empires. The archaeology of the nineteenth century often reflects the ideology and biases of European colonists.

■ Organizing Time

Throughout the nineteenth century, prehistoric artifacts poured into museums and other collections, but nobody knew how old these objects were or how to group them. The first step toward solving this problem was the development of the Three-Age system by the Danish antiquarian Christian Jürgensen Thomsen (Trigger 1989). In 1816, Thomsen was given the job of cataloguing collections for the newly founded National Museum of Antiquity. His solution was to divide the collections into the relics of three periods—the Stone Age, the Bronze Age, and the Iron Age—based on the material of manufacture. Thomsen assumed that he had arranged these periods chronologically, with the Stone Age being the earliest and the Iron Age the latest. Thomsen also recognized that some stone and bronze artifacts continued to be manufactured in later periods. He therefore augmented his classification with attention to the designs found on the objects.

■ The Establishment of Human Antiquity

Already in the early 1800s, scientists were beginning to talk about the evolution of life on Earth and even the possibility that humanity was the product of evolution.

Three-Age system A system developed by Danish antiquarian Christian Jürgensen Thomsen that catalogues artifacts into relics of three periods—the Stone Age, the Bronze Age, and the Iron Age—based on the material of manufacture.

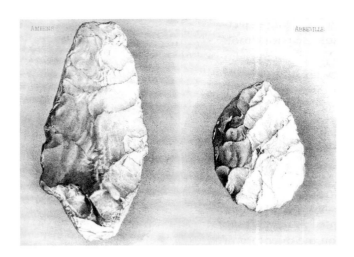

FIGURE 2.5 This lithographic print of handaxes collected by Boucher de Perthes was published in 1880

The French zoologist Jean Baptiste Lamarck developed an evolutionary framework for the history of life on Earth based on the inheritance of acquired characteristics. Lamarck was not alone. Many scientists were beginning to question a strict acceptance of the biblical chronology of life, which, according to Bishop James Ussher, placed creation at 4004 B.C. Because the early nineteenth century was a period of political struggle between Christianity and materialism, the resistance to evolution was fierce. Theologians objected strenuously to removing divinity from creation and ridiculed the idea that "man descended from the apes."

Beginning in the late 1850s, everything began to change (Grayson 1983). Within a number of years, the evidence for the existence of human remains together with the remains of extinct animals was irrefutable. In 1857, a Neanderthal skull was discovered near Düsseldorf (Germany), providing evidence of a premodern human. In 1859, the publication of Charles Darwin's *On the Origin of Species* put the theory of evolution on new and more solid ground.

The turning point in the recognition of the depth of human antiquity came from the interaction between two very different scientists (Cohen and Hublin 1989). Jacques Boucher de Perthes was a customs officer at Abbeville in northwestern France. Far from the centers of power in Paris and London, Boucher de Perthes wrote a series of idiosyncratic books describing his discovery of tools of human manufacture together with bones of extinct mammoths and rhinoceros in the deep gravel deposits of the Somme Valley (Figure 2.5). Alone, these books had little impact.

Unlike Boucher de Perthes, Charles Lyell was a powerful scientific figure and an authority in the field of geology. In 1859, Lyell visited Boucher de Perthes in Abbeville and became convinced of the authenticity of the association between tools that were clearly produced by humans and the remains of animals that had long been extinct. On the basis of this observation, Lyell concluded that human existence dates far back in geological time. When Lyell, who had been a critic of claims about evidence of early humans, presented his findings to the Royal Academy, the recognition of the depth of human antiquity shifted from a position held by a few mavericks to the consensus of the scientific establishment.

The vast new expanses of time opened up by these discoveries soon led to the division of Thomsen's Stone Age into two periods. In 1865, John Lubbock defined the **Neolithic** (New Stone Age) as the period in which there are polished stone tools and the **Paleolithic** (Old Stone Age) as the period during which humans lived with now-extinct animals. At the same time, excavations in southern France showed that Paleolithic sites included not only stone tools, but also art objects (see Figure 2.6).

■ Imperial Archaeology

The nineteenth century also saw an explosion of exploration in the expanding European empires. Often, this was the work of treasure hunters with little in the way of scruples. An extreme example is Giovanni Belzoni, a circus strongman turned Egyptian explorer. Belzoni writes of moving through a passageway "choked with mummies, and I could not pass without putting my face in contact with that of some decayed Egyptian. . . . I could not avoid being covered with bones, legs, arms

Neolithic The period in which there are polished stone tools. Also called the New Stone Age.

Paleolithic The period in which humans lived with now-extinct animals. Also called the Old Stone Age.

RELIQUÆ AQUITANICÆ.
(DORDOGNE)

B. PL.XXVIII.

FIGURE 2.6 An ivory tusk carved with a depiction of a mammoth from a Paleolithic site in southern France, published by Edouard Lartet and Henry Christy in 1875

and heads rolling from above. . . . The purpose of my researches was to rob the Egyptians of their papyri" (Fagan 1996, 77–78). In other cases, such as Champollion's decipherment of Egyptian hieroglyphs in 1822, the motivations were more scholarly. The German archaeologist Heinrich Schliemann's identification of the site of Hissarlik, Turkey, with Troy of the *Iliad* captured the imagination of the world (see Figure 2.7). Other archaeologists began to dig at the biblical-period foundations of Jerusalem and in the ancient cities of Mesopotamia. In far-flung colonies from Africa to Tasmania, archaeologists were also at work. In many areas, archaeologists created a picture of the "unchanging savage," which supported the racist underpinnings of colonial empires (Trigger 1989).

2.3 Developing Method and Theory

The basic tools of archaeology (including stratigraphic excavation and the quantitative analysis of artifacts) began developing during the early part of the twentieth century. Archaeological theory also began to develop during this period, particularly in the writing of V. Gordon Childe.

■ Stratigraphic Method and Culture History

By the end of the nineteenth century, archaeology was an established and increasingly professional discipline. The professionalization of archaeology saw the emergence of modern methods of excavation and analysis. In Egypt and Palestine, Sir Flinders Petrie pioneered the methods of stratigraphic excavation and seriation (see Figure 2.8). In North America, particular attention was given to the development of culture history through the elaboration of formal schemes for the classification of archaeological sites into culture groups. The resultant methods included the Pecos Classification in the southwestern United States and the Midwestern Taxonomic method. These developments were driven in part by the increasing amount of archaeological activity. In the United States, archaeology carried out under the Depression-era public works acts was a particular stimulus.

Although the focus on defining cultures generated an enormous amount of research, it also began to generate a degree of dissatisfaction. In 1948, Walter Taylor

FIGURE 2.7 Heinrich Schliemann displayed the treasures he recovered at Troy in this striking photo of his wife. Recent scholarship has shown that Schliemann's flair for the sensational often led to misrepresentation of his findings.

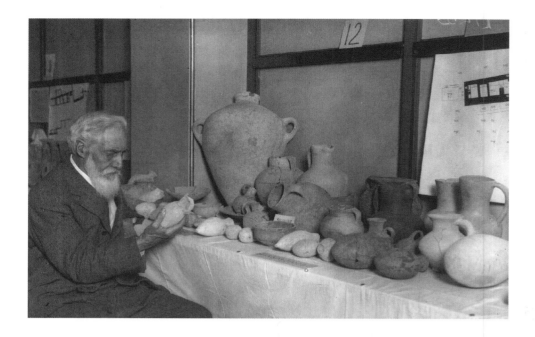

FIGURE 2.8 Flinders Petrie examining pots from an excavation. Petrie was one of the first archaeologists to use stratigraphy to create a chronology.

wrote, "The archaeologist, as archaeologist, is nothing but a technician" (Taylor 1948, 43). While they were focusing on classifying artifacts, archaeologists at times ignored the societies whose remains they were excavating. In some cases, the focus on defining the extent and spread of culture took on a more insidious tone. Gustaf Kossinna used a culture history approach to reinforce German nationalism, and his work became central to the ideology of Nazi Germany (Arnold 1990).

■ V. Gordon Childe

Although his only excavation was of a small village in Orkney, V. Gordon Childe is a towering figure in the history of archaeology (Harris 1994). Childe, shown in Figure 2.9, was born in Australia, but he lived most of his life in England. His early work was firmly within a culture history framework. He was aided in this work by what is said to have been a near-photographic memory. A powerful visual memory allowed him to make comparisons and recognize patterning in the archaeological collections across Europe.

FIGURE 2.9 V. Gordon Childe

In his later work, Childe went beyond mapping cultures to asking fundamental questions about the nature of prehistory. Archaeology showed him that across the globe, societies have undergone two revolutions. The first was the Neolithic Revolution, which led to the emergence of settled villages practicing agriculture. The second was the urban revolution, which led to the appearance of cities and complex forms of government. We can compare Childe's ideas with Thomsen's Three-Age system discussed earlier. Thomsen focused on the classification of objects and thus created major periods—the Stone Age, Bronze Age, and Iron Age. Similarly, Lubbock split the Stone Age into the Paleolithic and Neolithic. Childe shifted the focus from artifacts to societies of people living in a network of social and economic relations. The great changes we see in the archaeological record, Childe held, are evidence of changes in society because the material aspects of culture are intimately connected to social and economic relations. Thus, for Childe, the presence of bronze artifacts presupposes a society that was able to gain access to tin and copper and that could support specialists with the skills necessary to practice metallurgy.

Childe was a committed and politically active Marxist. In his writing, he stressed the social organization of production and revolutionary change in human societies. His ideas were influenced by his contacts with Soviet archaeologists and also drew heavily on the U.S. ethnographer Lewis Henry Morgan.

2.4 Archaeology as Science

Childe's work is significant in that he pushed archaeology away from defining itself in terms of the recovery and classification of artifacts and toward a focus on the study of ancient societies. This is a significant shift, and it has resulted in ongoing debates about how archaeology can go beyond describing objects to explore past societies.

■ Developing Scientific Methods

Beginning in 1949, the Cambridge-based archaeologist Graham Clark brought together botanists, zoologists, and archaeologists to excavate Star Carr, a prehistoric hunter-gatherer site in East Yorkshire, England. Because the site is waterlogged, many artifacts not usually found on archaeological sites, such as wood, are well preserved. Clark opened wide excavation areas at Star Carr, with the explicit goal of gaining insight into the subsistence practices of late prehistoric hunters. The term *subsistence* refers to the activities involved in procuring and processing food. Clark's student Eric Higgs extended Clark's emphasis on economy. Indeed, Higgs took the position that archaeology should concern itself only with economy. Higgs also pioneered methods for recovering botanical remains from archaeological sites.

Similar developments took place in the United States, stimulated by the work of the ecological anthropologist Julian Steward, who explored the relationship between nature and culture and developed the school of thought known as cultural ecology. In 1946, Gordon Willey carried out a pioneering survey project in the Virú Valley of Peru. The importance of this survey is that its goal was to gather evidence of settlement patterning that would provide information relevant to social organization.

Alongside the development of methodologies for the archaeology of economy and society found in the work of Clark and Willey, a number of archaeologists began to develop and stress the importance of statistical methods for archaeology. A.C. Spaulding argued, on the basis of pottery studies in the Lower Mississippi Valley and the southwestern United States, that archaeologists should not impose categories on material culture, but rather should discover clustering through statistical analysis of attributes. One of the important aspects of Spaulding's position is that he was championing a statistical method not because it was better for building chronologies—the goal of the culture history approach—but because his methods were necessary to explore how societies changed through time.

■ The New Archaeology

The rumblings of discontent with the culture history approach could be heard as early as 1948, with the publication of Walter Taylor's *A Study of Archaeology*. At the

New Archaeology (or **processual archaeology**) An approach to archaeology based firmly on scientific method and supported by a concerted effort aimed at the development of theory.

induction Drawing general inferences on the basis of available empirical data.

deduction Drawing particular inferences from general laws and models.

same time, Clark and Willey were working to develop scientific methods for the study of the economy and organization of ancient societies, and Spaulding was urging the adoption of statistical methods. One can easily imagine these trends causing a gradual eclipse of culture history by an increasingly sophisticated social and economic archaeology—but that is not what happened.

Rather than a gradual transition, what took place in the 1960s was a fierce confrontation initiated by a group of young archaeologists calling their approach the **New Archaeology** or **processual archaeology**. The catalyst in this movement was Lewis Binford. In a series of fiercely polemical articles, Binford pronounced that archaeology should be a science or it should be nothing at all. Clearly, he did not view the work of traditional archaeologists as science. Why was the debate so heated? Perhaps its tone was an extension of the excitement and vitality of campus life in 1960s America. Perhaps it was the sense that traditional archaeologists had a stranglehold on the field that could be loosened only by confrontation. It is clear that the tone of the debate reflected the fact that radically new ideas were being brought into archaeology. The New Archaeologists were the first to argue that the central problem of the field was not the need for more data or even better methods; rather, they questioned the way archaeologists could know the past. This is essentially an intellectual, or, as it has come to be known, a theoretical, problem.

Binford was an ideal ringleader for a gang of intellectual revolutionaries. A tireless master at the cut and thrust of debate (and not shy about drawing blood), he carried out wide-ranging research from the midwestern United States to the Arctic.

Binford set out a fundamental problem facing archaeologists. Their interest is the *dynamics* of past societies, but what they have to study are the *static* objects recovered in an excavation or a survey. Archaeologists tend to work by **induction**, drawing inferences on the basis of available data. James Deetz has described induction as "the archaeologist providing the flesh for the bare bones of his data" (quoted in Binford and Binford 1968, 17). Drawing on the work of the philosopher of science Carl Hempel, Binford saw induction as dangerously naïve. For archaeology to be a science, he believed, it must work by **deduction** from general laws and models. The fundamental methodology of archaeology should be testing hypotheses. This stress on hypothesis testing, which was meant to ally archaeology with the hard sciences such as physics, created a breach between the New Archaeologists and the rest of the discipline.

The excitement of the New Archaeology flowed from the argument that archaeologists were not limited to describing the archaeological record. Theory and method have the potential to enable archaeological research to extend into all realms of past societies. Binford (1968) expressed this potential when he wrote that "facts do not speak for themselves . . . data [will] tell us nothing about cultural process or past lifeways unless we [ask] the appropriate questions" (13).

The key to the optimism of the New Archaeologists was the linkage they made between material remains and other aspects of society (Watson, LeBlanc, and Redman 1984). To Binford, it was inconceivable that any cultural item functioned independently of nonmaterial aspects of society. Thus, the potential scope of archaeologists' knowledge of past societies would be almost limitless. Paradoxically, processual archaeology often involved an extremely reductive view of culture. In Binford's (1965) famous formulation, "Culture is man's extrosomatic [i.e., external to the body] means of adapting to the environment" (203). What is striking is that, in Binford's view, all aspects of symbolic behavior are relegated to insignificance.

As archaeological theory matured, the insistence of the New Archaeologists on strict adherence to hypothesis testing and their rejection of induction tended to moderate. This trend was strongly influenced by the work of Alison Wylie, who showed through careful analysis that all archaeologists have to use induction at some points in their research. By 1984, Patty Jo Watson, Steven LeBlanc, and Charles Redman, important proponents of the New Archaeology, recognized that archaeological research involves a "to-and-fro" between induction and deduction (Watson, LeBlanc, and Redman 1984, 60). Quoting Kent Flannery, who states that the New Archaeologists "assume that truth is just the best current hypothesis, and that whatever they believe now will ultimately be proved wrong" (Flannery 1967, 122), Watson, LeBlanc, and Redman stressed that the New Archaeology adopted a scientific approach to truth.

Because the search for covering laws in archaeology yielded at best only modest results, Binford returned to his initial question about how we can know about processes that took place in the past. In the absence of covering laws, Binford emphasized the importance of **middle-range research**, which allows us to make secure statements about past dynamics on the basis of observations made on archaeological material. The key to middle-range research is to look at processes that we can observe in the present and analyze the material patterning left by those processes. We can then develop hypotheses about the past that can be tested by reference to our observations in the present. As an example, Binford carried out a project in which he fed bones to hyenas and recorded the patterns of breakage and the markings on the bones. He could then compare these patterns with those found on early human sites to test the hypothesis that these sites were produced partially by carnivore activity.

■ Systems Theory

One direction pursued by the New Archaeologists is the application of **systems theory** to the study of past societies. A system is an interconnected network of elements that together form a whole. A classic example of a system is the combination of a thermostat and the furnace in a house. The ambient temperature affects the thermostat, which turns the furnace on and off. The heat of the furnace raises the temperature in the house, which in turn causes the thermostat to turn off the furnace. The thermostat and furnace together control the temperature through feedback within the system. When you set the temperature in your house, this system works to produce a steady state. Archaeologists argued that societies can be viewed as systems that normally operate at such a steady state. David Clarke and Kent Flannery were among those who went to great lengths to try to formalize the elements of archaeological systems. One attraction of the systems approach is that it made it possible to investigate periods of rapid change in the archaeological record in terms of feedback among elements of a complex system. As a result, change could be understood as the effect of internal processes—processes that took place within society. Although today formal systems theory plays a minor role in archaeology, the recognition of both the complexity of social systems and the interrelation of various aspects of the archaeological record is of critical importance. Systems theory has been particularly valuable in giving archaeologists tools to integrate evidence of ecological change into models of social change.

■ Cultural Resource Management

The development of the New Archaeology overlapped with changes in legislation that led to a significant increase in public archaeology and the emergence of cultural resource management (CRM; see Figure 2.10). Legislation protecting heritage sites dates back to the Antiquities Act of 1906, which states that the U.S. government has the responsibility to protect historic and prehistoric sites on land that it owns.

middle-range research Research investigating processes that can be observed in the present and that can serve as a point of reference to test hypotheses about the past.

systems theory An archaeological theory that views society as an interconnected network of interacting elements.

FIGURE 2.10 A modern salvage excavation in London. Note the context on a construction site and the combination of heavy equipment with more traditional recovery methods.

National Historic Preservation Act (NHPA), Section 106 The legislation that regulates cultural resource management archaeology.

However, the enactment of the **National Historic Preservation Act (NHPA)** in 1966, followed by a series of amendments to this act through the 1970s, marks a significant shift in policy. **Section 106** of the NHPA states, "The head of any Federal agency having direct or indirect jurisdiction over a proposed Federal or federally assisted undertaking . . . shall . . . take into account the effect of the undertaking on any district, site, building, structure, or object that is included in or eligible for inclusion in the National Register." Although this sounds like a limited mandate, the repercussions have transformed the practice of archaeology in the United States. Because almost all major construction projects involve some level of federal funding or licensing, Section 106 applies very broadly. The precise guidelines for compliance with Section 106 are set out in Title 36, Part 800 of the Code of Federal Regulations (C.F.R.). This regulation sets out the basis for the process followed by CRM archaeologists "to identify historic properties potentially affected by [development], assess its effects and seek ways to avoid, minimize or mitigate any adverse effects on historic properties" (36 C.F.R. § 800.1). Section 106 applies to all sites with potential to "yield information significant in prehistory or history" (36 C.F.R. § 800.1). Although CRM archaeology is based on federal legislation, enactment of Section 106 is regulated by State Historical Protection Offices (SHPOs) or, on tribal lands, by Tribal Historical Protection Offices (THPOs). In addition to Section 106, municipal or state legislation can further regulate the impact of development on archaeological sites. In recent years, the terms of Section 106 have shifted to place increased emphasis on consultation with local communities.

2.5 Alternative Perspectives

Lewis Binford proclaimed that archaeology should be a science based on deduction and hypothesis testing. The New Archaeologists worked to create the guidelines for an explicitly scientific approach to archaeology—what has come to be known as processual archaeology—an approach strongly associated with systems theory and with an emphasis on ecology. Although the emphasis on pure deduction was gradually toned down and the search for general laws was replaced by middle-range

TOOLBOX

Faunal Analysis and Taphonomy

Faunal analysts (also known as zooarchaeologists or archaeozoologists) study animal bones found on archaeological sites. The fundamental skill needed to practice faunal analysis is the ability to recognize the species of animal from the scraps of bone that survive in the archaeological record. Comparative collections of skeletons of modern animals are an essential tool in developing this skill and for confirming identification. But the work of the faunal analyst goes far beyond the technical demands of species recognition, or even the more complex tasks of identifying the age and sex of an individual. Faunal analysts bridge zoology and archaeology and seek to understand the interaction between humans and animals through prehistory.

Understanding the processes that have shaped the collections of bones recovered on archaeological sites is a critical first step in any faunal analysis. Taphonomy is the study of postdepositional processes that shape the archaeological assemblage. In many cases, determining whether humans were actually responsible for the accumulation of bones is a central concern, and taphonomy leads faunal analysts to a close consideration of the activities of scavengers such as hyenas. Excavating hyena dens, while an unpleasant and often smelly undertaking, can provide critical tools to evaluate faunal assemblages. Taphonomy can also contribute to understanding how carcasses were processed.

Faunal analysts have also been at the forefront of developing excavation methods that ensure complete recovery of an unbiased sample. These accomplishments are often remarkable. On some coastal sites, it has been possible to track the seasonality of human occupation by analyzing the ear stones, or otoliths, of fish that are less than 1 centimeter in length. Faunal analysts combine meticulous recovery and detailed observation with a knowledge of animal biology and behavior to provide critical insight into the archaeological record. ●

ADDITIONAL READING: Simon J. M. Davis. 1987. *The Archaeology of Animals*. New Haven, CT: Yale University Press. Elizabeth Jean Reitz and Elizabeth S. Wing. 1999. *Zooarchaeology*. Cambridge: Cambridge University Press.

FIGURE 2.11 Cleaning the upper canine tooth of a bear, discovered at the Lower Paleolithic site of Isernia de la Pineta, Italy

research, the basic premises of processual archaeology remained largely unchallenged until the mid-1980s, by which time processual archaeology had become the dominant approach to archaeological theory in the United States. Indeed, processual archaeology strongly influenced the development of CRM.

■ Postprocessual Archaeology

The central argument of processual archaeology is that archaeology should be a science, a discipline that emulates the hard sciences such as physics. The only apparent alternative to processual archaeology was culture history based on naïve induction. It took over 20 years for processual archaeology to be effectively challenged. The challenge came from British archaeologists led by Ian Hodder in a movement that came to be known as **postprocessual archaeology**. Hodder's challenge to Binford went to the core of processual archaeology. Why, Hodder asked, should archaeologists not choose to emulate historians rather than physicists? Perhaps archaeology is more similar to reading a text than carrying out an experiment. After all, is a science based on predicting the outcome of experiments appropriate to the study of processes that took place in the past? How can archaeologists ever replicate their results, as is expected of a laboratory scientist?

Hodder was not arguing for naïve induction or advocating a return to culture history. To parry Binford's reliance on the philosopher of science Hempel, Hodder drew on the theoretical writing of historians such as R.G. Collingwood, who espoused the idea that it is necessary for the historian to get at the "inside" of events. The historian should try to understand the past from the perspective of the people who lived through those events.

Binford had defined culture as a means of adaptation and had argued that there is no need to understand how the people themselves viewed their own culture. Following Binford, one can adopt an external approach—what anthropologists term an **etic** approach—and still get at a true understanding of the society. Hodder argued that culture must be understood as the result of the meaningful and purposeful actions of people and that only an internal understanding of these meanings—what anthropologists call an **emic** approach—produces a real knowledge of the past.

The strength of Hodder's position is readily apparent. Clearly, we all experience the world as meaningful and would have a difficult time thinking of the way we live as our "extrasomatic means of adaptation." Should we not assume that this was the case for people who lived in the past? Some cultural anthropologists have argued persuasively for an etic approach to living societies. For example, Marvin Harris has studied the taboo on eating cattle in Hindu societies and has argued that the emic understanding of this taboo in religious terms hides the fact that the taboo actually serves an important ecological function. However, Harris is certainly in the minority among people who study living societies.

The problem faced by archaeologists who embrace Hodder's position is that archaeologists do not work with living societies. Archaeologists cannot simply ask their informants what something means. To meet this challenge, Hodder emphasized the importance of context in providing clues to understanding the meaning of artifacts. As he writes, "As soon as the context of an object is known it is no longer totally mute" (Hodder 1986, 4). Where objects are found and what they are found with provide the basis for making interpretations about their meaning. To use a very simple example, if a type of object is found only in a tomb setting, this fact tells us something about the object's meaning.

But even allowing for the use of context, it is hard to see how one could try to "work from the inside" and still meet the New Archaeologists' criteria for scientifically valid deductive research. Not surprisingly, Hodder dismissed the position that the deductive method is the appropriate framework for archaeological research.

The goal of postprocessual archaeology is not to test hypotheses, but rather to offer interpretations based on contextual data. Some have argued that this means that "anything goes" and that all interpretations are equally valid. Unlike processual archaeology, which ultimately holds that proper scientific procedure will lead archaeologists to the truth about the past, postprocessual archaeology argues that the process of interpretation is ongoing. This does not, however, mean that all

postprocessual archaeology
A movement, led by British archaeologist Ian Hodder, that argues archaeologists should emulate historians in interpreting the past.

etic An approach to archaeological or anthropological analysis that does not attempt to adopt the perspective of the members of the culture that is being studied.

emic An approach to archaeological or anthropological analysis that attempts to understand the meanings people attach to their actions and culture.

hermeneutics A theory of interpretation that stresses the interaction between the presuppositions we bring to a problem and the independent empirical reality of our observations and experiences.

interpretations are equally valid. For example, our legal system is based on the ability of a judge or a jury to reach a consensual interpretation of events. Clearly, we care very much that these interpretations are sound and well grounded.

The analogy to a jury trial is useful in introducing the concept of **hermeneutics**, which is critical to the way that Hodder views archaeology. When a jury renders its verdict, there is a degree of finality to the decision. However, the verdict is not necessarily the end of the interpretation of the past events examined in the trial; such interpretation can continue in the courts if new evidence is found or out of the courts in the investigations of reporters and historians. Hermeneutics is a theory of interpretation that stresses the interaction between the presuppositions we bring to a problem and the independent empirical reality of our observations and experiences. Rather than coming to an archaeological situation with a hypothesis, in following a hermeneutic approach we come with preexisting knowledge and questions. Hermeneutic interpretation is an open-ended cycle of continual inquiry. Because this process results in an understanding that is continuously enriched through a confrontation with empirical reality, it is often depicted as a spiral—a process through which we arrive at a deeper understanding of the past (see Figure 2.12).

Postprocessual archaeologists have also taken the lead in seriously considering the position of archaeology in modern society and contemporary politics (Figure 2.13). If interpretation is the continuous confrontation of presuppositions with empirical reality, then how we arrive at our presuppositions about the past becomes far more important than it would be in a processual archaeological approach. With their stress on a pure scientific method, the New Archaeologists could do little but urge their followers to do their best to separate politics from archaeology. Postprocessual archaeologists have embraced the idea that archaeology is an activity that

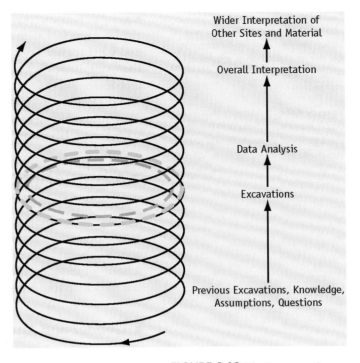

FIGURE 2.12 The hermeneutic spiral represents a process of continually refining knowledge through an ongoing process of confronting preexisting knowledge with new information

FIGURE 2.13 President Evo Morales Ayma of Bolivia giving a speech at his reelection ceremony at the start of his second term in the ruins of Tiwanaku. Why do you think he chose this site for his speech?

feminist archaeology An approach that focuses on the way archaeologists study and represent gender and that brings attention to gender inequities in the practice of archaeology.

agency theory A theory that emphasizes the interaction between the agency of individuals and social structure.

takes place in the present and that the archaeologist is a person working in a particular historical setting. In two books published in the late 1980s, Michael Shanks and Christopher Tilley went as far as to deny that archaeologists could ever do more than simply project the present onto the past and to assert that the major role of archaeology is to legitimate the modern political order (see Shanks and Tilley 1987a, 1987b). Although most of those in the field reject this argument, Shanks and Tilley were instrumental in spurring archaeologists to look critically at the history of the science in relation to factors such as colonialism, nationalism, and racism.

2.6 Branching Out

The struggle between processual and postprocessual archaeology shaped how archaeologists think about the past, as well as the process of learning about the past. However, archaeological theory today is characterized by an exciting diversity of approaches and has moved well beyond a simple dichotomy between these two schools of thought. What holds archaeological theory together is the shared sense of the relevance importance of the archaeological study of the past.

■ Gender and Agency

Feminist archaeology and agency theory are two approaches that have developed out of postprocessual archaeology. **Feminist archaeology** has brought new attention both to the way that archaeologists study and represent gender and to gender inequities in the practice of archaeology (Gero and Conkey 1991; see Figure 2.14). Archaeologists have had a tendency to treat society as homogeneous. Feminist archaeologists have drawn on studies by sociocultural anthropologists to show that the experience of individuals is shaped by their role in society. The challenge to archaeologists is how to study gender with the tools of archaeology. Studies focusing on identifying gender differences have looked at a wide range of topics, including stone tool production, textiles, and plant food processing. The difficulty is that identifying gender in these realms can be elusive. In cultures with written documents or art showing people at work, it has been possible to combine the information contained therein with archaeology to reach significant conclusions about gender in ancient societies. Studies of skeletal remains have also produced important insights into the relation between gender and other factors, such as diet, activity, and burial practices.

Feminist archaeology has also brought attention to the way that archaeologists represent gender. The invisibility of gender in archaeology has often masked a strong bias toward viewing men as the active and productive agents of change and women as passive "fellow travelers." One humorous example is found in the rather implausible title of one of Childe's books: *Man Makes Himself.* Feminist archaeologists have done important work identifying the pervasiveness of gender bias in archaeology and offering alternative images. In a number of intriguing studies, feminist archaeologists have used fiction as a way to bring attention to the active role of women in society (Spector 1991). Feminist archaeologists have made an important contribution by demonstrating that societies are not uniform. Archaeologists working with agency theory have taken this idea further by arguing that the basic unit of archaeology is not society, but individuals living in society (Dobres and Robb 2000). Based on the theory of practice developed by the sociologists Pierre Bourdieu and Anthony Giddens, **agency theory** emphasizes the agency of

FIGURE 2.14 Dorothy Garrod directed major Paleolithic excavations in Europe and the Middle East and was the first woman to hold the position of professor at Cambridge University

TOOLBOX

Archaeoacoustics

It is hard to imagine a world without sound, but archaeologists often feel limited to the visual and tactile aspects of culture. The discovery of bone flutes from the Upper Paleolithic of Germany (see Chapter 5) and the Neolithic of China (see Chapter 9) has drawn attention to the central importance of music in human experience. However, a small group of archaeologists has cast a far wider net. Researchers in the emerging field of archaeoacoustics aim to explore the archaeological record to understand the role of sound in human behavior (Scarre and Lawson 2006). Archaeoacoustics is one element of an "archaeology of the senses" that has developed out of postprocessual archaeology. Some of the first studies of ancient music focused on the lur, a wind instrument from the Scandinavian Bronze Age. Already in the 1960s John Coles (1979) was carrying out experiments to determine how this instrument would have sounded. More recent studies in archaeoacoustics include analysis of Mesoamerican hieroglyphic signs relating to sound (Houston and Taube 2000), studies of the acoustic properties of the ceremonial center of Chavín de Huántar in Peru (Burger 1992; see p. 386, in Chapter 14), and examination of the placement of rock art in relation to places with acoustic resonance (Waller 2006). One of the most interesting acoustic phenomena uncovered by archaeologists is the association of rock art with "rock gongs" found in both South Africa and India. These are rocks that produce a clear tone when struck (Boivin 2004; Parkington, Morris, and Rusch 2008). In the case of rock gongs, there is little question that people were drawn to a location for its aural qualities. One can clearly see the places where the rocks have been struck, and when this action is repeated, it produces a clear tone. In other cases, the connection between the acoustics of a place and the actions of people in the past is more tenuous, and the archaeologist has to take great care in drawing inferences about how sound shaped behavior. However, as Chris Scarre notes, "the study of archaeoacoustics has much to offer, and has scarcely begun" (Scarre and Lawson 2006, 9). ●

ADDITIONAL READING: Christopher Scarre and Graeme Lawson. 2006. *Archaeoacoustics*. McDonald Institute Monographs. Cambridge: Cambridge University Press.

FIGURE 2.15 Acoustics are critical at sites of public performance such as the Greek theater at Epidauros that is shown here. Archaeologists are beginning to explore acoustics in a broad range of contexts.

individuals—the purposeful actions of the people who lived in the past. Agency theory is a constant balancing act between the recognition that history consists of the choices and actions of individuals and an awareness that the choices people make are strongly shaped by structure, the social world, and material conditions in which they live.

Archaeologists working from a foundation of agency theory have tackled a wide range of topics. One of the most interesting directions this research has taken

Why Do I "Do" Archaeology?

JOE WATKINS, UNIVERSITY OF OKLAHOMA

Many of you who read this book will wonder how an American Indian became an archaeologist. Initially, I wanted to be a paleontologist and work in China with Roy Chapman Andrews, digging up dinosaur egg nests. One fateful day when I was 10 years old, I was walking with my Choctaw grandmother, and I found a projectile point made of milky quartz that was about 6,000 years old. My grandmother spoke at the most a hundred words of English, and I spoke fewer than a hundred words of Choctaw. I showed her the projectile point, and she told me, with the help of my cousin who translated, that it represented the unwritten history of the people who had lived there before the Choctaw were moved into Oklahoma. She said that, even though it wasn't our history, it was important that we save that unwritten history for the sake of our ancestors and for the descendants of the people who would come after us.

From then on, I was interested in finding ways of connecting the people from the past to those who are alive today. Archaeology has allowed me not only to maintain that connection between the past and the present, but also to cement my connections with the generations that lived in southeastern Oklahoma thousands of years ago.

I have been involved in all facets of archaeology. I have excavated sites in Oklahoma, Texas, and New Mexico, as well as in Europe. I have worked for the federal government recording sites in danger of being lost due to erosion and neglect. I have trudged ahead of a bulldozer, building fire lines during a forest fire in the Black Hills of South Dakota.

I currently teach at the University of Oklahoma, and now I'm more interested in how archaeology affects indigenous populations—the descendants of the people who left behind the sites archaeologists excavate and study. My research takes me to far-off places such as Australia, New Zealand, and Sweden and to some not-so-distant locations like Taos, Oklahoma, and Georgia. In these places, the people who have ties to the archaeological past do not necessarily control the land where those sites are located.

There are often conflicts between archaeologists and the descendants of the people they study. Many descendant populations are concerned about archaeologists digging up the graves of people of the past and placing them in museums or in storage. Archaeologists are not as likely to dig

is in reconsidering the nature of the landscape. By putting people at the center of the landscape, agency theorists have led archaeologists to investigate how ancient monuments were experienced by the people who built them and lived with them (Thomas 1996). Adopting an agency perspective also pushes archaeologists to look for particular variations in material culture that might express the actions of the individual. For example, in a detailed study of Mimbres pottery from the American Southwest (A.D. 1000–1300), Michelle Hegmon and Stephanie Kulow (2005) view the act of painting a design as agency and the overall style of the design as a form of structure. Potters work within a style, while expressing their individual agency in their painting. However, agency is not expressed only through personal style or deviation from social norms. Rosemary Joyce (Joyce and Lopiparo 2005) has pointed out that agency also involves recapitulating valued practices of the past and thus is responsible for the maintenance of tradition, as well as the development of innovation.

More recently archaeologists have begun to draw on queer theory to provide a theoretical perspective on difference among members of ancient societies (Geller 2009). The shift toward queer theory is linked to the political struggle for LGBT rights. On a practical level it is important for the archaeological community to recognize and work to combat the barriers that LGBT people face, particularly in archaeological field training (see From the Field, Chapter 13, p. 370). At a theoretical level there is a tension between the emphasis in earlier gender research to find up people's graves as they were in the past, and chief among the reasons for this is that people have complained about such actions. Researchers today are more aware of the ways their study of past peoples affects existing populations.

I do archaeology because it helps me connect with the people who lived in the past and with those who live today. It helps me understand the ways we are tied to those who have lived and died throughout written and unwritten history. Archaeology has given me a depth of experience that mere written history cannot, as well as the desire not only to learn more, but also to share what I have learned with those around me. I am an archaeologist, and I am an American Indian. While there might still be times when I am in conflict about being both, there is rarely a time when I am disappointed that I have chosen this field. And when I do question why I became an archaeologist, I remember my grandmother's words. ▲

evidence of women in the archaeological record and the growing sense that "binaries, such as male/female, man/woman, and gay/straight, simply do not make sense in other cultural contexts" (Aimers and Rutecki 2016, 13).

■ Evolutionary Archaeology

Evolutionary archaeology was developed by processual archaeologists who stress the importance of evolutionary theory as a potential unifying theory. Robert Dunnell pioneered this approach in his studies of archaeological systematics. In recent years, evolutionary archaeology has come to encompass a range of approaches, from ecological studies that look at changes in culture as changes in human adaptation to attempts to apply Darwinian theory to changes in the frequencies and types of artifacts found at a site (O'Brien and Lyman 2002).

In recent years there has been a growing drive to integrate an evolutionary perspective into medical practice and efforts to improve health and well-being (Stearns 2012). The Paleo diet craze has grown out of a popular sense that there is a mismatch between the ecological and adaptive contexts in which humans evolved and the way we live today. Although some of the more commercial incarnations of the Paleo diet are best thought of as "paleofantasies" (wrapped prepared snacks were definitely not a component of the early hominin landscape!) the question of mismatches has spurred a renewed interest in the archaeological study of nutrition and

evolutionary archaeology
A range of approaches that stress the importance of evolutionary theory as a unifying theory for archaeology.

biomechanics (Zuk 2013). The study of ancient DNA opens the potential to study how genetic variation in modern populations, including variable susceptibility to disease, is the legacy of diverse past cultural practices.

■ Niche Construction and the Anthropocene

As we come to terms with the threat posed by accelerated global warming, questions about the way in which humans have shaped the global ecosystem have great urgency. Some archaeologists and geologists suggest that we should recognize the modern era as a distinct geological epoch known as the Anthropocene. The Anthropocene is marked by "rapid global dissemination of novel materials including elemental aluminum, concrete, and plastics" and also the by-products of fossil fuel combustion, including "black carbon, inorganic ash spheres, and spherical carbonaceous particles" (Waters et al. 2016). While some argue for a rapid onset of the Anthropocene as recently as the 1950s, also known as "the great acceleration," archaeologists have tended to take a longer view of the Anthropocene, stretching back as far as the spread of modern humans and the extinction of megafauna approximately 50,000 years ago (Braje 2016).

Evolutionary archaeologists are engaged in exploring the relevance of niche construction theory, which emphasizes the active role of organisms. From the perspective of niche construction theory, "the selective environments of organisms are themselves partly built by the niche construction activities of organisms" (Laland and O'Brien 2010, 304). Humans adapt to an environment that they themselves influence. This insight is reshaping the way that archaeologists approach questions as varied as the origins of agriculture and the development of wealth and inequality.

2.7 Archaeology at the Trowel's Edge

Along with the growth and diversification of archaeological theory has come a sense of a disconnection between the way archaeologists write about their discipline and what they actually do. Ian Hodder (1999) has proposed that we change archaeological theory from a top-down approach to one that begins "at the edge of the trowel" (92). Drawing on the theory of hermeneutics, Hodder argues that archaeological theory should build on what archaeologists *actually* do rather than prescribing what they *should* do.

Archaeology has developed from the simple recognition of the extent of the human past to a discipline that involves intense debate about how we gain knowledge of the past. Archaeology today has a rich theoretical "tool kit"—a diversity of approaches that can be used to think about the past. This diversification of approaches has led to confusion, confrontation, and, at times, a degree of despair. Alison Wylie (1989) has given us a beautiful image comparing archaeology to sailing, wherein one tacks back and forth in the wind in order to make progress. Our subject matter is over 2 million years of human experience. Our evidence is all of the physical remains of that experience. Given the immensity of the venture, we are really in a very small boat on an enormous ocean. The ability to maneuver between approaches may be just what is needed in such a voyage.

SUMMARY

- The earliest use of archaeology to learn about the past was in Renaissance Europe. However, until the nineteenth century, there were no methods for determining the age of prehistoric artifacts, and in many cases, the human manufacture of artifacts was not recognized.

- The development of the Three-Age system of Stone, Bronze, and Iron Ages was a major accomplishment of nineteenth-century archaeologists.
- The recognition that tools of human manufacture were found in the same layers as the bones of extinct animals, together with the development of the theory of evolution, changed the scope of archaeological research.
- The professionalization of archaeology during the early part of the twentieth century led to a focus on culture history and stratigraphic method.
- V. Gordon Childe shifted the focus of archaeologists from changes in the material remains recovered on archaeological sites to what those remains told us about ancient and prehistoric societies.
- The New Archaeologists, also known as processual archaeologists, led by Lewis Binford, argue that archaeologists should follow an explicitly scientific method of testing hypotheses.
- One of the approaches widely used by the New Archaeologists is systems theory.
- The postprocessual archaeologists, led by Ian Hodder, argue that archaeology is closer to history than to the exact sciences. The postprocessualists emphasize the role of interpretation and context in archaeological research.
- Gender and agency theory are two of the approaches used by postprocessual archaeologists.

KEY TERMS

agency theory, 50
archaeological theory, 36
deduction, 44
emic, 48
etic, 48
evolutionary archaeology, 53
feminist archaeology, 50
hermeneutics, 48
induction, 44
middle-range research, 45

National Historic Preservation Act (NHPA),
     Section 106, 46
Neolithic, 40
New Archaeology/processual archaeology, 44
Paleolithic, 40
postprocessual archaeology, 48
systems theory, 45
Three-Age system, 39
thunderstones, 37

REVIEW QUESTIONS

1. What kind of impact do you think the establishment of human antiquity has had on the way we think about humanity?
2. Do you agree with the New Archaeologists' stress on the importance of scientific method in archaeology?
3. How does the regulation derived from Section 106 of the NHPA shape the process of CRM archaeological research described in Chapter 1?
4. What are the critiques raised by the postprocessualists? Do you think these critiques are valid?

PART TWO

HUMAN EVOLUTION

The study of human evolution draws insight from a multitude of disciplines, including paleontology, genetics, the reconstruction of past climates, and archaeology. This section of the book synthesizes the current state of research in human evolution with a strong emphasis on the unique perspective provided by archaeology. Particular topics are the timing of hominin dispersals and changes in adaptation and technology. After reading this introduction, you should understand:

- The place of humans in biological classification.
- The genetic evidence for the timing of the split between the human and chimpanzee lineages.
- The fossil record of hominoid phylogeny.

Introduction: Our Place in Nature

Charles Darwin is an odd choice for a hero. Plagued by everything from boils to self-doubt, he hardly fits the picture of a revolutionary figure. However, the theory of evolution developed in Darwin's *On the Origin of Species* is among the cornerstones of modern science. Almost all of Darwin's ideas were based on what he was able to observe on his voyage around the world on the *Beagle* and on walks around his country home in England. Darwin was obsessed with the question of how one explains the incredible variation in the living world. The theory of evolution begins with the observation that there is significant variety within populations. Whether one is looking at a bed of roses, a flock of pigeons, or a room of people, such variation exists. Darwin suggested that, if some variations offered advantages to survival, they might come to be prevalent. Drawing on an analogy to the way humans breed domesticated animals for certain traits, he proposed that natural selection would act on the variation within populations to favor organisms with traits that were adaptive. Over vast periods of time, natural selection in different settings would lead to the splitting of populations into distinct species. Darwin's conception of evolution derives much of its power from its simplicity. According to Darwin, the action of selection on variation over very long periods of time explains the spectacular variety of life on earth. Thus, the emergence of new species need not be explained by an appeal to metaphysics, but rather could be rendered intelligible through a detailed understanding of shifts in environments and adaptation over time.

In *On the Origin of Species*, Darwin wrote little about human evolution. Only at the end of the concluding chapter did he write that, on the basis of his theory, "light will be thrown on the origin of man and his history" (Darwin 1859). The theory of evolution is not a formulation that provides ultimate answers; rather, it is a doorway to an endlessly fascinating exploration of humanity and the natural world. The next four chapters examine what we have learned in the last 150 years about the evolutionary history of humans.

■ Phylogeny

Before turning to a consideration of human evolution, it is necessary to define some of the fundamental aspects of biological terminology and to situate humans within an evolutionary framework. The basic unit of biological classification is the **species**, which is defined as a group of organisms that can produce fertile offspring. A genus (plural *genera*) refers to a grouping of similar species. All living humans are members of the species *Homo sapiens*, which belongs to genus *Homo*. Similar genera are grouped into families and superfamilies, and similar families are grouped into orders. Humans, the great apes (orangutans, gorillas, and chimpanzees), and gibbons make up the biological superfamily Hominoidea, or the **hominoids**. Together with monkeys and prosimians (lemurs, lorises, tarsiers, and their relatives), the hominoids belong to the order Primates. Most primates are tree-dwelling animals. Primates rely heavily on sight in dealing with the environment and are highly social, with a tendency to live in groups.

TABLE II.1 BIOLOGICAL CLASSIFICATION OF HUMANS

Species	*Homo sapiens*	All living humans
Genus (pl. *genera*)	*Homo*	Humans and immediate ancestors
Superfamily	Hominoidea (hominoids)	Humans, orangutans, gorillas, chimpanzees, and gibbons
Order	Primates	Hominoids, monkeys, and prosimians

species A group of intimately related and physically similar organisms that can produce fertile offspring.

hominoids The biological superfamily that includes humans, great apes, and gibbons.

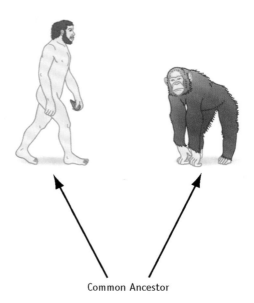

FIGURE II.1 In biological classification, chimpanzees and humans are closely related, reflecting their recent branching from a common ancestor

Common Ancestor

phylogeny The evolutionary history of a species.

ontogeny The growth and development of an individual organism.

Table II.1 gives a biological classification of humans. Biological classifications are not based only on the degree of similarity between species; rather, they are also meant to reflect the branching pattern of evolution. Popular media often misrepresent evolution as a linear process of progress through stages (see Figure II.2). Evolution is actually a process of splitting ancestral populations into distinct lineages. A common example of the popular misconception of evolution is found in the statement, "Humans evolved from apes." The correct statement is that humans and chimpanzees share a common ancestor, as is depicted in Figure II.1.

Reconstructing evolutionary history, or **phylogeny**, is based on a combination of information from fossils and genetics. The nature of the evidence provided by each of these sources differs. Genetic evidence is derived largely from living populations of humans and animals, although in a small number of cases it is possible to recover genetic material from fossils. Genetics provides insight into the evolutionary relationship between living species and the timing of the split between the lineages leading to those species (see Figure II.3). Fossils are the physical remains of prehistoric life. It is only through fossils that we can learn about our now–extinct human ancestors.

■ Genetic Evidence

The path of our growth and development as individuals (called **ontogeny**) is the result of the interaction between genetics and the environment. A copy of the DNA molecules that encode our genetic inheritance is contained in the nucleus of every one of our body cells. This **nuclear DNA** is a combination of genes inherited from each of our parents. **Mitochondrial DNA**, which is located outside of the cell nucleus, differs from nuclear DNA in that it is inherited exclusively from the maternal lineage. The DNA of all living humans is similar, so, genetically, humans are a quite homogeneous species.

FIGURE II.2 This image from Thomas Huxley's book *Evidence as to Man's Place in Nature*, published in 1873, presents a picture of evolution as a linear directional process. This image has had a powerful influence on popular perceptions of evolution.

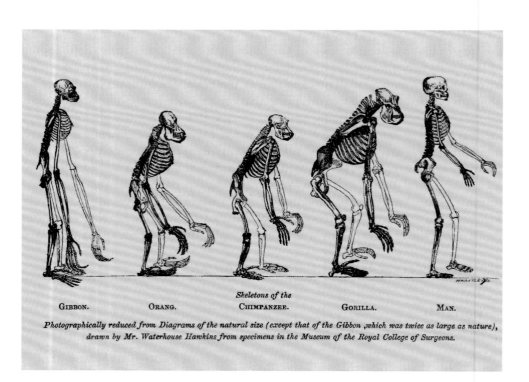

Sheletons of the

GIBBON.   ORANG.   CHIMPANZEE.   GORILLA.   MAN.

Photographically reduced from Diagrams of the natural size (except that of the Gibbon ,which was twice as large as nature), drawn by Mr. Waterhouse Hawkins from specimens in the Museum of the Royal College of Surgeons.

Constructing a phylogeny, or evolutionary history, of the hominoids (humans, great apes, and gibbons) on the basis of genetic evidence involves comparing the degree of genetic similarity between species. Most genetic phylogenies of the hominoids emphasize the high degree of similarity between humans and chimpanzees. Chimpanzees consist of two living species: common chimpanzees (*Pan troglodytes*) and pygmy chimpanzees (*Pan paniscus*). The degree of similarity of humans to gorillas (*Gorilla gorilla*) is only slightly lower than that of humans to chimpanzees. Orangutans (*Pongo pygmeaus*) are genetically less similar to humans than either chimpanzees or gorillas, and gibbons (*Hylobates*) are even more distantly related.

Based on genetic studies a degree of consensus has been reached over the timing of the divergence between the lineages of humans and the great apes (see Figure II.3). The split between the human and chimpanzee lineages is now placed between 4 million and 6 million years before the present. The split between the human and gorilla lineages is said to have taken place 6 million to 8 million years before the present, and that between the human and orangutan lineages is held to be 12 million to 15 million years before the present. However, based on new studies some geneticists are beginning to question this time scale, placing the split between the human and chimpanzee lineage back between 7 and 13 million years ago (Langergraber et al. 2012). These new genetic studies are also beginning to enable geneticists to make inferences about fluctuations over time in population size of the various hominoid lineages (Prado-Martinez et al. 2013).

■ The Fossil Record

Although genetic evidence provides a framework for the timing of the split of the lineages leading to living species, it does not provide information about the extinct species that make up these lineages. **Paleoanthropologists**—scientists specializing in the study of the hominoid lineage—rely on fossils to construct the evolutionary history of humanity. As Darwin recognized in *On the Origin of Species*, the study of the fossil record is like reading a book with many pages missing. Because the preservation and discovery of fossils rely heavily on chance, there are significant gaps in the fossil record. Of course, one of the exciting elements of paleoanthropology is the role new discoveries play in developing knowledge and challenging ideas.

The earliest fossils that appear to be ancestral to the order Primates date to the Cretaceous period, 90 million to 65 million years ago. A particularly important locality for the study of early primates is the Fayum Depression, south of Cairo, Egypt. The rich fossil remains recovered from the Fayum date to the Eocene and Oligocene periods (56 million to 23 million years ago). At that time, the Fayum, which is today a desert, was a marshland inhabited by a wide array of animals. Included in the Fayum assemblage are some of the earliest ancestors of monkeys. *Aegyptopithecus*, a fairly well-represented species from the Fayum, might be ancestral to old-world monkeys and apes.

The **Miocene era** (23 million to 5 million years ago) saw an explosion in the number of hominoid species. During this

nuclear DNA DNA located in the cell nucleus; combines from each parent.

mitochondrial DNA DNA located outside of the cell nucleus; inherited exclusively from the mother.

paleoanthropologist A scientist who studies the evolutionary history of the hominoids.

Aegyptopithecus A fossil primate that lived 56 to 23 million years ago.

Miocene era The period 23 million to 5 million years ago when there was an explosion in the number of hominoid species.

FIGURE II.3 Hominoid phylogeny based on molecular data. How does this differ from Huxley's image found in Figure II.2?

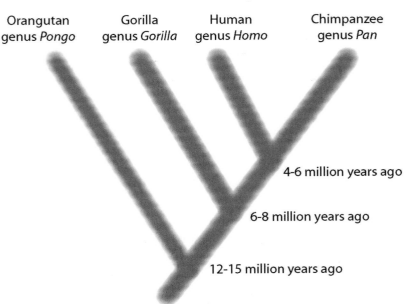

Orangutan genus *Pongo*   Gorilla genus *Gorilla*   Human genus *Homo*   Chimpanzee genus *Pan*

4-6 million years ago

6-8 million years ago

12-15 million years ago

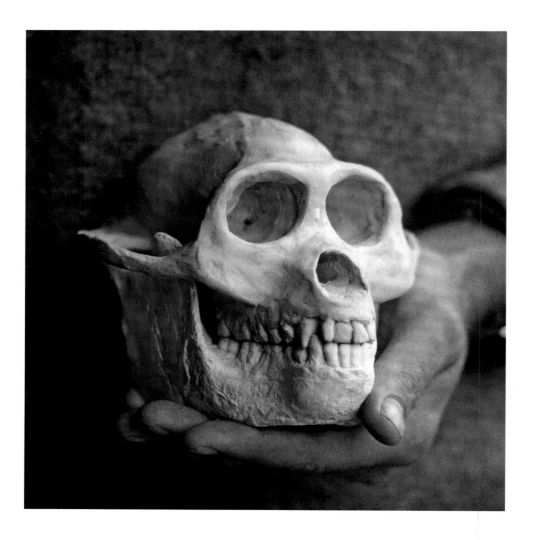

FIGURE II.4 Reconstructed skull of *Sivapithecus*, a Miocene hominoid dating from 12.5 million to 8.5 million years ago

period, hominoids filled many of the ecological niches now filled by monkeys. The range of Miocene hominoids is impressive. Species ranged from the size of a very small monkey to that of a gorilla (Figure II.4). One of the greatest challenges facing paleoanthropologists working with Miocene fossils is to determine where they fit on the hominoid evolutionary tree. Several Miocene species show traits that are characteristic of the orangutan, to the exclusion of the other hominoids. Thus, although it is possible to identify Miocene ancestors of modern orangutans, it is still difficult to identify a clear Miocene ancestor of the chimpanzee-human lineage. One of the major gaps in the fossil record is a representative of the common ancestor of humans and chimpanzees.

■ Culture and Human Evolution

One of the defining characteristics of biological evolution is that selection operates on traits that are transmitted genetically between generations. We pass our genes, not our experiences, on to our children. The early French zoologist Jean-Baptiste Lamarck famously made the argument that giraffes evolved long necks through the inheritance of acquired characteristics. This means that, as giraffes stretched their necks to reach the tops of trees, their necks grew longer, and the lengthened-neck trait was then passed on to the next generation. A more contemporary example would be to argue that the children of fans of loud music are born partly deaf because their parents' hearing was damaged when the parents stood near loud speakers. We now know that Lamarck made one of the great errors in the history of science: Traits acquired during life are not transmitted genetically to the next generation.

Throughout the animal world, we often find that acquired traits are in fact transmitted. However, their transmission takes place not through genetics, but rather through learning. Learning provides a mechanism for transmitting experience from generation to generation (see Figure II.5). We frequently refer to the learned behaviors found in human societies as culture. Is culture unique to humans? This is partly a matter of definition, but there is significant evidence that suggests that there is a patterning of learned behavior between chimpanzee groups that warrants the label "culture" (Whiten et al. 1999). Regardless of how one resolves this issue, it is unquestionable that the specific nature of human culture is unique in the animal world. Change in human culture has been both rapid and cumulative. There is a clear sense that developments in human culture build on themselves, creating a kind of "ratchet" effect. When we study human evolution, we are studying not only biological evolution, but also cultural evolution. The fascination inherent in the archaeology of human origins lies in the exploration of the relationship between biological and cultural evolution. Did biological evolution drive cultural change and innovation? Or is it possible that innovations in culture led to events in biological evolution?

Underlying these questions is one of the most engaging mysteries in biological science: Why is it that human culture is of a unique nature? One intriguing answer examines the solely human capability to recognize others as "beings *like themselves* who have intentional and mental worlds like their own" (Tomasello 1999, 5). As far as we know, this capability is not found in any other animals, although chimpanzees can recognize themselves in a mirror. Michael Tomasello (1999) argues that the capability to see another as like oneself opens the door to powerful new mechanisms of learning, in which humans learn by identifying with another rather than simply by observing.

Language is also critical to human interaction and plays an essential role in the transmission of cultural knowledge between generations. The timing of the

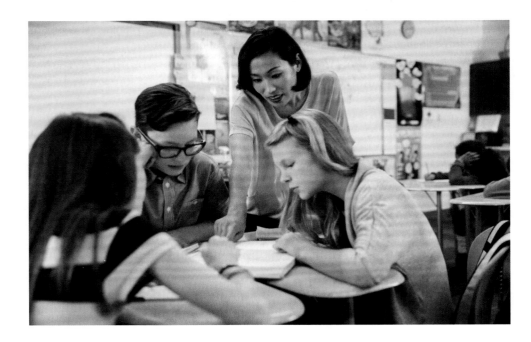

FIGURE II.5 A teacher working with eight- to nine-year-old children. How does the teacher guide the children's attention?

first appearance of language is a central topic in the archaeology of human origins. Unfortunately, language does not leave fossil evidence. We must infer what cultural behaviors would have required language. One intriguing idea is that the evolution of the human brain took place within the context of the evolution of language. Terrence Deacon (1997) has suggested that there was a coevolutionary relationship between language and the brain. If he is correct, the implication is that the archaeology of human origins traces the intricate give-and-take between genetic evolution and the evolution of culture. It is this interaction that makes the archaeology of human origins a unique and challenging field of study.

SUMMARY

- Reconstructing evolutionary history (phylogeny) is based on genetic and fossil evidence.
- Genetic evidence indicates a close relationship between humans and the great apes. Chimpanzees show the greatest genetic similarity to humans. On the basis of the genetic evidence, the split of the human and chimpanzee lineages is placed at 4 million to 6 million years ago.

- During the Miocene era (23 million to 5 million years ago), there was an explosion in the diversity of hominoids.
- Learning, self-recognition, and language are critical components of human culture and the transfer of cultural knowledge between generations.

KEY TERMS

Aegyptopithecus, 59
hominoids, 57
Miocene era, 59
mitochondrial DNA, 59
nuclear DNA, 59

ontogeny, 58
paleoanthropologist, 59
phylogeny, 58
species, 57

REVIEW QUESTIONS

1. What is the evidence for the timing of the split between the human and the chimpanzee lineages?
2. What are some characteristics of the Oligocene and Miocene hominoid fossil record?

3. What is the difference between biological evolution and cultural evolution?

EARLY HOMININS

The early hominin record includes species belonging to four distinct genera. After reading this chapter, you should understand:

- **The hominin radiation between 4 million and 2 million years ago.**
- **The major characteristics of Lower Paleolithic stone tool industries.**
- **The evidence for the origin of tool use.**
- **The debates about hunting and food sharing by early hominins.**
- **The evidence for the first dispersal of hominins out of Africa.**

Excavating an early hominin site in East Africa

3 TIMELINE

				Lokalalei ▲	
○ SITES				Gona ▲	Sang
○ ARCHAEOLOGICAL INDUSTRIES					
					PA
○ HOMININS					HOMO
			AUSTRALOPITHECUS		
millions of years ago	**3.5**	**3.0**	**2.5**		**2.0**

SITES DISCUSSED IN CHAPTER 3

● Dmanisi
● Nihewan
● Ubeidiya

Hadar ●
Lokalalei ●
Taï Forest ●
● Nariokotome
● Chesowanja
Olduvai Gorge ●
(DK1 & FLK)

Wonderwerk ● ● Swartkrans
Cave

PACIFIC
OCEAN

ATLANTIC
OCEAN

INDIAN
OCEAN

● Java
(Sangiran &
Perning)

▲ Nariokotome
▲ Ubeidiya
▲ Nihewan

ACHEULIAN

OLDOWAN

HOMO ERECTUS

1.5   1.0   0.5   0.0

hominins All the members of the human lineage after it split with the chimpanzee lineage.

Sahelanthropus tchadensis
A possible early member of the hominin lineage. Fossils of the species were discovered in Chad in levels dating to 7 million years ago.

Ardipithecus ramidus An early species in the hominin lineage. This species, which lived approximately 4.5 million years ago, is known from fossils discovered in 1992 at the site of Aramis in Ethiopia.

radiation A period in which there is a rapid increase in the diversity of a single lineage. During the period between 4 million and 2 million years ago, there was a radiation in the hominin lineage.

One and a half million years ago, a male *Homo erectus* lived in the Caucasus Mountains, in what is today the Republic of Georgia. When archaeologists discovered his skull at the site of Dmanisi, they were surprised to find that he had lost all but one of his teeth, years before he died at the age of 40 (Lordkipanidze et al. 2005). How did he survive without teeth? Did he rely on the compassion of members of his social group for food he could eat? The toothless man from Dmanisi raises many of the fundamental issues that occupy archaeologists studying early human ancestors. What was the nature of their society? How did they get food? How did they use tools? A total of five crania, shown in Figure 3.1, have now been found at Dmanisi. The recent discovery of a complete skull, including both the cranium and mandible, has only added to the questions raised by this site (Lordkipanidze et al. 2013). This skull, known as D5000, shows a combination of small brain size for *Homo erectus* and a face that juts forward.

In this chapter, we examine the archaeology of the early members of the hominin lineage. **Hominins** include all members of the human lineage after it split with the chimpanzee lineage. Until recently, hominins were referred to as hominids; however, the term *hominin* has now been adopted because it more properly fits with the rules of biological nomenclature (Wood and Richmond 2000). We begin by setting the stage for the study of early hominins by examining the fossil record, the geological context of early sites, and the definition of archaeological periods. With this background, the chapter moves on to three major themes in the archaeology of early hominins: tool use, adaptation, and social organization. Tool use is often thought to be a distinctive marker of the human lineage. We consider the evidence for tool use by animals and then move on to the timing and nature of the earliest archaeological evidence for tool manufacture. Beyond tool use, we are interested in the way that early hominins lived, including how they got their food and how their societies were organized. We focus on the evidence for hunting and food sharing by early hominins. Finally, the chapter turns to the archaeological evidence for the expansion of the hominin lineage beyond Africa and into Europe and Asia. One can imagine the toothless grin of the old man from Dmanisi as we struggle to understand the basic outlines of the lives of our early hominin ancestors.

FIGURE 3.1 The five skulls discovered at Dmanisi, shown here against a backdrop of the site, provide a rare view of the diversity of *Homo erectus*

3.1 The Fossil Record

The oldest fossils thought to belong to the hominin lineage are of ***Sahelanthropus tchadensis*** (Brunet et al. 2005; Zollikofer et al. 2005). The fossils of *Sahelanthropus* have been found in Chad in levels dating to 7 million years ago. A complete skull of *Sahelanthropus* has been discovered, but it is badly deformed, leaving room for differing interpretations of the species. Some have argued that *Sahelanthropus* is an African ape ancestor, while the discoverers of the fossil argue that it is in fact a hominin.

Ardipithecus ramidus is another early hominin (White, Suwa, and Asfaw 1994, 1995). This species, which lived approximately 4.5 million years ago, is known from fossils discovered beginning in 1992 at the site of Aramis in Ethiopia. A picture of this early human ancestor has begun to emerge from the dramatic discovery of the fairly complete skeleton of a female *Ardipithecus* (White et al. 2009; see Figure 3.2). This individual, nicknamed "Ardi," appears to have combined the ability to walk upright with anatomical traits, such as an opposable large toe, that would have facilitated climbing in trees. Ardi lacks anatomical features of the hands and wrists required for moving around on all four limbs using knuckle walking as is found in chimpanzees and gorillas. Ardi also differs from the great apes in that it lacks the pronounced canines found in these species. At this point, many questions remain about *Ardipithecus*, but the discovery of Ardi forces paleoanthropologists to reconsider the adaptations of the earliest members of the hominin lineage.

FIGURE 3.2 Reconstruction of *Ardipithecus ramidus*. The anatomy of *Ardipithecus* suggest that there were significant differences between the earliest hominins and the living great apes such as chimpanzees.

■ The Early Hominin Radiation

The period between 4 million and 2 million years ago saw an explosion in the diversity of hominin species (Wood and Richmond 2000). Such an event is known in evolutionary biology as a **radiation**. The hominin radiation that took place between 4 million and 2 million years ago included three distinct genera: *Kenyanthropus*, *Australopithecus*, and *Paranthropus*.

Despite the wide variation found in these three genera, there are certain broad similarities among them. Members of the three genera appear to have been distinct from living great apes in that they were adapted to walking upright. However, it is possible that some species were also adapted to moving easily through trees by climbing. It is notable that these hominins, like *Ardipithecus*, lacked the pronounced canine teeth characteristic of living great apes. The mean brain size for members of the three genera was consistently between 450 and 475 cubic centimeters, at the high end of brain size for living apes. Thus, within the hominin lineage, bipedalism (walking upright) and the loss of large canines preceded a significant increase in brain size. Table 3.1 presents some important aspects of *Kenyanthropus*, *Australopithecus*, and

TABLE 3.1 MEMBERS OF THE HOMININ LINEAGE DISCUSSED IN THIS CHAPTER

GENUS OR SPECIES	DATE	BRAIN SIZE	CHARACTERISTICS	FOUND IN
Australopithecus	4.0–2.5 million years ago	450–475 cc	Bipedal	East Africa, West Africa, and South Africa
Kenyanthropus	3.5 million years ago	450–475 cc	Similar to *Australopithecus*	East Africa
Paranthropus	2.5–1.4 million years ago	450–475 cc	Massive molars and chewing muscles	East Africa and South Africa
Homo habilis	2.5–1.6 million years ago	500–800 cc	Increased brain size	East Africa and South Africa
Homo erectus	1.9 million–45,000 (?) years ago	750–1,250 cc	Further increase in brain size, dispersal out of Africa	Africa, Asia, and Europe

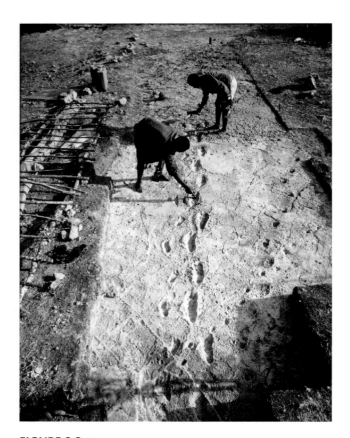

FIGURE 3.3 The footsteps at Laetoli preserved in a bed of volcanic ash, dated to 3.8 million years ago. Notice the hominin trackways and the tracks of other animals running off to the right.

Paranthropus, as well as of the two later species *Homo habilis* and *Homo erectus*. The evolution of the hominin lineage, and particularly the emergence of genus *Homo*, are linked with long-term climatic trends toward drier conditions and a shift from forests to grasslands (Bobe and Behrensmeyer 2004). At the same time there is evidence for rapid climatic fluctuations during this period. The variability selection hypothesis emphasizes the ability of species in the hominin lineage to adapt to environmental unpredictability (Potts 2013).

AUSTRALOPITHECINES. The **australopithecines** are known from as many as six distinct species. Australopithecine fossils are known from sites dating between 4 million and 1.8 million years ago (Leakey et al. 1995; Berger et al. 2010). Most specimens come from East Africa and South Africa; however, a new species, *Australopithecus bahrelghazali*, which lived 3.5 million years ago, was discovered in 1996 in Chad in Central Africa (Brunet et al. 1995). The nearly complete skeleton of an *Australopithecus afarensis* discovered by Donald Johanson in the Hadar region of Ethiopia, famously nicknamed Lucy after the Beatles song "Lucy in the Sky with Diamonds," provides the first evidence that australopithecines walked on two legs. Graphic evidence that the species walked upright is found in a trail of footprints left in volcanic ash at the site of **Laetoli** in Tanzania, shown in Figure 3.3 (Leakey and Harris 1987). A team of excavators working with Mary Leakey in 1978 discovered fossil footprints left by three individuals walking on a surface of volcanic ash. The prints at Laetoli clearly show that these three individuals were walking upright. Because the ash dates to 3.8 million years ago, the footprints were most likely produced by members of the species *Australopithecus afarensis*. The recent discovery of the remarkably well-preserved remains of an australopithecine child in the Dikka research area in Ethiopia sheds new light on this species (Alemseged 2006). Much of the skeleton shows apelike traits that suggest that australopithecines were adapted to climbing trees as well as to walking upright. A new species, *Australopithecus sediba*, recently discovered in South Africa, lived toward the end of the australopithicine lineage and displays some traits in common with genus *Homo*.

KENYANTHROPUS. *Kenyanthropus*, which dates to 3.5 million years ago, was first discovered in 2001 by Meave Leakey and her colleagues on the shores of Lake Turkana in northern Kenya (Leakey et al. 2001). *Kenyanthropus* is still poorly understood; however, in general terms, it seems similar to the australopithecines.

PARANTHROPUS. *Paranthropus*, also known as robust *Australopithecus*, is characterized by massive molars and muscles for chewing (Wood and Richmond 2000). Louis Leakey nicknamed the *Paranthropus boisei* skull he recovered at Olduvai Gorge in Tanzania "Nutcracker Man," and it is thought that the massive chewing mechanisms of these species are related to a diet that included seeds or fruits with a hard outer coating (Figure 3.4). The earliest known *Paranthropus* dates to 2.5 million years ago, while the most recent dates to 1.4 million years ago.

HOMO HABILIS. Contemporary with *Paranthropus* there was a very different hominin living in East Africa. This hominin lacked the heavy chewing muscles and large teeth

FIGURE 3.4 Louis Leakey examines the skull of a *Paranthropus*

characteristic of *Paranthropus* and had a larger brain, which had a volume of 500 to 800 cubic centimeters. This was the first primate with such a large brain and also the earliest species to be assigned to the genus *Homo*. **Homo habilis** is known from sites in East Africa dating to between 2.5 million and 1.6 million years ago, including Olduvai Gorge, Tanzania, and Koobi Fora, Kenya (Wood and Richmond 2000). Paleoanthropologists emphasize the diversity of this group of fossils and there are likely two contemporary lineages within this group (Antón, Potts, and Aiello 2014).

HOMO ERECTUS. The next member of genus *Homo* to appear in the fossil record is **Homo erectus**. The oldest evidence of *Homo erectus* dates to the period between 1.9 million and 1.5 million years ago. *Homo erectus* fossils are known from East Africa and South Africa, as well as from sites in Europe and Asia. Some paleoanthropologists separate the earliest *Homo erectus* fossils from sites in Africa into a distinct species called *Homo ergaster* (Wood and Collard 1999). It has recently been proposed that the fossils discovered at the Rising Star cave system in South Africa represent a new species designated as *Homo naledi* (Berger et al. 2015).

The discovery of the complete skeleton of a juvenile adolescent *Homo erectus* at the site of Nariokotome, Kenya, has provided a unique picture of this hominin species (Leakey and Walker 1993). The fossil found at Nariokotome is the skeleton of a boy who was approximately 160 centimeters (5 ft. 3 in.) tall when he died, roughly 1.5 million years ago (see Figure 3.5). Not only was he tall, but he was thin, with a body shape typical of tropical populations among modern humans. He lived on the rich floodplain grasslands along the banks of a channel of the Omo River, in a landscape that was mostly open grassland and swamps, with trees limited to the river's edge and high spots. It is unclear why the boy died. There is no evidence of any trauma or attack by a carnivore. The only evidence of pathology is a pocket of gum disease related to the loss of one of his milk teeth. It is possible that infection of this inflammation was the cause of death.

3.2 Setting the Scene

The lives of early hominins left behind few traces. The only remains are the stone tools and bones discarded as they moved around the landscape. The richest context for the recovery of early hominin archaeological sites is the **East African Rift Valley**. The stone tools found on early hominin sites are grouped as belonging to the Lower Paleolithic, or, as it is known in Africa, the Early Stone Age. The Oldowan and the Acheulian are the two main industries identified within the Lower Paleolithic.

■ The East African Rift Valley

The East African Rift Valley is a massive geological feature stretching from Malawi in southern Africa to Turkey and Syria in the Middle East. This formation can be thought of as an enormous trough that is in constant formation as the surface of the earth pulls apart along the rift. Three characteristics of the Rift Valley make it invaluable in the search for early hominin sites. The first is that, because it is a trough, it is filling up with sediments. It is thus a depositional

Homo habilis This hominin is the earliest species to be assigned to the genus *Homo*.

australopithecine A hominin genus that lived in Africa between 4 million and 1.8 million years ago.

▲▲ **Laetoli** A location in Tanzania where tracks of australopithecine footprints were found, showing that australopithecines walked upright.

Homo erectus The first hominin found on sites outside of Africa. The earliest known *Homo erectus* fossils date to the period between 1.9 million and 1.5 million years ago.

▲▲ **East African Rift Valley** A geological feature stretching from East Africa to the Middle East that is the richest context for the recovery of early hominin archaeological sites.

FIGURE 3.5 The skull of *Homo erectus* discovered at Nariokotome. Notice how low the cranial vault (forehead) is compared to that of modern humans.

Fraud—Piltdown and Kama-takamori

On December 28, 1912, the *Illustrated London News* announced "a discovery of supreme importance to all who are interested in the history of the human race." The discovery, made at the site of Piltdown in East Sussex, England, included fragments of a skull and jaw that appeared to be the oldest known fossils of a human ancestor. When the skull of Piltdown Man was reconstructed, a picture emerged of an individual with a large cranium similar to the skull of living humans. However, the jaw (mandible) was in many ways apelike. The Piltdown fossils became the basis for a new genus of human ancestor: *Eoanthropus*, or "dawn man."

In 1954, 42 years after the discovery, the fossil remains from Piltdown were unmasked as an elaborate fraud. The jaw was from a modern orangutan and had been stained to appear fossilized. The teeth had been filed down to alter their shape into a slightly more human configuration, and parts of the mandible had been deliberately broken off in order to make it more difficult to identify as the mandible of an ape. The skull fragments were from a modern human of recent archaeological origin. All of the bones found at Piltdown were deliberately introduced into the site.

Of course, the intriguing question is, who concocted and carried out this scheme? The most likely suspect is Charles Dawson, the amateur scientist and solicitor who discovered the fossils. However, Dawson did not have a clear motive, and many doubt that he had the expertise to make the fakes, as well as access to paraphernalia such as an orangutan jaw. It seems likely that Dawson was himself duped or had an accomplice. Among the list of suspects were two of the most prominent scientists of the day, Arthur Smith Woodward and Arthur Keith. Both had the expertise and access to the site, but their motive is unclear. Would they risk everything and sacrifice the most basic of scientific ethics in such an undertaking? The Catholic priest and paleontologist

Teilhard de Chardin has also been implicated as a suspect, particularly given the fact that he discovered some of the Piltdown fossils himself during brief visits to the site. Even Sir Arthur Conan Doyle, the author of the Sherlock Holmes mysteries, has been suggested as a suspect. To this day, the file on the Piltdown hoax remains open.

Frauds like Piltdown are exceptionally rare in archaeology. However, a similar scandal recently rocked Japanese archaeology. In 1993, Japanese archaeologists announced the discovery of stone tools at the Kama-takamori site in a context dated to roughly 500,000 years ago. The discovery was widely reported, primarily in the Japanese popular press, as the earliest evidence of human occupation of Japan. In 1995, a pit was found with 15 tools arranged in an oval, with 2 tools in the center, one made of a particularly beautiful white rock and the other of an unusual red rock.

In 2002, the archaeological community was stunned to learn that the artifacts at the Kama-takamori site had been deliberately planted by one of the excavators. Videotapes caught the excavator in the act of digging out a pit, planting the tools, covering them up, and then carefully tamping down the earth with his boot. The events at the site have cast confusion over the early prehistory of Japan, as this same excavator was involved in many projects.

It is important to distinguish between fraud, as practiced at Piltdown and Kama-takamori, and error. Fraud is inimical to scientific research, while error plays a large role in increasing our knowledge of the past. A fraud is an intentional attempt to deceive. An error is a false interpretation based on the best available evidence. Errors often form the basis for further testing and refutation of a scientific theory. ●

ADDITIONAL READING: Frank Spencer. 1990. *Piltdown: A Scientific Forgery*. Oxford, England: Oxford University Press.

FIGURE 3.6 A painting of the examination of the Piltdown skull. The painting underscores the fact that this forgery was perpetrated on the scientific establishment of the time.

environment that preserves archaeological and paleontological sites. Second, because it is tectonically active, there is a great deal of erosion. The result is the formation of badlands, landscapes in which enormous deposits of earth are cut by gullies and ravines (see Figure 3.7). Third, as a sort of icing on the cake, the Rift Valley is also volcanically active, so there are levels of volcanic ash, known as tuffs, that can be dated using the argon method (see the Dating Early Hominin Sites Toolbox on p. 80).

OLDUVAI GORGE. Of all the gullies and ravines of the East African Rift Valley, none is more impressive or more important for the study of human evolution than **Olduvai Gorge** in Tanzania. Olduvai Gorge has come to be synonymous with the names Louis and Mary Leakey. The Leakeys' decades of research at Olduvai revolutionized ideas of prehistory and brought attention to the tremendous potential of the East African Rift Valley for the study of early hominins. Two million years ago, in the area that is now Olduvai Gorge, there was a small lake surrounded by a grassland and marsh landscape within a large basin or depression. The lake was salty, but it supported a diversity of fish and reptiles, including crocodiles. The surrounding grassland and swamps of the basin supported mammals such as elephants, bovids (ancestors of cows), hippos, antelope, and hominins. Over time, the basin filled with sediments carried by wind and water until it was scarcely discernible on the landscape of the Serengeti Plain.

Two hundred thousand years ago, modern streams began to carve a canyon through the soft sediments filling the basin at Olduvai. Over time, this erosion created the spectacular landscape of Olduvai Gorge, a main gorge and side gorge that meet to form a Y shape. The erosion that created the gorge provides a point of access to the fossils and stone tools deposited around Lake Olduvai. Without the erosion, this critical evidence would remain inaccessible, locked under tens of meters of accumulated sediments. Research at Olduvai first involves walking along the gorge, looking for places where tools or fossils are eroding out of the cliffs. As one walks up the walls of the gorge, one is walking up through geological time. In the spots where material is found eroding out of the sections, it is possible in some cases to dig into the cliff face to expose ancient living surfaces.

The sequence at Olduvai Gorge is based on geological rather than archaeological strata. Bed I is the earliest unit, Bed IV is the latest, and overlying Bed IV is a unit known as the Masek Beds. Table 3.2 gives a chronology of the formation of the beds.

FIGURE 3.7 A view of the badlands landscape in the East African Rift Valley near Dikka, Ethiopia, where the fossil of an australopithecine child was discovered. The erosion of sediments is what allows archaeologists and paleoanthropologists to find hominin sites.

▓ Lower Paleolithic

The period during which early hominins began making stone tools is known as the **Lower Paleolithic**. In Africa, the Lower Paleolithic is often called the Early Stone Age. The Lower Paleolithic includes two major industries: the Oldowan and the Acheulian. An archaeological industry is a period characterized by a certain

Lower Paleolithic The period when hominins began producing stone tools.

TABLE 3.2 STRATIGRAPHIC BEDS AT OLDUVAI GORGE

Masek Beds	0.6–0.4 million years ago
Bed IV	0.8–0.6 million years ago
Bed III	1.15–0.8 million years ago
Bed II	1.7–1.15 million years ago
Bed I	1.9–1.7 million years ago

▲▲ **Olduvai Gorge** The most impressive and important location in the East African Rift Valley for the study of human evolution.

Following the Footsteps of Our Ancestors
ANDREW DU, RUTGERS UNIVERSITY

In the summer of 2007, I conducted fieldwork in northern Kenya as an undergraduate student on the Koobi Fora Field School, jointly run by Rutgers University and the National Museums of Kenya. The purpose of the field school is to inform students on the basic principles and field methods of paleoanthropology. Through hands-on learning in the field, students are trained in various subdisciplines such as archaeology, geology, paleontology, taphonomy, botany, ecology, and ethnography. The site we excavated was FwJj 14 East, located in Ileret, a semi-desert Plio-Pleistocene region on the eastern side of Lake Turkana. Ileret is an area well known for its abundance of hominin fossils, but at first sight to us students, Ileret could be described only as windy, sandy, and, above all else, hot. However, these minor discomforts were not enough to quell our passion for the field of human origins. We were all eager to excavate and do our part in contributing new finds and information to the paleoanthropological field.

FwJj 14 East is an absolutely extraordinary site. It is situated on the side of a badlands outcrop eroded away by a river feeding into the larger Il Eriet River. Of course, our field season was in the dry time of the year, so there were only vestiges of these rivers in the form of *lagas*, or dried-up riverbeds. In 2004, the field school discovered a fossil hominin right arm and, in 2006, a trail of footprints left by bovids, carnivores, birds, and hominins. Geological evidence indicates that the footprints were made in the muddy silts of a river floodplain. These strata of interest were tightly constrained between two volcanic ash layers, or tuffs, and using argon dating, the site was estimated to 1.5 million years ago, an exciting time period of climate variability, speciation, and cultural innovation. The objectives of the 2007 field season were to (1) excavate in the *laga* to see if any more hominin remains had eroded out from the outcrop and (2) extend the footprint trail and expose uncovered areas so they could be digitized with an optical laser scanner.

Daily routine consisted of rising from our tents at 7:00 a.m., eating breakfast, and walking over to the site. Excavations usually started at around 8:00, and we each fulfilled one of three roles. One person would excavate a 1 × 1 meter square in the *laga* using a trowel to scrape sandy sediment into a dustpan, which would then be emptied into a metal pan called a *karai*. Any large bone or artifact uncovered in the square would have its location recorded using a total station (an electronic theodolite that uses lasers to measure the position of objects), and it would subsequently be bagged. A second person would carry *karais* over to the sieve, keeping in mind which *karai* belonged to which square. A third person would sieve the sediment in search of any small fossils and artifacts, which would then be bagged indicating their respective square. Everyone was expected to keep a field notebook describing what they did that day in abundant detail. This was especially important for the excavator, who needed to record the specimen in three-dimensional coordinates.

Only a lucky few were allowed to brush off the footprints. I was one of these lucky few. Brushing off the footprints was a tedious task requiring finesse and patience. The footprints themselves were imprinted in a hard, fine-grained mudstone. This was overlaid by a layer of fine sand, which was brushed away using a chip brush. Occasionally, gravel infilled the footprints and required the use of a dental pick to remove it. Great care was needed when uncovering the footprints. If destroyed, they would be gone forever, so I had only one chance to

approach to making stone tools. Prehistorians working on very early periods tend to be cautious about using the term *culture* because it implies that the groups that lived during those periods resemble modern cultures in sharing a common set of beliefs and values and, in many cases, also a common language. We do not know whether that is true of the people who made Oldowan and Acheulian types of stone tools; therefore, the term *industry* is used.

THE OLDOWAN. The **Oldowan** was defined on the basis of the archaeological material from Olduvai Gorge Beds I and II, dated between 1.9 million and 1.7 million years ago, although the earliest age for the Oldowan has now been pushed back to approximately 2.5 million years ago, and a small assemblage of artifacts has been found in a context dated to 3.3 million years. The question of which hominin made

Oldowan Lower Paleolithic stone tool industry, dated between 1.9 million and 1.7 million years ago, characterized by choppers and flakes.

get it right. Immediately after brushing off the footprints, I had to quickly scan them lest the wind blow sand right back into them. Digitizing the footprints would allow them to be preserved forever and their dimensions to be precisely measured for later quantitative analysis.

Working on the footprints was an incredibly surreal experience. Here I was, physically touching the very ground where our hominin ancestors had once walked. Hominin body fossils are fascinating in their own right, but their remains are more akin to imagery evoked from graveyards and horror movies. Footprints are flesh put on the bone; there is something indescribably familiar about a hominin footprint. Footprints are a powerful symbol of nostalgia and presence. They abound in the forecourt of the Hollywood Chinese Theater, and they are an indelible reminder of humankind's first walk on the moon. The hominin footprints evoke all of these emotions and more—a deep connection with the remote past.

The footprints were also significant from an academic perspective. Hominin foot bones are extremely rare in the fossil record. In addition to being scarce, they cannot inform on important issues such as foot shape and gait. This is why

the hominin footprints at FwJj 14 East were such a momentous discovery, garnering recognition in the prestigious scientific journal *Science*. By applying statistical analyses to the laser scans of the footprints, our team was able to deduce that by 1.5 million years ago, hominins had evolved feet and a walking gait indistinguishable from ours today. Modern attributes included a midfoot arch, an in-line and robust big toe, and a heel-to-toe weight transfer. The footprints were attributed to *Homo erectus*, making them the oldest known footprints of our genus, *Homo*. The study shows that hominins by this time period possessed

a modern body size and a mode of bipedalism that enabled them to travel over long distances at lower energetic costs, thus expanding their home ranges.

It was exhilarating to be a part of such groundbreaking research, collaborating with some of the most prominent scientists in the field today. Being in the field was certainly an adventure, and the ever-present allure of discovering the unknown was undoubtedly captivating. This experience only reconfirmed my previous notions: I want to pursue a career doing research and fieldwork in paleoanthropology. ▲

FIGURE 3.8
Reconstruction of the Lower Paleolithic landscape at Koobi Fora

the Oldowan tools is not yet resolved. *Paranthropus*, *Homo habilis*, and *Homo erectus* all lived during the time Oldowan tools were manufactured. Fossils of all these hominins are found either on or near Oldowan archaeological sites.

Oldowan tools have been described as a least-effort solution to creating sharp-edged tools (Schick and Toth 1993). The basic distinction between Oldowan tools is that they are either flakes or cores. Flakes are slivers of rock that have been struck off of a stone. Cores are the pieces off of which flakes have been struck. The characteristic tool of the Oldowan is the chopper, the tool shown being used to smash a bone in Figure 3.9. To manufacture a chopper, one begins with a rounded stone and strikes a series of flakes off one edge. The process can be continued by flipping the stone over and striking a series of flakes off the same edge on the other side. When Mary Leakey began work at Olduvai Gorge, she identified choppers as tools and

FIGURE 3.9 An Oldowan chopper (right) and flake (left).

Acheulian Lower Paleolithic stone tool industry dated in Africa between 1.7 million and 200,000 years ago, characterized by bifacial tools including handaxes and cleavers.

bifaces Characteristic tools of the Acheulian. Bifaces include handaxes and cleavers.

FIGURE 3.10 An Acheulian cleaver (left) and handaxe (right). Archaeologists stress the symmetry of many Acheulian handaxes. The horizontal scale is in centimeters.

imagined them as being useful for butchering animals. However, when archaeologists began making Oldowan tools and using them to butcher carcasses, they found that choppers were not very useful for this task. These experiments demonstrated that it was the sharp-edged flakes that were most useful. As a result, it has been argued that the actual desired product was the flake and that the chopper was simply waste from manufacture. An alternative is that both flakes and choppers were used. The choppers might have been useful for working wood or breaking bones to get at marrow, while the flakes were used for butchery. Unfortunately, we have no preserved wood from Oldowan sites.

THE ACHEULIAN. The earliest **Acheulian** industries in East Africa date to the period between 1.7 million and 1.5 million years before the present. The earliest Acheulian site is Kokiselei 4, Kenya, which is dated to 1.76 million years ago. It is interesting that at Kokiselei 4, Oldowan tools were found together with Acheulian handaxes and the form of the handaxes is very crude. The date for the end of the Acheulian is currently unclear, but it is in the range of 400,000 and 200,000 years ago. Acheulian sites are found throughout Africa, including major sites in both eastern and southern Africa, as well as in Europe, the Middle East, and India. The Acheulian began at the same time as the first appearance of *Homo erectus* and the extinction of *Homo habilis*.

The characteristic tool of the Acheulian is the biface. Unlike the Oldowan flakes and cores, the Acheulian tool can hardly be described as a least-effort solution. The Acheulian **bifaces** are better described as the earliest evidence of design. Bifaces can be either handaxes, if they are pointed at the end, or cleavers, if they have a wide working end (see Figure 3.10). Bifaces were carefully and skillfully fashioned tools, not simply

TOOLBOX

Stone Tools

The archaeological study of stone tools is known as lithic analysis, and the manufacture of stone tools is known as knapping. When looking at stone tools, archaeologists see not only the formal properties of the artifact (color, shape, size, weight), but also evidence of how it was manufactured and used. To understand the process of knapping, archaeologists take great care to recover all stone artifacts, including waste products from manufacture.

Lower Paleolithic tools were made by delivering a sharp blow to a rock in order to break off a smaller piece, a technique known as percussion. The piece that is struck off is called a flake, and the piece from which the flake is struck is called the core. The goal of percussion is to produce either flake tools or core tools. In many cases, both flakes and cores were used as tools.

Flakes have several important features. The surface that is split off of the core, known as the ventral face, has a convex area called the bulb of percussion at the end where it was struck. This end is known as the proximal end of the flake. The bulb of percussion is produced when the force of the blow enters the rock. The force enters the rock as a cone, much like the cone produced when a bullet strikes glass or a stone is thrown into a body of water. The force from the blow ripples out from this initial cone, eventually splitting the flake from the core.

Percussion techniques can be classified on the basis of the way the blow is delivered. In *direct percussion*, it is delivered directly to the core. In *hard-hammer direct percussion*, a rock is used as a hammer. In *soft-hammer direct percussion*, either an antler or a piece of hardwood is used. Using a soft hammer allows the knapper to produce thin flakes with a less pronounced bulb of percussion. *Indirect percussion* involves the use of an intermediary device known as a punch between the hammer and the core. The advantage of indirect percussion is that the precise placement of the blow can be controlled. Indirect percussion is often used in making long blades or shaping arrowheads.

Pressure techniques follow the same principles as percussion, except that the force is applied by pressure rather than a blow. In practice, the knapper presses the tip of an antler or, in some cases, a copper tip against the edge of a tool to push off a flake. Pressure techniques involve the exertion of a great deal of force by the knapper, and usually the entire upper body is involved. Pressure techniques are normally used in the very fine shaping of tools. Because no blow is involved, the bulb of percussion is extremely diffuse, and very thin flakes can be removed.

In some cases, a flake would simply be used as struck. In other cases, however, a core or a flake was carefully modified to create a desired shape or edge. The careful secondary shaping of a core or flake is known as retouch.

It is critical that the knapper have control of the way the rock fractures. Many rocks are not suitable for these techniques because they either fracture along cleavage planes in the rock or crumble when struck. The stones used by knappers are brittle and fine grained and do not have internal features that determine the direction in which they break. A wide variety of rocks, including flint (also known as chert), basalt, and obsidian, fit these criteria and can be used to make stone tools. ●

FIGURE 3.11 Cores and flakes bear traces of the manufacture process such as retouch and the bulb of percussion

Core | Flake | Flake Ventral Surface
Retouch | Bulb of Percussion

cores. One aspect of their design is their symmetry with reference to a central axis. The actual function of bifaces has remained an enigma. Clearly, they were highly effective tools if hominins continued to use them for over 1 million years. The handaxe is perhaps the most successful tool humans have ever invented. But what was it used for? Recently, an archaeologist studied botanical remains known as phytoliths on handaxes from the site of Peninj, Tanzania (Dominguez-Rodrigo 2002). Phytoliths are mineral elements of plant cells that survive after the rest of the plant has disintegrated. The phytoliths adhering to the handaxes from Peninj suggest that these tools were used for woodworking. There is some evidence of worked wood at the Acheulian site of Kolambo Falls, Zambia.

3.3 The Origin of Tool Use

Tool use is often considered a trait that separates humans from animals, although research by ethologists—scientists who study animal behavior—casts doubt on tool use as a uniquely human behavior. Nonetheless, the development of stone tool technology marks an important point in human evolution. Stone tools dating to 2.4 million years ago are the earliest known archaeological artifacts. Recent research indicates that the manufacture of these early stone tools was a more complex process than previously imagined.

■ Tool Use by Animals

Most evidence for tool use and manufacture comes from studies of chimpanzees and the other great apes. However, surprising evidence for tool manufacture by birds has emerged in a study of crows on New Caledonia, a string of islands approximately 900 miles northeast of Australia. While observing the behavior of New Caledonian crows, Gavin Hunt noticed that the birds were carrying objects in their beaks and using the objects to extract insects from trees. There is also evidence for tool use in some dolphin populations. Dolphins in Shark Bay, Australia, use sponges that they wear on their beaks to scour the seafloor for prey (see Figure 3.12). Not all dolphins use sponges and there is evidence that this is learned behavior that takes place within social cliques (Mann et al. 2012).

Jane Goodall was among the first to document tool use by chimpanzees in the wild. The chimpanzee group she studied at Gombe in Tanzania used twigs, bark, or grass to fish termites and ants out of mounds (Goodall 1986). In subsequent years, tool use was discovered in a number of distinct groups of chimpanzees. Perhaps the most dramatic of these discoveries comes from the studies of the chimpanzees in the Taï Forest, Ivory Coast (Boesch and Boesch-Achermann 2000). The **Taï Forest** chimpanzees use stone hammers and anvils to break open hard nuts (see Figure 3.13). The tools are not manufactured, but rather are used as found. However, the use of these tools is a skilled activity that young chimpanzees acquire by observing their mothers over a period of years. The skills the young chimpanzees learn include both the selection of the right hammers and anvils and the appropriate use of force.

On their own, dipping for ants and cracking nuts seem like rather modest examples of tool use. However, an interesting pattern emerges when the distribution of chimpanzee tool use behaviors is examined across Africa (Whiten et al. 1999). The tools and the way they are used are not uniform across the continent, but rather are distinctive of particular groups. This pattern is true not only of tool use, but also of other behaviors, such as greeting and grooming. Ecological factors alone do not dictate where particular tools are used. For example, there are populations of chimpanzees living in West Africa that have access to the same nuts as those in the Taï Forest, but that do not use stone hammers to break the nuts. These groups either

Taï Forest A location where chimpanzees use stone hammers and anvils to break open hard nuts. The tools are not manufactured, but rather are used as found.

FIGURE 3.12 A dolphin in Australia carries a sponge to scour the seafloor

ignore the nuts completely or break them with their teeth, a far less efficient technique. These observations have led some ethologists to argue that chimpanzees have culture.

In 1990, a group of archaeologists and primatologists began an experiment to determine whether they could teach Kanzi, a pygmy chimpanzee born and raised at the Language Research Center at Georgia State University, to make stone tools (Schick et al. 1999; Toth et al. 1993). Kanzi was shown a box with a transparent door held closed by a piece of rope. A piece of fruit was placed inside the box, and Kanzi was shown that the rope could be cut with a stone flake struck off a rock with a hammer. The chimpanzee was then shown how to create sharp flakes by striking one piece of rock (a hammer) against another (a core). Kanzi was able to carry out this task; however, his preferred method was to smash a rock by throwing it onto the concrete floor of the laboratory. In all cases, the method of flake production was very crude. Still, Kanzi did manage to make some tools bearing a resemblance to the earliest tools produced by hominins.

Kanzi's skill at breaking rocks seems to indicate that the ability of chimpanzees to manufacture tools is at best quite limited. However, this test might actually have more to do with the qualities of the human hand than with any abstract conceptual abilities. Humans are unique in having a thumb and fingers that are able to rotate, allowing for a wide range of grips. Chimpanzee hands, like all ape hands, are largely limited to folding their fingers over objects or gripping small objects between the thumb and the index finger (Panger et al. 2002). Perhaps Kanzi's difficulties in stone tool manufacture reflect the limited range of grips he is capable of compared to those the human demonstrator is able to assume.

◼ The Archaeological Evidence

The earliest occupation at Olduvai Gorge, in Bed I, dates to approximately 1.8 million years ago. On the basis of discoveries made at **Hadar** and **Lomekwi 3**, it is now clear that the stone tool manufacture stretches back far earlier in time. The Hadar region, located in the East African Rift Valley in Ethiopia, has produced some of the

▲▲ **Lomekwi 3** A site in Kenya where stone tools dated to 3.2 million years ago have been found. These are the earliest stone tools to be discovered.

▲▲ **Hadar** A location in the East African Rift Valley where many important fossils, including the near-complete fossil of an australopithecine, and some of the earliest known stone tools have been discovered.

BKT-3 *2.33 ± 0.07 Ma (Ar/Ar)*

◆ ★ A.L. 666

20 —

BKT-2 *2.92 ± 0.03 Ma (Ar/Ar)*

0 —

★ Hominin Locality
◆ Artifact Locality

FIGURE 3.14 Stratigraphic context of the stone tools from the Hadar. Notice the position of the artifacts (indicated by a diamond) and the hominin fossil (known as A.L. 666 and indicated by a star). Both the tools and the hominin are above BKT-2 and below BKT-3. Dates are in millions of years ago (Ma). The vertical scale on the left is in meters.

▲▲ **Lokalalei** An archaeological site in Kenya dating to 2.3 million years ago. Analysis of refit cores from the site indicates that stone tool manufacture at this early date was more complex than anticipated.

FIGURE 3.15 A refit core from Lokalalei, Kenya, shows the complexity of the earliest stone tool manufacture. This refit includes a large number of flakes struck from a single core.

most important fossils of australopithecines, including Lucy. In the early 1990s, two teams discovered stone tools at sites in the Hadar in levels that date to approximately 2.5 million years ago. At the site of Lomekwi 3, Kenya, a small assemblage of tools has been found in a context dated to 3.2 million years ago. Currently Lomekwi 3 is the only site with evidence of tool manufacture from such an early period.

At the Gona site in the Hadar region, close to 3,000 stone tools were found in a single layer in two excavation areas covering an area of 22 square meters (Semaw 2000). The tools were discovered in a clay soil that showed no signs of river activity. Although the tools are simple, there is no question that they were manufactured by hominins. Given what is known about the geological context, it is not possible that any geological process produced the uniform patterns of flaking found on these tools. The major types of tools found are sharp-edged flakes and cores, including choppers.

The archaeological horizon at the Gona site is sandwiched between layers of volcanic ash known as tuff (see Figure 3.14) (Semaw et al. 1997). Fortunately, these tuff layers are ideal for argon dating. The BKT-2 tuff, which underlies the site, dates to 2.9 million years ago, while the BKT-3 tuff, which overlies the site, is dated to 2.3 million years ago. Therefore, the stone tools were produced and deposited during the time interval between 2.9 million and 2.3 million years ago.

Another team of researchers working near Gona has found a smaller assemblage of tools from a similar context (Kimbel et al. 1996). Adding to the interest of this discovery is a hominin fossil found at the same level. The fossil is a well-preserved maxilla (palate) that has been identified as belonging to the genus *Homo*. Due to the fossil's fragmentary nature, it was not possible to determine what species it belongs to, but given the age of the site, *Homo habilis* is the most likely candidate.

The tools from the Hadar site seem to be the simplest possible form, showing the least possible elaboration. Indeed, were it not for the geological context, one might even cast doubt on whether these tools are evidence of human manufacture.

Lokalalei, situated in the West Turkana region of northern Kenya, is yet another East African Rift Valley site to produce evidence of tool manufacture from an early date (Roche et al. 1999). Based on the argon dating method, **Lokalalei** is approximately 2.3 million years old, younger than the Hadar sites. At Lokalalei 2C, a horizontal area of 17 square meters has been excavated, and slightly over 2,000 stone flakes and cores were recovered from a single surface. A wide range of animal remains was also found, including 12 mammal species as well as reptiles and fish. There is no indication of cut marks or other signs of human activity on the animal bones.

In studying the stone tools from Lokalalei, Hélène Roche and her colleagues focused on trying to understand the process through which the tools were manufactured (Roche et al.1999). By carefully fitting the flakes back onto the cores from which they were struck, the researchers showed that the simple tools at Lokalalei were produced through a fairly elaborate process (Figure 3.15). The cores included not only coarse-grained cobbles from which only 2 or 3 flakes had been removed, but also more fine-grained cobbles and pebbles from which up to 30 flakes had been removed. The analysis of how the flakes were removed in these lengthy sequences demonstrates that the knapping was not random and haphazard, but rather followed a clear and consistent strategy. The complexity of tool manufacture at Lokalalei demonstrates that the first stone tools were not the simplest of all possible, only a step removed from the hammers used by the chimpanzees in the Taï Forest or similar to the flakes produced by Kanzi the chimpanzee. Some of the first tools manufactured by hominins thus involved a sequence of manufacture more complex than any process known from studies of animal behavior.

3.4 Hunting and Sharing Food

Western philosophy has developed two opposing pictures of "man in a state of nature." For Thomas Hobbes, humans were essentially violent, and it was only through the development of institutions that it was possible for humanity to tame its destructive nature. Other philosophers, such as Jean Jacques Rousseau, imagined a life of leisure and peace that was disrupted only by the development of social inequality. Prehistorians have carried this debate into the study of early hominins. While some archaeologists view early hominins as killer apes, others envision societies of hunter-gatherers sharing meat and other food.

■ Were They Hunters?

As a young professor of anatomy in South Africa, Raymond Dart was the first to identify the remains of an australopithecine. Dart subsequently became convinced that australopithecines used tools made of fractured pieces of bone. He labeled these tools the osteodontokeratic (bone, tooth, and horn) culture. The tools Dart identified included cutting tools, scoops, and spears. Dart developed a vision of australopithecines as brutal hunters "slaking their ravenous thirst with the hot blood of victims and greedily devouring livid writhing flesh" (Dart 1953, 209).

In the 1970s, archaeologists began to question Dart's interpretation with a series of studies into how bones are accumulated and what processes affect them after their burial. Such studies, known as taphonomic analyses, have included scrambling into hyena dens to collect bones gnawed by these carnivores. When bones from hyena dens were compared

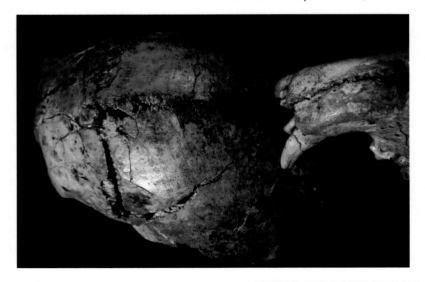

FIGURE 3.16 The hunted, not the hunter. The skull of an australopithecine from Swartkrans, South Africa, with a puncture wound that matches the spacing of the lower canines of a leopard.

TOOLBOX

Dating Early Hominin Sites

Precisely dating early hominin sites is extremely challenging. Archaeologists are often forced to rely on a combination of methods to arrive at a reliable age for a site. The main methods used to date early hominin sites are paleomagnetic dating and argon dating. Recently, a new method known as cosmogenic burial age dating has begun to have an impact, particularly on cave sites (Granger and Muzikar 2001).

Paleomagnetic Dating

Paleomagnetic dating is a method used to determine when sediments were deposited. The method dates the soils in which artifacts are found rather than the artifacts themselves. To use paleomagnetism for dating artifacts or fossils, one must be confident that these objects are in the context in which they were initially deposited. If this is not the case—for example, if artifacts have been transported by water and redeposited in a new location—then the paleomagnetic date will be for the redeposition event rather than the manufacture of the artifacts.

The scientific basis for paleomagnetic dating is the observation that the earth's geomagnetic field has repeatedly switched polarity. The current state of the earth's geomagnetic field is known as normal polarity. In periods of reversed polarity, the field was switched, so a compass that points north today would have pointed south. It has been possible to build up a chronology of these switches so as to divide geological time into a sequence of epochs of normal and reversed polarity.

When particles containing iron are deposited, they orient themselves in accordance with the earth's geomagnetic field. This orientation is preserved as long as the particles are not moved. Almost all soils on earth contain iron. By studying the orientation of their iron particles, a geophysicist can determine the direction of the earth's geomagnetic field at the time the soil was deposited. Thus, on most archaeological sites, it is possible to determine whether the site formed during a period of normal or reversed polarity.

In some cases, archaeologists working in recent periods have been able to use the paleomagnetic record of subtle shifts in the geomagnetic field to date artifacts or sites. The materials dated with these methods are usually hearths or pottery.

Argon Dating

Unlike paleomagnetic dating, argon dating provides a numerical age rather than assigning a deposit to an epoch or event. Argon dating works by means of an accumulation clock. The unit that is accumulating is ^{40}Ar, an isotope of the element argon. Isotopes are forms of a chemical element that have the same

FIGURE 3.17 Paleomagnetic time scale. Time in millions of years ago. Periods of normal polarity are in dark blue; periods of reverse polarity are in light blue.

with the bones Dart had identified as tools, it became clear that the "tools" were actually produced by carnivores' gnawing. It also turns out that the hominins at these sites were not the hunters, but rather the hunted. In a particularly vivid illustration, the puncture marks on the skull of a juvenile australopithecine from the site of Swartkrans closely match the spacing of the lower canines of a leopard (see Figure 3.16).

Some archaeologists began to question whether early hominins were even capable of hunting large animals. Lewis Binford vocally advanced the idea that early hominins were scavengers, living off carcasses left behind by carnivores or fallen through natural mortality. Binford left archaeologists with a tremendous challenge. Rather than being able to assume that the bones found on archaeological sites were number of protons and electrons, but vary in the number of neutrons in the nucleus. Because ^{40}K, an isotope of the element potassium, decays into ^{40}Ar at a constant rate, the rate at which ^{40}Ar accumulates is also a constant. The trick with any accumulation clock is that it must be set to zero at the point in time of interest. Argon diffuses rapidly at high temperatures, while potassium does not. This means that, when a material containing argon is heated, the argon will be diffused out of the material, while the potassium will remain stable. If a material containing both ^{40}Ar and ^{40}K is heated to a very high temperature, the resulting product will be a material containing ^{40}K and no ^{40}Ar. From that point on, ^{40}K will begin to decay, resulting in a steady accumulation of ^{40}Ar.

Fortunately for archaeologists, the magma that explodes out of volcanoes to form ash or lava is rich in potassium. The magma is superheated until it cools after eruption. As a result, any volcanic material can be dated by determining how much ^{40}Ar has accumulated since cooling. Time zero is the point of eruption, and the time since eruption is determined by measuring the accumulation of ^{40}Ar.

In potassium-argon dating, the measure of accumulation of ^{40}Ar is based on the ratio of ^{40}K to ^{40}Ar. The development of single-crystal argon dating has significantly improved the reliability of the argon method. With the use of lasers to vaporize the sample, it is possible to date single crystals of lava or ash by measuring the ratio of ^{39}Ar to ^{40}Ar. Argon dating has been critical to the study of human evolution, particularly at East African sites such as Olduvai Gorge. Unfortunately, in areas with limited volcanic activity, argon dating is not useful. ●

FIGURE 3.18
Eruption of ash from Mount St. Helens, Washington, in 1980. Such an eruption can blanket a wide area in a layer of ash that can be dated using the argon method.

the traces of human hunting, they now had to prove that those bones were neither scavenged nor brought onto the site by geological processes.

Before looking at the archaeological evidence, it is worth considering whether it is even plausible to think that early hominins were hunters. Here, again, information from the study of wild populations of chimpanzees is useful. There has long been a popular conception of chimpanzees as peaceful vegetarians, but we now know that this is far from the truth. Chimpanzees fight, often to the death, and hunt. The range of animals hunted by chimpanzees is quite limited, including small monkeys and very small antelope. Chimpanzees hunt without tools, but rely on cooperation to catch and kill animals. When the Taï Forest chimpanzees hunt monkeys,

▲▲ **FLK North (FLKN)** The site in Olduvai Gorge where the remains of an elephant were found together with stone tools.

some members of the group chase them up a tree, while others wait quietly in a strategic spot to catch the monkeys as they run away. The monkeys are usually killed by biting and then ripped apart and eaten on the spot. The hunters are males, and the distribution of meat from the hunt seems to be an important element of how particular males gain dominance in the group.

From the way chimpanzees hunt, it is safe to assume that early hominins might have hunted small animals. It should be kept in mind, however, that early hominins would have lacked the chimpanzees' prominent canine teeth and their ability to move rapidly through trees. What is most interesting about chimpanzee hunting is that it is a group activity characterized by cooperation. It is likely that early hominins were capable of similar behavior. The problem posed by Binford is that the animal bones found on early hominin sites are not only of small animals, but also of midsized animals, such as antelope, and very large animals, including hippopotamuses and elephants. Could early hominins armed with choppers and flakes have taken down such animals, even if they were working cooperatively?

It turns out that it is very difficult to prove archaeologically that animals were hunted rather than scavenged. Perhaps the clearest evidence would be a site with the remains of a single animal carcass and stone tools. One such site is **FLK North (FLKN)** in Olduvai Gorge, Bed I (see Figure 3.19). FLKN is a site with six distinct occupation levels. In the lowest, the nearly complete skeleton of an extinct elephant (*Elephas recki*) was found together with a small number of choppers and flakes. At least one cut mark from a stone tool has been found on the elephant bones. Fragments of a wide range of smaller animals were also found concentrated in the area around the elephant skeleton. This is clearly a butchering site, but the Leakeys were uncertain to what degree the kill was planned. One possibility is that the elephant was "deliberately driven . . . into a swamp to be slaughtered" (Leakey 1971, 64). However, it is also possible that the hominins came upon an elephant carcass that

FIGURE 3.19 The plan of the excavation of the FLK North site, Olduvai Gorge, showing the association between the stone tools and the elephant bones they then scavenged for meat. Even at a site as seemingly simple as FLKN, it is not possible to determine with certainty that the hominins were actually hunting.

Although the association of stone tools with the remains of very large animals such as elephants might best be explained as the result of hominin scavenging, the same is not clearly the case for midsized to large animals. Field studies of the bones left behind after carnivores finish with a kill have raised a significant challenge to the theory that early hominins were scavengers. In general, these studies show that very little is left behind and that most of the carcass is consumed. If the early hominins were collecting the leftovers from the meals of lions and other carnivores, their yield would have been very small.

The most promising studies of how early hominins acquired meat are analyses of the surface of the animal bones found on archaeological sites. If these bones are well preserved, they bear the marks of three distinct processes: (1) gnawing by carnivores, which leaves characteristic pit marks and striations; (2) butchery with stone tools, resulting in clearly identifiable cut marks (see Figure 3.20); and (3) smashing the bones to gain access to their marrow, which produces distinctive fracture patterns known as bulbs of percussion. By studying which bones show evidence of which kind of modification, researchers can develop a picture of meat processing that provides clues as to whether the animals were hunted or scavenged. Studies such as these point to a complex interaction among carnivores and early hominins.

Almost all early hominin sites with well-preserved bone surfaces produce evidence of carnivore gnawing, cut marks, and bulbs of percussion. The problem therefore is not whether both hominins and carnivores were involved in the formation of the recovered bone assemblage; rather, the difficulty lies in determining the order of events. Did carnivores kill the animals before hominins scavenged the remains, or did hominins kill animals whose remains were then scavenged by hyenas or other carnivores? What was the role of smashing bones for marrow in this process? In the current state of research, the answer to these questions remains contentious. Some archaeologists, pointing to cut marks on the most meat-rich bones, argue

FIGURE 3.20 A cut mark left by a stone tool on an animal bone found on an archaeological site. This photograph was taken with a scanning electron microscope (SEM).

home-base/food-sharing model
A model developed by Glynn Isaac that sees the sharing of meat at base camps as a fundamental part of the lives of early hominins.

▲▲ **DK** The site at Olduvai Gorge where a stone circle was found, suggesting evidence of a temporary structure built on a home-base site.

that hominins had access to fresh kills. This pattern would not be expected if the hominins had access only to scraps of flesh that a carnivore had left behind. However, other scientists, emphasizing the frequency of carnivore gnaw marks on the midshaft of long bones, maintain that hominins scavenged bones mostly for marrow. Such a pattern fits with studies of bone damage found when carnivores deflesh carcasses.

■ Living Floors and Base Camps

When chimpanzees hunt, they consume the meat on the spot. They do share parts of the carcass, and as ethologist Craig Stanford (1999, 201) has written, "meat eating is about politics as well as nutrition." For chimpanzees, the sharing of the meat plays an important role in creating the social structure of the group. Modern human groups that subsist on hunting and gathering place a great emphasis on sharing. On the basis of research on the !Kung San hunter-gatherers of Botswana, ethnographers have found that sharing is the fundamental ethos of such societies (Lee 2003). Unlike chimpanzee sharing, which takes place at the spot where the kill was made, sharing among hunter-gatherers takes place when meat is brought back to a camp. This distinction forms the basis of the **home-base/food-sharing model** developed by Glynn Isaac. According to this model, hominins created places on the landscape to which meat was brought for sharing among members of a community. According to Isaac (1978), it is the ability to share and cooperate, rather than the ability to kill, that is the driving force behind human evolution.

THE STONE CIRCLE AT DK. When Isaac developed his home-base/food-sharing model, he had in mind site **DK** in Bed I at Olduvai Gorge. Excavations at DK in

FIGURE 3.21 The stone circle at the DK site, Olduvai Gorge. Notice that part of the circle was destroyed in a trial excavation.

1962 uncovered a circle of lava blocks on what the Leakeys identified as an "occupation floor" (Leakey 1971)—a clearly defined level of animal bones and stone tools (see Figure 3.21). The circle measures roughly 4 meters in diameter. Blocks are piled around the circumference to a maximum height of approximately 30 centimeters, and there are scattered stones on the inside. The Leakeys interpret this circle as the remains of a temporary shelter or windbreak of branches, which were then covered with grass or skin. In the area in and around the structure, stone tools and animal bones were found. The density of these remains was greater outside the stone circle than inside.

DK offers a vivid picture of what an early hominin base camp would look like and suggests that these sites would have resembled the camps of modern human hunter-gatherers. However, there is some need for caution. The stone circle at DK was found in a level immediately above the volcanic bedrock—the same material out of which the circle is constructed. The Leakeys note that "the area immediately outside the circle is relatively clear of loose stones, which become more numerous again at a distance of approximately 2 feet (0.6 meters) from the outer circumference" (Leakey 1971, 24). Thus, the possibility that the stone circle is a natural feature cannot be completely ruled out. The animal bones recovered from the DK site included the bones of mid- and large-sized mammals, with crocodile and turtle bones predominating. Reanalysis of the animal bones from the site suggests that carnivores played a major role in the accumulation of these animal remains (Dominguez-Rodrigo, Egido, and Egeland 2007).

ASSESSING THE ARCHAEOLOGICAL EVIDENCE. As was the case with the distinction between hunting and scavenging, it appears that the answer to the question of which activities led to the concentrations of stone tools and animal bones found on archaeological sites is complex. In some cases, the association of stone tools and animal bones is the result of geological processes, primarily transport by rivers or streams. However, most other sites suggest an overlay of activities that took place at a single location. Such a situation is referred to as a **palimpsest**—an archaeological surface that is the result of multiple distinct occupations. A palimpsest exists on a site that was revisited on at least several occasions and is distinct from a base camp that a single group occupied continuously. From this perspective, the early hominin sites were built up over time as different butchery and meat-processing events took place. For example, at FLKN, the elephant butchery was distinct from the events that led to the deposition of the fragmentary remains of other animals. It is possible that the DK site is a palimpsest site rather than the base camp the Leakeys reconstructed. One problem with maintaining that DK is a base camp is that doubts have been raised about the evidence for the remains of a shelter at the site. Equally problematic is that the site is in close proximity to a source of freshwater. It seems unlikely that such an area, which would attract predators, would be selected as a place for sharing meat from kills.

But if these sites were not base camps, why did early hominins continuously return to the same spots on the landscape? The DK site is only one of a number of early sites with large concentrations of stone tools and animal bones. One possibility is that hominins were drawn by natural features, such as tree cover, that would have provided shelter from carnivores and scavengers. Richard Potts (1988) has suggested that stone tools might have been cached at certain locations and carcasses dragged to those locations for processing. This is certainly possible, but it does not explain every case. For example, at FLKN, only a small number of stone tools were found.

There is clear evidence that early hominins moved stone tools around the landscape, and the same appears to be true for parts of animal carcasses. However,

palimpsest An archaeological site produced by a series of distinct brief occupations.

it is still not possible to demonstrate unequivocally that the animal carcasses were coming into base camps, where the members of hominin groups shared the meat in the fashion that is so characteristic of societies of modern hunter-gatherers.

■ Fire and Symbolic Behavior

There is very little evidence for the controlled use of fire from Oldowan and Acheulian sites in Africa. At site FxJj 20 in the Okote member at Koobi Fora, two round features roughly 1 meter in diameter are thought to be evidence of the use of fire. The soil in these circles is reddish in color, and the magnetic properties of the soil suggest that it was burnt. At the site of **Chesowanja**, Kenya, dated to 1.4 million years ago, lumps of burnt clay were found in the same context as stone tools and animal bones. The excavators argue that these lumps are the remains of a hearth that has become broken up and dispersed. Because the possibility that the burnt clay was the result of natural fires cannot be ruled out, the lumps of clay from Chesowanja cannot be taken as unequivocal evidence that early hominins used fire.

At Wonderwerk Cave, traces of wood ash, burnt artifacts, and burnt bone have been identified in an Acheulian level dated to around 1 million years ago in an area over 30 meters from the cave entrance where natural fire would be unlikely to penetrate (Berna et al. 2012). The evidence from Wonderwerk provides the best evidence that already in the Acheulean hominins were transporting fire. But the role that fire played in early hominin society remains the subject of lively debate. Richard Wrangham (2009) has proposed that already 1.8 million years ago hominins were dependent on cooked meat as a regular component of their diet. Yet the traces of fire in the early archaeological record are rare and it is hard to reconcile the sparse record with such a dietary dependence. At Wonderwerk there is no evidence that hominins were intentionally producing fire at this site as opposed to collecting and transporting fire. The function of this early fire also remains unclear and there is no evidence that the fire at Wonderwerk was used to cook meat.

In an intriguing study of modern hunter-gatherers Polly Wiessner (2014) has demonstrated how the use of fire fundamentally shapes human society. In her study

▲▲ Chesowanja A site located in Kenya and dated to 1.4 million years ago that has produced tentative evidence for the use of fire by early hominins.

FIGURE 3.22 This photo shows how a fire at night forms the focal point for social life for a San group in the Kalahari, an experience many of us have shared when camping out with San hunter-gatherers in Botswana she found differences in the conversations that took place around the fire and those that took place in other settings (Figure 3.22). Weissner describes night activities as ones that "steer away from tensions of the day to singing, dancing, religious ceremonies, and enthralling stories, often about known people" (Wiessner 2014: 14027). Weissner's study makes it clear that the impact of the use of fire extends far beyond nutrition.

There is virtually no evidence for symbolic artifacts found in early Lower Paleolithic contexts. The discovery of a large group of hominin fossils deep in the Rising Star cave system in South Africa led the excavator to suggest that the location of these bones in a dark part of the cave system that today is only accessible through a narrow passage was the result of the transport of corpses below ground for burial (Dirks et al. 2015). Unfortunately, the precise age of these fossils, assigned to the new species *Homo naledi*, has not been determined, but based on the morphology of these fossils they are likely contemporary with early *Homo erectus*. If indeed it is true that this is an intentional burial context, Rising Star would provide very early evidence for ritual activity in the hominin lineage. However, it still remains to be determined whether taphonomic processes rather than intentional human action could account for the accumulation of bones in this unique context.

3.5 The Expansion of the Hominin World

By 1.4 million years ago, the hominin radiation was over. Of the four genera that flourished beginning 4 million years ago, only genus *Homo* survived. Within genus *Homo*, there was at this point only a single species, *Homo erectus*. By this time, a sophisticated tool technology, the Acheulian, had developed in Africa. Overlapping with the end of the hominin radiation, the hominin colonization of areas outside of Africa began. In a **dispersal** event, a single species dramatically expands its geographic range. Dispersal, which often involves a species moving into a new ecological niche, contrasts with radiation in that a single species expands both its geographical range and the range of ecological niches it inhabits. By contrast, in a radiation event, a wide diversity of new species evolves, each of which adapts to a particular ecological niche. What took place in the hominin lineage around 4 million years ago was a radiation. The first event of hominin dispersal began around 1.8 million years ago, soon after the first appearance of *Homo erectus* in Africa.

What is the significance of the spread of *Homo erectus* beyond Africa? We need to be careful to avoid seeing this process through the lens of the heroic modern image of the explorer. The dispersal of *Homo erectus* does not track the paths of individual wanderers; rather, it follows the expansion of populations into new ecological settings. What is it about *Homo erectus* that allowed this species to move into areas that earlier hominins did not occupy? Did *Homo erectus* possess some new ability that spurred its expansion? We will return to these questions at the end of the chapter, but first we must follow the archaeological evidence for the timing of the dispersal.

■ Ubeidiya and Dmanisi

The site of **Ubeidiya** is located south of the Sea of Galilee in Israel. The Sea of Galilee is part of the northern extension of the East African Rift Valley, and the setting of the site is not very different from that at Olduvai Gorge. When the site was in use, it was at the edge of a large freshwater lake in an area occupied by a wide diversity of mostly African species of animals. The stone tools from Ubeidiya also look much like the material from Olduvai. The lower part of the sequence includes tools characteristic of the Oldowan, including choppers and flake tools along with a small

dispersal An event where a single species dramatically expands its range.

▲▲ **Ubeidiya** One of the earliest archaeological sites outside of Africa, located in Israel south of the Sea of Galilee and dated between 1.4 and 1.0 million years ago.

number of crude handaxes. Ubeidiya is dated between 1.4 million and 1.0 million years ago.

The prehistoric site of **Dmanisi**, in the Republic of Georgia, was discovered during the excavation of a medieval village. When the excavators were clearing out the cellars that had been dug into the ground by the site's inhabitants, they found bones eroding out of the earthen walls. A paleontologist identified the bones as fossils dating to around 1.8 million years ago. In 1994, a limited paleontological project began to recover more of these fossils, which, to the surprise of the excavators, included a *Homo erectus* mandible (jaw). This spectacular discovery was followed by the identification of stone tools on the site and the recovery of three fairly complete crania of *Homo erectus*. Dmanisi is widely accepted today as the earliest evidence of human occupation outside of Africa. The hominin occupation at Dmanisi is dated between 1.85 and 1.77 million years ago (Ferring et al. 2011).

The nature of the hominin activity at Dmanisi remains unclear. None of the animal bones have signs of cut marks, and it does not seem likely that the hominins had anything to do with accumulating these bones. The stone tools are found widely dispersed on the site and are not found in association with the hominin and animal fossils. The fossils and some of the tools come from irregularly shaped pits in the soil. It is possible that these pits were formed by water action that created depressions into which hominin and animal carcasses tumbled. Alternatively, the pits could have been natural features altered and used as dens by carnivores. The site was located at the edge of a freshwater lake that would have been an ideal habitat for hominins.

The stone tools found at Dmanisi are mostly simple flakes (De Lumley et al. 2005; Ferring et al. 2011). There are none of the bifaces characteristic of the Acheulian industry. A small number of choppers have been found at the site.

■ East Asia

The discovery at Dmanisi of strong evidence for a hominin dispersal soon after the first appearance of *Homo erectus* in Africa is supported by recent research on sites in China and Indonesia. Like Dmanisi, the East Asian sites have produced no evidence of Acheulian technology. The early dates for sites in China and Indonesia are currently the subject of heated debate. However, if these early dates hold up to scrutiny, they suggest that the initial dispersal of *Homo erectus* was a remarkably rapid event.

JAVA. The first discovery of a *Homo erectus* fossil took place far from Africa, at the site of Trinil on the Indonesian island of Java. The Trinil fossil, discovered in 1892 by the Dutch paleontologist Eugene Dubois, created a sensation and much controversy. Many scientists were unwilling to accept Dubois's claim that he had found the "missing link" between apes and humans and argued instead that the fossil was either an ape or a human. Dubois was so infuriated by the controversy that he stopped allowing researchers direct access to the fossils, keeping them locked in a safe in his office.

Today, controversy again surrounds the *Homo erectus* from Java. There is little dispute about the taxonomic status of the fossils; all appear to belong to the species *Homo erectus*. The subject of contention now is the dating of the fossils, specifically those from the sites of **Sangiran** and **Perning**. These fossils are found in an early geological position within the Javan sequence known as the Upper Sangiran Formation. The date of this formation was long thought to be approximately 1 million years ago on the basis of paleomagnetism and the types of animal fossils found in the formation. In 1994, argon dates were published for the Upper Sangiran Formation at Sangiran and Perning that place the fossils at 1.8 million years ago. However, a number of archaeologists have questioned whether this date is accurate.

Although Java is now an island, it was not so throughout the Pleistocene era. A land bridge, known as the Sunda Shelf, connected Java to mainland Southeast Asia during periods of low sea level. One oddity of the early *Homo erectus* sites on Java is that none have produced evidence of stone tools. Still, it is not yet clear whether these hominins lacked stone tools or whether they made tools that have not been identified.

NIHEWAN BASIN. The **Nihewan Basin** in the Northern China Plain near Beijing is an area rich in paleontological sites. A number of sites with stone tools have been found at Nihewan in contexts that appear to be Early Pleistocene. Four of these sites have been dated by paleomagnetism to the period around 1.6 million years ago (Zhu et al. 2004). The stone tools from the Nihewan Basin are flakes, mostly made of poor raw material.

■ Summing Up the Evidence

The evidence from Ubeidiya and Dmanisi makes it clear that the initial hominin dispersal took place soon after the first appearance of *Homo erectus* in Africa. If one accepts the early dates from Java, it would appear that the initial dispersal was a widespread event. Whether it is best to reconstruct a single migration or multiple migrations is open to question. It is quite possible that the dispersal of hominins to Java followed a southerly route across the Arabian Peninsula and around the Indian subcontinent. Such a route would have required crossing the minor body of water known as the Straits of Bab el Mandeb at the mouth of the Red Sea.

It is particularly difficult to try to tie the hominin dispersal in with a particular climatic event. In a general sense, climatic instability might have played a role in the dispersal. Another possibility is that some aspect of technology gave these hominins the ability to adapt to new environments. Clearly, this ability is not tied to any particular type of stone tool, as these elaborate tools are lacking in all of the early sites. One interesting suggestion is that it was the development of technologies of food processing, particularly the use of fire, that led to the hominin dispersal (Wrangham et al. 1999). However, to date, none of the early sites outside of Africa have produced evidence for the use of fire.

Some archaeologists have suggested as an explanation of the dispersal the increased cognitive capacity of *Homo erectus*, reflected in a larger brain, which might have led to the development of new forms of social organization. Clive Gamble has argued that, before *Homo erectus*, the social organization of hominins required frequent face-to-face interactions. The cognitive ability of *Homo erectus* to retain information for increased periods of time allowed for the "stretching of society in time and space," as the social group could then maintain its coherence even when individuals met infrequently (Gamble 1993, 142). As a result, *Homo erectus* social groups would be able to survive in areas where seasonal scarcity forced the group to disperse across a wide territory during parts of the year. Groups of *Homo erectus* thus were able to survive in ecological niches that could not support earlier hominin species. One can easily imagine how such wide-ranging social groups would discover new territories, perhaps as young adults explored the edges of the range of the core group, leading to its expansion into previously uninhabited areas.

▲▲ **Nihewan Basin** A location in northern China where there is solid evidence of human occupation around 1.6 million years ago.

SUMMARY

- The hominin radiation between 4 million and 2 million years ago included four distinct genera.
- The earliest evidence for walking upright is found in *Australopithecus afarensis*.
- *Homo habilis* is characterized by an increased brain size relative to that of other early hominins.
- The earliest known *Homo erectus* dates between 1.9 million and 1.5 million years ago. *Homo erectus* is characterized by an increase in brain size compared with *Homo habilis*.
- Chimpanzee tool use includes fishing for termites and breaking nuts with stone hammers and anvils.
- The earliest evidence for hominin stone tool manufacture is found at the Gona site in the Hadar region of Ethiopia, dated to 2.5 million years ago.
- Analyses of stone tools from the site of Lokalalei indicate that the manufacture of the earliest stone tools was a complex process.
- There is debate over whether early hominins gained access to meat by hunting or by scavenging.

- The home-base/food-sharing model suggests that meat sharing at base camps played an important role in the lives of early hominins.
- A stone circle that might have been the base of a hut was found at the DK site, Olduvai Gorge. This type of site is predicted by the home-base/food-sharing model.
- The earliest tentative evidence for the controlled use of fire was found at Chesowanja, Kenya, a site dated to 1.4 million years ago.
- The earliest archaeological sites outside of Africa are Dmanisi, Georgia (1.8 million to 1.7 million years ago) and Ubeidiya, Israel (1.4 million to 1.0 million years ago).
- *Homo erectus* fossils found on the Indonesian island of Java at the sites of Sangiran and Perning have been dated to 1.8 million years ago. No other archaeological material has been found with these fossils.
- The oldest reliable evidence for human occupation of China is from the Nihewan Basin, dated to around 1.6 million years ago.

KEY TERMS

Acheulian, 74
Ardipithecus ramidus, 66
australopithecines, 69
bifaces, 74
Chesowanja, 86
dispersal, 87
DK, 84
Dmanisi, 88
East African Rift Valley, 69
FLK North, 82
Hadar, 77
home-base/food-sharing model, 84
hominins, 66
Homo erectus, 69

Homo habilis, 69
Laetoli, 69
Lokalalei, 78
Lomekwi 3, 77
Lower Paleolithic, 71
Nihewan Basin, 89
Oldowan, 72
Olduvai Gorge, 71
palimpsest, 85
radiation, 66
Sahelanthropus tchadensis, 66
Sangiran and Perning, 88
Taï Forest, 76
Ubeidiya, 87

REVIEW QUESTIONS

1. Why is the period between 4 million and 2 million years ago referred to as the hominin radiation?
2. Which hominin produced the earliest stone tools?
3. What is the significance of the discoveries made at FLK North, Olduvai Gorge?

4. What is the home-base/food-sharing model? Does the archaeological evidence support it?
5. Is the initial dispersal of *Homo erectus* best described as gradual or rapid?

FROM *HOMO ERECTUS* TO NEANDERTHALS

Neanderthals occupied Europe and the Middle East between 175,000 and 30,000 years ago. After reading this chapter, you should understand:

- The *oxygen isotope* glacial sequence.
- The spread of hominins through Europe and the characteristics of the European Lower Paleolithic.
- The major anatomical features that characterize Neanderthals.
- The three major theories of the evolution of Neanderthals.
- The evidence for Neanderthal stone tool technology, hunting, use of fire, burial of the dead, and artwork.

Extracting DNA from a Neanderthal fossil

4 TIMELINE

SITES

Gran Dolina (TD-6 level), Atapuerca

Gesher Benot Ya'akov

Isernia la Pineta

Bose

Boxgrove

Zhoukoukian

ARCHAEOLOGICAL INDUSTRIES

HOMININS

HOMO ERECTUS

thousands of years ago 800   700   600   500

SITES DISCUSSED IN CHAPTER 4

ATLANTIC OCEAN

Beeches Pit
Boxgrove
• Schöningen
• Biache Saint Vaast
La Cotte de Saint Brelade

Atapuerca

Gorham's Cave

• Mezmaiskaya

Gesher Benot Ya'akov
• Umm el Tlel
Kebara • Amud

INDIAN OCEAN

• Zhoukoudian

Bose •

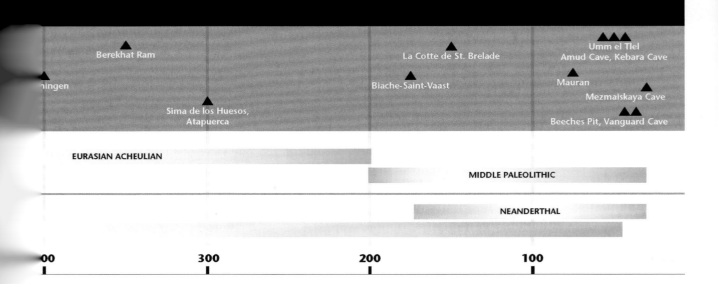

Berekhat Ram

La Cotte de St. Brelade

Umm el Tlel
Amud Cave, Kebara Cave

...ingen

Biache-Saint-Vaast

Mauran

Mezmaiskaya Cave

Sima de los Huesos,
Atapuerca

Beeches Pit, Vanguard Cave

EURASIAN ACHEULIAN

MIDDLE PALEOLITHIC

NEANDERTHAL

00   300   200   100

FIGURE 4.1 Marcelin Boule's reconstruction of a Neanderthal as a stooped hairy brute. Notice the club grasped firmly in the Neanderthal's right hand. Why do you think this detail is included?

The picture of Neanderthals as hulking ape-men dates back to 1908 and the discovery of the "Old Man of La Chapelle-aux-Saints." The La Chapelle fossil was the most complete skeleton of a Neanderthal ever recovered, and it provided a unique opportunity to understand the characteristics of this intriguing hominin. The task of analyzing the skeleton fell to Marcelin Boule, a prominent paleoanthropologist who came to the job convinced that Neanderthals were "a degenerate side branch of human evolution" (Bowler 1986, 88). Not surprisingly, the portrait that emerged from Boule's analysis was a hairy, stooped creature (see Figure 4.1). Subsequent studies show that Boule had largely ignored the effects of arthritis and other pathologies on the posture of the fossil from La Chapelle. Contemporary studies of Neanderthals paint a far more intriguing picture of a hominin that is in numerous respects similar to modern humans, but at the same time is distinctive. In many ways, the dramatic picture of Neanderthals as our apish ancestors has been replaced by the image of Neanderthals as an enigma.

In this chapter, we begin by examining the environmental record pertaining to the Pleistocene, or the Ice Age. We then pick up where we left off in the last chapter to follow the record for the continued spread of populations of *Homo erectus* into western Europe. We also look at new developments that begin to appear in the archaeological record toward the end of the Lower Paleolithic around 500,000 years ago. We then turn to the Neanderthal fossil record and offer an extended consideration of the archaeological record of Neanderthal behavior and society.

4.1 Defining the Ice Age

The evolution of Neanderthals took place within the context of the geological period known as the Pleistocene, or the Ice Age. The boundary between the **Pleistocene** and the preceding Pliocene era is fixed at almost precisely 1.8 million years ago, although geologists are considering moving the boundary back to 2.6 million years ago. The Pleistocene is characterized by periods with a significant buildup of ice sheets, known as glacial eras, and periods during which the ice sheets subsequently retreated, known as interglacial eras.

Geologists first developed a record of Pleistocene climate change on the basis of features of the landscape. One such feature is the terminal moraine, a characteristic raised ridge that formed at the point where the glacial ice sheet reached its maximum extent. Cape Cod in Massachusetts is a classic example of a terminal moraine. By looking at such features in both North America and Europe, geologists developed a glacial chronology for the Pleistocene involving four major cycles of advance and retreat of the ice sheets. In Europe, the four major glacial advances were named, from earliest to latest, Günz, Mindel, Riss, and Würm. In North America, the last two glacial advances are known as the Illinoian and the Wisconsin.

The bottom of the sea might seem to be an unlikely place to search for a record of the advance and retreat of ice sheets, but analyses of cores drilled from the ocean floor have revolutionized our view of Pleistocene climate change. The development of glaciers is only one element of a global process. As glaciers build up, water is locked up in ice at the expense of water otherwise held in the oceans. When glaciers advance, sea levels drop, and when glaciers retreat, sea levels go up. During

Pleistocene The geological era that began 1.8 million years ago, characterized by the frequent buildup and retreat of continental ice sheets.

some past periods of glacial advance, the global sea level was close to 140 meters below what it is today (Rohling et al. 1998). Today's sea level reflects the fact that we are living in an interglacial period.

Analysis of cores drilled from the seafloor allows scientists to measure and date fluctuations in the amount of water in the ocean and thus develop a global "thermometer" for the Ice Age. The secret behind this thermometer is foraminifera, tiny organisms that live on the surface of the ocean. The skeletons of these organisms are made of calcium carbonate, which absorbs oxygen from seawater and drifts to the seafloor after the organisms die. Over millennia, the seafloor deposits incorporate a continuous stratigraphic sequence of foraminifera. A core drilled out of the seafloor can recover a sequence of foraminifera covering millions of years. Such sequences can be dated by the uranium series method.

Foraminifera absorb two isotopes of oxygen. ^{18}O is the heavier isotope and ^{16}O is the lighter. During periods of glacial buildup, the oceans become isotopically heavy because ^{16}O is drawn off with the moisture that builds the ice sheets. During glacial periods, the oceans have a high ratio of ^{18}O to ^{16}O. The reverse is true during interglacial periods, when sea levels rise. Measuring the ratio of ^{18}O to ^{16}O in the foraminifera collected in deep-sea cores provides a record of the advance and retreat of glaciers during the Pleistocene. The record provided by sea cores is very different from the model of four major glacial periods. The picture that emerges is of an

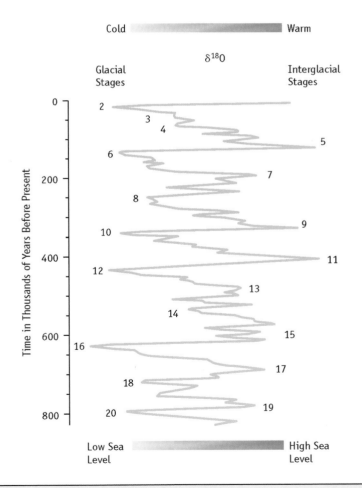

FIGURE 4.2 The oxygen isotope curve provides a record of Pleistocene climate change by measuring shifts in the ratio of oxygen isotopes in foraminifera, microscopic organisms that live on the surface of the ocean

Colder Climate ⟶ More Ice on Land ⟶ Less Water in the Ocean ⟶ High Ratio of ^{18}O to ^{16}O
Warmer Climate ⟶ Less Ice on Land ⟶ More Water in the Ocean ⟶ Low Ratio of ^{18}O to ^{16}O

oxygen isotope curve The record of fluctuations in global climate during the Pleistocene.

▲▲ **Gran Dolina, Atapuerca** A cave in Spain where stone tools and hominin remains dated to 800,000 years ago were found. These artifacts are the oldest reliable evidence of human occupation of western Europe.

▲▲ **Bose** A site in southern China that produced a stone tool industry that includes handaxes dated to 800,000 years ago.

unstable climate with many glacial and interglacial periods over the last 1.8 million years. In the last 700,000 years, there have been eight full glacial-interglacial cycles (see Figure 4.2). The climate record produced by the analysis of deep-sea cores is known as the oxygen isotope curve. Glacial and interglacial events are given numbers, from the most recent (we now live in Oxygen Isotope Stage 1) to the oldest. If one looks closely at the **oxygen isotope curve**, it becomes evident that the extent of glaciation and the rapidity of climate change vary considerably. For instance, the boundaries between Stages 5 and 6 and Stages 9 and 10 are examples of particularly abrupt climate change.

4.2 Before the Neanderthals

In the last chapter we examined the evidence for the initial dispersal of *Homo erectus*. To understand the evolution of Neanderthals, we need to know more about what happened after this initial dispersal. We need to know when hominins first spread into western Europe. We also need to know about the Lower Paleolithic cultures of Europe and Asia. Finally, we want to know about developments toward the later stages of the Lower Paleolithic. Did hominins intensify the use of fire? Is there evidence for changes in the way tools are used? Is there artwork? Are there burials?

■ The Initial Occupation of Western Europe

Although Dmanisi, at the eastern edge of Europe, has evidence of occupation going back approximately 1.7 million years, hominin sites more than 500,000 years old in western Europe are rare. However, the 500,000-year barrier has been dramatically shattered by research at a system of caves located at **Atapuerca** in north-central Spain. The construction of a railroad through the hill at Atapuerca exposed the **Gran Dolina**, a massive cave filled with 18 meters of deposits. Archaeologists perched on an elaborate system of scaffolding have swarmed over the Gran Dolina sequence, digging into 11 archaeological levels that have been dated by paleomagnetism and electron spin resonance. In the TD-6 level, dated to 800,000 years ago, a rich collection of stone tools and fossil bones was recovered along with 30 hominin fragments (Carbonell et al. 1999). There is growing evidence for hominin occupation in Spain as early as 1 million years ago (Toro Moyano 2010).

The stone tools from Gran Dolina TD-6 are flakes and cores. The hominin remains from TD-6 have been classified as a new species, *Homo antecessor*. Because most of the remains are fragmentary and the single fairly complete skull is of a juvenile, further discoveries are needed to confirm the identification of the species.

Another early site in western Europe is Isernia la Pineta in Italy, dated to more than 700,000 years ago (Peretto 2006). In the Sett. I t.3a level, a dense occupation layer of stone tools and animal bones was found covering an area of 24 square meters. Over 1,000 stone tools were discovered, mostly simple flakes made on poor-quality stone. The animal bones include the remains of bears, elephants, rhinos, bison, and deer.

■ The Acheulian in Europe and Asia

In East Asia, chopper and flake tools characterize most Lower Paleolithic sites. Paradoxically, the earliest date for an Acheulian industry anywhere outside of Africa is at the site of **Bose** in China (Yamei et al. 2000). Bose is also the only site in China where handaxes have been uncovered. The artifacts at Bose are found in a river terrace in a stratigraphic unit that varies between 25 and 100 centimeters in thickness. Argon dating of tektites (small fragments of glass formed by meteor impacts) found with the tools has dated the site to 800,000 years ago. As with volcanic ash and lava, argon dating determines when the glass formed.

Other than Bose, the earliest well-dated Acheulian site outside of Africa is **Gesher Benot Ya'akov**, Israel, located to the north of the Sea of Galilee in the northern extension of the East African Rift Valley. Dated to 780,000 years ago, Gesher Benot Ya'akov is similar to African Acheulian sites. Bifaces are made on very large flakes, and handaxes and cleavers are common. The excavations at Gesher Benot Ya'akov have also produced limited evidence for the use of fire and for the cracking of nuts.

It is beginning only 500,000 years ago that Acheulian sites became common across Europe, in the Middle East, and on into the Indian subcontinent—the geographic region known as Eurasia. There is regional variation in the **Eurasian Acheulian**, but taken as a whole, these industries show some significant contrast with the African Acheulian. Cleavers are almost completely absent from the Eurasian Acheulian, and handaxes are the major type of biface.

Another characteristic of the Eurasian Acheulian is that the handaxes were often part of a tool kit that also included retouched flakes—flakes that were modified after being struck off the core. The characteristic type of flake tool is the sidescraper, in which one or two edges of the flake have been regularized and strengthened by retouching (see Figure 4.3).

Boxgrove, located in West Sussex in southern England, is among the earliest known Acheulian sites in Europe and one of the most extensively excavated (see Figure 4.4). On the basis of the animal species represented in the faunal assemblage, the site is dated to 500,000 years ago (Roberts and Parfitt 1999). The hominin occupation of Boxgrove appears to have been close to the shore of a small lake near the sea. The stone tools include the debris from handaxe manufacture, which, when

Eurasian Acheulian A stone tool industry found on sites throughout the Middle East and Europe beginning 500,000 years ago. The handaxe is the characteristic tool of this industry.

▲▲ **Gesher Benot Ya'akov** An Acheulian site in Israel dating to 780,000 years ago that has produced limited evidence for the use of fire and for the cracking of nuts.

▲▲ **Boxgrove** One of the oldest known Acheulian sites in Europe; located in England and dated to 500,000 years ago.

Cagny-l'Epinette
0   5 cm
Level I1

FIGURE 4.3 Handaxe (left) and flake tool (right) from the Lower Paleolithic site of Cagny-l'Epinette, France

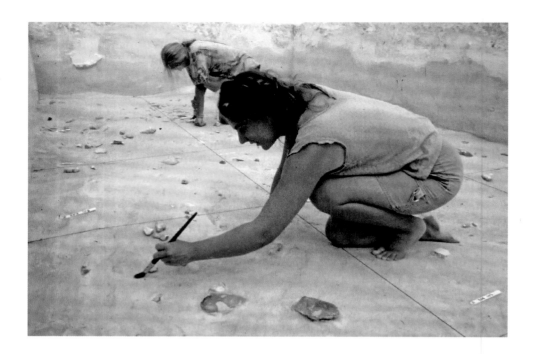

FIGURE 4.4 Excavation at Boxgrove. Notice how artifacts are left in place as they are exposed, providing a clear view of a broad horizontal surface.

refit, provides a detailed picture of the process involved in making these tools. The handaxes found at Boxgrove were shaped with both hard and soft hammers.

Experiments in which an experienced butcher was given a replicated handaxe to use showed that these tools would have served very well to skin and butcher carcasses. Animal bones from the site, including the bones of a large horse, have traces of tool cut marks, and whether or not these animals were hunted, hominins did have early access to the carcasses. No evidence for the use of fire or of a base camp has been found at Boxgrove.

Not all sites in Europe dating later than 500,000 years ago have produced handaxes. The **Clactonian** is an industry in England of simple flake tools contemporary with the Acheulian. Some have argued that Clactonian sites are simply Acheulian handaxe manufacturing sites from which the finished products are absent. This idea has been refuted, and it is now clear that the Clactonian is distinct from the Acheulian. In eastern Europe, a number of Lower Paleolithic sites have produced flake tool industries. Vértesszölös is a particularly rich site located in Hungary dated to 350,000 years ago. The stone tools at Vértesszölös are choppers and retouched flakes.

The variation in Lower Paleolithic industries is modest compared with that found in later periods, but is nonetheless real. The patterns of variation that do exist confound some of our expectations and prove difficult to explain. One would expect that all groups would rapidly adopt the Acheulian technology. However, this was clearly not the case. The site of Bose has produced the oldest known handaxes outside of Africa. However, handaxe manufacture never became widespread among early hominins in East Asia. In Europe, Acheulian industries appeared only 500,000 years ago, hundreds of thousands of years after the first arrival of hominins. Even after the widespread appearance of handaxes in Europe and western Asia, there were industries, such as the Clactonian, that did not involve handaxe manufacture.

■ Changes within the Lower Paleolithic

Clactonian A simple flake tool industry contemporary with the Acheulian in England.

During the stage of the Lower Paleolithic, beginning around 500,000 years ago there are a series of subtle new features in the archaeological record. The limited collection of European and African hominin fossils from this period are often grouped under the species *Homo heidelbergensis*; however, many question whether this in fact a single species (Rightmire 1998). In Asia *Homo erectus* appears to continue through this period. **Zhoukoudian** is a series of caves in Longgu-shan, or Dragon Bone Hill, outside of Beijing (Peking), China (see Figure 4.5). Since excavations began at the cave known as Locality 1 in the early 1920s, the remains of more than 40 *Homo erectus* individuals and over 100,000 stone tools, all choppers and flakes, have been recovered. The hominins from Zhoukoudian, also known as Peking man, are at the center of one of the unsolved mysteries of archaeology. After Japan attacked Pearl Harbor in World War II, an attempt was made to get the fossils out of Peking, which was under Japanese occupation. In the confusion of war, the fossils were lost, and no trace of them has ever reappeared. Fortunately, accurate casts of most of the fossils were saved.

Locality 1 at Zhoukoudian is an absolutely massive site. The scale of the early excavations was more like a mining operation than what we expect from a modern archaeological project. The total depth of the deposits at Locality 1 is 48 meters, which has been divided into 17 layers. The dating of the site is extremely complex; however, most studies agree that the hominin occupation occurred between 500,000 and 300,000 years ago. Recent dating of Zhoukoudian by the newly developed cosmogenic burial age dating method suggests that the site might actually be as much as 750,000 years old (Shen et al. 2009).

Locality 1 at Zhoukoudian has long been thought to provide the earliest evidence for the use of fire. The most important evidence comes from Layer 10, which has been described as an ash layer. However, recent research has demonstrated that there is no ash in Layer 10 and that what had been identified as ash is actually organic material brought in by a river that ran through the cave (Goldberg et al. 2001). Similar conclusions have been reached concerning the evidence of burning in Layer 4. The only evidence suggestive of the controlled use of fire by hominins at Zhoukoudian Locality 1 is the occurrence of burnt bones together with stone tools. Although evidence of fire has been identified at the Acheulian site of Gesher Benot Ya'akov in Israel, in general terms the use of fire during the Lower Paleolithic was rare. The most compelling evidence for the use of fire in the Lower Paleolithic comes from the site of Beeches Pit in England, which is dated to 400,000 years ago (Preece et al. 2006). At **Beeches Pit**, there are clearly discrete areas where a concentration of charred bones and stone tools was found (see Figure 4.6). However, the possibility of natural fire cannot be completely ruled out, since burnt lizard and rat bones were found along with the bones of large mammals. There is nonetheless strong support for controlled use of fire by the hominins occupying the site. The evidence of fire is found only in strata in which artifacts are present, and it is restricted to small, shallow depressions. At Qesem Cave in Israel, occupied around 300,000 years ago, excavations have uncovered the remains of hearths that included preserved wood ash (Karkanas et al. 2007).

Anatomical studies of living humans, including detailed studies of the biomechanics of baseball pitching (Figure 4.7), suggests that modern humans have evolved

FIGURE 4.5 Historical photo of the site of Zhoukoudian at the time of the discovery of a *Homo erectus* fossil

FIGURE 4.6 Horizontal exposure of hearths at the site of Beeches Pit. The hearths are visible as clearly delineated areas of black sediment.

▲▲ **Schöningen** The location in Germany where 400,000-year-old wooden spears were discovered.

FIGURE 4.7 A pitcher throwing a baseball draws on an evolutionary legacy that makes such a powerful gesture possible

adaptations for throwing (Roach et al. 2013). When a pitcher's arm is cocked, energy is stored and then released during the throw. Studies of fossils suggest this anatomical adaptation is found in *Homo erectus*. The archaeological record is beginning to yield evidence for the emergence of thrown weapons such as spears.

Excavations in a coal mine at **Schöningen**, Germany, have uncovered three spruce spears together with a rich collection of stone tools and animal bones dated to 400,000 years ago (Thieme 1997). The unique context of this site allowed for the preservation of these wooden artifacts (see Figure 4.8). The spears vary between 1.8 and 2.2 meters in length and between 29 and 47 millimeters in diameter. Another piece, which is pointed on both ends (as opposed to the spears, which are pointed at only one end), is 0.8 meters long. The spears are well made and balanced, but do not appear to have had a stone tip or any decoration. The excavator interprets them as projectiles.

At the site of Kathu Pan, South Africa, the stone tools from a level dated to 500,000 years ago seem to anticipate the kinds of technological advances that are found in Europe with the advent of the Neanderthals. Among the tools uncovered at Kathu are pointed flakes. The tips on some of these tools were fractured by high-velocity impact identical to the fractures found on replicated spear tips used in experiments (Wilkins et al. 2012). The Kathu Pan evidence suggests that beginning 500,000 years ago hominins in Africa used stone-tipped spears.

There is very little evidence of either artwork or ritual behavior in Lower Paleolithic contexts. Two exceptions to this generalization deserve particular mention. The first is a small pebble of volcanic rock found at the Lower Paleolithic site of Berekhat Ram, Golan Heights (see Figure 4.9). The excavator of Berekhat

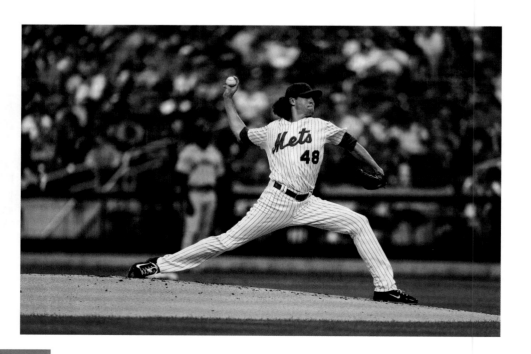

Ram discerned signs of work on this stone and identified it as a representation of a human female. Because the site is more than 230,000 years old, the stone is possibly the earliest evidence of human representation. Subsequent research has confirmed that the pebble was indeed worked by the incision of a single line. Whether the intention was to create a figurine remains unclear (d'Errico and Nowell 2000). A very intriguing discovery is a shell from a site in Indonesia dated between 540,000 and 430,000 with a simple grid design incised on the outside surface (Joordens et al. 2015). This discovery points to how poor our knowledge is of the Lower Paleolithic of Southeast Asia and the need for further research to contextualize this surprising artifact.

The only significant evidence for special treatment of the dead during the Lower Paleolithic comes from a cave at Atapuerca known as Sima de los Huesos, which is dated to 300,000 years ago. In this pit, the complete remains of 27 hominin individuals were recovered (Carbonell et al. 2003). Only one stone tool, a well-made quartz handaxe, has been found in the cave. There is no evidence of human occupation of Sima de los Huesos, nor is there evidence that it was an accessible cave. It appears to have been a crevice in the rock, in which the inhabitants were cave bears and other carnivores. The excavators argue that the hominins were not brought to the cave by carnivores and that the cave was not a natural crevice into which they fell. Rather, they interpret Sima de los Huesos as a place where corpses were placed as part of a funerary ritual, and they construe the handaxe to be a funerary offering. Unlike the scenario suggested for the much earlier Rising Star Cave in South Africa, where the bodies are thought to have been placed deep in the ground, it is thought that at Sima de los Huesos the corpses were thrown into this chasm. The excavators suggest that the large number of corpses reflects a burial of the victims of an ecological crisis. There is evidence of carnivore gnawing on almost half of the human bones. These gnaw marks include the actions of a small fox-sized animal and a larger lion-sized animal. There is no evidence that the corpses were buried. It is interesting that one of the skulls from Sima de los Huesos has traces of two blows delivered to the upper forehead, which appear to be the result of fatal blows from a single weapon (Sala et al. 2015).

4.3 Neanderthals

All living humans are members of the species *Homo sapiens*, also known as modern humans. Neanderthals are at once similar to modern humans and yet highly distinctive (Figure 4.10). The significance of the similarities and differences between Neanderthals and our own species is the focus of intense debate. Some scientists argue that the similarities are so strong that Neanderthals must be merely a subspecies—*Homo sapiens neanderthalensis*—of our own. Others argue that despite the similarities, the

FIGURE 4.8 400,000-year-old wooden spears and faunal remains discovered at the site of Schöningen, Germany

FIGURE 4.9 The Berekhat Ram figurine. The groove running around the top part of the stone appears to be artificial. Height: 3.5 cm.

FIGURE 4.10 Neanderthal skulls from the sites of La Chapelle-aux-Saints, France (top) and La Ferrassie, France (bottom). Notice that the skull is long and the face juts forward.

differences warrant the creation of a distinct species—*Homo neanderthalensis*—for the Neanderthals. Table 4.1 lists some important attributes of Neanderthals.

The similarities between modern humans and Neanderthals are rooted in their shared ancestry. Unfortunately, there is some controversy surrounding the identification of the last common ancestor of modern humans and Neanderthals. Three scenarios (shown in Figure 4.11) have been posed for the evolution of Neanderthals:

1. Neanderthals and modern humans each evolved separately from populations of *Homo erectus*, possibly through local intermediate species. According to this scenario, the evolution of Neanderthals and modern humans took place in parallel, in separate geographic areas. Evidence for the evolution of modern humans in Africa will be discussed in the next chapter. Neanderthals, a species (or subspecies) adapted to cold climates, evolved in Europe.

2. The common ancestor of modern humans and Neanderthals was a distinct species that itself evolved from *Homo erectus* and lived between 700,000 and 300,000 years ago. One candidate for this critical intermediate position is *Homo heidelbergensis*.

Neanderthals and modern humans then each evolved separately from this intermediate species in parallel, in separate geographic areas.

3. Neanderthals and modern humans did not evolve in isolation; rather, there was a constant exchange of genetic material, or gene flow, between the two populations. This possibility cannot be ruled out; however, some degree of isolation must have existed in order for Neanderthals to evolve some of

TABLE 4.1 NEANDERTHAL TRAITS

GENUS OR SPECIES	DATE	BRAIN SIZE	CHARACTERISTICS	DISTRIBUTION
Homo neanderthalensis or	175,000–30,000 years ago	1,200–1,700 cc	Muscular and adapted to the cold	Europe and the Middle East
Homo sapiens neanderthalensis				

FIGURE 4.11 Three scenarios for the evolution of Neanderthals

their characteristic skeletal traits. According to this model, Neanderthals and modern humans are members of a single species.

The distinctiveness of a Neanderthal skeleton makes it easy to identify. The skull is elongated compared with the skull of a modern human, with an occipital bun at the back and a large, projecting nose in front. The forehead is sloping and the chin almost absent. As in *Homo erectus*, there is a brow ridge over the eyes; however, in Neanderthals, this ridge is double arched. The skull is not as thick as that of *Homo erectus*, but is still thicker than the norm among living humans. The molars of Neanderthals were large, and the front teeth show marks of wear, indicating the regular use of the incisors as tools in preparing food or gripping hides. The Neanderthal body is stocky and similar in proportion to modern humans adapted to cold climates. Particularly notable are a broad rib cage and bowed, long bones. The muscle insertions are well developed, and the bones are generally robust. Although Neanderthals were completely bipedal, the way they walked was slightly different from that of modern humans.

The overall impression one forms of Neanderthals is that they were very strong and well adapted to cold climates. Among the features tied to a cold-weather adaptation are the projecting face and large nose. These features distinguish Neanderthals from both *Homo erectus* and modern humans. Studies of fossil remains of Neanderthal children indicate that many of the characteristic Neanderthal features developed quite early in childhood.

The brains of Neanderthals were within the size range of those of modern humans, between 1,200 and 1,700 cubic centimeters. This is considerably larger than the brain of *Homo erectus*. If Neanderthals and modern humans each evolved independently from *Homo erectus*, then the increase in brain size took place as a parallel process in the two lineages. Alternatively, the large brains of Neanderthals and modern humans could be derived from a large-brained common ancestor such as *Homo antecessor*—or the parallel evolution of larger brains could be the product of gene flow.

The evolution of the brain in the Neanderthal lineage is critical to assessing Neanderthal behavior. If Neanderthals evolved larger brains independently from modern humans, then there is a possibility that, despite being the same size, modern human and Neanderthal brains are significantly different in organization and cognitive capacity. The idea that Neanderthals might have differed cognitively from modern humans has intrigued many researchers. One proposal is that Neanderthals lacked the cognitive capacity for language, as well as the anatomical apparatus to produce speech. Much of this argument is based on the shape of the Neanderthal cranium base, which is flat in comparison to the flexed morphology of modern human skulls. But because the soft tissue of the larynx is not preserved in the fossil record, it is difficult to make conclusive statements about Neanderthals' ability to speak. The only skeletal element incorporated into the musculature of the larynx is a very small bone called the hyoid. The discovery of the complete hyoid of a Neanderthal at the site of Kebara Cave in Israel has produced no evidence supporting the argument that Neanderthals were physically incapable of speech (Arensburg 1989). The Kebara hyoid is identical to modern human hyoids, an unlikely coincidence if the morphology of the Neanderthal larynx had been significantly different (see Figure 4.12).

■ Neanderthal Genetics and the Denisovans

In 1999, scientists announced that they had succeeded in extracting and sequencing mitochondrial DNA from a Neanderthal fossil (Krings et al. 1999). Subsequently,

FIGURE 4.12 The Neanderthal hyoid bone from Kebara. The hyoid bone is found in the larynx and connects to the muscles used in producing speech. The Kebara hyoid is identical to the hyoid bone found in modern humans. The width of the Kebara hyoid is 4.5 cm.

nuclear DNA from a Neanderthal specimen from the site of Vindija Cave, Croatia, was extensively sequenced by two research teams (Green et al. 2006; Noonan et al. 2006). One team was able to sequence 62,250 base pairs of the Neanderthal genome and derived a date of 700,000 years ago for the last common ancestor of Neanderthals and modern humans. The other team sequenced over 1 million base pairs and arrived at a date of 500,000 years ago for the split between the modern human and Neanderthal lineages. In 2008, the complete mitochondrial DNA sequence for the Vindija Neanderthal was published, followed in 2010 by the draft sequence of the Neanderthal genome (Green et al. 2008). The comparison of this sequence with modern human mitochondrial DNA confirms the early date for the divergence of the Neanderthal and modern human lineages at roughly 650,000 years ago. The mitochondrial DNA sequence also suggests that the population size of Neanderthals was small.

Genetic sequencing of a fossil finger bone found in the Denisova Cave in Siberia, dated between 50,000 and 30,000 years ago, suggests that there was an Asian species that was genetically distinct from both Neanderthals and modern humans (Reich et al. 2010). This is the first case where we know of a species based on genetic analysis rather than from fossil discoveries. Many question remain about this enigmatic species, which has come to be known as the Denisovans, and currently their anatomy is only known from a single finger bone and two teeth. The teeth, one of which is shown in Figure 4.13, do show distinctive morphology that supports the genetic evidence (Sawyer et al. 2015). It is interesting that there are also Neanderthal fossil remains found in Denisova Cave. Fossils of both species are found in different subphases of Layer 11 but it is not clear that the Denisovans and Neanderthals were there at precisely the same time. The genetic sequence of the toe of a Neanderthal woman found at Denisova suggests that this woman's parents were closely related, perhaps even half siblings sharing the mother (Prüfer et al. 2014). The analysis also suggests that there was limited gene flow between Neanderthals and Denisovans.

■ Chronology and Ecology

The oldest fossil that can be clearly classified as a Neanderthal was discovered at **Biache–Saint–Vaast** in northern France. Biache has been dated to 175,000 years ago by means of thermoluminescence. A possible older date has been proposed for a Neanderthal fossil, found at the Ehringsdorf site in eastern Germany, which has been dated between 200,000 and 250,000 years ago. The Biache and Ehringsdorf

▲▲ **Biache-Saint-Vaast** The site in France where the oldest known fossil of a Neanderthal, dated to 175,000 years ago, was found.

FIGURE 4.13 Comparison of one of the teeth from Denisova with a Neanderthal tooth from Krapina and a recent modern human tooth. This comparison shows the distinctive tooth morphology of the species that has come to be known as the Denisovans.

Denisova 4   Neandertal   Recent

(Krapina D109)

10 mm

Religion and Evolution

The struggle between evolution and religion predates the publication of Charles Darwin's *On the Origin of Species*. Paralyzed by fear of the implications of his ideas and of the reception they would receive, Darwin delayed the publication of his theory for years (Desmond and Moore 1992). Many of the archaeologists who first took up the study of human evolution during the late nineteenth century were motivated by an intense antipathy to religion. Perhaps the most outspoken was the French prehistorian Gabriel de Mortillet, who viewed religion as a brake on the progress of humanity.

It is curious that, in the early twentieth century, prehistoric archaeology came to be dominated by a group of Jesuit priests. These priests recognized the power of evolutionary theory and enthusiastically engaged in pioneering research in all aspects of archaeology and paleontology. The most active archaeologist in this group was the Abbé Henri Breuil, who pioneered the study of Paleolithic cave art. The Jesuit prehistorians also attempted to reconcile evolutionary theory with Catholic theology. Pierre Teilhard de Chardin developed an elaborate interpretation of evolution as a process directed by divine intervention and tending toward the unity of mankind. De Chardin was "rewarded" for his creativity by a lifetime church ban on the publication of his writings.

In the United States, evolution has played a particularly central role in drawing the line between church and state. The celebrated Scopes "monkey trial" pitted Clarence Darrow in defense of the teaching of evolution against William Jennings Bryan (Larson 1997). At issue in this case was the violation of a Tennessee law against the teaching of evolution in a public school by a schoolteacher named John Scopes. The

Scopes trial became the "trial of the century" and inspired the play and movie *Inherit the Wind*. The fight between Darrow and Bryan resonates to this day in court cases about the teaching of creationism and intelligent design in public schools. Courts have decided that both creationism and intelligent design are religious doctrine rather than science and therefore should not be taught in public schools. However, one would have to be extraordinarily naïve to think that the issue will not reappear in U.S. courts and legislative bodies.

Why has evolution attracted such conflict? After all, it is one among many scientific theories. Even within biology, other influential theories, such as the role of DNA in inheritance, have not produced similar controversy. We can trace this question back to Charles Darwin. Why did he delay publishing his breakthrough? These are difficult and profound questions that go to the very core of the nature of science and

the meaning of religious belief. The power of evolutionary theory is that it provides a framework for understanding the development of the natural world without recourse to a deity. Until Darwin published his book, there was no convincing way of explaining the diversity of life on earth without relying on divine intervention. Darwin set out a way to look at the natural world that does not require a God. For people who draw on faith as a cornerstone of their lives, this can clearly be an unsettling concept, and the passion of the resulting debate is understandable.

As an archaeologist, I do not feel a need to struggle with these issues on a daily basis. I do not find that studying human evolution removes all meaning from the world. On the contrary, I find that the theory of evolution is a key to unlocking the complexity of the world around us. Recognizing that variability is produced by history is a fundamentally enriching insight. ●

FIGURE 4.14 Abbé Henri Breuil was a pioneering prehistoric archaeologist and a Jesuit priest

▲▲ Mezmaiskaya Cave The
location that has produced the most
recent Neanderthal fossil, dated to
30,000 years ago.

Middle Paleolithic The
archaeological period during which
Neanderthals occupied Europe.

prepared-core technology
The dominant approach to tool
manufacture during the Middle
Paleolithic; a technique in which the
person making the tools carefully
shaped the core to control the form
of the flakes produced.

fossils suggest that Neanderthals first appeared in Europe in the latter part of inter-glacial Oxygen Isotope Stage 7.

The most recent date for a Neanderthal fossil is roughly 30,000 years ago, from sites such as the **Mezmaiskaya Cave**, Russia, the source of one of the Neanderthal fossils from which DNA was successfully extracted. Neanderthals thus lived through two complete glacial cycles, beginning with interglacial Oxygen Isotope Stage 7 and ending with glacial Oxygen Isotope Stage 3. Neanderthals survived through rapidly changing climatic conditions, including the deep glacial advances of Oxygen Isotope Stage 6 and the very warm conditions of the early part of interglacial Oxygen Isotope Stage 5.

Neanderthal fossils have been found across a wide area stretching from western Europe to central Asia. The southern limit of the distribution of Neanderthal fossils is in the Middle East. No Neanderthal fossils have been found in either Africa or East Asia. Neanderthal fossils and archaeological remains have been found in a wide range of ecological zones, including open temperate grasslands in northern Europe and Mediterranean-climate woodlands in the Middle East.

4.4 Aspects of Neanderthal Culture and Adaptation

Neanderthals are often portrayed as loutish brutes, and the word *Neanderthal* has become an insult indicating a lack of intelligence or culture. Our fascination with Neanderthals might be the result of their status as both similar to and different from living humans. Archaeological research presents a subtle picture of Neanderthal culture and adaptations. The archaeological period during which Neanderthals occupied Europe and the Middle East is known as the **Middle Paleolithic**.

■ Stone Tools

Neanderthals only rarely made handaxes. After having been a central part of the hominin tool kit for over a million years, handaxes rapidly disappeared from the archaeological record around 200,000 years ago. Rather than fashioning bifacial tools from cobbles or very large flakes, Neanderthals made tools by retouching the edges of flakes. The flakes used by Neanderthals as tools were not made haphazardly. The dominant approach to tool manufacture during the Middle Paleolithic is known as **prepared-core technology**, a technique in which the person making the tools carefully shaped the core to control the form of the flakes produced.

Within the narrow range of Neanderthal stone tool technology, there is surprising diversity. With some important exceptions, the Lower Paleolithic is characterized as showing a great deal of uniformity across broad geographical areas and long time scales. This is not the case for the stone tool industries made by Neanderthals, which show a great deal of variation, both in the location and nature of the retouching and in the shape of the flakes on which the tools were made (Figure 4.15). The study of variation in Middle Paleolithic stone tools has played a critical role in developing archaeological methods of artifact analysis. Understanding these tools is key to understanding Neanderthal adaptation, culture, and cognition.

FRANÇOIS BORDES AND NEANDERTHAL ETHNICITY. In the early twentieth century, excavations of Neanderthal sites in Europe were undertaken on a massive scale. Layers were described on the basis of particularly characteristic artifacts that became known as "fossil directors." In most cases, the bulk of the material recovered was

FIGURE 4.15 The typology of Middle Paleolithic retouched flakes is determined by the location and shape of retouched edges: single convex sidescraper (left), transversal sidescraper (center), and convergent double sidescraper (right). Grey lines indicate the location of retouch.

simply discarded as irrelevant. This approach to the excavation of Middle Paleolithic sites changed drastically due to the pioneering efforts of the French prehistorian François Bordes, who worked to improve excavation methods and to create a more fine-tuned stratigraphic division of sites. In his excavations at the sites of Combe Grenal and Pech de l'Azé, he divided the stratigraphic sequence into dozens of well-defined levels (Bordes 1972; see Figure 4.16). He was also dissatisfied with the characterization of the archaeological content of a layer on the basis of so small a number of tools as the fossil directors. By creating a detailed list of tool types (a typology) and counting how many of each type were found in a particular level, Bordes was able to quantify the totality of the tools found in that level.

On the basis of his excavations and quantitative studies, Bordes identified a series of distinct types of Middle Paleolithic industries. He found that in southern France these industries did not form a chronological sequence; rather, within a single site, they were found in alternating levels. Bordes interpreted the Middle Paleolithic industries as the product of distinct ethnic groups. He maintained that the stratigraphic evidence showed that these different groups lived contemporaneously in southern France.

THE BINFORD-BORDES DEBATE. Attacking Bordes's interpretation was a temptation Lewis Binford (1983) could not resist. Binford had spent time in France with Bordes while his wife, Sally, worked on analyzing the stone tools from her excavations of a Middle Paleolithic site in Israel. Both Binfords had enormous respect for Bordes's analysis but found his interpretation fundamentally flawed. Binford could not accept that variation in the types of tools found on sites was the result of ethnicity during the Middle Paleolithic. He argued that it was far more plausible that the tools found in a level reflected the activities that took place there. Different tools would be used depending on the purpose of the site, whether for the preparation of hides, for butchery, or, as Bordes joked back, for peeling carrots. For Binford, the idea of Neanderthal ethnicity was an illusion built of Bordes's biases.

DISSENTING VOICES. As Binford and Bordes squared off, the study of Middle Paleolithic stone tool variability became an archaeological cause célèbre, pitting the "traditional" European archaeologists against the brash American New Archaeologists. Ultimately, it became a classic debate over the relative importance of culture and biological adaptation in archaeology. However, a number of studies emerged that undermined some of the central arguments of both Binford and Bordes.

FIGURE 4.16 The stratigraphic sequence from Combe Grenal, France. Sixty-two occupation levels were identified, allowing François Bordes to examine patterns of change in archaeological industries through time. The labels on the left refer to the type of industry identified within each layer. How would you describe the sequence of archaeological industries in this figure?

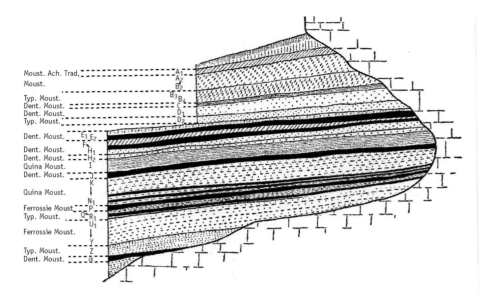

Paul Mellars (1996) studied the sequences from southern France and reached the conclusion that the variants Bordes identified are, for the most part, found in a chronological sequence. Contrary to Bordes, Mellars did not find evidence that these variants were contemporaneous. Bordes's vision of neighboring ethnic groups is not supported by these data. Binford's picture of sites reflecting particular activity areas suffers as well unless one imagines that a "hide-working period" was followed by a "butchery period."

Philip Chase (1986) studied the sequence of animal remains from the site of Combe Grenal. His studies failed to identify any relationship between the types of animals found or the way the bones had been processed and the type of industry. Chase's analysis further undermines Binford's position.

THE FRISON EFFECT. The debate between Binford and Bordes centered on the shared premise that the typology developed by Bordes was valid. On this shared basis, the two researchers went on to argue whether variation in the types of tools found was the result of ethnicity or site function. Bordes's typology is a list of tools based on subtle variations on the locations of retouch. The main type of tool is the sidescraper, which is simply a flake with retouch along the side. Sidescrapers are subdivided into flakes with retouch on one edge (simple sidescrapers), flakes with retouch on two edges (double sidescrapers), and flakes with retouch on two edges that meet (convergent sidescrapers), as shown in Figure 4.15. These categories of tools are then further subdivided according to the shape of the edge.

To Bordes, tool types were fixed entities representing the goal of their manufacture. In the 1980s, American archaeologist Harold Dibble (1987) developed an elegant critique of the Bordes typology. Dibble pointed out that stone tools have a lifetime of use, or use-life, that includes resharpening. This quality of stone tool technology is known as the **Frison effect**. During its use-life, a single piece might pass through several forms as it undergoes resharpening. Dibble argued that this is exactly what happened with sidescrapers during the Middle Paleolithic. The types of tools that Bordes saw as desired end products were actually stages in a process of a tool's use-life. A flake could begin as a single scraper, become a double scraper, and then become a convergent scraper as it passed through successive stages of resharpening. Or, as shown in Figure 4.17, a simple sidescraper could be transformed into a transversal sidescraper.

Frison effect Due to resharpening, the process through which the shape of a stone tool changes during its use-life.

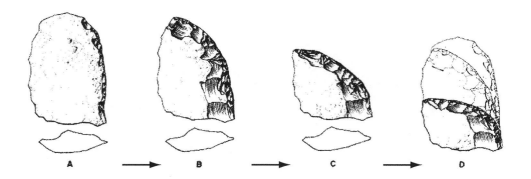

FIGURE 4.17 The scraper reduction model proposed by Harold Dibble. As the scraper is used and resharpened, its shape, and therefore its typological category, changes. In this case, a simple sidescraper (A) is transformed through a series of stages (B, C) into a transversal sidescraper (D).

Dibble argued that Bordes was wrong in his view of Neanderthal society, saying that, as Binford had argued, ethnicity was an illusion. Perhaps all variability could be accounted for by the degree to which tools were exhausted. In place of Binford's site function model, Dibble proposed that variability in Middle Paleolithic stone tool industries could be explained on the basis of access to raw material and the degree of mobility of the inhabitants of the site. The farther the sites were from sources of raw material, the more the scrapers would be retouched. The more mobile a group of hunter-gatherers was, the more likely the members of the group would be to maintain their tool kit, and, in turn, the more likely the number of pieces intensively retouched would be to increase.

THE *CHAÎNE OPÉRATOIRE*. Dibble put the argument against Neanderthal ethnicity on new and more solid ground. By going to the root and challenging the very basis of Bordes's method, he managed to cast doubt on the entire theory. The French riposte came rapidly. To arrive at the types of flakes found on Neanderthal sites, one has to know what one is doing. The same, then, must have been true of Neanderthals. But what did they know?

The answer to this question crystallized in the study of stone tools from the site of Biache-Saint-Vaast carried out by Eric Boëda (1995). It was clear that the stone tools at Biache-Saint-Vaast were produced by a prepared-core method called the **Levallois method**, recognizable from its characteristic products. The flakes produced by this method are very large and regular and usually have quite a sharp cutting edge (see Figure 4.18). Like Dibble, Boëda was interested in getting at the process behind these types of tools, but for him, the process was one of manufacture rather than resharpening.

It is useful to think of flint knapping as similar to a game of pool. In both pool and knapping, it is necessary to have a strategy, and this strategy involves controlling angles. In pool, it is the angles between the balls on the table and the angles between those balls and the pockets. In making stone tools, the control of angles allows the knapper to remove flakes of a desired shape and size. Of course, in both knapping and pool, it is also necessary to have the skill to put a plan into action! Boëda suggested that in the Levallois method, the knapper conceives of the core as two surfaces that meet at a plane of intersection. The surfaces are hierarchically related, with each playing a different function. The upper surface is the one from which the desired flakes are struck, while the lower surface provides the platform that receives the hammer blows for the removal of these flakes. The knapper controls the shape of the Levallois flakes by shaping the convexity of the upper surface. By following these rules Neanderthals were able to control the form of flakes produced.

As Boëda and his colleagues applied this insight to Middle Paleolithic sites across Europe and the Middle East, it became apparent that there might indeed

Levallois method A particular prepared-core technology used during the Middle Paleolithic that can often be recognized on the basis of tortoise-shaped cores.

be Neanderthal ethnicity, but not in the way Bordes had thought. The methods used in making flakes and the resulting types of flakes vary significantly across time and space. Researchers now realize that there is much greater diversity in the way Neanderthals made stone tools than they had imagined. One important example is a group of sites in northern Europe that have produced evidence for the manufacture of elongated flake tools known as blades (Conard 1990). Nowadays, *Neanderthal ethnicity* refers to strongly held traditions in the way stone tools are manufactured. These traditions require that knowledge and skill be transmitted between generations by learning.

SUMMING UP THE STONES. Dibble and Boëda have pushed the study of Middle Paleolithic stone tools into an entirely new realm, one in which the focus of study is a process rather than a finished object. The stone tool analyst becomes more like an ethologist watching behavior than an art historian appreciating objects. This is not to imply that consensus reigns. Ironically, the debate between Dibble and Boëda is every bit as intense as the debate between Binford and Bordes. However, it is likely that both archaeologists have seized on a critical piece of the puzzle. Boëda has demonstrated that Neanderthal stone tool manufacture was highly sophisticated learned behavior. At the same time, Dibble has alerted us to the critical importance of raw material and mobility in identifying which tools will be found on a site.

Studies of Neanderthal teeth have found scratches on the outside surface of the front teeth that are the result of teeth serving as a "third hand" while using stone tools (Estalrrich and Rosas 2013). It appears that Neanderthals would grasp material in their teeth while pulling the other end with one hand and using the other hand to cut or scrape the material. At Sidron Cave in Spain the pattern of the scratches indicates that this group of Neanderthals were right-handed. Neanderthal back teeth (molars and premolars) have been found with grooves near the base that were left by the habitual use of a wooden toothpick (Frayer and Russell 1987).

TOOLBOX

Isotope Analysis

At least when it comes to bones and teeth, you are what you eat. The bone and dental chemistry of humans and animals is determined largely by their diet. As a result, the chemistry of bones and teeth can be used as a source of data for reconstructing diet. However, identifying diets using bone chemistry can succeed only if the consumers ate foods that had a particular chemical signature. One type of chemical signature is the relative frequency of two isotopes of the same element.

The ratio of carbon-13 (^{13}C) to carbon-12 (^{12}C) varies in plants with different photosynthetic pathways. The ratio of carbon-13 to carbon-12 is expressed as the value δ^{13}C, which is the deviation from an international standard. Trees, bushes, and shrubs (δC_3 plants) have a low ratio of carbon-13 to carbon-12. Grasses from the tropics and subtropics, including maize, sorghum, and sugarcane (C_4 plants) have a high ratio. In the study of early hominins, carbon isotopes suggest a mixed diet of C_3 and C_4 plants.

The amount of ^{15}N increases between plant food and meat. As one rises within the food chain, the amount of ^{15}N increases. Analyses of Neanderthal fossils from three sites in Belgium and one in Croatia show that the ^{15}N found in the bones of Neanderthals is equaled only by the ^{15}N found in the bones of predators.

Isotope ratios of elements including oxygen can be used to track the movement of people. Where the isotope ratios of these elements do not match the isotope ratios in local water sources there is reason to suspect that the individuals in question moved in the course of their lives. Because the timing of the mineralization of teeth takes place by age 13, and the age of mineralization of each tooth is known, the oxygen isotope signature of a series of teeth can reveal where a person lived during childhood, while the oxygen isotope signature of the bones provides information about where a person lived later in life (White et al. 1998). An analysis of skeletons from the neighborhood of Tlailotlacán in the Mesoamerican city of Teotihuacán showed that people living in this part of the city spent at least part of their childhood in the Oaxaca region (see Chapter 13). ●

ADDITIONAL READING: Margaret J. Schoeninger. "Stable Isotope Analyses and the Evolution of Human Diets." *Annual Review of Anthropology* 43 (2014): 413–430.

FIGURE 4.19 Diagram showing the relationship between carbon and nitrogen isotopes and diet

◼ Hunting

Some authors, notably Binford, have questioned whether Neanderthals were hunters. However, the discovery of a series of sites at which archaeological material is associated with a large number of animal carcasses leaves little doubt that Neanderthals were capable of hunting large game. Whether they also relied on scavenging remains an open question.

The site of **La Cotte de St. Brelade** is located on what are today the Jersey Islands in the English Channel. When the site was occupied during glacial Oxygen Isotope Stage 6, the Jersey Islands were connected to continental Europe due to lower sea levels. Excavations uncovered the remains of at least 20 mammoths and 5 woolly rhinos at the foot of a steep rock face (Scott 1986). These animals were deliberately led to stampede over the cliff face and fall to their deaths, where Neanderthal occupants butchered them. However, the topography above the cliff is very uneven, so there is reason to question the animals found at La Cotte de St. Brelade were actually killed in a stampede (Scott et al. 2014). Nonetheless it seems clear that Neanderthals were hunting very large animals at this site.

Four Middle Paleolithic sites in southern France have produced evidence of specialized hunting of bovids, both aurochs and steppe bison. At Mauran, a 25-square-meter excavation produced a minimum number of individuals (MNI) count of at least 136 bison. The excavators do not think that this was a mass kill site, but rather a seasonal occupation where animals were hunted and butchered. The dating of Mauran is the subject of some controversy; however, a date of roughly 75,000 years ago, in Oxygen Isotope Stage 5, appears most likely.

From the discovery of the wooden spear at the Lower Paleolithic site of Schöningen, we can assume that such tools were used, although they are rarely preserved. Graphic proof that Neanderthals used stone-tipped spears in hunting has been found at the Middle Paleolithic site of Umm el Tlel in Syria (Boëda et al. 1999). Umm el Tlel is an open-air site with 57 levels of Middle Paleolithic occupation and excellent preservation of animal bones. The site has not been precisely dated, but it is over 50,000 years old. At Umm el Tlel, a fragment of a Levallois point was found embedded in the cervical vertebra (neck bone) of a wild ass. The point had clearly entered the bone while the animal was alive, and the blow most likely immobilized it. The excavators have demonstrated that the spear had to have entered the animal with considerable force and was more likely to have been thrown than thrust.

Rare evidence of exploitation of fish, shellfish, and other marine resources by Neanderthals comes from a series of sites on the coast of Gibraltar. At Vanguard Cave in Units C and D, dated by radiocarbon to 42,000 years ago, a hearth was found with approximately 150 mussel shells along with seal and dolphin bones. Two of the seal bones have clear cut marks. Bones of terrestrial mammals, including deer and boar, were also found in this context, indicating a very broad diet for the Neanderthal occupants of the site (Stringer et al. 2008).

RECONSTRUCTING DIET. The evidence for Neanderthal hunting is overwhelming, but it provides little information about the role of meat in the diet. Studies of the bone chemistry of Neanderthal fossils from Belgium, France, and Croatia suggest that Neanderthals were essentially meat eaters (see Toolbox on Isotope Analysis). In ecological terms, these studies have demonstrated that Neanderthals were at the top of the food chain, or at a high trophic level. The chemical signature of Neanderthal bones matches that of predators such as lions and wolves (Bocherens et al. 2001).

Although some isotope studies suggest that meat made up as much as 97% of the Neanderthal diet (Balter et al. 2002), studies of the calculus adhering to

Neanderthal teeth provides evidence for the use of plant food. Dental calculus is a deposit of calcium phosphate that adheres to tooth enamel. We are familiar with calculus as the plaque that is scraped off our teeth on visits to the dentist. As dental calculus forms, microscopic bits of organic materials are cemented onto the teeth and wrapped in a calcium phosphate cocoon. Dental calculus found on Neanderthal teeth from El Sidrón Cave in Spain incorporated traces of conifer wood that provide supporting evidence for Neanderthal use of toothpicks (Radini et al. 2016). Alternatively, the inner bark of trees might have been a component of the Neanderthal diet (Sandgathe and Hayden 2003). A biochemical analysis of the dental calculus from El Sidron found evidence for cooked plant food and inhalation of smoke from wood fire (Hardy et al. 2012). The traces of plant foods in the El Sidron dental calculus included chemical compounds found in bitter-tasting non-dietary plants such as yarrow and chamomile. This discovery suggests that Neanderthals might have been using plants for their medicinal properties.

■ Site Organization and the Use of Fire

The evidence from animal bones and from the chemical analysis of Neanderthal fossils demonstrates that Neanderthals were hunters. Neanderthal sites include specialized kill sites, such as Mauran, but most appear to fit well with Glynn Isaac's (1978) concept of a base camp (see Chapter 3). These sites are sheltered locations to which meat and other resources would have been brought for consumption. Many of the Neanderthals' base camp sites are located in caves, which serve as excellent depositional contexts with well-preserved archaeological remains. Many Neanderthal sites show evidence of intensive occupation and a deep accumulation of archaeological layers. Microscopic analysis of the sediments found in Middle Paleolithic cave sites shows that, although some of the fill is made up of sediments blown into the cave, a large proportion of the deposits, including charcoal, bone fragments, and fragments of stone tools, are the products of human activities.

Although alignments of stones are occasionally reported, evidence for any kind of construction at Neanderthal sites is rare. A possible exception is a circle of large mammoth bones found at the site of Moldova in the Ukraine, a configuration that has been interpreted as the remains of a hut. The careful horizontal excavation of cave sites has begun to show that there is spatial organization to Neanderthal habitations. **Kebara Cave**, Israel, is a Neanderthal cave site dating to approximately 50,000 years ago (Bar-Yosef et al. 1992). The horizontal excavation of the central part of the cave indicates that the main living surface was relatively clean, while the sides of the cave were refuse areas into which bones were tossed. A feature found in the central area appears to have been a pit used for the collection of discarded material. At Bruniquel Cave in southern France, archaeologists have made the stunning discovery that 175,000 years ago Neanderthals built circular structures deep in the cave using stalagmites as building materials (Jaubert et al. 2016). Fires were lit in these structures but the function of this activity remains unknown.

The most significant features found at Kebara Cave were hearths. In horizontal excavation, these hearths were poorly defined, and no stones were used to delimit a fireplace. Vertical excavation of the site produced a section that is striped black and white. Microscopic analyses of these deposits show that they are the remains of numerous simple fires. The black layers are charcoal, the white layers ash. Similar evidence of an extensive use of fire is found on most Neanderthal sites. In addition to burnt sediments, burnt flint and bone are very common. Neanderthals were also able to make adhesives by extracting resin from birch bark, a process that would have required careful control of fire (Mazza et al. 2006).

▲▲ **Kebara Cave** A site in Israel where excavations have produced important evidence about the nature of Neanderthal occupation of caves, as well as one of the most complete skeletons of a Neanderthal.

TOOLBOX

Geoarchaeology and Micromorphology

Geoarchaeology is the interdisciplinary field of study that brings the methods of the geological sciences to bear on archaeological research. From a geoarchaeological perspective, one sees familiar archaeological phenomena in a completely different way. Understanding the geology of a survey region is the first step in identifying localities where archaeological deposits are preserved and visible. Geoarchaeologists also play a fundamental role in identifying the sources for the raw materials used to make artifacts, including rocks for stone tools, clays for pottery, and ores for metal artifacts.

Soil micromorphology is a method used by geoarchaeologists to conduct a detailed examination of the deposits that make up an archaeological site. Micromorphologists begin their research by carefully removing a block of sediment from a stratigraphic profile. The block is encased in plaster or tape for transport to a laboratory, where it is placed in a vacuum chamber and impregnated with silicon. Once the silicon has hardened, a thin slice can be taken from the sample for examination under a microscope. Micromorphologists have shown that a single depositional unit is in fact made up of a very large number of discrete events. The power of micromorphology is that it can reveal how a feature formed. For example, the process can identify rodent activity and the multiple events involved in resurfacing floors. In Paleolithic archaeology, micromorphology is a valuable tool for identifying the often ephemeral traces of occupation left by hunter-gatherers. At Kebara Cave in Israel, micromorphology has demonstrated that the stratigraphy of the Middle Paleolithic occupation consists of hundreds of individual hearths built up one on top of another. Micromorphological analysis at Kebara Cave has also shown that a high percentage of the sediments are anthropogenic—microscopic pieces of bone, charcoal, and stone tools brought in by the Neanderthals who occupied the site. ●

ADDITIONAL READING: Paul Goldberg and Richard Macphail. 2006. *Practical and Theoretical Geoarchaeology*. Malden, MA: Blackwell.

FIGURE 4.20 Thin section taken by micromorphologists from the hearth deposits of Kebara Cave. The black areas are charcoal, and the white streaks are the remains of ash.

Neanderthal base camps were apparently modest encampments that included central living areas with hearths and peripheral areas that were used as dumps. There is no evidence that the hearths were maintained or constructed. One significant complication in the study of Neanderthal cave sites is that the caves were shared (although not at the same time) by Neanderthals, hyenas, and, in some cases, cave bears. Distinguishing which aspects of the bone assemblage are the results of Neanderthal activity is critical.

Amud Cave, Israel (Hovers, Kimbel, and Rak 2000).

■ Treatment of the Dead

The discovery of intact Neanderthal skeletons in cave sites rapidly led archaeologists to conclude that Neanderthals buried their dead, in turn leading to speculation that the Neanderthals had a concept of an afterlife. Although in many cases the evidence for Neanderthal burial can be questioned (Gargett 1989), in a number of instances it is clear that the corpse was placed into a pit dug into the ground. Particularly clear evidence was found at Kebara Cave, where the outline of the burial pit could be traced stratigraphically. Moreover, if Neanderthals were not burying their dead, it is hard to understand why complete skeletons are recovered with no evidence of disturbance by scavengers.

At Kebara Cave, the burial pit is shallow, and there is no evidence of any ritual beyond placing the body in the pit. More extravagant claims, however, have been made about a number of other sites. One such claim asserts that a Neanderthal at Shanidar Cave, Iraq, was buried with flowers (Leroi-Gourhan 1975). The claim is based on an analysis of pollen recovered from soil collected near the skeleton. However, significant questions remain about the association of the soil with the skeleton and the source of the pollen.

One of the few sites to have produced detailed evidence of an object deliberately buried with a Neanderthal is **Amud Cave**, Israel (Hovers, Kimbel, and Rak 2000). At Amud Cave, a Neanderthal infant was found in a natural niche in the side of the cave, together with the upper jaw (maxilla) of a red deer, which was resting against the child's pelvis (see Figure 4.21). The excavators carefully considered the possibility that the bone was beside the infant simply by chance. After all, the child was found in a site full of animal bones and stone tools. However, the excavators concluded that such a scenario was undermined by the fact that this maxilla was the only such specimen found on the site, despite the fact that deer bones were common. They thought it an extremely unlikely coincidence that a unique specimen would appear in a clear burial context and concluded that the maxilla had been placed with the infant deliberately. The excavators did not speculate on the meaning of this gesture.

On the basis of the evidence from sites such as Kebara Cave and Amud Cave, it appears that Neanderthals did at times bury their dead in small pits, perhaps placing objects in the pits with the deceased. However, such a reverent approach to the dead is not always found on Neanderthal sites. Analyses of the Neanderthal skeletal remains from the sites of Moula-Guercy, France, and Krapina, Croatia, show clear evidence of cut marks that are likely the

FIGURE 4.21 The Amud Neanderthal child with an associated deer maxilla

Infant Skull

Deer Maxilla

A Paleoepiphany

LYNNE SCHEPARTZ, HEAD OF THE DIVISION OF BIOLOGICAL ANTHROPOLOGY, SCHOOL OF ANATOMICAL SCIENCES, UNIVERSITY OF THE WITWATERSRAND

I remember the feeling as if it had just happened. It's not the kind of experience you forget. I had gone up to Israel from Kenya, where I had been conducting dissertation research on later Pleistocene hunter-gatherers and the biological effects of changing to herding lifeways. It was a terrific project, but like most research, it involved boring, meticulous data collection in a fascinating location. Sitting measuring teeth and bones all day for several months had burned me out. I was in serious need of a break.

And so I found myself flying up to Cairo, taking an early morning bus across the blazing Sinai Desert, and making my way to the Middle Paleolithic site of Kebara Cave. One of the project directors, Ofer Bar-Yosef, had invited me to join the excavations on my way home. I wasn't finished with my research in Africa, but I couldn't think of a better way to recharge my brain. It didn't matter that I had never

been to Egypt or Israel. There were friends awaiting me there, and it was my first chance to participate in a paleoanthropological excavation.

The Kebara project was unlike any other I had ever worked on. It was run by a group of top Israeli and French Paleolithic archaeologists, paleoanthropologists, paleozoologists, and geoarchaeologists, and the diggers were all graduate students. French was the main common language, and my command of it was not stellar. But everyone was very friendly, and it was exciting to listen in on all the conversations and debates about Neanderthals and the development of the Upper Paleolithic. During the day, the cave was as quiet as a library, with all workers intent on their tasks. Mine was to excavate in the deepest level of the cave, expanding the 1-meter-square test pit of an earlier researcher, Moshe Stekelis. He had found the remains of a Neanderthal baby by the

back wall in the 1960s. I was working with a Swiss student, and things were awfully tight in that square meter. We were to dig only another half meter to the north. Eventually, the student went to dig in another area, and I kept on in the pit. I was encountering exciting stuff—Mousterian flint artifacts and hearths full of burnt animal remains from Neanderthal dinners. This was what I had read about in the publications of Garrod and Bate, and here I was finding it myself! Because of my inexperience and my intense interest in bones, it was slow going. I took meticulous notes on sediment changes and called on the geologists for frequent advice, learning as I dug. I remember the French project director, Bernard Vandermeersch, coming over to visit me and exclaiming, "Enough of these animals! Find me the man!" He would not be disappointed.

Not long before the excavation was scheduled to close, I came upon

result of cannibalism (see Figure 4.23). The Moula–Guercy Neanderthal remains had been treated like all other animal bones. Evidence of butchery includes cut marks from defleshing and percussion marks from smashing the bones to obtain marrow (Defleur et al. 1999).

■ Artwork

There is currently no known artwork from Middle Paleolithic Neanderthal archaeological sites. Occasionally, archaeologists have claimed to have found bones with signs of incisions. However, in every case, it has been shown that the incisions were the result of gnawing by carnivores or some other natural process. One of the most spectacular recent claims was about a cave bear bone with two holes in it found at the site of Divje Babe I Cave in Slovenia. The claim was that the bone had been fashioned to be a musical instrument, perhaps a flute. However, a comparison of the bone in question with others from a natural accumulation of cave bear bones shows that similar holes can occur as the result of gnawing by carnivores. Thus, it is unlikely that the piece was actually manufactured by Neanderthals. The most convincing a layer of rock-hard sediments that I could not trowel through. I asked if anyone wanted to swap squares, but there were no takers, so I got a small hammer and chisel and began to break up the deposits. Inside was a complete human hand bone—a metacarpal. I called the directors over, and they agreed that it could be a more recent bone that had been transported down a rodent burrow, but they suggested that I clean the area for a photo. One sweep of the brush revealed an entire mandibular tooth row in the far corner of the excavated area—and this led to more and more bones. I couldn't contain my excitement, and my shouts echoed throughout the cave. It turned out that the half meter I was excavating held most of a Neanderthal burial! And it wasn't just any Neanderthal burial: It was that of a very well-preserved young male. Although it was mysteriously missing the skull and one leg, the delicate

structures of the pelvis had been spared. Moreover, the burial contained an astonishing new discovery never seen before in Neanderthals: the extremely fragile hyoid bone from the throat. I was lucky enough to meet this Neanderthal, nicknamed "Moshe," after Professor Stekelis had just barely missed discovering him two decades before, some 60,000 years after the Neanderthal's death.

Some paleoanthropologists devote their entire careers to discovering an important fossil or to making an exciting observation about human evolution. There seem to be two types of paleoanthropologists: those who work primarily on specimens in laboratories or museums and those who work in the field. I wanted to be a field person, but it meant gaining experience. Kebara was my entrée to that world. ▲

FIGURE 4.22 Lynne Schepartz (in brown shirt) at Kebara in 1987

evidence of Neanderthal art consists of a simple grid pattern incised into the bedrock of Gorham's Cave in Gibraltar that is older than the levels of sediment, which are dated to 39,000 years ago (Rodríguez-Vidal et al. 2014).

There is evidence that Neanderthals used mineral colors. On a number of Neanderthal sites, small blocks of red ochre and black manganese are found in archaeological contexts. Some of these pieces show clear signs of scraping by a stone tool. The function of these colorants remains an enigma, as no painted objects have ever been found. Some scientists have speculated that the Neanderthals would have painted their bodies or even practiced tattooing.

■ Neanderthal Society

If Glynn Isaac's model is correct, then the existence of Neanderthal base camps suggests that Neanderthals, like modern hunter-gatherers, lived in societies characterized by sharing. Certainly, there is no evidence from Neanderthal sites of any markers of status or wealth. There is also almost no evidence at all, with the exception of the possible grave offering at Amud, of any kind of ritual object.

FIGURE 4.23 A Neanderthal skull from the site of Krapina in Croatia with cut marks. Although cut marks are often interpreted as evidence of cannibalism, some researchers think that the cut marks found on the Krapina Neanderthal fossils are the result of ritual preparation of the skeleton before burial.

Understanding the structure of Neanderthal societies remains difficult. Although some evidence of reverence toward the dead exists in the form of burial, there are also clear cases of cannibalism. We can say little about gender roles in Neanderthal societies or about how a social hierarchy was established. The studies of stone tool manufacture do show that technical knowledge was passed between generations and that there is a persistence through time in local traditions of tool manufacture. Whether this translates into ethnicity is questionable. We know of no objects with which Neanderthals could have displayed their group identity. Whether the colorants found on Neanderthal sites were used for such a purpose is a matter of speculation.

There is no clear basis for determining Neanderthal group size; however, the overall sense is that, given the small size of most sites, the groups occupying them must have been relatively small as well. What is striking is that, while many sites are quite small, they show signs of intensive activity. In cave sites, this activity led to the buildup of deep stratigraphic deposits. One possibility is that Neanderthals were far more sedentary than modern human hunter-gatherers. Perhaps the reason the cave sites show such a buildup of sediments is that they were inhabited continuously. Such a pattern of occupation would be in sharp contrast to the high-mobility strategies practiced by recent hunter-gatherer groups.

Looking at the remains of small animals from the site of Hayonim Cave, Israel, Mary Stiner came up with an ingenious method of exploring Neanderthal group size and mobility (Stiner et al. 1999). Stiner found that Neanderthals at Hayonim Cave ate certain tortoises that were easy to collect, but that matured slowly. Surprisingly, she found that the tortoises consumed were quite large and did not exhibit the reduction in size that would take place with heavy exploitation. On the basis of her observations, Stiner suggests that Neanderthal populations were "exceptionally small and that [they] . . . did not spend much time foraging in any one vicinity" (Stiner et al. 1999, 193). If there had been large populations or permanent settlements, one would expect to see more of an impact on the tortoises. Stiner's results appear to contradict the picture of Neanderthals as quasi-sedentary hunter-gatherers, showing them instead as highly mobile hunter-gatherers living at an extremely low population density.

SUMMARY

- Global climate during the Pleistocene fluctuated between glacial and interglacial episodes. The fluctuations are recorded in the oxygen isotope curve.
- The earliest evidence of human occupation of western Europe is the TD-6 level of the Gran Dolina site at Atapuerca, which is dated to 800,000 years ago.
- The Eurasian Acheulian is found across Europe, the Middle East, and the Indian subcontinent beginning 500,000 years ago. With the exception of Bose, China, there is little evidence of Acheulian sites east of India.
- There is little evidence of artwork or human burial during the Lower Paleolithic.
- Neanderthals share many features with modern humans, including a large brain size. There are also distinctive Neanderthal features, many of which are adaptations to cold weather.
- The pattern of similarities and differences between modern humans and Neanderthals has led to debate over the evolutionary relationship between the two groups. The main question is whether there was gene flow between populations of modern humans in Africa and populations of Neanderthals in Europe or whether the two populations were two distinct species that evolved in isolation from *Homo erectus* or an intermediary species.
- Neanderthals occupied sites over a wide range of ecological settings, including fully glacial and interglacial Europe.
- There is clear evidence that Neanderthals hunted large animals. Stable-isotope analysis indicates that meat was a major component of the Neanderthal diet.
- Neanderthal sites have no constructed features; however, evidence of the intensive use of fire is often found.
- Analyses of variability in Middle Paleolithic stone tool assemblages have produced a wide range of interpretations.
- Neanderthals appear to have buried their dead in some cases and practiced cannibalism in others. At one site, there is evidence that a Neanderthal child was buried with the jaw of a red deer.
- There is no evidence of Neanderthal (Middle Paleolithic) artwork.

KEY TERMS

Amud Cave, 115
Beeches Pit, 99
Biache-Saint-Vaast, 104
Bose, 96
Boxgrove, 97
Clactonian, 98
Eurasian Acheulian, 97
Frison effect, 108
Gesher Benot Ya'akov, 97
Gran Dolina, Atapuerca, 96

Kebara Cave, 113
La Cotte de St. Brelade, 112
Levallois method, 109
Mezmaiskaya Cave, 106
Middle Paleolithic, 106
oxygen isotope curve, 96
Pleistocene, 94
prepared-core technology, 106
Schöningen, 100
Zhoukoudian, 99

REVIEW QUESTIONS

1. What are the three theories of Neanderthal phylogeny? Which view does the DNA evidence from Neanderthal fossils support?

2. How do the results of archaeological research affect our understanding of Neanderthals?

3. Why are Middle Paleolithic stone tools the subject of intense debate among archaeologists?

THE ORIGIN OF MODERN HUMANS

Modern humans first appeared in Africa between 200,000 and 100,000 years ago and replaced Neanderthals in Europe between 40,000 and 27,000 years ago. The arrival of modern humans in Europe was marked by a dramatic change in material culture known as the Middle to Upper Paleolithic transition. After reading this chapter, you should understand:

Hafting an experimental replica of a Solutrean point

- **The chronological and archaeological relationship between Neanderthals and modern humans in the Middle East.**

- **The major characteristics of the Middle Stone Age.**

- **The three main models for the replacement of Neanderthals by modern humans.**

- **The major characteristics of the Upper Paleolithic.**

5 TIMELINE

thousands of years ago	200	175	150	125

SITES — Pinnacle Point, Herto

ARCHAEOLOGICAL INDUSTRIES — MIDDLE STONE AGE, MIDDLE PALEOLITHIC

HOMININS — NEANDERTHALS

SITES DISCUSSED IN CHAPTER 5

Sungir

Hohlenstein
Arcy-sur-Cure
Saint Césaire
Hohle Fels
Lascaux
Chauvet
Côa Valley
Abrigo Lagar
Velho
Zafarraya

Dolní Věstonice
Vindija
Peştera cu
Oase

Skhul
Qafzeh

Herto

Katanda

ATLANTIC
OCEAN

Border Cave

Klasies River Mouth
Blombos
Pinnacle Point

Klasies
Qafzeh and Skhul

Blombos

Katanda

Chauvet   Vindija
St. Césaire, Peştera cu Oase   Abrigo Lagar Velho
Hohlenstein   Dolní Věstonice
Hohle Fels   Zafarraya   Lascaux

UPPER PALEOLITHIC

MODERN HUMANS

100   75   50   25

modern human A member of the species *Homo sapiens*, which includes all living humans.

Homo sapiens The species name for modern humans.

A visit to Lascaux Cave in southwestern France begins with a descent into inky blackness. Visitors, limited to a small number in order to preserve the cave, are asked to dip their feet into a pan filled with disinfectant and are then ushered through a door into a chamber shrouded in darkness, where they wait until the guide is ready. A switch is thrown, and in the dazzle of newly erupting light, all eyes are drawn upward to gaze in awe at scenes of massive bulls painted onto the cave walls 15,000 years ago. The wonder of Lascaux Cave is so powerful that it stuns even the most jaded (see Figure 5.1). One feels an instinctive connection to the people who shared our drive to represent the world—to make art of our experience. How did humanity move from the age of *Homo erectus* and Neanderthals to the explosion of creativity found on the walls of Lascaux Cave? This question has both inspired and vexed archaeologists for close to a century as they have struggled to understand the origin of modern humans and the fate of Neanderthals.

We begin this chapter with an examination of the biological definition of modern humans. We then move to Africa to trace the earliest evidence for modern human fossils and explore what archaeology can tell us about these earliest members of our species. Next, we pause to consider the relationship between modern humans and Neanderthals in the Middle East before continuing on to Europe and the momentous question of the last Neanderthals. We will then be in a position to consider the revolution in human culture that led to the painted cave of Lascaux.

5.1 What Is a Modern Human?

The term **modern human** refers to all members of the biological species ***Homo sapiens***, including all living humans. On both genetic and anatomical grounds, some authors argue that the similarity among human populations requires that all humans be included under a single subspecies, *Homo sapiens sapiens*. Studies of the genetic diversity of living humans indicate a very low degree of species diversity. Most of the genetic variation within living humans is found within members of a single population rather than between populations. The low genetic variation within modern humans reflects a relatively recent common ancestry.

FIGURE 5.1 A panoramic view of Lascaux Cave, France

Characteristics of the skull that distinguish modern humans from earlier species include a large brain (1,200–1,700 cc), a globular braincase, a vertical forehead, reduced brow ridges, and a pronounced chin. Teeth tend to be smaller. Modern human bodies have a reduced body mass, a narrow trunk, and a unique pelvic shape. There is, of course, considerable variability among living humans, both as individuals and as populations; however, the anatomical traits that define *Homo sapiens* are characteristic of all living human populations.

5.2 Early Modern Humans in Africa

Modern humans first appeared in Africa between 200,000 and 100,000 years ago, during Oxygen Isotope Stages 6–3. The oldest known fossils clearly ascribed to *Homo sapiens* were discovered in the Middle Awash region of Ethiopia (White et al. 2003). At the **Herto** site, an adult skull, a partial juvenile skull, and a fragmentary adult skull were found eroding out of a level argon dated between 160,000 and 154,000 years ago (see Figure 5.2). The complete skull has a large brain, 1,450 cubic centimeters, and lacks any of the specialized traits that characterize Neanderthals. Newly discovered fossils from the site of Jebel Irhoud, Morocco push the first appearance of modern humans back to a date around 300,000 years ago (Richter et al. 2017).

Fragments of fossils that are clearly modern humans have also been found in South Africa at the sites of **Klasies River Mouth** and **Border Cave** (Deacon and Deacon 1999). In both cases, the fossils are dated to between 120,000 and 70,000 years ago. The collection of fossils from Klasies River Mouth includes bits of a skull, a jaw, an arm, and a foot. The morphology of all these fossils fits within the range for modern humans.

■ The African Middle Stone Age

The Acheulian industries in Africa were replaced between 300,000 and 200,000 years ago by a group of industries known as the **Middle Stone Age**. The Middle Stone

▲▲ **Herto** A site in Ethiopia where the oldest known fossil of a modern human was discovered, dating to between 160,000 and 154,000 years ago.

▲▲ **Klasies River Mouth** A Middle Stone Age site in South Africa that has produced remains of modern humans and that offers evidence of hunting and the intensive use of fire.

▲▲ **Border Cave** One of the South African sites where fossils of modern humans dated to between 120,000 and 70,000 years ago were discovered.

Middle Stone Age The archaeological period of the earliest modern humans in Africa. The Middle Stone Age began between 300,000 and 200,000 years ago and ended around 40,000 years ago.

FIGURE 5.2 The Herto fossil. The significant features demonstrating that this is a modern human include the rounded form of the skull and the absence of forward projection in the face.

Age, which ended roughly 40,000 years ago, is the archaeological context for the earliest modern humans.

STONE TOOLS. The technology of stone tool manufacture in the Middle Stone Age in Africa has many similarities to that of the European Middle Paleolithic. For example, it is now recognized that the Levallois method was widely used in Africa during the Middle Stone Age. However, when one looks at the African continent as a whole, it becomes evident that the Middle Stone Age includes a greater degree of variation than is found in the Middle Paleolithic. Also, types of tools are found in the Middle Stone Age that are absent from the Middle Paleolithic.

Across Africa, a number of distinct Middle Stone Age industries have been identified (McBrearty and Brooks 2000). The **Aterian** is a North African stone tool industry distinguished by the presence of points with a pronounced tang—a small projection located at the base of the point and used to secure the point to a spear or handle. Aterian tools also include finely made bifacial tools that served as knives or hunting points.

The **Sangoan/Lupemban** is a Middle Stone Age industry found in Central and East Africa. Characterized by very crude heavy-duty tools, the Sangoan/Lupemban might be indicative of an adaptation to a heavily wooded environment.

The **Howiesons Poort** is an industry that has been identified in South Africa. Among the sites on which Howiesons Poort tools have been discovered is Klasies River Mouth. The tools found on Howiesons Poort sites include very small crescent-shaped implements known as microliths, which would have been used as part of a complex tool made by putting together a number of pieces (see Figure 5.3). The most likely function of these tools is as an element of spears or arrows.

Aterian A North African stone tool industry distinguished by the presence of points with a pronounced tang—a small projection located at the base of the point and used to secure the point to a spear handle.

Sangoan/Lupemban A Middle Stone Age industry found in Central and East Africa. Characterized by very crude heavy-duty tools, the Sangoan/Lupemban might be indicative of an adaptation to a heavily wooded environment.

Howiesons Poort A Middle Stone Age industry found in southern Africa that is characterized by small crescent-shaped stone tools.

FIGURE 5.3 Experimental hafting of Howiesons Poort microliths. Spears tipped with these types of points would have been very effective hunting tools.

BONE TOOLS. Katanda is a site located on cliffs overlooking the Semliki River in the Democratic Republic of the Congo (Yellen et al. 1995). Dating of the site has been complicated; however, all methods agree on a date that is earlier than 75,000 years ago, and the stone tools are characteristic of the Middle Stone Age (Brooks et al. 1995). The excavations at Katanda uncovered 10 remarkable barbed bone points, along with a smaller number of unbarbed bone points and a piece identified as a bone knife (see Figure 5.4). These are the oldest tools of this kind known in the world. Although barbed points are often used on harpoons, the excavators believe that the grooves on the base of the points suggest that they were mounted on spears.

Bone points have also been found in Middle Stone Age sites in South Africa. At the site of Blombos Cave, located at the southern tip of Africa, 21 bone tools were found, including 2 points and a number of awls (Henshilwood and Sealy 1997). The Middle Stone Age levels at Blombos Cave have been dated to 77,000 years ago by thermoluminescence.

ADAPTATION. The remains of large game are found on Middle Stone Age sites, where it appears that hunting took place. At Klasies River Mouth, a stone tool was found embedded in the vertebrae of a bovid. Middle Stone Age sites, including Klasies River Mouth, also show evidence of the kind of intensive use of fire documented at Kebara Cave and other Neanderthal sites.

At Klasies River Mouth and a number of other Middle Stone Age sites, large quantities of shellfish were found, along with seal bones. In contrast, the use of marine resources is rare on Neanderthal sites. At a site on the Buri Peninsula on the coast of the Red Sea in Eritrea, Middle Stone Age tools were found embedded in a coral reef deposit (Walter et al. 2000). Clearly, those who wielded these tools were people living at the edge of the sea, and it is likely that they were exploiting shellfish and other marine resources. Katanda has produced impressive evidence of fishing. Among the faunal remains recovered were many bones of large catfish weighing over 35 kilograms. At the site of **Pinnacle Point** on the coast of South Africa, there is evidence that mollusks were part of the diet as early as 160,000 years ago (Marean et al. 2007). The excavators suggest a link between this expansion of hominin diet and the harsh conditions of glacial Oxygen Isotope Stage 6.

▲▲ **Katanda** A Middle Stone Age site in the Democratic Republic of the Congo where bone barbed points have been found.

▲▲ **Pinnacle Point** A site on the southern coast of South Africa that has produced evidence that mollusks were part of the diet of modern humans as early as 160,000 years ago.

FIGURE 5.4 Bone tool from the Middle Stone Age site of Katanda. This tool has a series of barbs and incisions that appear to have been used to connect it to a haft. The length of this piece is 14.2 cm.

ART. In 1999 and 2000, two pieces of ochre with incised designs were found at **Blombos Cave**, South Africa, in a Middle Stone Age level dated to 77,000 years ago (Henshilwood et al. 2002). Ochre is a soft, red, iron-rich rock often used as a pigment. More than 8,000 pieces of ochre, many with traces of use, have been found in the Middle Stone Age levels at Blombos Cave.

As shown in Figure 5.5, the pieces of incised ochre are small—between 5 and 7 centimeters long. The incisions are a set of hatched lines on one face of the piece. These modest artifacts are the earliest evidence in the archaeological record of a hominin marking a pattern. Incisions have been found on 13 other pieces of ochre at Blombos in levels dating back as far as 100,000 years ago, shown in Figure 5.6. These remaining pieces are either fragments or lacking in clear patterns.

But what are these objects? The Blombos Cave artifacts have received considerable attention as the earliest evidence of human artwork or symbolic behavior. *Symbolic behavior* suggests that these artifacts are meant to represent something, while *artwork* implies that the incisions to the artifacts were made with an aesthetic goal in mind. This is a lot of baggage for a series of lines scratched into small pieces of ochre. Untangling the significance of the simple pattern of lines found at Blombos Cave remains one of the most difficult challenges facing Paleolithic archaeologists.

Pieces similar to the Blombos ochre have been found at the site of Klein Kliphuis, South Africa, which is tentatively dated between 80,000 and 50,000 years ago. At the sites of Diepkloof and Klipdrift, both in South Africa, excavators recovered fragments of ostrich eggshell with incised decorations in Howiesonspoort levels dated to 60,000 years ago (Henshilwood et al. 2014; Mackay and Welz 2008; Texier et al. 2010). Subsequent excavations in the 100,000-year-old level at Blombos

FIGURE 5.5 One of the incised pieces of ochre from Blombos. This photograph shows all of the sides of this piece. The incised pattern is limited to one narrow face (third from the top).

1 cm

uncovered two caches of artifacts that appear to be tools for processing ochre, together with a large shell that might have been used to store pigment, which are shown in Figure 5.6 in the process of excavation (Henshilwood et al. 2011). At Pinnacle Point, pieces of ground ochre have been found in the level dated to 160,000 years ago, although the incisions on these pieces lack the clear patterns shown in the ones from Blombos (Marean et al. 2007). Taken together, these discoveries place the Blombos incised ochre in a broader context, but do not resolve the questions surrounding these artifacts.

A collection of pierced shells was also found at Blombos Cave. Pierced objects have been reported from a number of Aterian sites in North Africa, and a number of late Middle Stone Age sites are reported to have included beads. A particularly interesting discovery is a painted slab with the depiction of an animal, found in the Apollo 11 Cave in Namibia. The slab is reported to come from a Middle Stone Age context, but the date provided is between 28,000 and 26,000 years ago, which raises some questions about this attribution.

■ Comparing the Middle Stone Age and the Middle Paleolithic

A comparison of the Middle Stone Age archaeological record left by modern humans in Africa with the Middle Paleolithic record left by Neanderthals in Europe points to both similarities and differences. As regards the similarities, in both cases (1) stone tools were made mostly by using a prepared-core technology, (2) there is variability between stone tool industries, and (3) evidence supports both hunting and the intensive use of fire. One difference is that the amount of variability in the Middle Stone Age stone tool industries is greater than that of their Middle Paleolithic counterparts. Another is that in the Middle Stone Age there are elaborate bone tools, as well as clear evidence of fishing and collecting shellfish, two elements that are rare in the Middle Paleolithic. Finally, there is modest evidence of artwork in the Middle Stone Age, while such evidence is absent in the Middle Paleolithic.

The significance of the differences between the Middle Stone Age and the Middle Paleolithic remains elusive. Why didn't Neanderthals make bone tools? Carving a point out of bone appears no more complicated than chipping a point from flint. And what is the meaning of the shellfish and fish remains found on Middle Stone Age sites? Why didn't Neanderthals exploit similar resources wherever they were available in Europe? The Blombos incised ochre is clearly important, but do these small pieces with their simple abstract design truly mark the entrance of humanity into the realm of symbolism?

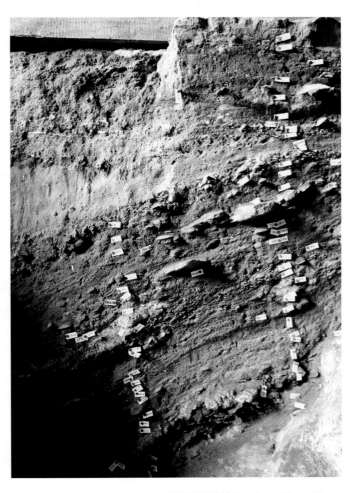

FIGURE 5.6 Stratigraphic profile of Blombos Cave showing the sequence of deposits with each distinct level marked with a tag. The incised ochre was found midway down the profile shown here. The total depth of this profile is approximately 2.5 meters.

5.3 Early Modern Humans in the Middle East

The Middle East is the crossroads of the continents, lying at the geographic intersection of Europe, Asia, and Africa. As a result, the Middle East plays a critical role

▲▲ Qafzeh Cave One of the sites in Israel where modern human skeletons were found in a Middle Paleolithic context.

▲▲ Skhul Cave One of the Middle Paleolithic sites in Israel where modern human skeletons have been found.

in research on the origin of modern humans. Middle Stone Age modern humans in Africa were contemporaneous with European Middle Paleolithic Neanderthals. The critical problem is determining what happened in the region where these two populations might have overlapped and coexisted.

Excavations at **Qafzeh Cave**, located in the hills of northern Israel just outside of Nazareth, uncovered a number of skeletons in Middle Paleolithic levels (Vandermeersch 1981). Although from their context, one might expect that these bones would be the skeletons of Neanderthals, as was the case at other Middle Paleolithic sites in the region, the Qafzeh skeletons are modern humans. A similar discovery was made at **Skhul Cave** on the Mediterranean coast. The Skhul and Qafzeh discoveries raise several critical questions. The first question is whether there are characteristics that distinguish the archaeological remains found on these sites from the remains found on Neanderthal sites. The second question is what the chronological relationship is between Neanderthals and modern humans.

■ The Archaeological Record

Surprisingly, there is little that distinguishes the archaeological material found at Qafzeh and Skhul from the remains found on Neanderthal sites in the Middle East—sites such as Kebara Cave, Tabun Cave, and Amud Cave in Israel; Shanidar Cave in Iraq; and Dederiyeh Cave in Syria. Both Neanderthals and modern humans made stone tools typical of the Middle Paleolithic, often using the Levallois method. Neither group produced bone tools or very much in the way of art; the only exception is a piece of flint with an incised pattern found at Qafzeh Cave. Both groups buried their dead in shallow pits with little in the way of burial goods. The discovery of a deer maxilla with a Neanderthal child at Amud is paralleled by the placement of a deer antler in a burial of a modern human at Qafzeh and a boar jaw found with a modern human buried at Skhul. Both groups lived in small sites where evidence indicates the extensive use of fire.

■ Chronology

Although the Middle Paleolithic cave sites in the Middle East all have deep stratigraphic sequences, none have produced fossils of both modern humans and Neanderthals. Thus, the chronological relationship between Neanderthals and modern humans in the region cannot be determined on the basis of stratigraphy. Until the 1980s, there was no method for dating the sites, and the general sense was that the Neanderthal sites must be early ones and that Skhul and Qafzeh, with their modern human fossils, must be more recent. Many paleoanthropologists believed that modern humans likely had evolved from Neanderthals; therefore, Neanderthal sites must be earlier than modern human sites. With the development of electron spin resonance and thermoluminescence dating methods in the 1980s, it finally became possible to date the Middle Paleolithic cave sites (see the Luminescence Dating Toolbox on p. 129). The results came as a shock: Skhul and Qafzeh date from between 120,000 and 80,000 years ago, while most of the Neanderthal sites produced dates that cluster in the range between 60,000 and 50,000 years ago (Valladas et al. 1988).

■ Assessing the Middle Eastern Pattern

The Middle Paleolithic of the Middle East confounds our expectation of the relationship between Neanderthals and modern humans. There is no obvious difference

TOOLBOX

Luminescence Dating

Luminescence dating methods are critical for the study of the later stages of human evolution. The luminescence methods that are most widely used are thermoluminescence (TL), electron spin resonance (ESR), and optically stimulated luminescence (OSL). TL dates burnt stone tools made of flint, ESR dates animal teeth, and OSL dates either quartz or feldspar grains in sediments.

All minerals consist of atoms and molecules arranged in a three-dimensional lattice known as a crystal. Inevitably, flaws arise within the structure of a crystal. These flaws serve as traps that accumulate electrons over time. The rate at which electrons are trapped is a function of the natural background radiation. The rate at which electrons are accumulated in a year is known as the annual dose rate and is specific to a given locality. Thus, every time one uses a luminescence dating method, the annual dose rate at the precise location of the find must be measured. The annual dose rate can be measured with a tool called a dosimeter.

When a sample of a mineral is heated, the trapped light energy, or luminescence, is driven out of the crystals. The amount of this energy can be measured precisely. The measure of the trapped luminescence is known as the accumulated dose. If one knows the accumulated dose and the annual dose rate, it is fairly simple to divide the accumulated dose by the annual dose rate to determine how long the mineral has been accumulating light energy.

The problem is that crystals begin trapping energy the moment they are formed. Thus, as with argon dating, the critical factor is finding a mechanism that zeroes the clock at exactly the point in time one is interested in dating.

TL dating of flint is based on the observation that heating flint to between 400 and 600 degrees centigrade effectively drives off the accumulated energy, thus resetting the clock to zero. After the rock is heated to a temperature in that range, the crystals again begin to accumulate energy at the annual dose rate. When one finds a stone tool that was burnt, the equation accumulated dose divided by annual dose rate will provide a measure of the date when the tool was burnt. If one is confident that the burning took place at the time the site was inhabited, usually as the result of the tool falling into a fire, then the foregoing equation yields a date for the occupation of the site. Fortunately, beginning in the Middle Stone Age and the Middle Paleolithic, burnt stone tools are common on archaeological sites.

TL can also be used for more recent periods to date the manufacture of pottery. The principle in the dating of pottery is that firing a ceramic vessel effectively zeroes the clock. Thermoluminescence dating of pottery has been particularly useful in detecting forged artifacts.

OSL works on the same principles as TL. Among the grains that make up most sediments are crystals of quartz and feldspar. It has been observed that exposure of these grains to sunlight effectively drives out the trapped light energy and zeroes the clock. Thus, the relationship accumulated dose divided by annual dose rate produces a date for when the sediments were last exposed to the sun, thereby effectively dating the time the site was buried.

ESR works on the same principles as TL and OSL. The main application of ESR is dating the enamel layer of teeth. Tooth enamel is made up of the mineral hydroxyapatite. Because mineral crystals form during the life of the animal, the accumulation of light energy begins when the animal is alive. The beauty of this method is that there is no need to reset the clock to zero because the accumulation of light energy begins only at the point in time one is attempting to date. ESR can be used on teeth covering the entire range of hominin evolution. ●

ADDITIONAL READING: R. E. Taylor and Martin J. Aitken, eds. 1997. *Chronometric Dating in Archaeology*. New York: Plenum Press.

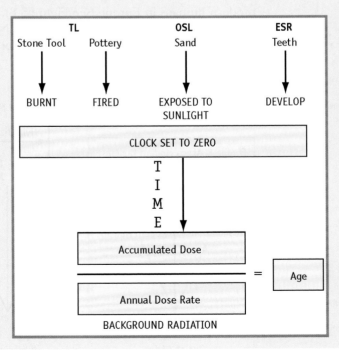

FIGURE 5.7
Luminescence dating methods work on the principle of measuring the accumulated dose and dividing this by the annual dose rate to arrive at an age determination

Upper Paleolithic The archaeological period that saw the earliest occupation of Europe by modern humans.

Middle to Upper Paleolithic transition The archaeological period that saw the appearance of modern humans in Europe. It includes the development of new types of stone and bone tools and the dramatic appearance of a wide range of symbolic artifacts.

in the behavior and technology of modern humans and Neanderthals living in the Middle East during the period between Oxygen Isotope Stages 5 and 3. As far as the current state of our knowledge goes, all that separates the behavior of these two species during that period is a single incised piece of flint. But what is even more puzzling is that the fossils of modern humans are actually older than those of Neanderthals.

The Middle Eastern sequence provides clear evidence that Neanderthals were not a primitive precursor of modern humans, but rather a population that evolved parallel to them. Geographically, the Middle East is located between the European range of the Neanderthals and the African range of early modern humans. In ecological terms, the range of Neanderthals was centered in Eurasia and the range of modern humans in Africa. In periods when the Neanderthal range expanded, Neanderthal remains are found in the Middle East. When the modern human range expanded out of Africa, fossils of modern humans are found in the Middle East. There is no evidence that the modern human range expanded into Europe earlier than 60,000 years ago. However, around 40,000 years ago, Neanderthals became extinct in the Middle East as part of a process that swept modern humans into Europe.

5.4 The Arrival of Modern Humans in Europe and the Fate of the Neanderthals

Extinction is an integral element of evolution. However, when extinction strikes a member of the hominin lineage, we often struggle to understand what happened. Nowhere is this problem more acute than in the case of the Neanderthals, who disappeared from Europe between 40,000 and 27,000 years ago and were replaced by populations of modern humans. The **Upper Paleolithic** is the archaeological period that corresponds to the first occupation of Europe by modern humans. The **Middle to Upper Paleolithic transition** is marked by a dramatic change to material culture. Three major theories relate to the replacement of Neanderthals by modern humans in Europe (see Figure 5.8).

The *out of Africa hypothesis* argues that Neanderthal populations in Europe were replaced by invading populations of modern humans during the period between

FIGURE 5.8 Three scenarios for the fate of the Neanderthals

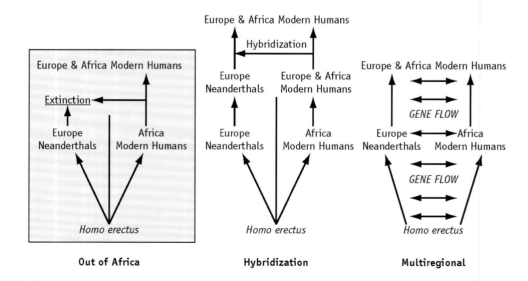

40,000 and 30,000 years ago. The archaeological transition is the direct result of this replacement. Neanderthals were a distinct species that evolved parallel to modern humans and then became extinct.

The *hybridization hypothesis* proposes a middle ground by acknowledging the evidence for an influx of modern humans into Europe, but not accepting extinction of the Neanderthals as a result of that influx. Rather than becoming extinct, Neanderthals "disappeared" as a result of substantial interbreeding with modern humans. The archaeological transition is seen as the result of interaction between Neanderthals and modern humans.

The *multiregional hypothesis* is rooted in the idea that, beginning with the first spread of *Homo erectus* out of Africa, there was continuous gene flow between populations. Therefore, positing Neanderthals as a discrete, isolated species is an artificial rendering of their lineage. Neanderthals evolved locally into modern humans as the result of a continuous gene flow between European and African populations. The multiregional hypothesis sees the Middle to Upper Paleolithic transition not as a local European phenomenon, but rather as part of a global process in the evolution of modern humans.

■ The Fossil Record

The fossil evidence appears to increasingly support the out of Africa position. Early fossils of modern humans have now been found in Africa at Klasies River Mouth and Herto. In Europe, there is no tendency toward modern human traits within late Neanderthal populations. The skeleton of a Neanderthal discovered at **Saint Césaire** in France and dated to 36,000 years ago by thermoluminescence is in every sense a classic Neanderthal (Day 1986). The earliest well-dated modern human remains from Europe are those of a jawbone found in **Peştera cu Oase Cave** in Romania (Trinkaus et al. 2003). This mandible was collected by spelunkers among the scattered bones of cave bears. The mandible itself has been dated to 36,000 years ago by Accelerator Mass Spectrometry (AMS) radiocarbon dating.

The persistence of Neanderthal traits poses an immense problem for proponents of the multiregional hypothesis. This evidence is not problematic for proponents of the hybridization hypothesis, who expect Neanderthal traits to have persisted until there was an influx of modern humans. The hybrid hypothesis predicts that after the influx of modern humans there would be skeletons that show a mixture of Neanderthal and modern human traits. Such hybrid skeletons would be evidence of Neanderthal and modern human interbreeding.

The difficulty with the hybrid hypothesis is that there is little agreement about how to identify a hybrid skeleton. A particularly important case is the skeleton of a child discovered in Portugal at the site of **Abrigo Lagar Velho** (Duarte et al. 1999). Dating to 24,500 years ago, the skeleton was found with Upper Paleolithic tools. The analysis of the skeleton led a group of paleoanthropologists to conclude that it presents "a mosaic of European early modern human and Neanderthal features. . . . This mosaic indicates a mixture between regional Neanderthals and early modern humans" (Duarte et al. 1999, 7604). However, this assessment was rapidly contested by two paleoanthropologists who concluded that "this is simply a chunky . . . child, a descendant of the modern invaders who had evicted the Neanderthals" (Tattersall and Schwartz 1999, 7119). Part of the difficulty with the Abrigo Lagar Velho skeleton is that it is a child. However, the fact that paleoanthropologists studying the skeleton have taken contrasting positions suggests that there is still a fundamental lack of agreement on how to identify hybridization between Neanderthals and modern humans.

▲▲ **Saint Césaire** A site in France where a Neanderthal was found dating to 36,000 years ago.

▲▲ **Peştera cu Oase Cave** The site in Romania where the oldest modern human remains in Europe, dating to 36,000 years ago, were found.

▲▲ **Abrigo Lagar Velho** A site in Portugal where the skeleton of a modern human child dating to 24,500 years ago was discovered. The discovery is thought by some to support the hybridization model.

Modern Human Origins and Questions of Race

There is a degree of irony to the fact that Darwin's engagement in the struggle to end slavery was an important factor leading him to develop his theory of evolution (Desmond and Moore 2009). Darwin's writings on variation had the potential to strike a fatal blow to racism. Unfortunately, this element of Darwin's work was often suppressed, and perceived splits within the human lineage formed the basis for labeling races as either more or less "evolved." Evolutionary theory was also used to support programs of eugenics, in which people viewed as showing "degenerate" traits were discouraged from having children or even, in extreme cases, sterilized. Earnest Hooton, a professor at Harvard University in the 1930s, argued that criminals were degenerate evolutionary throwbacks. He wrote that "a biological purge is the essential prerequisite for a social and spiritual salvation. . . . We must stop trying to cure malignant biological growths with patent sociological nostrums. The emergency demands a surgical operation" (Hooton 1937, 295). This chilling language presages the role that racial theory played in Nazi policies of extermination during the Second World War (Proctor 1988).

In the aftermath of the Second World War, the anthropological community turned strongly against the concept of race. Subsequent research on living populations has emphasized the essential unity of the human species (Lewontin 1982). Nonetheless, race remains a powerful and volatile issue in contemporary society. It is against this backdrop that the out of Africa model emerged in the late 1980s, providing both archaeological and genetic evidence of a very recent common ancestry for all living humans. As the media picked up on the story, they often highlighted the discovery's social implications.

Some archaeologists and biological anthropologists were concerned by the tone of discussions of modern human origins. Proponents of the multiregional model found themselves targeted as racists or felt that the scientific debate was being judged on political rather than scientific merits (Wolpoff and Caspari 1997). Others argued that the entire discussion of modern human origins tended to adopt a racist tone by viewing human variation in terms of "types" (Lieberman and Jackson 1995).

When we study human origins, we explore who we are by going back in time. It is almost inevitable there will be a political dimension to some aspects of this research. The question is how we deal with areas where research touches on issues that also have an ethical or moral dimension. ●

FIGURE 5.9 Charles Knight's classic painting of the Paleolithic artist at work. What assumptions did Knight make about the people who painted in these caves?

■ Genetic Evidence

Another important line of evidence in the debate over the fate of the Neanderthals comes from studies of the genetic diversity of living humans. The analysis of DNA from Neanderthal fossils was discussed in the last chapter. The analysis of the DNA of living humans offers strong evidence in support of the out of Africa hypothesis (Cann 2002). These studies work in a fashion similar to the genetic analysis of the split between the lineages of great apes and humans. Most studies look at mitochondrial DNA, which is inherited exclusively from the mother. Analyses of the mitochondrial DNA of living humans concur in identifying Africa as the place of origin of all living humans and a recent dispersal of humans out of Africa. A study published in 2000 based on the comparison of the complete DNA sequences of 53 individuals from diverse origins places the date for the spread of humans out of Africa within the last 100,000 years (Ingman et al. 2000).

Studies of the Y chromosome add important information about the male lineage. The results of these studies agree with the results of the analysis of mitochondrial DNA in identifying Africa as the region of origin for all living humans and a date for the dispersal of humans from Africa within the last 100,000 years. However, recent evidence from the sequencing of the Neanderthal genome supports the argument that there was interbreeding between modern humans and Neanderthals (Stringer 2012). People living outside of Africa are estimated to derive 1–4% of their DNA from Neanderthals. The timing of the gene flow between Neanderthals and modern humans appears to be between 37,000 and 86,000 years ago. (Sankaraman et al. 2012).

■ Archaeological Evidence

The fossil evidence and genetic evidence combine to strongly support the out of Africa model. Proponents of the multiregional hypothesis are faced with the difficulty of explaining both the existence of classic Neanderthals, such as those at Saint Césaire, dating to less than 40,000 years ago, and the genetic evidence from genetic studies. The fossil evidence poses less of a difficulty for the hybridization hypothesis, and the genetic evidence increasingly suggests that there was gene flow between Neanderthal and modern human populations.

Before examining the archaeological data, it is important to consider the nature of archaeological evidence. In a famous debate with a French colleague, Sally Binford made the pertinent observation that "stone tools don't mate." This is a rather obvious point, but one that is nonetheless critical. The fossil record and the genetic evidence reflect patterns of mating and biological reproduction. The transmission of culture takes place not through a process of cell replication, but through learning. Archaeology can inform us about interaction, but not about interbreeding.

European archaeologists have had a strong tendency to see the transition from the Middle to Upper Paleolithic as a local process. Several archaeological industries have been identified as transitional between the Middle and Upper Paleolithic. In eastern Europe, the transitional industry is known as the **Szeletian** and is characterized by bifacial points. The **Ulluzian** is a transitional industry in Italy in which arched-backed knives and some bone points are found.

The best-documented transitional industry is the **Châtelperronian**, found in France and northern Spain. The exact date of the Châtelperronian is the subject of debate; however, it clearly falls between 40,000 and 35,000 years ago. Châtelperronian stone tools are characterized by a type of knife known as a Châtelperronian point. Otherwise, the stone tools are similar to those found at Middle Paleolithic sites.

At the site of **Arcy-sur-Cure** in northern France, excavators discovered a rich collection of ornaments and bone tools in a Châtelperronian level (White 1992). The ornaments include grooved and perforated canine teeth from fox, wolf, bear, hyena, and deer species and grooved and perforated incisors from bovid, horse, marmot, bear, and reindeer species (see Figure 5.10). There are also small ivory beads. The 142 bone tools found include points, awls, and pins. The site of Quinçay is the only other Châtelperronian industry in which ornaments have been found.

Szeletian An archaeological industry found in eastern Europe during the transition between the Middle Paleolithic and Upper Paleolithic. Bifacially retouched tools are characteristic of the Szeletian.

Ulluzian An archaeological industry found in Italy during the transition between the Middle Paleolithic and Upper Paleolithic. Arched-backed knives are characteristic of the Ulluzian.

Châtelperronian An archaeological industry found in France and northern Spain identified as transitional between the Middle Paleolithic and Upper Paleolithic.

▲▲ **Arcy-sur-Cure** A site in northern France where excavators discovered a rich collection of ornaments, bone tools, and Châtelperronian stone tools.

FIGURE 5.10 Châtelperronian bone bead manufactured from a reindeer metapodial from Arcy-sur-Cure, France

All available evidence indicates that the Châtelperronian industry was produced by Neanderthals. The Saint Césaire Neanderthal previously discussed was found in a Châtelperronian level. Identification of the Neanderthals as the hominin responsible for the Châtelperronian is supported by the discovery of several teeth identified as Neanderthal in the Châtelperronian levels of Arcy-sur-Cure.

There is considerable debate over the interpretation of the Châtelperronian industry. Critical to this debate is the chronological position of the Châtelperronian in relation to the earliest Upper Paleolithic industry, known as the Aurignacian. In all but two sites, the **Aurignacian** is found stratigraphically above the Châtelperronian. In the two exceptions, a Châtelperronian level is sandwiched between Aurignacian levels. This situation, described as the interstratification of Châtelperronian and Aurignacian levels, suggests that these two cultures lived at the same time in France and northern Spain. A large-scale radiocarbon dating study of Middle Paleolithic, early Upper Paleolithic, and transitional sites suggests an overlap lasting between 2,000 and 5,000 years between the Middle Paleolithic and transitional industries, which are both associated with Neanderthals, and the early Upper Paleolithic, associated with modern humans (Higham et al. 2014).

If Neanderthals and modern humans lived in the same region at the same time, then the possibility of interaction exists. Some archaeologists suggest that the ornaments found at Arcy-sur-Cure are evidence of this interaction. They also suggest that these ornaments were made by Neanderthals copying the behavior of modern humans. Others go further and propose the possibility of exchange between Neanderthals and modern humans. Such a scenario would make the hybridization hypothesis plausible.

Aurignacian The earliest Upper Paleolithic period. Aurignacian industries have been found on sites across Europe and the Middle East.

▲▲ **Zafarraya Cave** A site in Spain where the discovery of Neanderthal remains dated between 33,000 and 27,000 years ago suggests that, at least in this area, Neanderthals survived long after the arrival of modern humans in Europe.

▲▲ **Vindija Cave** A site in Croatia where Neanderthal remains were discovered that have been dated to 29,000 years ago.

■ The Last Neanderthals

The case of the Châtelperronian industry suggests that in some areas Neanderthals were not rapidly replaced by incoming hordes of modern humans, but rather that these two populations might have coexisted for considerable lengths of time. In other areas, it appears that Neanderthals continued to live as they had, with no evidence of interaction with or replacement by modern humans for very long periods. These areas are what biologists call refugia—isolated areas where no widespread evolutionary change has occurred. Two refugia that have been identified are the Iberian Peninsula (Spain and Portugal) south of the Ebro River and Croatia. In these areas, Neanderthals appear to have survived in isolation from modern humans for a considerable length of time. In Spain, the site of **Zafarraya Cave** has produced Neanderthal remains and a Middle Paleolithic industry dated between 33,000 and 27,000 years ago (Hublin et al. 1995). In Croatia, two Neanderthal fossils from the site of **Vindija Cave** have been directly dated to 29,000 years ago by AMS radiocarbon dating (Smith et al. 1999).

■ Summing Up the Evidence

Of the three models describing the fate of the Neanderthals, the multiregional hypothesis appears least likely. The absence of any trend toward modern human morphology among late Neanderthals and the genetic evidence based on both mitochondrial DNA and Y chromosome DNA argue against a local evolution of Neanderthals into modern humans.

The fossil and genetic evidence offers strong support for the out of Africa model. Clearly, modern humans evolved in Africa long before they appeared in Europe. The fossils found with the early Upper Paleolithic industries are distinctly modern humans and could not have evolved from local Neanderthals. The genetic evidence supports Africa as the region of origin for all living humans and also supports a dispersal of modern humans after 100,000 years ago.

The archaeological evidence, along with recent genetic evidence, presents a more nuanced picture that might offer support for the hybridization theory, which is also supported by new genetic evidence. The arrival of modern humans was a dramatic event, but it did not signal the immediate disappearance of Neanderthals. In some areas, transitional industries such as the Châtelperronian developed that might provide evidence for interaction between Neanderthals and modern humans over a long period of time. In Spain and in Croatia, refugia areas have been identified where Neanderthals survived for thousands of years after the first arrival of modern humans in Europe. The archaeological evidence suggests that the arrival of modern humans in Europe did not spell the instant demise of Neanderthals.

5.5 The Upper Paleolithic

The first modern human hunter-gatherer societies that lived in Europe are known collectively as the Upper Paleolithic. The Upper Paleolithic is dramatically different from the preceding Middle Paleolithic.

■ Chronology

The stone tool industries of the Upper Paleolithic show a clear pattern of change through time (see Table 5.1). For western Europe, the broad chronological framework is well developed. The earliest Upper Paleolithic industry is the Aurignacian, dated to between 40,000 and 26,000 years ago. Aurignacian sites are found throughout Europe, and later-stage Aurignacian sites are also found in the Middle East. The characteristic tools of the Aurignacian are microliths known as Dufour bladelets, which would have been used as elements in complex tools, and a characteristic bone point known as a split-based point.

TABLE 5.1 UPPER PALEOLITHIC INDUSTRIES IN WESTERN EUROPE

INDUSTRY	DATE	CHARACTERISTICS
Aurignacian	40,000–26,000 years ago	Bladelets and split-based bone points
Gravettian	26,000–23,000 years ago	Small hunting points
Solutrean	23,000–20,000 years ago	Bifacial points
Magdalenian	20,000–11,000 years ago	Bone harpoons

The Gravettian dates to between 26,000 and 23,000 years ago and is found across much of Europe. The characteristic tools of the Gravettian are small hunting points. The following period, the Solutrean, dates between 23,000 and 20,000 years ago. The latter dates correspond to Oxygen Isotope Stage 2 and the height of the Last Glacial Maximum. The Solutrean is limited mostly to France and Spain and is characterized by the presence of beautifully thin bifacial points—pieces that have been thinned by removing flakes from each face not by striking the rock, but by applying pressure with an antler to push off remarkably delicate flakes.

The final industry of the Upper Paleolithic is the Magdalenian, which dates to between 20,000 and 11,000 years ago. The characteristic artifacts of the Magdalenian are a vast array of bone tools, including harpoons.

■ Stone and Bone Tools

The Upper Paleolithic industries include microliths and bone tools, unknown in the repertoire of the Middle Paleolithic. It is interesting that both of these types of tools are known from the Middle Stone Age of Africa—bone tools from Katanda and Blombos and microliths from the Howiesons Poort period.

In the Upper Paleolithic, many tools were made on blades, defined as flakes (pieces detached from a core) that are twice as long as they are wide (see Figure 5.11). The dominant types of tools are endscrapers, which are blades that have been retouched at the end, and burins, which are flakes or blades off of which a flake, known as a burin spall, has been removed along one edge. The removal of a burin spall produces a sharp-angled bit at the end of the tool, which has been likened to the burin tools used in engraving.

Perhaps the most striking aspect of Upper Paleolithic stone and bone tool industries is the presence of sophisticated points used as light projectiles. By the Gravettian industry, there is clear evidence that an atlatl, or spear thrower, was in use. An atlatl is a hooked piece of bone, ivory, or wood used to launch a light spear.

A number of archaeologists have studied the movement of the raw materials used in stone tool manufacture. During the Upper Paleolithic, raw materials, including the famous "chocolate flint" found in Poland, were moved across long distances. This pattern is interpreted as evidence of long-distance trade networks.

The bone tool industry encompasses a wide range of items, including hunting tools. In the later part of the Upper Paleolithic, there is also evidence of a well-developed tool kit for sewing, including fine bone needles (see Figure 5.12).

■ Human Burials

Human burials are absent from the Aurignacian. Beginning in the Gravettian, burials of individuals or groups are found with rich ornamentation. Some of these burials raise questions about the extent of inequality in Upper Paleolithic societies. At Sungir in Russia, for example, two children were found buried in a context dated to 24,000 years ago (Formicola and Buzhilova 2004). The children were buried in a large, shallow grave and covered with red ochre. The

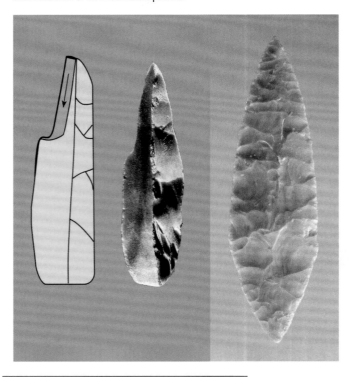

FIGURE 5.11 Stone tools characteristic of the Upper Paleolithic. Left: Burin with an elongated flake known as a burin spall removed along the edge, creating a pointed working end. This piece is a blade because it is twice as long as it is wide. The sketch on the far left shows the burin spall removal. Right: Bifacial point characteristic of the Solutrean period.

wealth of artifacts found in these burials includes thousands of ivory beads (probably the remains of beaded clothes), long mammoth-tusk spears, ivory daggers, pierced fox canines, antler rods, bracelets, ivory carvings of animals, disc-shaped pendants, and ivory pins.

At the site of Dolní Věstonice in Moravia, a triple burial was discovered in a context dated to 28,000 years ago (Bahn 2002). The three individuals, all young adults between 17 and 20 years old, face south and are positioned in a striking tableau. The central skeleton is the most gracile and is most likely female. She lies on her back, and her pelvic area is covered in red ochre. To her left, a heavily built male was buried lying face down, with his head turned away from the central figure and his hand apparently clasping hers. His head had been smashed. To the woman's right, a second male was buried with his hands positioned on her pelvis. A large piece of wood had skewered his body through to his sacrum. Burial offerings included wolf- and fox-tooth pendants and small ivory beads. The excavator proposed that the triple burial reproduces the failed birth of a child, the male figure on the right being a medicine man attempting to aid in the delivery and the man on the left attempting to provide comfort.

In the Sungir burial, a tremendous wealth of objects is buried with young children who would not have had a chance to accumulate such wealth through their own efforts. The practice suggests that some individuals in that society were born into positions of high status. At Dolní Věstonice, the triple burial raises the question of the connection between the three young people and why they were afforded such extraordinary treatment.

Detailed analysis of the skeletal remains has uncovered a surprising link between the two sites. Both the woman from Dolní Věstonice and one of the children from Sungir show evidence of pathology. The Sungir child's skeleton displays a marked bowing and shortening of the femur, while the skeleton of the woman from Dolní Věstonice exhibits deformities to her skull and her torso. Taken together, these discoveries suggest that individuals with visible pathologies might have held a particular status in some Upper Paleolithic societies.

FIGURE 5.12 Bone tools from the site of La Madelaine, France, dating to the Magdalenian period. Notice that the tools include harpoons used for either hunting or fishing, as well as awls and a sewing needle.

■ Artwork

The hallmark of the Upper Paleolithic is the dramatic appearance of a wide range of art objects. This richness of the repertoire of symbolic artifacts is in sharp contrast to the almost total absence of such artifacts at Middle Paleolithic sites.

MOBILIARY ART. The earliest Upper Paleolithic artwork is found in the Aurignacian levels of sites in southern Germany dated between 40,000 and 36,000 years ago.

TOOLBOX

Use-Wear Analysis

Figuring out how a particular stone tool was used is not as easy as it may seem. Archaeologists have developed a method known as use-wear analysis by means of which they infer the function of a tool on the basis of microscopic traces of wear left on its edge. There are two approaches to use-wear analysis: Low-power use-wear analysis documents damage to the edge of the tool that is visible below 70-power magnification. High-power use-wear analysis examines polishes that form on the surfaces near the edge of the tool. These polishes are usually visible only at very high magnification or under a scanning electron microscope.

Use-wear analysis hinges on experiments that provide the analyst with a reference collection. The analyst uses a stone tool for a particular task, such as scraping a hide or butchering a carcass, and the wear observed on the tool can then serve as a key to understanding the wear patterns found on an archaeological sample.

One of the most compelling use-wear studies was an analysis of Solutrean points carried out by the French archaeologists Jean-Michel Geneste and Hugues Plisson. The strength of this study is that it combined multiple lines of evidence to reach the conclusion that these delicately made tools were the tips of projectiles used for hunting. The first step of the study was to produce replicas of Solutrean points and use them for a variety of tasks, including shooting at a target with a longbow, a spear thrower, and a crossbow. The crossbow was particularly valuable, allowing for control of the speed of the arrow. Points were also used for a variety of other tasks, such as cutting and butchery. The patterns of breakage and wear found on the experimental tools were then compared with the assemblage of shouldered points found at the site of Combe Saunière in southwestern France. The comparison of the experimental and archaeological tools enabled the archaeologists to identify the way the tools were used by Solutrean hunters. ●

ADDITIONAL READING: Jean-Michel Geneste and Hugues Plisson. 1993. "Hunting Technologies and Human Behavior: Lithic Analysis of Solutrean Shouldered Points." In *Before Lascaux: The Complex Record of the Early Upper Paleolithic*, edited by Heidi Knecht, Anne Pike-Tay, and Randall White. Boca Raton, FL: CRC Press. Danielle A. Macdonald. 2014. "The Application of Focus Variation Microscopy for Lithic Use-Wear Quantification." *Journal of Archaeological Science* 48: 26–33.

FIGURE 5.13 High-power use-wear analysis examines polishes on the surface of a stone tool to determine how it was used. The image in the upper right shows use-wear polish on the edge of a bladelet, shown on the left. Note that the use-wear image is at high magnification and covers only a small part of the edge of the tool (indicated by the black box). A new method in use-wear analysis is using digital microscopy to create a 3D map of the edge of the tool, as shown in the bottom right image (Macdonald 2014).

▲▲ **Hohlenstein** A site in Germany where a lion-headed figure was found in levels with an Aurignacian industry.

The most spectacular discovery is a representation of a lion–headed man found at the site of **Hohlenstein** (see Figure 5.14). What is particularly striking about this piece of artwork is that it is a depiction not simply of the world as it is, but of the world of imagination. Similar carvings of animals and human figures are found at

Vogelherd and Geissenklösterle, also located in southern Germany (Conard 2003). Recent excavations at the neighboring site of **Hohle Fels** have produced one of the most intriguing pieces of mobiliary art from the Early Aurignacian (Conard 2009). This nearly complete figure of a woman is less than 10 centimeters high (see Figure 5.15). The figure lacks a head, but there is a ring above the shoulders that has been polished, suggesting that the figure may have been suspended as a pendant. The figure has large breasts, and although the carving is quite crude, the genitals are depicted in detail, as are the five fingers on each hand. The entire surface of the figure is covered with patterns of lines, reminiscent of patterns found on animal figures from neighboring sites. The legs are short and pointed. The figure was found in several fragments at the base of over 1 meter of deposits dating to the Aurignacian that were in the process of a meticulous excavation. A large suite of radiocarbon dates from this level produced a range of dates, but the most likely age for this figure is between 40,000 and 35,000 years ago.

Portable art objects such as those from Vogelherd and Hohlenstein are found throughout the Upper Paleolithic. Gravettian period objects that have become known as Venus figurines are found in sites across Europe (see Figure 5.16). The **Venus figurines** vary from a highly abstract to a more detailed representation of the female body. The faces are rarely depicted in any detail and in many cases are simply blank. The feet are always absent and in some cases have been deliberately broken off. The meaning and function of these pieces are the subject of a great deal of speculation.

Bone flutes are known from the Gravettian levels of the cave of Isturitz in southern France. It is interesting that two of these flutes are made of vulture bones. One flute was also recovered from the Aurignacian levels at Isturitz, and fragments have been found in the Aurignacian of Geissenklösterle (d'Errico et al. 2003). The most dramatic evidence for music in the early stages of the Upper Paleolithic comes

FIGURE 5.14 The Hohlenstein ivory figure of a human with a lion's head dating to the Aurignacian period. The height of this figure is 28 cm.

0 [scale] 1 cm

FIGURE 5.15 Front and side views of the recently discovered female figurine from the Aurignacian levels of Hohle Fels. Are there points of similarity between this figure and that of the lion-headed man found at Hohlenstein (Figure 5.14)? How does the Hohle Fels figurine compare to the Gravettian Venus figurine shown in Figure 5.16, which is from a later time period?

▲▲ **Hohle Fels** A site in Germany where bone flutes and a female figurine have been discovered in levels dating to the Aurignacian.

Venus figurines Portable art objects that are found with the Gravettian industry and that depict the female body.

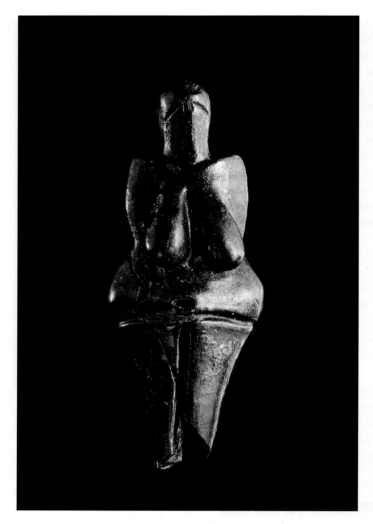

FIGURE 5.16 A Venus figurine dating to the Gravettian period from the site of Dolní Věstonice. The schematic representation of the face, large breasts, and hips and the absence of feet are features found on many Venus figurines. The height of this figure is 11 cm.

FIGURE 5.17 A well-preserved flute found in the Aurignacian levels of Hohle Fels. The boxes provide detailed views of the marks left when shaping the flute and the finger holes. Note the two parallel lines in box c. These markings might have been used to determine the placement of the finger holes.

from the excavations of the Aurignacian levels at Hohle Fels, Germany—the same site that has recently produced the earliest Upper Paleolithic sculpture of a woman (Conard, Malina, and Munzel 2009). Like the Isturitz flutes, the flute from Hohle Fels, shown in Figure 5.17, was produced from the radius of a large vulture. With a wingspan of over 2 meters, vultures have large hollow bones well suited for making flutes. The flute has five holes, and two V-shaped notches have been carved into one end, evidently to serve as the mouthpiece. There are thin markings around each of the holes, clearly to indicate where they were to be placed. The meticulous excavation procedures at Hohle Fels assure that the context of the flute at the base of the Aurignacian sequence is secure.

Some of the Upper Paleolithic mobile art is carved onto tools. Particularly notable are Magdalenian atlatls with fine engravings. Some pieces are decorated not only with depictions of animals, but also with arrays of dots and lines. Alexander Marshack (1972) has argued that these pieces were lunar calendars. While detailed analyses

A First-Person Account of the Bruniquel Horse Engraving Discovery

LAURA M. KAAGAN, PHD

My "home" museum was the Natural History Museum (NHM) in London. I had already spent months studying the fossil mammal collections in the Department of Palaeontology, looking for remains of British horses to measure, study, photograph, and earmark for radiocarbon dating as part of my PhD research. For my studies, I needed a comparative collection—one from continental Europe with a good number of bones to compare with the small, but important, collections I was finding in UK museums.

One September morning in 1994, I was going through a well-curated faunal collection, the 1864 de Lastic Collection. This collection was from a French site called Bruniquel (or "Roc du Courbet"), a Late Magdalenian "cave" (or rock shelter) in southwestern France explored first by Vicomte de Lastic Saint-Jal in the 1860s and later by Sir Richard Owen, who had purchased the faunal remains and Paleolithic artifacts for the British Museum.

Drawers full of horse bones awaited, and I worked my way systematically through this large collection of more than 30 individuals, measuring and inspecting bones and teeth, making meticulous notes, taking standardized measurements (width, depth, length), and noting any striking features, breaks, cut marks, preservation, and anomalies. Suddenly, I came upon a small sample of splint bones (the bones that sit on either side of the hind cannon bone or metatarsal). I noticed that some of the bones had cut and chop marks on them, so I took a closer look. One particular bone, a complete fourth metatarsal splint bone, looked interesting.

On measuring the bone, I noticed that it had been worked, with some regular marks on the flatter (dorsal) surface. I took a second look with my small magnifying glass. I could see an outline of what looked like an engraving—it was an animal's head engraved on the bone. "It couldn't be a horse, could it?" I wondered. My heart started beating a little faster. To my astonishment, I noticed that the museum label with catalogue number was still attached, overlying the engraving. This probably meant that it had not been noticed previously by other workers. What a moment! Was I the first person to view this engraving, perhaps since its burial in a cave in southwestern France thousands of years ago?

To be completely sure of what I had found, I alerted the Curator of Fossil Mammals at the NHM, Andrew Currant. After giving it a gentle cleanup and carefully removing the ID label, we could see much more clearly—and magnificently—this new horse find: an engraved horse's head on a splint bone from a prehistoric wild horse.

Although I discovered the engraving long after excavation and acquisition, which is in itself not a rare thing, it was found among curated material that had already been painstakingly pored over and catalogued, as is evidenced by Owen's interest and effort in recording and interpreting the collection. My fresh study led me to discover a "hidden" artifact, previously unnoticed by other researchers.

This unique find gives hope to all researchers that, if they look hard enough, an unexpected find may be just around the corner. This find connects me, and other researchers like me, directly to the material—to a time and place, a window onto another world—making our work more personal and bringing the research to life. A chance find like this enables us to make a unique contribution to world knowledge. Not only does this new find enhance an already impressive collection of art objects (e.g., engravings of reindeer and horses on bones and antlers) recovered from Bruniquel that have already been recorded, but also it is another good example of a "naturalistic" depiction, in typical Magdalenian style, of a Late Pleistocene wild horse, further adding to the record of wild horses depicted in Ice Age iconography. ▲

FIGURE 5.18 Bone with the horse-head engraving (NHM 38475) from Bruniquel discovered at the Natural History Museum in London

carried out by Francesco d'Errico (1995) do not support the identification of these pieces as lunar calendars, they do support the idea that the incisions were not simply decorative (see Figure 5.19). D'Errico concludes that the marks were used to store information, but does not speculate as to what that information might have been.

CAVE ART. The spectacular paintings discovered at Lascaux Cave in France and other sites such as Altamira in Spain are both awe-inspiring and enigmatic. The paintings were made by people who penetrated below the surface of the earth with only crude oil lamps for light. These people covered the walls of caves with sensitive depictions of the animal world, often using the irregular features of the cave to accentuate aspects of the animals' bodies. They also left stencils of their hands on the cave walls, outlined by colorants they spat out of their mouths. In these handprints, fingers are often missing, most likely because they were deliberately held clenched by the artist. Not only did these people paint the caves, but also they incised the outlines of animals, often overlaying image over image in a dizzying mat of lines. Oddly, depictions of human figures are extremely rare in caves. Most of the paintings are of animals; abstract forms such as grids and dots are also found.

FIGURE 5.19 Diagram of the La Marche antler. This piece is one of the most elaborate examples of Upper Paleolithic art, with a complex array of lines that might have served as a form of notation. The results of analysis by Francesco d'Errico demonstrate that these marks were made in groups using a series of different tools. Capital letters indicate groups of marks made by the same tool. Small letters and arrows show where the antler was turned.

The earliest known painted cave is also one of the most recently discovered. **Chauvet Cave**, shown in Figure 5.20 on page 138, was a chance discovery made by amateur spelunkers (Clottes, Bahn, and Arnold 2003). Imagine their shock when they looked around by the light of their torches and saw walls covered with panthers, battling rhinos, aurochs, and bears. An extensive program of radiocarbon dating at Chauvet Cave indicates that there were two periods of cave painting. The earlier phase was between 37,000 and 33,000 years ago. It was during this period that most of the black paintings were drawn on the cave walls. The later phase between 31,000 and 28,000 years ago corresponds to charcoal markings on the cave walls (Quiles et al. 2016). The tradition of cave painting continues throughout the Upper Paleolithic. Both Lascaux and Altamira, which are among the most famous painted caves, date to the Magdalenian period.

Archaeologists have struggled to arrive at an understanding of the paintings in Upper Paleolithic caves. This is one of the most difficult tasks an archaeologist can undertake because the goal is to recover the lost meaning of the paintings.

Hunting Magic. One possibility is that the paintings were elements of magic associated with hunting. Perhaps they were a form of sympathetic magic, whereby the hunter would first create an image of the animal and then be able to succeed in the hunt. Perhaps such magic even had a rational aspect: The paintings might have been plans for hunts or records of successful hunts. Proponents of the hunting magic hypothesis point to images of objects piercing the bodies of animals and to various geometric forms that can be interpreted as traps or pens.

Fertility Magic. Another explanation emphasizes aspects of the cave paintings related to fertility. Some of the arguments for this position are quite far-fetched and even suggest that many of the animals appear pregnant. Nonetheless, representations of females and of geometric forms resembling the vulva are found in the caves. Moreover, the female figure is frequently represented in mobiliary art, such as the Venus figurines of the Gravettian period.

Shamans and Trances. Both the hunting magic and the fertility magic hypotheses emphasize the potential role of cave paintings as elements of magical practice. The conception of magic in these explanations is that it helps people arrive

▲▲ **Chauvet Cave** The earliest known painted cave, dated to between 38,000 and 33,000 years ago. It is located in France.

FIGURE 5.20 Paintings of rhinoceroses and lions at Chauvet Cave. How would you describe the organization of this scene?

at an end or addresses their anxiety about the outcome of an unpredictable undertaking. Another approach to magic stresses the individual mystical experience of the sorcerer or shaman, who acts as an intermediary between humans and the supernatural realm. A number of archaeologists link the practice of cave paintings to shamanism and trances. The existence of images of humans transforming into animals, such as the lion-headed man figurine from Hohlenstein, suggests that shamans may have played a role in Paleolithic society. Certainly, the very act of entering caves to create a painted world suggests that cave painting had a powerful spiritual component. However, whether one can explain the paintings as direct representations of what shamans visualized while in a trance or under the influence of hallucinogens remains open to question.

Mythogram. The theories just discussed view the painted cave as the accumulation of numerous unconnected events. People went down into caves to practice magic or to experience a trance. A rather different perspective is proposed by archaeologists who see the cave as a structured whole. From this perspective, the caves, in their entirety, are to be read as a "mythogram" expressing a sophisticated metaphysical system. Such a hypothesis raises a number of questions: Why would people create a mythogram in a deeply buried cave? Why are the images overlain, sometimes many times over? Nonetheless, there is value to approaching caves as a whole entity that expresses fundamental ideas held by the group.

Artwork made on objects that cannot be transported is not limited to the insides of caves. In the Côa Valley, Portugal, incised drawings of animals on exposed slabs of rock have been dated to the Upper Paleolithic (Zilhao 1998). Luckily, these unique drawings were discovered before the completion of a dam in the valley. Intense lobbying by the archaeological community led the Portuguese government to halt construction of the dam and create a park in the Côa Valley.

BODY ORNAMENTATION. Bone beads, pierced animal teeth, and pierced shells are found throughout the Upper Paleolithic. It is assumed that these objects were worn as necklaces or attached to clothing. Studies of impressions found on burnt clay at the site of Dolní Věstonice have identified woven textiles and basketry made from plant fibers. In an innovative study, Olga Soffer has identified depictions of headgear and other clothing on the Gravettian Venus figurines (Soffer, Adovasio, and Hyland 2000). A rather unusual line of evidence links the development of clothing with the spread of modern humans (Kittler, Kayser, and Stoneking 2003). Human body lice evolved from head lice and are adapted to living in clothing. A genetic analysis of human lice places the origin of body lice at around 70,000 years ago and indicates that body lice probably first evolved in Africa. Kittler and colleagues suggest these data indicate that clothing was a surprisingly recent innovation. However, it remains unclear whether body lice are adapted to any type of clothing, including hides, or whether they are specifically adapted to textiles.

■ Site Structure

A number of open-air Upper Paleolithic sites have produced evidence of huts. Often, the existence of huts is inferred from the distribution of artifacts. At Mezherich in the Ukraine, a large circular mass of mammoth bones has been interpreted as the remains of a structure. Extensive horizontal excavations of open-air Magdalenian sites in the Paris Basin have allowed archaeologists to reconstruct the locations of tents that have left no physical trace. The distribution of animal bones and artifacts makes it possible to determine where the walls of tents once stood. In a particularly innovative study, data on the spatial distribution of artifacts and a large number of refit cores at the site of Etiolles have been combined to produce a picture of the organization of stone tool manufacture. This study demonstrated that the most experienced knappers worked on the best materials in close proximity to a central hearth, while less expert knappers worked on lower-quality flint at the edges of the habitation (Pigeot 1987). At the site of Pincevent, James Enloe (1992) was able to use refit animal bones to track the sharing of meat between habitations.

Although some Upper Paleolithic sites are quite large, there is no evidence that any of them included more than two or three structures at any given time. Margaret Conkey (1980) has interpreted some late Upper Paleolithic sites as aggregation sites where hunter-gatherer groups from a large territory would come together for a brief time.

■ Subsistence

There is clear evidence that the Upper Paleolithic inhabitants of Europe were hunters. There is also limited evidence of fishing, particularly in the later part of the Upper Paleolithic. Upper Paleolithic hunters often focused on herd animals, including reindeer. Unfortunately, we know little about how plant resources were utilized during this period.

Some archaeologists see evidence that some Upper Paleolithic societies engaged in the management or control of animals. One possibility is that some groups mapped their own mobility onto the seasonal movements of a particular herd of animals; evidence of this practice is found among modern Lapp reindeer herders (Ingold 1980). There is very limited evidence to support the argument that humans controlled animals during the Upper Paleolithic in a way that anticipates their domestication. One of the most controversial pieces of evidence is an incised rock from the site of La Marche (Bahn 1978). As with many Upper Paleolithic engraved plaques, this piece is covered in a dense network of overlapping lines, so the actual depiction must be extracted by the archaeologist. The La Marche plaque clearly shows the head of a horse with a diagonal line crossing the muzzle (see Figure 5.21). Paul Bahn has suggested that what is shown is a horse wearing a halter. Randall White (1989) has sharply disputed this interpretation, pointing out that similar lines are found on Magdalenian depictions of bison. White similarly disputes the validity of the evidence in support of the view that Upper Paleolithic hunters mapped their movements onto those of particular herds.

FIGURE 5.21 The engraved picture of a horse head from La Marche with possible evidence of a harness. A picture of the slab (a) shows the complexity of the piece. The drawing of the horse with a harness (b) was pulled out of the overlapping scenes engraved on the rock.

a.

b.

5.6 Explaining the Upper Paleolithic

The richness and diversity of Upper Paleolithic material culture stands in stark contrast to that of the Middle Paleolithic. It seems obvious that this contrast must have something to do with the replacement of Neanderthals by modern humans in Europe. Many of the characteristics of the European Upper Paleolithic are anticipated

FIGURE 5.22 Later Stone Age rock art from Wildebeest Kuil, South Africa

by the Middle Stone Age of Africa. For example, the use of bone tools and microlithic stone tools is found in the Middle Stone Age. The discoveries at Blombos Cave demonstrate that art was not completely absent from this period.

Nonetheless, nothing in the Middle Stone Age record prepares us for the cave paintings and portable art of the European Upper Paleolithic. Perhaps there has simply not been enough excavation on Middle Stone Age sites. This certainly is a possibility. New discoveries in Africa have had a tendency to bring major surprises. However, given what we know today, archaeologists are forced to grapple with the problems posed by the Upper Paleolithic: Why did this industry appear when it did? Why did modern humans replace Neanderthals?

Because of the discoveries at Herto, Klasies River Mouth, Qafzeh, and Skhul, it is not possible to say that something about modern humans inevitably produces complex material culture. In Africa, modern humans produced Middle Stone Age industries for close to 100,000 years. In the Middle East, modern humans produced Middle Paleolithic industries for close to 50,000 years. Richard Klein has developed a bold explanation for this pattern: Klein suggests that around 50,000 years ago, there was a genetic mutation within modern human populations living in Africa (Klein and Edgar 2002). This mutation did not lead to a change in the morphology of the skeleton or the size of the brain, but it did cause changes in the organization of the brain, giving modern humans the cognitive capacity for language. Armed with this new capacity, the affected populations experienced explosive growth and expansion. Modern humans replaced Neanderthals because modern humans had the cognitive capacity for language. Modern humans made symbolic artifacts because humans who use language will inevitably make such objects.

One of the strengths of Klein's proposal is that he sees the Upper Paleolithic as part of a global transformation of human culture. He links the Upper Paleolithic with the emergence of the African Later Stone Age, which also saw an increase in the use of clearly symbolic objects (see Figure 5.22), and with the colonization of Australia and the Americas.

Klein's scenario is plausible, but difficult to prove. How does one identify a mutation that had no effect on skeletal form? How do we know that the modern humans at Herto did not have language? One of the major challenges facing Paleolithic archaeologists is to devise alternative hypotheses for the replacement of Neanderthals by modern humans and for the dramatic innovations found in the Upper Paleolithic.

SUMMARY

- The earliest modern human fossil was found at the site of Herto, Ethiopia, and was dated to between 160,000 and 154,000 years ago.
- The Middle Stone Age is characterized by (1) a wide diversity of stone tool industries produced by using prepared-core technologies, (2) evidence of sophisticated bone tools, (3) hunting and the use of fish and shellfish, and (4) modest evidence of artwork.
- Modern humans are found at the sites of Skhul and Qafzeh, Israel, in layers with a Middle Paleolithic industry dating between 120,000 and 80,000 years ago. This date is earlier than that of the Neanderthal sites in the Middle East.

- The three theories of the relationship between modern humans and Neanderthals are the multiregional hypothesis, the out of Africa hypothesis, and the hybridization hypothesis.
- The earliest modern human fossil in Europe dates to 36,000 years ago, while the most recent Neanderthal fossil dates to between 33,000 and 27,000 years ago.
- The Middle to Upper Paleolithic transition corresponds to the appearance of modern humans in Europe and includes the development of new types of stone and bone tools and the dramatic appearance of a wide range of symbolic artifacts.
- One explanation for the Middle to Upper Paleolithic transition and the replacement of Neanderthals by modern humans is that modern humans were unique in possessing the cognitive capacity for language.

KEY TERMS

Abrigo Lagar Velho, 131
Arcy-sur-Cure, 133
Aterian, 124
Aurignacian, 134
Blombos Cave, 126
Border Cave, 123
Châtelperronian, 133
Chauvet Cave, 143
Herto, 123
Hohle Fels, 139
Hohlenstein, 138
Homo sapiens, 122
Howiesons Poort, 124
Katanda, 125
Klasies River Mouth, 123

Middle Stone Age, 123
Middle to Upper Paleolithic transition, 130
modern human, 122
Peştera cu Oase Cave, 131
Pinnacle Point, 125
Qafzeh Cave, 128
Saint Césaire, 131
Sangoan/Lupemban, 124
Skhul Cave, 128
Szeletian, 133
Ulluzian, 133
Upper Paleolithic, 130
Venus figurines, 139
Vindija Cave, 134
Zafarraya Cave, 134

REVIEW QUESTIONS

1. What is the significance of the discoveries made at the Qafzeh and Skhul Caves?
2. How does the Middle Stone Age archaeological record compare with the Middle Paleolithic archaeological record?
3. Why is the modern human skeleton discovered at Abrigo Lagar Velho thought to be significant?
4. How does Klein explain the replacement of modern humans by Neanderthals and the Middle to Upper Paleolithic transition? What are the strengths and weaknesses of his hypothesis? Can you think of any alternatives?

THE PEOPLING OF AUSTRALIA AND THE NEW WORLD

The dispersal of modern humans is a global process reaching across Australia and the Americas. After reading this chapter, you should understand:

- **The debates over the timing of the initial occupation of Australia and the Americas.**

- **The migration routes followed by the first humans moving into Australia and the Americas.**

- **The relationship between human occupation of Australia and the Americas and the extinction of megafauna.**

Australian rock art site

6 TIMELINE

SITES

Nauwalabila I

Cuddie Springs

Pedra Furada

Lake Mungo

ARCHAEOLOGICAL INDUSTRIES

HOMININS

| thousands of years ago | 55 | 50 | 45 | 40 | 35 |

- Broken Mammoth
- Kennewick
- Colby Site
- Olsen-Chubbuck
- Fulsom
- Wilson-Leonard
- Meadowcroft Rockshelter
- Blackwater Draw
- Watson Brake
- Newnans Lake

ATLANTIC OCEAN

PACIFIC OCEAN

- Caverna de Pedra Pintada
- Pedra Furada
- Quebrada Tacahuay
- Monte Verde

Solomon Islands

OCEANIA

- Ngandong
- Flores
- Nauwalabila
- Gunbilngmurrung
- Samoa
- Tonga

- Cuddie Springs
- Lake Mungo

Olsen-Chubbuck

Pedra Pintada

Newnans Lake

Monte Verde (MVII level)

Wilson-Leonard

Watson Brake

Meadowcroft Rockshelter

Quebrada Tacahuay

CLOVIS

FOLSOM

LAPITA

NENANA

MO FLORESIENSIS

25   20   15   10   5

FIGURE 6.1 Folsom point with associated bones from Folsom, New Mexico

George McJunkin was a quintessential scientific outsider. An African-American rancher born into slavery, McJunkin became an avid amateur scientist with wide-ranging interests, including astronomy, archaeology, and fossil bones (Preston 1997). In 1908, while fixing a fence after a storm, McJunkin noticed bones eroding out of a gully near Folsom, New Mexico. It was only in 1926, however, four years after McJunkin died, that Jesse Figgins of the Denver Museum of Natural History began excavations at Folsom. In his first season excavating there, Figgins found a distinctive spearpoint together with bison fossils. This spearpoint was thin and finely worked, with a long channel, or flute, running from the base toward the tip (see Figure 6.1). Figgins's discovery was met with skepticism, but doubt evaporated in 1927 when another spearpoint was found lodged between the ribs of a bison skeleton. The discoveries at Folsom proved that humans had been in North America for at least 10,000 years. Finding a spearpoint embedded in the remains of a large animal also suggested that early occupants of the Americas were specialized big-game hunters.

In this chapter, we focus on the debates surrounding the initial human occupation of Australia and the Americas. The only hominins known from these continents are *Homo sapiens*. Migration routes into both Australia and the Americas led through East Asia, so it is important to review the current understanding of modern human origins in that area first. With this background, it is possible to move on to consider the timing of the occupation of Australia and the likely migration routes. We also consider the significance of the recent discovery of a new species belonging to the genus *Homo* on the island of Flores in Indonesia. Beyond tracking when and how people first arrived in Australia, we examine the role of humans in the extinction of megafauna on the continent and the evidence for the development of cave painting in the Australian context. We then move on to the debates concerning the timing and migration routes taken by the first people to arrive in the Americas. Here, too, we consider the role of humans in megafauna extinctions.

The question of when people first arrived in Australia and the Americas is the subject of intense scientific controversy. It is important to recognize that it is also a subject of great sensitivity to indigenous people. The archaeological debate is framed entirely on the basis of scientific inquiry, which is often in conflict with beliefs. The question of when humans first arrived can conflict with an indigenous people's convictions that their people have been in a place since creation. Bridging these disparate worldviews requires care and respect. Although archeologists have only recently begun dealing with this conflict, they have already made great strides. The development of postprocessual archaeology, which acknowledges alternative narratives and viewpoints, provides room for dialogue and constructive disagreement. Issues relating to the treatment of human remains that indigenous groups claim as ancestral require particular care.

6.1 Modern Humans in East Asia

Populations of *Homo erectus* had arrived on the Indonesian island of Java perhaps as early as 1.8 million years ago, and by 1.6 million years ago, they were well established in China. However, what happened to East Asian populations of *Homo erectus* while modern humans were evolving in Africa and Neanderthals were evolving in Europe remains unclear. On the one hand, some paleoanthropologists argue, as part of the multiregional hypothesis, that there was a local East Asian evolution of modern humans from *Homo erectus* parallel with the evolution of modern humans in Africa. On the other hand, proponents of the out of Africa hypothesis argue vehemently that in East Asia populations of *Homo erectus* persisted until they were replaced by modern humans from Africa. Both sides of the debate recognize that they are relying on inadequate data.

One critical piece of evidence has emerged from the dating of *Homo erectus* fossils from the island of Java. Electron spin resonance and uranium series dating of animal teeth found with *Homo erectus* fossils at the site of **Ngandong** have produced dates that range between 46,000 and 27,000 years ago (Swisher et al. 1996). If this age is correct, it indicates that populations of *Homo erectus* remained in East Asia far later than anywhere else in the world. This evidence offers strong support for the out of Africa hypothesis. However, these dates are not universally accepted, as some scientists doubt that the animal teeth were actually found in the same deposits as the hominin fossils.

The questions concerning the fate of *Homo erectus* and the initial appearance of modern humans in East Asia provide a rather uncertain backdrop to the debates surrounding the peopling of Australia and the New World (North and South America). The Paleolithic of East Asia is a critical area of research that is likely to see dramatic developments in coming years.

6.2 Australia

During periods of glacial advance and low sea level, Australia, Tasmania, and New Guinea were connected in a landmass known as **Sahul**. A similar landmass known as **Sunda** connected much of Southeast Asia, including Vietnam, Malaysia, the Philippines, and much of Indonesia. As shown in Figure 6.2, Sunda and Sahul are separated by a string of islands known as Wallacea, where the channels between the islands are too deep to have been dry land at any time for the past 50 million years. The **Wallace Line**, which runs through Wallacea, separates the unique animals and plants of Australia from the animal and plant communities of Southeast Asia. In order to reach Australia, humans had to cross the Wallace Line by sea.

The discovery of stone tools on the island of Flores in Wallacea suggests that *Homo erectus* was able to cross bodies of water. The levels in which stone tools are found are dated to between 900,000 and 800,000 years ago, when *Homo erectus* was the only hominin in Southeast Asia. Some authors have argued that the evidence from Flores demonstrates that *Homo erectus* was able to make and use watercraft. However, *Homo erectus* was not the only mammal species to arrive in Flores between 900,000 and 800,000 years ago. At the same time, a species of large elephant (*Stegadon*) and a species of large rat also made their first appearance on the island. These animals could not have arrived by a land bridge connecting Flores to Sunda, as it is clear that no such land bridge ever existed. It is suggested that a combination of low sea level and favorable currents enabled such animals to reach Flores. It is quite likely that *Homo erectus* could have arrived through similar circumstances.

Continued excavations on Flores at the site of Liang Bua have stunned the scientific community with the discovery of tiny hominins so unique that they have been given their own species name: *Homo floresiensis* (Brown et al. 2004). The hominin remains date to the period between 60,000 and 100,000 years ago (Morwood et al. 2004; Sutikna et al. 2016). The body of *Homo floresiensis* is quite small, and its brain is 380 cubic centimeters, about the size of a grapefruit, which is below the range of any other member of genus *Homo*. It appears likely that the unique characteristics of *Homo floresiensis* are the result of the long-term isolation of a population of *Homo erectus* on the island of Flores for hundreds of thousands of years. There is a

▲▲ **Ngandong** A site on the island of Java where the most recent known fossil of *Homo erectus* was found, dating to between 46,000 and 27,000 years ago.

▲▲ **Sahul** The landmass that encompassed Australia, Tasmania, and New Guinea during periods of low sea level.

▲▲ **Sunda** The landmass that connected much of Southeast Asia during periods of low sea level.

▲▲ **Wallace Line** The line that runs through Wallacea and separates the unique animals and plants of Australia from the animal and plant communities of Southeast Asia.

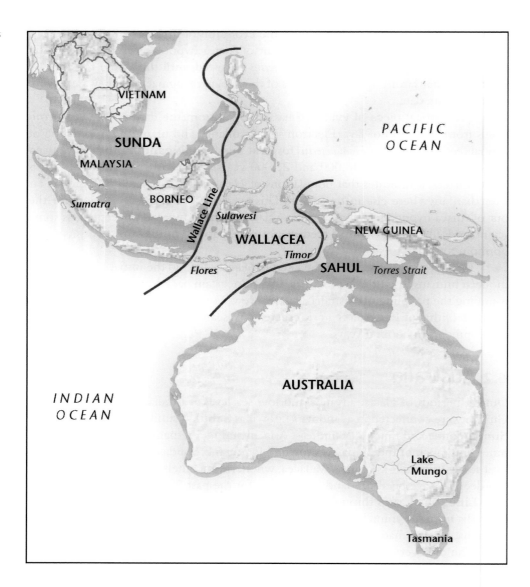

FIGURE 6.2 Map of the landmasses of Sunda and Sahul that existed during periods of low sea level. The areas exposed by low sea levels are indicated in purple.

general tendency for isolated island populations to evolve into species with reduced body size (Van den Bergh, de Vos, and Sondaar 2001).

The stone tool industry from Liang Bua associated with *Homo floresiensis* is, like the human fossils themselves, somewhat odd and difficult to characterize (Moore et al. 2009). The methods of manufacture are very simple, and the retouched tools are not highly standardized. What is somewhat surprising is that there is a tendency to use flakes as cores. This is a technology used in the Acheulian of Africa to produce large bifacial tools, but on Flores, the flakes produced are quite small. The stone tools are associated with faunal remains dominated by the bones of pygmy elephants and Komodo dragons (see Figure 6.3). Figure 6.4 shows that there are clear cut marks on the elephant bones. It is likely that the Komodo dragons, fierce predators, were vulnerable to hunting when they were inactive due to either nighttime cold or high midday temperatures (Van den Bergh et al. 2009).

Some paleoanthropologists remain unconvinced that *Homo floresiensis* is a distinct species, arguing that the fossils discovered are modern humans with a pathology known as microcephaly, which results in a small brain (Martin et al. 2006). However, the discovery of fossils very similar to *Homo floresiensis* at the open-air site

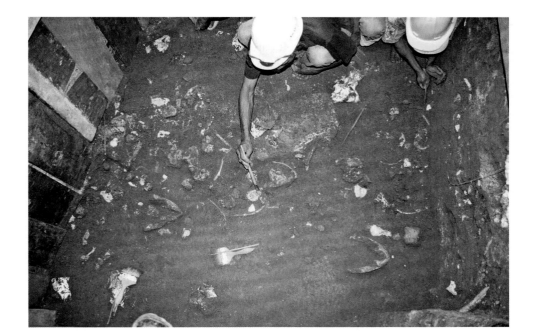

FIGURE 6.3 Excavating a dense concentration of elephant bones at Liang Bua, Flores

A

1 cm

B

1 cm

FIGURE 6.4 Cut marks on elephant bones from Liang Bua, Flores

of Mata Menge, also on Flores, offers strong support for the distinctiveness of this island population (van den Bergh et al. 2016). The stratum the Mata Menge fossils were found in is dated to approximately 700,000 years ago based on Argon dating of overlying and underlying strata (Brumm et al. 2006). The Mata Menge fossils are associated with simple flake tools like those found at Liang Bua.

There is no evidence that *Homo erectus* ever crossed Wallacea into Sahul. Nor is there evidence of an influx of mammals across the Wallace Line into Sahul at any time during the Pleistocene, as is found on Flores. Two possible routes for crossing Wallacea into Sahul have been identified. The northern route follows a string of small islands between the Indonesian island of Sulawesi and western New Guinea, known today as Irian Jaya. The southern route follows a series of small islands between Java and Timor, with a sea crossing between Timor and northern Australia. Both routes require sea voyages of greater than 10 kilometers and the settlement of a series of islands. Although the southern route is the most direct, it would have required a sea voyage of approximately 90 kilometers.

▲▲ **Nauwalabila I** The site that offers the earliest secure evidence of human occupation of Australia, dating to between 60,000 and 53,000 years ago.

▲▲ **Lake Mungo** One in a series of dried-out lakes located in southern Australia where evidence of human occupation dates to between 50,000 and 46,000 years ago.

megafauna Species of large animals that became extinct in many areas of the world, including the Americas and Australia, toward the end of the Pleistocene.

■ Dating the Earliest Human Occupation

A series of sites in Australia is now well dated to between 60,000 and 50,000 years ago. Thus, the arrival of humans in Australia predates the arrival of modern humans in Europe by at least 10,000 years.

The site of **Nauwalabila I**, located in Arnhem Land in northern Australia, is a rock shelter with 3 meters of archaeological deposits (Bird et al. 2002). The deepest levels have been dated by thermoluminescence and optically stimulated luminescence to between 60,000 and 53,000 years ago. Unfortunately, attempts to radiocarbon date these levels have failed. The archaeological remains from the lowest levels are mostly flake stone tools, including a thick retouched scraper. Two pieces that apparently served as grinding stones were also found.

Lake Mungo is one of a series of dried-out lakes known as the Willandra Lakes, located in southern Australia near the city of Canberra (Bowler et al. 2003). Two human burials and numerous stone tools have been discovered eroding out of the Lower Mungo Unit along the edge of the dried-out lake bed. The deposits in which these skeletons were found have been dated to 40,000 years ago by optically stimulated luminescence. The earliest stone tools at Lake Mungo have been dated to between 50,000 and 46,000 years ago. The stone tools found at Lake Mungo are simple flake tools and cores similar to those found at Nauwalabila I. A number of hearths were found, and the animal bones that were recovered include a large number of fish remains.

The evidence for human occupation of Australia before 60,000 years is scant. The Jinmium Cave site in Arnhem Land has produced thermoluminescence dates of 116,000 years ago for deposits with archaeological material (Spooner 1998). However, these dates have been contested and are not widely accepted. Current data suggest that human occupation of Australia began roughly 60,000 years ago and that the spread of humans across the continent was fairly rapid. The Lake Mungo dates indicate that humans had spread to southern Australia within 10,000 years of their initial arrival on the continent.

The current understanding of the timing of the first arrival of modern humans in Australia suggests that by 60,000 years ago they were capable of sea voyages and had already spread far beyond Africa. Some archaeologists remain skeptical about these dates and question how modern humans could have arrived in Australia before reaching Europe (O'Connell and Allen 1998). For others, the early Australian dates offer support for the multiregional hypothesis. Such an early date for modern humans in Australia might support the idea that they evolved locally in East Asia. Yet another possibility is that there were multiple dispersals of modern humans out of Africa. The modern human populations that arrived in Australia might have followed the same coastal route used by *Homo erectus* to get to Java. We are left wondering about the voyagers who set off across the seas to arrive in Australia. What kind of boats did they use? What compelled them to take this voyage into an unknown land?

■ Megafauna Extinction

Throughout the world, there was widespread extinction of animal species at the end of the Pleistocene Ice Age. Particularly hard hit were large animals, collectively known as **megafauna**. Some have suggested that the extinction of megafauna was largely the result of hunting by modern humans; others argue that a more broadly based ecological explanation is needed.

The unique animal communities of Sahul fit the pattern of widespread extinction toward the end of the Pleistocene. Of 24 genera of Australian land animals with a body weight greater than 45 kilograms, 23 became extinct at the end of the Pleistocene. These large animals included marsupials such as the rhinoceros-sized kangaroo *Procoptodon* (see Figure 6.5), mammals, and a large flightless bird, *Genyornis newtoni*. The date of the extinction of these species is the subject of debate. The dating of 700 *Genyornis newtoni* eggshells indicates that this species disappeared suddenly around 50,000 years ago (Miller et al. 1999). A project dating paleontological sites indicates that the large placental and mammalian animals became extinct around 46,000 years ago (Roberts et al. 2001). This study was restricted to sites in which articulated animal bones were found (i.e., a part of the skeleton was found with bones in their proper anatomical positions). When focusing on articulated skeletons, there is a high degree of confidence that the bones are in their original geological context and that dating the sediments provides an accurate date for the bones. Some sites have produced unarticulated bones of megafauna in contexts dated considerably later in time. One of the most important of these sites is Cuddie Springs in southeastern Australia (Field et al. 2001). At Cuddie Springs, stone tools were found together with the bones of extinct megafauna in layers dated to between 36,000 and 27,000 years ago. There is some question as to whether these bones are in their original place of deposition, and it has not yet been possible to date the bones directly.

The preponderance of the data suggests that the extinction of Australian megafauna was an event that took place across the continent between 50,000 and 40,000 years ago. Thus, the event took place within 10,000 to 15,000 years of the first arrival of humans on the continent. It is difficult to explain why an extinction took place at this time. Although there was a major climatic change in Oxygen Isotope Stage 2 (the Last Glacial Maximum) around 20,000 to 15,000 years ago, the extinction appears to have preceded the change by more than 20,000 years.

The fact that the megafauna extinction took place during the first 10,000 years after the first arrival of humans in Australia suggests that human activity caused the extinction. However, evidence for the hunting of megafauna by humans is practically nonexistent. Cuddie Springs is one of the few sites to produce an association of stone tools and the bones of extinct animals. There is no evidence from stone tools that the first inhabitants of Australia had highly sophisticated hunting weapons. Harpoons and spear throwers developed only much later in Australian prehistory.

There is little evidence that the first inhabitants of Australia hunted large game or had a highly developed tool kit for hunting. It is therefore extremely unlikely that these people hunted the megafauna to the point of extinction. Some archaeologists

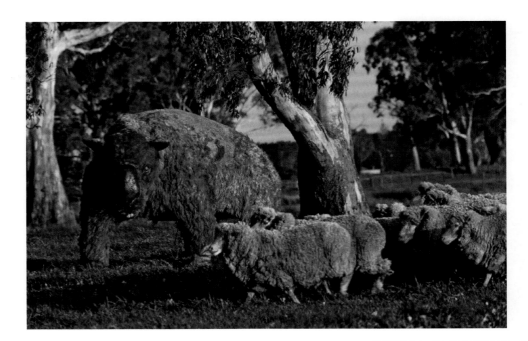

FIGURE 6.5 In an odd juxtaposition, a herd of sheep grazes around a model reconstruction of an extinct giant marsupial

fire-stick farming A term used by Rhys Jones to describe the aboriginal use of fire in Australia.

▲▲ **Gunbilngmurrung** A site in Australia where a beeswax figure of a turtle was found, which has been radiocarbon dated to 4,000 years ago.

have suggested that human activity altered the ecology of Australia in a manner that disrupted the highly specialized adaptations of the megafauna. One possible factor would have been human use of fire in hunting. Rhys Jones has described the aboriginal use of fire in Australia as **fire-stick farming**. Early European travelers in Australia described the active use of fire by aboriginal societies. For example, in 1848, Thomas Mitchell wrote, "Fire is necessary to burn the grass and form those open forests in which we find the large forest-kangaroo; the native applies that fire to the grass in certain seasons; in order that a young green crop may subsequently spring up, and so attract and enable him to kill and take the kangaroo with nets" (quoted in Lourandos 1997, 97). If the first inhabitants of Australia used a similar strategy, then, over a period of 10,000 years, it might have resulted in the alteration of the ecology to the point where the megafaunal species became extinct.

■ Rock Art

Among archaeologists, Australia is known as a continent in which a hunter-gatherer way of life persisted until contact with Europeans. This characterization of Australia does little to express the diversity and richness of aboriginal societies. Ethnographers often point to the nonmaterial aspects of aboriginal Australian culture, particularly the highly developed mythological and ritual traditions. Aspects of aboriginal mythologies have found expression in the spectacular artwork painted on thousands of rock shelters across the continent; Figure 6.6 shows an example of rock art. Many of these sites were painted recently or are still revisited and painted today. Archaeological research has begun to provide evidence that this practice is of great antiquity.

Rock art in Australia takes many forms (Chaloupka 1993). One particularly interesting form is that of drawings made by applying beeswax to a rock-shelter wall. At the site of **Gunbilngmurrung** in western Arnhem Land, a beeswax figure of a turtle has been radiocarbon dated to 4,000 years ago (Watchman and Jones 2002). The turtle is drawn in "X-ray style," with some of the internal bone structure depicted. As at most Australian rock art sites, paintings at Gunbilngmurrung are found one on top of another. The beeswax turtle clearly lies above six older sets of figures drawn with red ochre that appear to be more than 4,000 years old.

In an ingenious application of optically stimulated luminescence dating, archaeologists have managed to date mud wasp nests overlying paintings on rock shelters in Arnhem Land. In one cave, a nest overlying a mulberry-colored human figure was dated to 16,400 years ago. The human figure itself overlies a hand stencil that must be of even greater antiquity (Roberts et al. 1997).

■ Voyaging On

The spread of people across the islands of Micronesia and Polynesia (see Figure 6.7) began at least 35,000 years ago. Some of the earliest islands settled would have been visible from New Guinea. But by 29,000 years ago, there is evidence of voyagers occupying New Britain Island, which is not visible from either New Guinea or a previously occupied island. There is clear evidence from 20,000 years ago onward of human occupation across the Solomon Islands and the

FIGURE 6.6 Rock art from the site of Ubirr, Kakadu National Park, Australia. This figure gives a good sense of the range of equipment carried by aboriginal Australian hunter-gatherers.

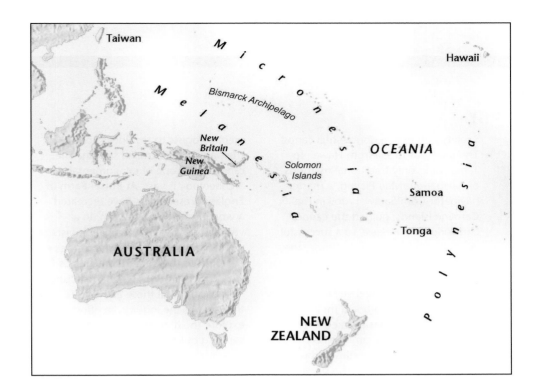

FIGURE 6.7 Map of Oceania showing the limits of Micronesia and Polynesia

▲▲ **Lapita** A culture that spread across a vast area of Melanesia beginning 3,500 years ago and reached as far as the islands of Samoa and Tonga.

Bismarck Archipelago, a massive area that is more than 1,000 kilometers in length. Settlement of these islands was not the result of a one-time chance voyage. Obsidian from sources in New Britain is found across the islands, as are bones of a tree-dwelling marsupial indigenous to New Guinea, which provides evidence of sustained trade between islands.

Although it is clear that these societies had mastered seafaring, there is not yet evidence for people venturing farther out into Melanesia until 3,500 years ago, when the **Lapita** culture spread across the region. The Lapita brought with them a new way of life that included a distinctive style of pottery (shown in Figure 6.8),

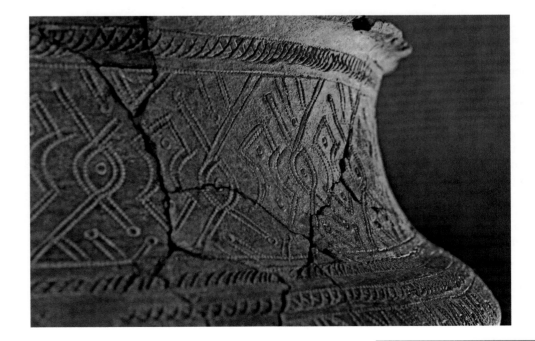

FIGURE 6.8 Decorated Lapita pottery from the Republic of Vanuatu

TOOLBOX

Experimental Archaeology

Voyaging across the sea figures prominently in Polynesian oral history; however, many anthropologists have viewed these voyages as myths rather than stories based on actual experience. There is good reason for skepticism. Hawaiian oral history speaks of repeated trips between Hawaii and an ancestral land that appears to be Tahiti. Is such a voyage conceivable in a canoe without a compass? The trip from Hawaii to Tahiti covers over 3,620 kilometers of open sea, but the actual distance is quite a bit farther, since it is necessary to curve eastward against the trade winds and currents that flow across the course. Archaeologists came to view the ancient Polynesians as hapless sailors blown off course until they reached fortuitous landfall.

A set of experiments has led to a reversal of opinion about the voyaging of ancient Polynesians and the veracity of Polynesian oral history. The first experiment was a computer simulation. In 1973, Michael Levison and colleagues used a computer model of Pacific Ocean currents and wind speeds to run over 100,000 simulations of what would happen to a vessel drifting away from various Polynesian islands. They found that, while hitting an island by drifting from east to west was possible, drifting from west to east and hitting an island was virtually impossible. Perhaps most significantly, the computer simulation showed that out of 16,000 trials from various Polynesian islands, none reached Hawaii. The implication is that Hawaii was reached by sailors who set their course intentionally.

In 1976, to push the experiment a step further, Ben Finney and colleagues formed the Polynesian Voyaging Society and built a double-hull canoe. The goal was to sail from Hawaii to Tahiti using only traditional methods of navigation. Mau Piailug, a master navigator from Satawal Atoll in the Caroline Islands, guided the canoe, christened the *Hokuile*, to a successful landfall in Tahiti. Since that time, the *Hokuile* has continued to voyage across the Pacific. The experiment successfully showed that controlled voyaging across Polynesia using traditional methods was possible and has sparked a rebirth of pride and interest among Polynesian and Hawaiian communities in their legacy of sea voyaging. The project has also led to a complex "dialogue developing between indigenous peoples in search of their own past and anthropologists seeking to reconstruct ancient practices" (Finney 1991, 398).

Finney's research is an example of an application of experimental archaeology, which allows archaeologists to test ideas about the past in a controlled setting. The range and scope of experimental archaeology is vast. At Butser Farm in England, researchers have recreated a working Bronze Age farm. In a very different setting, archaeologists working in engineering laboratories have tested the fracture mechanics that underlie stone tool manufacture. At the root of all these activities is the spirit of the inquiry, an effort to explore the dynamics of the past by carrying out experiments in the present. Experimental archaeology is closely associated with ethnoarchaeology, taphonomic analysis, and other aspects of archaeological methodology that use studies set in the present as a source of insight into the dynamics that formed the archaeological record. ●

For more information on the Polynesian Voyaging Society, see http://pvs.kcc.hawaii.edu/index.html.

FIGURE 6.9 A crew steers a voyaging canoe off the Hawaiian islands

large village settlements, and subsistence based on farming and fishing. Both archaeological and linguistic evidence places the origins of the Lapita people in Taiwan and the islands of Southeast Asia. The Lapita migration eventually covered an area 7,240 kilometers across, reaching eastward as far as Samoa and Tonga. What drove these voyagers not only to discover, but also to settle new lands? It does not appear that population pressure can account for this expansion. It would be virtually impossible for population growth rates to even keep up with, let alone fuel, the rapid rate of colonization. An intriguing idea is that Lapita social structure was the underlying cause for their migration. Patrick Kirch suggests that the Lapita had very strict rules of inheritance that heavily favored the firstborn. Kirch (1997) writes that "in such societies, junior siblings frequently adopt a strategy of seeking new lands to settle where they can found their own 'house' and lineage, assuring their own offspring access to quality resources" (65). Similar social dynamics, along with developments in the technologies of seafaring, might have also underlain the final stage of expansions into eastern Polynesia (including Hawaii) and New Zealand. Further research is needed to refine the chronology for the initial occupation of these islands, but the oldest dates are currently between 1,000 and 1,500 years ago, which suggests that there was a significant hiatus between the Lapita expansion across to Samoa and Tonga and the complete colonization of the Polynesian islands.

Clovis first model The Clovis culture, dated to 13,500 to 12,500 years ago, is the first human occupation in the Americas.

pre-Clovis model Human occupation of the Americas predates 13,500 years ago.

early arrival model Human occupation of the Americas began as early as 30,000 to 40,000 years ago.

Blackwater Draw A site near Clovis, New Mexico, where spearpoints were found in levels below Folsom points.

Clovis culture The period many North American archaeologists view as the initial human occupation of the Americas, dated to between 13,400 and 12,700 years ago.

6.3 The New World

Despite decades of intensive research, the timing of the first arrival of humans in the New World (North and South America) remains the topic of heated debate. There are three models for human occupation of the Americas. The **Clovis first model**, long dominant among North American archaeologists, views the Clovis culture, dated to between 13,500 and 12,500 years ago, as the initial human occupation of the Americas. Recently, a large number of archaeologists have come to support the **pre-Clovis model**, according to which the initial human occupation of the New World dates back earlier than 13,500 years ago. The **early arrival model**, which argues for human presence in the New World by 30,000 years ago, is a minority position.

■ Clovis First

In 1932, archaeologists excavating in **Blackwater Draw** near the town of Clovis, New Mexico, discovered the remains of bison in a level with Folsom points. Below this level, evidence of an earlier occupation was found. In this earlier level, spearpoints were found that were slightly different from the Folsom points. Clovis points, as these earlier forms came to be known, are fluted like the Folsom points, but the resulting channel does not extend the entire length of the point. Figure 6.10 shows a Clovis point. At Blackwater Draw, Clovis points were found together with mammoth and horse bones.

Clovis points have subsequently been found on a large number of sites across North America. These discoveries have led many archaeologists to conclude that the remains found at Clovis are characteristic of the earliest human occupation of the Americas.

CLOVIS CULTURE AND CHRONOLOGY. The definition of **Clovis culture** is based largely on the

FIGURE 6.10 Clovis point that has been carefully shaped by bifacial flaking. Notice the small flutes off the base of the point.

Beringia A land bridge that connected Asia and North America during periods of low sea level.

ice-free corridor A potential migration route for populations expanding out of Beringia, running between the Cordilleran and Laurentide glaciers.

form of spearpoints. In the midcontinental United States and eastern Canada, Clovis points are absent, but similar pieces known as Gainey points are found on many sites. Besides spearpoints, other stone tools found on Clovis sites include blades and multi-functional tools made on flakes. Apart from these stone tools, few cultural remains are found. Built features are not known, and the main features identified are hearths. A deep feature found in the Clovis levels at Blackwater Draw has been identified as a well that might have been excavated in response to drought conditions (Haynes et al. 1999).

The main type of bone tool found on Clovis sites is a rod-shaped object probably used as part of the haft of a spearpoint. A worked bone discovered at the Murray Spring site in Arizona is described as a shaft wrench because of the hole bored in one end. This is the only such object known from a Clovis site; engraved or incised objects are rare. At the Gault site in Texas, limestone slab with geometric decorations have been found (see Figure 6.11), but it is not clear that they are from the Clovis level (Haynes 2002). The discovery of Clovis tools at a red-ochre mining site known as Powars II in Platte County, Wyoming, suggests that colorants might have been used during the period (Stafford et al. 2003). At El Fin del Mundo in northwestern Mexico a Clovis site was found with the remains of a gompathere, a now-extinct elephant (Sanchez et al. 2014). El Fin del Mondo is one of the earliest Clovis sites, dated to around 13,400 years ago.

The chronological range for Clovis sites is between 13,400 and 12,700 calendar years ago (Miller, Holliday, and Bright 2014). Some archaeologists argue that the Clovis lasted only about 200 years and began about 13,000 years ago, but this is difficult to reconcile with sites like El Fin del Mundo (Waters and Stafford 2007). The dates 11500–10500 B.P. are often given for the Clovis period; however, these are uncalibrated radiocarbon dates.

FIGURE 6.11 This engraved stone slab from the Gault site, Texas, is a rare example of an incised artifact from a Clovis site

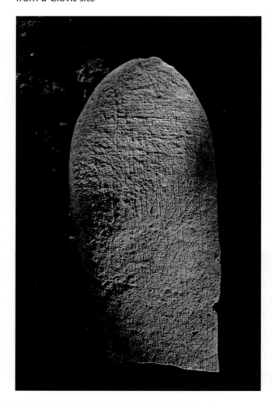

MIGRATION ROUTES. When global sea levels dropped during periods of glacial advance, the Bering Strait that separates Siberia from Alaska became dry land. The resulting land bridge that connected Asia to North America is part of the region known as **Beringia**. It is likely that the first inhabitants of the New World crossed into North America across this land bridge. The area of Beringia includes eastern Siberia, Alaska, and parts of the Yukon, as well as the land that today is submerged under the Bering Strait. Beringia was not covered by glaciers, but was a steppe landscape with a rich cover of sage and grass that supported extensive populations of mammals, including mammoth, horse, and bison. Figure 6.12 illustrates the changes in sea level in Beringia between 21,000 and 10,000 years ago.

The continental ice sheets that covered much of Canada during the last period of glacial advance (the Wisconsin glaciation, or Oxygen Isotope Stage 2) consisted of the Cordilleran glacier in the west and the more massive Laurentide glacier in the east. Proponents of the Clovis first model have argued that toward the end of the last glaciation, a gap existed between the Cordilleran and Laurentide glaciers. This gap formed an **ice-free corridor** that funneled people down from Alaska to the Great Plains, from where they spread rapidly across North America. Recent research has cast doubt on whether such an ice-free corridor existed in time to serve as a migration route for the Clovis people (Mandryk et al. 2001). Even if such an unimpeded corridor did exist, it is doubtful that it would have provided conditions in which people could have survived.

The Archaeological Evidence. If indeed the Clovis people moved into Alaska from Siberia and then migrated rapidly down an

FIGURE 6.12 Maps showing changes of sea level in Beringia between 21,000 and 10,000 years ago

Coastline 21,000 Calibrated Years BP

Ice cover

Coastline 12,000 Calibrated Years BP

Coastline 10,000 Calibrated Years BP

ice-free corridor, one would expect to find a well-developed tradition of fluted points in Siberia and Alaska before 13,500 years ago, the date of the earliest Clovis sites.

The earliest well-dated site in Beringia is the Broken Mammoth site in central Alaska (Yesner 2001). The stone tools at this site are characteristic of the **Nenana** culture, which dates to between 14,000 and 12,800 years ago. Nenana stone tools include small, bifacially flaked triangular points and knives. Among bone and ivory tools are an eyed needle and points. The preservation of animal remains at the Broken Mammoth site is excellent. A wide range of species is found, including large game (bison and elk), carnivores (bear, wolf, and fox), small game (squirrel, hare, marmot, and otter), and birds (goose, duck, and ptarmigan). Stone tools similar to

Nenana The earliest culture in Beringia, dating to between 14,000 and 12,800 years ago.

TOOLBOX

Radiocarbon Calibration

In Chapter 1, the basic principles of radiocarbon dating were introduced. The essential facts are that the ratio of carbon-14 to nonradioactive carbon is the same throughout the carbon exchange reservoir, which includes the atmosphere, oceans, and biosphere, and that carbon-14 decays at a constant rate. W. F. Libby, who discovered radiocarbon dating, believed that the carbon ratio was not only constant throughout the earth, but also constant through time. He has been proven wrong. Most dramatically, modern burning of fossil fuels and atomic weapons testing have increased the amount of carbon-14 in the reservoir. Also, detailed analyses of tree ring–dated samples indicate that there have been significant fluctuations in the concentration of carbon-14 over the past 50,000 years. Apart from contributions from burning fossil fuels and testing atomic weapons, there is a gradual trend of reduction in the concentration of carbon-14 over time. Overlying this decline is an extraordinarily complex pattern of fluctuations, known as "wiggles." The long-term trend is thought to be related to a reduction in the strength of the earth's magnetic field, while the wiggles appear to be related to solar activity.

Because the ratio of carbon-14 to nonradioactive carbon is not stable over time, radiocarbon years do not map directly onto calendar years. If we think of the decay of radiocarbon as a stopwatch that begins at the death of an organism, the problem is that the starting line is set by the concentration of radiocarbon and this starting line has been redrawn over and over again.

How have archaeologists dealt with this complication? Calibration is a complex issue that draws archaeologists into realms of statistics that are beyond the scope of this text. The essential tools used to connect radiocarbon time with calendar time are calibration curves created by dating tree-ring sequences that have already been independently dated by dendrochronology (Chapter 9). Calibration curves present the radiocarbon date for samples of known calendar age. For example, a tree ring known to be 6,900 years old produces a radiocarbon date of 6,000 years. Because the carbon exchange reservoir is global, this relationship will stand for all organisms that died in that particular calendar year. Conversely, one can conclude that a sample with a radiocarbon age of 6,000 years is actually 6,900 calendar years old. The calendar age is known as the calibrated date. All dates in this book are calibrated dates.

It is important to emphasize that, in practice, calibration is extremely complex, largely because of the aforementioned wiggles, which often result in a single radiocarbon age corresponding to more than one calendar age on the calibration curve. Resolving these conflicts is among the most mathematically challenging aspects of archaeology. ●

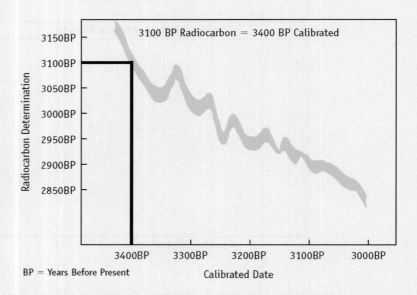

FIGURE 6.13 Radiocarbon calibration diagram. To arrive at a corrected radiocarbon date, draw a horizontal line from a radiocarbon determination on the *y*-axis to the point where it intersects with the calibration curve (the wiggly blue line). Draw a vertical line from this point down to the *x*-axis to arrive at the calibrated date. How do the wiggles on the calibration curve complicate finding a calibrated date?

those uncovered at the Broken Mammoth site are found at the site of Ushki on the Siberian side of the Bering Strait. At neither site is there evidence for fluted points. In subsequent periods, the stone tools of Siberia and Alaska are characterized by the production of very small microblades. This toolmaking tradition did not spread into areas to the south of the coast of British Columbia. Fluted points are found in Alaska; however, most do not come from sites that have been dated. It seems that the appearance of fluted points in this area is considerably later than the Clovis period. The discovery of three infants' burial, one in a cremation deposit and two in an underlying burial pit, at the Upward Sun River site in Alaska sheds new light on the prehistory of Beringia in the periods immediately following Clovis (Potter et al. 2014). The Upper Sun River site is dated to 11,500 years ago and was a summer occupation where the faunal remains include squirrels and salmon, as well as traces of a larger mammal that was most likely bison or wapiti. Found lying next to one of the infant burials was a cache of hunting tools, including three large bifacial points and four antler rods. The presence of such an impressive group of grave goods with an infant burial raises interesting questions about social organization among the early hunter-gatherers of Beringia. Finding such indicators of wealth with an infant or child burial suggests that some aspects of status might have been inherited. Surprisingly, genetic analysis showed that the two buried infants had unrelated mothers (Tackney et al. 2015). Because this genetic analysis focused only on mitochondrial DNA we do not yet know whether they had the same father.

■ Pre-Clovis

In the years following the discoveries made at Folsom and Blackwater Draw, many claims have been made for sites predating the earliest Clovis occupation or sites contemporary with Clovis that are difficult to reconcile with the Clovis first hypothesis. The case for the pre-Clovis model is strengthening with new discoveries at sites across North and South America. Among the sites that have produced evidence supporting a pre-Clovis occupation of the New World are Meadowcroft Rockshelter, Pennsylvania; Monte Verde, Chile; Pedra Pintada, Brazil; Quebrada Tacahuay, Peru; and the Page-Ladson site, Florida. The pre-Clovis hypothesis is also supported by reconstructions of a possible migration route along the Pacific coast.

MEADOWCROFT ROCKSHELTER. One of the most compelling claims for pre-Clovis occupation of North America comes from excavations of the **Meadowcroft Rockshelter** in western Pennsylvania. Excavations have uncovered 11 natural levels in the shelter (see Figure 6.14). Stratum IIa, near the base of the sequence, has produced a series of radiocarbon dates ranging between 23,000 and 15,500 years ago in association with stone tools. These dates have been disputed by archaeologists who claim that the carbon used in dating the site has been contaminated by "old" carbon carried by groundwater from coal beds in the surrounding bedrock.

MONTE VERDE. The site of **Monte Verde**, excavated by Tom Dillehay, is on the banks of Chinchihuapi Creek in southern Chile (Dillehay 1989). Located near the southern tip of South America, this site would seem to be an unlikely spot to find the earliest occupation of the New World. However, the discoveries made at Monte Verde pose

▲▲ **Meadowcroft Rockshelter** A site in Pennsylvania where evidence was found supporting pre-Clovis occupation of the New World.

▲▲ **Monte Verde** A site in Chile where evidence of human occupation 15,000 years ago supports the argument that Clovis culture does not represent the first occupation of the Americas.

FIGURE 6.14 Excavations at Meadowcroft Rockshelter, Pennsylvania, have exposed a deep stratigraphic sequence with ages between 23,000 and 15,500 years ago for the basal levels

Pedra Pintada A site in the Brazilian Amazon that demonstrates there were groups contemporary with the Clovis culture that were living in South America in a rain forest environment.

FIGURE 6.15 Stratigraphic profile and radiocarbon dates from Pedra Pintada. The diagram shows the stratigraphic context of the radiocarbon samples. Note that the dates shown are uncalibrated radiocarbon dates and are therefore later than the dates of the occupation of the site given in the text. Why do you think the excavators ran so many radiocarbon samples?

INITIAL B	EARLY	
10,250 ± 70	10,110 ± 60	10,260 ± 70
10,350 ± 70	10,120 ± 70	10,290 ± 70
10,390 ± 70	10,180 ± 60	10,290 ± 70
10,410 ± 70	10,190 ± 50	10,301 ± 70
10,470 ± 70	10,190 ± 60	10,330 ± 70
	10,210 ± 70	10,360 ± 60
	10,210 ± 60	10,370 ± 60
	10,220 ± 60	10,420 ± 70
	10,250 ± 70	

Legend	
Rock	Charcoal
Lithic	Root
Shell	Seed
Leaf	Palm
Stick	Wood

the most serious threat to the Clovis first hypothesis. The archaeological component at Monte Verde that the excavators designate as MV-II has produced a series of radiocarbon dates that give an average of 15,000 years ago, at least 1,500 years older than Clovis. The MV-II component is overlain by a level of peat dated to between 14,000 and 12,500 years ago.

Much of the debate concerning Monte Verde is due to the extremely unusual nature of the site. The preservation of organic remains is extraordinary. Not only were the bones of animals found, but also there are even traces of meat. Among the artifacts are a small number of stone tools, including projectile points. The bulk of the artifacts, however, are made of organic material, including rope and wood. Much of the evidence for human occupation comes from the discovery of objects (e.g., plant remains and unmodified stones) that the excavators argue were transported to the site by humans. The excavators have also identified the remains of huts built of organic materials. Perhaps the most unusual evidence found at Monte Verde is the trace of a human footprint.

The clearly dated MV-II horizon presents a significant challenge to the Clovis first model. It is not surprising, particularly given Monte Verde's unexpected location and the unusual nature of its artifacts, that Dillehay's announcement of the site's discovery was met with considerable skepticism (Fiedel 1999). Doubts were raised concerning the site's stratigraphy and the validity of the artifacts. In 1997, a prominent group of prehistorians visited Monte Verde and formed a commission to judge the validity of Dillehay's claim (Meltzer et al. 1997). Although they were not able to see the actual site, which had been destroyed by road construction, they were able to see all of the artifacts, detailed excavation records, and the regional geology. At the end of the trip, the commission published an article stating that Dillehay's identification of Monte Verde as a site of human occupation dating to 15,000 years ago was valid. The commission's report was met with criticism and even hostility, and one member of the commission recanted his support for Dillehay. In subsequent attacks, many important questions have been raised about Dillehay's interpretation of Monte Verde. However, the existence of strong evidence that humans were in southern Chile 15,000 years ago has given new life to the idea that perhaps Clovis does not represent the initial occupation of the New World.

CAVERNA DE PEDRA PINTADA. At present, Monte Verde remains the only site in South America that has produced widely accepted evidence for pre-Clovis occupation of the Americas. However, other discoveries in South America also cast doubt on the Clovis first model. Working in the Brazilian Amazon, Anna Roosevelt excavated the cave of **Pedra Pintada**, located in the Monte Alegre region of the Lower Amazon (Roosevelt et al. 1996), a region rich in caves, many of which bear traces of decoration. Pedra Pintada has a stratigraphic sequence 2.25 meters in depth from the surface to bedrock. Figure 6.15 shows the stratigraphy of Pedra Pintada, along with associated radiocarbon dates. Fifty-six burnt remains of seeds were dated from Layers 16 and 17, near the base of the deposits (see Figure 6.16). The dates obtained range between 13,000 and 11,500 years ago. This occupation is thus roughly contemporary with Clovis.

The stone tools from the early levels at Pedra Pintada include triangular bifacial points, as well as tools made on flakes, as shown in Figure 6.17. Hundreds of lumps of red pigment were found in Layers 16 and 17, but it was not possible to determine whether the paintings on the cave walls date to the same early period. The preservation of plant remains on the site is excellent, and there is evidence that the early occupants of the cave ate a wide range of plant foods, including fruits, palm, and Brazil nuts. The most abundant animal bones were those of fish, of both small and large species. There were also the remains of large and small land mammals.

The discoveries at Pedra Pintada demonstrate that, either at the same time or slightly after the Clovis occupation of North America, people lived in the Brazilian tropical rain forest, subsisting not on megafauna, but on a wide range of resources, including plants and fish. Unlike Monte Verde, Pedra Pintada is not claimed to be earlier than Clovis. However, the results of this excavation cast doubts on a simple model for the initial occupation of the New World by Clovis hunters. Roosevelt concludes that the initial occupation of the Americas was more complex than the Clovis first model recognizes and that Clovis was "only one of several regional traditions" (Roosevelt et al. 1996, 381).

QUEBRADA TACAHUAY. Further support for Roosevelt's argument comes from excavations at Quebrada Tacahuay, near the coast of Peru (Keefer et al. 1998). Limited excavations at this site have produced a small number of stone tools from a level dated between 12,700 and 12,500 years ago. These stone tools were found together with a large collection of animal bones in the remnants of hearths. The dominant faunal species are seabirds and marine fish. The dominant species of fish is the anchovy, which, due to its small size, suggests the use of nets. Some remains of marine mollusks were also found. Evidence of cut marks and burning was discovered on the bird bones, and there is some evidence for burning on the fish remains. The discoveries at Quebrada Tacahuay indicate that people in Peru were hunting seabirds and fishing, possibly with the use of netting, roughly contemporaneously with the Clovis occupation of North America.

PAGE-LADSON SITE. The excavators at the Page-Ladson site, which is submerged at a depth of 9 meters in a Florida sinkhole, work underwater using scuba gear (Halligan et al. 2016). The site contains a long stratigraphic sequence stretching back over 17,000 years. In Unit 3c, dated to between 14,700 and 14,400 years ago, two in situ stone tools including a simple biface were found. This occupation was located at the edge of a pond that dried seasonally. There is clear evidence in the form of dung, footprints, and faunal remains that mastodons frequented this pond at the same time as humans. Artifacts were also found in the overlying Stratum 4 dated to between 14,400 and 12,500 years ago.

COASTAL MIGRATION. One obvious objection to Monte Verde is that it seems implausible that people coming from Siberia would reach Chile before arriving in the Great Plains, particularly if the ice-free corridor between the Cordilleran and Laurentide glaciers was the only route connecting Beringia with areas to the south. The discovery

FIGURE 6.16 The Brazil nut is among the plant foods recovered in excavations at Pedra Pintada

FIGURE 6.17 Stone tools from Pedra Pintada, Brazil

2 cm

at Monte Verde suggests that decades of intensive research in North America have missed evidence of thousands of years of human occupation.

In the 1970s, K.R. Fladmark advanced a model of human migration into the Americas along the west coast rather than through an ice-free corridor (Fladmark 1979). This **coastal migration** model has recently gained widespread attention. One attraction is that it would make an early occupation of Chile more plausible. If the first occupants of the New World were adapted to coastal environments, they might have moved relatively rapidly down the coasts of North and South America. With geologists increasingly casting doubt as to whether an ice-free corridor was ever a viable migration route, interest in coastal migrations has grown.

Still, there are objections to a coastal route for human occupation of the New World. In parts of Alaska, there may have been glaciers blocking the coast, so that travel would have required the use of boats. Moreover, there is no evidence to date of any early sites on the west coast from Alaska to California.

Reconstructing the contours of the west coast of North America during the end of the Wisconsin glaciation is complex. On the one hand, the drop in sea level due to the formation of glaciers led to the exposure of extensive areas of the continental shelf. On the other hand, in the northwestern coast, the weight of the glaciers actually lowered the landmass in places, causing sea levels to be higher than they would otherwise be. Recent studies suggest that despite the weight of the glaciers, the sea level during the end of the Wisconsin glaciation was considerably lower than it is today. The exposed coastal region was rich in natural resources and largely free of glaciers. The difficulty is that, if there was a migration along the coast, most of the relevant archaeological sites would be submerged today.

In summarizing a coastal migration model, E.J. Dixon proposes that any "human colonization of the Americas suggested by the most current data [consists of] coastal migration with inland movement and settlement within broad environmental zones . . . that extend from north to south throughout the Americas" (Dixon 2001, 292). Like Roosevelt, Dixon sees the initial occupation of the Americas as a complex process of groups of people adapting to different environments. Unlike the traditional model, which sees people moving through an ice-free corridor before being "dumped" onto the Great Plains, Dixon sees a process of people migrating along the coast and branching off to inhabit inland regions they encountered along the way. Clovis would simply be one of these branches.

■ Early Arrival Model

The pre-Clovis model differs significantly from the Clovis first model in the precise timing of the initial occupation of the New World and the migration routes used to reach the areas south of the glaciers. However, both models agree that human occupation of the Americas took place during the later stages of the last period of glacial advance (the Wisconsin glaciation, or Oxygen Isotope Stage 2). Thus, the consensus of the archaeological community is that, with the exception of Antarctica, the Americas were the last continents to be occupied by humans. Whether these people followed a coastal route or an ice-free corridor, their voyage breached one of the last true frontiers.

A small number of archaeologists argue that the initial human occupation of the Americas was actually much earlier. Proponents of an early arrival model place the first appearance of humans in the Americas as early as 50,000 years ago, in Oxygen Isotope Stage 3. One impediment to this model is that human occupation of Beringia at that early date was extremely limited. Recent discoveries in Siberia have begun to push back the date for the initial occupation of western Beringia.

Repatriation of Indigenous Burial Remains

On January 9, 1877, at least 83 Northern Cheyenne were massacred by U.S. government troops near Fort Robinson, Nebraska. Remains of 17 of the Northern Cheyenne, including those of a three-year-old child, were collected for study by the U.S. Army medical examiner and were subsequently transferred to the Smithsonian National Museum of Natural History. Over 100 years later, on October 9, 1993, the bones from the Fort Robinson massacre were returned to the Northern Cheyenne for reburial (Thornton 2002).

In 1996, a human skeleton was discovered washing out of the bank of the Columbia River near the town of Kennewick, Washington. When a flint arrow was found embedded in the pelvis, it became clear that this was not a normal forensics case. Radiocarbon dating of the bones showed that Kennewick Man was 9,200 years old, one of the earliest known human remains in the Americas. The Army Corps of Engineers, which controls the land where the skeleton was found, decided to repatriate the bones to the Confederated Tribes of the Umatilla Indian Reservation for reburial. Outraged archaeologists filed suit in federal court to block the reburial and allow for scientific study of the skeleton. How, the archaeologists asked, could the Umatilla claim direct descent from an individual who lived over 9,000 years ago? How could the loss of such a valuable scientific specimen possibly be justified? As of 2005, the archaeologists have prevailed in court, but it is unlikely that this is the final word on the disposition of Kennewick Man.

Few would dispute the right of the Northern Cheyenne to bury their dead, but at the same time, many find the reburial of ancient skeletons such as that of Kennewick Man to be a tragic loss of knowledge. The scope of the problem cannot be overstated; estimates place the number of aboriginal human remains in North American institutions at between 100,000 and 200,000 individuals (Isaac 2002). Indigenous communities insist that the scientists must understand the pain and destruction caused by the excavation and collection of the remains of their ancestors. But the archaeological and scientific communities, of course, have a tremendous stake in this dispute. Claims for the reburial of human remains and restrictions on the study of skeletons strike at the core of the archaeological enterprise.

The dispute over repatriation is ultimately a political issue, and the U.S. government has crafted an impressive mechanism for regulating competing claims. A measure known as the Native American Graves Protection and Repatriation Act (NAGPRA) was voted into law in 1990. Senator John McCain eloquently expressed the need for NAGPRA, stating: "The subject of repatriation is charged with high emotions in both the Native American community and the museum community. I believe this bill represents a true compromise" (quoted in McKeown 2002, 108).

NAGPRA applies to all federal agencies and all museums that receive federal funds. The basis of the law is the right of Indian tribes and Native Hawaiian organizations to request the repatriation of burial remains, funerary offerings, sacred objects, and objects of cultural patrimony. There are also provisions requiring consultations with Indian tribes and Native Hawaiians concerning the disposition of human and cultural remains discovered on federal lands.

The implementation of NAGPRA is often complex. Although cases such as Kennewick Man have led to intense disputes between indigenous groups and archaeologists, such acrimony has proven to be the exception rather than the rule. The general consensus is that the impact of NAGPRA has been positive. The clear legal language provides a framework for archaeologists to redress historic wrongs. Many archaeologists have found that the implementation of NAGPRA has led to a new level of engagement between themselves and indigenous communities. ●

ADDITIONAL READING: Cressida Fforde, Jane Hubert, and Paul Turnbull, eds. 2002. *The Dead and Their Possessions: Repatriation in Principle, Policy, and Practice*. Vol. 43 of *One World Archaeology*. London: Routledge.

FIGURE 6.18 Sitka Wolf Clan members examine the Penn Museum's collections from the Northwest Coast as part of a repatriation process

The Yana River site, dated to 30,000 years ago, is the earliest evidence for human occupation of eastern Siberia. The intriguing discovery of a well-preserved mammoth found on the shore of Yenisei Bay in the Central Siberian Arctic in a level dated to 45,000 years ago suggests that humans were present in the Arctic at this very early date (Pitulko et al. 2016). No stone tools were recovered at Yenisei Bay, but the mammoth bones showed traces of trauma from hunting—including breaks from a blow to the head from a spear—and the tusk showed traces of processing for ivory.

Archaeologists working in the Old Crow Basin in the Canadian Yukon claimed to have found evidence of human activity dating as far back as 40,000 years ago. However, direct radiocarbon dating of a number of bone tools from the basin has shown that they are actually less than 3,000 years old (Nelson et al. 1986). Currently, it is claimed that two bones found in contexts dating to 40,000 years ago at Old Crow show evidence of being cut by a stone tool, and a number of bones are held to have been flaked by humans (Morlan 2003). Neither of these claims is widely accepted, and there is as yet no clear evidence for human occupation of western Beringia (Alaska and the Yukon) before the end of the last glacial advance.

A number of claims have been made for evidence of early human occupation of South America. At Monte Verde, Dillehay found objects that might be tools in Level MV-I, which is below Level MV-II, discussed earlier. MV-I is dated to 33,000 years ago. The evidence of artifacts from that level has not been widely accepted, and Dillehay himself expresses some reservations about this claim.

The boldest claim for early human occupation of the Americas comes from the excavators of the site of **Pedra Furada** in Brazil (Guidon et al. 1996). Excavations in the rock shelter at the site uncovered burnt patches associated with pieces identified as stone tools. Radiocarbon dating placed the earliest levels at Pedra Furada between 48,000 and 35,000 years ago. The excavators argue that the burnt patches are evidence of controlled use of fire by humans. Critics have countered that these patches are equally consistent with natural bush fires. The major point of contention is whether the pieces identified as stone tools are actually the result of human manufacture. Most of the tools are quartzite cobbles that have been very simply chipped and whose source is a geological deposit found at the top of the cliff, 100 meters directly above the site. The actual sediment of the site is made up of cobbles and soil that plunged down from the top of the cliff over the course of millennia, probably during periods of heavy rainfall.

David Meltzer, James Adovasio, and Tom Dillehay (1994) have suggested that the chipping found on the stones recovered at Pedra Furada is the result not of human activity, but of the impact of the cobbles as they fell down the cliff and were smashed on the ground. The researchers suggest that the cobbles are "geofacts"—objects created by geological forces—rather than artifacts made by humans. The excavators—Fabio Parenti, Michel Fontugue, and Claude Guérin—have reacted with outrage to this suggestion, stating that the patterns of chipping found at Pedra Furada are too complex to have been created by a natural process. Resolving the question of whether humans were involved in the burnt features and stone tools found at Pedra Furada is of critical importance.

■ The Solutrean Hypothesis

The lack of evidence of antecedents of the distinctive Clovis points in Siberia and Alaska casts some doubt on the Clovis first model. Added to this doubt are the

Mawlukhotepun—Working Together

SUSAN BLAIR, UNIVERSITY OF NEW BRUNSWICK

Karen Perley and I met on a bright sunny day in late August 1996 near the banks of the Jemseg River in central New Brunswick. Our meeting place was an old farmer's field next to the river, overgrown with alders and wildflowers and alive with grasshoppers, frogs, and snakes. The provincial Department of Transportation had plans to begin clearing this area for the new Trans-Canada Highway within the year. This rerouting of the highway was long overdue and would replace the narrow, winding, windblown road along the banks of the Saint John River with a broad, four-lane, modern highway.

Under our feet, we were told, was an archaeological site.

I was a recently graduated archaeologist, and Karen was an educator, grandmother, and traditional person from Tobique First Nation. With us were Patrick Polchies of Kingsclear First Nation, provincial archaeologist Dr. Chris Turnbull, and highway engineers. We were being given an opportunity to participate in what grew to be the largest archaeological salvage ever undertaken in Atlantic Canada. Over the next eight months, we struggled through a Maritime winter, devising ground-thawing units that were laid in succession in long, tunnel-like tents. As we excavated, we realized that the deposits that we had thought would be localized, shallow, recent, and disturbed were in all ways more complicated. Furthermore, a precipitous construction schedule left us little time to excavate, let alone adequately consult and communicate with the descendants of the creators of the site, the Wolastoqiyik. We hired First Nations crew and crew leaders and established advisory committees and processes of notification. Nonetheless, throughout the fall, there was growing concern in First Nation communities and protest about the project and the

appropriateness of archaeology itself. There were also unfounded rumors that we were excavating burials.

My archaeological training had only partially prepared me for this experience. I had learned to think critically about science and the role of authority in the process of exploring about the past, but I had little idea of how I could transpose these concepts into practice. How should I balance the role of project leader with a reflexive theoretical stance?

Karen guided me through these challenges by refocusing me on the specific and immediate challenges of communication and practice. Our oblong test units looked like burial plots. Our practice of marking artifacts with clear polish and ink was being viewed as an assault on the objects themselves. Elders needed to feel welcomed and comfortable.

Karen brought us to her community and culture and taught us basic principles to guide our work. *Mawlukhotepun*—"working together"—reflected the true spirit of collaboration and partnership between equals. *Kcit'mitahoswagon*—"respect"—governed not only our interactions with individuals, but also our relationship to their culture, history, and ideas.

Weci apaciayawik—"so that it will come back"—firmly rooted the idea that we must return something for everything gained from our work. In a profound way, these teachings led me to reconsider my role as team leader, technical expert, and archaeologist. Working together meant relinquishing authority and control. Respect meant hearing instead of telling. Commitment to archaeology meant an obligation to living and breathing people and their communities. In Karen's words, "Archaeology should not be only about the past and the dead but should also represent the present and the living. When you include First Nations

FIGURE 6.19 The Jemseg Crossing site in New Brunswick where excavations led to the emergence of cooperation and efforts at mutual understanding between archaeologists and members of the local First Nations communities

perspectives in science, you breathe life into it, you give it a voice, you give it Spirit. Their knowledge provides a window through which to see what was happening in their past."

Years on, the Jemseg Crossing project remains for many of us a transformative experience. We finished the project, though not as we had intended. We continued our work with written assurances that the project would not impact on burials. We found living floors, hearths, pottery, and stone tools, evidence of food preparation and storage, eating, socializing, and toolmaking extending over thousands of years. At the same time, we built bonds of friendship and mutual respect.

Near the end of the project, we found a small, basin-shaped pit, quite unlike anything else we had seen. Although it did not contain artifacts, it was coated with red ochre, a mineral commonly used in burials in the northeast. Despite comparative archaeological and ethnographic research, chemical testing, and radiometric analysis, I was unable to determine that it categorically was not a burial, and so, on April 14, 1997, the planned route of the highway was shifted southwest, bypassing the site entirely. ▲

Solutrean hypothesis The proposal that the origin of the Clovis culture was in the migration of groups from the Solutrean of southern France.

Kennewick A site in Washington where skeletal remains were found, dating to 9,200 years ago. Control and ownership of the remains have been the subject of controversy.

Beringian Standstill Hypothesis The idea based on genetic analysis that the founder populations for the occupation of the Americas was isolated in eastern Beringia for thousands of years before dispersal into the Americas.

aforementioned questions raised about the viability of an ice-free corridor as a migration route connecting Beringia with the regions to the south of the Cordilleran and Laurentide glaciers. According to the **Solutrean hypothesis**, proposed by Dennis Stanford and Bruce Bradley (2000), the origin of the Clovis people was not Siberia, but rather western Europe. This is a very unlikely scenario, as it would require a lengthy crossing of the North Atlantic. Stanford and Bradley point to similarities in the fine bifacial flaking of spearpoints in the Clovis period of North America and in the Solutrean period of the Upper Paleolithic of Spain and France. Their proposal, however, does not explain why these similarities could not be the result of parallel invention. As has been pointed out by Lawrence Straus (2000), there are considerable differences between Solutrean and Clovis points—notably, a lack of fluting in the Solutrean. Moreover, the Solutrean industry ends around 5,000 years before the beginning of the Clovis.

■ The Skeletal and Genetic Evidence

Only a small number of human skeletal remains have been recovered from sites in the Americas that are older than 9,000 years. No significant human remains have been found from either Clovis or pre-Clovis contexts. All of the human skeletal remains found in the Americas can be assigned unambiguously to *Homo sapiens*.

The small number of human skeletal remains that have been found in contexts slightly later than Clovis has recently become the focus of controversy. On the basis of analyses of the shape of the skulls of these individuals and comparisons with the shape of the skulls of modern populations, some scientists have argued that they are distinct from modern populations of Native Americans. The description of a skeleton discovered in **Kennewick**, Washington, that is dated to 9,200 years ago, as Caucasoid has led to an intense dispute in which the critical issue is ownership and control of the skeleton. The intensity of the political debate has clouded the question of what the recovered human remains tell us about the initial human occupation of the Americas. The discovery of a near-complete skeleton dated between 13,000 and 12,000 years ago in the Hoyo Negro underwater cave system in Mexico provides a new glimpse at the morphology of early humans in the Americas (Chatters et al. 2014). Genetic analysis of both the Kennewick Man and the Hoyo Negro skeleton clearly group these individuals with Native Americans (Rasmussen et al. 2015).

The genetic study of living Native American populations along with archaeological samples is beginning to yield strong support for the pre-Clovis model. These studies are unanimous in showing an East Asian origin for all American populations, although most recognize waves of migration from East Asia subsequent to the initial peopling of the Americas. One idea supported by the genetic data is known as the "**Beringian Standstill Hypothesis.**" According to this hypothesis, a human population was isolated in eastern Beringia beginning as early as 25,000 years ago. Around 16,000 years ago, with the retreat of the ice sheets that made a Pacific coastal route accessible, this population spread into the Americas and rapidly dispersed (Llamas et al. 2016). The size of the founder population isolated in eastern Beringia is thought to have been quite small, numbering in the tens of thousands. After rapid dispersal, populations were geographically isolated and evolved the genetic differentiation found among living Native Americans. The genetic studies also vividly demonstrate the degree of impact that European colonialism had on Native American communities, resulting in the loss of much of the genetic diversity found in archaeological samples.

Clovis Adaptations and Megafauna Extinction

The discovery of spearpoints together with the remains of now-extinct megafauna at both Folsom and Blackwater Draw suggested that the earliest inhabitants of the New World were specialist big-game hunters (see Figure 6.20). It is clear from a number of sites beyond Blackwater Draw that Clovis people were able to hunt very large animals, including elephants. The Colby site in Wyoming has produced a number of mammoth bones with clear evidence that they were hunted and possibly that the meat was stored for later consumption. Because the widespread extinction of megafauna in the Americas correlates with the Clovis period, it would seem obvious that the large animals must have been killed off by Clovis hunters. Seventeen genera of North and South American megafauna, including elephants (mastodons and mammoths), horses, and camels, became extinct between 13,250 and 12,900 years ago. Other species, such as ground sloths, become extinct slightly later.

Although Clovis people hunted large animals and many of these became extinct soon after the earliest Clovis sites were established, some archaeologists doubt whether overhunting was the cause of widespread extinction of megafauna. In examining the archaeological record, Donald Grayson and David Meltzer (2002) found that only 14 sites show clear evidence of Clovis hunting of megafauna. In every case, the hunted animals were elephants, either mastodons or mammoths. For example, at the Mannis site on the coast of Washington, a fragment of what appears to be a bone point was found embedded in the vertebra of a mastodon (Waters et al. 2011). The Mannis mastodon dates to 13,800 years ago, which is slightly earlier than the Clovis period. No stone tools were found at the Mannis site. Clovis people were clearly superbly equipped hunters capable of killing very large animals. The question that remains unresolved is whether this killing resulted in the widespread extinction

FIGURE 6.20 One possible cause for the extinction of North American megafauna is hunting by humans. In this painting, hunters armed with spears and spear throwers stalk a mammoth mired in a bog.

of megafauna. There is also some question as to why Clovis and other Paleoindian groups hunted large game. Although there is a tendency to assume that the explanation must be rooted in subsistence, it is also true that depending on large game for survival is a very risky strategy, as a steady supply of food depends on successfully killing large animals. One intriguing idea is that the hunting of large animals had more to do with the social dynamics of Clovis society, and particularly the role of the successful hunter, rather than the demands of survival (Speth et al. 2013).

Another point of contention is whether Clovis hunters specialized exclusively in hunting large game. A number of sites have produced evidence of hunting of smaller game, including reindeer, by people using Clovis or Gainey points (Storck and Spiess 1994). It is interesting that turtles are a common component of the animal remains found at Clovis sites. At the Blackwater Draw, a turtle roasting pit was reported with a stack of six or seven turtles (Meltzer 2009, 275).

A novel proposal links the extinction of megafauna with an extraterrestrial impact event. No impact crater has been identified, but there is evidence in levels overlying Clovis sites of features such as nanodiamonds and traces of iridium that are linked to impact by meteors or other extraterrestrial materials (Firestone et al. 2007). One possibility is that a massive impact caused widespread burning and sudden climatic change, which in turn caused the extinction of megafauna. The end of the Clovis period is correlated with the onset of the Younger Dryas cold event, which in North America is characterized by "black mat" layers that might be evidence of widespread burning. The possibility that the extinction of megafauna was caused by a catastrophic event is intriguing, but there is some reason for caution. One problem is that the type of evidence of extraterrestrial impact found in the layers overlying Clovis sites could be "the result of constant and certainly non-catastrophic rain of sand-sized micrometeorites into Earth's atmosphere" (Pinter and Ishman 2008, 37). There are three further problems: The available evidence suggests the disappearance of megafauna was gradual; there is no indication of a decrease in human population size at the end of the Clovis period; and the "black mat" layers are formed by a higher water table rather than by burning (Buchanan, Collard, and Edinborough 2008; Haynes 2008).

■ Beyond Clovis

Due to the complexities of radiocarbon calibration, it is difficult to mark the precise timing of the transition from the Clovis to the Folsom. The approximate dates for the Folsom are 12,600 to 12,200 years ago (Surovell et al. 2016). However, the data do seem to support a rather abrupt end to the Clovis, followed directly by the onset of the Folsom. Most archaeologists stress the continuities that link the Clovis and Folsom, along with a series of other regional cultures referred to collectively as the Paleoindian time period. Despite these continuities, there are shifts in later Paleoindian adaptation and technology, including increased evidence for mass kill sites and for hunting of small game, as well as changes in the technology of projectile point production. The Paleoindian time period is followed by the Archaic. We will return to the Archaic in Chapter 8 in the context of discussion of the origins of agriculture, but a brief consideration of recent discoveries in Texas, Florida, and Louisiana will provide a sense of the importance of this period.

LATE PALEOINDIAN AND ARCHAIC SUBSISTENCE AND TECHNOLOGY. In the late Paleoindian period, there is clear evidence for mass kill sites. At the Olsen-Chubbuck site in Colorado, Joe Ben Wheat excavated a continuous bed of bison bones lying in a small arroyo, or dry stream bed (see Figure 6.21). The hunters had stampeded the animals into this narrow gorge, killing almost 200. Many of these animals show evidence of systematic butchery; however, the sheer mass of the kill resulted in the hunters leaving some carcasses untouched— particularly those buried in the pileup. Most of the artifacts recovered at the Olsen-Chubbuck site are points. The form of the points indicates that the site belongs to the Cody Complex, which dates to approximately 10,000 years ago. It is interesting that, despite the clear evidence for bison kill sites, the species did not become extinct.

Late Paleoindian technology shows an impressive development of the tools used for hunting. Folsom points are among the most sophisticated stone tools ever made. In the first step of their manufacture, the knapper thinned the point by applying pressure along the edges with the tip of an antler, forcing off wafer-thin flakes. This process, known as pressure flaking, requires a high degree of skill and takes significant effort to complete. Once the point was exquisitely thinned, one step remained before it was ready. The knapper took the point and drove a long, thin flake off the base. The point was then flipped and the same procedure repeated on the other side. The result was a shallow channel, or flute, running from the base of the point to near the tip on both faces. One aspect of the process that has puzzled archaeologists is exactly how the flute was produced. Some experimental archaeologists have suggested that a lever-type device was used in fluting the point.

An even more puzzling issue is why the flute was made to travel the entire length of the point. Consider that, before the flute was produced, a major effort had been expended in carefully thinning the point with pressure flaking. All of this work was put at risk not once, but twice, as the point was subjected to the pressure required to produce the flutes. On archaeological sites, points broken during the process of fluting are common. Why take this risk with artifacts that were already suitable for use as hunting points?

A number of answers have been proposed to solve the riddle of the Folsom flute. One obvious possibility is that the flute was designed to fit a specific type of haft. Perhaps the points were designed to fit into a socket at the end of a spear shaft. Another functional explanation is that the flutes enhanced the ability of the point to penetrate an animal. However, some archaeologists question functional explanations for fluting and stress possible symbolic significance of the fluting as part of hunting rituals. None of these explanations account for the seeming inefficiency of investing so much energy in producing a hunting tool. One novel explanation advanced recently by Stanley Ahler and Phil Geib (2000), illustrated in Figure 6.22, is that the goal of fluting was to produce a tool that could be continually resharpened as the tip was damaged during hunting. According to Ahler and Geib's theory, the investment of both effort and risk in fluting a Folsom point was balanced by the gain in efficiency from a point that could be continually resharpened.

A chance discovery in the mountains of Wyoming has provided a unique glimpse into other strategies used by late Paleoindian hunters (Frison et al. 1986). In the Absaroka Mountains east of Yellowstone National Park, hikers came across a folded net that had been preserved by overlying deposits of packrat feces. Radiocarbon

FIGURE 6.21 Excavation of a bison mass kill at the Olsen-Chubbuck site, Colorado

FLUTE

Cross-Section

a

b

c

FIGURE 6.22 Diagram showing the reduction of Folsom points (a) through use, as proposed by Ahler and Geib. Note that the hafted point (b) has been shortened by resharpening and rehafted (c). A photo of a Folsom point is shown in Figure 6.1.

▲▲ **Wilson-Leonard site** A site in Texas with a stratigraphic sequence that includes both Paleoindian and Archaic occupations.

FIGURE 6.23 Stratigraphy of the Wilson-Leonard site. Note that the Wilson component (Unit I*si-c*) is located stratigraphically above the bone bed (Unit I*si*) and below the Late Paleoindian (Unit II). Based on this stratigraphic profile, why is the burial thought to date to the Wilson occupation?

dating has determined that this net is roughly contemporary with the Olsen-Chubbuck site, dating to the Late Paleoindian, 10,000 years ago. The precise dimensions of the net cannot be determined, but it is about 1.5 meters long and half a meter high. The effort involved in making the net is impressive, requiring over 2,000 meters of juniper cordage. The net was probably used to hunt mountain sheep that are found in the Absaroka Mountains. The mesh is too large for it to have been used in hunting smaller animals such as rabbits.

THE PALEOINDIAN TO ARCHAIC TRANSITION. Already in the late 1950s, Gordon Willey and Philip Phillips (1958) proposed a series of criteria that distinguish the Archaic and the Paleoindian periods. In the Archaic, adaptations shifted toward an increased reliance on small animal and plant foods. Technologies for food processing, including grinding stones and stones used for cooking, also developed. Sites indicate reduced mobility, and there is systematic burial of the dead. Typologically, the Archaic is identified by stemmed, corner-notched, or side-notched projectile points. Archaic points have a clearly defined tang at the base that indicates a change in the way they were attached to the shaft of projectiles (spears, darts, or arrows). This list of traits is useful for distinguishing between the Paleoindian and Archaic periods, but leaves open the question of the nature and causes of the transition. Recent research in Texas has shed new light on the nature of the transition. The **Wilson-Leonard site** is located 65 kilometers north of Austin on a tributary of the Brazos River (Bousman et al. 2002). Excavations at this site have produced a stratigraphic sequence in which an Archaic level, known as the Wilson component, lies between two Paleoindian occupations (see Figures 6.23 and 6.24). The sequence has a large number of radiocarbon dates that place the Archaic occupation between 11,500 and 10,250 years ago. The faunal remains indicate that these were generalized hunters who focused on rabbit, hare, turtle, deer, and occasionally bison. Unlike other Archaic sites in the region, the Wilson-Leonard site produced few ground stone tools or other evidence for the

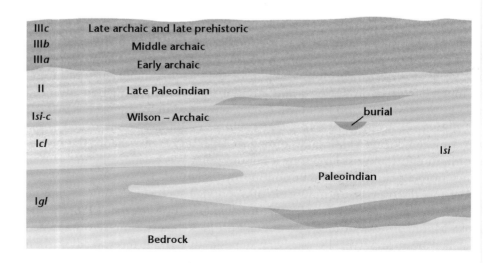

IIIc	Late archaic and late prehistoric
IIIb	Middle archaic
IIIa	Early archaic
II	Late Paleoindian
Isi-c	Wilson – Archaic
Icl	
Igl	

burial

Paleoindian

Isi

Bedrock

FIGURE 6.24 Projectile points from the Wilson-Leonard site. Notice the difference between the Paleoindian points with concave bases (Unit I*si* and Unit II) and the stemmed points characteristic of the Archaic (Unit I*si-c*).

FIGURE 6.25 The remains of an Archaic period canoe in situ at the site of Newnans Lake, Florida

processing of plant foods. One burial was found in the Archaic occupation. The excavations at Wilson-Leonard demonstrate that the transition from the Paleoindian to the Archaic was a lengthy process and that Archaic and Paleoindian groups overlapped chronologically. These discoveries point to the need for further research into this important element of the prehistory of North America.

SHELL MOUNDS AND CANOES. During the Middle and Late Archaic of the southeastern United States, beginning approximately 8,000 years ago, there is an increasing emphasis on collecting shellfish. In some cases, shell middens, large mounds of discarded shell, formed. In the spring of 2000, a drought in northern Florida led to the lowering of **Newnans Lake**, located 9 kilometers east of Gainesville. As the lake waters receded, a trove of 41 Late Archaic canoes emerged (see Figure 6.25). These canoes, ranging from 4.5 to 8.5 meters in length, were made of fire-hollowed logs. Most have slightly upward-sloping ends. A low partition or "thwart" was found on 19 of the canoes. Canoes are rarely preserved in the archaeological record, but the discovery at Newnans Lake underscores the diversity of Archaic adaptations and emphasizes the importance of freshwater resources.

MOUND BUILDING. Recent research has demonstrated that the practice of mound construction has deep roots in the Archaic. The site of **Watson Brake** is a series of mounds and ridges constructed on the floodplain of the Ouachita River in Louisiana (Saunders et al. 1997). A combination of radiocarbon and luminescence dating securely places this site in the Middle Archaic between 5,400 and 5,000 years ago. Building on the discoveries at Watson Brake, archaeologists have begun to turn their

▲▲ **Watson Brake** A series of mounds in Louisiana built between 5,400 and 5,000 years ago that provide the earliest evidence of monumental construction in eastern North America.

▲▲ **Newnans Lake** A lake in Florida where a large number of Archaic canoes have been recovered.

attention from a narrow focus on those aspects of the Archaic related to subsistence toward an examination of the social forces within Archaic society. As Kenneth Sassaman (2005) has written, "The next generation of researchers must jettison the received wisdom of their forebears who, in canonizing the Archaic as the antecedent to 'complex' society, perpetuated the myth that little of interest took place. Clearly this was not the case" (102). We will return to the topic of Archaic monumental construction when we examine the site of Poverty Point, Louisiana, in Chapter 8.

SUMMARY

- Human migration to Australia required the crossing of the Wallace Line by boat.
- The earliest evidence of human occupation in Australia is dated between 60,000 and 53,000 years ago.
- The extinction of Australian megafauna appears to have taken place approximately 46,000 years ago.
- Human occupation of the Americas followed the Beringia land bridge, which was exposed during periods of low sea level.

- There is considerable debate as to whether the Clovis culture represents the initial occupation of the Americas or whether there was an earlier migration, represented by sites such as Monte Verde.
- The first people to arrive in the Americas migrated south from Beringia either through an ice-free corridor or along a coastal migration route.
- The extinction of American megafauna took place around 13,000 years ago.

KEY TERMS

Beringia, 160
Beringian Standstill Hypothesis, 170
Blackwater Draw, 159
Clovis culture, 159
Clovis first model, 159
coastal migration, 166
early arrival model, 159
fire-stick farming, 156
Gunbilngmurrung, 156
ice-free corridor, 160
Kennewick, 170
Lake Mungo, 154
Lapita, 157
Meadowcroft Rockshelter, 163
megafauna, 154

Monte Verde, 163
Nauwalabila I, 154
Nenana, 161
Newnans Lake, 175
Ngandong, 151
Pedra Furada, 168
Pedra Pintada, 164
pre-Clovis model, 159
Sahul, 151
Solutrean hypothesis, 170
Sunda, 151
Wallace Line, 151
Watson Brake, 175
Wilson-Leonard site, 174

REVIEW QUESTIONS

1. How and when did people first arrive in Australia? What is the importance of Lake Mungo in understanding the spread of humans in Australia?
2. Was the process of megafauna extinction similar in Australia and the Americas?
3. What is the significance of Monte Verde to debates about the initial occupation of the Americas? What

additional information is provided by the excavations at Caverna de Pedra Pintada?
4. What are the alternative migration routes for the initial occupation of the Americas?

PART THREE
PERSPECTIVES
ON AGRICULTURE

The development of agriculture involved a profound reorientation in the way humans relate to plants and animals, along with equally significant changes in human society and technology. Because the transition to agriculture took place independently in several distinct regions, we can take a comparative approach to the origins of agriculture in order to gain a broad understanding of this process. In doing so, we learn that the shift to an agricultural way of life often spanned a period of several thousands of years and that the details of the process differ significantly among regions.

The development of agriculture has been linked to a trend toward the separation of humanity from nature. Recent perspectives on the domestication of plants and animals challenge this assumption. After reading this introduction, you should understand:

- The ideas of Lewis Henry Morgan and V. Gordon Childe about the origin of agriculture.
- The challenge to these ideas posed in the writing of David Rindos, Tim Ingold, and Marshall Sahlins.
- The major components of the Neolithic Revolution.

Introduction: Definitions of Agriculture

Almost the entire evolutionary history of genus *Homo* has taken place within a hunting-and-gathering context. It was only 15,000 years ago that societies of modern humans in different areas of the world began to shift to an agricultural way of life. The transition from hunter-gatherer societies to agricultural societies is one of the most profound and significant events in prehistory. The origins of agriculture can be viewed as a broad phenomenon that can be broken into three components.

1. **Domestication**. A relationship between humans, on the one hand, and plants and animals, on the other. Figures III.1 and III.2 on next page give a sense of the variability that exists in the cultivation of domesticated crops.

2. **Technology**. The tools used for daily tasks, including tools used for harvesting and processing food and installations for storage.

3. **Community**. The development of settled villages and a constructed landscape.

The development of agriculture involves important shifts in social organization, leadership, and the relationship between kin groups and property. The shift to agricultural society also had significant effects on cosmology—the way people saw themselves in relation to supernatural forces. The historical photograph of the Walpi Pueblo in Figure III.3 gives a sense of the size and organization characteristic of farming villages.

Early anthropologists and archaeologists saw the development of agriculture as the natural result of an inherent human tendency to move toward more advanced ways of life. Today, most archaeologists reject both the association between agriculture and progress and the use of progress to explain changes in prehistory. We are left with the challenge of discovering the diverse pathways that societies around the world took toward agriculture and of grappling with the question of what caused those societies to change.

■ Early Perspectives

> *Mankind are the only beings who may be said to have gained an absolute control over the production of food. (Morgan 1877, 24)*

The pioneering American anthropologist **Lewis Henry Morgan** wrote that, through the invention of agriculture, humans placed themselves outside of the world of nature and moved toward "human supremacy on the earth" (Rindos 1984, 9). In his book *Ancient Society*, published in 1877, Morgan labeled the transition to agriculture as the shift from a period of "savagery" to one of "barbarism." Among the defining aspects of barbarism, he included the invention of pottery, the domestication of animals and plants, and the construction of buildings out of mud brick. In his writing on barbarism, Morgan emphasized that the transition to agriculture was a stage in the progress of humanity.

> *The escape from the impasse of savagery was an economic and scientific revolution that made the participants active partners with nature instead of parasites on nature.*
> *(Childe 1942, 55)*

domestication The relationship between humans, on the one hand, and plants and animals, on the other, in which the humans play an integral role in the protection and reproduction of plants and animals.

technology The tools used for daily tasks, including farming, food processing, and food storage.

community The term applied to the changes in society and settlement patterns in the transition to an agricultural way of life.

Lewis Henry Morgan A nineteenth-century American anthropologist who viewed the transition to agriculture as marking the boundary between the period of "savagery" and the period of "barbarism."

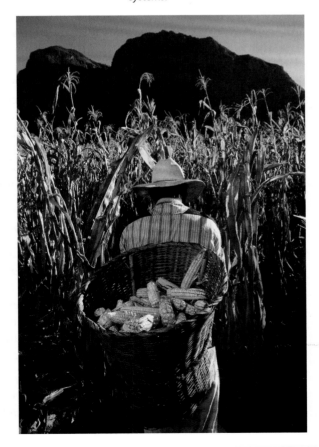

FIGURE III.1 A farmer harvesting maize. This picture shows the close relationship between the farmer and plants in traditional agricultural systems.

In the 1940s, V. Gordon Childe synthesized the existing archaeological information to reformulate Morgan's ideas about the origin of agriculture. He coined the term **Neolithic Revolution**. For Childe, the most important result of the Neolithic Revolution was the ability to actively control food production. This led to an increase in the food supply, which in turn supported an increase in population, resulting in the development of settled villages.

The concepts developed by Morgan and Childe remain essential to the study of prehistory. Few archaeologists question the revolutionary effects the development of agriculture had on human society, and understanding the Neolithic Revolution remains central to the study of prehistory. However, although Morgan's and Childe's contributions are widely recognized, most of their specific ideas about the nature of the shift to agriculture are the subject of debate and criticism.

■ Humanity and Nature in the Shift to Agriculture

Both Morgan and Childe viewed the development of agriculture as a shift in the relationship between humanity and the natural world. Morgan believed that "barbaric" society had set itself in a position of supremacy above nature. Childe saw Neolithic societies as "active partners with nature" rather than "parasites on nature." Both Childe and Morgan seem to imply that humans consciously removed themselves from nature by inventing agriculture. Today, such a concept is contested by archaeologists and anthropologists working from a wide range of perspectives.

The idea that we as a culture, a nation, or a species are in conscious control of our environment and thus of our destiny is one part truth, one part rhetoric, and two parts wishful thinking.
(Rindos 1984, 6)

Neolithic Revolution The term V. Gordon Childe used to describe the transition to agriculture as an event that affected every aspect of human society.

FIGURE III.3 Historical photograph of the Walpi Pueblo, Arizona

For **David Rindos**, the development of agriculture was a coevolutionary process involving a symbiotic relationship between plant and animal species in which each species contributes to the other's support. Symbiotic relationships with plants and animals are not unique to humans and are widespread in the natural world. For example, there is a symbiotic relationship between ants and acacia trees. The ants live in the acacias, harvesting the trees' sugars and leaves while feeding on insects that would otherwise destroy the trees. If the ants are removed, other insects attack the trees, which then rapidly die. The relationship is a symbiotic one in which the ants receive nutrients and shelter and the acacias receive protection from harmful insects. Nobody would argue that this biological process involves a conscious decision on the part of either the ants or the trees. Rindos argued that the domestication of plants by humans was a similar coevolutionary process.

Rindos's view on the origins of agriculture was based on biological theory. Working from a different perspective, anthropologist **Tim Ingold** (2000) has also argued against agriculture as the removal of humans from nature. Ingold begins by looking at the way modern hunter-gatherer societies see the world. He finds that these people do not make the kinds of distinctions between the natural and human worlds that are so critical to Childe's and Morgan's account. Ingold sees the domestication of animals as a shift from a world where relationships are based on trust to one where they are based on domination. The relationship between hunter-gatherers and animals is based on trust in a powerful natural world that will provide for people in return for human respect and propitiation (see Figure III.4). Social relations between humans are formed on the same basis of trust because there is no essential distinction between the human and animal worlds. A hallmark characteristic of hunter-gatherer social relations is sharing based on trust.

For Ingold, the shift from hunting to agriculture involves a move from trust to domination that pervades all aspects of human life. Thus, in agricultural societies, animals are dependents of humans. Animals no longer present themselves; instead,

David Rindos An archaeologist who saw agriculture as the result of a coevolutionary process involving a symbiotic relationship between plant and animal species.

Tim Ingold An anthropologist who views the shift from hunting to agriculture as a shift from trust to domination.

FIGURE III.4 Rock art from Valtorta, Spain. This painting illustrates Ingold's conception of hunting as a relationship of trust between the hunter and the prey.

the herdsman makes life-and-death decisions about them. Similar concepts of domination and control pervade the social life of humans with the development of owned property and social hierarchy. But Ingold stresses that the shift from trust to domination does not involve a separation of humanity from nature, as envisioned by Morgan and Childe. Rather, the development of agriculture involves a "change in the terms of engagement." Not until the recent development of industrialized agriculture did animals become merely objects of human control.

Niche construction theory, discussed in Chapter 2, provides an additional basis for viewing agriculture as part of a broad continuum of "human efforts to restructure biotic communities" (Smith 2007). The interaction between Native Californians and plants that served for both basketmaking and food provide a sense of the extent of human niche construction even in the absence of agriculture (Anderson 1997, 1999). Basketry was, and remains, an essential technology for Native Californians and creating baskets required access to very large quantities of branches of trees such as redbud, wild lilac, sumac, and willow. However, mature branches from mature trees lack the qualities needed for basketmaking. Native Californians encouraged the growth of new branches known as epicormic shoots by controlled burning or pruning. In controlled burns and pruning, Native Californians restructured the plant community to provide the materials necessary for basketry. Burning, along with methods of tillage, were used similarly by Native Californians to encourage the growth of tubers such as mariposa lilies and golden broiaea that were an essential source of fod. Collecting epicormic shoots and geophytes are excellent examples of the extent of niche construction that can develop in non-agricultural societies.

■ Agriculture and Progress

> *There is also a Zen road to affluence. . . . That human material wants are finite and few, and technical means unchanging but on the whole adequate. . . . That, I think, describes the hunter.*
> (Sahlins 1972, 2)

Today, it is quite jarring to read Morgan and Childe describe hunter-gatherer societies as savages. The term clearly embodies a value judgment, as does the term *barbaric* for farming societies. Both characterizations are repugnant to contemporary anthropologists, who see them as dehumanizing (Figure III.5). Moreover, the entire notion of linking the transition to farming to the idea of progress has become extremely problematic. In a clever turn of phrase, anthropologist **Marshall Sahlins** (1972) has called hunter-gatherers the "original affluent society." Through a careful comparison of ethnographic studies of hunter-gatherer and farming communities, Sahlins has shown that, contrary to our expectations, hunter-gatherers spend less time working for their food than agriculturalists. Hunter-gatherers actually have far more leisure time than farmers. In a similar vein, on the basis of a study of human skeletal remains from prehistoric sites, Mark Cohen (1977) has demonstrated that early agriculturalists were not as healthy as hunter-gatherers. Because of increased crowding in permanent villages, agricultural societies were vulnerable to outbreaks of disease. Also, their health suffered from a decrease in the quality of their diet. As a result of studies such as these, many archaeologists question whether the development of agriculture was the result of people choosing or inventing a "better" way of life.

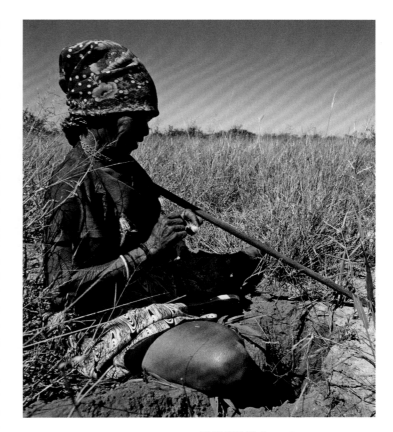

FIGURE III.5 A Nharo woman in the Northern Cape Province of South Africa collecting plant food. How does this image compare to the image you have of hunter-gatherers?

■ Searching for Explanations

If agriculture is not inherently advantageous, why did it develop? Kent Flannery once crystallized the difficulty of answering this question, saying, "If you asked me 'Why did agriculture begin?' I'm not sure what I'd give you as a cause" (quoted in Hayden 1990, 31). In the chapters that follow, we will pursue the trail of empirical evidence that archaeologists have uncovered and continue to uncover. Central to the study of agricultural origins is the recognition that plants and animals have been domesticated independently in numerous locations. The major centers for the independent domestication of indigenous plants and animals were the Middle East, southern China, northern China, Africa, the Andes, and central Mexico (see Figure III.6). Other regions where there was limited independent domestication of plants include eastern North America and New Guinea. Because agriculture developed independently in at least six regions, archaeologists can explore whether there were regularities in its unfolding.

Archaeologists make a distinction between areas where agriculture developed independently and areas into which agriculture spread. The spread of agriculture is increasingly recognized as a process that is as complex and worthy of study as the original domestication of plants and animals. The origin of agriculture is a complex topic that involves both empirical and theoretical components. The essential theoretical issue that faces archaeologists is how to approach the origins of agriculture as a process. How and why did societies across the globe shift from a hunter-gatherer way of life to living in settled farming communities?

One approach to this question has been to look for an external trigger that played a role in the shift to agriculture. An obvious candidate for such a trigger is

Marshall Sahlins An anthropologist who described hunter-gatherers as the "original affluent society."

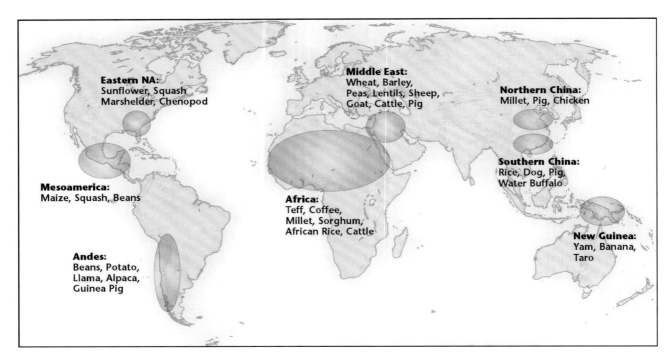

FIGURE III.6 Map of the major centers of domestication

climate change. Another factor that might have triggered the shift to agriculture is an increase in population. Research by **Ester Boserup** suggests that population growth might actually be an underlying cause, rather than an effect, of agriculture. Boserup's (1965) studies suggest that subsistence systems—the ways people get their food—tend to be the result of population pressures.

A major breakthrough in the study of agricultural origins has been the recognition that it is unlikely that searching for a single external trigger will produce a satisfying explanation. Following an approach based on systems theory, archaeologists have shifted to developing models of how the interaction between a number of factors might have led to the adoption of agriculture (Bender 1975). For example, Lewis Binford examined the interaction between increasing population size and fluctuating climatic conditions (Binford and Binford 1968). A particularly intriguing model developed by Brian Hayden focuses on the interaction between surplus food and social organization. Hayden begins by arguing that not all hunter-gatherer societies are the same. *Generalized hunter-gatherers* rely on scarce or unpredictable resources and, as a result, live at low population densities. In such societies, competition over food resources will be detrimental to the group and therefore maladaptive. *Complex hunter-gatherers* use more reliable and abundant resources (such as salmon, cod, insects, rodents, grass seeds, and nuts) and therefore can live at higher population densities. Because overexploitation of these resources is practically impossible, competition can develop and will largely take the form of feasting events. It is the "competition between individuals using food resources to wage their competitive battles," says Hayden (1990), that "provides the motive and the means for the development of food production. . . . Aspiring accumulators can be expected to exert all their ingenuity to bribe, coerce, cajole, and con other members of the community into supporting competitive feasts and producing as many delicacies or other high-quality foods as possible for feasts" (35–36).

An interesting aspect of Hayden's model is that it builds on changes in hunter-gatherer adaptations, which then interact with social factors to push societies toward

Ester Boserup An economist whose research suggests that increased population size might have been the cause of the shift to agriculture.

agriculture. In every case study that we examine in the coming chapters, we will see that increasing complexity in hunter-gatherer adaptations precedes the shift to agriculture. Such societies of hunter-gatherers are often labeled "Archaic" in the Americas and "Epipaleolithic" or "Mesolithic" in other parts of the world. Kent Flannery (1973) has emphasized that a common characteristic of these societies is that they relied on a **broad spectrum adaptation**, which included a wide range of plant and animal foods.

broad spectrum adaptation
Exploitation of a wide range of plant and animal resources characteristic of many hunter-gatherer societies that preceded the shift to agriculture.

In examining the case studies in the coming chapters, no particular model for the origins of agriculture is adopted. We will find much support for Barbara Bender's (1975) conclusion that "there is no single hypothesis that will explain the shift to food production in different parts of the world" (215). There is considerable variation in the pathways different societies took in adopting farming.

■ Agriculture and Progress Revisited

Progress has been rejected as an *explanation* for why agricultural societies came into being; however, there does seem to be an element of progress, or at least directionality, built into our conception of the origins of agriculture as a process. For example, Hayden (1990) discusses a shift from generalized hunter-gatherers, to complex hunter-gatherers, to farmers. Flannery (1973) emphasizes broad spectrum adaptations as a precondition for agriculture.

Systems theory, as presented in Chapter 2, should not allow for such a "ratchet effect." The feedback loop between your furnace and your thermostat is a self-regulating system that has no direction; it simply adjusts to changes in temperature. The directionality inherent in the shift to agriculture poses a significant theoretical challenge. A similar challenge plagues evolutionary biologists struggling to explain how evolution can have direction without recourse to models that view progress as explaining evolution (Nitecki 1988). Several concepts from evolutionary biology are useful to our study of agricultural origins. The first is that directionality and progress are distinct. Stephen Jay Gould has argued that directionality is the essential element of any historical process. Notably, Gould (1988) states that "history must be more than a string of isolated, if distinctive, events strung together one after the other" (333). The essence of historical processes is that they unfold in time. Our task in examining case studies of agricultural origins is not only to look at how various aspects of agriculture are related, but also to understand the *process* of agricultural origins. We will be interested in both the tempo of this process (e.g., was it a revolution, as Childe proposed?) and the relationships among events.

In one of the classic articles of evolutionary biology, Gould and his colleague Richard Lewontin (1979) used the essentially historical nature of evolutionary processes to launch an attack on what they called the "Panglossian paradigm." Dr. Pangloss is a character from a satire by Voltaire who elaborates ridiculous explanations of how everything in the world is for the best. Gould and Lewontin argue that evolutionary biologists think much as Dr. Pangloss does, explaining every aspect of organisms as the best possible adaptation. To counter the Panglossian paradigm, Gould and Lewontin use an illustration from architecture. At the Cathedral of San Marco in Venice, small triangular spaces between arches are used for a perfectly fitted painted scene (see Figure III.7). One might think that these triangular spaces were built for the needs of the painter, but that is not the case. The spaces, known by the architectural term *spandrels*, are created by the intersection of two rounded arches that meet at a right angle. The critical point is that the paintings in the spandrels are adapted to an existing structure. It is useful to keep Dr. Pangloss and the spandrels of San Marco firmly in mind as we move through the world of agricultural origins. We

FIGURE III.7 In this photograph of the interior of the Cathedral of San Marco, an angel fills the space created by a spandrel

are looking at the way changes built on preexisting conditions, just as the painters of the cathedral took advantage of spaces that were structurally essential to the building; thus, we must be wary of explaining every aspect of society as adaptive.

In the next three chapters, we will explore a series of case studies in the shift to agriculture. The focus will be on examining the relationships among domestication, technology, and community, as well as the role of external triggers, including climate changes and increases in population. The picture that emerges is one of tremendous diversity in the way agricultural societies developed. Agriculture came into being because of the actions of people, and the changes unleashed by the process shook the foundations of the world in which those people lived. The shift from hunter-gatherer societies profoundly affected every aspect of human life, from the diversity of the ecosystem to the way people experienced the supernatural. Living as we do in a rapidly changing world, we are in a good position to have some empathy for and insight into such an experience. The development of agriculture is a process with immediate relevance to the upheavals that we experience today. The origins of agriculture point to the essential link among aspects of experience we often treat as distinct. Social change, technological innovation, ecological impact, and religious experience are all inextricably linked in a process that produced a truly revolutionary change in human societies. From thousands of years away, we look back at this process and try to piece together the evidence that survives. What was it like to be part of the generations that experienced the Neolithic Revolution? What role did individuals play in effecting the large-scale changes they lived through? Similar questions might be asked about our own experience living a in a world of change.

SUMMARY

- To many early archaeologists and anthropologists, including Lewis Henry Morgan and V. Gordon Childe, the origin of agriculture involved the separation of humanity from nature.

- More recently, anthropologists and archaeologists working from a diversity of perspectives have challenged the traditional understanding of the origins of agriculture.

- Ester Boserup has proposed that the development of agriculture was a response to an increase in population.
- Childe labeled the development of agriculture the Neolithic Revolution, one that includes changes in three major aspects of human society and adaptation: domestication, technology, and community (the process of settling down).
- Plants and animals have been domesticated independently in numerous locations.

KEY TERMS

broad spectrum adaptation, 185
community, 179
David Rindos, 181
domestication, 179
Ester Boserup, 184

Lewis Henry Morgan, 179
Marshall Sahlins, 183
Neolithic Revolution, 180
technology, 179
Tim Ingold, 181

REVIEW QUESTIONS

1. Why are contemporary archaeologists and anthropologists critical of Morgan's and Childe's conception of the origin of agriculture?
2. How do Rindos's ideas about the origins of agriculture differ from Ingold's?

3. Why did Childe choose to describe the origin of agriculture as the Neolithic Revolution?

TOWERS, VILLAGES, AND LONGHOUSES

In the Middle East, the domestication of plants and animals took place within the context of large villages. After reading this chapter, you should understand:

- **The emergence of settled villages in the Middle East.**

- **The domestication of plants and animals in the Middle East.**

Neolithic architecture at the site of Basta, Jordan

- **The relationship among domestication, villages, and technology in the development of agriculture in the Middle East.**

- **The questions surrounding the spread of agriculture to Europe.**

7 TIMELINE

Ohalo

○ SITES

ARCHAEOLOGICAL INDUSTRIES

KEBARAN AND GEOMETRIC KEBARAN

thousands of years ago   **25**   **20**

SITES DISCUSSED IN CHAPTER 7

Talheim

Lepenski Vir

Black Sea

Mallaha

Kefar Hahoresh • Ohalo

Netiv Hagdud

Jericho • Ain Ghazal

Çatalhöyük

Göbekli Tepe

Jerf el Ahmar

Abu Hureyra

Nahal Hemar

Wadi Mataha

Wadi Mataha

Jericho Tower
Netiv Hagdud
Jerf el Ahmar

Abu Hureyra

Kefar Hahoresh
Göbekli Tepe

Çatalhöyük

Lepenski Vir

Mallaha

Ain Ghazal

EARLY NEOLITHIC

PRE-POTTERY NEOLITHIC A (PPNA)

LATE NEOLITHIC

NATUFIAN

PRE-POTTERY NEOLITHIC B (PPNB)

LINEAR BAND KERAMIK (LBK)

10

5

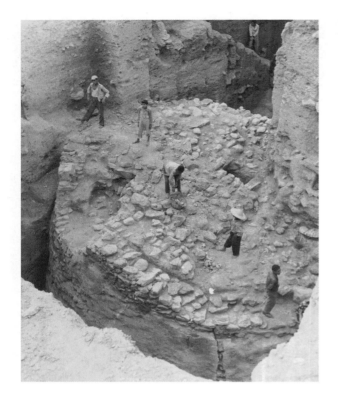

FIGURE 7.1 Photograph of the Jericho tower during excavation. Notice the opening in the top of the tower that leads to a stairway.

The ancient mound, or *tel*, of Jericho is a powerful lure to archaeologists. The famous walls of Jericho, toppled in the biblical book of Joshua, are exactly the type of concrete evidence archaeologists should easily be able to identify and recover. The British archaeologist Kathleen Kenyon sank massive trenches through the tel of Jericho, documenting the stratigraphic sequence and revealing the history of the site. Surprisingly, Kenyon recovered no evidence of a settlement dating to the biblical period. Why these remains are absent is unclear. Perhaps the story of Joshua is more myth than reality. Or maybe the settlement of Jericho described in the book of Joshua was in a different, as yet undiscovered, location.

As Kenyon penetrated the deepest archaeological deposits at Jericho, she uncovered a wall and a tower that astounded the archaeological community (see Figure 7.1). These constructions were far older than Joshua; in fact, they were the oldest known monumental architecture ever discovered. The tower and wall at Jericho were built 12,000 years ago, during the Early Neolithic period.

The tower of Jericho is only one of a string of discoveries that have shed dramatic light on the origins of agriculture in the Middle East. In this chapter, we examine the shift from hunter-gatherer to agricultural societies in the Middle East. The domestication of plants and animals in this region took place within the context of large and dense villages. The adoption of agriculture resulted in a transformation of all aspects of life. These profound changes affected not only social relations between people, but also the way people conceived of the supernatural. In the last section of the chapter, we explore the spread of domesticated plants and animals into Europe.

7.1 Setting the Scene

The Middle East includes a wide range of climates. A ribbon of Mediterranean climate extends today from Israel and Jordan in the south, up into Turkey, Syria, and Lebanon in the north, and into northern Iraq and western Iran to the east. Together, these regions form an area known as the **Fertile Crescent**, characterized by dry summers and winter rains with enough precipitation to support vegetation ranging from woodlands to open-park woodlands. Along with trees such as oak and pine, large stands of wild cereals, including wheat, barley, and rye, dot the countryside. To the south and the east of the Fertile Crescent, the Mediterranean open-park woodlands grade into steppe environments that in turn grade into true deserts.

The archaeological record clearly shows that the shift to an agricultural way of life in the Middle East was a process rather than a revolution. The transition to agriculture can be traced through a number of stages (see Table 7.1):

▲▲ Fertile Crescent A ribbon of Mediterranean climate that arcs across the Middle East. It is characterized by dry summers and winter rains with enough precipitation to support vegetation ranging from woodlands to open-park woodlands.

TABLE 7.1 CHRONOLOGY OF THE TRANSITION TO AGRICULTURE IN THE MIDDLE EAST

STAGE	PERIOD	DATE (YEARS AGO)
1	Kebaran and Geometric Kebaran	25,000–15,000
2	Natufian	15,000–12,000
3	Early Neolithic	12,000–8,500
4	Late Neolithic	8,500–7,000

ARCHAEOLOGY *in the world*

Political Borders and Archaeology

Politics and archaeology frequently intersect in the Middle East. Sites like Masada, where a group of Jewish rebels made a futile last stand against the Roman army, have become powerful symbols for the modern state of Israel (Zrubavel 1995). As Palestinians reach for statehood, archaeology has also been an important tool for exploring identity and asserting a presence that has often been overlooked or even suppressed. In Jordan, archaeology has had strong sponsorship from the royal family. The Syrian government has used traveling exhibits of archaeological finds as an opportunity to expand the narrow perspectives Americans hold about their country.

Prehistoric archaeology, including the study of the origins of agriculture, has relatively little political significance. But this does not mean that prehistoric archaeology has escaped the influence of politics. Steven Rosen (1991) has shown that national borders have had a major influence on the reconstruction of the prehistory of the region, even though these boundaries were irrelevant for ancient hunter-gatherer and early farming communities. The modern borders strongly affect where archaeologists can work and even where they can visit. A UN diplomat tells of having breakfast in Tel Aviv, Israel; lunch in Amman, Jordan; and dinner in Damascus, Syria, before getting back to Tel Aviv after dinner. All of this travel was possible thanks to a diplomatic passport. However, an Israeli archaeologist who has lived in Israel his whole life is unable to visit Syria, and a Syrian archaeologist who has lived her whole life in Syria is unable to visit Israel. The result is a lack of communication and a fragmentation of the archaeological record. There are cultural groupings in the Epipaleolithic that closely map onto national borders. These are modern impositions on a prehistoric landscape, filters that distort our view of the past.

The signing of a peace agreement between Israel and Jordan has eased travel between these two countries, but ongoing tensions and outbreaks of violence have kept interaction to a minimum. Nonetheless, the increased ease of travel has led to an improved understanding of the connections between Israel and Jordan in prehistory. The influence of national borders on our view of prehistory is not unique to the Middle East; it is simply heightened and thus more visible in this politically sensitive region. Prehistoric archaeologists have a natural interest in open borders. In many ways, the emphasis on understanding local archaeological developments from a global perspective, which is the core of prehistoric archaeology, is a very useful counterbalance to tendencies to use archaeology to promote nationalist agendas. One hopes that in the future prehistoric archaeologists might contribute to building bridges across our fragmented modern landscape (Scham and Yahya 2003). ●

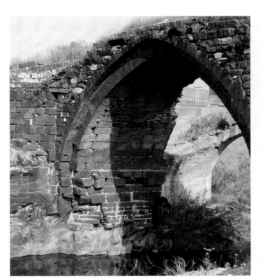

FIGURE 7.2 The site of Gesher/'Jesir al-Majami, a bridge spanning the Jordan River that dates back to the Roman period, is a focus of the PUSH Project. The PUSH Project works to promote dialogue and cultural understanding of shared heritage among Israelis, Jordanians, and Palestinians.

Reproduced with the permission of the PUSH Project.

1. During the Kebaran and Geometric Kebaran periods, hunter–gatherers living in the region subsisted on a wide range of plant and animal resources. There is no evidence of domesticated plants or animals during those periods, and the remains of brush huts are the only evidence of architecture.

2. During the Natufian period, constructed architecture and increased elaboration of material culture appear. There is no evidence that agriculture had yet become widespread.

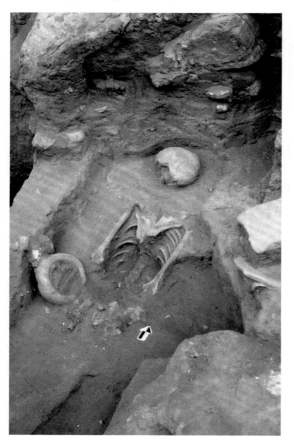

▲▲ **Ohalo** A Kebaran site in northern Israel with excellent preservation of organic remains.

FIGURE 7.3 The excavation of the Wadi Mataha burial. At this stage of the excavation, the body's legs have been removed. Note how the shoulder bones (scapula) are overlapping. What does this tell us about the way the body was buried?

3. In the Early Neolithic period, people lived in villages and began to farm a range of cereals and pulses (lentils and peas). Subsequently, they also began to domesticate goats.

4. During the Late Neolithic period, the earliest pottery manufacture appears. In most areas, the sites of this period are smaller and less densely packed than those of the end of the Early Neolithic. Sheep, goats, cattle, and pigs were fully domesticated.

7.2 Stage 1: Kebaran and Geometric Kebaran

Most sites dating to the Kebaran and Geometric Kebaran periods are small hunter–gatherer encampments with few remains other than stone tools and animal bones. The recent discovery of **Ohalo**, a Kebaran site with excellent preservation of organic remains, has shed new light on that period.

■ Technology

Sites belonging to the Kebaran and Geometric Kebaran are easily identified on the basis of their characteristic stone tools (Goring-Morris and Belfer-Cohen 1998). The tools from these periods are made mostly on small blades known as bladelets. In the Geometric Kebaran, bladelets are often shaped into geometric forms such as triangles and rectangles.

■ Settlements

Most sites from the Kebaran and Geometric Kebaran periods are the remains of small camps left by highly mobile hunter-gatherers who did not live year-round in one location. Ohalo, in northern Israel, has provided a unique glimpse of a Kebaran occupation site (Nadel 2002). Soon after it was abandoned, the encampment at Ohalo was submerged beneath the waters of the Sea of Galilee. Because the deposits were not exposed to air, the preservation of organic remains is extraordinary. A recent period of drought led to an unprecedented lowering of lake levels that exposed the site. Archaeologists were able to open up a horizontal 2,000-square-meter area at Ohalo and unearth the remains of six brush huts that could be traced as shallow oval depressions in the ground between 3 and 4.5 meters in length.

The artifacts recovered at Ohalo include a large collection of stone tools dominated by retouched bladelets. Tools were also made of bone, mostly in the form of awls. The only personal ornaments recovered were shell beads that had been transported from the Mediterranean Sea coast. An adult male was buried near the huts at Ohalo. The skeleton was found lying on its side in a semi-flexed position. No burial items were found with the skeleton; however, the excavator believes that a stone circle found near the burial might have some ritual significance.

Burials from the Kebaran and Geometric Kebaran sites are rare. A puzzling Geometric Kebaran burial was excavated at the site of Wadi Mataha in southern Jordan (see Figure 7.3). Wadi Mataha was a very small camp site during that period, so the discovery of a

The Author on His Fieldwork at Wadi Mataha

The Nabateans were some of the greatest architects of the ancient world. They carved massive tombs out of the sandstone outcrops around Petra in southern Jordan and also built palaces, theaters, and an entire city in this now-desolate region. Petra is starkly beautiful. The Nabatean monuments combine the geological beauty of the sandstone with the grandeur of monumental architecture. The Nabateans sculpted the landscape to gather every drop of water to support agriculture, but after the collapse of their kingdom, the irrigation system fell into disrepair, and subsequent soil erosion has left much of the bedrock exposed and the land incapable of supporting large-scale agriculture.

Umm Sayhun, the Bedouin village overlooking Petra, is a very modest village, mostly small, square houses with dusty yards and the occasional animal roaming the streets. Many of the houses appear unfinished, with rebars left poking out of the flat roofs. When I worked at Petra, we lived in Dakhlala's house, a relatively grand and massive structure at the edge of town. Dakhlala was responsible for a good amount of the reconstructive stone masonry in Petra, and he had adorned his own house with some of the simple geometric patterns found on the ancient sandstone monuments.

I had come to Petra with Joel Janetski of Brigham Young University via a rather roundabout route. Joel is a specialist in early agricultural societies of Utah and learned from a colleague who worked on the Nabateans of Petra that there might be an interesting prehistoric site tucked in this 2,000-year-old city. Joel needed a specialist in Near Eastern prehistory, and that is how I landed at Dakhlala's house.

We were looking for the Natufians, who lived in this area more than 10,000 years before the Nabateans. We worked on a slope of a tributary of the Wadi Mataha (which gave the name to the site) that was littered with artifacts characteristic of the Natufians. But would we discover anything more than a scatter of surface finds? Our first full season after Joel's initial test of the site yielded a windfall of finds, including the walls of a Natufian structure and the Geometric Kebaran burial described on page 184. We returned for two more seasons, which expanded our coverage and confirmed that we did in fact have the earliest architectural remains in southern Jordan. We are still hard at work on the analysis of the material we recovered during our excavations. This is perhaps the greatest challenge in archaeology—not making the discoveries, but finishing the publication. ▲

FIGURE 7.4 Excavation of one of the Natufian structures at Wadi Mataha. The floors of the structures were poorly defined, so it was necessary to map every artifact and piece of fallen rock.

somewhat elaborate burial feature was a surprise (Stock et al. 2005). The individual at Wadi Mataha was a young adult male buried with his face pointed down and his arms and legs "hog-tied" behind his back. A stone bowl with the bottom broken out was found with the human remains, as was a long flint blade. The man's skull had been broken open sometime soon after death, leaving a large hole slightly above the forehead.

Natufian Societies in the Middle East that practiced a broad-spectrum subsistence strategy that relied on a wide range of resources.

▲▲ **Mallaha** A Natufian site in northern Israel with the remains of oval stone structures.

lunate Tiny, crescent-shaped stone tool characteristic of the Natufian.

On the basis of the discoveries at Ohalo and Wadi Mataha, it is very difficult to understand the spiritual world of the people of the Kebaran and Geometric Kebaran periods. The burial at Ohalo, located within the camp, would fit with a burial ritual that serves to form a spiritual link between a group and its place of habitation. The situation at Wadi Mataha is quite different, and it is difficult not to see the burial as a violent event. Art objects from either period are rare; the only known examples are two crudely incised pebbles.

■ Domestication

There is no evidence of either animal or plant domestication during the Kebaran or Geometric Kebaran period. The people at Ohalo lived near the edge of a lake with access to a wide range of resources. The plant remains recovered are wild grasses (including wild barley and wild wheat), fruits, nuts, and water plants. The most common mammal bones are from gazelles, but the remains of deer, wild pig, wild goat, hare, red fox, and wildcat are also found. From a single hut, nearly 10,000 fish bones, mostly of carp and cichlids, were found. The remains of over 77 species of birds, including grebes, ducks, geese, quail, and birds of prey, were also found at Ohalo.

7.3 Stage 2: The Natufian

The **Natufian** societies of the Middle East constructed the earliest stone buildings in this area of the world and developed an impressive range of art objects and personal ornaments. However, there is no evidence that the Natufians domesticated any plants or herd animals. The Natufian settlements at sites such as **Mallaha** were small villages with up to a dozen structures.

We are still far from understanding the causes underlying the innovations found in the Natufian period. It is possible that an increase in population led to an increase in the size and complexity of settlements, but even if this was the case, we are left to question the reasons for an increase in population. Toward the end of the Natufian, coinciding with a period of climatic stress known as the Younger Dryas, there was a reduction in the size and number of Natufian settlements.

FIGURE 7.5 Small, crescent-shaped lunates are the characteristic tools found on Natufian sites. How might such small tools have been used?

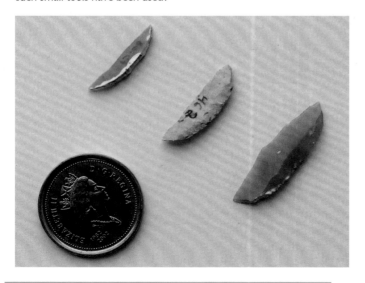

■ Technology

The technology of the Natufian shows a great deal of continuity with that of preceding periods. The stone tools continue to be made on small bladelets. The characteristic shape of tools in the Natufian is seen in the crescent-shaped bladelet known as a **lunate** (Bar-Yosef and Valla 1991). It is assumed that, like the bladelet tools of the preceding periods, lunates served as elements in hunting tools or as parts of tools made up of many small pieces (see Figure 7.5). At the site of Wadi Hammeh in Jordan, a series of bladelets was found mounted in a bone haft of what appears to be a knife or a sickle (Edwards 1991). Some lunates show a type of luster known as sickle polish, which forms only when stone tools are used to harvest grasses.

The Natufians were the first people in the Middle East to invest a great deal of energy in the manufacture of ground stone tools. Among such tools found on Natufian sites are mortars, pestles, and grooved stones known as shaft straighteners (see Figure 7.6) decorated with a simple meander pattern. In some cases, the tools have been found far from the source of the stone, indicating that they were traded across long distances. Long-distance trade is also indicated by the abundance of Red Sea and Mediterranean Sea shells and shell beads found on Natufian sites, which are often quite distant from the sea.

■ Settlements

The transition to village life began during the Natufian. Structures consist of undressed stones piled to form walls that are often preserved to a height of up to 1 meter. The structures are ovals or open semi-circles. The floors of the structures are covered with refuse, including stone tools and debris and animal bones (see Figure 7.7). It is hard to imagine these surfaces being used as houses for families, although it is not clear what other function they might have had. It is usually suggested that the stone walls would have supported a superstructure made of wood and brush.

The size of Natufian sites ranges from large villages, such as Mallaha or Wadi Hammeh, with up to a dozen structures, to much smaller sites. There is considerable debate as to whether these sites were occupied year-round.

During the later part of the Natufian, there is a marked reduction both in the number and in the size of the sites. The contraction in Natufian settlements is correlated with a brief period of climatic stress known as the **Younger Dryas**, a global event often characterized as a "little Ice Age." Recent research suggests that the onset of the Younger Dryas was extremely rapid and that major shifts in climate would have taken place within a single generation. In the Middle East, the effect of the Younger Dryas was to reduce the areas suitable for human occupation. From the change in the size and density of the settlements, it is clear that the Younger Dryas had a significant effect on Natufian society.

FIGURE 7.6 Fragment of a ground stone artifact known as a shaft straightener from the site of Wadi Mataha. Note the groove in the upper surface and the incised decoration around the base.

Younger Dryas A period of global climatic stress that had a significant impact on Natufian society.

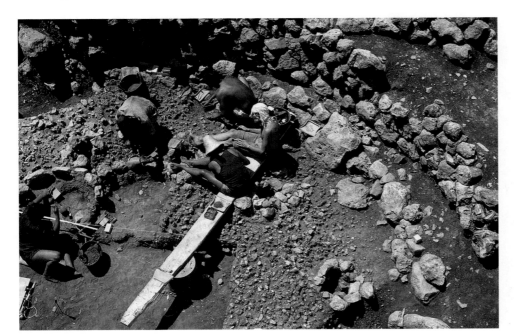

FIGURE 7.7 Excavation of a large Natufian structure at the site of Mallaha, Israel. The excavators sit on planks so as not to disturb the floor of the structure that is covered with debris. In addition to the circular wall of the structure, several postholes lined with stones are visible.

Burials are commonly found on Natufian sites, often under the floors of houses. In some cases, in a practice that is elaborated in the subsequent Neolithic periods, the skull has been removed prior to burial. Objects found in some Natufian burials include shell necklaces and head coverings.

■ Domestication

Unfortunately, it has rarely been possible to recover plant remains from Natufian sites. An important exception is the site of **Abu Hureyra**, located on the Upper Euphrates River in Syria. Abu Hureyra is a site with multiple levels of occupation that span the sequence from the Natufian through the Neolithic. Excavations in the earliest levels at Abu Hureyra uncovered a culture parallel to the Natufian, but with subtle differences. For example, the houses at Abu Hureyra were sunken pits rather than built walls. An ambitious program of flotation for burnt seeds at Abu Hureyra was richly rewarded with a spectacular assemblage of botanical remains. The analysis of the recovered seeds indicates that the people living at Abu Hureyra, like the people at Ohalo, exploited a wide range of plants. Such a broad spectrum strategy is not surprising, as it is an effective way for hunter-gatherers to minimize the risk that any particular resource will be temporarily scarce. The plant species do not show clear evidence of having been domesticated.

With some exceptions, the animal bones found on Natufian sites are dominated by gazelle bones. At Abu Hureyra, 80% of the bones identified were from gazelle. At the same time, Natufians continued to hunt a wide range of animals, including wild sheep, goats, and cattle. At sites such as Mallaha, which is located near a marsh, birds were hunted as well.

FIGURE 7.8 Burial of a dog together with a human from the Natufian site of Mallaha. Archaeologists have interpreted this burial as evidence that dogs were domesticated during the Natufian.

The Natufians did not domesticate any herd animals. (Gazelles have actually never been completely domesticated.) Interestingly, there is evidence that Natufians had domesticated, or at least tamed, dogs. At two sites—Hayonim Terrace and Mallaha—dog skeletons were found buried with human remains (see Figure 7.8). These burials signify that dogs were brought into human society. There is also some indication that the snouts of dogs found on Natufian sites are smaller than the snouts of wild dogs (Dayan 1994). This change in morphology is consistent with the early stages of domestication.

Genetic studies support a date for dog domestication in the period between 11,000 and 16,000 years ago (Freedman et al. 2014). This analysis does not identify where domestication took place but suggests a single center of domestication; however, a global study of modern village dogs suggests that dog domestication took place in central Asia (Shannon et al. 2015). The genetics study of dogs is complicated by evidence that there was continuous interbreeding between wolves and domesticated dogs. A particularly interesting genetic study compared the entire genome of wolves and dogs to understand what traits were selected for in the process of domestication (Axelsson et al. 2013). There is a clear signal that genes that are related to starch digestion were selected for in domesticated dogs, suggesting that selection for this trait allowed domesticated dogs to thrive on a starch-rich diet that living with people made available.

7.4 Stage 3: The Early Neolithic

The Early Neolithic is divided into two major periods: the Pre-Pottery Neolithic A, which dates between 12,000 and 10,800 years ago, and the Pre-Pottery Neolithic B, which dates between 10,800 and 8,500 years ago. The beginning of the Pre-Pottery Neolithic A corresponds with the end of the Younger Dryas event, while the Pre-Pottery Neolithic B corresponds to a period of improved climate.

■ Technology

For archaeologists, the major marker that distinguishes the Early Neolithic from the Natufian is a gradual shift away from tools made on bladelets to a tool kit made on blades with a particular emphasis on arrowheads (see Figure 7.9). By the Pre-Pottery Neolithic B, arrowheads were made on skillfully manufactured blades. Blades are also used for sickles, as is indicated by the frequent presence of sickle polish. Ground stone axes and adzes, tools with a beveled edge, suitable for working wood or clearing trees are an important addition to the Early Neolithic tool kit. Grinding stones used for processing grain are also found in extremely large quantities on Early Neolithic sites.

The use of plaster is highly developed during the Pre-Pottery Neolithic B period. Manufacturing plaster involves burning large quantities of limestone. Plaster was used to line the floors of houses and for a ritual purpose that will be described shortly. In some cases, plaster was used to build simple basins and bowls.

■ Settlements

During the Pre-Pottery Neolithic A, the size of settlements increased, and the first evidence of communal structures appeared. Houses continued to be circular, but settlements were larger than Natufian ones. At the site of **Netiv Hagdud** in the Jordan Valley, the remains of at least three houses were found in an excavation covering 500 square meters, less than 10% of the total area of the settlement (Bar-Yosef et al. 1991). Although population sizes are difficult to estimate, it seems likely that Netiv Hagdud housed somewhere between 20 and 30 families. Beyond the size of the settlement, there are other contrasts between Netiv Hagdud and large Natufian sites such as Mallaha. A rapid accumulation of sediments on Early Neolithic sites points to the extensive use of mud-brick architecture. At Netiv Hagdud, there was a buildup of close to 4 meters of sediment over a period of 200 to 300 years. The floors of the structures on Early Neolithic sites are well maintained, and debris tends to be concentrated in refuse pits. Storage pits, which are rare on Natufian sites, are common at Netiv Hagdud and other Early Neolithic sites.

The appearance of communal structures is the most striking aspect of the Pre-Pottery Neolithic A. The most spectacular of these structures is the tower discovered in the Pre-Pottery Neolithic A levels at Jericho. The 9-meter-high tower is made of undressed stones and mud brick and is attached to the inside of a massive wall. A staircase built inside the tower runs from the base to a hole in the flat platform at the top. The **Jericho tower** is the earliest known large-scale piece of architecture in the Middle East. Estimates for the time taken to build the tower and the attached wall range

▲ Netiv Hagdud A Pre-Pottery Neolithic A site in the Jordan Valley that was a village of between 20 and 30 houses.

Jericho tower A 9-meter-high structure made of undressed stone and mud brick dating to the Pre-Pottery Neolithic A.

FIGURE 7.9 Neolithic arrowheads from the site of Nahal Hemar, Israel

FIGURE 7.10 View of the site of Jerf el Ahmar showing houses surrounding a central circular structure

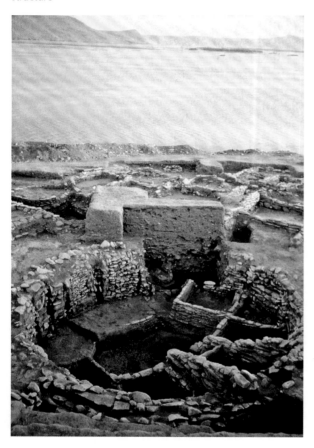

between 10,000 and 15,000 working days (Bar-Yosef 1986). Kenyon (1981) interpreted the tower as part of a defensive wall, which she thought ran around the Neolithic village. Because only a small portion of the Neolithic site was excavated, there is no way of knowing whether the bit of wall found attached to the tower does in fact run around the site. In any case, it seems extremely unlikely that the tower could have served a military purpose, as it is built on the inside of the wall. The interpretation of the tower is made more difficult by the fact that 12 skeletons were found at the base of the staircase. The skeletons were inserted when the staircase began to collapse. Among the suggestions for the purpose of the tower are (1) that the tower and the wall served for flood protection and (2) that the entire installation had a cultic function, as its construction and use appear to have been a community effort.

Excavations on Pre-Pottery Neolithic A sites in Syria have also uncovered evidence of communal structures. At the site of **Jerf el Ahmar**, on the Upper Euphrates River in Syria, the excavators found that although the Pre-Pottery Neolithic A houses appear to be located somewhat randomly across the site, there is a sense of community planning. As Figure 7.10 shows, houses are grouped around larger buildings that are built into the ground (Stordeur 1999). The excavators suggest that these buildings played a communal role in the small Early Neolithic village at Jerf el Ahmar. In one case, the skeleton of an individual lying splayed on his back with his head removed was found in the central chamber of one of these larger buildings. Soon after this person died, the building was destroyed and burnt. The discoveries at Jericho and Jerf el Ahmar indicate that the organization of Pre-Pottery Neolithic A society allowed the community to act as a group. It is intriguing that much of the evidence of community-level activity is found in structures with ritual functions associated with evidence of violence. We are left to question the role that ritual and violence played in knitting these early communities together.

During the Pre-Pottery Neolithic B period, there was a shift from round houses to rectangular ones, and the size of settlements increased significantly. The shift to rectangular houses allowed sites to be more densely packed than they had been in the Pre-Pottery Neolithic A. The villages of the Pre-Pottery Neolithic B are quite large and often show a high degree of planning. Excavators estimate that in the Early Neolithic levels of Abu Hureyra, there were up to 1,440 houses with a population of about 5,000 people (Moore, Hillman, and Legge 2000). As seen in Figure 7.11, the houses in the areas excavated were

FIGURE 7.11
Reconstruction of the Pre-Pottery Neolithic B village at Abu Hureyra, Syria. This picture shows the extent to which the landscape of the early Neolithic was shaped by human construction and activity.

TOOLBOX

Harris Matrix

Any process that has led to the accumulation of material on an archaeological site is considered to be a depositional event. Because deposition on archaeological sites is not continuous, archaeologists can define depositional units. What makes the concept of depositional units confusing is that these units can be of many types, including walls, floors, and the fill of pits. The job of the archaeological stratigrapher is to place these units into a matrix of relationships. Many archaeologists use a formal system called a Harris matrix to represent the network of relationships between depositional units (Harris 1989). Much of the challenge of stratigraphy comes from the fact that we do not actually observe the creation of the site. Instead, we observe changes in the composition and color of deposits as we excavate. The excavator's art is to determine whether a change in color or soil texture represents a new depositional unit.

Building a Harris matrix is based on identifying one of three possible relationships between depositional units:

1. Units can have no stratigraphic connection. For example, if there is a floor on the inside of a wall and a road on the outside, there is no direct stratigraphic relationship between the road and the floor.
2. Units can be in superposition. For example, if a wall is built over the remains of another wall, then the two units are in superposition.
3. Units can be correlated as parts of what was originally part of a single feature. For example, if there was a large pit house that was cut in half by the excavation of a foundation trench for a wall, then the two halves of the pit (which would be identified in the field as two separate depositional units) would be correlated as part of a single feature.

On the basis of these three types of relationships, it is possible to build a formal matrix expressing the stratigraphic relationships between all of the depositional units on a site.

The life of a mud-brick house provides a useful example of the range of processes that result in depositional units. The following is a list of depositional units that might be found in such a house:

1. The wall built into the foundation trench.
2. The fill placed between the edges of the trench and the base of the wall.
3. A pile of dirt excavated from the foundation trench and dumped in a pile outside of the house.
4. The material incorporated into the dirt floor of the house during the life of the building.
5. A pile of garbage built up against the outside wall of the house.

6. The mud bricks that have collapsed after the abandonment of the house.
7. Garbage that accumulated in the remains of the house after its abandonment.

It is possible to put all of the units of the abandoned mud-brick house in a sequence except for the garbage pile outside the house and the dirt pile from the digging of the foundation trench. It is possible to say that the garbage pile appeared later than the wall. However, because there is no stratigraphic connection between the inside and the outside of the house, it is not possible to determine the stratigraphic relationship between the pile outside the house and any of the features on the inside. The dirt pile from the digging of the foundation trench is in no stratigraphic relationship with any of the other depositional features. ●

1. House walls
2. Fill of foundation trench
3. Dirt from digging foundation trench
4. Floor
5. Garbage outside the house
6. Mud brick collapse
7. Garbage fill

FIGURE 7.12 Diagram and Harris matrix of a mud-brick house closely packed together and had a regular orientation. There is no evidence that the site was protected by a defensive wall.

Estimates for the size of Abu Hureyra place it at the high end of Early Neolithic sites in the Middle East. However, sites that could have easily housed hundreds or even thousands of people are common. Excavations at the site of Badja in southern Jordan have shown that houses during the later part of the Early Neolithic were two or even three stories high (Gebel et al. 1997). At Badja, the size of the settlement was limited by its rather precarious setting on cliffs above a deep gully. It appears that people responded to this limitation by crowding their houses closely together and building upward. Why people chose to live in such an inaccessible setting is an intriguing question.

During the Pre-Pottery Neolithic B, people lived in dense villages where their social life and interactions were constrained within a grid of houses. Life in these villages also required institutional structures to maintain social order. Hunter-gatherer societies, which are highly mobile, can resolve disputes simply by breaking into smaller groups, or "fissioning." The people living in villages like Abu Hureyra would not have had this option. Moreover, life in a densely packed village would have led to inevitable tensions over issues of inheritance and property rights. Discovering how Early Neolithic societies resolved these conflicts is a challenging archaeological problem, but one that is essential to resolve.

It is somewhat surprising that there is no real evidence for a social hierarchy in early Neolithic villages. Most houses look more or less the same, as do most burials. There is no sense that the regular layout of the sites reflects the decisions of a central authority.

■ Ritual

Jacques Cauvin and Trevor Watkins (2000) have eloquently called the Early Neolithic period the "birth of the gods," and a staggering array of symbolic artifacts has been found on Early Neolithic sites. Ritual objects appear to have operated at many levels, including everyday household objects and objects of display found in sacred precincts or temples. Within both houses and temples, there was also a domain of bodies and objects built into walls and buried under floors. It seems clear that, as they walked the streets of their villages, these people negotiated not only a world of constructed architecture, but also a world charged with deities, both visible and hidden. The archaeological evidence for Early Neolithic ritual activity can be broken down into three broad categories (based on ideas in Verhoeven 2002 and Naveh 2003): hidden, displayed, and daily life.

HIDDEN RITUALS. Many of the ritual objects found on Early Neolithic sites are hidden away in pits or under floors. The most striking hidden objects are **plastered skulls**. The removal of skulls from human skeletons is found as far back as the Natufian. On Pre-Pottery Neolithic B sites, excavators have discovered skulls on which a plaster face has been modeled. Both plastered and unplastered skulls are found below the floors of houses or in small caches.

An analysis of one of the skulls from the site of Kefar Hahoresh has provided a particularly detailed picture of the process of creating a plastered skull (Goren, Goring-Morris, and Segal 2001). In most cases, the mandible or jawbone was removed before the face was modeled. The first stage was to plug up the recesses in the skull, including the eye sockets and nasal passages. The face was then modeled onto the skull, but the position of the features was adjusted upward. Thus, the eyes were built up on the forehead, the nose over the eye sockets, and the mouth over

plastered skulls Human skulls on which a plaster face has been modeled; found buried beneath floors on sites dating to the Pre-Pottery Neolithic B period.

the nasal passage. As a result, the faces of the plastered skulls have an oddly shortened appearance. The analysis of the Kefar Hahoresh skull has shown that the process of modeling a plaster skull took place in several stages and included a range of types of plaster, as well as other materials (see Figure 7.13).

Careful stratigraphic analysis has indicated that in some cases plastered skulls were removed from their hiding places below the floors of houses and then carefully redeposited. Some archaeologists argue that this practice was an aspect of ancestor worship and that it was through reverence for the ancestor that Early Neolithic societies maintained cohesion. At Kefar Hahoresh, much of the excavated area is taken up by a dense deposit of human skeletal remains, hardly consistent with a normal habitation site. The excavator of Kefar Hahoresh has argued that it was a ritual site serving to bring together various communities in the region.

At the site of Ain Ghazal in Jordan, a collection of plaster figures—one of which is shown in Figure 7.14—was discovered in two pits (Rollefson 1998). How these figures relate to the Pre-Pottery Neolithic B plastered skulls is an

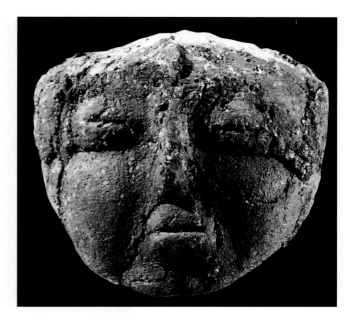

FIGURE 7.13 The plastered skull from Kefar Hahoresh

enigma. Another puzzling site is a small cave known as Nahal Hemar, located in a remote region south of the Dead Sea (Bar-Yosef 1985). In this cave, a wide range of artifacts was found, such as beads, bone tools, and arrowheads. Due to the dry conditions, textiles, including the remains of a cap and a bag, were recovered, along with a painted stone mask and a skull. The face of the skull was not decorated, but a net pattern had been applied to the cranium. What the function of this collection of artifacts was and, perhaps more importantly, how they got to where they were found are two questions that remain difficult to answer.

At the site of Badja in southern Jordan, the excavator has found a series of unused axes carefully hidden within the walls of a house. The excavator suggests that these beautifully crafted hidden objects would have had a magical function.

DISPLAY RITUALS. The Pre-Pottery Neolithic A tower of Jericho and the central structure at Jerf el Ahmar were meant to be seen. It seems quite likely that, regardless of their practical functions, these structures also stood as visible symbols of the community. During the Pre-Pottery Neolithic B, visibly special buildings are found on a number of sites.

At the site of Göbekli Tepe, on the Euphrates River in eastern Turkey, a series of buildings has been found built around monumental T-shaped pillars quarried as a single block from the bedrock (see Figure 7.15). Some of these pillars are carved with either human or animal figures (Schmidt 2001). At the nearby site of Navali Çori, a series of large stone sculptures has been uncovered that includes depictions of humans, birds, snakes, and birds combined with humans. Most of these sculptures come from a structure identified as a temple. The faunal remains from Göbekli Tepe are dominated by gazelle, which appear to have been hunted in the mid-summer to autumn. An isotope analysis suggests that this is a period of the year when large herds of migratory gazelle passed through the area (Lang et al. 2013). This is also a time of the year when plant foods such as wild pistachios and almonds were available in large quantity in the area around the site. Thus the monumental architecture at Göbekli Tepe might be linked with seasonal gatherings of people drawn by the rich resources available in this area during the mid-summer to autumn.

FIGURE 7.14 Plaster figure from Ain Ghazal after restoration

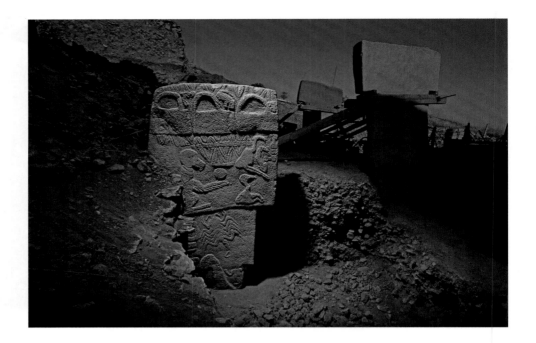

FIGURE 7.15 One of the massive T-shaped pillars from the site of Göbekli Tepe during excavation

The majority of the display items found in the Pre-Pottery Neolithic B would not have been visible from any great distance. They are thus quite different from the Jericho tower. Many authors have argued that the context for display in the Pre-Pottery Neolithic B was within temples or sacred precincts. This is a very important point because it suggests that access to visible signs of divinity was controlled. Perhaps the elite of Early Neolithic society was a ritual elite.

In some cases, there is evidence for the display of skulls, objects that are normally found in hidden contexts. At the site of Çayanu in eastern Turkey, the remains of 450 individuals have been recovered from a single structure known as the skull room, mostly from pits (Schirmer 1990). However, 49 burnt skulls were also found in contexts that suggest they fell off shelves when the building was burnt.

RITUALS OF DAILY LIFE. On several Early Neolithic sites, a large number of simple clay figurines have been found. Although some archaeologists suggest that the statuettes were children's toys, it appears more likely that they had symbolic meaning. These objects are usually found distributed among houses, together with domestic debris.

■ Domestication

Excavations at the Pre-Pottery Neolithic A site of Netiv Hagdud recovered the remains of barley with a tough **rachis**—the part of the plant that holds the seed to the stalk. In wild grains, the rachis is brittle and shatters easily, allowing seeds to disperse. For agriculturalists, it is desirable to have a plant with a tough rachis so that the seed remains on the plant until it is harvested. A plant with a tough rachis is truly domesticated in that it depends on human intervention for successful reproduction. Figure 7.16 illustrates the differences between a brittle rachis and a tough one.

Although the discovery at Netiv Hagdud was interpreted at first as evidence of domesticated plants in the Pre-Pottery Neolithic A, it now appears that this conclusion is not warranted (Bar-Yosef et al. 1991). Within wild populations of barley, a

rachis The part of a cereal plant that holds the seed to the stalk and keeps the seed on the plant until it is harvested.

small percentage of plants have a tough rachis, so the small number of remains of apparently domesticated barley found at Netiv Hagdud could have been collected from wild stands along with a wide range of wild plants.

Harvesting of grains did take place during the Pre-Pottery Neolithic A, as is attested by botanical remains, grinding stones, and sickles. However, it does not appear that these plants were farmed. The wild forms of plants, including wheat and barley, were harvested, but there is no indication that seeds were stored and planted. In accordance with the criterion developed by Rindos (see p. 181), cereals exploited during the Pre-Pottery Neolithic A were not domesticated, as the plants did not depend on their relationship with humans for protection or reproduction. There is no evidence of domesticated animals other than dogs during the Pre-Pottery Neolithic A. Gazelles remained the main species hunted, together with a wide range of other animals, including fish and birds.

A series of dried figs recovered from the Pre-Pottery Neolithic A site of Gilgal, located in the Jordan Valley near Netiv Hagdud, provides the earliest compelling evidence of plant domestication in the Middle East (Kislev, Hartmann, and Bar-Yosef 2006). These figs, like modern domesticated ones, are not capable of reproduction without human intervention. Although this intervention is simple, involving merely the cutting and planting of branches, it clearly meets the definition of domestication.

Farming developed across the Middle East during the Pre-Pottery Neolithic B. A wide range of domesticated crops is found, including cereals (emmer wheat, einkorn wheat, and barley), pulses (lentil and pea), and legumes (bitter vetch and chickpea). The domesticated grains show an increase in the size of individual grains and a shift to a tough rachis. The large number of grinding stones found on Pre-Pottery Neolithic B sites give a clear sense of the important role of grains in the diet during this period.

Animal domestication developed somewhat later than plant domestication. The later part of the Pre-Pottery Neolithic B shows evidence of the domestication of sheep and goats. Sheep were domesticated in the northern mountainous regions of Turkey, Iraq, or Iran, their natural habitation zone. Establishing the location and timing for the domestication of goats is quite complex, as wild goats are found across the entire region of the Middle East. By the end of the Pre-Pottery Neolithic B, pigs and cattle were domesticated. The evidence for domesticated animals in this phase includes a reduction in animal sizes, an overrepresentation of the bones of young males, and the discovery of animals such as sheep outside of their natural range. The domestication of sheep and goats appears to have followed a falloff in gazelle populations.

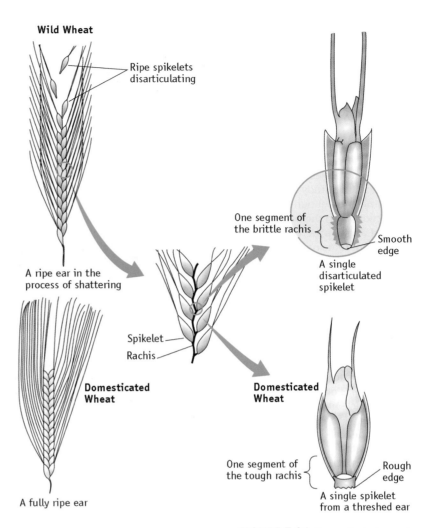

Wild Wheat

Ripe spikelets disarticulating

A ripe ear in the process of shattering

Domesticated Wheat

A fully ripe ear

Spikelet
Rachis

One segment of the brittle rachis

Smooth edge

A single disarticulated spikelet

Domesticated Wheat

One segment of the tough rachis

Rough edge

A single spikelet from a threshed ear

FIGURE 7.16 Domesticated cereals such as wheat and barley develop a tough rachis that holds seeds to the plant until threshing after harvest. Wild cereals have a brittle rachis that allows for easy dispersal of the seeds.

TOOLBOX

Paleoethnobotany

Paleoethnobotanists grasp at the most ephemeral of archaeological remains. Paleoethnobotany is defined as "the study of past cultures by an examination of human populations' interactions with the plant world" (Hastorf and Popper 1988, 1). In rare cases, plant remains are exquisitely preserved. Dry climates, such as the highland caves of Mexico, can preserve the desiccated remains of plants that would otherwise rapidly disintegrate. By contrast, waterlogged conditions, including bogs and deposits sealed under water, can preserve botanical remains because of the absence of oxygen. An example of such anaerobic preservation is the remains of brush huts at the site of Ohalo, Israel, which were sealed below the waters of the Sea of Galilee.

All botanical remains that can be seen without magnification are known as macrobotanicals. Most macrobotanicals are not preserved. An important exception is the charred remains of burnt seeds, plant parts, and wood found on the majority of archaeological sites. The problem for paleoethnobotanists is that these tiny, fragile specimens are usually found dispersed across the site, closely bound in the soil matrix. Trying to recover such plant remains is a literal case of grasping at straws. To get around this problem, paleoethnobotanists have developed a recovery method known as flotation. The basic principle behind flotation is simple: Burnt macrobotanical remains will float in water, whereas the soil matrix will sink; therefore, if soil is vigorously mixed with water, the macrobotanicals will float free of the soil matrix. The paleoethnobotanists can then skim off the charred seeds, stalks, and wood for analysis.

Paleoethnobotanists have developed elaborate flotation machines that allow large amounts of soil to be processed. After macrobotanicals are skimmed off, they need to be carefully dried and then laboriously sorted. Paleoethnobotanists can identify species of seeds and other plant parts and can also usually distinguish between domesticated and wild plants. By looking at where different types of plant remains are found, paleoethnobotanists can also contribute to understanding the spatial organization of activities on a site—for example, identifying areas where food was prepared. ●

FIGURE 7.17 Using flotation to recover charred plant remains at the site of Jerf el Ahmar, Syria

FIGURE 7.18 Charred barley seeds recovered from the site of Tel Kerma

7.5 Stage 4: Late Neolithic

At the end of the Pre-Pottery Neolithic B, there is a sharp reduction in the number of large village sites across most of the Middle East. Some archaeologists argue that the collapse of the Early Neolithic settlement system was the result of ecological degradation caused by deforestation. At the same time that the settlement system collapsed, there were significant changes in technology, including the introduction of pottery, and in the production of symbolic artifacts.

■ Technology

Pottery manufacture developed in the Middle East during the Late Neolithic. Among the vessels that have been found are small bowls and jars, as well as pots used for cooking. There is significant variation in the forms of vessels and in the way they are decorated in different regions and within different periods (see Figure 7.19). Two of the main methods of decoration were burnishing the clay to produce a polished surface and using red pigments in painted designs. All pots were built by hand without the use of a potter's wheel and were fired at a low temperature. At the same time that pottery was developed, the wide-scale production of plaster was abandoned.

There was also a significant shift in stone tool manufacture during the Late Neolithic. The skillful production of blades disappeared, and arrowheads became rare. Most stone tools found on Late Neolithic sites are expedient tools made of locally available materials with a minimal investment of energy. Sickle blades remain common and often have a serrated edge created by a series of notches.

■ Settlement and Ritual

The end of the Pre-Pottery Neolithic saw a decline in the number and size of sites. By the end of this period, which is often labeled Pre-Pottery Neolithic C, most of the large sites in Israel, Jordan, Syria, and eastern Turkey were abandoned. The Late Neolithic in these areas is characterized by a limited number of large sites and small dispersed hamlets. The large sites differ from those of Pre-Pottery Neolithic B in that they are not densely packed with structures.

The seeming collapse of the Pre-Pottery Neolithic B settlement system presents a challenge for archaeological interpretation. One possibility is that the collapse was the result of a human-induced ecological crisis. The large populations concentrated in Pre-Pottery Neolithic B villages along with their herds of domesticated animals might have degraded their environments to the point where such population densities could no longer be supported. One important culprit in this scenario is the large-scale production of plaster, which could have led to extensive deforestation.

An alternative perspective sees the end of the Pre-Pottery Neolithic B settlement system not as a collapse, but rather as a shift toward a way of life focused on the grazing of herds of domesticated animals. The dispersed settlement system found in the Late Neolithic might reflect a population that had shifted to living scattered across the landscape rather than huddled in large villages.

FIGURE 7.19 Neolithic ceramics. 1: Unpainted jar. 2–5: Sherds of vessels with red painted decoration. Note the incised decoration on 4. 6: Sherd of a black burnished vessel.

▲▲ **Çatalhöyük** A Late Neolithic site in Turkey that includes rooms decorated with elaborate frescoes.

FIGURE 7.20 Fresco painted onto a plaster wall at the site of Çatalhöyük. How would you describe the interaction between the human figures and the large bull at the center?

The symbolic system of the Early Neolithic seems to have collapsed along with the settlement system by the time of the Late Neolithic. Among the most striking symbolic artifacts of the Late Neolithic are small figurines that tend to be of stylized humans rather than animals. Skull removal and ornamentation is not found on Late Neolithic sites.

In central and western Turkey, there is a continuity in dense village settlement through the Late Neolithic. It is during this period that the settlement of **Çatalhöyük** developed on the Konya Plain of central Turkey. Excavations at the site have revealed a densely occupied settlement dating between 9,000 and 8,000 years ago (Cessford 2001; Mellaart 1967). The excavations at Çatalhöyük uncovered a series of rooms richly decorated with frescoes depicting scenes of leopards, bulls, and goddesses, as well as geometric designs. A particularly striking image found in these rooms is that of vultures, at times depicted circling around headless human figures. Figure 7.20 shows a fresco from Çatalhöyük that depicts a large bull surrounded by human figures. Bulls' heads and other figures were often modeled in relief, and bulls' horns were set into the plaster bulls' heads. Arrangements of bulls' horns were also found on benches running through the rooms, and human burials were commonly found beneath the benches.

James Mellaart, the first excavator of the site, interpreted the decorated rooms at Çatalhöyük as shrines or temples. This interpretation is consistent with that of Pre-Pottery Neolithic B structures from sites such as Göbekli Tepe and Navali Çori. However, of the 139 rooms Mellaart excavated, more than 40 were interpreted as shrines. It appears that ritual spaces at Çatalhöyük were widely distributed. Alternatively, it could be that the structures Mellaart interpreted as shrines were actually houses and that ritual and elaborate symbolism were an integral part of daily activity rather than something set apart.

The actual interpretation of the symbolism found at Çatalhöyük has provided rich grounds for speculation. The discovery of a significant number of goddess figurines at the site has drawn the attention of archaeologists who argue that Neolithic society was focused on a goddess cult. Çatalhöyük has attracted the attention of Ian Hodder, who has reopened excavations at the site in order to gain a broader contextual understanding of the ritual activity and symbolism.

■ Domestication

During the Late Neolithic, there is a continuous decline in the role of hunting for subsistence. Evidence of the domestication of animals during the Late Neolithic includes changes in the shape of horns in goats. A recent study has found that even at Çatalhöyük, despite the heavy symbolic emphasis on bulls, the main source of meat was domestic goats. Late Neolithic societies also continue to rely on the full range of plants domesticated during the Early Neolithic.

7.6 Assessing the Neolithic Revolution

The evidence from the Middle East demonstrates that there is a great deal of value in Childe's concept of a Neolithic Revolution. By the end of the Pre-Pottery Neolithic B, every aspect of life in the Middle East had been transformed as a result of the adoption of a village farming way of life. However, the shift to agriculture in the Middle East was not a sudden process as predicted by Childe. Rather, the beginning of the shift dates back to the Natufian period with the construction of small settlements, which then grew during the Pre-Pottery Neolithic A phase of the Early Neolithic, when there is evidence of community planning and monumental architecture. The people who lived during this phase had begun to rely heavily on cereals, but had not domesticated either plants or animals. Plant and animal domestication began in the Pre-Pottery Neolithic B phase of the Early Neolithic, together with an increase in the size and density of settlements. Pottery was introduced only in the Late Neolithic, when there was a *decrease* in the size and density of settlements in much of the region.

The Middle East affords important insights into the reasons for the adoption of agriculture. There is some evidence that the climatic stress of the Younger Dryas corresponding to the end of the Natufian and the beginning of the Pre-Pottery Neolithic A was a trigger in the development of villages. Most strikingly, agriculture developed as a consequence of people living in villages. In other words, villages preceded agriculture in the Middle East.

7.7 The Spread of Agriculture to Europe

In classic fictional mysteries, all of the clues are exposed, but the pattern stubbornly refuses to emerge. The spread of agriculture from the Middle East is as obvious and elusive as any work of fiction. The facts are clear. The origins of European domesticated plants and animals can be traced to the Middle East. There is no evidence of indigenous domestication of plants and animals. Instead, the spread of the Middle Eastern domesticates can be tracked as they move across Europe in what some archaeologists characterize as a "Wave of Advance" (Renfrew 1990). By 8,500 years ago, domesticated plants and animals had begun to spread into southeastern Europe. Around 7,500 years ago, farming spread into central and western Europe. By 6,000 years ago, people in most of western Europe, including southern Scandinavia, Britain, and Ireland, were practicing agriculture.

The clarity of the pattern has led many archaeologists to claim that a massive movement of populations is the explanation for the spread of agriculture into Europe. According to this perspective, incoming farmers gradually replaced the hunter-gatherer societies of Europe. The driving force behind the expansion is thought to be the population increase associated with farming. One fascinating line of research links the expansion of populations of farmers into Europe with the spread of the Indo-European language family. Indo-European languages include all the European romance languages, such as French, Portuguese, Italian, and Spanish; the Germanic languages, such as English, German, and Dutch; the Slavic languages, such as Russian, Polish, and Czech; Asian languages such as Farsi, Hindi, and Bengali; several Baltic and Balkan languages, such as Latvian, Lithuanian, and Albanian; and a number of more dispersed languages, such as Sanskrit and the ancient language Hittite, spoken in the area that is now Turkey. The **language dispersal hypothesis**, as this idea has come to be known, views the spread of agriculture as the movement of people carrying with them an entire way of life, including farming, religion, and language (Renfrew 1990).

language dispersal hypothesis
The theory that the spread of agriculture across Europe was the result of the migration of farmers who spoke Indo-European languages.

The language dispersal hypothesis is a bold concept, reminiscent of the out of Africa hypothesis discussed in Chapter 5. Farming is linked with people and language. The spread of agriculture into Europe involves the replacement of hunter-gatherers by farmers. In this model, the hunter-gatherers emerge as passive and defenseless in the face of the gradual wave of advancing farmers.

However, there is increasing evidence that the millennia leading up to the shift to agriculture saw dramatic shifts in European hunter-gatherer societies that preceded the arrival of farming. These societies, collectively labeled as Mesolithic, practiced a broad spectrum adaptation similar to that found in the Natufian of the Middle East (Perlès 2001). In the Mesolithic levels of the Franchthi Cave, Greece, occupied around 11,000 years ago, there is evidence that the occupants hunted red deer, cattle, and pigs and also collected land snails and shellfish. Wild plants, including pistachios, almonds, pears, wild oats, and wild barley, were also collected. There is also evidence of long-distance sea travel. Obsidian was brought to the site from the island of Melos, a 100-kilometer sea voyage from the mainland. Tuna are also found in large quantities, indicating offshore fishing.

Paleoenvironmental studies along the coast of England are producing strong evidence that Mesolithic hunter-gatherers used fire to shape their landscape (Brown 2005). Charcoal is ubiquitous in sediment profiles dating to the period of Mesolithic occupation. The prevalence of charcoal cannot be explained on the basis of natural phenomena such as lightning strikes. Similar use of fire by Australian hunter-gatherers is known as fire-stick farming (see the discussion on p. 156). Burning would have increased the fodder available to wild animals, which could then be hunted, and would also have increased the availability of wild plants for collecting. The evidence of burning by Mesolithic hunter-gatherers in England muddies the clarity of the division between hunter-gatherers and farmers. Clearly, the hunter-gatherers in what is now England were capable of actively manipulating aspects of their environment.

The most impressive Mesolithic site is **Lepenski Vir**, located next to a whirlpool in the Iron Gates gorges of the Danube River in Serbia. Lepenski Vir consists of a series of trapezoid-shaped structures associated with a large number of burials and sculptures that mix human and fish attributes (see Figure 7.21). Untangling the relationship among the sculptures, burials, and other household features such as hearths remains a major challenge (Boric 2005; Srejovic 1972). The Danube would have been a rich source of fish, particularly sturgeon, and it is not surprising that the faunal remains from the earliest levels are dominated by fish bones. In the final stages of occupation, there appears to have been a shift to increased reliance on hunting deer. The dates for the occupation of Lepenski Vir range between 8,400 and 7,600 years ago. These dates overlap with the time of the arrival of Neolithic agriculturalists, indicating that in the later phases of the village the Mesolithic hunter-gatherers of Lepenski Vir lived alongside farming communities.

Domesticated plants and animals spread into Europe from the Middle East. However, there is also little doubt that the Mesolithic societies were capable of adopting these plants and animals into their broad spectrum adaptations. Genetic studies of skeletal remains found on European archaeological sites indicate that the spread of agriculture into Europe involved the influx of new populations, but also that there was not a simple replacement of Mesolithic hunter-gatherers (Fu et al. 2012). Analysis of Mesolithic hunter-gatherer skeletons shows a dominance of a single line of descent known as Haplogroup U. Haplogroup U is present among European Neolithic samples but is found in lower frequency, while another line of descent known as Haplogroup H is dominant. Haplogroup H is completely absent from the Mesolithic sample. These data indicate the influx of a new population with

FIGURE 7.21 Fish-like sculpture from the Mesolithic site of Lepenski Vir

the onset of the Neolithic, as indicated by the appearance of Haplogroup H, that did not completely replace the Mesolithic population, as indicated by the persistence of Haplogroup U.

The farming communities that emerged around 7,200 years ago in central and western Europe are known as the **Linear Band Keramik**, or LBK, culture. LBK societies cultivated Middle Eastern plants and herded Middle Eastern animals, but they lived in communities unlike any found in the Middle East. LBK villages consist of longhouses built of massive timbers. The houses reached up to 30 meters in length. LBK houses are evidence of far more than simply changes in technology or construction. The large size of these houses must reflect the nature of the households that lived in them, suggesting that during the LBK period extended kinship groups lived together.

Wooden-lined wells are a striking feature found at a number of LBK sites (Tegel et al. 2012). At Altscherbitz, Germany, it was possible to use 3D laser scanning of individual worked planks to reconstruct the complex carpentry involved in building the well lining (Figure 7.22). At the bottom of the Altscherbitz well, shown in Figure 7.23, there was extraordinary preservation of plant remains, including einkorn and emmer wheat, peas, lentils, and linseed (used for oil). There were also wild fruits, including strawberries, apples, and raspberries, and hazelnuts, along with black henbane, which is a strong hallucinogenic.

Excavations on LBK sites have produced graphic evidence of warfare that resulted in mass killings, suggesting that this new agricultural way of life included a high level of violence. At **Talheim** in southern Germany a large pit was found with the remains of 11 men, 7 women, and 16 children. Blows to the head had killed 20 of these people, and 2 adults had been shot in the head by arrows. At Schöneck-Kilianstädten, also in Germany, the bodies of 26 individuals were found in a trench in the middle of the village (Meyer et al. 2015). The skeletons show evidence of blunt force trauma to the head and arrow injuries. Young females were absent, perhaps indicating these members of the community were abducted. There is also evidence that the victims' legs were broken in acts of systematic torture or mutilation.

In September 1991, two hikers discovered a corpse stuck in the ice in the Alps near the Austrian-Italian border. Subsequent investigation showed that their find was no ordinary corpse: It was the mummified remains of a man who had died on this spot near the end of the Neolithic period, slightly over 5,000 years ago (Spindler 1994) (see Figure 7.24). His body and clothing had been preserved under the ice, providing a unique perspective on aspects of Neolithic culture that are rarely preserved. He wore a cap, a shirt, and leggings made of fur; a loincloth and shoes made of leather; and a grass cloak. He carried a bag with embers to start fires, as well as what are apparently medicinal plants. His gear included a retoucher to repair his flint tools as needed. His skin bears tattoos on his wrist, spine, knee, calf foot, and ankle.

Since his discovery, Ötzi the Iceman, as he came to be known, has been the subject of

Linear Band Keramik The culture of the earliest farming communities that emerged around 7,200 years ago in central and western Europe; also referred to as LBK culture.

▲▲ **Talheim** An LBK site in Germany where a pit containing a mass grave was discovered.

FIGURE 7.22 3D reconstruction of the Neolithic well at Altscherbitz based on laser scans of the individual worked planks

FIGURE 7.23 Organic remains and broken ceramic vessels at the base of the Neolithic well at Altscherbitz

FIGURE 7.24 Dagger and scabbard found with Otzi the Iceman. Note the remarkable preservation of wood and organic material.

what is perhaps the most detailed study any human body has received. Not even the single fingernail that survived has escaped scrutiny. Analysis of the fingernail found evidence of periods of stress in the months before the Iceman died. Sequencing of his DNA shows that he was lactose intolerant (Keller et al. 2012).

Yet as the details build up, an air of mystery still surrounds the Iceman. Who was he, and why was he up in the mountains? Was he a shepherd? A shaman? An outcast? There are many clues, but no clear answers. We do know that he experienced violence immediately before his death: An arrowhead was found lodged in his left shoulder, and he appears to have incurred a deep slash wound to one of his hands a few days before he died (Nerlich et al. 2003). One possibility is that he fled to the mountains to escape an attack on his village, perhaps an attack like the event that produced the mass graves at Talheim and Schöneck-Kilianstädten.

■ Summing Up the Evidence

LBK culture is highly uniform across its entire distribution and appears to have spread across Europe very rapidly (Dolukhanov et al. 2005). Those who view agriculture as the expansion of populations point to these features and argue that the LBK is best explained as the result of people moving with their way of life. However, the novelty of LBK community structure suggests that it represents a local innovation rather than an idea that came with new groups of people. This new way of life also appears to have brought with it an intensification of warfare and violence.

SUMMARY

- There is no evidence for the domestication of plants or animals during the Kebaran and Geometric Kebaran periods.
- Excavation of the waterlogged site of Ohalo in the Sea of Galilee has revealed the remains of a series of brush huts.
- The characteristic stone tool of the Natufian period is the lunate, a small, crescent-shaped bladelet. Some lunates have sickle polish. Other characteristic Natufian artifacts include decorated ground stone artifacts and shell beads.
- Natufian sites include the remains of circular stone-built structures and burials.
- There is no evidence of the domestication of plants from the Natufian period. Dogs were the only animal domesticated during the period.
- During the Early Neolithic, large settled villages developed. Some of these sites show evidence of large communal structures, such as the tower at Jericho and the semi-subterranean buildings at Jerf el Ahmar.
- Numerous ritual objects, including plastered human skulls, are found on Early Neolithic sites.

- Plant domestication developed sometime in the Early Neolithic during the Pre-Pottery Neolithic B period. Among the plants domesticated were wheat, barley, lentils, peas, bitter vetch, and chickpeas.
- The domestication of sheep and goats developed during the Early Neolithic, after the domestication of plants.
- The earliest pottery is found in the Late Neolithic.
- There was a reduction in the number of large village sites across much of the Middle East during the Late Neolithic.
- In contrast to the general pattern, the site of Çatalhöyük in Turkey developed into a major center during the Late Neolithic Period.
- The origin of agriculture in Europe is based on the adoption of Middle Eastern domesticated plants and animals.
- The distinctive site structure of the Linear Band Keramik early agricultural villages suggests a shift not only in technology but also in social structure.
- There is significant evidence for violence and warfare found on Linear Band Keramik sites.

KEY TERMS

Abu Hureyra, 196
Çatalhöyük, 206
Fertile Crescent, 190
Jerf el Ahmar, 198
Jericho tower, 197
language dispersal hypothesis, 207
Lepenski Vir, 208
Linear Band Keramik, 209
lunate, 194

Mallaha, 194
Natufian, 194
Netiv Hagdud, 197
Ohalo, 192
plastered skulls, 200
rachis, 202
Talheim, 209
Younger Dryas, 195

REVIEW QUESTIONS

1. Can the development of agriculture in the Middle East be described as a "Neolithic Revolution"?
2. In what ways does the Natufian period differ from the preceding Kebaran and Geometric Kebaran periods?

3. What is the evidence and significance of ritual behavior during the Early Neolithic?
4. What are the opposing views of how agriculture came to be adopted in Europe? Why is the LBK significant to this debate?

MOUNDS AND MAIZE

Maize was domesticated in Mesoamerica and was subsequently adopted by societies throughout the Americas. After reading this chapter, you should understand:

- The archaeological record of the domestication of maize, beans, and squash in Mesoamerica.

- The impact of the adoption of maize agriculture on the Archaic societies of the southwestern United States and northern Mexico.

- The complex interaction between the indigenous domestication of plants and the adoption of maize in eastern North America.

- The context of the mound construction of the Adena and Hopewell cultures.

Engraving by Theodor De Bry of the Algonquin village of Secotan, printed in 1590

8 TIMELINE

 SITES

Guilá Naquiz
domesticated squash

ARCHEOLOGICAL
PERIODS

thousands of years ago 10   9   8   7

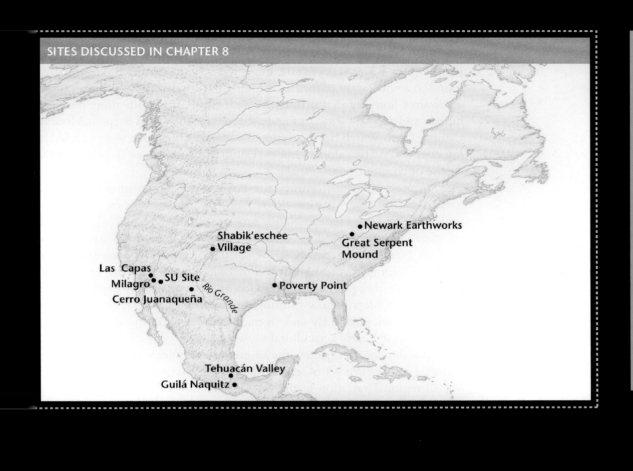

SITES DISCUSSED IN CHAPTER 8

- Newark Earthworks
- Shabik'eschee Village
- Great Serpent Mound
- Las Capas
- SU Site
- Milagro
- Cerro Juanaqueña
- Rio Grande
- Poverty Point
- Tehuacán Valley
- Guilá Naquitz

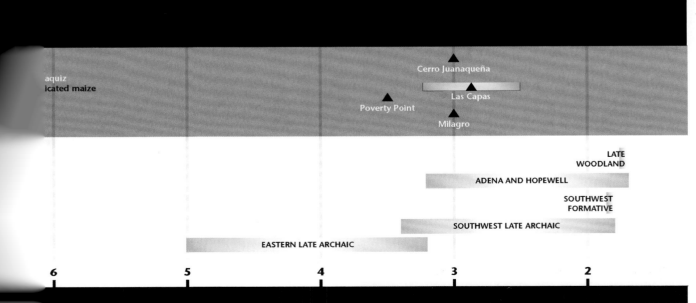

aquiz
icated maize

Cerro Juanaqueña

Las Capas

Poverty Point

Milagro

LATE WOODLAND

ADENA AND HOPEWELL

SOUTHWEST FORMATIVE

SOUTHWEST LATE ARCHAIC

EASTERN LATE ARCHAIC

6   5   4   3   2

As European settlers spread westward across North America, they encountered the remains of massive artificial earthworks (Silverberg 1986). These monuments of a remote and mysterious past fired the imagination of colonial Americans. The earthworks were astonishing in their size and density. One mound at Miamisburg, Ohio, was 20 meters high and 200 meters in circumference. In the Ohio River Valley alone, there were 10,000 mounds. The earthworks were found in a wide array of forms, including flat-topped mounds, conical mounds, and enclosures. Some of the earthworks, such as the Wisconsin effigy mounds, included human and animal forms. In Figure 8.1, we see the Great Serpent Mound in Adams County, Ohio, which has the figure of an undulating snake with a curled tail stretching over 200 meters along a hill overlooking Brush Creek (Squier and Davis 1848). At the open mouth of the snake is an oval mound.

In the nineteenth century, the belief was widespread that the earthworks of eastern North America were the remains of a mysterious race of mound builders with no relation to modern Native Americans (Silverberg 1986). The mound builders were often portrayed as "civilized" in contrast to the perceived "savagery" of modern Native Americans. Theories of the origins of the mound builders ranged from the Vikings to the Lost Tribes of Israel. The fate of the mound builders was imagined as either migration to Mexico or defeat in bloody battle. The idea of a race of mound builders is now thoroughly discredited. Rather than searching for lost tribes, archaeologists today seek to trace the economic and social context of mound building among early agricultural societies.

It is difficult to organize the origins of agriculture in Mesoamerica and North America into a clear set of stages. The picture that emerges from recent research is one of regional variation in the pathways taken in the shift to an agricultural way of life. Perhaps the most surprising development is the genetic and archaeological evidence that suggests that domesticated bottle gourds are found in the Americas as early as 10,000 years ago (Erickson 2005), although a more recent analysis suggests the equally surprising scenario that wild bottle gourds floated to South America

FIGURE 8.1 The Great Serpent Mound, Ohio

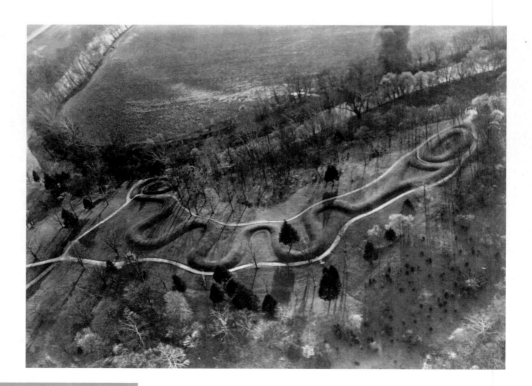

from Africa and were subsequently domesticated (Kistler et al. 2014). In this chapter, we begin in Mesoamerica before moving to the American Southwest and then to eastern North America. Mesoamerica has been studied primarily as the area where major food crops, including maize, squash, and beans, were domesticated. The development of new dating methods has radically altered the chronology for the domestication of these plants. Although we know quite a bit about the timing of crop domestication, many questions linger. Currently, we know little about the social context of domestication in Mesoamerica.

The uptake of maize agriculture in the American Southwest was geographically variable. In some areas, large villages with features such as terrace walls and irrigation canals appeared at the same time as the first domesticated maize. However, in other parts of the Southwest, the impact of maize agriculture was minimal. In explaining this variation, archaeologists working in the American Southwest have emphasized the ecological variability of the region and have developed models based on optimal foraging theory.

In eastern North America, we trace a complex situation involving the local domestication of plants, followed by the addition of maize to an already established farming way of life. Archaeologists in eastern North America have struggled to explain the early and pervasive appearance of earthen mounds long before the appearance of large villages. In grappling with the social meaning of these monuments, archaeologists have drawn on a variety of theoretical frameworks, including agency theory.

We end the chapter by following a debate among archaeologists working in eastern North America over the question of who actually domesticated plants. The context for this debate is feminist archaeology, but the questions raised go to the very core of the origins of agriculture.

8.1 Plant Domestication in Mesoamerica

The Pueblo societies of the American Southwest express the centrality of maize or corn to both their subsistence and their spiritual life with the simple phrase "Corn is our mother" (Ford 1994). Maize plays a similar central role in many indigenous farming communities throughout the Americas. Archaeologists and botanists have traced the origins of maize back to **teosinte**, a wild grass found in the highlands of Mexico. Teosinte produces two rows of small, triangular-shaped seeds encased in a thick glume (see Figure 8.2). Maize seeds are usually several times larger than teosinte seeds and grow in four or more rows (Harlan 1995). Teosinte also differs from corn in that the rachis, the part of the plant that holds the seeds, is brittle, so the seeds disperse at maturity.

The identification of teosinte as the wild ancestor of maize has been the subject of debate. However, the genetic relation between the two plants is now well established. It is even possible that the shift from the one to the other took place rapidly (Eubanks 2001). Genetic analysis of modern populations of maize suggests that there was a single center of domestication for this crop, probably located in the highlands of Mexico (Matsuoka et al. 2002).

Archaeological research on the origins of agriculture in Mesoamerica has focused on the excavation of dry caves in the highlands of Mexico, where plant remains are well preserved. The picture that has emerged from the cave excavations is that plants, including maize, squash, and beans, were domesticated in Mexico by groups of mobile hunter-gatherers. The domestication of plants appears to have had little effect on these societies beyond providing an additional resource for

teosinte A wild grass found in the highlands of Mexico; the wild ancestor of maize.

FIGURE 8.2 Wild teosinte with two rows of small triangular seeds

subsistence. However, it is possible that the archaeological emphasis on highland caves has biased our understanding of the impact of agriculture.

Excavations by Richard MacNeish in a series of caves in the Tamaulipas Mountains and in the **Tehuacán Valley** and by Kent Flannery at the cave site of **Guilá Naquitz** in the Oaxaca Valley have produced a long record of occupation by prehistoric hunter-gatherers who gradually incorporated domesticated plants into their subsistence base. The highland valleys of Tehuacán (1,000–1,500 meters above sea level) and Oaxaca (2,000 meters above sea level), shown in Figure 8.3, might not be the actual location where any of the Mesoamerican crop species were initially domesticated (Piperno and Flannery 2001). The sites were chosen for excavation because of their long sequences of occupation and excellent preservation of plant remains.

The identifiable plant remains excavated at the highland dry cave sites are too small to be dated directly with conventional radiocarbon dating methods. However, it was possible to date other organic remains, such as wood charcoal, and to build an absolute chronology of the stratigraphic sequence. The age of identifiable plant remains was then determined based on the level in which they were recovered.

The stratigraphic sequences at Guilá Naquitz and the Tehuacán Valley sites are relatively shallow and compacted. At Guilá Naquitz, five levels were identified. The top of the sequence is Zone A, a 20-centimeter-thick level dated to a little over 1,000 years ago. Below Zone A is a series of levels labeled Zone B to Zone E, which date between 12,700 and 7,800 years ago. The entire thickness of Zone B to Zone E is approximately 60 centimeters, covering a period of over 4,000 years (Flannery 1986). When one considers that plant remains are often extremely small and deposits shallow, it is perhaps not surprising that the stratigraphic method of dating plant remains from dry caves has turned out not to be dependable.

The development of **Accelerator Mass Spectrometry (AMS) radiocarbon dating** has made it possible to date identifiable plant remains. When plant remains from Guilá Naquitz and the Tehuacán Valley are directly dated using AMS radiocarbon dating, the ages obtained are often different (in most cases, younger) than what is expected based on the age of the level from which the sample was recovered.

On the basis of AMS radiocarbon dating, squash has been identified as the earliest plant to be domesticated in Mexico. The type of squash domesticated in Mesoamerica, *Curcubita pepo*, is the ancestor of the vast array of squash we eat today, including pumpkin, zucchini, and acorn, marrow, and spaghetti squash. Squash seeds recovered from Zones C and B at Guilá Naquitz have been directly dated to between 10,000 and 8,300 years ago (Smith 1997). The seeds are larger than those of wild squash. The thickness and color of the rind also distinguish the domesticated variety

FIGURE 8.3 The landscape in the highlands of the Oaxaca Valley from the wild one. It is only in Zone B, which dates to around 8,000 years ago, that there is an increase in the thickness of the squash rinds and a change in color from green to orange. On the basis of these results, it appears that the domestication of squash was a prolonged process that began 10,000 years ago with selection for larger seeds. Over the next 2,000 years, farmers selected for an increase in the thickness of the rind and a change in its color.

The oldest directly dated maize was also found at Guilá Naquitz. The stratigraphic context for these maize samples is an ephemeral occupation between Zone A and Zone B. Two fragments of maize cobs from this context were directly dated to 6,250 years ago. The maize from Guilá Naquitz has a tough rachis and is thus clearly domesticated. It is interesting that one cob has two rows, like teosinte, while the other has four rows, as is found in most maize.

The earliest maize from the Tehuacán Valley, directly dated to 5,500 years ago, is of the four-row variety. The long sequence from the Tehuacán Valley sites illustrates a gradual increase through time in the size of the cobs and the number of kernels.

Studies of modern domesticated beans suggest that both common beans and lima beans were domesticated independently in the Andes and Mesoamerica (Smith 1995). The oldest direct date on a domesticated bean from Mexico is approximately 2,500 years ago, for a single bean from Coxcatlán Cave in the Tehuacán Valley. It is likely that beans were domesticated at a far earlier date, possibly at the same time as maize. Chili peppers were domesticated in either central or eastern Mexico but the timing of domestication remains unclear (Kraft et al. 2014).

Turkeys were the only animals domesticated in Mesoamerica. It is unclear when the domestication of turkeys took place.

8.2 Maize Agriculture in the American Southwest

Domesticated maize was grown in the highlands of Mexico by 6,250 years ago. Maize and squash agriculture spread to northern Mexico and the southwestern United States during the Southwestern Late Archaic period (ca. 3,400 years ago) (Cordell 1997). The initial impact of maize and squash agriculture varied across the region. In some areas, there is evidence of increased sedentism, while in others, it appears that agriculture did not substantially alter the lives of Late Archaic hunter-gatherers.

On a steep hill overlooking the Río Casas Grandes in northwest Chihuahua, Mexico, near the New Mexico border, archaeologists have found dramatic evidence that some Late Archaic farmers shifted to village life (Hard and Roney 1998). At the site of **Cerro Juanaqueña**, archaeologists have traced over 8 kilometers of terrace walls and 100 rock rings. Although the construction of these features is simple, it represents a considerable investment of energy. The excavators estimate that the construction of the walls found at the site involved moving 20,000 metric tons of rock and soil, which would have taken 16 person-years of labor.

Excavation of three of the stone circles at Cerro Juanaqueña has failed to yield evidence of their function. Excavation of the terraces has yielded a wide array of domestic debris, including ground stone and chipped stone tools, ashy soil, and burnt and unburnt animal bones. On one terrace, postholes outlining the remains of a structure were found. The excavators believe that the function of the terraces was to provide a level surface for the construction of houses. Four maize kernels from Cerro Juanaqueña have been directly AMS radiocarbon dated to an average date of 3,070 years ago. The arrowheads found at the site are forms belonging to the Late Archaic, which is consistent with the radiocarbon dates.

▲▲ **Cerro Juanaqueña** An early agricultural site in northern Mexico with extensive evidence of terracing and other stone-built features.

TOOLBOX

AMS Radiocarbon Dating

In previous chapters, the basic methods of radiocarbon dating and calibration were introduced. The principles of radiocarbon dating are that (1) the ratio between radioactive carbon-14 and stable carbon atoms is constant throughout the carbon exchange reservoir, which includes the atmosphere, the oceans, and the biosphere; and (2) carbon-14 decays at a known rate. When an organism dies, it is removed from the carbon exchange reservoir, and the concentration of carbon-14 in the remains of the organism decreases at a fixed rate. By measuring the concentration of radiocarbon in a sample, it is possible to calculate the time since the death of the organism. Calibration becomes necessary because the concentration of carbon-14 in the global carbon reservoir fluctuates over time.

But how is the concentration of carbon-14 measured? The initial method was to measure the radioactivity of a sample as an indirect measure of its carbon-14 concentration. The problem with this method is that the concentration of carbon-14 in the carbon reservoir is very low. Therefore, in order to measure the carbon-14, large samples are needed. Thus, there was a limitation on the type of samples that could be dated. Also, very old samples in which most of the carbon-14 had already decayed could not be dated.

Accelerator Mass Spectrometry (AMS) radiocarbon dating is a solution to this problem. AMS radiocarbon dating combines ingenuity and power to directly count the carbon isotopes in a sample. The first step in developing AMS radiocarbon dating draws on the following principle of physics: When an electrically charged particle travels through a magnetic field, it follows a curved path, and the amount of curvature is related to the mass of the particle. Specifically, the lower the mass, the greater the curvature. Using this method, a scientist should be able to take a sample of (radioactive) carbon-14 mixed with nonradioactive carbon-13 and carbon-12 isotopes (which are lighter than carbon-14), sort them into separate streams, and literally count their atoms. However, to count the small number of carbon-14 atoms, tremendous energy is needed, so an atomic accelerator is used to blast the carbon-14 atoms through the system at an acceleration of 8 million volts.

The impact of AMS radiocarbon dating has been almost as dramatic as the initial impact of radiocarbon dating. It is now possible to directly date small samples, including seeds and residues. Samples can be dated more quickly than with conventional methods, and in some cases, it is possible to date very old samples in which the surviving concentration of carbon-14 is extremely low. ●

FIGURE 8.4 Diagram of an accelerator used for AMS radiocarbon dating. Note how different isotopes of carbon are separated at the end of the line.

Although a small amount of maize has been found in excavations at Cerro Juanaqueña, seeds from wild plants, including chenopodium, gourds, and grasses, dom-
inate the plant remains found on the site. The faunal remains indicate that animals
such as jackrabbit, cottontail rabbit, mule deer, and pronghorn antelope were hunted.
There is no evidence of significant fishing, despite the proximity of the site to the
Río Casas Grandes. Almost 600 grinding slabs and basins have been found, indicating
that grinding seeds or grain was a very important activity at the site. The only pottery
found is from later occupations limited to two small areas of the site. Three additional
large Late Archaic sites have been reported in the vicinity of Cerro Juanaqueña.

Moving to the northeast from Cerro Juanaqueña, archaeologists have found
that people living in the Jornada Mogollon region along the Río Grande did not
significantly engage in agriculture until A.D. 1000. There is a 2,000-year gap in
the onset of agriculture over a distance of less than 100 kilometers between the
Río Casas Grandes, where Cerro Juanaqueña is located, and the Jornada Mogollon
region. Robert Hard and John Roney (2005) explain this pattern in terms of **optimal foraging theory**. According to this theory, humans act on the basis of rational
self-interest to maximize efficiency in collecting and processing resources. Hard
and Roney argue that, in the Río Casas Grandes region, maize agriculture offered
a higher rate of return than many low-ranked resources that were exploited during
the Late Archaic, such as grama grass and dropseed grass. These grasses are described
as low-ranked resources because they offer little return of energy for the input of
energy required to collect and process them. The Jornada region has lower rainfall
than the Río Casas Grandes, resulting in low returns and high risk for maize agriculture. At the same time, the availability of shrubs such as mesquite and saltbush, as
well as other plants, offered resources with higher rates of return. Optimal foraging
explains the early uptake of maize agriculture at Cerro Juanaqueña as the result of
rational decision making based on the available resources. The delay in the development of maize agriculture in the Jornada region was the result of similar rational
decisions, reflecting differences in local ecology.

Maize agriculture associated with large settlements
is also found in the area around Tucson, Arizona. At the
Milagro site, the Late Archaic people lived in pit houses
and appear to have stored maize in bell-shaped pits. The
plant remains recovered at Milagro include domesticated
maize, along with wild plants such as amaranth, chenopod, and grass seeds. The faunal remains recovered at the
site include jackrabbit and possibly deer. Two radiocarbon
dates place the occupation of Milagro at 2,950 years ago.

Large-scale cultural resource management projects
outside Tucson have produced spectacular insights into
the agricultural settlements of the Late Archaic period
(Mabry 2005). Terrace walls associated with maize remains
have been excavated at the Tumamoc Hill site. At the **Las
Capas** site, a sequence of canals was discovered dating
to between 3,250 and 2,500 years ago (Figure 8.5). The
canals carried water at least 2 kilometers from the Santa
Cruz River to irrigated fields. These features indicate that
the adoption of maize agriculture in this region involved a
significant investment of labor. Some of the sites excavated
in the area around Tucson include over 100 pit houses
(although not all of these were occupied simultaneously),
as well as large communal structures. Figure 8.6 shows a

optimal foraging theory A theory
based on the assumption that the
choices people make reflect rational
self-interest in maximizing efficiency
when collecting and processing
resources.

▲▲ **Milagro** An early agricultural
village located outside Tucson,
Arizona.

▲▲ **Las Capas** A site near Tucson,
Arizona, where an Archaic village
and canal system have been
discovered.

FIGURE 8.5 Stratigraphic profile
at the Las Capas site showing the
section of an irrigation ditch. The
ditch is visible as a concave feature in
the dark sediments at the base of the
profile.

Irrigation
Ditch

FIGURE 8.6 View of the Las Capas site near Tucson, Arizona. The site is located on the median strip of a highway.

view of the structures excavated at the Las Capas site.

Maize agriculture spread to the higher altitudes of the Mogollon Highlands and the Colorado Plateau at roughly the same time as the occupation of Milagro and Cerro Juanaqueña. In these regions, the adoption of agriculture did not result in the development of villages (Plog 1997). However, the storage areas, garbage pits, and remains of fireplaces found in the excavation of cave sites indicate that the use of caves intensified with the adoption of agriculture (Cordell 1997).

Because of the dry conditions in the highland caves, the remains of basketry and other organic materials are superbly preserved. A particularly rich collection of organic remains was recovered at White Dog Cave, Arizona, named for one of the mummified dog burials found at the site (Cordell 1997; Kidder and Guernsey 1919). The organic artifacts recovered at White Dog Cave include a net made of fine fiber string that is over 200 meters long and 1 meter wide and a range of baskets decorated in woven or painted designs.

A number of human burials were also excavated at White Dog Cave. Women were buried with necklaces of beads made of stones, shells, and seeds. Men were buried without clothes, while women were buried in loose-fitting aprons made of soft fiber. Both men and women were buried wearing sandals made of yucca fiber and with robes made of animal skins. Babies were found wrapped in soft rabbit-skin blankets and diapers made from juniper bark. Mobile cradles for infants were also found at the site.

■ The Formative Period

Although some pottery, including figurines from Milagro and Las Capas and vessel fragments from Las Capas, has been found on Late Archaic sites, the widespread introduction of pottery into the American Southwest occurred around 1,800 years ago at the beginning of the Formative period. It is interesting that the introduction of pottery overlaps with the introduction of domesticated beans in this region. By this time, sites with architecture in the form of pit houses are common across the Southwest. These houses were usually square or rectangular and were excavated as much as 1 to 2 meters below the surface (Plog 1997). The superstructure was usually built of wooden beams, brush, and soil.

The number of houses found on Formative-period sites varies from 1 or 2 to as many as 25 to 35. Although storage pits are common on most sites, their placement varies (Plog 1997). The Shabik'eschee Village site in Chaco Canyon, New Mexico, is an unusually large one where the remains of 60 pit houses have been excavated. There is some question whether the entire site was occupied at any one time (Wills and Windes 1989). A large number of carefully constructed storage pits were found at Shabik'eschee, all located outside the houses.

The SU site in central New Mexico is a large Formative-period settlement with 40 pit houses. At this site, the storage pits are located inside the houses. The contrast between the location of storage pits in Shabik'eschee Village and that at the SU site has been interpreted as reflecting differences in the ownership of food stores. The placement of pits outside houses suggests communal ownership; the placement of pits inside suggests household ownership.

At both Shabik'eschee Village and the SU site, unusual structures were found that appear to have played a communal function. At Shabik'eschee Village, one structure was five times the size of other pit houses and was surrounded by a bench. At the SU site, one structure was unusually large and lacked the internal storage pits found in other structures.

Regional variation in the impact of maize agriculture in the American Southwest continued into the Formative period. In Utah, the Fremont culture, dated between A.D. 700 and A.D. 1200, challenges archaeologists to explain the variations in adaptation after the introduction of maize agriculture. What is particularly striking about the Fremont is "the diversity it presents in the importance of maize farming relative to hunting and gathering" (Barlow 2002, 68). Renee Barlow has analyzed the yield of maize agriculture practiced by modern Guatemalans using traditional methods and has come to the conclusion that intensive agriculture produces little food in return for the energy expended in growing, collecting, and processing the plants. Less formal methods of maize agriculture, in which fields rotate frequently, produce a lower total yield, but a greater yield per unit of energy expended. On the basis of optimal foraging theory, Barlow suggests that Fremont farmers adapted the intensity of their reliance on maize agriculture to the availability of other, higher-ranked food resources. When resources such as game or pine nuts were available, maize would be exploited using only low-yield methods, which require a low investment of energy. When highly ranked resources were scarce, intensive maize agriculture became worth the energy investment. The variation in the Fremont reflects the variation in rational choices made by people living in different ecological settings.

Locally domesticated turkeys are an interesting component of the fauna recovered from Formative sites in the Southwest (Lipe et al. 2016). Genetic analysis has identified a locally domesticated matrilineage, known as Haplogroup H1, that is distinct from both wild turkeys and the Mesoamerican domesticated turkeys. Turkeys were raised both as a source of food, perhaps as a response to the depletion of wild game as village size expanded, and also for their feathers, which were used for textiles. Isotope analysis of turkey bones shows that these animals were fed heavily on maize and illustrates the relationship between domesticated crops and animals. It is estimated that a turkey would have required a significant amount of maize, almost a third of what a person would need for their annual diet. Surprisingly, genetic analysis demonstrates that domesticated turkeys belonging to Haplogroup H1 were raised alongside wild turkeys belonging to a distinct lineage, Haplogroup H2. No differences were found in the treatment of wild and domesticated birds and they were all fed on a maize diet. Both lineages supplied birds that were used in ritual internments, as shown in Figure 8.7, that might have been spring rituals for the new harvest.

FIGURE 8.7 Turkey burials within a structure at the Champagne Spring site, Colorado

TOOLBOX

Hand-Built Pottery

The pottery produced by the indigenous societies of the American Southwest is the antithesis of modern mass-produced ceramics. The first step in producing hand-built pottery is to mine the clay and mix it with water. In some cases, inclusions such as sand, straw, or even crushed sherds of broken pots are added to the clay paste. Forming a vessel often begins by making a shallow bowl from a ball of clay. The walls of the vessel are then built up with either coils or slabs of clay. Next, a paddle may be used to smooth and sometimes thin the walls of the vessel. Afterward, the vessel is left to partially dry before surface decoration is added. Many fine-ware pots are dipped in a slip—a slurry of fine-grained clay, often mixed with iron-rich clay. A slip mixed with minerals can also be used to paint designs on pots. Pots can be polished by burnishing the semi-dry surface with a smooth stone that compresses the clay particles. After the surface of the vessel has been treated with slip, paint, or burnishing, the pot is again left to dry. Once completely dry, pots are stacked and heated in an open fire or in a kiln. If the fire is smothered and the pots are heated without access to oxygen, the surface will be black. If the fire is allowed to burn freely, the iron in the clay will oxidize, and the surface will be red.

Over the centuries during which southwestern potters have hand-built clay vessels, they have used these basic processes to produce a wide array of shapes and surface treatments. Many such vessels raise hand-built pottery to a fine art. The Mimbres potters created beautiful bowls with simple, yet powerful scenes painted in black against a white background. More recently, Pueblo potters have explored the range of surface treatments that can be achieved by combining burnishing with carefully controlled firing. Maria Martinez of the San Ildefonso Pueblo is among the most celebrated modern ceramic artists. Her creations include vessels with patterns formed by setting highly polished designs against a matte unpolished background. Many of these vessels are a deep black color, which is achieved by smothering the pot while it is firing. ●

FIGURE 8.8 A Mimbres bowl from New Mexico

■ Summing Up the Evidence

New discoveries have established the onset of intensive maize agriculture in northern Mexico and the American Southwest during the Late Archaic period, approximately 3,000 years ago. Agricultural societies lived in large villages and built large-scale features, including terraces and canals. However, the uptake of maize agriculture was not uniform across the region during the Late Archaic and in the Formative period. In responding to the challenge of understanding this diversity, archaeologists have turned to optimal foraging theory to explain the variation in adaptation as a rational response to differing ecological conditions.

The AMS radiocarbon dating of maize from the highland caves of Oaxaca and the Tehuacán Valley has shown that the time between the domestication of maize and its spread to northern Mexico and the American Southwest is shorter than had previously been thought. Some archaeologists have argued that the spread of maize

FIGURE 8.9 A: A pot made by Maria Martinez. The following photographs show the process she used to make this type of vessel. B: Preparing the clay. Notice the pots drying in the background. C: Using coils of clay to build up the vessel walls. D: Smoothing the vessel walls. E: Burnishing a pot with a smooth stone. F: Removing finished pots from the fire.

(top left): Maria Montoya and Julian Martinez (San Ildefonso Pueblo, Native American, ca. 1887–1980; 1879–1943). "Jar" ca. 1939. Blackware. 11? × 13 in. (dia.). The National Museum of Women in the Arts, Washington, DC. Gift of Wallace and Wilhelmina Holladay.

agriculture was the result of the movement of populations of farmers northward (Matson 2003). This is a controversial proposal, however—one that is difficult to assess on the basis of the available data.

8.3 Eastern North America

The development of agriculture in eastern North America involved both the domestication of a wide range of local plants and the adoption of maize. The initial domestication of plants in this area took place during the Eastern Late Archaic period (5,000 to 3,200 years ago). (For a discussion of other aspects of the Archaic period, see Chapter 6.) The intensification of agriculture and the first appearance of maize in the region occurred during the florescence of the Adena and Hopewell traditions of the Early and Middle Woodland period (3,200 to 1,700 years ago). However, maize played a minor role in people's diet, and settlements remained small and dispersed for almost 1,000 years after the plant was first adopted in eastern North America. Intensive maize agriculture and large settled villages became established only at the beginning of the Late Woodland period.

■ The Indigenous Domestication of Plants

A wide range of plants, including squash, chenopod, marsh elder, and sunflower, were domesticated by the Late Archaic hunter-gatherer groups of eastern North America (Smith and Cowan 2003). The domestication of squash in the region was independent of the earlier domestication of the plant in Mexico. Chenopodium was independently domesticated in South America, Mexico, and eastern North America. Eastern Late Archaic sites that have produced the remains of domesticated plants include both rock shelters and open-air sites. At the Riverton site in Illinois, remains of sunflower, chenopod, *C. pepo* squash, and bottle gourd were found in a site covering about 2 acres with extensive midden deposits. The excavations uncovered the remains of 10 clay floors of small structures (Smith 2011).

Along with the presence of domesticated plants, the Eastern Late Archaic is characterized by an increasingly narrow subsistence base, particularly in areas with rich supplies of shellfish. Large accumulations of discarded shells are found on sites known as **shell middens**. Some of these sites, such as the Indian Knoll site on the Green River

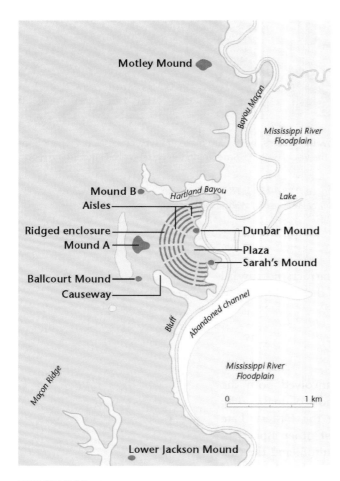

FIGURE 8.10 Plan of Poverty Point

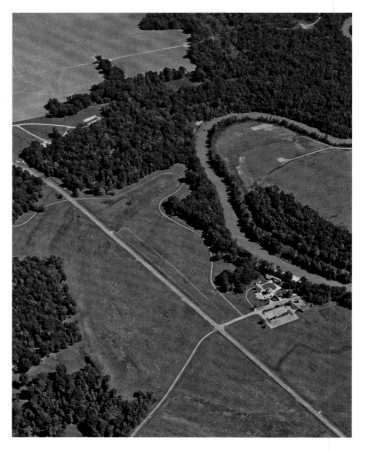

FIGURE 8.11 Oblique aerial view showing the semicircular rings at Poverty Point, Louisiana

in Kentucky, are quite large. At the Indian Knoll site, thousands of burials were recovered, along with the traces of structures built of posts (Brose, Brown, and Penney 1985).

Crude ceramic vessels first appeared in eastern North America 5,000 years ago in the Stalling Island culture of the Savannah River Valley, Georgia. The material culture of the Late Archaic also includes a wide range of ceremonial objects and ornaments. There is evidence of trade in various minerals, including galena (lead), hematite (iron oxide), jasper, native copper, and slate, over very long distances.

The Late Archaic **Poverty Point** site in Louisiana, dated to between 3,600 and 3,200 years ago, is a massive planned construction that raises many questions about subsistence and social organization during that period. The site consists of a series of six concentric embankments 2 meters high and over 20 meters across that form a semicircle more than 1 kilometer wide (Figure 8.10). Aerial photography (Figure 8.11) and Geographical Information System (GIS) analysis (Figure 8.12) provide a sense of how this site fits within the landscape. Along with the embankments, there is a series of massive mounds, some of which appear to be in the shape of birds.

The purpose of the embankments remains unclear. If they were house platforms, then Poverty Point was an extremely large, exquisitely planned village. However, plowing has largely removed any evidence that might have remained of houses. The density and diversity of cultural materials found on Poverty Point support the identification of the site as a village. Most of the finds are objects of daily life: net sinkers for fishing, stone tools for hunting animals and gathering plants, soapstone and pottery vessels, and more. But the most compelling evidence that Poverty Point was a village comes from the extensive deposits of refuse. As Jon Gibson (2000) summarizes the situation, "Claims that Poverty Point was a vacant ceremonial center are simply not tenable given the extensive midden and its secular-looking trash" (105).

Stones for tool manufacture are not available in the area around Poverty Point. It is therefore not surprising that stone tools were brought onto the site from

▲▲ Poverty Point A Late Archaic site in Louisiana with a series of six concentric embankments.

FIGURE 8.12 Perspective map of Poverty Point created using GIS software

nonlocal sources. However, the quantity of material and the distance to the sources are astounding. It has been estimated that 70 metric tons of stone were brought onto the site. The distance of the site from the sources of the material makes this figure even more staggering: Burlington chert and galena (lead) ore were brought from quarries near St. Louis, 450 miles from Poverty Point; hematite, crystal quartz, slate, volcanic rocks, and other minerals came from the Ouachita Mountains in Arkansas, 150 miles away; other types of chert came from Kentucky, 365 miles away; and soapstone came from Alabama and Georgia, 400 miles from Poverty Point. These distances are those of the most direct route; if people were traveling by river, then the figures would be roughly doubled.

The stones were brought to Poverty Point either as finished tools or as pieces that had been roughed out. Cherts were used for hunting points, hoes, and knives; hard minerals were used to make net sinkers for fishing; and soapstone was used for cooking vessels. In most cases, archaeologists expect to trace a "down the line" pattern for trade items, meaning that the quantity of a given item will decrease as the distance from the source increases. Generally, this rule works for the Late Archaic, but Poverty Point stands out from the pattern. There is something about the activities that took place at that site that led to the deposition of enormous quantities of artifacts at a great distance from their source.

One possible explanation for what took place at Poverty Point can be found by returning to Hayden's (1990) model for the origins of agriculture, which stresses the importance of competitive feasts. Perhaps Poverty Point was not a large village, but rather the focal point of feasting events, drawing in people from a very wide region—people who were not otherwise living together in village communities. Is it possible that in the Late Archaic of eastern North America, monumental construction preceded large settled villages? The same issue will emerge when we turn to the monuments of the Hopewell. The essential question is whether the early farming communities of eastern North America could have found an alternative pathway to creating farming communities—a pathway that relied on the construction of massive earthworks instead of large villages.

Although the Late Archaic was clearly a period of significant change in the societies of eastern North America, the impact of domesticated plants on subsistence was minimal. Collecting wild plant foods and hunting wild animals continued to form the basis of subsistence. One source of evidence relevant to the role of domesticated plants in the diet is the human fecal remains, or coprolites, found on archaeological sites. Although coprolites are certainly not the most glamorous aspect of archaeological research, studying them provides a unique insight into the human diet. Studies of coprolites from two sites in Kentucky dated to 3,400 years ago demonstrate a great deal of variability in the diet (Gremillion 1996). In some samples, domesticated plants were dominant, whereas in others, they were a smaller component. These findings suggest that cultivated crops played a variable role in the diet during the initial period of plant domestication.

■ The Adena and the Hopewell

Adena A period of intensive mound building in the Ohio River Valley; it corresponds to the Early Woodland culture.

Hopewell A period of intensive mound building in the Ohio River Valley; it corresponds to the Middle Woodland culture.

Most of the mounds in Ohio and surrounding areas date to the Early and Middle Woodland period between 3,200 and 1,700 years ago (Gremillion 2003). In the Ohio River Valley, the Early Woodland corresponds to the **Adena** culture, and the Middle Woodland corresponds to the **Hopewell** culture. In both the Adena and the Hopewell cultures, there is evidence of elaborate burial practices, including the construction of mounds, and extensive trade networks. Figure 8.13 shows an example of Hopewell art.

The earliest ceramics in the Northeast date to the Early Woodland in a style known as known as Vinette 1. These are coarse open vessels that are found in low numbers. A combination of isotope and lipid analysis of Vinette 1 potsherds suggests that these vessels were used to process fish oil, which in historic periods was a commodity valued for exchange among indigenous communities (Taché and Craig 2015).

Careful excavations of Hopewell mounds have shown that some were erected over structures built of bent poles (Brown 1979). Multiple human remains were placed in these structures before they were filled in and covered by a mound of earth. In some cases, bodies were laid out to decompose before burial, and the bones were either left in their original position or gathered together into bundles after decomposition. In other cases, the bodies were cremated in ceramic basins or placed in pits dug into the floors of the structures. There is also evidence that in some cases burials were excavated into mounds, while in others new structures for burial or cremation were built on top of mounds and were subsequently covered over by a secondary mound (Brose, Brown, and Penney 1985).

FIGURE 8.13 A bird claw cut from a sheet of mica. This is a masterpiece of Hopewell art.

Hopewell material culture includes impressive art objects made of copper, mica, and polished stone. Expertly crafted objects that were traded over long distances are found in many Hopewell burials. It is likely that objects such as hard stone pipes in the form of animals and large plaques made of sheets of mica were produced by craft specialists. Such discoveries suggest that elite members of these societies controlled a network of trade in prestige objects.

In his classic work on eastern North American prehistory, James Griffin (1967) suggested that there were Hopewell villages near the massive earthworks. Griffin had in mind not only the mounds, but also the earthen enclosures found at sites such as the Liberty Earthworks near Chillicothe, Ohio. At the Liberty site, there are two circular enclosures, one over 200 meters in diameter and the other over 500 meters, as well as a square enclosure covering 11 hectares (Squier and Davis 1848). However, materials collected from the farm that now includes the Liberty Earthworks have not yielded any remains of a large village until the late Middle Woodland period, toward the end of the Hopewell culture (Coughlin and Seeman 1997).

There is evidence that some of the earthworks were occupied. The massive Newark Earthworks, shown in Figure 8.14, have largely been engulfed by the city of Newark, Ohio. The construction of a new highway that goes through the earthworks led to a salvage project in which the remains of two Hopewell houses were identified, together with evidence of domestic activities (Lepper and Yerkes 1997). Despite this evidence, some archaeologists have suggested that, rather than residing in large villages, the people of the Hopewell culture lived dispersed across the landscape in small farmsteads (Dancey and Pacheco 1997). According to this model, known as the **vacant center pattern**, the earthworks served as the symbolic and ceremonial core of a community that lived across a wide area.

Christopher Carr and Troy Case (2006) have challenged archaeologists to think about the Hopewell phenomenon from an agency perspective. Adopting such a perspective requires that we shift our focus from the community as a whole to the individuals who make it up. However, these individuals are conceived not as the rational calculators of optimal foraging theory, but rather as persons negotiating

vacant center pattern The model that sees the Hopewell earthworks as the empty core of a dispersed settlement system.

FIGURE 8.14 Map of the Newark Earthworks, Ohio, published by E. G. Squier and E. H. Davis in 1848. Squier and Davis's drawings are a critical resource, since many of the features they record have subsequently been destroyed.

their place in the world within the context of overlapping structures of power. On the basis of careful analysis of the iconography of Hopewell figurines, Carr and Case argue that there were different types of leaders in Hopewell society, including both shamans and others with more secular sources of power. Carr and Case raise the possibility that, rather than a series of households held together by a ceremonial core in the form of a particular earthwork, what actually existed was a situation in which each individual might have connections to multiple earthworks.

Given both the widespread modern destruction of the earthworks and their massive scale, it remains difficult to determine whether they were the locations of large villages. Adding to the difficulty of assessing the nature of Hopewell settlements is the low archaeological visibility of many Hopewell habitation sites. Because of the massive buildup of river-borne alluvial sediments in the Ohio River Valley, Hopewell sites located in the valley are deeply buried and not easily discovered by archaeologists (Stafford and Creasman 2002).

Early and Middle Woodland subsistence included the cultivation of indigenously domesticated plants (Smith 1995). The earliest direct AMS radiocarbon dates of maize in eastern North America are between 2,000 and 1,800 years ago, from three Middle Woodland sites in Tennessee, Illinois, and Ohio. However, maize remains rare and does not appear to have played a major role in the diet. Throughout the Woodland period, hunting and collecting wild plants continued to be key elements of subsistence alongside the cultivation of domesticated plants.

■ Intensification of Maize Agriculture

At the end of the Middle Woodland period, around 1,700 years ago, the extensive trade networks of the Hopewell culture and the construction of massive earthworks came to an end. At the same time, there was an increase in the number of large settled villages. By the beginning of the Late Woodland, maize is found as far north as Ontario (Crawford, Smith, and Bowyer 1997). Although maize was cultivated throughout much of eastern North America by 1,700 years ago, the isotope analysis

Who Owns the Past?

Who owns the past? This is a rather vague question, but for archaeologists, it takes on a very concrete meaning. For example, the Metropolitan Museum of Art in New York recently returned the Euphronios vase, a 2,500-year-old Greek vessel with exquisite paintings of mythological scenes, to Italy because it was resolved that the vase had been illegally acquired. In this case, the Metropolitan Museum's claim of property rights to an artifact was found to be legally faulty; therefore, the object was returned to the Italian government, whose claims to property rights were supported by international law.

But should laws of property rights always determine who owns archaeological artifacts or sites? What happens when property rights clash with other claims to ownership and access? This question is particularly pertinent in the United States, where property rights are highly prized. The Newark Earthworks provide an illustration of this problem. Squier and Davis documented the Newark Earthworks in 1848 in their study of Ohio Valley mounds (Figure 8.14). In 1853, the local agricultural society purchased the northwestern part of the earthworks, and in 1891, the land was sold to the City of Newark for State Encampment Grounds. The state militia used the Encampment Grounds for a number of years before the land was leased to its current tenants, the Moundbuilders Country Club. In 1933, the deed to the property was transferred to the Ohio Historical Society.

It is quite incredible that one of the most impressive monuments in the Americas is today a golf course. Two events have brought renewed attention to the earthworks. The first was an unsuccessful attempt by the country club to build a new clubhouse that would have damaged the mounds. The second was the identification of a lunar orientation for the octagon-shaped enclosure. Archaeologist Chris Scarre (1999) has included the Newark Enclosures among his 70 wonders of the ancient world. But for the club manager, it is the right of the club to limit access to this site because the club holds the lease (Maag 2005). As with many significant archaeological sites, the planning for the long-term conservation of the Newark Earthworks is an extremely delicate undertaking. The Ohio Historical Society has set out a management plan for the site that does include removing the golf course. In the meantime, procedures have been put in place to provide at least limited access to visitors wishing to experience this spectacular site. ●

FIGURE 8.15 The return of the Euphronios vase to Italy

FIGURE 8.16 The Newark Earthworks are today the location of a country club golf course

of human skeletal remains provides strong evidence that maize did not come to play a major role in the diet until around 1,000 years ago. Grasses from the tropics and subtropics, including maize, sorghum, and sugarcane (C_4 plants), have a high ratio (see Isotope Analysis Toolbox, Chapter 4, p. 111). The only C_4 plant that contributed to the diet of the people of the Woodland period in eastern North America is maize. By analyzing the $\delta^{13}C$ value for Woodland-period skeletal remains, it is possible to determine the role that maize played in those people's diets. The shift to a high $\delta^{13}C$ value in human skeletal remains takes place only during the period around 1,000 years ago, approximately 700 years after the initial introduction of maize into eastern North America. This finding indicates that there was a considerable length of time between the first planting of maize in eastern North America and the adoption of this plant as an essential food source.

■ The People behind the Transition

Archaeologists studying the development of agriculture have a tendency to forget to include people in the process. The dating of the initial domestication of various crops and the description of archaeological sites provide an essential framework for understanding the transition to agriculture; however, it is necessary to go beyond this framework to consider what led people to adopt a radically new way of life.

Patty Jo Watson and Mary Kennedy have linked the seeming invisibility of people in the origins of agriculture to gender bias in our conception of the past. According to Watson and Kennedy (1991), in the anthropological literature "men are strong, dominant protectors who hunt animals; women are weaker, passive, hampered by their reproductive responsibilities, and hence, consigned to plant gathering" (256).

Watson and Kennedy have identified strategies that have been used by archaeologists to maintain gender bias in their explanations of the origin of agriculture. The first strategy is to view its development as a passive process that simply happened as the result of the unconscious ecological consequences of human actions. Bruce Smith's coevolutionary model for the indigenous domestication of plants in eastern North America is an example of such an approach (Smith and Cowan 2003). According to Smith, climate change led to an increased permanence of human settlements in eastern North America. This shift to more permanent settlements led to gradual ecological changes that resulted in the emergence of domesticated plants over a period of several thousand years.

Smith outlines five major stages in the process. In the first stage, the garbage heaps around long-term human occupations provided an excellent ecological niche for weedy plants that thrived on the availability of sunlight and fertile soil. In these contexts, seeds that sprouted and grew quickly had a selective advantage. Seeds that sprout and grow quickly would be large and have a thin coat. In the second stage, people tolerated edible plants and removed useless or harmful ones. In the third stage, people began to encourage and systematically harvest useful plants, while carefully weeding out useless ones. In the fourth stage, seeds of the useful plants were planted deliberately every year. In the fifth stage, plants that were clearly morphologically domesticated emerged.

Smith's model for plant domestication sets this process within a well-constructed ecological framework. The model fits with the kind of evolutionary approaches advanced by Rindos. However, Watson and Kennedy (1991) argue that "the built-in mechanisms adduced [in the model] carry plants and people smoothly and imperceptibly . . . with little or no effort on anyone's part. The plants virtually domesticate themselves" (262). The formulation "women = plants = passive" is maintained.

Whereas Smith views domestication of plants as a passive process, Guy Prentice has proposed that domestication might have been the result of intentional actions by individuals. Prentice argues that the introduction of domesticated squash into eastern North America was carried out by male shamans who would have used gourds as rattles or ritual containers. Prentice (1986) writes of the shaman, "He would have

"Towns They Have None": In Search of New England's Mobile Farmers
ELIZABETH S. CHILTON, UNIVERSITY OF MASSACHUSETTS, AMHERST

I am a professor and director of the Center for Heritage and Society. When I began my graduate studies at UMass Amherst, I was very interested in the Late Woodland period (A.D. 1000–A.D. 1600) and Contact period (A.D. 1600–A.D. 1700) in the Massachusetts portion of the Connecticut River Valley in the western part of the state. In particular, archaeologists had long been looking for large Late Woodland–period villages. On the basis of previous experience with research on the neighboring Iroquoian tribes, archaeologists expected to find large sedentary villages as a result of the adoption of maize horticulture around A.D. 1000. Nevertheless, when I came to UMass in 1988, no large Late Woodland villages had yet been found in the region.

In 1989, a local farmer reported that he had found a large number of ceramics on a forested hill surrounded by a floodplain in the valley of the Deerfield River, a major tributary of the Connecticut River. Subsequent excavation at the Pine Hill site in 1989, 1991, 1993, 1995, and 1997 as part of the UMass Amherst Archaeological Field School revealed that this was indeed an important Late Woodland site. We uncovered fragments of more than 300 Late Woodland–period vessels, a large number of lithic artifacts, and 22 large pit features, which likely served for food storage and/or refuse disposal. Radiocarbon dates firmly placed most of the activity at the site during the Late Woodland period.

Despite the fact that we had excavated quite a few of these Late Woodland pit features and had identified food remains (e.g., small and large mammal bones, charred nutshells and seeds), until 1995 we had not found a single kernel of maize. This surprised us, since elsewhere in New England maize had been dated to the start of the Late Woodland period. One day at the

site, a student excavating the plow zone from a 2 × 2 meter test unit suddenly said, "Hey, Elizabeth, I found a weird blueberry thing." I looked at it and immediately recognized it as a charred maize kernel! Later that summer, we discovered the first pit feature on that site to yield maize kernels, approximately 200 in all! Still, 200 maize kernels are equivalent to only about one cob of Northern Flint, eight-row maize (Chilton, Largy, and Curran 2000). We have many more nutshells and small animal bones than maize kernels.

Now, digging conditions on this site were quite grueling, despite the fact that we were in Massachusetts. There was standing water in an oxbow near the Deerfield site; therefore, the mosquitoes were far more intense than any pest I encountered when I did some work in Belize after graduating from SUNY Albany in 1986. We were bitten through our clothes, on our lips and eyelids, and on our fingers. On top of that, we did not have ready access to restrooms, and there was a fair bit of poison ivy. The digging itself was quite easy—the soils are

sandy from the postglacial lake deposits. But digging in a forested environment provides its own challenges in the form of tree roots and rodent activity.

After several years of excavating the Pine Hill site and after conducting a detailed analysis of the attributes of the ceramics for my dissertation, we came to the conclusion that it was a Late Woodland–period site that was repeatedly occupied on a seasonal basis, primarily in the late summer to early fall (Chilton 1999, 2002). This conclusion dovetails nicely with archaeological evidence from throughout the Connecticut River Valley, which suggests that, although New England peoples had adopted maize by A.D. 1000, it did not significantly alter their seasonal mobility, nor did it significantly change their diet. Archaeological evidence indicates that maize may have become more important across New England around A.D. 1300. Nevertheless, year-round villages like those of the Iroquois have not been found in New England. Instead, New England peoples offer us a clear example of mobile farming. ▲

FIGURE 8.17 Pine Hill site, UMass Amherst Archaeological Field School, 1993 (Elizabeth Chilton, shown left)

the greatest knowledge of plants" (113). Here, the domestication of plants is seen as an active process, and, tellingly, the agent is explicitly male.

As a counterbalance to existing models for the role of women in the development of agriculture, Watson and Kennedy (1991) propose a model for the adoption of maize in eastern North America that emphasizes the active role of female gardeners. The introduction of maize, which is a tropical grass, into the northern latitudes of North America is an impressive event. The spread of maize into northern latitudes involved a transition from midwestern 12-row maize to a variety known, due to the smaller number of rows per cob, as eastern 8-row, or Northern Flint, maize. Watson and Kennedy propose that the women in eastern North America, who already had extensive experience growing indigenous cultivated plants, actively experimented with the midwestern 12-row maize to develop a variety that was better suited to the soils and climates of their region. The result was the development and spread of eastern 8-row maize. According to this proposal, then, the adoption of maize agriculture in eastern North America was an achievement of the active intervention of women.

■ Summing Up the Evidence

The transition to agriculture in Mesoamerica and North America was a complex process. In the southwestern United States, maize agriculture was either adopted by groups of Archaic hunter-gatherers, who appear to have had no previous experience with domesticated plants, or possibly spread by populations of farmers moving in from the south. The impact of the adoption of agriculture on these societies varied. In some cases, notably at Cerro Juanaqueña and the sites around Tucson, large villages developed, while in other areas, people continued to live in temporary camps. This regional variability continued into the Formative period. Archaeologists have tried to explain the pattern that developed in terms of optimal foraging theory.

In eastern North America, hunter-gatherer groups had domesticated a number of plant species long before the introduction of maize agriculture. Intensively occupied sites are already found in the Late Archaic and, in the case of the Poverty Point site, had reached an impressive size and degree of planning. In the Early and Middle Woodland Adena and Hopewell cultures, massive earthworks were constructed, and there is evidence for specialized craft manufacture and long-distance trade in high-status items. However, the nature of the settlement systems remains poorly understood. The possibility remains that in eastern North America monumental architecture preceded settled villages. The initial introduction of maize at the end of the Middle Woodland period had little impact on the diet. Studies of bone chemistry indicate that it took approximately 700 years before maize came to play a major role in the diet.

The spread of agriculture is as complex a process as the initial domestication of plants and animals. It is clear from the study of North America that local societies adapted agriculture into their lives in different ways. Rarely did the initial introduction of agriculture have an immediate transformative effect on those societies. As discussed in the last chapter, research in other areas, such as Europe, where agriculture was introduced rather than developed indigenously, similarly points to the active role played by the indigenous societies of hunter-gatherers in the adoption of this practice.

SUMMARY

- The wild ancestor of maize is teosinte, a wild grass found in the highlands of Mexico.
- The three major crops domesticated in Mesoamerica are maize, squash, and beans. No animals were domesticated in the region.
- Evidence for the initial domestication of plants in Mesoamerica comes mostly from excavations of highland caves in the Tehuacán and Oaxaca Valleys.
- The earliest domesticated squash dates to between 10,000 and 8,300 years ago. The earliest domesticated maize dates to 6,250 years ago.
- Cerro Juanaqueña, in northern Mexico, is a large Archaic-period site with evidence of extensive terrace walls and maize agriculture.
- Archaic-period villages with evidence of maize agriculture have been found at the Milagro and Las Capas sites in Arizona.

- Archaic-period sites in the Mogollon Highlands and the Colorado Plateau have also produced evidence of domesticated maize. However, there is no evidence of Archaic-period villages in these areas.
- Pottery first appeared widely in the American Southwest during the Formative period, around 1,800 years ago.
- Among the plants that were domesticated indigenously in eastern North America were squash, chenopod, marsh elder, and sunflower. This domestication took place between 5,000 and 3,500 years ago.
- Extensive earthworks were built in Ohio and surrounding areas during the Early Woodland period (Adena culture) and Middle Woodland period (Hopewell culture).
- The earliest maize in eastern North America dates to the Middle Woodland period. However, there is evidence that maize did not play a major role in the diet until about 700 years after its introduction.

KEY TERMS

Accelerator Mass Spectrometry (AMS) radiocarbon dating, 216
Adena, 226
Cerro Juanaqueña, 217
Guilá Naquitz, 216
Hopewell, 226
Las Capas, 219

Milagro, 219
optimal foraging theory, 219
Poverty Point, 225
shell middens, 224
Tehuacán Valley, 216
teosinte, 215
vacant center pattern, 227

REVIEW QUESTIONS

1. What is known about the initial domestication of squash and maize?
2. What impact did the spread of maize have on Southwest Archaic societies? Was the effect the same throughout the region?

3. What was the social and economic context surrounding the construction of the Adena and Hopewell mounds?
4. What is the basis for Watson and Kennedy's critique of models for the origin of agriculture in eastern North America? What model do they propose?

A FEAST OF DIVERSITY

By comparing case studies, it is possible to learn whether the shift to agriculture always followed a single path. This chapter examines the origins of agriculture in Africa, New Guinea, the Andes, and East Asia. After reading this chapter, you should understand:

- The role of pastoralism and the timing for the introduction of pottery in Africa.

- The nature and significance of the archaeological site at Kuk Swamp, New Guinea.

- The relationship between the origin of village life and domestication in the Andes.

- The evidence from the two centers of domestication in China.

A field of quinoa growing in the Andean highlands

9 TIMELINE

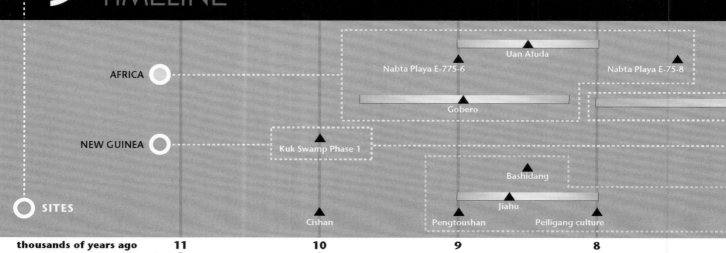

	AFRICA			Nabta Playa E-775-6	Uan Afuda		Nabta Playa E-75-8
				Gobero			
	NEW GUINEA	Kuk Swamp Phase 1			Bashidang		
					Jiahu		
SITES		Cishan		Pengtoushan		Peiligang culture	
thousands of years ago	11		10		9		8

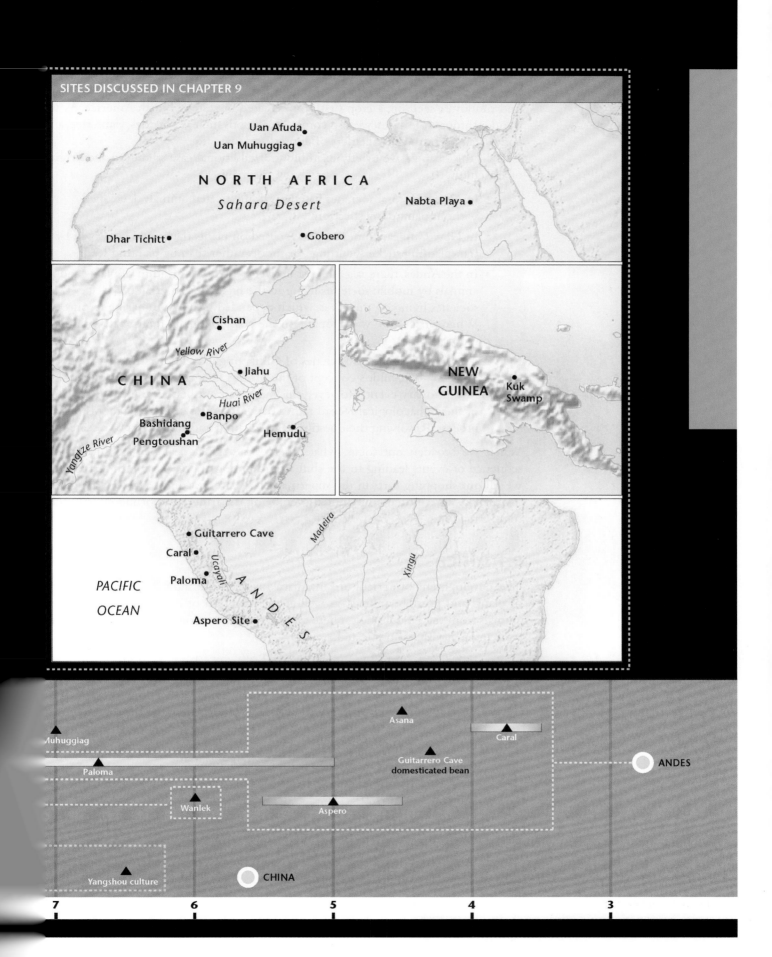

Uan Afuda
Uan Muhuggiag

NORTH AFRICA
Sahara Desert

Nabta Playa

Dhar Tichitt
Gobero

Cishan
Yellow River

CHINA
Jiahu

Huai River
Banpo
Bashidang
Pengtoushan
Hemudu
Yangtze River

NEW GUINEA
Kuk Swamp

Guitarrero Cave
Madeira
Caral
Ucayali
Paloma
A N D E S
Xingu

PACIFIC OCEAN

Aspero Site

Muhuggiag

Asana
Caral
Paloma
Guitarrero Cave
domesticated bean
ANDES
Wanlek
Aspero
Yangshou culture
CHINA

7   6   5   4   3

A visit to the supermarket is also a trip around the world. In the produce section, we find corn and squash, plants domesticated in Mesoamerica; the bakery section is filled with breads baked from wheat, domesticated in the Middle East; at the butcher, we find the meat of cattle and pigs (as well as the occasional sheep and goat), also domesticated in the Middle East; and down the aisle, we find sunflower seed oil, a crop first domesticated in eastern North America. As we wander through the aisles, we also come across foods such as potatoes, yams, rice, and coffee that point to other centers of domestication.

In this chapter, we briefly examine four additional case studies in the origins of agriculture:

- In Africa, pastoral societies based on domesticated animals developed without plant domestication.
- In New Guinea, domestication focused on plants that could be grown by transplanting suckers, cuttings, or shoots rather than by planting seeds.
- In the Andes, there is a contrast between the domestication of plants and animals by mobile societies living in the highlands and that by village societies living on the coast, which depended heavily on marine resources. When agriculture was adopted on the coast, the main focus was a nonfood crop: cotton.
- The early agricultural societies of China might yield the strongest support available for Childe's concept of the origins of agriculture as a rapid and revolutionary event. However, this picture might be the result of limitations of the archaeological record rather than a reflection of the actual historical process. Resolving the question is an exciting and active area of research.

When we broaden our focus, what emerges is a great deal of flexibility in the sequence of events leading to the shift from hunting and gathering to farming. As we fill our shopping carts in the supermarket, we are not only sampling the global diversity of agricultural crops, but also enjoying the fruits of a cornucopia of social transformation.

9.1 Africa

The development of agriculture in Africa involved the indigenous domestication of plants and possibly animals, as well as the adoption of domesticated plants and animals from the Middle East. There are three major regions in Africa where plants were indigenously domesticated.

- In Ethiopia and Eritrea in northeast Africa, a wide range of plants was domesticated, including grains such as teff and finger millet, which are essential to the local diet (D'Andrea et al. 1999). A local domesticate that has had a more global impact is coffee. Unfortunately, the timing and process of the domestication of all these plants are poorly understood.
- In central Africa, two critical cereals—pearl millet and sorghum—were domesticated. It is most likely that pearl millet was first domesticated in the Sahara, but the location where sorghum was first domesticated is not known.
- In west Africa, African rice (*Oryza glaberrima*) was domesticated (Linares 2002).

In addition to these indigenously domesticated plants, African agricultural systems incorporated domesticated plants introduced from the Middle East, including wheat, barley, and lentils. Among the domesticated animals introduced to Africa from the Middle East were sheep and goats. However, there is considerable debate over the origin of domesticated cattle on the continent. Although there is some genetic evidence supporting the argument that cattle were independently domesticated in Africa, the preponderance of evidence is that the animals were introduced from the Middle East.

The **Sahara Desert** is the most dominant feature of the North African landscape today. The current arid environment in the Sahara developed only within the last 4,000 to 5,000 years. Between 14,000 and 4,500 years ago, there was considerably more rainfall in the Sahara, allowing for extensive human occupation (Muzzolini 1993).

◼ Villages of Hunter-Gatherers

During the period of increased rainfall in the Sahara, small villages of hunter-gatherers developed across northern Africa. The sites resemble the Natufian societies of the Middle East in several ways—their size, the nature of their structures, the exploitation of a wide range of resources, and the use of grinding stones. However, there are also significant differences between the African and the Natufian sites. The most striking difference is that pottery is commonly found on the African sites. In the Middle East, pottery was developed only during the Late Neolithic. Another feature found on African sites that is lacking from the Natufian sites is a large number of storage pits.

One of the most complete pictures of an early village of hunter-gatherers in North Africa comes from excavations at **Nabta Playa** in the Egyptian Western Desert (Wendorf and Schild 1998). This area is barren today, but when it was occupied, it was a small lake surrounded by grasslands. Site E-75-6 was a village of 15 square or circular huts built in two rows that was occupied 9,000 years ago. Storage pits are found next to the remains of each structure. Pottery, in the form of small jars with impressed designs, is also present, although it is rare. A large range of plant remains has been recovered from this site, where the inhabitants focused particularly on the collection of wild sorghum.

Excavations at the cave site of **Uan Afuda** in Libya have given a unique perspective on the preagricultural societies of the Sahara. Uan Afuda was occupied between 9,000 and 8,000 years ago. The spectacular preservation on the site has allowed the excavators to recover wooden artifacts, basketry, and a rich array of charcoal and seeds. The botanical remains at the site indicate that the people living there exploited a wide range of resources. One of the most interesting discoveries was a 10-centimeter-deep bed of animal dung and plant remains found in the back of the cave. Analysis of the dung indicates that it is from wild barbary sheep, a North African species that was never domesticated. The excavators argue that such an accumulation of dung does not form from sheep visiting a cave site. It appears that the early occupants of Uan Afuda were keeping wild sheep in a pen at the back of the cave. This discovery suggests that, although these people had not domesticated sheep, they were practicing a form of animal management by capturing live animals and keeping them corralled in a cave.

Excavations at the site of **Gobero**, in the southern Sahara in Niger, have uncovered a cemetery and associated evidence of habitation dating to 9,700 to 8,200 years ago (Sereno et al. 2008). The site was located on a peninsula in a large lake, and fish appear to have made up a large part of the diet (see Figure 9.1). Artifacts recovered include barbed bone points, bladelets, and pottery. Due to an increasingly arid climate, the site was abandoned a little over 8,000 years ago.

▲▲ **Sahara Desert** The most dominant feature of the North African landscape today. Between 14,000 and 4,500 years ago, there was increased rainfall in the area, allowing for human occupation.

▲▲ **Nabta Playa** An area in the Egyptian Western Desert that was the location of a series of preagricultural and early agricultural sites located along the edge of a lake.

▲▲ **Uan Afuda** A preagricultural site in the Sahara that yielded evidence that wild sheep were kept in pens in the back of a cave.

▲▲ **Gobero** A site in the Sahara alongside an ancient lake where a hunter-gatherer occupation dating to between 9,700 and 8,200 years ago has been discovered.

FIGURE 9.1 A view of the site of Gobero, Niger. Between 9,700 and 8,200 years ago, this barren desert was the site of a hunter-gatherer village at the edge of a lake.

■ Pastoralists

In much of North Africa, domesticated animals were introduced before domesticated plants. Domesticated cattle, sheep, and goats appear to have been incorporated into mobile hunter-gatherer societies (see Figure 9.3). Mobile societies with an economy focused on maintaining herds of domesticated animals are known as **pastoral societies** (Holl 1998a).

Based on excavations at Nabta Playa, Fred Wendorf and his colleagues have argued that cattle might have been domesticated independently in Egypt as early as 10,000 years ago. This theory has not been widely accepted. However, it is clear that by 8,000 years ago, domesticated cattle, sheep, and goats had been introduced into societies that still did not exploit domesticated plants. Site E-75-8 at Nabta Playa has produced vivid evidence of the reliance on cattle roughly 7,500 years ago. At this site, a series of cattle burials was found under piles of stones known as tumuli (Wendorf and Schild 1998). Recent excavations in the Fayum where sediments were carefully screened to find small faunal remains show that in the Nile Valley fish were a major food resource alongside early domesticated animals (Linseele et al. 2014).

The earliest evidence of domesticated animals in the Central Sahara, at the site of Uan Muhuggiag, is dated to 7,000 years ago (Holl 1998b). As with Nabta Playa, there is no evidence of domesticated plants. The site of Gobero was reoccupied 7,200 years ago as climate conditions improved. By 6,000 years ago, the occupants added a small component of domesticated cattle to their subsistence base, although they continued to rely heavily on fishing.

■ The First Farmers

Unfortunately, the development of village farming communities in Africa is poorly understood. In Egypt, the earliest evidence for domesticated plants dates to approximately 7,000 years ago. Wilma Wetterstrom has suggested that these resources were at first adopted by hunter-gatherers to provide a "backup" for brief periods of drought or low Nile floods. Once domesticated plants were introduced, large villages developed rapidly in the rich environment of the Nile Valley.

pastoral societies Mobile societies with an economy based on herds of domesticated animals.

Ethiopian Farmers Yesterday and Today

CATHERINE D'ANDREA, SIMON FRASER UNIVERSITY

People often ask, "Why would you go to Ethiopia to do archaeology? Don't Ethiopians have more pressing issues to deal with, like drought and food shortages?" The short answer is yes, there are more significant developmental priorities, but in fact cultural resource management is a high priority for Ethiopia and many other developing nations because they are often more vulnerable to the loss of precious cultural heritage. It's true that Ethiopia is actively working on improving the infrastructural and agricultural sectors of its economy, but heritage preservation is also of major importance, and the country's potential to develop a tourism industry holds great promise.

I became interested in developing an archaeological survey project after completing five years of ethnoarchaeological research on traditional farming societies in northern Ethiopia. This work involved documenting several aspects of traditional lifeways—including nonmechanized crop processing, cooking, and house construction—to be used as guides to understanding the archaeological record.

As I read more about the late prehistoric archaeology of Ethiopia, I noticed that much of the research has focused on the ancient capital cities of Yeha and Aksum, which were important urban centers of two ancient Ethiopian polities, the pre-Aksumite and Aksumite kingdoms (800 B.C.–A.D. 700). We know a fair amount about the origin and development of these societies, which were major trading partners for the Romans, but what was the contribution of rural populations to the origin and development of these ancient kingdoms? We decided to try to answer this question by developing a survey project in a region of eastern Tigrai known as Gulo-Makeda.

Conducting a ground survey in a country like Ethiopia is quite physically demanding. Located in the East African Highlands, the landscape has a spectacular, rugged, rocky mountainous topography. Some of our survey transects were over 3,000 meters above sea level. Although our surveyors are in excellent physical condition, we are not trained rock climbers, so we have to be aware of our limitations. We continually combat physical fatigue, as well as thirst and heat (not to mention clashes with cactus patches, wayward bulls, and misplaced military ordnance), while hauling several kilos of stone tools and ceramic artifacts in our backpacks. Our work takes us to rural areas sometimes far away from main roads, and we tend to attract the attention of curious individuals, especially children, who immediately offer to help us collect artifacts. Because of their intimate familiarity with their environment, the children know exactly what we are looking for and quickly spot the differences between ancient and modern pottery fragments. Meeting and working with villagers has been one of the most rewarding and interesting aspects of our fieldwork, as well as a lesson in hospitality. We are frequently invited to visit people's homes, where we are invariably offered food and drink, even if there is only one piece of bread in the house. People also perform a coffee ceremony—a uniquely Ethiopian tradition in which fresh coffee beans are roasted and pounded in front of us.

Our foot surveys and GPR (ground-penetrating radar) work indicate that, far from being a rural hinterland, Gulo-Makeda was a significant regional center that had large-scale buildings and artifacts, indicating the presence of local elites who may have been involved in international trade. Many of the larger sites were likely chosen for settlement because of their proximity to water runoff sources and their location along major trade routes running between the cities of Yeha and Aksum and the Red Sea coast. Gulo-Makeda was an especially significant region during the Classic Aksumite period (A.D. 150–350). We are now eagerly planning to test some of what we have learned from surveys by conducting excavations at several sites in Gulo-Makeda. ▲

FIGURE 9.2
Attracting the attention of curious individuals, especially children, while collecting artifacts (mostly stone tools and pot sherds) from a 10 × 10 meter controlled collection unit at an archaeological site in eastern Tigrai, Ethiopia

FIGURE 9.3 Rock art painted by pastoralists in the Sahara showing cattle being herded. Can you make any observations about herd structure or social organization based on this image?

In western Africa, the earliest evidence of plant domestication is the imprint of domesticated millet grains found in the village sites of the Dhar Tichitt region of Mauritania around 3,500 years ago. Sorghum appears to have been introduced at a somewhat later date.

■ Summing Up the Evidence

There is a great deal that we still need to learn about the origins of agriculture in Africa. However, even given the preliminary nature of the archaeological record, we can observe some interesting patterns. Pottery was introduced at the beginning of the sequence in Africa, whereas it is found only in the Late Neolithic in the Middle East. Pastoral societies in Africa developed thousands of years before fully agricultural villages did. In Africa, as in the Middle East, small villages predate the domestication of plants and animals. The evidence for a particular focus on wild sorghum at Nabta Playa and the penning of wild sheep at Uan Afuda is particularly intriguing.

9.2 New Guinea

During glacial periods, New Guinea, Australia, and Tasmania formed a single landmass known as Sahul. Today, New Guinea is a large island divided into the independent country of Papua New Guinea in the east and the Indonesian province of Irian Jaya in the west. The New Guinea highlands run the length of the island at an elevation between 1,300 and 2,500 meters.

Ethnographers studying the modern agricultural societies of New Guinea have emphasized the centrality of pigs and sweet potatoes—not only for subsistence, but also in developing a social hierarchy (see Figure 9.4). The exchange of pigs is an essential element of political power. Sweet potatoes are an important part of the diet of pigs; therefore, accumulating sweet potatoes is an essential element in gaining political power (Golson and Gardner 1990). Surprisingly, neither sweet potatoes nor pigs were domesticated indigenously in New Guinea, and both were introduced fairly recently. Sweet potatoes were domesticated in South America and were probably introduced into New Guinea after they were brought to the Philippines by Spanish sailors sometime in the sixteenth century (Gichuki et al. 2003). The timing of the introduction of domesticated pigs to New Guinea is poorly understood.

Recent genetic research indicates that a large number of plant species were domesticated indigenously in New Guinea. These crops include yams, bananas, taro, and possibly sugarcane (Lebot 1999). None of these crops are cereals, and traditional agricultural processes in New Guinea involve transplanting suckers, cuttings, or shoots rather than planting seeds.

■ Clearing Forests and Draining Swamps

The earliest evidence of human occupation of New Guinea is found at coastal sites on the Huon Peninsula, dated to 40,000 years ago (Groube et al. 1986). The earliest occupation of the highlands is found at the sites of Kosipe and Yuku, which are dated to approximately 30,000 years ago (Bulmer 1976). Animal bones recovered from these sites indicate that a wide range of animals was hunted. There is no evidence of domesticated plants or animals. The exact date for the introduction of ground stone tools in the highlands is unclear; however, polished axes dating to 10,000 years ago are found on a number of sites.

FIGURE 9.4 Sweet potato farming in New Guinea. In modern societies in New Guinea, sweet potatoes play an important role in social hierarchy.

Most of the archaeological sites in the highlands are cave sites. However, at Wanlek, the remains of a 6,000-year-old village, including remains of circular houses and a large central structure, were excavated. The artifacts recovered at Wanlek include polished stone axes, but no pottery. On archaeological sites in the highlands, no pottery is found that dates to earlier than 800 years ago.

The main evidence for the development of agriculture in highland New Guinea comes from the excavation of ancient field systems at the **Kuk Swamp** in the Wahgi Valley (Denham 2003). The major features found at Kuk Swamp are drainage canals, pits, and earth mounds (see Figure 9.5). These features are the result of efforts to drain the swamp and create beds for planting crops. The age of the features at Kuk Swamp is based on radiocarbon dating of wood charcoal found in the fills of channels. Canals from the earliest phase at Kuk Swamp, radiocarbon dated to approximately 10,000 years ago, are limited in size and extent. In the second phase, dated to 6,500 years ago, there are regularly distributed earth mounds and channels across the site. In the third phase, dated to 4,000 years ago, a network of drainage ditches was excavated through the site. Subsequently, the network of channels became denser and more regular. Around 3,000 years ago, the maintenance of agricultural fields at Kuk Swamp appears to have come to an end.

Starch grains on stone tools from the first two occupations have been identified as taro, which does not grow naturally in the highlands and therefore must have been planted at Kuk Swamp. There is also evidence of banana cultivation beginning around 6,500 years ago. Phytoliths of bananas are found throughout the Kuk Swamp sequence. Phytoliths are mineral structures that build up on plant tissue. In the early phase of the occupation of Kuk Swamp, the presence of banana phytoliths is expected because wild banana trees would have grown in the forest environment that was found in the region at that time. However, around 6,500 years ago, the environment around Kuk Swamp changed to grassland, in which a high percentage of banana phytoliths would not occur without human intervention. Therefore, the presence of large quantities of banana phytoliths in the swamp deposits after 6,500 years ago is evidence that people were planting banana trees. Features similar to those found at Kuk Swamp have been

FIGURE 9.5 Maps showing the development of agricultural ditches and mounds at Kuk Swamp, New Guinea

Plan of Phase 2: 6950-6440 Calibrated Years BP

Plan of Phase 1: 10220-9910 Calibrated Years BP

TOOLBOX

Pollen, Phytoliths, and Starch Grains

Paleoethnobotanists are not limited to the macrobotanical remains recovered through flotation. In their efforts to understand human interactions with plants, paleoethnobotanists also draw on microbotanicals, the preserved microscopic remains of plant material.

Pollen grains, produced by the male reproductive organs of plants and trees, can be used to reconstruct past climate conditions. Pollen is best preserved in freshwater lakes and ponds, where the grains are embedded in the continuous buildup of sediments on the lake bottom. The continuous sequences recovered from these contexts allow botanists to track changes in the makeup of plant communities over time. One major change that can be tracked is the shifting ratio between pollen from trees and pollen from grasses. By looking at changes in this relationship, it is possible to determine periods when local ecology shifted from woodlands to open grasslands. Often, pollen can also be recovered from archaeological sites, providing a window into the ecological setting.

Phytoliths are silica structures that build up along plant cell walls. The source of the silica is groundwater that is pulled into the plant during its life. The form of the phytolith is shaped by the morphology of the plant; as a result, it is possible to identify types of plants on the basis of their phytoliths. Commonly preserved on archaeological sites, phytoliths can be used to reconstruct the ecological setting of a site. Sometimes phytoliths are found adhering to artifacts, and in these cases, the phytoliths can provide an insight into how a tool was used.

Paleoethnobotanists have begun to explore starch grains found adhering to artifacts. In some cases, the grains have been shown to be remarkably resilient, surviving for thousands of years. Starch grain analysis has the potential to provide critical data about how tools were used. In one instance, the analysis of starch grains on pottery vessels recovered in Egypt allowed archaeologists to trace the process of beer production. ●

ADDITIONAL READING: Dena F. Dincauze. 2000. *Environmental Archaeology: Principles and Practices.* Cambridge: Cambridge University Press.

FIGURE 9.6 Scanning electron microscope photograph of pine pollen

FIGURE 9.7 Scanning electron microscope photograph of potato starch grains

Humboldt Current A current that brings cool waters from the south up along the Andean coast, accounting for the remarkable wealth of marine resources in the area.

▲▲ **Guitarrero Cave** A site in the Andean highlands of Peru where excavations uncovered the earliest evidence of domesticated beans dating to 4,300 years ago.

found on other sites, such as Kana, which is also located in the Wahgi Valley (Muke and Mandui 2003). However, as there is very little evidence from the excavation of village sites from these early periods in highland New Guinea, there is little basis for reconstructing the social context of early agriculture. It appears that the transition to agriculture in New Guinea was quite gradual and that only plants were involved. New Guinea is unique in that no cereal crops were domesticated. The development of ground stone tool technology appears to be related to agriculture; however, pottery was introduced quite late and did not have any role in early agricultural systems.

9.3 The Andes

The Andes are the second-highest mountain chain in the world, with peaks reaching close to 7,000 meters above sea level. The Andean highlands can be divided into four zones based on altitude (Quilter 1989; see Figure 9.8). In the Quechua zone, between 2,300 and 3,500 meters above sea level, corn grows well. In the Suni zone, between 3,500 and 4,000 meters, a range of crops indigenous to the Andes is grown. The most important of these crops are a cereal called quinoa and root crops, including potatoes, oca, and olluco. The Puna zone, between 4,000 and 4,800 meters, is an open grassland used for grazing llamas and alpacas. The high peaks of the Cordillera zone, above 4,800 meters, are not exploited for agriculture. To the east, the Andean highlands drop off rapidly into the Amazon rain forest, the archaeology of which, unfortunately, remains poorly understood (Raymond 1988).

To the west, the Andes descend gradually to the Pacific coast. The coastal region is a barren desert bisected by numerous rivers running down from the mountains (Burger 1992). Agriculture is limited to the river valleys. The desert is also broken by llomas—patches nurtured by mist from coastal fog where dense vegetation grows during the winter. The coast itself is remarkably rich in marine resources, including small fish such as anchovies, large fish, ocean birds, marine mammals, and shellfish such as clams and mussels. The wealth of resources along the Andean coast is due to the **Humboldt Current**, which sweeps cool waters up the coast of South America, bringing nutrients to the surface.

■ Domestication in the Andean Highlands

Excavations at **Guitarrero Cave** in the Andean highlands of Peru uncovered domesticated beans, which subsequently were dated to approximately 10,000 years ago (Smith 1980). But it was not the beans themselves that were dated; rather, it was charcoal recovered from the same level as the beans. When one of the beans was dated directly using Accelerator Mass Spectrometry (AMS) radiocarbon dating, it turned out to be only 4,300 years old (Kaplan and Lynch 1999). Apparently, the beans came from a higher level in the stratigraphic sequence at Guitarrero Cave and were perhaps moved by burrowing animals.

The redating of the beans from Guitarrero Cave has thrown all early dates for domesticated plants in the Andean highlands into question. At Panaulauca Cave, a small number of quinoa seeds have been found in layers dating to between 5,700 and 4,500 years ago (Smith 1995). Until these seeds are dated directly, the timing for the domestication of quinoa remains open to question. The earliest evidence for domesticated potatoes from sites on the Peruvian coast dates to between 4,000 and 3,000 years ago (see Figure 9.9). It is unlikely that these are the earliest domesticated potatoes, as the coast is not the region where wild forms of potatoes grow. An added problem is that distinguishing domesticated quinoa and potatoes from wild forms is

FIGURE 9.8 Topographic map of the Andes showing the dramatic changes in elevation moving west to east from the narrow band along the Pacific coast rising to the to the highlands and then over into the Amazon Basin

difficult. With quinoa, a thin seed coat means the grain is domesticated. With potatoes, the shape and size of the starch grains are used to distinguish between wild and domesticated forms.

The domestication of **llamas** (Figure 9.10) and **alpacas** in the Andean highlands is fairly well documented (Lavallée 2000). Both animals are camelids. The ancestral species of llamas are guanacos; the wild ancestors of alpacas are vicuñas. It is difficult to distinguish between domesticated and wild camelids on the basis of the shape and size of their bones. However, at a number of cave sites in the Andean highlands, the percentage of camelids relative to deer increases steadily throughout the period between 10,000 and 5,000 years ago, a trend that appears to indicate a gradual shift toward camelid domestication. Beginning around 7,000 years ago, the number of

llamas Camelid animals domesticated in the Andean highlands; *guanacos* are the ancestral species of llamas.

alpacas Camelid animals domesticated in the Andean highlands; *vicuñas* are the ancestral species of alpacas.

FIGURE 9.9 Illustration of Inca farmers digging up potatoes, from a sixteenth-century Spanish document. The domestication of potatoes in the Andes dates back at least 3,000 years.

FIGURE 9.10 A woman with a herd of llamas in the Andean highlands very young camelids increased sharply. This pattern is interpreted as the result of disease, which struck closely packed herds of domesticated animals. Another line of evidence for domestication is found at the Asana site near Lake Titicaca. In a level dated to 4,500 years ago, chemical analysis of the soils indicated that there had been a high concentration of dung in an area surrounded by postholes. The excavators interpret this feature as the remains of a corral for domesticated camelids. The other domesticated animal in the Andes is the guinea pig. Little is known about when guinea pigs were first domesticated, but it appears to have been considerably later than camelids.

No village sites from these early periods have been excavated in the Andean highlands. Currently, it appears that the domestication of plants and animals took place in the context of mobile hunter–gatherer societies.

■ Coastal Villages

By 8,000 years ago, small settled villages had developed in the lloma fog meadows on the Peruvian coast (Pineda 1988). The inhabitants of these villages were hunter-gatherers who relied heavily on the rich coastal marine resources.

The village of **Paloma**, which was inhabited intermittently between 8,000 and 5,000 years ago, provides a broad view of one of these early preagricultural villages (Quilter 1989). Houses were built of reeds and grasses over a structure of wooden poles. The total population of the villages is unclear, but it appears to have been in the range of 10 families at any given time. A large number of burials were excavated at Paloma, mostly in pits dug into the floors of houses, with grave offerings placed near the skeleton. An analysis of the burials demonstrated an overall uniformity in the treatment of the dead, although males tended to be buried toward the center of houses, suggesting that they might have had a higher status than females.

The Paloma site provides a vivid demonstration of the centrality of marine resources to these early village communities. Analysis of the faunal remains from the site showed that 98% of the individuals recovered were marine animals and shellfish (Reitz 1988). The dominant species were anchovies. Only a small number of land mammals' remains were found; these include spider monkeys, camelids, and deer.

The skeletal remains also afford evidence of the intensive exploitation of marine resources at Paloma. Eight skeletons were found with auditory exostoses, a growth in the inner ear caused by spending long periods in cold water. Burial 159 at Paloma presents particularly graphic evidence of the relation

▲▲ **Paloma** A preagricultural village site on the coast of Peru.

FIGURE 9.11 Burial 159 from the Paloma site, Peru. The left leg is missing, and the pelvis shows marks consistent with attack by a shark.

Cotton Preceramic The period beginning 5,700 years ago when sites with monumental architecture flourished on the coast of Peru.

these people had with the sea. Burial 159 is a young man in excellent health, except for a missing leg (see Figure 9.11). This man was buried in an elaborate cane structure tied with cord along with a number of burial offerings. A series of cut marks was found on the man's pelvis, indicating "the likelihood that his leg was removed by a shark" (Quilter 1989, 59).

A wide range of plant resources from the llomas, including seeds, fruits, and tubers, was exploited by the people living at Paloma. The only clearly domesticated plants were cultivated gourds. Beans and squash might have been cultivated, but there is no evidence that they played a significant role in the diet.

■ The Cotton Preceramic

Approximately 5,700 years ago, large sites with monumental architecture began to appear on the coast of Peru. These belong to a period called the **Cotton Preceramic**, in recognition of the prevalence of cotton seeds and the absence of pottery. The sites from the Cotton Preceramic reach up to 58 hectares at El Paraíso and 65 hectares at Caral (Quilter et al. 1991; Solis, Haas, and Creamer 2001). At the site of Aspero, a large flat-topped pyramid known as Huaca de los Ídolos is dated to between 5,500 and 4,500 years ago. At Caral, there are six large artificial mounds, the largest of which measures 160 meters by 150 meters and is 18 meters high, dated to between 4,000 and 3,500 years ago (Solis et al. 2001). Figure 9.12 shows one view of the Caral site.

There has been considerable debate concerning the economic basis of the large Cotton Preceramic sites. Because the site of Aspero is located on the coast, it has been suggested that these sites were based on fishing and collecting marine resources rather than on agriculture. Subsequent studies have shown that in fact the bulk of the diet of Cotton Preceramic sites consisted of fish and shellfish. Even at the site of Caral, located 23 kilometers from the coast, almost all of the faunal remains recovered were of clams, mussels, anchovies, and sardines (Solis et al. 2001). However, at both Caral and the coastal site of El Paraíso, a wide range of domesticated plants—including gourds, squash, chili peppers, and beans, as well as the tubers achira and jicama—was grown. The dominant crop species was cotton, which was used for making nets and textiles.

FIGURE 9.12 The Preceramic mounds at Caral with the Andean foothills in the background

■ The Role of El Niño

The Humboldt Current, which brings cool waters from the south up along the Andean coast, is responsible for the wealth of marine resources that allowed villages such as Paloma to thrive without agriculture. The large centers of the Cotton Preceramic also relied heavily on the rich marine resources brought by the Humboldt Current. **El Niño** is a severe reversal of the Humboldt Current that occurs every 25 to 40 years. When major El Niño events strike, there is a massive decline in fish and shellfish populations on the coast, as well as torrential rains on the shore, which cause massive flooding and mudslides (Burger 1992). It is hard to imagine how villages like Paloma would have survived such events.

Studies of the shellfish found on archaeological sites have led scientists to argue that El Niño events began only around 6,000 years ago (Sandweiss et al. 2001). According to this model, El Niño events between 6,000 and 3,000 years ago were less frequent than they are today. The onset of El Niño appears to correlate with the beginning of the Cotton Preceramic. It is possible that the climatic uncertainty of the arrival of El Niño played a role in pushing the development of large centers with a partial reliance on agriculture.

■ Summing Up the Evidence

The domestication of plants and animals in the highlands of the Andes appears to have had little impact on the way people lived. Early agricultural sites are either small cave sites or open-air ones, with little evidence of architecture. However, the absence of early agricultural villages in the highlands might be the result of a bias in the types of sites that have been excavated. Archaeologists have focused largely on dry cave sites with well-preserved organic remains.

On the coast, settled villages preceded the adoption of agriculture. These villages were small collections of huts showing little evidence of social inequality. The adoption of domesticated plants took place on the coast in the context of increased settlement size and the emergence of monumental architecture. Because of the availability of rich coastal marine resources, agriculture played only a minor role in the subsistence of Cotton Preceramic settlements. The dominant crop was cotton, used for making fishing nets and textiles. The adoption of agriculture on the Andean coast might have been a reaction to the climatic uncertainty introduced by the onset of El Niño.

9.4 East Asia

The two most significant plants domesticated in East Asia are **rice** and **millet**. Today, rice feeds half of the world's population. The wild ancestor of rice is the species *Oryza rufipogon*, and all domesticated Asian rice belongs to the species *Oryza sativa*. (Note that this species is distinct from African rice and from the plant we call wild rice.) *Oryza rufipogon*, the wild ancestor of rice, was a plant that thrived in seasonally flooded areas. The earliest stages of domestication might have involved the construction of temporary dams to expand the lands that were seasonally inundated (Smith 1995).

One strain of rice, *Oryza sativa japonica*, was domesticated in southern China in the **Yangtze and Huai River Valleys**. Other plants domesticated in southern China include water caltrop and fox nut, both of which grow, like rice, in inundated fields. Among the domesticated animals in southern China are dogs, pigs, and water buffalo. Genetic evidence suggests that another strain of rice, *Oryza sativa indica*, was

El Niño A severe reversal of the Humboldt Current that causes a massive decline in marine resources along the Andean coast.

rice A major cereal crop domesticated in southern China in the Yangtze and Huai River Valleys.

millet A cereal crop domesticated in northern China in the region around the Yellow River Valley.

▲▲ **Yangtze and Huai River Valleys** The area of southern China where rice was domesticated.

▲▲ **Yellow River Valley** The area in northern China where millet was domesticated.

Jomon Japanese preagricultural societies that lived in large villages and produced elaborate pottery.

independently domesticated in the region between India and Thailand (Londo et al. 2006). There is not yet any archaeological evidence for rice domestication from this region.

Two types of millet—broomcorn and foxtail millet—were both domesticated in northern China in the region around the **Yellow River Valley**. Both species of millet are highly drought-resistant cereals. Animals domesticated in northern China include pigs and, possibly, chickens.

■ Early Pottery

By 10,000 years ago, societies of hunter-gatherers across East Asia were utilizing a wide range of wild resources and living in permanent or semipermanent settlements. Many of these groups produced pottery (see Figure 9.13). The **Jomon** societies of Japan, dated to between 13,000 and 2,500 years ago, produced elaborate pottery and lived in villages that included as many as 50 pit houses (Imamura 1996). The subsistence of the Jomon was based on hunting and gathering, with a particular emphasis on fish and shellfish. Rice and millet agriculture was introduced into Japan only during the Late Jomon period, around 3,000 years ago (D'Andrea et al. 1995). Isotope and lipid analysis of charred remains found in Jomon pottery indicates that these vessels were used for processing fish, as is the case for the Vinette 1 pottery of eastern North America (Craig et al. 2013; Lucquin et al. 2016).

The earliest known pottery in East Asia is found at Xianrendong Cave, Jiangxi Province, China in levels dated to 20,000 years ago (Wu et al. 2012). It does not appear that people living in China during this period lived in large settlements like those found in Jomon-period Japan.

In northern China, little is known about preagricultural societies. The reason for this paucity of knowledge is a massive buildup of windblown sediments known as loess, which has buried sites from these periods deep underground.

FIGURE 9.13 Jomon pottery from Japan

■ The First Farmers

There is debate among archaeologists working in China as to where to place the boundary between the collection of wild rice and full domestication (Liu et al. 2007). There is general agreement that this was a gradual process and that collecting wild foods remained important throughout the Neolithic. The earliest evidence of rice farming is found on village sites in the Yangtze and Huai River Valleys. The site of **Pengtoushan** is a village dated to approximately 9,000 to 8,000 years ago that has produced evidence of cultivated rice, although it is unclear if rice was fully domesticated (Higham and Lu 1998). The excavations at Pengtoushan recovered traces of houses surrounded by a protective ditch. The neighboring site of Bashidang has also produced a large quantity of charred rice (Pei 1998). Bashidang appears to have been occupied slightly after Pengtoushan. The village at Bashidang covered an area of 30,000 square meters. A wide range of wild animal bones was recovered at Bashidang, indicating that hunting continued to be important for subsistence.

In the Huai River region, the village site of Jiahu, occupied between 9,000 and 8,000 years ago, covered an area of roughly 55,000 square meters (Zhang et al. 1999). Excavations have uncovered a total of 45 houses, storage pits, and graves. As at Bashidang, a range of wild animals was hunted. The excavations at Jiahu recovered six complete flutes made from the long bones of the red-crowned crane. These flutes are so well preserved that a musician was able to use one of them to play a Chinese folk song, "The Chinese Small Cabbage." The excavators point out that in ancient China music was a part of nature and was associated with government.

Until recently, the initial stages of millet farming were thought to date to approximately 8,000 years ago in what is known as the Peiligang culture. But research at the site of **Cishan**, located in northern China, has now pushed back the date for the initial domestication of millet to roughly 10,000 years ago, based on direct AMS radiocarbon dating of plant remains (Lu et al. 2009)—see Figure 9.14. Cishan was a village at least 400 meters square that was occupied over a period of 3,000 years.

▲▲ **Pengtoushan** A site in southern China that has produced some of the earliest evidence of domesticated rice, dating to approximately 9,000 years ago.

▲▲ **Cishan** A site in northern China that has yielded dates of 10,000 years ago for domesticated millet.

FIGURE 9.14 Modern broomcorn millet. Research at the site of Cishan, China, has demonstrated that this crop was domesticated by 10,000 years ago.

TOOLBOX

Residue Analysis

When animals are exploited for milk and wool, they are more than just a source of meat. Andrew Sherratt (1983) has argued that the exploitation of domesticated animals for secondary products such as milk and wool transformed the economy of early farming societies. Herds of animals became a walking source of wealth.

But how can we tell whether an animal was milked? One approach is to look for evidence of dairying in the population structure of the herd. If dairying was economically significant, one would expect a culling of young males. However, this approach provides evidence that is at best indirect. In 2003, a group of biochemists published dramatic results of a new method that allowed them to identify the biochemical traces of milk residues on pottery sherds from the Neolithic in Britain (Copley et al. 2003). These results provide direct evidence that milk was an important aspect of the early farming communities of Britain.

The milk residues found in this study are lipids that have survived for approximately 6,000 years. The first stage of analysis is to get the lipids out of the pot sherd. Sherds are cleaned thoroughly, and then a sample weighing 2 grams is ground to a powder and soaked in a solvent in an ultrasonic bath. Next, the solvent, which now contains the lipids, is evaporated, leaving the lipids behind. The chemical composition of the lipids is determined with a mass spectrometer. The critical step in developing this method was finding a signature that would distinguish between adipose (body) fat and milk fat. Fortunately, such a marker, based on differences in ratios of carbon isotopes, was found.

Biochemical methods have also been used to identify the processing of plants. In one notable study, a chemical analysis of pottery sherds from the Neolithic site of Jiahu, China, found evidence of a fermented beverage made of rice, honey, and fruit (McGovern 2004). ●

FIGURE 9.15 Neolithic storage jar from the site of Jiahu, China, with the result of a mass spectrometry analysis of the chemical composition of the residues found inside the vessel

THE DEVELOPMENT OF FARMING SOCIETIES. The Peiligang culture of the Yellow River developed into the Yangshao culture 6,500 years ago (Debaine-Francfort 1999). The **Yangshao culture** is particularly well represented at **Banpo**, a village site that consisted of both round semi-subterranean houses and rectangular houses built on ground level. A range of wild plants and animals, including fish, fruits, and nuts, was exploited. Millet was fully domesticated, as were dogs and pigs. The repertoire of pottery vessels found at Banpo is particularly impressive and includes vessels with elaborate painted decorations (see Figure 9.16).

In southern China, the **Hemudu** site provides a picture of a village based on rice cultivation contemporaneous with Banpo (Smith 1995). The excavations at Hemudu have uncovered 4 meters of superbly preserved archaeological deposits. The houses at Hemudu were skillfully built of wood and raised on piles above the waters of a river or pond that existed on the spot. Because the site is waterlogged, the wooden houses are well preserved. Enormous quantities of rice, along with the bones of domesticated dogs, pigs, and water buffalo, were also recovered at Hemudu. The people living at Hemudu also continued to exploit wild plants and animals.

Chinese archaeologists have been particularly interested in understanding the social life of early farming villages (Pearson and Underhill 1987). As a result, many of the early village excavations are on a very large scale. The tendency in China is to view early agricultural societies as matrilineal clans organized around maternal lineages. Over time, these societies are seen as having evolved into patrilineal, property-owning families. The logic behind this theory is that women played a decisive role in raising and tending plants and would therefore have wielded power in early agricultural societies. Attempts have been made to use the distribution of burial practices within village sites to gain a fuller understanding of their social organization. One of the burial features that has been emphasized is that young girls found in Yangshao cemeteries were richly adorned.

Archaeology and the Environment

Archaeology is the only discipline capable of providing empirical evidence about the long-term environmental effects of human actions. In recent years. archaeologists have documented the impact of climate change on ancient civilizations (deMenocal 2001) and cases of environmental degradation linked to overexploitation of resources. Global warming has placed the environment at the top of the international political agenda. Yet archaeologists are rarely active voices in environmental policy debates. Peter Mitchell (2008) has raised the question of what archaeologists should be doing in response to the urgency of environmental issues, particularly global warming. He argues that archaeologists should be focusing on research that can provide substantive data relevant to contemporary concerns about the environment.

But what exactly is the archaeological perspective on the environment? Archaeologists tend to emphasize that culture and environment are closely linked. Moreover, archaeologists tend to be cautious about the concept of pristine environments, stressing that even landscapes that appear untouched have been shaped by human activity. Karl Butzer (1996) writes that because "contemporary ecosystems are the product of millennia of co-evolution between environmental components and human activities ecological issues are sufficiently complex to demand a new and greatly expanded medium of interdisciplinary interaction and collaboration. Archaeology should, indeed must, be a major player" (142).

Frances Hayashida (2005) warns the archaeological community to expect their data and interpretations to be misrepresented in the political arena. Hayashida identifies three dangers:

1. Archaeological interpretations will be used to depict indigenous practices as ecologically detrimental.

2. The recognition that few landscapes are truly pristine can be used to excuse modern destruction.

3. Modern development might be justified as mimicking natural processes or ancient practices.

But Hayashida (2005) ends this list of potential hazards with a call to action: "Only by taking active roles can we shape how our research results are interpreted in public discourse and applied to policy outcomes" (57). The time when archaeologists sit on the sidelines of debates about the environment appears to be coming to a close. ●

FIGURE 9.17 This terraced landscape on the island of Sifnos in the Cyclades, Greece, illustrates the coevolution of the environment and human activities

■ Summing Up the Evidence

In China, as in Africa, pottery manufacture predates the development of agriculture. Hunter-gatherers living in large settlements with constructed houses are found in Japan, as they are in both the Middle East and Africa. Although the earliest stages of agriculture in China are poorly understood, it appears that the domestication of both plants and animals happened at the same time. As in the Middle East, the adoption of agriculture was accompanied by an increase in the size of sites. In China, domestication took place independently in two centers, with rice domesticated in the south and millet in the north. The overlap in domesticated animal species suggests that there was some connection between these two centers of domestication.

The earliest agricultural sites in China are large sedentary villages. The excavations at Pengtoushan, Bashidang, and Jiahu have uncovered the remains of large settlements with some evidence of defensive ditches. If these sites were inhabited soon after the initial domestication of rice, then southern China would provide a case in which domestication is linked directly with the formation of large villages. However, research on the preceding periods is in its early stages and researchers working in China stress that the transition from collecting wild rice to full domestication was gradual, so the validity of this conclusion remains open to question.

9.5 Questioning the Neolithic

Julian Thomas (1999) has written, of the origins of agriculture, that it was a "messy and fragmented series of developments, and any attempt to define a particular set of attributes as constituting the Neolithic will be arbitrary in the extreme" (13). The evidence in this chapter supports the view presented by Thomas and contrasts sharply with Childe's view of the Neolithic Revolution as a sudden transformation of human society that took place in much the same way around the globe.

In all regions, the transition to agriculture was a gradual process. This fact has led Bruce Smith (2001) to argue that it is necessary to consider a territory "in between" hunting and gathering, on the one hand, and farming, on the other. The route taken in traversing this intermediate territory was extremely varied. Settled villages preceded agriculture in the Middle East, Africa, and the Andean coast, but, apparently, not in New Guinea, the Andean highlands, or Mesoamerica. Pottery can develop very early in the process, as it did in Africa and China, or very late, as it did in the Middle East, New Guinea, the Andes, and Mesoamerica. Plants can be domesticated before animals (Middle East and New Guinea), after animals (Africa and the Andes), or at the same time as animals (China), or animals might play a very minor role (Mesoamerica).

The development of agriculture is a complex process involving changes in the biology of plants and animals, human subsistence strategies, human social organization, and the way people think about their place in the world. Perhaps it should not come as a surprise that this transition can follow many trajectories, depending on the plant and animal species involved, the characteristics of the local environment, and the particularities of cultural practices. In a sense, the diversity found in the archaeological record forces us to recognize the need for multiple perspectives on the origins of agriculture.

SUMMARY

- Indigenous plant domestication in Africa took place in three major regions: Ethiopia and Eritrea, central Africa, and West Africa.
- At Nabta Playa, a village of circular huts with storage pits and pottery vessels is dated to 9,000 years ago.
- Pottery developed in North Africa before the domestication of plants and animals.
- Domesticated animals were introduced into North Africa by pastoral societies before the adoption of domesticated plants.
- Yams, bananas, and taro were domesticated indigenously in New Guinea.
- The main evidence for the development of agriculture in New Guinea comes from the excavation of ancient field systems at the Kuk Swamp site. There is evidence of artificial drainage systems at Kuk Swamp beginning 10,000 years ago.
- Because of the Humboldt Current, the Andean coast is extraordinarily rich in marine resources.
- Domesticated beans from Guitarrero Cave, Peru, have been directly dated to 4,300 years ago. The earliest evidence for domesticated potatoes is between 4,000 and 3,200 years ago.
- There is evidence for the domestication of llamas and alpacas beginning 6,000 years ago.
- By 8,000 years ago, small villages relying on marine resources had developed along the Andean coast.
- During the Cotton Preceramic, large sites, including monumental mounds, were built on the Andean coast. Among the domesticated crops from these sites were gourds, squash, and beans. The most significant crop was cotton.
- Rice was domesticated in southern China in the Yangtze and Huai River Valleys. The Pengtoushan site has produced the earliest evidence of domesticated rice.
- Millet was domesticated in northern China in the region around the Yellow River.
- The Jomon societies of Japan were hunter-gatherers who lived in small villages and made pottery.
- The Banpo site in northern China and the Hemudu site in southern China are large villages with extensive evidence of both plant and animal domestication.

KEY TERMS

alpacas, 245
Banpo, 252
Cishan, 251
Cotton Preceramic, 248
El Niño, 249
Gobero, 237
Guitarrero Cave, 244
Hemudu, 252
Humboldt Current, 244
Jomon, 250
Kuk Swamp, 242
llamas, 245

millet, 249
Nabta Playa, 237
Paloma, 247
pastoral societies, 238
Pengtoushan, 251
rice, 249
Sahara Desert, 237
Uan Afuda, 237
Yangshao culture, 252
Yangtze and Huai River Valleys, 249
Yellow River Valley, 250

REVIEW QUESTIONS

1. Do any aspects of the pattern of domestication in the Middle East fit in with the case studies in this chapter?
2. In what ways was the origin of agriculture in New Guinea unique?
3. What does Bruce Smith mean by a territory "in between" hunting and gathering, on the one hand, and farming, on the other? What are some examples of such "in-between" societies?
4. What generalizations can be made about pottery and the origins of agriculture?

PART FOUR

THE DEVELOPMENT OF SOCIAL COMPLEXITY

In the previous section, we examined the shift to an agricultural way of life. In this final section, we visit different societies in many parts of the world and consider the increasing inequality among members of these societies that developed as they grew larger. Power and access to resources came to be controlled by a smaller segment of the population, leading to the emergence of state societies. After reading this introduction, you should understand:

- Fried's and Service's categories for the forms of social organization.
- Childe's 10 criteria that define urban societies.
- Explanations for the emergence of social complexity.

Introduction: Defining Social Complexity

In the modern world, institutionalized power is a basic fact of life. With the exception of a small number of disputed territories, the deep oceans, and Antarctica, the entire globe is carved up into sovereign entities in which a central government holds authority. The way this authority is exercised and its limits vary considerably; however, the existence of centralized authority is a global phenomenon that shapes the world we live in (Figure IV.1). A linked aspect of the modern world is economic inequality and the concentration of wealth in the hands of a small percentage of the population. In recent years, outrage over the degree of economic inequality has fueled political action and revived hopes for finding a way to create complex urban societies in which wealth is shared equitably.

FIGURE IV.1 The Canadian-American border between Maine and Quebec

Centralized government or authority and marked economic inequality are relatively recent developments in human society. Gaining an understanding of how these conditions came into being is one of the central themes of archaeological research. Through much of the early history of archaeology, the origin of central authority and of concentrated wealth was couched within the broader framework of the progress of humanity. Lewis Henry Morgan and V. Gordon Childe considered what was often called the origin of civilization to have been the inevitable next step in the upward movement of humanity following on the origins of agriculture. From such a perspective, the source of central authority explains itself: People would naturally aspire to live within more advanced and highly developed societies. It is notable that V. Gordon Childe did not think that our destiny is to live within the structures that emerged in prehistory. Rather he studied the past to help develop an understanding of how to build a different future.

Today, most archaeologists have a more subtle understanding of the development of politically complex human societies. Although it is recognized that centralized authority is essential in order for people to live in large urban centers and for significant developments to occur in culture and technology, there is also a clear sense of the costs of such authority. Political complexity is inevitably linked with increased social inequality and limitations on personal autonomy. While early archaeologists might have questioned what allowed societies to "advance" to civilization, archaeologists today are more likely to ask about the forces that pushed societies toward increasing social inequality. The critical issue underlying much contemporary research is how centralized authority gained legitimacy. An authority has **legitimacy** when its right to power is accepted. One question is, to what degree is the legitimacy of authority the result of consensus or coercion? In a system grounded in consensus, members of society believe in the rights of the centralized authority; in a system based on coercion, people are forced to accept this authority. In most cases, legitimacy is the result of a combination of consensus and coercion.

■ Categorizing Political Complexity

A number of anthropologists have developed schemes for categorizing the types of social organization found in societies around the world. These schemes provide an

legitimacy A quality or status achieved when the right of a centralized authority to have power is accepted. Legitimacy can be based on consensus or on coercion.

egalitarian society A society in which the only differences in status are based on skill, age, and gender.

ranked society A society in which there is a hierarchy of prestige not linked to age, gender, or ability.

stratified society A society in which access to key resources is linked to prestige.

state A society in which power is organized on a supra-kin basis or by a bureaucracy that uses force.

essential framework for guiding research endeavors dealing with the development of political complexity. The goal of such schemes is not to encompass the tremendous variation that characterizes human societies, but rather to provide a model of commonalities in the way that political complexity develops.

Morton H. Fried (1967) defined four types of societies: egalitarian, ranked, stratified, and state. In **egalitarian societies**, the only differences in status between members are based on their skill at subsistence activities (such as hunting), their age, and their gender. A person's status is determined by a combination of these factors. Production in egalitarian societies takes place within households, with each one carrying out more or less the same tasks. Exchange tends to be casual and based on reciprocity.

In an egalitarian society, there are as many positions of prestige as there are people to fill them. In a **ranked society**, there are fewer positions of prestige than there are people to fill them, and there is a hierarchy of prestige that is not linked to age, gender, or ability. The basis for prestige is often a simple attribute, such as birth order. In such a society, the firstborn son might have higher prestige than his siblings. Although there is a hierarchy in a ranked society, there is no real political power or exploitation. The role of a person occupying a high-status position is to collect rather than expropriate, to redistribute rather than consume.

In ranked societies, there are individuals with high prestige, but little real power. These "big men" or "chiefs" serve as the focal point of a system of collecting and redistributing resources, but they do not expropriate or consume more than their neighbors who have lower prestige. By contrast, in a **stratified society**, all people do not have equal access to key resources. Rather, access is tightly linked to prestige: People of high prestige have unimpeded access to these resources, while people of low prestige encounter impediments. In stratified societies, as in ranked societies, the number of high-prestige positions is limited on the basis of criteria other than age, gender, and ability. Because of the unequal access to key resources, including food and shelter, stratified societies are characterized by a growth of exploitation, which can take the form of demands on labor, institutional slavery, or more complex systems based on a division of labor among groups of specialists. Organization is based not only on the household and kin group, but also on communities of people drawn from different households and kin groups.

Fried (1967) defined **states** as societies in which power is organized on a "supra-kin" basis. The essential task of the state is to use its power to maintain the social hierarchy that has escaped from its grounding in the kin group. Characteristics of state societies include population control through the fixing of boundaries, the development of a legal system, the maintenance of military and police forces, taxation, and conscription. For Fried, the evolution of political complexity is a gradual process in which the basic unit of organization shifts from the family and kin group to large, supra-kin communities. This process also sees increases in control of access to key resources and in centralized political power.

A similar scheme developed by Elman Service (1971) divides societies into bands, tribes, chiefdoms, and states. Service's definitions of *band* and *tribe societies* correspond roughly to Fried's egalitarian and ranked societies. For Service, chiefdoms are societies characterized by an intermediate level of social complexity, where centralized leadership is based on heredity. However, leaders in these societies have little ability to use force to maintain order, relying on religious authority as their source of power (Service 1975). State societies are sharply different from chiefdoms in that government and law are backed by force. Service summarizes his view of the state as a society integrated by a bureaucracy that uses force (Service 1971, 167). The state has a legitimate monopoly over the use of force. This does not mean that state societies are inherently violent. Rather, it is through the monopolization and controlled use of force that the rulers of state societies are able to maintain peaceful order among a large population. The role of force is to allow the bureaucratic elite to integrate society.

Both Fried and Service see the development of political complexity as the movement of authority from the kin group to a government that is not based on kinship. Fried tends to emphasize the emergence of inequality as high status becomes increasingly concentrated in the hands of a smaller number of people. (See Figure IV.2 for an example of the way that high status can be indicated.) Service highlights the emergence in state societies of a control over the legitimate use of force.

■ Defining Cities

V. Gordon Childe (1942) chose to sidestep the search for the early state by shifting the emphasis from political institutions to the cities that characterize **urban society**. In the modern world, urban centers are characterized by high population density, as well as by a high degree of planning (Figure IV.3). Childe developed 10 criteria that archaeologists could use to identify urban societies in the archaeological record: urban centers, surplus production and storage, taxes to a deity or king, monumental architecture, a ruling class, writing systems, exact and predictive sciences, sophisticated art styles, foreign trade, and specialist craftsmen. In the same way that he saw the origins of agriculture as the Neolithic Revolution, Childe saw the development of state societies as the Urban Revolution. Once again, all aspects of human life were transformed by interlocking changes in economy and society.

FIGURE IV.2 Maori women from New Zealand. Their high status is indicated by their feather cloaks and jade pendants.

The advantage of Childe's list of criteria is that they are likely to leave visible traces in the archaeological record. However, a number of these criteria are poorly defined. For example, how big does a settlement have to be to count as an urban center? Furthermore, Childe did not make it clear why these criteria are relevant, other than the fact that they are archaeologically visible. One solution to this problem is to define the urban center in terms of its place in a regional settlement system. Henry Wright and Gregory Johnson (1975) have emphasized that in urban societies there is a hierarchy with at least three different levels of settlement size. This hierarchy is significant because it reflects a differentiated administrative structure. In a clever turn of phrase, Norman Yoffee (2005) points out that the birth of the city was also the origin of the countryside. The movement of people and power into cities inevitably restructured the lives of people living in towns and villages.

■ A Comparative Approach to State Formation

Inequality is an essential element of all human societies. Even in those societies that Fried describes as egalitarian, there are differences in status based on skill, age, and gender. The categories developed by Fried and Service are useful tools, but they should not trick us into believing that the emergence of inequality followed a single trajectory in all societies. For example, the societies of the northwest coast of North

urban society A society in which people live in large cities. V. Gordon Childe developed 10 criteria defining an urban society.

FIGURE IV.3 Midtown Manhattan. This picture illustrates the density and organization that characterize modern urban centers.

FIGURE IV.4 Totem poles in a Northwest Coast village on Charlotte Island, British Columbia

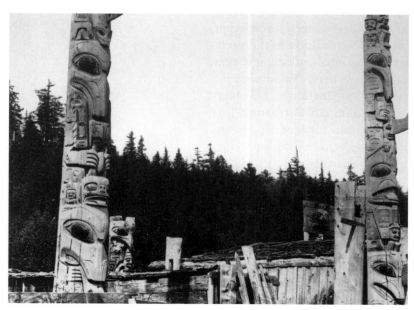

America offer a fundamental challenge to our expectation that the emergence of political complexity builds on the economy of a village farming way of life. These complex hunter–gatherer societies had a subsistence base that included a broad range of marine and terrestrial resources, lived in villages (see Figure IV.4), and had a complex social hierarchy that included the institution of slavery. Perhaps any attempt to shoehorn societies into a category such as a chiefdom or a state is misguided. One could argue that it would be better to study social complexity as a continuum or, alternatively, to focus on the internal logic of each individual society.

There certainly are dangers to taking a comparative approach to the emergence of political complexity. While recognizing these dangers, Bruce Trigger (2003) has written an eloquent defense of comparative studies:

> The most important issue confronting the social sciences is the extent to which human behavior is shaped by factors that operate cross-culturally as opposed to factors that are unique to particular cultures. . . . Given the biological similarities and the cultural diversity of human beings, how differently are they likely to behave under analogous circumstances? The answer to this question is crucial to understanding human behavior and cultural change and shaping the future course of human development. (3)

Adopting a comparative approach allows archaeologists to explore the regularities associated with the formation of states, regardless of the context in which that formation occurs, and at the same time to appreciate the unique features of the process in particular regions.

State societies can be divided into primary states, which form without external influence from neighboring state societies, and secondary states, which form under the influence of neighboring state societies. As with the origins of agriculture, the transition to state societies is a process that took place independently in a number of regions. Increasingly, archaeologists are paying close attention not only to the processes leading to the formation of states, but also to those that cause them to collapse (Diamond 2005).

In some cases, states began aggressive campaigns of expansion, resulting in the formation of empires (Alcock et al. 2001). **Empires** are political entities that bring together a diverse and heterogeneous group of societies under a single ruler. Often, empires rely on the brutal use of military power to achieve domination. This power is vividly depicted in the sculpture of the temples of the Assyrians (Figure IV.5), who expanded out of Mesopotamia to control a large part of the Middle East. Empires also require the development of methods of communication to allow for the rapid transmission of information. Communication enables the core of the empire to control events far from the center. The inequality between a core region and peripheral ones is characteristic of empires. The flow of goods and resources moves from the periphery to the core, usually in the form of tribute.

The archaeology of empires requires research covering an immense geographic area. One of the most interesting aspects of this study is exploring how the core maintained control and domination over the periphery. Archaeologists must look at sites at the core and at the periphery, while paying attention to the two linchpins of the empire: communication and force. Excavations and surveys of roads and military camps are a common part of the archaeology of empires.

FIGURE IV.5 Relief showing the Assyrian attack of the town of Lachish

■ Ecology and Society

Karl Wittfogel (1957) proposed a theory of early state formation that emphasized the importance of large-scale irrigation systems. Wittfogel argued that the need to organize large groups of workers to build and maintain irrigation canals allowed the formation of a hierarchical form of government he labeled "oriental despotism."

Wittfogel's model is an example of a prime-mover model—one in which a single factor is seen as the cause of a phenomenon. In this case, the organization of large-scale agriculture leads to the formation of a centralized bureaucratic government. Robert Carneiro (1970) has proposed a model of state formation that considers the interaction among geography, population increase, and violence. Carneiro emphasizes that early state societies tend to develop in circumscribed areas—that is, areas surrounded by natural barriers or frontiers with neighboring groups. A population increase in a circumscribed area leads to increasing pressure for resources, which in turn will lead to increased violence between communities. Carneiro argues that it is within the context of this competitive violence that power will become increasingly centralized. Unlike Wittfogel's model, the circumscription model proposed by Carneiro suggests that it is the interaction among multiple factors that leads to the development of state societies.

■ The Source of Power

Exploring early state societies is essentially a search for the roots of power—the glue that held these large-scale, highly differentiated societies together. How did some people gain the ability to control the actions of others? The critical characteristic of power in state societies is that it comes to reside in institutions, as well as developing around charismatic individuals.

A number of archaeologists have suggested that the control of information was a major element in the formation of state societies. The rise of a centralized bureaucracy rested on the ability to gather, control, and record information. The development of specialized craft production involved the transmission of elaborate technical skill and knowledge among a small group of people. The development of

empires A political entity that brings together a diverse and heterogeneous group of societies under a single ruler.

FIGURE IV.6 Modern symbols of power. Queen Elizabeth II and Prince Philip open Parliament.

writing systems and mathematical knowledge gave the centralized government the ability to control resources and people.

Theories of the origin of the state tend to focus on factors drawn from Western economics. Access to resources, control of labor, population size, competition, access to information, and bureaucracy are among the factors that are often stressed as underlying the power of the centralized government of early states. Another approach is to ask how the people themselves saw the world in which they lived. From this perspective, it is likely that part of the power of rulers flowed from their possession of unique symbols of power and an intimate connection to the gods. The power of special objects—be they banners, thrones, or scepters—to invoke fear, awe, or loyalty is a force that must be kept in mind when trying to understand how centralized bureaucracies came to have legitimacy in the eyes of their subjects (Figure IV.6).

In the coming chapters, we will explore the emergence of state societies from a comparative perspective. We will begin with four societies that afford clear evidence of a complex social organization without the institutionalization of power that is characteristic of state societies. From this foundation, we will move on to examine early states in chapters organized geographically. Our own experience living in a world structured by complex local and global political interrelationships serves as the backdrop to all of these case studies. We are essentially examining how the world we inhabit came into being.

SUMMARY

- Archaeologists today see the development of political complexity as a process that requires explanation and cannot be viewed as the natural result of progress. Political complexity is linked with increased social inequality and limitations on personal autonomy.
- An authority has legitimacy when its right to power is accepted. Legitimacy can be based on coercion or consensus (or both).

- Morton Fried developed a system of classifying human societies into egalitarian, ranked, stratified, and state societies. For Fried, state societies are defined as the organization of society on a supra-kin basis.
- Elman Service divides human societies into bands, tribes, chiefdoms, and states. For Service, state societies are defined as a system that implements bureaucratic government by force.

- V. Gordon Childe developed a definition of urban societies based on 10 criteria.
- Karl Wittfogel explained the emergence of states as a response to the need to organize large groups of workers for public-works projects.
- Robert Carneiro argued that states developed in circumscribed settings as a response to the warfare generated by population growth.
- Empires are political entities that bring together a diverse group of societies under a single ruler.

KEY TERMS

egalitarian society, 260
empire, 263
legitimacy, 259
ranked society, 260

state, 260
stratified society, 260
urban society, 261

REVIEW QUESTIONS

1. How does Fried's system for classifying societies differ from Service's?
2. Why is it important for archaeologists working on state societies not to focus exclusively on the excavation of tombs and palaces?
3. How do Wittfogel and Carneiro explain the development of state societies? Why is such an explanation needed?

COMPLEXITY WITHOUT THE STATE

Some of the most impressive archaeological sites in the world were produced by societies that Morton Fried would describe as ranked or stratified and Elman Service would describe as chiefdoms. After reading this chapter, you should understand:

- The development of Stonehenge and the social and economic context surrounding the construction of this monument.

- The evidence for the function and political organization of Pueblo Bonito and Cahokia.

- The current theories of the organization of the society of Great Zimbabwe.

Stonehenge viewed from above

10 TIMELINE

AFRICA SITES				
U.S. SITES				
GREAT BRITAIN SITES		Durrington Walls		
		Amesbury Archer		
PHASES	STONEHENGE PHASE 2 BURIALS AND TIMBER			
	STONEHENGE PHASE 1 EARTHWORK CIRCLE		STONEHENGE PHASE 3 STONE MONUMENT	
thousands of years ago	5		4	3

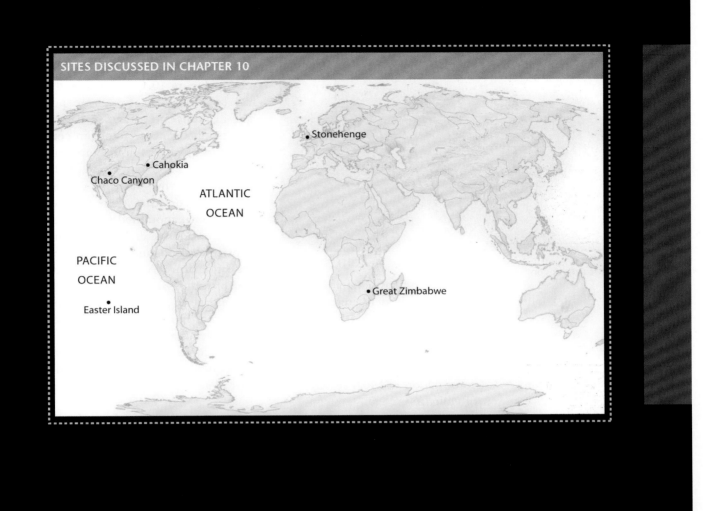

SITES DISCUSSED IN CHAPTER 10

- Cahokia
- Chaco Canyon
- Stonehenge
- Great Zimbabwe
- Easter Island

ATLANTIC OCEAN

PACIFIC OCEAN

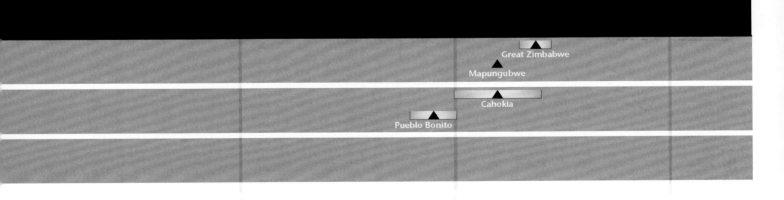

Great Zimbabwe

Mapungubwe

Cahokia

Pueblo Bonito

FIGURE 10.1 Moai statues on Easter Island

Easter Island is a speck of land thousands of miles from any other inhabited island. The monumental stone heads known as Moai that dot the island embody the enigma that is at the heart of this chapter (see Figure 10.1). Easter Island has never had large cities or even large populations. The island has no particular material wealth, and its inhabitants were not in contact with any of its neighbors until Europeans reached there in 1722. So how—and, perhaps more importantly, why—did the people of Easter Island construct these massive monuments? What motivated them to quarry the rock laboriously, drag the massive stones across the island, and set them up on elaborate platforms? Archaeological research on Easter Island has gone a long way toward providing an answer to these questions. Competing leaders erected the Moai during periods of prosperity. Competition between chiefs fueled a cycle of construction of monuments. Some archaeologists argue that in the fragile island ecology of Easter Island this competitive cycle had disastrous consequences, resulting in deforestation and the decimation of resources (Flenley and Bahn 2003). During the subsequent period of ecological distress, the construction of Moai ceased and appears to have been replaced by increased levels of violence.

Societies that have developed a degree of political complexity, but that lack a fully developed state bureaucracy, often produce archaeological sites that strike us as enigmatic or even mysterious. These sites are frequently characterized by elaborate and well-planned construction, yet yield little evidence of a ruling elite. In this chapter, we examine the archaeological record of Stonehenge, Chaco Canyon, Cahokia, and Great Zimbabwe. All of these sites are the ruins of structures built by societies that Fried would define as ranked or stratified and Service would describe as chiefdoms. None have produced evidence of the centralized bureaucracy that characterizes the state. In this chapter, we explore these spectacular sites in order to gain insight into the social life of pre-state complex societies.

10.1 Stonehenge

Stonehenge, a ring of massive standing stones on the Salisbury Plain in southern England, has been the subject of contemplation and wonder for centuries (see Figure 10.2). William Wordsworth wrote about the site in a poem:

> Pile of Stone-henge! so proud to hint yet keep
>
> Thy secrets, thou that lov'st to stand and hear
>
> The Plain resounding to the whirlwind's sweep,
>
> Inmate of lonesome Nature's endless year;

The construction of Stonehenge has been variously attributed to Romans, Druids, Danes, and Greeks (Castleden 1993). For some, Stonehenge is the product of mystical forces or "earth mysteries" (Chippindale et al. 1990). Archaeological research has demonstrated that Stonehenge is not a single monument, but rather the site of a sequence of monuments built over a period of more than 1,000 years. Research

▲▲ **Stonehenge** A ring of massive standing stones on the Salisbury Plain, England, that was constructed beginning in the Early Neolithic and ending in the Early Bronze Age.

on the region surrounding Stonehenge has documented an entire landscape upon which monuments were constructed. As a result, Stonehenge can now be grounded within a long process of development and within a broad regional context. Still, the wealth of archaeological research at Stonehenge and in the surrounding region has not dispelled all the enigmas. Understanding the social and economic organization of the people who built Stonehenge still poses significant challenges.

■ The Development of Stonehenge

Archaeological research at Stonehenge has demonstrated that the site developed through a series of stages beginning in the Late Neolithic (5,000 years ago) and ending in the Early Bronze Age (3,500 years ago) (Cleal, Walker, and Montague 1995; Souden 1997). Understanding Stonehenge requires an understanding of the long process through which the site came into being. Figure 10.3 illustrates the major stages of construction of Stonehenge.

PHASE 1: THE EARTHWORK CIRCLE. The first monument at Stonehenge was a round ditch excavated to enclose an area 110 meters in diameter. Slight embankments were built up on both the inside and the outside of the ditch. Wooden posts were erected in a ring of holes known as the Aubrey holes, which were dug along the inside of the ditch. Animal bones, including a cow jaw and an ox skull dating to Phase 1, were found buried in the ditch. Phase 1 dates to the Late Neolithic, roughly 5,000 years ago.

PHASE 2: BURIALS AND A TIMBER STRUCTURE. During Phase 2, the ditch and the Aubrey holes were largely filled in. Human remains dating to Phase 2, including remains from cremated burials, are found in the fill of both the ditch and some of the Aubrey holes. A structure of standing timber posts was constructed near the center of the monument. Phase 2 dates to the Late Neolithic, between 5,000 and 4,500 years ago. The recent reappraisal of the site (Parker Pearson et al. 2009) suggests that most of the burials actually date to Phase 1.

FIGURE 10.3 Phases in the
construction of Stonehenge

Phase 1: The Earthwork Circle.

Phase 2: Burials and a Timber Structure.

Phase 3a: The Bluestones.

Phase 3b: Sarsen Circle and Trilithons.

bluestones A ring of standing
stones at the center of Stonehenge.
The source of the stones is over 240
kilometers from Stonehenge.

PHASE 3: STONE MONUMENT. The monumental standing stones that are the most impressive aspect of Stonehenge were erected in a series of six subphases during the Early Bronze Age, between 4,500 and 3,500 years ago.

Phase 3a: The Bluestones. The **bluestones**, shown in Figure 10.4, were set up in either a circular or a semicircular formation at the center of the monument in a series of holes known as the Q and R holes. The bluestones, which stand between 2 and 2.5

FIGURE 10.4 The bluestones are
the smaller standing stones in the
inner circle surrounded by the far
larger sarsen stones

meters high, are not the most impressive stones at the site, but they do raise many questions. The geological source of these stones is not in the vicinity of Stonehenge; it lies in the Preseli Mountains in Wales, over 240 kilometers away. Moving these stones from Wales to the Salisbury Plain would have required an enormous effort. Some archaeologists have argued that the bluestones had been transported to southern England by glacial activity during the Pleistocene. However, the identification of a bluestone quarry in Wales that was active in the Early Bronze Age provides strong evidence that in fact the bluestones were transported by people (Parker Pearson et al. 2015). Why these particular stones would have had a value to justify such an effort remains an open question. Recent research suggests that the bluestones might have been brought to Stonehenge as early as the first construction phase, perhaps from an earlier monument in Wales to mark a migration (Parker Pearson et al. 2009). It is calculated that each stone weighed two tons and could have been carried on poles by 60 people with each person bearing a weight of no more than 30 to 50 kilograms.

Phase 3b: Sarsen Circle and Trilithons. The **Sarsen Circle**, constructed of massive blocks, was set up in the central area of the site. The blocks were of sarsen stone, a very hard sandstone found 30 kilometers from Stonehenge. In a staggering triumph of engineering, the circle of sarsen stones was capped by lintels made of solid blocks. These lintels and their supporting stones were fit together with carved joints. Inside the Sarsen Circle, another set of sarsen monoliths known as the **trilithons** was arranged in a horseshoe oriented toward the northeast. The trilithons were set up in five pairs, each capped by a lintel. The trilithons are truly massive, reaching a maximum height of 7 meters.

Phases 3c–f: Rearranging Bluestones and Digging Holes. The construction of the Sarsen Circle and the trilithons was the most intensive phase at Stonehenge. There followed a series of three phases in which the bluestones were reorganized and a series of holes was dug in concentric circles around the site. In the final configuration, one set of bluestones was arranged in the shape of a horseshoe on the inside of the trilithons, and another was erected between the trilithons and the Sarsen Circle. Two concentric rings of pits were excavated around the outside of the monument.

■ A Constructed Landscape

Stonehenge was not an isolated monument. Numerous different types of earthen mounds and enclosures were built on the Salisbury Plain during the Late Neolithic and the Early Bronze Age (see Figure 10.5). One of the most impressive features is the Avenue, a path bounded by ditches and embankments that runs for over a kilometer between the Avon River and Stonehenge. Although the function of the Avenue appears to have been to guide people toward Stonehenge, other features on the site have a less clear purpose. The most massive of these is the Cursus, a slightly raised earthen platform that runs for almost 3 kilometers in an east–west alignment. The entire landscape of the Salisbury Plain was sculpted by these massive earthen constructions (Thomas 1991). New excavations at the Cursus have shown that this feature might actually predate the first phase of construction at Stonehenge (Thomas et al. 2009).

■ The Context of Stonehenge

Stone monuments constructed during the Late Neolithic and Early Bronze Age are found in many parts of western Europe. However, even within this context, Stonehenge stands out as a marvel of engineering and a true enigma. What was its

Sarsen Circle A circle of massive upright sandstone blocks capped with lintels set up in the central area of Stonehenge.

trilithons Three pairs of upright sandstone blocks capped with lintels at Stonehenge located within the Sarsen Circle.

FIGURE 10.5 Map of Stonehenge landscape

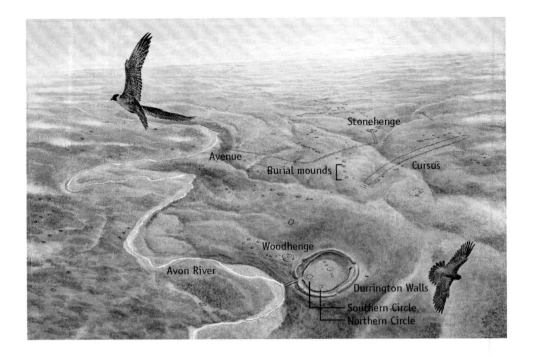

function within the lives of the people who built it? Many have argued that the monument is aligned to allow for the prediction of celestial events. It seems beyond question that it was a construction of religious significance. Almost no domestic remains have been discovered during excavations at the site. Moreover, in the region as a whole, domestic remains are limited to small pits with artifacts and refuse and the faint traces of houses built of wooden posts (Hunter and Ralston 1999). The people who built Stonehenge were agriculturalists who raised wheat and grazed cattle. There is botanical evidence that in the Late Neolithic the Salisbury Plain became an increasingly open landscape used mostly for grazing. Recent excavations at the site of **Durrington Walls**, located 2.8 kilometers from Stonehenge, have revealed the exciting discovery of a series of houses that appear to be part of a village dating to the Late Neolithic (Parker Pearson et al. 2005). However, analysis of plant and animal remains from Durrington Walls suggest that this might not have been a normal village (Craig et al. 2015). Evidence for cooking plant foods is rare. In the large quantity of animal bones recovered, mostly of pigs but also some of cattle, there were few neonatal bones. The absence of bones of newborn animals does not fit with expectations if herds were raised on-site. It appears likely that Durrington Walls was a feasting site, perhaps linked to the early phases of the construction of Stonehenge.

The construction of Stonehenge required the ability to organize a large group of people for work beyond their basic subsistence activities. This labor force had to be coordinated and guided by clear planning. The accomplishment of transporting and erecting the 7-meter-high trilithons and then capping them with a lintel stone is quite impressive. These feats of engineering and organization were achieved by people who did not live under a state bureaucracy. The leaders who directed these projects are invisible to us today. Their authority would have rested not on an absolute control based on force, but rather on the "soft power" that comes from the redistribution of surplus goods and the status that comes from holding an inherited position in society.

▲▲ **Durrington Walls** A site on the Avon River near Stonehenge with three monumental timber circles and evidence of occupation.

Colin Renfrew (1984) has argued that Stonehenge was built by people living in chiefdoms and that the increasing scale of the monument over time reflects the increasing size of territories controlled by a single chief. Renfrew (1984) recognizes that a critical weakness in his argument is the absence of "direct evidence among the artifacts found for personal ranking, as indicated by distinctive dress, ornament, or possessions" (243). However, in 2002, archaeologists working on a rescue excavation before a housing development was to be constructed found a pair of burials that fulfill Renfrew's prediction: The people who built Stonehenge did include elites marked by ornaments and possessions.

The **Amesbury Archer**, as the main burial came to be known, was found 3 miles from Stonehenge (see Figure 10.6). He lived during the Early Bronze Age, corresponding to Phase 3 in the construction of Stonehenge. A recent program of radiocarbon dating indicates that the Amesbury Archer lived during Phase 3c–f, after the Sarsen Circle and trilithons had been erected (Parker Pearson et al. 2007). Objects found with the burial include two slate wrist-guards, a bone pin, two copper knives, five pots, boar tusks, a cache of flints, arrowheads, a shale belt ring, and two gold earrings. No other burial with a similar wealth of grave goods has been discovered from this period. Nearby, a second burial was found of an individual with more modest grave goods that include gold earrings. The goods found with these two burials are precisely the kind of display items that Renfrew would expect in the burials of the leaders of a chiefdom. However, the Amesbury Archer also raises questions. Isotopic analyses of the skeletal remains indicate that the Archer grew up not in the vicinity of Stonehenge, but rather far off in the Alps. Why did he move such a long distance? How did he gain status in a society he was not born into?

Amesbury Archer A burial with a range of elite burial goods found near Stonehenge.

■ What Did Stonehenge Mean?

It might seem that there must be an explanation for Stonehenge, that it is a mystery waiting to be unlocked. There is no lack of explanations for the monument; they range from the construction of a prehistoric observatory to fantasies of a Druid sanctuary (Chippindale et al. 1990). Certainly, there is some truth behind these ideas: Stonehenge must have had a ritual function, and many aspects of the arrangement of the standing stones correspond to celestial orientations. However, Barbara Bender (1992) has criticized such explanations as attempts to "freeze" the past that lack a sense of an ongoing historical process. Bender's critique is particularly relevant to the site of Stonehenge, a monument that came into being as part of a process lasting over 1,500 years. According to Julian Thomas (1996), "Stonehenge never had a meaning" (62). Over more than 80 generations, Stonehenge became the landscape within which people lived. The essential explanation of the monument is that it does not have a single explanation; rather, it must be understood as the long-term unfolding of a society's relationship to the landscape.

But can we say *anything* about what Stonehenge meant? Determining the meaning of ancient monuments is treacherous terrain, since we are essentially trying to gain insight into prehistoric beliefs. Ian Hodder (1990) has placed Stonehenge within the broader context of monument building in the Neolithic of western Europe. He sees the emergence of large monuments as part of the

FIGURE 10.6 The Amesbury Archer with associated grave goods

expansion of the household to include a larger group of people spread over a wider area. For Hodder, Stonehenge is one of many monuments that recreate the household at the level of a regional landscape. Bender (1992) takes a somewhat different approach, seeing the scale of construction at Stonehenge and the surrounding area as producing a fusion of nature and culture. Over the generations, the constructions at Stonehenge became elements of a developing landscape, where the lines between nature and culture were blurred. One intriguing idea is that, for Stonehenge and the surrounding earthworks such as the Avenue, the act of producing and experiencing the landscape was as important as the enduring monument. Bender points to the digging and refilling of holes and the way the earthworks would have channeled people's movements. She also suggests that the shaping of the landscape might have expressed and strengthened conceptions of gender and power in society.

Mike Parker Pearson and Ramilisonina (1998) have developed an interpretation of Stonehenge that builds on recent research at the site of Durrington Walls (see Figure 10.7). Like Stonehenge, Durrington Walls sits on the Avon River, but in every other respect, these sites are opposites. At Durrington Walls, there is evidence of occupation, including houses, while at Stonehenge, no domestic debris has been recovered. Durrington Walls has three monumental circles, but these were built of timber rather than standing stones. Radiocarbon dating now shows that Durrington Walls and Phase 3b at Stonehenge, the period of the construction of the trilithons and Sarsen Circle, are contemporary. Parker Pearson and Ramilisonina have suggested a connection between the two sites, saying that Durrington Walls was the land of the living, while Stonehenge was the domain of the ancestors. At Stonehenge, the wood circle at Durrington Walls was transformed into stone, a material that represented the builders' ancestors. If Parker Pearson and Ramilisonina's interpretation is correct, it might explain why the builders of the Sarsen Circle used mortise and tenon as well as tongue-and-groove joints to fit the lintels onto the upright stones. These are techniques used in woodworking, and their use at Stonehenge is puzzling. Perhaps the explanation of this feature is symbolic rather than technological—perhaps Stonehenge was built as a stone replica of a wooden structure. Parker Pearson and Ramilisonina (1998) believe that Stonehenge would

FIGURE 10.7 Excavation of a series of postholes at the site of Durrington Walls marking the fence that surrounded a house visible as a faint square outline. The red earth is the hearth or fireplace that was in the center of the house.

Cultural Resource Management Archaeology in the Southwest

DR. SARAH HERR, RESEARCH ARCHAEOLOGIST, DESERT ARCHAEOLOGY, INC., TUCSON, AZ

What I particularly enjoy about my job as a project director for Desert Archaeology is that it combines research, teamwork, and a feeling of relevance. For the past 13 years, a large component of my job in applied archaeology has been to manage the cultural resources needs on a highway realignment project on National Forest land through the mountains of central Arizona. The archaeological sites are small and the artifacts are plain, so the region has not attracted much attention from archaeologists. Because federal dollars and federal land are involved, however, Section 106 of the National Historic Preservation Act requires that the state's department of transportation consider the effects of this new highway on the historical resources. Therefore, before each 3- to 4-mile-long section of highway is constructed, we do the archaeological, ethnographic, and historical investigations, as needed.

This project is located about 200 miles away from my home, so during field seasons we work four 10-hour days. Every Sunday night crew members from all over the state meet at the designated project hotel. Then every morning we travel another 20 miles to our sites. Thursday after lunch, we go back to the hotel, hurl our belongings into the car, and get on the highway, knowing every truck stop that sells ice cream even as we try to get home by dinnertime.

I direct a field crew that, during the course of a field season, will work at anywhere from 1 to 17 sites. The crew is comprised of field directors (skilled archaeologists who oversee the excavation at each site), crew members, assistants, and a backhoe driver. The crew members include people who have just graduated with an associate's or a bachelor's degree in archaeology and are gaining experience and money as they decide whether to enter a master's program. They also include "shovel bums," people who might live in their cars, going from project to project across the country. I hire underemployed White Mountain

Apache tribal members from the adjacent reservation as assistants. The land I am working on is their ancestral land. They get a steady paycheck for several weeks, and we learn from their tremendous knowledge of the landscape and its resources. In the fall, I'll walk onto a site and hear the crew calling the rutting elk and talking with the backhoe driver about their favorite way to cook venison. They show me how oak galls become children's toys and a certain red berry that is called "Apache koolaid."

For every day we spend in the field, about four days are spent in the office analyzing and interpreting artifacts and writing about the results. Here, my team is specialists who interpret the ceramics, flaked stone, ground stone, animal bone, charred plant remains, radiocarbon samples, and pollen that we have collected. While the fieldwork told us about the major period of occupation at any site, the

detailed analyses tell us about the activities of daily life. They might reveal the presence of a specialized projectile point industry or identify a headdress made out of a deer skull. They also discover diagnostic artifacts that identify ephemeral occupations such as Archaic houses or later Apache ramadas, as we realize that small groups of people returned to the same place every three or four generations, living on top of the sites of earlier people.

I like that, even as I fulfill a public need to help make Arizona's highways safer for travel, I can offer experience to crew members who are exploring archaeology as a career and jobs to Apache men and women who need the money to support their families. My research is informed by the crew's understanding of the site deposits and landscapes and by the views of specialists as I write a history of the people who once lived in this poorly known place. ▲

FIGURE 10.8 Giving a tour to Apache cultural advisors, with Forest Service archaeologist and ethnographers

Photograph by T. J. Ferguson.

▲▲ Chaco Canyon A canyon in New Mexico that became the center of a regional settlement network and the site of the construction of large, multistoried structures, known as Great Houses, beginning around A.D. 800.

Great Houses Large, multistoried structures located at Chaco Canyon, New Mexico, that became the center of a regional settlement network beginning around A.D. 800.

have stood empty after its construction, that "its inhabitants were the spirits of the ancestors" (319).

■ Summing Up the Evidence

Archaeological research has demonstrated that Stonehenge came into being over a period of more than 1,500 years. It is therefore very unlikely that the site has a single meaning or explanation. The source of power underlying the construction of the site did not rest on control based on force, as is often found in state societies. The Amesbury Archer provides the first direct evidence of the elites of Early Bronze Age society in the region. Although the cultural context of Stonehenge remains enigmatic, the new excavations at Durrington Walls have opened up a promising new line of research on the cultural landscape of Stonehenge.

10.2 Pueblo Bonito, Chaco Canyon

Beginning around A.D. 700, there is evidence for an increased level of social complexity across the American Southwest (Plog 1997). In the arid deserts of southern Arizona, sites with platform mounds and ball courts have been attributed to the Hohokam culture. The largest Hohokam site is Snaketown, located in the Phoenix Basin. At the height of its development in the eleventh century, Snaketown had a population of 300 to 600 people and two large ball courts. The Hohokam developed large-scale irrigation projects to pull water from the Salt and Gila Rivers to agricultural fields.

The ancestral Puebloan cultures flourished in what is now the Four Corners region, where Arizona, New Mexico, Utah, and Colorado meet. Beginning around A.D. 800, **Chaco Canyon** in the San Juan Basin of New Mexico became the center of a regional settlement network and the site of the construction of spectacular multistoried structures known as **Great Houses**. Understanding the organization of Chaco society and the function of the Chaco Great Houses is one of the most exciting challenges in the study of the prehistory of North America.

The current environment of Chaco Canyon "does not exactly correspond to most people's concept of Eden" (Sebastian 1992, 9). Chaco Canyon covers an area 30 kilometers long and between 0.5 and 1 kilometer wide and is between

FIGURE 10.9 Satellite image of Chaco Canyon

90 and 180 meters deep. Rainfall, vegetation, surface water, and game are all sparse (see Figure 10.9). The inhabitants of the canyon responded to this challenging environment by developing dams and canals to control runoff water from torrential summer rains.

■ The Development of Pueblo Bonito

Pueblo Bonito, a massive multistory complex of 650 rooms covering almost 2 acres, is the largest Great House in Chaco Canyon (see Figure 10.10). The rooms are arranged in a semicircle enclosing a central plaza, which is divided roughly in half by a wall running in a north–south direction (see Figure 10.11). The rooms that make up the Great House include a large number of subterranean circular chambers known as **kivas**, structures that have religious significance in modern Pueblo villages.

Archaeological research at Pueblo Bonito has demonstrated that the massive Great House was built up over centuries (Windes 2003). The excellent preservation of wooden beams in the dry environment of Chaco Canyon has allowed archaeologists to use dendrochronology, or tree-ring dating, to develop a tight sequence of events. The construction of Pueblo Bonito began around 1,200 years ago (A.D. 800), and the complex reached its full size over the next 200 to 300 years (A.D. 1000–A.D. 1100). Subsequently, there was a reduction in the extent of occupation, and building activity slowed before the site was abandoned about 750 years ago (A.D. 1250).

■ The Function of Pueblo Bonito

Archaeologists working at Pueblo Bonito have struggled to determine the function of this impressive site (Neitzel 2003). The construction of a complex of hundreds of rooms suggests that the site was a very large settlement, and population estimates for the site have ranged as high as 1,200 people. However, excavations have uncovered a surprisingly small number of fireplaces and few remains of domestic activities. These observations, along with the layout of the site and the large number of kivas, have led some to argue that Pueblo Bonito was essentially a ceremonial center and that it rarely had a population of much more than 100.

Two large mounds of cultural debris and earth reaching 6 meters in height and located in front of the plaza are an important source of information on the function of Pueblo Bonito (Cameron 2002). Similar mounds, known as berms, are a common feature of Great Houses from the Chaco period. A unique feature of the Pueblo Bonito berms is that they were

▲▲ **Pueblo Bonito** A massive 650-room complex, the largest Great House in Chaco Canyon.

kivas Subterranean circular chambers found on sites in the American Southwest.

FIGURE 10.10 View of Pueblo Bonito. This photograph shows the semicircular plan of the site with a central plaza divided by a wall and flanked by rooms and circular kivas.

FIGURE 10.11 Reconstruction of Pueblo Bonito drawn in 1878. How did the artist view the site?

plastered, so they could have served as a platform for ceremonies. Excavation of the berms here and at other sites has produced massive quantities of ceramics. The types of vessels found suggest that they are the refuse of ceremonial feasting rather than of normal daily activities.

The function of Pueblo Bonito might have changed over time (Neitzel 2003). Its initial occupation conforms to the size and organization of a residential site. It is possible that between A.D. 800 and A.D. 1000 it was the residence of an elite group. With the expansion around A.D. 1000, the focus of the site shifted toward ceremonial function. Of course, it is possible that throughout its occupation Pueblo Bonito served as both an elite residence and a ceremonial center; it appears that at A.D. 1000 the balance of activity shifted toward the ceremonial aspect. The connection between an elite residence and a ceremonial center indicates that the elite's power was at least partly the result of their special role in religious ceremonies.

■ Evidence for Elites

The sheer scale of the construction at Pueblo Bonito suggests some form of political leadership. To get a sense of the size of the undertaking, consider that over 200,000 trees were used to make the floors and roofs of the Great House. One estimate places the amount of labor involved in its construction at 800,000 person hours (Metcalf 2003).

Archaeological evidence for social inequality at Pueblo Bonito is restricted largely to the finds made in two small rooms at the north end. Although a number of rooms at the site included burial remains, those at Room 33 are unique (Akins 2003). Here, the disarticulated remains of 16 individuals were found above a wooden plank floor. Below the floor, two male burials were found together with lavish offerings. Altogether, the burial offerings found in Room 33 included over 50,000 pieces of turquoise in the form of beads, pendants, and mosaic inlays. Such a concentration of turquoise is unknown in any contemporary context. Not far away, in Room 38, a rich deposit of beads, pendants, and mosaic pieces made of jet, a hard black stone, was discovered (see Figure 10.12). Although no human burials were found in

FIGURE 10.12 Pottery in the form of a human head from Room 38, Pueblo Bonito

TOOLBOX

Remote Sensing

Methods of remote sensing, including aerial and satellite photography, play a critical role in discovering sites and orienting exploration. Satellite imagery can cover large geographical regions. In recent years, methods of satellite imagery have come to rely heavily on sensors that detect features invisible to the human eye. Radar imaging from satellites is able to detect large-scale buried features. In research in the eastern Sahara Desert, archaeologists have used space shuttle radar images to trace the remains of buried river systems associated with Paleolithic sites. Some sensors can detect minute variations in the surface temperature of the earth, thus providing an index of the characteristics of the soil. In Chaco Canyon, New Mexico, a Thermal Infrared Multispectral Scanner (TIMS) flown by NASA was used to detect a road system dated to between A.D. 900 and A.D. 1000.

Photography from aircraft or balloons can reveal buried features, raised mounds, or wall systems. Most aerial photographs used by archaeologists are taken at an oblique angle to further enhance the visibility of features. Aerial photographs are particularly useful in giving a view of an area that would be too large to excavate. Photographs of ancient cities often reveal the complete urban plan, including roads and fortification walls. Aerial photographs have even been used successfully in making the outlines of ancient field systems visible to archaeologists. In a small number of cases, aerial photography has revealed construction on a scale that is too large to be seen from the ground. The most spectacular of these types of construction are the Nazca Lines in Peru, which consist of representations of animals made by clearing paths on the desert floor. The form of these alignments is visible only from the air. In recent years archaeologists have begun to use airborne LIDAR to map landscapes that are covered by vegetation. LIDAR uses radar to penetrate below the vegetation cover to produce a map of the ground surface. This method has already had a significant impact on our understanding of the Maya cities and the structure of Angkor Wat. ●

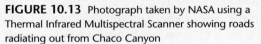

FIGURE 10.13 Photograph taken by NASA using a Thermal Infrared Multispectral Scanner showing roads radiating out from Chaco Canyon

FIGURE 10.14 Aerial photograph of Guatacondo in the Atacama Desert of Chile, A.D. 200 to A.D. 500. Notice how structures that have not been excavated are visible in this photograph.

Room 38, it also contained 14 skeletons of macaws, colorful birds native to the Gulf Coast of Mexico.

The discoveries in Rooms 33 and 38 at Pueblo Bonito make it clear that wealth was not equally distributed among members of society. It is interesting that turquoise, jet, and macaws were traded over very long distances. The concentration of large quantities of these objects in two rooms suggests that the elite of Pueblo Bonito society exercised some degree of control over trade networks.

Studies of residues on pottery vessels for Pueblo Bonito and other southwestern sites have found very prevalent evidence for drinking cacao and *Ilex vomitoria*, a variety of holly used to make a caffeinated drink (Crown et al. 2015). In analysis of the residues using a mass spectrometer, three chemical compounds—methylxanthine, theobromine, and caffeine—were detected. Cacao is native to Mesoamerica and *Ilex vomitoria* is local to the Southwest, so both had to be traded into Chaco Canyon. It is likely that these stimulating drinks would have been consumed in a communal ritual context.

■ The Chacoan Network

The large number of trade items found in Rooms 33 and 38 at Pueblo Bonito indicates that the site was part of a larger network. Within Chaco Canyon, archaeologists have identified a system of roads connecting the Great Houses. Research using satellite imagery has provided clear evidence that the system of roads stretched far beyond the limits of the canyon. A series of photographs taken by NASA with a Thermal Infrared Multispectral Scanner (TIMS) detected over 200 miles of roads radiating out from Chaco Canyon.

The road system links Chaco Canyon with sites covering a large part of what is today the Four Corners region of the American Southwest. Sites in this region tend to share similarities in architecture, which, together with the road system, suggests that they were linked into what has been called the **Chacoan Network**. Although Chaco Canyon was clearly the center of this network, there is no evidence that the people living there had control over the outlying settlements. However, more than just high-status trade items such as turquoise, jet, and macaws flowed into the Great Houses at Chaco. It has long been recognized that much of the pottery recovered at Chaco Canyon was not produced locally, but was brought to the site from outlying areas in the Chacoan Network. A study of maize kernels suggests that some of the food consumed at Chaco Canyon was not grown locally. By looking at the isotopes of the element strontium in maize kernels found at Chaco Canyon, researchers have shown that at least some of the maize was grown in areas over 80 kilometers away (Benson et al. 2003).

The riddle of the Chacoan Network is, what made it run? What compelled people to bring food and pottery into Chaco Canyon from surrounding areas? What gave the people living at Pueblo Bonito the ability to control large quantities of high-status trade items? One possibility is that these items were brought to Chaco Canyon as taxes collected by a central authority backed by the threat of force. The problem with such a scenario is that there is no evidence of such an authority or even of very large populations in Chaco Canyon. Another possibility is that the power of the people living at Chaco Canyon was the result of the centrality of the canyon in the ritual and religious life of the people living within the greater Chacoan Network. The flow of goods into Chaco Canyon might have been the result of cycles of ceremonial feasting in which large groups of people congregated in the canyon for very brief periods, bringing from their homes food and utensils that were then discarded in the refuse piles such as the berm in front of Pueblo Bonito.

■ The Rise and Fall of Chaco Canyon

The location of the elaborate structures like Pueblo Bonito in the highly arid environment of Chaco Canyon has led archaeologists to look for a connection between

Chacoan Network A road system that links Chaco Canyon with sites covering a large part of what is today the Four Corners region of the American Southwest.

TOOLBOX

Dendrochronology

Almost all archaeological dating methods provide a date with a margin of error. Dendrochronology, or tree-ring dating, is the only method capable of absolute precision. Dendrochronologists use the annual rings laid down by trees as they grow to build a clock that today reaches back 10,000 years. How does this clock work? The principles are simple. Each year, as trees grow, they add on a single ring of new wood immediately under the bark. These annual rings are clearly visible in sections cut through a tree trunk. As the rings accumulate, they form a pattern that we can think of as the tree's fingerprint.

The ring pattern of a tree is a record of the fluctuating climatic conditions experienced as it grew. Within the same climatic region, trees of the same species experience similar growth conditions. This uniformity allows dendrochronologists to match up the ring patterns from different trees. Ultimately, by overlapping the ring patterns of trees stretching back in time, it is possible to build up a long-term chronology. The first tree used is a living one, anchoring the chronology in the present. The beginning of the growth of this tree might overlap with a beam found in a historic house, allowing the chronology to be pushed back. This historic beam might be found to overlap with the ring pattern of a tree recovered from an ancient bog, pushing the chronology still further back in time. Once a chronology has been built up, any new piece of wood can be precisely dated by finding the closest match between its ring pattern and the fluctuating pattern found in the long-term chronology.

Dendrochronology has played a critical role in dating the prehistory of the American Southwest. The method has also provided the essential scale for calibrating radiocarbon dates. Although dendrochronology does achieve absolute precision, this does not mean that archaeologists do not need to be very careful in using the data obtained. The ring pattern of a tree can be fit into a long-term chronology to anchor its growth and death precisely in time. However, archaeologists need to be certain that the wood from the tree was used soon after its death. If, for example, wood was salvaged from an old building, the dates provided by dendrochronologists could be far older than the date of the archaeological occupation. As with all dating methods, knowledge of the context in which the sample is found is critical. ●

ADDITIONAL READING: M. G. L. Baillie. 1995. *A Slice Through Time: Dendrochronology and Precision Dating.* London: Batsford.

FIGURE 10.15
Measuring the pattern of annual growth rings in a section cut through a tree trunk provides the basis for dendrochronology

fluctuations in climate and the rise and fall of the Great Houses. The relationship between climate and the end of the occupation of these houses is clear and direct (Sebastian 1992). A devastating drought beginning in A.D. 1130 made continuing intensive occupation untenable (Benson and Berry 2009). As a result, construction of the Great Houses came to an end, and occupation was abandoned. By the time the drought had ended, the Chacoan Network had collapsed, and Chaco Canyon never regained its central role.

The link between climate and the rise of Chaco Canyon is more complex than the connection between climate and the end of its occupation. A number of archaeologists have suggested that the Chacoan Network developed as a means of buffering risk in an uncertain environment. Given the low rainfall in the region around Chaco Canyon, there was always a risk of local crop failure. If each group lived in isolation, then crop failure would lead to starvation. However, if groups were linked through a network in which exchange regularly took place, any group that experienced a failure of its crops could trade for food with other members of the network whose crops had not failed. The existence of a network for the redistribution of food and other goods thus acted as a buffer between the uncertain environment and local communities.

Lynne Sebastian (1992) has argued that this explanation for the rise of Chaco Canyon is wrong. She points out that the Great Houses were built during a period with relatively high rainfall. Why would a buffering mechanism develop when climate pressures were reduced? As an alternative, Sebastian suggests that during the periods beginning around A.D. 1000 there was an increase in annual rainfall, which allowed for an agricultural surplus. The accumulation of surpluses in the hands of local elites led to a cycle of competition. The elaborate construction at Pueblo Bonito and the concentration of rare trade goods such as turquoise and jet are expressions of this competition. For Sebastian, it is the existence of an agricultural surplus, rather than the threat of agricultural failure, that led to the spectacular developments in Chaco Canyon.

■ Summing Up the Evidence

The Great Houses of Chaco Canyon were the hub of an extensive Chacoan Network. Whether this network was a buffer against stress or the result of surplus production remains the subject of debate. Excavations at Pueblo Bonito have demonstrated that there was a considerable concentration of wealth in the hands of an elite. This wealth included trade goods drawn from a very large area. At the same time, excavations indicate that the Great Houses were not densely settled towns, but rather ceremonial centers that were probably permanently occupied only by a small group. Given the effort expended in the construction of the Great Houses, the concentration of wealth in burials, and the evidence for the influx of goods to Chaco Canyon from the Chacoan Network, it is clear that the leaders of this society were extremely powerful. However, there is no evidence that their power rested on the monopolization of force. One possibility is that the power of the leaders flowed from the centrality of Chaco Canyon in ritual and ceremony.

10.3 Cahokia

Two hundred years ago, while traveling along the Mississippi River near what is now St. Louis, the explorer Henry Brackenridge (1814) encountered the great mound at **Cahokia** and was led to exclaim, "What a stupendous pile of earth!" (187). The principal mound at Cahokia is spectacular. **Monk's Mound**, as it has come to be known, rises over 30 meters high in a series of four terraces, covers an area of more than 60,000 square meters, and contains over 600,000 cubic meters of earth (see Figure 10.16).

Exploring the area around Cahokia, Brackenridge (1814) found that the "great number of mounds, and the astonishing quantity of human bones . . . announce that this valley was at one period filled with habitations and villages" (271). The site at Cahokia is the largest known settlement of the Mississippian Period (A.D. 1000–A.D. 1400) in eastern North America. Archaeologists now understand Monk's Mound to be the center of an enormous site covering roughly 4.5 kilometers. At a very brisk pace, it takes about an hour to walk across the site.

▲▲ **Cahokia** A large settlement dating to the Mississippian Period located just outside of St. Louis.

Monk's Mound A massive earthen pyramid occupying the core of the ancient settlement of Cahokia.

FIGURE 10.16 Aerial view looking from the back of Monk's Mound, Cahokia, across the Grand Plaza

■ The Layout of the Site

Cahokia is located in the floodplain of the Mississippi River near St. Louis. This area, known as the American Bottom, is rich in meandering stream channels, wetlands, and swamps. Monk's Mound is located to the south of Cahokia Creek, forming the northern limit of a large flat area known as the **Grand Plaza**, which was cleared and leveled to create an open area at the core of the site. Smaller mounds bound the eastern, southern, and western edges of the Grand Plaza (see Figure 10.17). Both geophysical survey and excavation have demonstrated that a wooden wall known as a palisade surrounded the Grand Plaza and mounds.

The settlement at Cahokia consisted of a series of small clusters, with the Grand Plaza and the mounds of "Downtown Cahokia" at the center. It is likely that

Grand Plaza An artificially cleared and leveled area at the core of Cahokia located just to the south of Monk's Mound.

Key:
1. Monk's Mound
2. Grand Plaza
3. West Plaza
4. East Plaza
5. Cahokia Creek

Mound 71

1 km.

N

FIGURE 10.17 Satellite image showing the major landscape features in Cahokia

Mound 72 A mound at Cahokia where excavation uncovered an individual buried on a bird-shaped platform made of shells, as well as mass burials of apparently sacrificial victims.

swamps and wetlands broke up the landscape. Unfortunately, the size of the site and the poor preservation of domestic structures make it difficult to determine the density and distribution of houses. As a result, estimates of the population of Cahokia range anywhere from 4,000 to 40,000 (Milner 1998). Although Cahokia was a large population center, it is not clear that the term *city* or *metropolis* accurately describes it. More likely, the site was a series of dispersed living areas centered on the monumental core of Monk's Mound and the Grand Plaza.

■ Evidence of Inequality

Understanding the political organization of Cahokia poses an enormous challenge. Clearly, there was some mechanism in society that made it possible to construct a mound on a scale unparalleled anywhere else in eastern North America. Just as clearly, a large number of people, whether in the thousands or tens of thousands, lived at the site. For some archaeologists, Cahokia was a chiefdom on the verge of becoming a state (Young and Fowler 2000). From this perspective, Cahokia's elite ruled not only over the site itself, but also over the surrounding settlements in the American Bottom (Pauketat 2004). Others argue that Cahokia's elite were simply the most powerful among many competing chiefdoms and that their power was limited.

The most vivid evidence of social inequality within Cahokia society comes from the excavation of **Mound 72**, located to the south of "Downtown Cahokia." Mound 72 is relatively unimpressive; what brought it to the attention of archaeologists is the fact that it is aligned directly with the western edge of Monk's Mound. Students excavating the mound were surprised to come across a cache of hundreds of complete arrowheads (Young and Fowler 2000). As they continued excavating, they found that the arrowheads were part of an elaborate burial complex. The central figure was a man laid face up on a bird-shaped platform made of over 20,000 cut shell beads. A number of other people were buried alongside this individual, together with a rich array of goods, including hundreds of arrowheads and polished granite discs. Other discoveries at Mound 72 suggest the possibility that victims were killed to accompany the main burial. In one area, the bodies of four men were laid out with their arms overlapping those of the others. All four skeletons were missing their heads and hands. In a nearby pit, the skeletons of over 50 young women were found. Strontium isotope analysis shows that out of a sample of 17 skeletons analyzed from this pit, all but two were women who were local to Cahokia (Slater et al. 2014). The discoveries made at Mound 72 indicate that wealth was concentrated in the hands of a small number of people within the community living at Cahokia. Twenty thousand shell beads and hundreds of arrowheads represent an enormous amount of skilled workmanship. The mass burials of young women and the series of headless and handless buried males raise the possibility that the elite of Cahokia had control not only over material wealth, but also over the lives of their subjects.

■ Feasting

Excavations below Mound 51, located to the east of the Grand Plaza, provide a different perspective on the social life of Cahokia that complements the dramatic discoveries from Mound 72 (Pauketat et al. 2002). Mound 51 was excavated in 1961 when it was in the process of being destroyed by residents of a nearby subdivision. Below the mound, archaeologists found a well-stratified sequence that was rich in botanical and faunal remains and pottery. This material is not ordinary residential debris, but rather the refuse from large-scale feasting that took place in the Grand

Plaza. The quantity of material found suggests that these feasting events were massive. The excavators have extrapolated the amount of material in the pit by multiplying the density of objects per cubic meter in the excavated unit by the estimated volume of the entire pit. They calculate that there were over 18,000 ceramic vessels, more than 5,000 deer, and over a half-million tobacco seeds within one stratigraphic zone.

The excavations below Mound 51 indicate that the Grand Plaza at Cahokia was the site of massive feasting events. The number of people who could have fit within the palisades has been estimated at 30,000 (Dalan 2003). The Grand Plaza appears to have served as the site of communal feasts involving people from Cahokia and the surrounding region. If so, the power of the elite of Cahokia might have stemmed from their ability to organize large numbers of people through feasting events rather than through a bureaucracy exercising the threat of force. One interesting possibility is that the Grand Plaza served as the setting for sporting events. The polished granite discs found in Mound 72 fit with ethnographic descriptions of a game known as chunkey, as shown in Figure 10.18, played with discs that were rolled along a line and struck with thrown spears (Young and Fowler 2000).

Two discoveries in the Mound 51 excavations cast light on the religious system of Cahokia. The most common bird bones were those of swans and prairie chickens. Both species are rarely found in excavations of sites contemporary with Cahokia. In Mound 72, the burial of the main individual on a shell platform in the shape of a bird also suggests that birds had particular significance in Cahokia society. This interpretation is supported by the discovery, during excavations in Monk's Mound, of a small sandstone plaque depicting a birdman, shown in Figure 10.19.

The excavations at Mound 51 also produced a significant amount of red cedar branchlets and cypress wood chips. It has been suggested that both of these types of wood had ritual significance. Large poles of red cedar, including an enigmatic ring of poles known as "woodhenge," were used at Cahokia in special buildings.

■ Summing Up the Evidence

The elites of Cahokia were able to mobilize large numbers of people. The bulk of Monk's Mound and the expanse of the Grand Plaza are evidence of large-scale work parties. The burial goods in Mound 72 are the product of a great deal of effort by skilled artisans. The remains found below Mound 51 indicate that there were feasting events in the Grand Plaza involving thousands or even tens of thousands of people. The political force that made this organization possible remains unclear. Was it the "soft power" of the chief, or did the elites of Cahokia also have recourse to the controlled use of force that characterizes the state? Many archaeologists see Cahokia as a society on the verge of forming a state. Unlike the societies that built Stonehenge and Pueblo Bonito, the people who built the monuments at Cahokia lived in a large, densely populated center. The sacrificial victims in Mound 72 also seem to indicate a degree of power

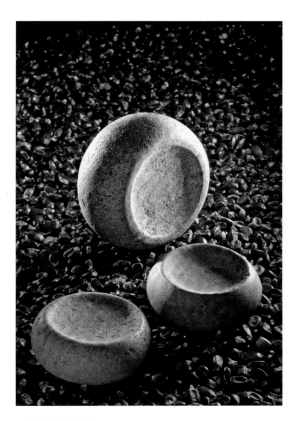

FIGURE 10.18 Chunkey stones found at Cahokia

FIGURE 10.19 Tablet of the "birdman" found at Cahokia

▲▲ **Great Zimbabwe** A large
settlement in modern Zimbabwe
that includes the remains of
impressive stone enclosures and was
built between A.D. 1300 and A.D.
1450.

dhaka A mixture of clay and gravel
that was used for building huts at
Great Zimbabwe.

that goes a long way toward the kind of authority found in the hands of the rulers of state societies.

10.4 Great Zimbabwe

When early European explorers visited **Great Zimbabwe**, they were convinced that they had found the palace of the Queen of Sheba. It has taken decades of archaeological research to firmly discredit such fantasies that "sustain a 'colonial' interest in denying the local people a claim in their history" (Pikirayi 2001, 24). Great Zimbabwe is now understood as evidence of local development of political complexity in southeast Africa during the period between A.D. 1300 and A.D. 1450 (see Figure 10.20).

■ The Layout of the Site

Great Zimbabwe is located in the modern state of Zimbabwe. The region around Great Zimbabwe is agriculturally productive and capable of supporting large herds of cattle. Great Zimbabwe also sits within an area rich in mineral resources, particularly gold.

The architecture of Great Zimbabwe consists of large enclosures surrounded by walls standing up to 10 meters high, built of carefully dressed granite blocks. Circular huts built of a mixture of clay and gravel known as **dhaka** were constructed inside the enclosures. Unfortunately, early excavations at the site focused on the search for evidence of the supposed foreign origin of the builders, resulting in the destruction of much of the archaeological sequence of the dhaka structures built within the enclosures. Careful excavations of some of the remaining deposits have shown that the structures were frequently rebuilt, leading to the rapid buildup of deposits that reach a depth of 5 meters.

Great Zimbabwe stretches across two hills and an intervening valley. The earliest occupation of the site was on the northern hill, known as the Hill Complex, which consists of a large enclosure on the western end and a series of smaller

FIGURE 10.20 View of Great Zimbabwe from the Hill Complex across to the Great Enclosure enclosures to the east. The western enclosure is roughly 50 meters across. It is estimated that there was space for around 20 dhaka huts within the enclosure. The eastern enclosure in the Hill Complex appears to have had a ritual function. A series of tall, monolithic stones carved with the figures of birds and crocodiles was found in this area (see Figure 10.21).

When the site expanded, a new enclosure, known as the Great Enclosure, was built on the southern hill. The Great Enclosure is approximately 100 meters across and could have contained over 40 dhaka huts. The most striking architectural feature of the Great Enclosure is a conical stone tower 5 meters in diameter and 10 meters in height (see Figure 10.22). Probes into the tower proved that it is solid.

The enclosures running down the sides of the hills and into the valley are smaller and more modest in construction than the Hill Complex and the Great Enclosure. It is estimated that they could each have contained about 10 dhaka huts.

FIGURE 10.21 One of the bird sculptures from Great Zimbabwe

■ The Organization of Great Zimbabwe Society

There is no evidence that the walls of the enclosures at Great Zimbabwe served a defensive function. There is no source of water within the Hill Complex, and there is no sign that the walls were damaged in a conflict. The walls appear to have been built to screen the activities of elites from the view of people outside the enclosure. Moreover, the enclosure walls on the Hill Complex and the Great Enclosure would have been visible from a distance. In some cases, this visibility was enhanced by mounting monolithic stones on top of the walls.

Many questions remain to be answered about Great Zimbabwe. As with Cahokia, there is considerable controversy over the size of the population. Low estimates put Great Zimbabwe's population between 1,000 and 2,500 people, while others claim it was between 11,000 and 18,000.

The degree to which the elite of Great Zimbabwe had control over the rest of society and the extent to which they ruled over the surrounding region are unclear. More trade items, including glazed pottery from Iran and China and glass beads from Syria, are found here than at any other site in the region. These artifacts indicate that the elite of Great Zimbabwe played a critical role in the trade networks that stretched from the gold mines of southern Africa as far as China.

The evidence from the site of **Mapungubwe** in northeastern South Africa puts Great Zimbabwe into a broader perspective and suggests that the rise of social complexity in this region was not simply the result of developing trade networks (Huffman 2009). Mapungubwe provides the earliest evidence for the type of large enclosures found at Great Zimbabwe (see Figure 10.24). Around A.D. 1220, a large community moved to Mapungubwe from a settlement known as K2 about a kilometer away. By A.D. 1250, these people had begun to build stone-walled enclosures around the elite living quarters, a pattern not found at K2. Archaeological evidence for rainmaking rituals is found on sites in the hills around Mapungubwe. When the enclosures were built, the use of the surrounding hills for rainmaking ceremonies came to an end. The enclosure built at the top of the hill at Mapungubwe directly overlies a ritual site. It appears that, as the power of the rulers increased, they expropriated the powers of

▲▲ Mapungubwe A predecessor to Great Zimbabwe; located in South Africa, it features an elite residence situated within a walled compound.

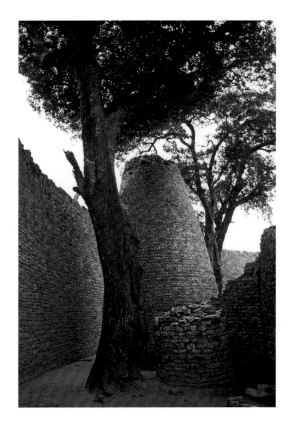

FIGURE 10.22 The tower in the Great Enclosure at Great Zimbabwe. Note that during occupation the enclosure was filled with dhaka huts.

The Trade in African Antiquities

The systematic looting of archaeological sites in Africa has been described as a "horror in the making" (Schmidt and McIntosh 1996, 45). Nowhere is this problem worse than in Mali, around the ancient urban center of Jenne-Jeno, where sites are plundered for their terracotta and metal artifacts. The destruction of the cultural heritage of Mali is fueled by a lucrative market for antiquities in Europe and North America. Collectors are willing to pay very high prices for sculptures and other precious artifacts that serve as marks of prestige and wealth. But for archaeologists, the plunder of archaeological sites results in the irreparable loss of all contextual information. These objects, ripped from their context, lose much of their historical value.

In 1970, the United Nations Educational, Scientific and Cultural Organization (UNESCO) passed a historic legal convention to stem the illegal trade in antiquities. This convention seeks to bar the import and export of cultural property without authorization from the country of origin. The burden of responsibility for stopping the looting of sites lies not only with local authorities, but also with the governments of countries into which the antiquities are transported.

The scale of the illegal trade in antiquities places a heavy ethical burden of responsibility on archaeologists. Their expertise is often sought out by collectors and dealers who want to authenticate objects in their possession. Archaeologists are tempted to cooperate not only out of financial self-interest, but also from a desire to see objects that otherwise will disappear into the hands of collectors without documentation. Increasingly, archaeologists have come to understand that it is important to resist this temptation (Schmidt and McIntosh 1996).

Stemming the trade in antiquities is imperative. The antiquities market has developed sophisticated methods for moving artifacts around the world in violation of the UNESCO convention. International policing agencies such as Interpol are increasingly involved in trying to track and recover looted artifacts. How do archaeologists fit into this complex situation? One part of the answer is that archaeologists must work to raise awareness of cultural heritage as a fundamental human right. ●

ADDITIONAL READING: Peter R. Schmidt and Roderick J. McIntosh, eds. 1996. *Plundering Africa's Past*. Bloomington, IN: Indiana University

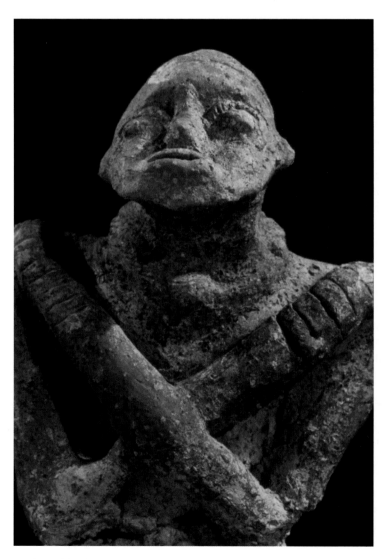

FIGURE 10.23 Rare example of a terracotta figurine recovered from controlled archaeological excavations at the site of Jenne-Jeno. Because the provenience of this artifact is known, it provides important information on the chronology and society of Jenne-Jeno. This information is lost for similar artifacts that have been looted from the site.

rainmaking, becoming ritual as well as political leaders. It is likely that the placement of the hill complex at Great Zimbabwe reflects a similar association between the ruler and rainmaking.

■ Summing Up the Evidence

Great Zimbabwe emerged as an important node in a far-flung trade network that tied the gold mines of Africa with markets as distant as China. The elite of Great Zimbabwe lived within great enclosures that screened their lives from the rest of society and sent a visible message of their power and standing. By considering the evidence from the site of Mapungubwe, it is possible to suggest that there was also a sacred aspect to the power of the rulers of Great Zimbabwe that was associated with rainmaking ceremonies.

10.5 Comparative Perspectives

A comparison of Stonehenge, Pueblo Bonito, Cahokia, and Great Zimbabwe brings out the diversity of societies that Fried would define as ranked or stratified and Service would describe as chiefdoms. Stonehenge was built by people who lived in small, dispersed hamlets that have left few archaeological traces. Pueblo Bonito and the other Great Houses in Chaco Canyon were at the core of a settlement network that stretched across a wide region of what is today the American Southwest. Both Cahokia and Great Zimbabwe were large population centers inhabited by thousands, if not tens of thousands.

These case studies also bring out the difficulty of understanding the political organization of non-state complex societies. The prestige of the elites is clear in most cases. At Pueblo Bonito and Cahokia, the burial of individuals with large quantities of goods presents a vivid picture of social inequality. At Great Zimbabwe, the height of the walls of the enclosures projects the power of the elite, as well as their separation from the rest of society. The monumental nature of these four sites also leaves no doubt about the ability of the elites to organize labor on a massive scale. However, the source of the power of the elites remains less clear. The critical question is whether the elites had control based on the use of force or whether they managed society by other means, such as religious authority or the organization of ceremonies and feasting. The enigma of Stonehenge, Pueblo Bonito, Cahokia, and Great Zimbabwe is not only a question of engineering, but also one of social organization. One ultimately asks how and why a group of people came together to create these structures. In each case, this is a question that will continue to motivate archaeological research well into the future.

FIGURE 10.24 The main hill at Mapungubwe where the ruler constructed his enclosure over a site used for rainmaking rituals

SUMMARY

- Stonehenge is located on the Salisbury Plain in southern England. This impressive monument was built up in stages beginning in the Late Neolithic and ending in the Early Bronze Age.
- Stonehenge was part of a landscape marked by many monumental constructions, including earthen mounds and enclosures.
- Excavations at Durrington Walls have uncovered the remains of a settlement near Stonehenge.
- The Amesbury Archer burial provides rare evidence for elite status contemporary with the later stages of the construction of Stonehenge.
- Beginning around A.D. 800, Chaco Canyon, New Mexico, became the center of a regional network and the site of the construction of multistoried structures known as Great Houses.
- Pueblo Bonito is the largest of the Chaco Canyon Great Houses, with 650 rooms covering almost 2 acres.
- Population estimates for Pueblo Bonito range between 100 and 1,200 people. It is possible that the site's primary function was as a ceremonial center and that only a small number of people lived there permanently.

- A small number of rooms in Pueblo Bonito have a concentration of high-prestige items.
- Chaco Canyon was connected by roads to a network of sites known as the Chacoan Network, which covered a large part of the Four Corners region of what is today the American Southwest.
- Cahokia is the largest known settlement dating to the Mississippian Period (A.D. 1000 to A.D. 1400) in eastern North America.
- Monk's Mound is a massive structure that lies at the core of Cahokia, overlooking a large open area known as the Grand Plaza.
- Excavations at Cahokia have uncovered evidence of human sacrifice and material wealth in a burial mound and the remains of large-scale feasting near the Grand Plaza.
- Great Zimbabwe was a large settlement built between A.D. 1300 and A.D. 1450.
- Large enclosures that appear to have housed the elite of Great Zimbabwe are located on hills on the east and west ends of the site. The power of the elite of Great Zimbabwe was derived from their control over long-distance trade routes.

KEY TERMS

Amesbury Archer, 273
bluestones, 270
Cahokia, 282
Chaco Canyon, 276
Chacoan Network, 280
dhaka, 286
Durrington Walls, 272
Grand Plaza, 283
Great Houses, 276

Great Zimbabwe, 286
kivas, 277
Mapungubwe, 287
Monk's Mound, 282
Mound 72, 284
Pueblo Bonito, 277
Sarsen Circle, 271
Stonehenge, 268
trilithons, 271

REVIEW QUESTIONS

1. How did Stonehenge fit into the surrounding landscape? Is it associated with a large settlement or other monuments?
2. What similarities and differences are there between Pueblo Bonito and Cahokia?

3. What evidence is there that part of the power of elites in the complex societies discussed in this chapter rested on their control over trade routes? What other sources of power emerge from these case studies?

CITIES, PYRAMIDS, AND PALACES

EARLY STATES OF MESOPOTAMIA, EGYPT, AND THE AEGEAN

The early state societies of Mesopotamia and Egypt provide a study in contrasts. In Mesopotamia, cities were at the center of the state, while in Egypt, monumental mortuary complexes were critical to the emergence of social complexity. After reading this chapter, you should understand:

- The evidence for urbanization in early Mesopotamia.
- The development of royal mortuary complexes in ancient Egypt.
- The nature of bureaucracy and social inequality in both Egypt and Mesopotamia.
- The basic characteristics of Minoan and Mycenaean society, including questions about interactions between polities.

Statue of Mycerinus found at Giza

11 TIMELINE

	5000 BC	4500 BC	4000 BC	3500 BC
EGYPT SITES				
EGYPT PERIODS			PREDYNASTIC	
MESOPOTAMIA SITES				Uruk
				URUK
MESOPOTAMIA PERIODS		UBAID		
AEGEAN SITES				
AEGEAN PERIODS				

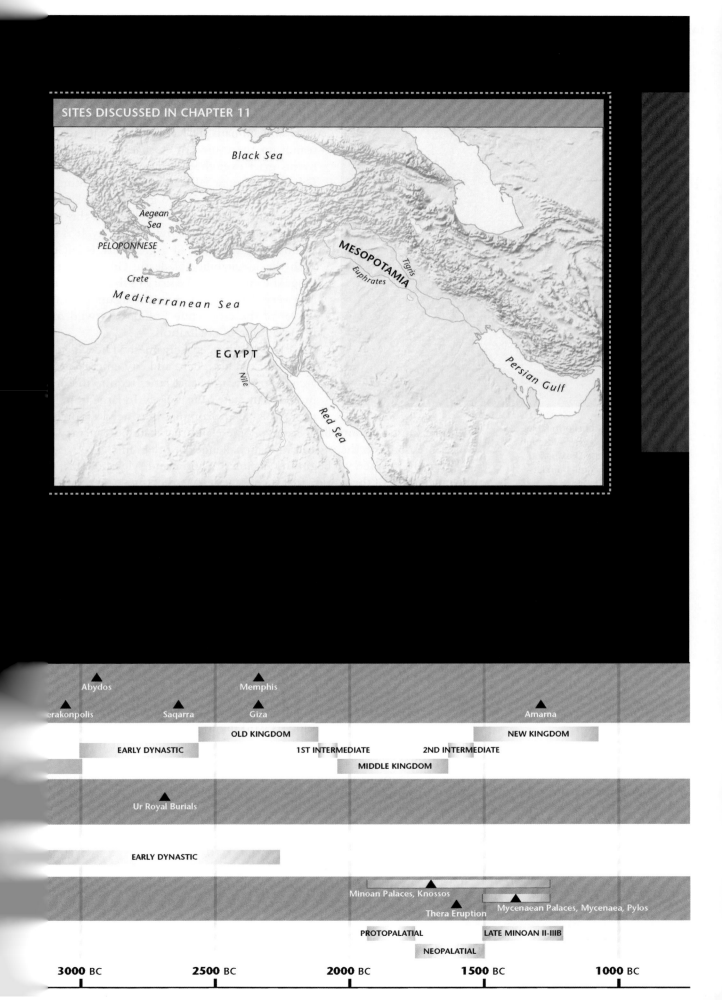

SITES DISCUSSED IN CHAPTER 11

Black Sea

Aegean
Sea

PELOPONNESE

Crete

Mediterranean Sea

MESOPOTAMIA

Tigris

Euphrates

EGYPT

Nile

Red Sea

Persian Gulf

Abydos

Memphis

erakonpolis

Saqarra

Giza

Amarna

OLD KINGDOM

NEW KINGDOM

EARLY DYNASTIC

1ST INTERMEDIATE

2ND INTERMEDIATE

MIDDLE KINGDOM

Ur Royal Burials

EARLY DYNASTIC

Minoan Palaces, Knossos

Thera Eruption

Mycenaean Palaces, Mycenaea, Pylos

PROTOPALATIAL

LATE MINOAN II-IIIB

NEOPALATIAL

3000 BC   2500 BC   2000 BC   1500 BC   1000 BC

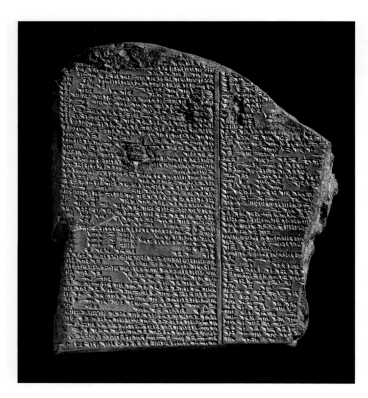

FIGURE 11.1 Cuneiform tablet of *The Epic of Gilgamesh*. Although the epic is set in the Uruk period, all known copies come from later contexts. The text was preserved partly because it was used as an exercise for students learning cuneiform writing.

© *The British Museum.*

The *Epic of Gilgamesh* is a poem recounting the exploits of the king of the city of Uruk, located in ancient Mesopotamia (see Figure 11.1). Gilgamesh is a partly historical and partly mythical figure whose adventures carry him through a world of both gods and humans. The core of the tale is Gilgamesh's search for the source of eternal life, which is triggered by his grief over the death of his companion, Enkidu. Gilgamesh's quest takes him to Utnapishtim, the survivor of the great flood, who gives him a plant that grants immortality. Gilgamesh tragically loses this plant and is left to struggle with his own mortality. It is telling that in this story the king of a great city is left to struggle with the inevitability of death; Gilgamesh is a human king. The epic is also the story of the friendship between two very different characters. Gilgamesh embodies the power of the city, while Enkidu is a wild man, a man living outside of civilization.

Did Uruk need Gilgamesh? Did Gilgamesh need Uruk? Or did both hero and city emerge as one? Many archaeologists argue that cities require the organization provided by state bureaucracy. In large population centers, roads need planning, laws need enforcement, and violence must be controlled. Some people claim that state bureaucracy developed only in response to the organizational challenges of urban life.

In this chapter, we begin in Gilgamesh's homeland, Mesopotamia, which saw the emergence of the world's first state societies. We then move on to ancient Egypt, where the spectacular mortuary complexes of the pyramids provide the clearest evidence for emerging social complexity. We then briefly consider the archaeological record of early state formation in Africa beyond the Nile Valley, with particular focus on the site of Jenne-Jeno in Mali. We conclude by examining the emergence of the great palaces of Minoan and Mycenaean Greece, the setting for the myth of the Minotaur.

11.1 Mesopotamia

Mesopotamia, meaning the land between the two rivers, covers the region along the course of the Tigris and the Euphrates Rivers (see Figure 11.2). The heartland of Mesopotamia is in southern Iraq, where the two rivers flow into the Arabian Gulf. However, Mesopotamia also extends to the north into Syria and Turkey and to the east into Iran. Archaeologists working in Mesopotamia have recovered a rich and complex archaeological record, as well as documents that include the earliest written epics and legal systems in the world (Hallo and Simpson 1971). The earliest stages of state formation appear to have been focused in southern Mesopotamia, also known as Sumer.

◢◣ Mesopotamia A region along the course of the Tigris and Euphrates Rivers centered in modern Iraq.

◢◣ Tigris and Euphrates Rivers Two large rivers that were the focus for the development of Mesopotamian civilization.

■ The Physical Setting

The **Tigris and Euphrates Rivers** flow through a geological depression formed where the Arabian Shield plows into and under the Asian Shield. This powerful geological process has pushed up the Zagros Mountain chain that runs along the

FIGURE 11.2 Map of Mesopotamia.

eastern edge of the Tigris River floodplain. As they flow through the area defined by the geological depression, the Tigris and Euphrates deposit their load of waterborne silts on the valley floor.

There are three important consequences of the geological position of Mesopotamia. The first is that many early sites are deeply buried by the deposit of river silts. As a result, little is known about the Paleolithic and Neolithic periods of the Tigris and Euphrates River Valley. The second consequence is that there are no mineral resources in southern Mesopotamia. The only locally available building materials are reeds from marshes and the ubiquitous mud (see Figure 11.3). The third consequence of the geological situation of the Tigris and Euphrates Rivers is that the soils of Mesopotamia are extremely fertile. This fertility is in sharp contrast to the desert regions along the western edge of the Euphrates River floodplain.

In southern Mesopotamia, crops can be grown only with irrigation, which draws water from the rivers out onto agricultural fields. Dry farming, which depends on rainfall, is possible only in areas with over 200 millimeters of rain per year. The 200-millimeter isohyet (a line on a map that connects areas of equal rainfall) defining the limit of the dry farming region runs through northern Iraq and Syria.

Many of the early cities of southern Mesopotamia lie in what today appears to be a desert wasteland. Archaeological surveys, along with aerial photographs, have shown that when these sites were occupied, they lay

FIGURE 11.3 Photograph of marsh settlements in southern Iraq. The setting of many of the early cities of southern Mesopotamia resembled this marsh.

The Catastrophe of Warfare: Iraq and Syria

The devastation of the Iraq Museum in the days following the U.S.-led invasion of Iraq was a traumatic event. Pictures of looted storerooms and display cases provoked fears that the cultural heritage of Iraq had been irreparably damaged. The exact extent of the loss and the precise sequence of events are still being determined years later. It is likely that the repercussions of this tragedy will shape the field of archaeology for decades to come.

Before trying to assess the implications of the events in Iraq, it is important to give some details about what happened to the Iraq Museum. Press stories have varied enormously, and much remains unknown. However, Matthew Bogdanos, the U.S. marine charged with investigating the events, has presented a useful timeline and parameters of the looting. On Tuesday, April 8, 2003, three days after first reaching Baghdad, U.S. forces entered the area around the museum. At that point, the museum became a battleground, as Iraqi troops took up positions in it and the staff was forced to leave. With two exceptions, U.S. troops refrained from shelling the museum, and damage from military operations was minimal. On April 12, the museum staff returned, and after that time, no

further looting took place. On April 16, U.S. forces entered the museum. The looting appears to have taken place between April 8 and April 12. There were three separate episodes. In the public galleries, 40 objects were stolen; the looters were organized and careful in their choices. In the aboveground storage rooms, there was extensive looting, apparently carried out by a disorganized mob. The number of objects stolen from these storage rooms is hard to calculate, but is in the thousands. In the basement, a collection of small valuable objects, including thousands of cylinder seals, was stolen. This appears to have been an inside job, and the objects chosen were both valuable and easy to transport. Close to 10,000 objects were taken from the basement storage.

Colonel Bogdanos, together with Italian and Iraqi colleagues, set up a project that combined amnesty and seizure, resulting in the return of close to 2,000 objects, mostly from the aboveground storage and the gallery. The objects returned include many of the most famous pieces, including the Warka Vase. Sadly, the devastation of Iraq's antiquities goes beyond the museum: There are extensive reports of large-scale looting of archaeological sites and regional museums.

The brutal warfare that erupted in Syria in the spring of 2011 has led to unspeakable violence against the civilian population. When faced with such a scale of human suffering it is hard to focus on the toll taken on archaeological heritage. The destruction of archaeological heritage is perhaps to be expected in such a conflict, but in Syria the use of the intentional destruction of archaeological heritage by forces aligned with the Islamic State (ISIS or ISIL) marks a new and distressing development. The propaganda value of destroying cultural heritage had already been vividly demonstrated in 2001 when the Afghan Taliban destroyed the monumental sandstone Buddhas at Bamiyan, but the Islamic State has used the destruction of archaeological heritage for propaganda purposes at a scale that was previously unimaginable. The Islamic State has relied on digital media to directly broadcast video of destruction of museums and monuments. None of these images are reproduced here. Archaeologists are forced to grapple with a new problem: What do we do when expressing our outrage at acts of destruction just plays into the propaganda aims of the perpetrators?

The impact of the war in Syria extends well beyond the selected

either within or at the edges of extensive marshlands. However, as the Euphrates River shifted course, ancient cities were left isolated far from the river channel. The degraded state of the modern landscape is also the result of the farming practices of the early inhabitants of the cities, which caused salt to be concentrated in soils near the surface. As a result of this process of salination, crops can no longer be grown in the fields that once supported great cities.

■ Chronology

Most Paleolithic and Neolithic sites in southern Mesopotamia are inaccessible to archaeologists because they are deeply buried by the accumulation of river silts. The earliest well-represented period in southern Mesopotamia is the Ubaid, between broadcast acts of propaganda (full information can be found at www.asor-syrianheritage.org). All parties to the conflict have engaged in looting sites, although in the areas controlled by the Islamic State this looting has become regulated and sanctioned as a means to generate money, reaching a scale that UNESCO describes as "industrial" (Casana 2015). As always, the trail of guilt in such acts of looting extends from the archaeological sites, through middlemen in neighboring countries, and on to gallery owners and collectors living mostly in the West. As war has raged across Syria another casualty has been the archaeological storerooms with their carefully catalogued collections of artifacts, faunal remains, and botanical samples. Many of these have been destroyed, damaged, or repurposed for military functions. The loss to the archaeological record is immense. Tragically, the violence perpetrated by the Islamic State has extended to the murder of Khaled al-Asaad, an 81-year-old archaeologist who would not provide information about the artifacts they wished to sell or destroy.

The events in Iraq and Syria highlight the political significance of archaeological remains and force archaeologists to reconsider the degree to which they can sequester themselves from current events. Archaeologists are left with a number of troubling questions. Perhaps the most important is what role archaeologists play in the international antiquities market and how they can help fight against the growing market for illegal objects. Although the looting in Iraq was carried out locally, the devastation of the museum ultimately points to a network of dealers who are able to move antiquities across international borders and into the hands of collectors. But archaeologists have more to do than just fight the antiquities trade. Archaeologists are also challenged to think of how to rebuild and to help to build a future of civil society built on a deep respect for all aspects of human rights, including the right to preserve and explore our shared archaeological heritage. ●

FIGURE 11.4 U.S. tank stationed in front of the Baghdad Museum

5000 B.C. and 4000 B.C. The first urban sites appeared in the subsequent **Uruk period**, between 4000 B.C. and 3200 B.C. The Uruk is followed by the **Early Dynastic period**, during which a series of city-states developed in southern Mesopotamia. The rulers of these city-states are known from written documents recovered on archaeological sites. The Early Dynastic period drew to a close when Sargon of Akkad unified southern Mesopotamia under his rule in 2350 B.C.

■ Uruk

The site of **Uruk** in southern Iraq is the oldest known city in the world. It grew from the unification of two towns dating to the Ubaid period built along opposite banks of a channel of the Euphrates River. During the Uruk period, the city grew to

Uruk period The period between 4000 B.C. and 3200 B.C. during which the first cities in Mesopotamia were developed.

Early Dynastic period The period that follows the Uruk period, during which southern Mesopotamia was home to a series of city-states.

▲▲ **Uruk** The oldest known city in the world, located in southern Iraq.

cover an area of 2.5 square kilometers and had an estimated population of between 20,000 and 40,000 (Nissen 2002). Surveys in the area around Uruk show that the city was by far the largest site in a landscape densely settled with smaller towns and villages.

Excavations at Uruk have focused on the two massive temple precincts located in the center of the city, where a sequence of temple structures stretching back to the Ubaid period has been uncovered. The city of Uruk grew around these central temple precincts. The temples were built of limestone and bitumen, both of which would have been imported from outside of southern Mesopotamia. Many of the temple structures were built on platforms, evidently the precursor of the stepped pyramid or **ziggurat**, which is at the center of Mesopotamian temple precincts from later periods (see Figure 11.5). The structures were often elaborately decorated. One method of decoration was to insert colored clay cones into mud-brick walls to form a mosaic.

Unfortunately, we know little about the organization of the city of Uruk outside of the temple area. From excavations at other sites, we know that houses were usually built around a central courtyard and were sometimes grouped together into large enclosures (Postgate 1994, 91). It is likely that these were the houses of extended families. Surprisingly, few palace structures have been found from early cities in southern Mesopotamia. Extensive surveys around Uruk have provided some information about the regional setting of this city. On the basis of these surveys, it appears that the growth of the urban center took place at the expense of rural villages. By the Early Dynastic period, there was a sharp dropoff in the number of village sites, suggesting that a migration occurred from these to the urban center.

■ Government

Mesopotamian society revolved around three sources of authority: the temple, the palace, and the city council. The temple was a permanent installation at the heart of the city, and the deity to which the temple was dedicated was a basic element of the city's identity. The temple compounds were quite large; they included land and fulfilled economic functions (see Figure 11.6). Excavations of temple complexes have uncovered the remains of both workshops and storage rooms.

During the Uruk and Early Dynastic periods, the relationship between the palace and the temple was complex and remains poorly understood. It is possible

ziggurat A stepped pyramid found in many Mesopotamian temple precincts.

that the chief priest of the temple was the ruler of the city. The duties of the king, or *ensi*, included maintenance of the temple and military leadership of the city. Kingship was not determined strictly by descent, and there is evidence that the king was selected by a city council. Unfortunately, little is known about the powers of this council.

During the Early Dynastic period, there were over 30 independent cities in southern Mesopotamia. Although they cooperated on military and economic ventures, there were also rivalries, and not all rulers were equal.

The Code of Hammurabi, which dates to the period around 1800 B.C., is the most extensive of a series of early Mesopotamian legal documents. The laws set out in this code cover a wide range of domains, including the penalties for perjury, robbery, and murder; the regulations surrounding adoption, marriage, and the ownership of slaves; and more mundane issues, such as the cost of hiring an ox or an ass. From the Code of Hammurabi, it appears that the king had jurisdiction over the regulation of commercial activities, punishment for violent acts, and aspects of family life.

■ Surplus and Specialization

The growth of the cities of Mesopotamia was based on the production of agricultural surplus. This surplus depended on irrigation agriculture, which required the organization of large work crews to build and maintain canals. Already by the Uruk period, there were people who specialized in various aspects of craft production. One of the most interesting artifacts found on Uruk sites is also one of the most modest. Bevel-rim bowls are small, undecorated vessels made of a very coarse clay fabric (see Figure 11.7). Both complete and broken sherds of bevel-rim bowls are found in enormous quantities on Uruk-period sites. It is possible that these bowls were simply the Styrofoam cups of the Uruk period—cheap and easy-to-manufacture containers that were rapidly discarded. However, archaeologists have puzzled over their function and particularly the regularity of their size. Why would such simple vessels be consistently made the same size?

One proposal is that **bevel-rim bowls** were vessels in which grain rations were distributed to workers. The standardized size would then reflect the basic ration for a day of work. If this proposal is correct, it implies that the rulers had tight control over the distribution of agricultural surplus to workers. Some archaeologists have pointed out that the shape of the bowls is not appropriate for carrying around a ration of grain. Imagine thousands of laborers carefully trying to avoid spilling any grain from their bowls as they carried their rations home. An alternative is that these vessels were used as molds for baking bread. If this is the case, then the bevel-rim bowls indicate that baking in the Uruk period was carried out by specialists who produced bread in very large quantities, perhaps to be paid out as a ration for work.

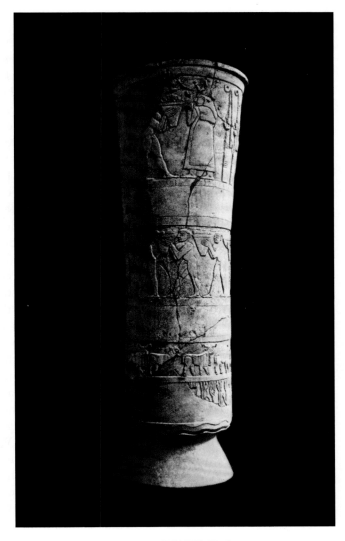

FIGURE 11.6 The Warka vase, showing a procession of offerings being brought to the temple

bevel-rim bowls Small undecorated vessels made of coarse clay that are ubiquitous on Uruk-period sites.

FIGURE 11.7 Bevel-rim bowls, the Styrofoam cup of the Uruk world

▲▲ **Royal Tombs at Ur** Tombs dating to the Early Dynastic period in which the dead were buried with a spectacular array of precious artifacts and sacrificial victims.

■ Inequality

Mesopotamian society included kings, priests, craft specialists, merchants, laborers, and slaves. There were clear disparities in wealth and privilege among the various members of society. It appears that clothing and hairstyle were often used to mark status. The king in the Uruk period is often shown wearing a flat hat and a netted skirt. Slaves are described as bearing a distinguishing mark known as an *apputum*, which might have been a particular hairstyle.

In the 1920s, Leonard Woolley excavated a cemetery at the site of Ur that provides a vivid picture of the wealth and power of the rulers of an Early Dynastic city (Zettler, Horne, and Hansen 1998). The cemetery includes hundreds of burials, most of which are simple interments of individuals with a few pottery vessels. The chambers known as the **Royal Tombs at Ur** present a startling contrast. These tombs contain staggering deposits of wealth, including tools, jewelry, musical instruments, and vessels made from a wide range of metals (gold, silver, copper, and electrum) and precious stones (lapis lazuli, carnelian, steatite, and calcite). These materials were brought to Ur from considerable distances: Lapis lazuli comes from Afghanistan and carnelian from Pakistan. The Royal Tombs are associated with chambers that Woolley called death pits; they contained the skeletons of men and women together with the remains of oxen attached to carts (see Figure 11.9). These people and animals appear to have been slaughtered as part of the burial ritual. Many of the skeletons are still adorned with lavish jewelry and ornaments; many clutch weapons in their hands. Among the most famous objects is the headdress of one of the main figures, which consists of leaves made of thinly hammered gold (see Figure 11.10). Other impressive artifacts include a series of lyres inlayed with elaborate scenes and a sculpture of a ram peering out from behind some branches.

Unfortunately, Woolley preserved very few of the skeletons from Ur, which he discarded because they were highly fragmented. Two skulls, one of a man wearing a helmet and the other of a richly adorned woman, are among the small surviving assemblage of skeletons from the Royal Tombs (Baadsgaard et al. 2011). Analysis of these skulls using a CT scan shows puncture holes in both skulls consistent with blunt trauma from a bronze axe (Figure 11.8). Not only does this study show that these attendants were violently killed, but there are also indications that the skeletons were heated before burial, perhaps as part of a procedure to preserve the body. Traces of a dusting of cinnabar, a form of mercury that can be used as a preservative, were also found around the skulls, adding support for the idea that the attendants were killed, preserved, and only then buried with the ruler.

FIGURE 11.8 CT scans of two skulls from Ur showing evidence of blunt force trauma, marked as the depression on the image on the left and radiating fracture on the image on the right. The image on the left is the skull of a young woman wearing an elaborate golden headdress and earrings. The image on the right is of a male wearing a copper helmet.

It is probable that the rich burial goods and the sacrificial victims found in the Royal Tombs were meant to accompany the deceased to the afterlife; perhaps the goods were used to provide offerings to the gods. The woman buried with the elaborate headdress shown in Figure 11.10 appears to be a queen by the name of Puabi. Another tomb is thought to have been the burial chamber of a king.

The Royal Tombs illustrate the wealth concentrated in the hands of the king and his close family. This wealth included access to large quantities of precious materials imported from a wide geographical region outside of the areas directly controlled by the Mesopotamian state. How did the king come to be the focal point of such an extensive trade network? One possibility is that he controlled the production of textiles in Mesopotamia. The surplus textiles produced were traded for the precious material that the king used as the expression of his power.

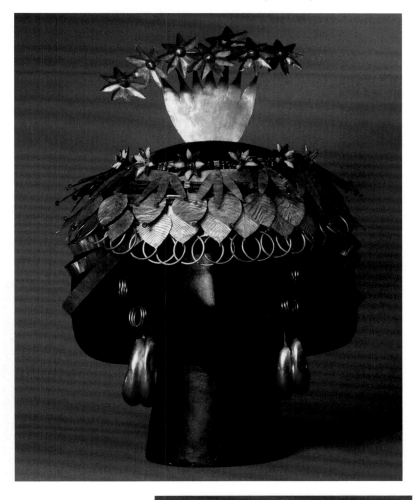

The king not only controlled the flow of precious materials, but also was able to sponsor the highly skilled artisans who produced the spectacular objects found in the burials. The sacrificial victims point to another facet of the ruler's power: the ability to control the life and death of his subjects. It is hard not to conclude from the Ur burials that Mesopotamian rulers had immense power. The riddle remains why so much wealth was buried with the dead. Such a squandering of resources seems at odds with

cuneiform A writing system in which signs were impressed in wet clay. Cuneiform was used to write a range of languages, including Sumerian and Akkadian.

cylinder seals One of the methods developed by Mesopotamian scribes to mark ownership

the accumulation of power found in Mesopotamian kingship. Why sacrifice not only people, but also prestigious objects? One possibility is that the destruction of wealth fueled the continuing effort to accumulate more of it, an effort that was the key to the ruler's power. This power might have been based not simply on a wealth of goods, but also on the ability to maintain a system of trade, tribute, and specialized craft production that continuously created wealth.

Perhaps it is wrong to look at the Royal Tombs from only an economic perspective. Looking back to *The Epic of Gilgamesh*, we see that, despite his power as the ruler of Uruk, Gilgamesh struggled with his own mortality. It seems likely that the elaborate rituals of the Ur Royal Tombs tapped into the same desire for immortality.

■ The Development of Writing

The origins of some of the symbols used by Mesopotamian scribes have been traced to clay tokens found on Neolithic sites in the Zagros Mountains. The **cuneiform** writing system in Mesopotamia first developed during the Uruk period (see Figure 11.11). Mesopotamian scribes wrote on clay tablets, using a stylus to impress the signs into the wet clay (Walker 1987). The cuneiform writing system originated as a pictographic script in which each picture represented a term or concept. By the Early Dynastic period, the symbols were increasingly stylized and were used to represent syllables. The cuneiform script was used to write in several different languages. During the Uruk and Early Dynastic periods, the main written language was Sumerian. During later periods, the cuneiform script was also used to write texts in Akkadian, a Semitic language related to modern Arabic and Hebrew, and Hittite, an Indo-European language.

Mesopotamian scribes also developed elaborate methods for making seals. The seals were carved in hard stone, which could then be pressed onto clay or mud to mark ownership by a person or group. An important function of seals was to ensure that, once closed, a room or vessel remained undisturbed. These early precursors of our tamper-proof lids were frequently applied to clay plugs, sealing vessels and closures on doors. **Cylinder seals** first appear in the Uruk period (see Figure 11.12). They were made by carving scenes onto cylinders of stone. The cylinder seal was then rolled

FIGURE 11.11 Early cuneiform tablet. The dots and semicircles are numbers, and most individual compartments refer to a quantity of a commodity. The signs are still visibly pictographic, some depicting bowls or jars. Note the compartment in the lower right-hand corner that includes a series of signs with no numbers. What do you think this could refer to?

FIGURE 11.12 Cylinder seal. The original seal is shown on the left. The right side shows the impression produced when the seal is rolled across soft clay.

Picture Desk, Inc./Kobal Collection.

across fresh clay or mud, leaving behind an impression. The carving of cylinder seals quickly became a highly developed art. Working on a miniature scale, Mesopotamian seal carvers illustrated vivid scenes from daily life and mythology.

The earliest cuneiform documents were developed to record ownership and economic transactions, not unlike our receipts and contracts. On sites dating to early in the Uruk period, hollow clay balls filled with small clay tokens are found. The surface of the clay balls, known as bullae (singular: *bulla*), is covered with impressions from seals and marks recording numbers (see Figure 11.13). In at least one case, the number on the bulla is known to correspond to the number of tokens in the interior. Bullae were a concrete method of recording a transaction. Each object is represented by an actual token, and the tokens are enclosed in a clay "envelope" that was then sealed. The earliest written documents, which date to the end of the Uruk period, mirror the function of the bulla, but eliminate the need for the concrete tokens. If bullae are one level of abstraction from reality—the sealed tokens representing real objects—the earliest written documents take this abstraction one step further, replacing the tokens with marks in clay. The development of syllabic script extended the economic functions that texts could fulfill still further. One of the most interesting types of documents from the Early Dynastic period is the kuduru texts, which record transactions involving the exchange of land for goods such as bread, oil, beer, cloth, and silver. The kuduru make it clear that land was privately owned in Early Dynastic Mesopotamia and give insight into the relative values of commodities. The economy of early Mesopotamian cities included the wealth of the king and the temple, as well as private wealth. Written documents played an essential role in the operation of this complex system of ownership and exchange.

Over the course of more than 2,000 years, the use of the cuneiform writing system was expanded to include texts as varied as epics, histories, dictionaries, and mathematical treatises, as well as letters, treaties, and accounts.

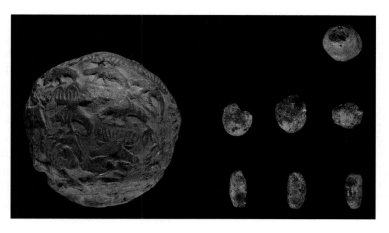

FIGURE 11.13 Bullae, like the example shown here on the left, are clay envelopes that enclose small tokens like those shown on the right. The surface of the bulla was marked with seals before the clay dried.

■ Warfare and Expansion

From the wealth and power displayed in the Royal Tombs of Ur, one might assume that early Mesopotamian cities were highly militaristic societies. Cities were walled, and the texts often speak of wars between them. Perhaps even more telling are cylinder seals from the Uruk period depicting bound prisoners. However, the tools of war were limited, and the conflicts described in the texts appear to be more a display of power than battles resulting in massive numbers of casualties. The main tools of war were axes, spears, arrows, and carts drawn by asses or oxen. The earliest mention of a standing army comes from the time of Sargon, when there is mention of an army of over 5,000 soldiers. In later periods, the power of the Mesopotamian military expanded significantly, allowing for far-ranging campaigns of conquest in foreign lands.

Given the apparently limited extent of military might during the Uruk and Early Dynastic periods, the discovery of Uruk colonies far from southern Iraq has come as a surprise. The most completely excavated Uruk colony is the site of **Habuba Kebira**, located on the upper reaches of the Euphrates River in northern Syria (see Figure 11.14; Algaze 1993). Habuba Kebira was occupied only during the

▲▲ **Habuba Kebira** An Uruk colony located on the upper reaches of the Euphrates River in northern Syria.

FIGURE 11.14 The town of Habuba Kebira, Syria. The Euphrates runs along the east side of the site; the other sides were fortified by a city wall. Notice the major road running north–south through the site and the crossroad running from the city gate.

Uruk period, and there has been very little subsequent accumulation of sediments. As a result, archaeologists have been able to open up a large horizontal excavation, uncovering an almost complete plan of the settlement. The site of Habuba Kebira is a walled town of densely packed houses running for about half a kilometer along the banks of the Euphrates. All of the artifacts found on the site are made in the styles found in the Uruk heartland in southern Iraq. Bullae with Uruk seal impressions and a temple in classic Uruk style have also been found on the site. There is very little evidence of artifacts made in the styles of the surrounding local communities. Habuba Kebira and similar sites present a challenging enigma. They are clearly evidence of the expansion of people out from the Uruk heartland, but there is no evidence that the expansion was a military one. Some archaeologists have argued that Habuba Kebira was a trading post or a settlement built to protect trade routes for critical mineral resources coming from northern Syria and Turkey. However, it remains unclear whether the people coming from southern Iraq actually dominated and controlled these exchange routes or whether there was a more subtle relationship between the people coming from the southern cities and local groups.

Recent excavations at the Uruk-period site of Hamoukar in Syria provide some of the first evidence that the Uruk expansion involved violent conflict (see http://oi.uchicago.edu/research/projects/ham/). The excavators have found evidence for the bombardment of the site by clay slingstones, leading to the collapse of walls and an ensuing fire.

■ Summing Up the Evidence

The development of state societies in southern Mesopotamia is closely linked with the emergence of large urban centers. The Royal Tombs at Ur give a sense of the extensive power of the ruler of the early Mesopotamian cities. The rapid expansion of Uruk-period settlements into northern Mesopotamia provides an indication of the dynamism of these early cities. Much of the power of the cities and their rulers can be linked to economic factors, the organization of large-scale irrigation systems, and the control of surplus production of textiles. The development of the cuneiform writing system served the need of this economy to control and regulate trade and ownership. However, the growth of the Mesopotamian cities was not simply the product of economic forces. In fact, the core around which the city grew was not the palace, but the temple precinct. Still, in ancient Mesopotamia, the boundary between the temple and the palace is difficult to draw. Ultimately, the strength of the early Mesopotamian state seems to flow from a blending of the power of the temple and that of the palace.

11.2 Egypt

The splendor of the temples and tombs of ancient Egypt has long evoked wonder and mystery. Some people have even been led to mystical interpretations of ancient Egypt, seeing monuments such as the pyramids at Giza as evidence of supernatural or extraterrestrial activity. Archaeological research has uncovered a very different perspective. As scientists unearth pot sherds and domestic remains and trace the processes by which monuments were constructed, a picture of the intensely human aspect emerges. Ancient Egypt is not the product of otherworldly forces. The monuments that amaze us are the result of human effort and imagination on an enormous scale. Perhaps the most awesome feature of the pyramids is not their sheer size, but rather the chisel marks left on the stones over 4,000 years ago. These marks open up the real mysteries of the pyramids: How were people motivated to undertake such a venture? How were they organized? How were they fed? These questions lead to the core of the issues surrounding the origin of the state.

▲▲ **Nile Valley** A swath of lush vegetation descending from the highlands of Ethiopia and standing in sharp contrast to the surrounding desert.

■ The Setting

The Nile descends out of the highlands of Ethiopia to cut a dramatic swath through the deserts of the Sudan and Egypt (see Figure 11.15). Until the construction of the Aswan Dam in the 1960s, the annual flooding of the Nile deposited rich alluvial silts across the valley floor. The contrast between the lush vegetation of the **Nile Valley** and the surrounding desert is stark (see Figure 11.16). One can literally place one

FIGURE 11.15 Map of Egypt

FIGURE 11.16 The lush Nile Valley contrasts sharply with the surrounding desert

▲▲ **Upper Egypt** The southern
Egyptian Nile River Valley ending
in a series of cataracts, or rapids, in
the area around the modern border
between Egypt and Sudan.

▲▲ **Lower Egypt** The northern
part of the Egyptian Nile River Valley,
including the Nile Delta.

foot in agricultural fields and the other in desert sand. Egypt is thus an extreme case of circumscription in which the limits of inhabitable land are clearly defined.

Egypt is divided into **Upper Egypt** in the south and **Lower Egypt** in the north. To the north of Cairo, the Nile Valley spreads into several branches, forming the Delta region as it flows toward the Mediterranean Sea. To the south, the limit of Upper Egypt is defined by a series of cataracts or rapids in the area around the modern border between Egypt and Sudan. Aside from the Nile Valley and the Delta, the major inhabitable areas in Egypt are a number of small oases in the Western Desert and the Fayum Depression located just south of Cairo.

The unusual geography of Egypt played a major role in defining the nature of ancient Egyptian society. Because the area was protected by deserts to the east and west and cataracts to the south, the threat of foreign invasion was minor. Almost all human settlement was located along the Nile Valley. The Nile served as a means of transportation, allowing for the easy movement of people and goods north and south along the river. The annual flooding of the Nile served to replenish the soil, so the problems of salination found in southern Mesopotamia are not endemic to Egypt. The richness of the flood also meant that massive irrigation projects were not necessary. The Nile Valley, like Mesopotamia, is completely lacking in mineral resources. However, the surrounding deserts contain sources of metals, including copper and gold, and building materials—including limestone, alabaster, and granite—that the Egyptians exploited heavily.

■ Chronology

The shift toward state society in Egypt began during the Predynastic period, the political organization of which remains poorly understood. However, it appears that by the late Predynastic period three kingdoms had formed along the Nile Valley. The earliest evidence for the unification of Egypt under a single ruler is a slab of

FIGURE 11.17 The Narmer Palette shows Narmer wearing the crowns of Upper and Lower Egypt. How is the power of Narmer shown through this artifact?

carved slate known as the **Narmer Palette**, discovered at the site of Hierakonpolis in Upper Egypt.

The Narmer Palette shows scenes of conquest by a king named Narmer (see Figure 11.17). The rule of Narmer marks the end of the Predynastic period and the beginning of the Early Dynastic period. Significantly, on one side of the palette, Narmer is shown wearing the white conical crown of Upper Egypt, while on the other, he is shown wearing the red crown of Lower Egypt. The depiction of Narmer with these two crowns indicates that he ruled the entire Nile Valley.

The chronology of Egyptian kings is known from documents and monuments. The classical historian Manetho (300 B.C.) devised the system of grouping kings into dynasties. Egyptian dynastic history, outlined in Table 11.1, can be divided into three cycles of integration and collapse (Hallo and Simpson 1971). During periods of integration (Early Dynastic/Old Kingdom, Middle Kingdom, New Kingdom), Egypt was controlled by a single centralized authority. During periods of collapse (First Intermediate, Second Intermediate, Third Intermediate), competing centers of authority emerged, and competing dynasties, with control over only a part of the country, ruled simultaneously.

A constant dynamic in Egyptian dynastic history is a struggle for dominance between Upper and Lower Egypt. The **First Dynasty** was based in **Hierakonpolis** and **Abydos** in Upper Egypt. In the Second Dynasty, the site of the royal cemetery shifted to Saqqara in Lower Egypt. During the Old Kingdom, kingship was firmly established at Memphis in Lower Egypt. In the New Kingdom, the center of power shifted to Luxor in Upper Egypt.

Although Egypt was relatively well protected from foreign invasion, incursions from the north and south did take place, particularly during the periods of collapse. During the Middle and New Kingdoms, Egypt embarked on ambitious military campaigns in the north, ultimately coming into conflict with Mesopotamian powers. During those same kingdoms, Egypt also came to play an active role in trade networks connecting the lands of the eastern Mediterranean and the Aegean.

■ Government and Writing

The ultimate source of the power of the Egyptian king was his identification as a divinity. The king in Egypt was the human incarnation of the falcon god Horus, the paramount god in the Egyptian pantheon. Upon his death, the king became the incarnation of the god Osiris, the god of the dead. The king also had a special relationship to the sun god Ra; however, the way this relationship was expressed varies among documents.

Narmer Palette An artifact discovered at the site of Hierakonpolis; its two sides show the unification of Upper and Lower Egypt under King Narmer.

First Dynasty The dynasty based in Hierakonpolis and Abydos in Upper Egypt.

▲▲ **Hierakonpolis** Along with Abydos, one of the two centers of Egypt during the late Predynastic period and the First Dynasty.

▲▲ **Abydos** The site of the royal cemetery of Egypt during the First and Second Dynasties.

TABLE 11.1 CHRONOLOGY OF ANCIENT EGYPT

PERIOD	DATES	DYNASTY	MAJOR SITES
Predynastic	4500 B.C.–3000 B.C.		
Early Dynastic	3000 B.C.–2575 B.C.	1–3	Hierakonpolis, Abydos, Saqqara
Old Kingdom	2575 B.C.–2134 B.C.	4–8	Giza, Memphis
First Intermediate	2134 B.C.–2040 B.C.	9–11	
Middle Kingdom	2040 B.C.–1640 B.C.	12–14	
Second Intermediate	1640 B.C.–1532 B.C.	15–17	
New Kingdom	1532 B.C.–1070 B.C.	18–20	Thebes, Amarna
Third Intermediate	1070 B.C.–712 B.C.	21–25	

Source: Lehner 1997.

ma'at A concept that combines the virtues of balance and justice; it was of central importance to Egyptian society.

The power of the king was tightly linked to the critical Egyptian concept of **ma'at**, which combines the virtues of balance and justice. In Egyptian thought, chaos and disorder were viewed as catastrophic, and the role of the king was to ensure the preservation of *ma'at*. The breakdown of centralized rule during periods of collapse is described in Egyptian documents as a fundamental, even cosmic, calamity.

It is quite a distance from the lofty concepts of divine kingship and *ma'at* to the more mundane business of organizing a large kingdom. It is clear, for example, that the divine status of the ruler did not prevent palace intrigue and, in some cases, even murder. The king controlled the state through the agency of armies of scribes (Kemp 2006). During the harvesting and processing of cereals, scribes intervened at every stage to measure output and deter theft. The yield of the harvest was measured in the field, during transport, and at delivery. The quantities of bread and beer produced from grain were carefully measured before being distributed as rations.

A picture of the role of the scribe is found on the bottom register of a scene painted in an Old Kingdom tomb from Saqqara. Egyptian tombs were often painted with detailed depictions of daily life meant to magically provide for the deceased in the afterlife. The Tomb of Ty at Saqqara gives particularly detailed pictures of a bakery/brewery. In the bottom register, a line of scribes is shown at work. Scribes are depicted as an integral element of the operation of a bakery (see Figure 11.18). An individual to the left of the scene depicted here is shown being brought to the scribes for discipline.

There is a clear sense that in ancient Egypt the extended family remained an essential social unit. Some even go as far as to suggest that the conception of kingship was based on an extension of the household. A study of graffiti left by workers on blocks in the Giza pyramids affords a unique insight into the organization of labor in the Old Kingdom (Roth 1991). Workers were organized into large labor groups, perhaps by clan or extended family. This evidence challenges the idea that the state represents a rupture with social organization based on kinship.

FIGURE 11.18 Scene from the Tomb of Ty at Saqqara showing a scribe overseeing part of the process of bread baking

The Egyptian bureaucracy often operated by breaking tasks into equivalent parts. This practice is preserved in an unfinished chamber located below the pyramid of Cheops at Giza. The chamber is reached by descending a long passageway that stretches deep below bedrock. For reasons that are not clear, this chamber was abandoned in the midst of quarrying and was never completed. Walking around, one can follow the hammer blows of the workers as they labored to hollow out the subterranean room. One can see that the chamber has been divided in half and then in half again, with two sets of two teams working in parallel. This simple tactic appears to have been widely used by Egyptians to organize large-scale construction projects.

FIGURE 11.19 The boat cemetery from the First Dynasty at Abydos. These vessels were buried as part of the mortuary ritual for the kings of the First Dynasty.

The hieroglyphic writing used by Egyptian scribes is based on a combination of logograms (signs that represent a whole word), phonograms (signs that represent sounds), and determinatives (signs that indicate the exact meaning of a word). Documents were written in ink on paper made of papyrus, a reed native to the Nile Valley. Unfortunately, few of these documents survive from early periods. Because hieroglyphics were not suited for the rapid writing of administrative documents, an alternative script, known as hieratic, was developed by the Fourth Dynasty. Hieroglyphics remained in use primarily for inscribing monuments.

■ The Pyramids

The pyramids of Old Kingdom Egypt are among the most impressive monuments ever built. These spectacular structures were constructed on the desert fringe far from major settlements. The pyramids were temples to the deceased king, who was the incarnation of the god Osiris. Veneration of the king required both preservation of his corpse and provision for his needs in the afterlife. The mortuary temples of Egypt were not the core around which the city developed, but rather a distinct center of power.

THE DEVELOPMENT OF MORTUARY ARCHITECTURE. The development of royal mortuary architecture in Egypt has its roots in the Predynastic period. By the Early Dynastic period, elaborate royal burial structures were built at the site of Abydos. The first pyramid was the stepped pyramid at Saqqara, built in the Third Dynasty. This structure was soon followed by the construction of true pyramids, culminating in the Great Pyramid at Giza.

Hierakonpolis and Abydos. The earliest structure identified as a royal tomb is Tomb 100 from the site of Hierakonpolis, which dates to the end of the Predynastic period. Tomb 100 is a mud-brick structure with crude wall paintings that include depictions of a figure smiting an enemy. It is interesting that the wall paintings of Tomb 100 include depictions of two boats, possibly reflecting the beliefs that led later kings to bury boats next to their tombs.

During the First and Second Dynasties, the royal burial ground moved to the desert cemetery of Abydos (Kemp 2006). The tombs at Abydos are simple brick chambers built into pits dug into the ground. Above the burial chamber, a square mud-brick enclosure was erected and then filled in with earth and gravel. A pair of

TOOLBOX

Tracking Trade Routes

Tracking trade routes is essential to understanding how politically complex societies interact with their neighbors. Archaeologists can trace trade routes on the basis of the physical properties of artifacts. For example, on Egyptian sites dating to the New Kingdom, pottery vessels from Cyprus and the Aegean can easily be identified on the basis of their distinctive shape and surface finish. However, in many cases, it is necessary to employ more complex methods to identify the source of archaeological artifacts.

For objects made of clay, petrographic analysis is often used to identify the place where the artifact was produced. Petrography is a branch of geology that focuses on the identification of minerals and rocks on the basis of their physical properties. Archaeological petrographers identify the minerals that have been added to clay during its manufacture. Petrographic analysis involves taking a very thin slice from a piece of pottery and polishing it until it is so thin that light can travel through it. This thin section is then studied under a petrographic microscope, which allows light to pass through the sample. By combining evidence of size, color, and the way light is refracted through the thin section, the petrographer can identify the mineral component of the pottery vessel. By comparing the mineral composition of the specimen to geological maps, he or she will often be able to determine where a pot was manufactured.

Petrographic analysis has been applied to the study of diplomatic letters discovered in

FIGURE 11.20 One of the Amarna letters. Although written in cuneiform, these are letters between the Egyptian ruler and vassal states to the north.

stone markers inscribed with the name of the king was placed in front of the tomb, and a separate small temple was built close to the valley floor. Recent excavations of the burial enclosures related to King Aha at Abydos have made some surprising discoveries. The burial enclosure appears to have been purposefully destroyed shortly after construction. Outside the enclosure, a number of subsidiary burials have been excavated that appear to provide evidence of human and animal sacrifice to accompany the deceased king to the afterlife (O'Connor 2009). Archaeologists have also recently uncovered an enigmatic fleet of buried boats at Abydos, shown in Figure 11.19.

Saqqara and Dahshur. By the Third Dynasty, the royal burial site had shifted to **Saqqara**, located outside of Cairo. The first pyramid is the stepped pyramid constructed by **King Djoser** of the Third Dynasty (Lehner 1997). At Saqqara, an the New Kingdom Egyptian city of Amarna (Goren et al. 2004). Although found in Egypt, these documents were written on clay tablets in Akkadian, the language of Mesopotamia, using cuneiform script. During the New Kingdom, cuneiform was used as the medium for diplomatic communication. The letters are from neighboring kings seeking alliances with Egypt. Unfortunately, some information about the geographical location of the kings sending the letters is unclear. A petrographic analysis project treated these tablets as clay artifacts and managed to link some of the tablets to the places they were made on the basis of the mineral component of the clay.

Neutron activation analysis is another method for finding the source of ceramic artifacts. Rather than looking at the mineralogy of materials added to the clay, neutron activation focuses on the chemical characteristics of the clay itself. With the help of a nuclear reactor, it is possible to create a profile of the rare elements that are present at very low levels in the clay. This profile can serve as a chemical fingerprint for the clay a pot was made from that can be matched with the fingerprint of known geological clay sources. Neutron activation analysis was used to trace a unique pot, known as the "Dolphin Vase" and found on the Middle Kingdom Egyptian site of Lisht, back to its place of manufacture near the modern city of Gaza (McGovern et al. 1994). Rare element analysis can also be carried out with instrumentation known as an inductively coupled plasma mass spectrometer or ICP-MS. ●

FIGURE 11.21 Petrographic thin section of a pottery vessel from Jordan. The white speckled masses are pieces of calcite.

enclosure wall surrounds a large open-air courtyard, in the middle of which stands the stepped pyramid (see Figure 11.22). The royal tomb is located in a granite vault in an elaborate network of chambers branching off from a central shaft below the pyramid. The pyramid itself was built in a series of stages. It appears to have been originally conceived as a simple, if massive, filled enclosure like those found at Abydos. Only after building was under way did the project evolve into the construction of a pyramid.

Three engravings found in the Djoser complex depict the Sed festival, an event during which the king would run a course in an important ritual of renewal. The king's performance was essential to maintaining order in the world. The architecture

FIGURE 11.22 Aerial photo of the Djoser complex. The pyramid complex is contained within an enclosure wall.

Cheops A Fourth Dynasty Egyptian king who constructed the first and largest pyramid ever built at Giza.

Cepheren A Fourth Dynasty Egyptian king who constructed a pyramid at Giza that was slightly smaller than the one constructed by Cheops. The Great Sphinx is located alongside the Cepheren valley temple.

Mycerinus The last Fourth Dynasty Egyptian king to build a pyramid at Giza; it was smaller than the other pyramids and at least partially sheathed in polished granite.

Giza The site of the pyramids of Cheops, Cepheren, and Mycerinus—monuments representing the apex of pyramid construction in Old Kingdom Egypt.

of the Djoser complex actually replicates in stone the course that the living king would have run during the Sed festival. It is notable that because of the high enclosure walls, this symbolic ritual ground was hidden from view. Although the portion of the stepped pyramid visible beyond the enclosure would have been impressive, the fundamental characteristic of the Djoser pyramid complex is that it encloses and hides sacred space.

The first true pyramid was built by King Snefru of the Fourth Dynasty at the site of Dahshur, just south of Saqqara. Snefru actually attempted this construction three times before succeeding in building a true pyramid. The first attempt, at the site of Meidum, appears to have collapsed during construction. Snefru then moved to Dahshur, where he built the bent pyramid that began at a very steep slope of approximately 60 degrees (Lehner 1997). Midway through construction, the slope was decreased to approximately 44 degrees, resulting in a pyramid with a pronounced "bend." The final pyramid built by Snefru was the Red Pyramid, a true pyramid 105 meters high.

Giza. Pyramid building reached its apex with the Fourth Dynasty kings—**Cheops, Cepheren**, and **Mycerinus**—who built their pyramids at **Giza**. Subsequent dynasties put far less effort into the construction of monumental pyramids, although the tradition persisted well into the Middle Kingdom. The Giza pyramids are very different in conception from the Djoser pyramid complex. At Giza, there is no enclosure wall hiding the sacred ground. The Giza pyramids are one element of a complex made up of four parts (see Figure 11.23). The first element is the valley temple, constructed near the Nile Valley. The second element is a massive causeway connecting the valley temple to the desert plateau on which the pyramids were built. This causeway is also connected to the third element of the complex, the mortuary temple, which is built up against the pyramid. The final and most visible element of the complex is the pyramid itself. The three royal pyramids at Giza are surrounded by subsidiary structures, including secondary pyramids, massive fields of bench-shaped "mastaba" tombs of nobility, and long pits in which boats were buried.

FIGURE 11.23 Aerial photograph of the Giza pyramids

Key:
1. Cheops pyramid
2. Cheops mortuary temple
3. Cheops causeway
4. Cepheren pyramid
5. Cepheren mortuary temple
6. Cepheren causeway
7. Cepheren valley temple
8. The Great Sphinx
9. Mycerinus pyramid
10. Mycerinus mortuary temple
11. Mycerinus causeway
12. Mycerinus valley temple
13. Mastaba fields
14. Lehner excavation area

The pyramid of Cheops, the first constructed at Giza, is also the largest ever built. The pyramid of Cheops rises to a height of 146 meters and contains an estimated 2,300,000 blocks of stone (see Figure 11.24). This monumental building task appears to have been accomplished during a reign that lasted 32 years. Ironically, the only royal statue that remains of Cheops is a crude stone figure less than 8

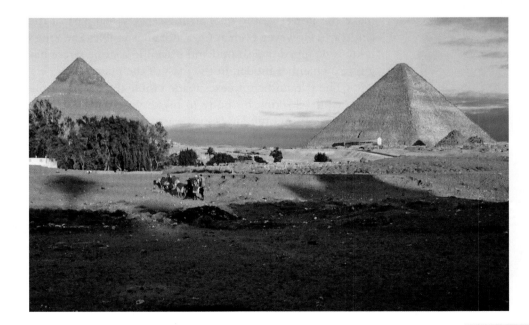

FIGURE 11.24 View of the Cepheren (left) and Cheops (right) pyramids from the south

centimeters high. Originally, the Cheops pyramid was sheathed in a casing of fine polished limestone. It is hard to imagine the effect this massive gleaming edifice would have had, emerging from the flat, dull landscape of the desert plateau. The burial chamber of the Cheops pyramid is hidden within the body of the pyramid at the top of a massive ramp. The actual burial chamber is constructed of massive granite monoliths transported from Upper Egypt. Standing in the burial chamber today, one is struck by the complete absence of ornamentation. The body of the king, presumably wrapped in a shroud, was laid to rest in a sarcophagus embedded in the floor of the burial chamber. The sarcophagus was then enclosed in the massive granite walls of the chamber, which itself is buried deep within the pyramid structure.

The Cepheren pyramid is slightly smaller than the Cheops pyramid. Some of the original casing stones are still preserved on the upper part of the Cepheren pyramid, providing an idea of what these monuments looked like when they were first constructed. Cepheren's image is well preserved in a series of powerful sculptures discovered in his pyramid's valley temple. One of the most famous features at Giza is the Great Sphinx, the figure of a cat with a human head, carved into the bedrock of a small hill adjoining the Cepheren valley temple (see Figure 11.25).

Mycerinus was the last king to build a pyramid at Giza. His effort was more modest than those of his predecessors. The most impressive aspect of the Mycerinus pyramid, which is only 65 meters high, is the fact that it was at least partially sheathed in polished granite. Some of the most beautiful Old Kingdom sculptures are figures of Mycerinus that were recovered from his valley temple. These figures convey the sense of quiet power that is the hallmark of Old Kingdom art.

FIGURE 11.25 The Great Sphinx was carved from a small limestone hill. The layers of rock vary in hardness, resulting in uneven weathering of the Sphinx's body.

THE PYRAMIDS AND THE STATE. The stepped pyramid of Djoser at Saqqara is cloaked in an enclosure wall. The great power of the pyramid complex was visible only to those allowed into the enclosure. The conception of the pyramid complex first developed by Snefru at Meidum and Dahshur and then brought to full fruition at Giza is radically different. At these sites, the complex sits on sacred ground, but the monumental pyramids are an inescapable presence visible to all. The Giza pyramids project the power of the king and make the power of the state an inescapably real part of the landscape. However, even at Giza, not all is visible: The king's body is wrapped in a shroud and placed in a stone sarcophagus in a chamber hidden in the mass of the pyramid.

The pyramid complexes made visible the power of the king, while cloaking his body in mystery. At the same time, the construction of the pyramids was an undertaking of such immensity that it became a substantial aspect of what the state did. One of the most fascinating questions in archaeology is how the early Egyptian state was able to mobilize the labor to build these spectacular monuments.

Beginning in the 1980s, excavations to the south of the Great Sphinx have begun to pick up traces of the massive organization of labor involved in constructing the pyramids (see "The Author on His Fieldwork Excavating at Giza" on p. 316). The discovery of breweries and bakeries to the south of the pyramid complex suggests that at least some of the workers were paid in the form of food rations. The organization required in building the pyramids involved not only labor to construct the structures, but also people to produce food for the labor force.

■ The City

The Egyptian king ruled over the entire Nile Valley. Egypt was a territorial state rather than a city-state. The fundamental expression of the state was the unification of Egypt, embodied by the figure of the king wearing the crowns of Upper and Lower Egypt. The monumental core of the early Egyptian state was not embedded in an urban center.

The largest settlements known from the Early Dynastic and Old Kingdom periods are best characterized as large towns rather than cities. However, it is possible that the picture of Egypt as a state without cities is partly the result of the limitations of archaeological recovery. At many sites, the Early Dynastic and Old Kingdom levels are far below the water table and cannot be reached by excavation. This is true of Memphis, the Old Kingdom capital of Egypt, where excavations have not been able to penetrate below the New Kingdom occupation.

AMARNA. A unique picture of an Egyptian city is preserved at the New Kingdom site of **Amarna** in Upper Egypt (Kemp 2006). Amarna was founded as a new capital city by the heretic king **Akhenaten** (1363 B.C.–1347 B.C.). Akhenaten put in place a reform of Egyptian religion, discarding much of the traditional pantheon and focusing on the visible disc of the sun, known by the Egyptians as Aten. In addition to instituting religious reform and founding a new capital, Akhenaten developed a new art style in which he and his queen, Nefertiti, were depicted with oddly elongated features.

After Akhenaten's death, his religious reforms were rejected, his monuments smashed, and his city at Amarna abandoned. Because Amarna was not subsequently reoccupied, it has provided archaeologists an opportunity to map extensive horizontal exposures of a fortified city stretching for over a kilometer along a major ceremonial road. Excavations of workshops, houses, and bakeries have provided unique insights into life in an Egyptian city. The question that lingers is whether cities like Amarna existed during earlier periods of Egyptian dynastic history or whether urban centers developed only during the New Kingdom.

■ Summing Up the Evidence

The Egyptian state challenges the expectations archaeologists have formed of state societies. The most obvious challenge is that there is at present no evidence that the early Egyptian state was an urban society. No cities are known from the Old Kingdom. Indeed, not only are cities absent, but the focal point of the state was the construction of massive funerary monuments that were set out in the desert margins. However, there is also a more subtle challenge: What we know about social organization suggests that, in Egypt, kinship continued to play an important role long after the formation of the state.

The pyramids of Giza lead us to question the source of the legitimacy of this early state society. These monuments are spectacular feats of engineering, organization, and sheer human effort. We have begun to gain an understanding of how the labor was organized, but the question remains of how these people were motivated to participate in such an undertaking. Is it possible that the state was powerful enough to coerce such a massive labor force? There is no evidence to support such a hypothesis, although, undoubtedly, not everybody participated willingly. There is

▲▲ Amarna A city built by the heretic king Akhenaten and abandoned after his reign. Excavation of this city has provided a unique horizontal exposure of an Egyptian urban center.

Akhenaten A religious reformer who built the city of Amarna.

The Author on His Fieldwork Excavating at Giza

In 1988, I stood on the Giza Plateau in Egypt to try to help answer a fundamental question: Where did the workers who built the pyramids live? We hoped that by looking at the plateau as an archaeological landscape, we might be able to unlock the answer to questions about the organization of the society that built these monuments. I was at the site thanks to Mark Lehner. Mark had spent years working at Giza before returning to the United States for graduate school. He enlisted me, along with a group of other graduate students, to join him on his new project, and we, of course, jumped at the opportunity.

Mark drew on his intimate knowledge from over a decade of experience at Giza and tried to figure out where on the crowded Giza Plateau there might be space for a settlement. The first location we studied was a bowl-shaped depression to the south of the pyramids. Examination of this area quickly showed that it had never been inhabited. Mark then turned to a second area behind

the Cepheren pyramid, where the archaeologist Flinders Petrie in the late nineteenth century had found a series of large rectangular rooms or galleries. Our excavations, directed by Nick Conard, uncovered the same galleries found by Petrie and showed that this was a truly massive structure, longer than a football field. However, there was no sign of habitation in the rooms—only scant traces of manufacturing. It appears that the spaces were storerooms and workshops.

Mark then turned to a third area near the shallow depression where he had begun his search. Here, a massive wall separated the sacred space of the plateau from the area beyond. One of my most vivid memories is watching as more than 40 men came over this monumental wall, ready to work. I knew little Arabic, and there was very little basis for the considerable trust Mark had placed in me to supervise them. We quickly got to work, burning off scrub and measuring out excavation units. We soon began to pick up the traces

of occupation, particularly vessels used for brewing beer and baking bread. By the end of the second season, we had uncovered a bakery, and our Egyptian colleagues, led by Zahi Hawass, had found a large burial ground.

My responsibilities alternated between excavation and work in the storerooms, which were located in the middle of the Mastaba field. We were inundated by pot sherds and struggled to keep up with the sorting and cataloguing of the finds. We worked with inspectors from the Egyptian Antiquities Organization, who taught me a great deal about pottery—and also about how I was perceived as an American. One day, after we had been working together long enough for them to know me fairly well, I was trying to explain to them how the television show *Dallas* gave an unrealistic view of the United States and its people; after all, they knew me, and I was nothing like that. Their response was to emphatically insist that I was exactly like one of the characters from the show!

good reason to think that the people's belief in the king as the actual incarnation of divinity essential for the maintenance of *ma'at* played a key role in the creation of the Egyptian state. It is hard not to conclude that the people who built the pyramids at Giza did so, at least in part, because they believed that they were building the tomb of a living deity.

11.3 Africa beyond the Nile Valley

The development of African states was not restricted to the Egyptian Nile Valley. However, the formation of indigenous African states remains poorly understood (Connah 1987). In the Sudan, a series of complex societies developed along the Nile in what is known as Nubia. In the Ethiopian highlands, an impressive kingdom developed around the city of Axum, which flourished during the first millennium A.D., contemporary with the Roman Empire. Axum is famous for its standing stones carved in the shape of multistory buildings (see Figure 11.28). The tallest of these monuments, carved from a single block of stone, rises 21 meters. Along the East African coast, stretching from Somalia in the north to Mozambique in the south,

What I found striking about working at Giza was the focus that Mark was able to keep on understanding the plateau as a complete entity. I learned that a successful project requires a clear goal and that one cannot simply hope to get direction from what one digs up. Once the bakery was excavated, Mark was faced with a problem: He could continue to dig, structure by structure, but using traditional archaeological methods, he would never get an idea of the area as a whole. So he launched a bold campaign of horizontal excavation, stripping the overlying sands from a massive area with the help of heavy equipment. These excavations are still in progress, but already the traces of a palace and workshop complex have been uncovered. These traces provide a picture of the royal establishment at Giza and the workshops that would have produced the food to supply a large workforce.

But where was the workers' village? One possibility is that such a village lies below the modern town Nazlet el Seman, which borders the excavated areas. However, as Mark and his team have continued stripping the overlying sands from areas beyond the palace complex, the remains of modest irregular structures have begun to appear. Perhaps they have finally found the elusive traces of the pyramid builders. (For more on the Giza Plateau Mapping Project, see www.aeraweb.org.) ▲

FIGURE 11.26 Excavation of a bakery in the area south of the Giza pyramids

a series of cities developed contemporary with medieval Europe. These cities were active in extensive trade networks connecting southern Africa with the Middle East and Asia.

When European explorers reached the coast of West Africa, they found well-established cities. One of the most impressive was Benin, in what is today Nigeria. Benin is celebrated for its remarkable brass plaques, many of which have been acquired by Western museums. Some have questioned whether cities such as Benin developed indigenously in West Africa or whether they emerged as the result of an external stimulus, first from Islamic North Africa and then from Europe.

Excavations at the site of **Jenne–Jeno**, located in the Middle Niger Valley in Mali, have demonstrated that urban centers in West Africa predate extensive external contacts (McIntosh and McIntosh 1993). The city of Jenne is known from historical sources as an important trade center for caravans coming from Timbuktu to the north. The region around Jenne is very fertile, and the river is rich in a wide array of fish. Jenne-Jeno is a site 3 kilometers from modern Jenne. The mound at Jenne-Jeno rises 8 meters and covers over 330,000 square meters. Excavations have uncovered three major phases of occupation beginning around 250 B.C. and lasting through

▲▲ **Jenne-Jeno** The site of an urban center in Mali, West Africa, that predates extensive external contact.

Archaeology and Genetics

Rapid advances in biotechnology have begun to have a significant impact on archaeology. As discussed in Chapter 4, genetic research has already had an impact on our understanding of human evolution, particularly the phylogenetic relationship between Neanderthals and modern humans (see pp. 101–103). When geneticists turn to more recent samples, the risk of contamination from modern DNA becomes acute. To overcome this challenge, careful protocols have been developed to minimize the risk of contamination and to provide researchers with tools to detect when contamination has taken place.

One of the most impressive genetic studies to emerge is the sequencing of nearly the entire genome of a man who lived in Greenland 4,000 years ago from a single hair recovered on an archaeological site locked in permafrost (Rasmussen et al. 2010). This study is far more than a demonstration of technical wizardry. The genome of this person sheds light on the earliest human occupation of the Arctic and resolves questions that have challenged archaeologists for decades. It can now be said with a high degree of certainty that the initial occupants of the Arctic came from Siberia rather than from within North America. Moreover, this discovery offers strong evidence that the modern Inuit populations of the North American Arctic and Greenland are the descendants of a second wave of human migration.

Another fascinating application of genetics is a study of a series of Egyptian mummies thought to be members of the family of Tutankhamun (Hawass et al. 2010). Although the tomb of Tutankhamun was found intact, many questions about this New Kingdom ruler remain. Great care was taken in the genetic analysis to avoid contamination, including repeating the study in two separate labs and testing the genetic markers from the mummies against the genetic markers of the scientists. The analysis determined that Tutankhamun's father, the heretic king Akhenaten, and Tutankhamun's mother were brother and sister. The identification of inbreeding within Tutankhamun's lineage accounts for the presence of a genetic walking impairment, a condition known as Köhler disease II, that was detected in a radiological analysis of his mummy. This genetic disease was likely a contributing factor to Tutankhamun's death at a young age. It is interesting that the radiological examination of Tutankhamun and the members of his lineage did not find any evidence of the genetic disorder known as Marfan syndrome. Marfan syndrome produces a feminine physique, and some archaeologists have suggested that the unusual art style characteristic of Akhenaten's reign was actually an accurate representation of a person with this condition. We now know that in fact the representations of Akhenaten are not a realistic depiction of his physique. The genetic analysis of Tutankhamun's mummy also recovered evidence of malaria, a subject we will return to in the Tracking Ancient Diseases Toolbox in Chapter 14, p. 404. ●

ADDITIONAL READING: M. Rasmussen et al. 2010. "Ancient Human Genome Sequence of an Extinct Palaeo-Eskimo." *Nature* 463: 757–62.

Z. Hawass et al. 2010. "Ancestry and Pathology in King Tutankhamun's Family." *Journal of the American Medical Association* 303(7): 638–47.

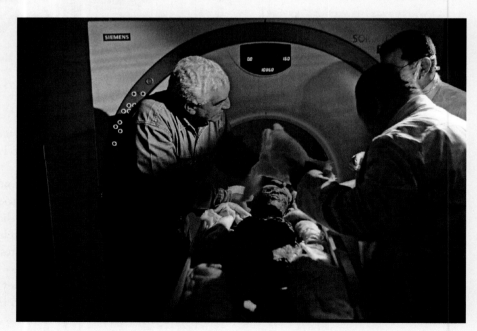

FIGURE 11.27 Preparing the mummy of Tutankhamun for a CT scan. The combination of radiographic and genetic analysis of this mummy has produced new insight into the genealogy and health of the rulers of New Kingdom Egypt.

A.D. 800. By A.D. 300, the entire area of the site appears to have been densely inhabited. Population estimates for the site range from 7,000 to 16,000. There is considerable evidence of local iron smelting and other specialized craft activity. The city was surrounded by a mud-brick wall; however, there is no evidence that the houses were laid out along a regular grid. Surveys in the region around Jenne-Jeno have shown that the area was dotted with a range of sites of different sizes.

Only a small area of Jenne-Jeno has been excavated, making it difficult to come to any conclusion about the social organization of the city. The excavators of the site, Susan Keech McIntosh and Roderick McIntosh, have found no evidence of either a clearly defined elite or a special elite area of the site. Roderick McIntosh (1998) has developed a picture of Jenne-Jeno as a city ruled by overlapping sources of authority rather than the centralized authority found in other early state societies.

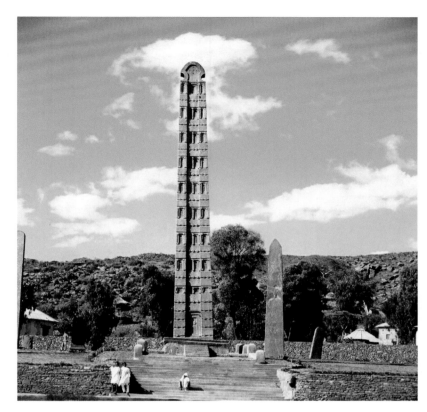

FIGURE 11.28 One of the monumental stelae at Axum, Ethiopia

11.4 The Aegean

On a spring day in 1900, Arthur Evans stood on the hill of **Knossos** on the island of Crete and began the excavations that were to transform our knowledge of ancient Greece. Greek mythology told the story of King Minos of Crete and the terrible secrets of his labyrinth, where the Minotaur, a man-eating monster who was half man and half bull, lived imprisoned in the twisted complex built by Daedalus. Perhaps Evans imagined Daedalus and his son flying away from Knossos on wings made of wax and feathers before Icarus, flying too close to the sun, melted his wings and plunged to his death.

Evans's excavations at Knossos uncovered a large palace adorned with frescoes showing incredible scenes of bull-leaping festivals, helping to raise the curtain on a previously unknown civilization—the **Minoan** culture of Crete. Over a century after Evans sank his first pit at Knossos, fundamental questions remain about the organization of Minoan society, as well as about the relationship of the Minoans with their neighbors in the Aegean, particularly the **Mycenaeans** of the Peloponnese Peninsula and central Greece.

■ Setting and Chronology

The homeland of the Minoan culture was the island of Crete, while Mycenaean societies developed on the Peloponnese Peninsula in southern Greece and to the north in central Greece (see Figure 11.29). The islands of the Cyclades also played an important role in the development of these societies, as did the area of western Turkey known as Asia Minor. Both the Peloponnese Peninsula and Crete are characterized by a varied topography with high mountain peaks and small open plains.

Knossos A site excavated by Arthur Evans that is the largest Minoan settlement.

Minoan A Bronze Age society located on the island of Crete.

Mycenaean A Bronze Age society that developed on the Peloponnese Peninsula and in central Greece.

FIGURE 11.29 Map of the Bronze Age Aegean

Although the earliest occupation of many Minoan and Mycenaean sites dates back to the Neolithic, the Bronze Age was the period during which complex social institutions developed. The emergence of centralized power structures began in Crete around 1900 B.C., during the Protopalatial and Neopalatial periods. It was almost 500 years until similar institutions developed among the Mycenaeans, around 1500 B.C. After this time, during a period known as the Late Minoan II–IIIB, there is evidence in Crete for strong Mycenaean influence on Minoan society.

■ Comparing Palaces

Archaeologists have tended to paint a picture of the Minoans and Mycenaeans as polar opposites, with the Minoans playing the role of peace-loving flower worshipers and the Mycenaeans cast as aggressive warriors. It is true that, while the Minoans appear to have left their settlements exposed, the Mycenaeans often surrounded their citadels with massive fortification walls, including the monumental **Lion Gate** at Mycenaea (see Figure 11.30). However, the picture of the Minoans and Mycenaeans as archetypical opposites does little to help us understand why these societies differed and obscures their similarities.

Minoan and Mycenaean society consisted of a series of autonomous political units. Colin Renfrew (1986) refers to such units as **early state modules**. The interaction between early state modules, or what Renfrew calls **peer polity interaction**, has the potential to fuel the development of social complexity, since change within each polity has an effect on its neighbor. John Cherry (1986) has argued that the development of the Minoan states fits very well with the model of peer polity interaction. Recently a number of archaeologists have questioned whether the

Lion Gate An important example of Mycenaean defensive architecture.

early state modules Colin Renfrew's term to describe autonomous political units.

peer polity interaction Colin Renfrew's term to describe the full range of exchanges taking place between autonomous sociopolitical units.

hierarchical organization characteristic of state society actually existed on Minoan Crete. The concept of **heterarchy** has been advanced as a better framework for understanding the organization of Minoan society. Carole Crumley (1995) defines heterarchy as "the relation of elements to one another when they are unranked or when they possess the potential for being ranked in a number of different ways" (3). She illustrates the concept of heterarchy by pointing out that oak trees and symphonies are both highly structured, and yet neither is hierarchically organized. In the context of Minoan Crete, the concept of heterarchy means that complex social organization may be developed in the absence of a clearly defined ranking of members of society.

The core of both Minoan and Mycenaean states was the palace. Minoan palaces are massive and elaborate constructions that might have been the inspiration for the myth of the labyrinth (see Figure 11.31). The center of the palace and the heart of its function is the central court. Bull games, feasting, dancing, and other public events are thought to have taken place in these open spaces, buried deep within the palace structure. Estimates for the number of people who would have participated in these rituals range between 1,500 and 5,000.

The core of the Mycenaean state was also the palace. The most completely preserved example of a Mycenaean palace was excavated at the site of Pylos. Here, the center of the structure is a large room known as a **megaron**, with a central hearth and four central pillars (see Figure 11.32). An open court for public gatherings, on a smaller scale than the central courts in Minoan palaces, was located in front of the megaron. Both the Minoan and the Mycenaean palaces were lavishly painted. One striking difference between these palaces is the presence of elaborate funerary rituals on Mycenaean sites and the absence of large tombs on Minoan sites like Knossos.

The palaces were more than simply the setting for spectacle. They were also the seat of the administration of the Aegean early state societies. This pairing of spectacle and administration is very interesting. It also lends support to the kind of dynamics Renfrew and Cherry discuss as characteristic of peer polity interaction, which include competition, emulation, symbolic entertainment, and exchange. Until the middle of the Neopalatial period, the only documents that survive from Crete are in scripts, Linear A and Cretan hieroglyphics, that have not been deciphered. The Mycenaean script, **Linear B**, was used to write a form of the Greek language that has been deciphered, providing insight into the function of the Minoan and Mycenaean palaces. Linear B was subsequently adopted on Crete as well; in fact, it is possible that it was first developed by Mycenaeans living in Crete.

The title of the ruler in the Linear B tablets is the **wanax**, but little detail is given on the powers of this position. What is apparent is that the wanax controlled vast quantities of resources. In the Linear B tablets from Knossos, there is mention of

FIGURE 11.30 A historic photograph of the Lion Gate at Mycenaea gives a sense of the scale of the fortification walls surrounding Mycenaean citadels

Deutsches Arch. Inst. Lion's Gate—Athens. Deutsches Archaologisches Institut, Athens, D-DAI-ATH-Mykene 63.

heterarchy The relationship of elements to one another when they are not ranked.

megaron A large hall located at the center of the Mycenaean palace.

Linear B A script used to write the Mycenaean language; texts in Linear B are a major source of information about the organization of Aegean society.

wanax The title of the ruler in Linear B texts.

FIGURE 11.32 Reconstruction of Pylos megaron

800 tons of harvested wheat and 80,000 to 100,000 sheep that would have been valued primarily for their wool (Killen 2007, 115). These very large quantities fit with the archaeological data from the excavation of the palace storerooms at Knossos, which included both large storage vessels known as pithoi and built storage facilities (see Figure 11.33). Beyond simply housing commodities, there is evidence from both texts and archaeology that the palaces played an important role as workshops for the production of goods, including fine textiles.

The palaces of the Late Bronze Age Aegean controlled the production of basic commodities, housed the manufacture of finished goods, and hosted large-scale spectacles and feasts. However, the palaces were part of a broader cultural landscape. Estimates for the population of Minoan and Mycenaean settlements are difficult to determine with a high degree of accuracy. Current estimates place the population of Knossos at around 15,000. Knossos was the largest settlement in Crete, so this can be taken as a maximum size for a Minoan town.

Archaeological research in the Aegean includes a heavy emphasis on the use of surveys to gain an understanding of the countryside beyond the palace and surrounding settlement. For example, a survey in the Pediada region, a rich agricultural area to the south of Knossos, has found an increase in settlement density in the period contemporary with the full development of the palace (Panagiotaki 2004). During this period, settlements with Knossos-style luxury products are found lining the communication routes to Knossos. The survey results suggest that this region was drawn into the provisioning of agricultural commodities for the palace at Knossos. The mechanisms that connected the palaces to their hinterland were varied. In some cases, during the Late Minoan II–IIIB period, the Linear B texts refer to taxes, while in other cases, they refer to land owned by the palace.

FIGURE 11.33 One of the storage rooms at Knossos with large ceramic storage vessels known as pithoi

■ Violence and Warfare

Determining the actual nature of conflict in ancient societies is often difficult and requires a thorough understanding of the technology of warfare. For the Bronze Age Aegean, there is evidence of both military conflict and ritualized contests, including the boxing matches and bullfights depicted in palace frescoes (see Figures 11.34 and 11.35). Experimental archaeology has provided new insight into

FIGURE 11.34 Bullfight fresco from Knossos

FIGURE 11.35 A row of warriors shown on a Mycenaean pottery vessel. Notice the weapons that include shields and spears, as well as the elaborate uniforms worn by the warriors.

the fighting capacity of Late Bronze Age Aegean swords and in turn a new perspective on the structure of Minoan and Mycenaean society. These swords tend to be 50 centimeters or longer, straight, with a central midrib and sharp edges. Archaeologists have studied the typology of these artifacts, but have rarely asked what it would be like to wield them as weapons. This is the question that Barry Molloy (2008) examined in his experimental study. He began by developing his own skills through two years of martial arts training with swords; he then carried out a series of tests using replicas of archaeological weapons. A great deal of skill was needed to effectively use these swords, and there was a risk of breakage during combat if the weapon was misused. To work effectively, the sword must be drawn in a whip-like motion at the same time the blow is delivered. Tests on linen, leather, and metal armor showed that thrusting attacks penetrated only the first two, while the swords were unable to penetrate the metal armor. Tests of the swords on recently slaughtered pigs gave a sense of how the blades would have cut into unprotected flesh during battle. Molloy (2008) concludes that

> only very effectively executed strikes would inflict serious injury, such as severing tendons or arteries. . . . Other less effective strikes would nonetheless cut the flesh, resulting in loss of blood, wearing down combatants over a longer duration of fighting. The combat skills of the prehistoric warriors needed to have been sufficiently developed to allow these strikes to be executed repeatedly in a single combat event with limited risk to the weapon itself. (126)

These results indicate that warfare in Minoan and Mycenaean society would be a test of skills and that the combatants would have a fair chance of surviving violent encounters. The sense of controlled violence in combat, and the training that it would have required, adds a vivid feel of what lay behind peer polity interactions in the Late Bronze Age Aegean.

■ The Eruption of Santorini and Its Impact

At the site of **Akrotiri** on the island of **Thera**, visitors can walk through a Late Bronze Age Cycladic town that has been preserved under the ash deposited by the volcanic eruption that devastated the island (also known as Santorini). A large-scale program of radiocarbon dating indicates an age slightly earlier than 1600 B.C. for the eruption of Thera (Manning et al. 2006). However, the stratigraphic context of Minoan pottery found in Egypt leads some archaeologists to argue for an age of 1500 B.C. The excavations at Akrotiri provide a unique picture of life in a Late Bronze Age Cycladic town and also give important evidence about the expansion of Minoan influence from Crete into the Cycladic islands. The frescoes recovered at Akrotiri are both beautiful and informative (see Figure 11.36). One set of paintings gives an unparalleled view of Minoan ships and includes possible evidence of conflict at sea. However, Thera has sparked a debate that reaches far beyond Akrotiri and that is fundamental to the archaeology of Minoan Crete. There is no question that the eruption of Thera was a massive event, but archaeologists differ greatly in their opinions of its impact on the palaces and towns of Crete. For some, the volcanic eruption was merely a loud noise that the inhabitants of Crete would have heard from a distance. Others see the eruption as ushering in a rapid decline in the power of the Minoan elites. About a century after the eruption of Thera, there

Akrotiri A Bronze Age town on the island of Thera that was buried by a catastrophic volcanic eruption.

Thera A Cycladic island that was devastated by a major volcanic eruption during the Bronze Age.

FIGURE 11.36 Fresco from the site of Akrotiri

was an increase in Mycenaean influence on Crete, and Knossos appears to have emerged as a paramount center for the entire island. But was Thera a causal factor in these changes? If so, where are the archaeological indications for massive destruction caused by the eruption? And why is there a hiatus of a century between the volcanic eruption and its impact?

Geoarchaeological research at the site of Palaiakastro on the eastern coast of Crete has produced evidence that the eruption of Thera might have caused a massive tsunami that would have led to widespread destruction, at least on the eastern coast (Bruins et al. 2008). At Palaiakastro, volcanic ash reworked by water was found in buildings well away from today's shoreline. Chemical tests confirm that the source of this ash is the Thera eruption. In exposed sections along the coastline, deposits of cultural material such as ceramics, building stones, and animal bones are found at 1.5 meters above sea level. Based on the geoarchaeological data, it is suggested that, as a result of the eruption of Thera, a tsunami as high as 9 meters hit the eastern coast of Crete. If true, this would indicate that the eruption had a catastrophic impact on the people living at Palaiakastro and other towns along the eastern coast of Crete. However, to date there is little evidence for a tsunami on other coastal Minoan sites.

Even if this evidence of a tsunami holds up, it does not completely explain the impact of the Thera eruption on Minoan society, as there is no widespread evidence for upheaval across Crete until approximately 100 years after the volcanic eruption. One possibility is that the eruption led to the destruction of Minoan naval forces, leaving the island vulnerable to attack by Mycenaeans. Another possibility revolves around the source of authority of the rulers of Minoan Crete. If the Thera eruption did lead to calamity, this could have shaken people's faith in their leaders' ability to provide safety and stability (Driessen and Macdonald 1997). The result of such a crisis might have been a gradual shift to a more bureaucratically centralized way of life.

■ Summing Up the Evidence

The development of social complexity in Minoan and Mycenaean Greece might have been the result of peer polity interactions between multiple early state modules.

However, archaeologists are increasingly questioning whether the model of a hierarchical state fits with the evidence from Minoan Crete. For both Minoans and Mycenaeans, the palace was the core of the state. These massive complexes served as large-scale storage facilities, the seat of administration, and the site of public spectacle. The nature of violence and warfare, particularly among the undefended Minoan centers, is an intriguing question. Experimental study of swords suggests that combat was highly skilled and perhaps not always lethal. One of the major questions facing archaeologists working in the region is the impact of the eruption of Thera. This debate includes both empirical questions, such as the validity of the evidence for a tsunami, and more interpretive questions that examine how such a disaster would influence the nature of Minoan social organization.

SUMMARY

- Mesopotamia covers the area along the course of the Tigris and Euphrates Rivers, a region where large-scale agriculture is possible only with irrigation.
- Urban sites appear in Mesopotamia during the Uruk period, 4000 B.C. to 3200 B.C. These cities were developed around temple precincts dating back to the earlier Ubaid period.
- The cuneiform writing system developed in Mesopotamia to record economic information. Cuneiform came to be used for a wide variety of texts, including epics and legal codes.
- The Royal Tombs at Ur demonstrate the power and wealth of early Mesopotamian kings.
- There is little evidence of extensive warfare in early Mesopotamia; however, Uruk sites such as Habuba Kebira did develop far to the north on the Euphrates River.
- The Nile Valley, a highly fertile agricultural land bounded by desert, is divided into Upper Egypt in the south and Lower Egypt in the north.
- The shift toward complex societies in Egypt began during the Predynastic period. Egyptian dynastic history can be divided into three cycles of integration and collapse.
- The Egyptian king was the human incarnation of the god Horus and was responsible for preserving *ma'at*—balance and justice.
- Scribes played a critical role in maintaining the organization of Egyptian society.
- The earliest royal tombs are found at Hierakonpolis and Abydos. The stepped pyramid constructed by Djoser at Saqqara was the first Egyptian pyramid.

- The first true pyramid was constructed by Snefru at Dahshur. Pyramid building reached its apex in the three pyramids at Giza constructed during the Fourth Dynasty.
- No cities are known from the Old Kingdom of Egypt. The most completely documented Egyptian city is the site of Amarna, built by the heretic New Kingdom king Akhenaten.
- The site of Jenne-Jeno in the Middle Niger Valley was a large city occupied between 250 B.C. and A.D. 800.
- Mycenaean complex societies developed in the Peloponnese Peninsula in southern Greece and to the north in central Greece beginning around 1500 B.C.
- Palaces were at the core of both Minoan and Mycenaean society.
- Colin Renfrew proposed peer polity interaction among early state modules as the dynamic underlying the development of social complexity in the Aegean.
- Some archaeologists are beginning to question whether Minoan and Mycenaean societies fit with the idea of hierarchical states, suggesting that these societies are better understood in terms of heterarchy.
- Experimental archaeology has demonstrated that warfare using Aegean swords required considerable skill and would not have always been lethal.
- The eruption of Thera, an island in the Cyclades, resulted in the destruction of the town of Akrotiri. The nature of the impact of the Thera eruption on Minoan Crete remains the subject of debate.

KEY TERMS

Abydos, 307
Akhenaten, 315
Akrotiri, 324
Amarna, 315
bevel-rim bowls, 299
Cepheren, 312
Cheops, 312
cuneiform, 302
cylinder seals, 302
Early Dynastic period, 297

early state modules, 320
First Dynasty, 307
Giza, 312
Habuba Kebira, 303
heterarchy, 321
Hierakonpolis, 307
Jenne-Jeno, 317
King Djoser, 310
Knossos, 319
Linear B, 321

REVIEW QUESTIONS

1. Why are the Royal Tombs at Ur significant for understanding early Mesopotamian society?
2. What was the role of writing in early Mesopotamia and Old Kingdom Egypt?
3. What can we learn about the process of state formation by comparing Mesopotamia and Egypt?
4. What is peer polity interaction, and how is it applied to early Aegean states?

LOCATING THE SOURCE OF AUTHORITY

EARLY STATES IN ASIA

The early state societies of the Indus Valley and China challenge us to understand the sources of authority underlying state formation. The influence of the Chinese Empire across Asia provides an opportunity to consider the relationship between the core areas of state development and their peripheries. After reading this chapter, you should understand:

- The archaeological evidence for urbanism and the questions regarding social inequality in the Harappan civilization.
- The evidence from surveys and excavation for the emergence of state societies in China.

Figure of an archer from the Xian Tomb

- The role of influence from China on the development of social complexity in Japan, the response of the people living in the Tarim Basin to their position on the Silk Route, and the emergence of the city of Angkor.

12 TIMELINE

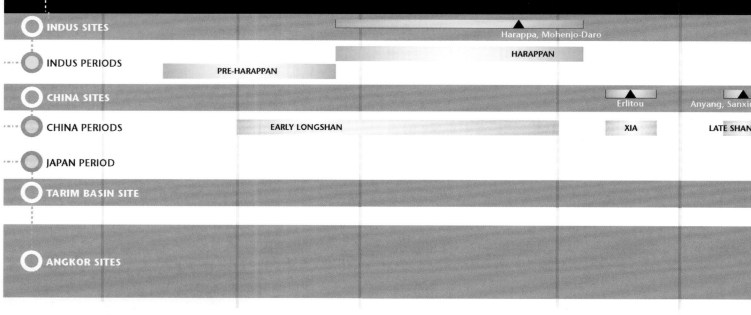

INDUS SITES			Harappa, Mohenjo-Daro		
INDUS PERIODS				HARAPPAN	
	PRE-HARAPPAN				
CHINA SITES				Erlitou	Anyang, Sanxin
CHINA PERIODS	EARLY LONGSHAN			XIA	LATE SHAN
JAPAN PERIOD					
TARIM BASIN SITE					
ANGKOR SITES					

3500 BC	3000 BC	2500 BC	2000 BC	1500 BC

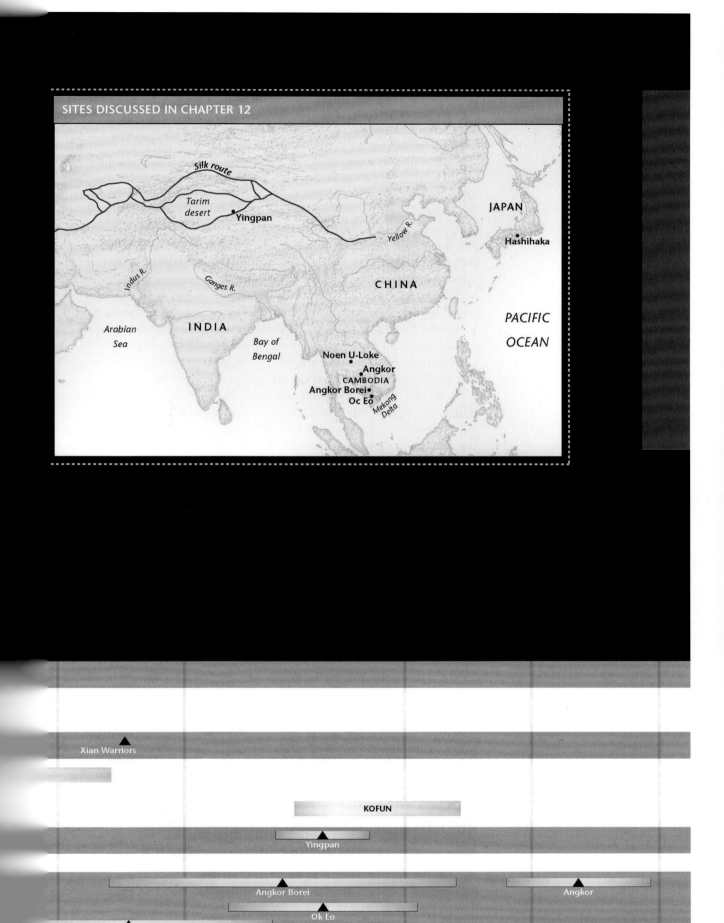

SITES DISCUSSED IN CHAPTER 12

Silk route

Tarim desert

Yingpan

Yellow R.

JAPAN

Hashihaka

Indus R.

Ganges R.

CHINA

Arabian Sea

INDIA

Bay of Bengal

PACIFIC OCEAN

Noen U-Loke

Angkor

CAMBODIA

Angkor Borei

Oc Eo

Mekong Delta

Xian Warriors

KOFUN

Yingpan

Angkor Borei

Angkor

Ok Eo

00 BC

0

500 AD

1000 AD

1500 AD

ometime around 221 B.C., Ying Zheng, the First Emperor of Qin, began to assemble an army unlike any the world had ever seen. This army—over 7,000 men with bronze swords, halberds, daggers, axes, crossbows and bows, 130 chariots, and close to 700 horses—was not meant for the world of the living. Ying Zheng's army is made of clay, beautifully sculpted life-sized models of soldiers set in formation to stand guard against the enemies the emperor would face after his death, perhaps the spirits of the armies he had massacred in wars of conquest (Figure 12.1). A chance discovery in 1974 near the city of Xian led to archaeological excavations that have brought to light the First Emperor's army, much of it still standing intact after more than 2,000 years. In the Royal Tombs of Ur and the pyramids of Giza, we have already seen the efforts of rulers to continue their dominance in the afterlife. The paradox at the core of *The Epic of Gilgamesh*—that power among the living does not conquer death—would have been familiar to the First Emperor, who is said to have searched in vain for a secret source of immortality. The terracotta army—row after row of intricately molded, yet mute figures—is among the most spectacular archaeological sites in the world. The tomb of the First Emperor is an ultimate expression of the power of administration in which "the realm of the future became peopled by officials, servants and armies, unlike the afterlife populated by gods and spirits described by so many of the world's religions" (Rawson 2007, 145). In the terracotta army of Xian, we see the extension of the institutions of social complexity into the realm of the afterworld on a monumental scale.

In this chapter, we will trace the early stages of state formation in the Indus Valley and China. The Indus Valley presents a fascinating quandary, a clearly urban society without clearly visible elite. In China, we will examine the large urban center of Anyang, but we will also look at recent archaeological research, much of it based on intensive surveys, that is leading to a nuanced picture of state formation in China. It is important to remember that the well-ordered soldiers of the terracotta army, each with a distinctive hairstyle indicating status and ethnicity, are—despite the realism of the individuals depicted—ultimately a fiction. Where the rulers of states and empires might have seen order and discipline, the reality was often far more complex. Similarly, archaeologists have learned that, although models for the social

FIGURE 12.1 The Emperor's army at Xian

structure of early states and theories of state formation are essential, the archaeological reality will continuously challenge our expectations. Following the examination of the origins of the state in China, we will consider how interactions with China shaped neighboring societies. Our inquiry will stretch to the Tarim Basin in central Asia and across the sea to Japan. We end by considering the developments that led to the emergence of the great city of Angkor, Cambodia.

▲▲ Indus Valley An area extending along the course of the Indus River that covers much of modern Pakistan and the Kutch and Gujarat Provinces of India.

12.1 The Indus Valley

The Harappan civilization developed along the Indus Valley in modern-day Pakistan at approximately the same time that the Great Pyramids were built in Egypt (see Figure 12.2). The defining characteristic of this civilization is the presence of well-planned cities—notably, the urban centers of Harappa and Mohenjo-Daro. However, monumental architecture is virtually absent from the Indus Valley, as is any evidence for the elaboration of the power of the ruler through intricate mortuary rituals. The Harappan civilization remains wrapped in enigma and mystery. The rulers remain largely faceless and nameless, and perhaps most intriguing, the Harappan script remains one of the few undeciphered ancient languages.

■ The Setting and Chronology

The Indus River descends from the Himalaya Mountains and winds through 3,000 kilometers of modern Pakistan before flowing into the Arabian Sea. The Indus is among the most powerful rivers in the world, with twice the annual flow of the Nile and three times the combined flow of the Tigris and the Euphrates (Jarrige 1989). The Indus is also an unpredictable river that frequently changes its course. During the time of the Harappan civilization, the Ghaggar-Hakra River, which is now dry, flowed to the east of the Indus.

The rich agricultural lands of the **Indus Valley** are bounded on the west by the highlands of Baluchistan and on the northwest by the highlands of Afghanistan. To the east, the Indus Valley is bounded by the Great Thar Desert. The Harappan civilization extended across the entire Indus Valley, covering an area of almost half a million square miles. In the southeast, Harappan sites are found along the coastal regions of Kutch and Gujarat (Allchin and Allchin 1982). Trade networks connected the Harappan civilization by sea to the Arabian Peninsula and Mesopotamia and overland to Iran and Afghanistan. The Indus Valley has been identified as the land of Melluha, mentioned in Mesopotamian texts as an important trading partner.

Excavations at the site of Mehrgarh in the Baluchistan foothills to the west of the Indus Valley have produced important information on the Neolithic and later prehistoric societies of the region (Jarrige 1989). The agriculture of Mehrgarh was based on plants and animals first domesticated in the Middle East, including wheat, barley, sheep, goats, and cattle. These plants and animals continued to form the basis of agriculture during the Harappan period. In Level IIa at Mehrgarh, which dates to around 5500 B.C., buildings consisting of a series of square cells have been excavated. The excavators interpret these structures as silos for storing surplus crops.

FIGURE 12.2 Map of the Indus Valley

Harappan period The period between 2600 B.C. and 1900 B.C. during which urban centers developed in the Indus Valley.

The earliest evidence for extensive settlement of the Indus Valley comes from the Pre-Harappan period, between 3300 B.C. and 2600 B.C. Sites dating to this period include large towns surrounded by fortification walls. It is unclear whether these walls were for defense from human invaders or for protection against river floods and erosion. During the Pre-Harappan period, there was an increase in the uniformity of material culture across the Indus Valley.

The **Harappan period** lasted for 700 years, from 2600 B.C. to 1900 B.C. The beginning of this period is marked by the expansion of a small number of sites into major urban centers. The material culture of the Harappan period is extremely uniform across the entire Indus Valley. The end of the period is the subject of considerable debate. Some archaeologists believe that invading forces—perhaps even the Aryan invaders described in the sacred Hindu texts of the Rig-Veda—destroyed the Harappan people. The main evidence for this interpretation consists of groups of skeletons found in the final levels of Mohenjo-Daro. In one staircase, 13 skeletons of adults and children were found, while in another area the sprawled skeletons of three men, one woman, and one child were discovered (Agrawal 1985). A recent reanalysis of the skeletons from Mohenjo-Daro suggests that these people may have died from an outbreak of malaria rather than as the victims of a conquering army (Bahn 2002). Many archaeologists today emphasize that the decline of the Indus civilization was a gradual process (Kenoyer 1998). Following the collapse of the Harappan civilization, there was a decline in the size of sites in the Indus Valley and an increased diversity of material culture within the region. When large urban centers were reestablished in the Indian subcontinent over a century later, they were built along the Ganges River system in India.

■ The City

In the 1850s, British railway engineers began construction of a railway link between Lahore and Multan in what was then the Punjab Province of the British Empire (Kenoyer 1998). Searching for material for the railway beds, these engineers seized on the idea of using crushed brick rubble from mounds they found along the path of the railroad. Archaeologists were both powerless to stop the destruction and

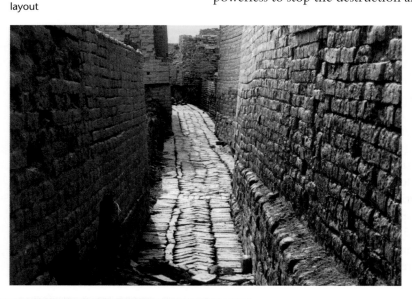

FIGURE 12.3 A view down one of the streets of Mohenjo-Daro gives a sense of the regularity of this city's layout

FIGURE 12.4 Site plan of a neighborhood in Mohenjo-Daro, Pakistan

5 m.

N

TOOLBOX

Space Syntax

Buildings are objects we build, as well as places we inhabit. Architecture blurs the line between artifact and landscape. Archaeologists have many ways to study architectural remains. One approach is to look at the activities that took place within a structure by analyzing the distribution of artifacts or the microstratigraphy of floor deposits (Steadman 1996). From this perspective, how we use space determines its nature.

A different, complementary perspective explores how architectural space can shape social life. The complex spaces that make up the cities of Harappa and Mohenjo-Daro are examples of structures that constrain and shape action.

Space syntax is a methodology for studying the configuration of architectural space. It was first developed by architects and city planners, but is increasingly used by archaeologists (Cutting 2003). Space syntax can be applied at any level, from a single structure to a complete settlement. The methodology works with floor plans or city plans to create a graph that represents the relationship between spaces (Bafna 2003). At least in the first stage of analysis, the size of the rooms and other qualities of these spaces are put aside to focus on the access between spaces. Figure 12.5 provides an illustration of the use of space syntax analysis to create a graph for a simple structure with eight rooms. The plan on the left shows the layout of these rooms; the dotted lines indicate the links between spaces. The numbers indicate the "depth" of the space or the extent to which it is linked to other spaces. The number 4 signals connection to only one other space and is the maximum possible depth, essentially a dead end. The number 3 indicates two links, one of which is a dead end; the number 2 signifies two links to spaces that lead on to other rooms; and the number 1 stands for the lowest measure of depth, a highly integrated space. On the right is a "justified access graph," showing the relationship of these spaces. The isolation of the one dead-end space is very apparent in this graph, as is the presence of two widely accessible spaces within the structure.

The fundamental idea of space syntax analysis is that these characteristics would shape the nature of social relations that took place within this structure. By reducing architectural space to a graph, patterns emerge that might otherwise be obscured, and comparisons between types of architecture become possible. ●

FIGURE 12.5 Space syntax

---

puzzled by the absence of Buddhist-period remains from the mounds. It took over 50 years for archaeologists to understand that these sites were the remains of a previously unknown civilization (Marshall 1928).

Harappan cities have a number of common features. Houses and other structures are laid along a regular grid of streets that run through the city (see the reconstruction in Figure 12.3 and the site plan in Figure 12.4). The most striking aspects of Harappan cities are the sense of order and the emphasis on hygiene. Elaborate drains are found leading from the houses to covered channels that run through the streets and out of the city (Jansen 1989). Water was supplied by wells lined with fired bricks, and structures were built of fired bricks of a uniform size. The normal brick size was $28 \times 14 \times 7$ centimeters (Allchin and Allchin 1982). Most of the Harappan

Harappa One of the two major urban centers of the Harappan period.

Mohenjo-Daro One of the two major urban centers of the Harappan period.

Great Bath An impressive structure built around a rectangular basin at the site of Mohenjo-Daro. It is one of the few monumental structures found on a Harappan site.

▲▲ **Dholavira** A Harappan site in the Gujarat, India, that shows neighborhoods separated by walls and large water tanks.

Harappan script A script that has not yet been deciphered and is known mostly from small carved stone sealings used to mark vessels and bundles.

settlements were small villages. Only five cities greater than 80 hectares are known. The largest Harappan cities were the sites of **Harappa** and **Mohenjo-Daro**.

Both Harappa and Mohenjo-Daro were built on a series of walled mounds. Most archaeologists argue that the cities consisted of an elite area on a high mound or citadel at the western side, overlooking a lower town where the non-elite members of society lived. Excavations along the edge of the high mound at Mohenjo-Daro suggest that the citadel buildings were constructed on a massive mud-brick platform. Although the mounds that make up Harappa and Mohenjo-Daro had walls, it is not clear whether they were designed for military defense. There is no evidence of warfare at either site, with the possible exception of the skeletons of Mohenjo-Daro.

At Mohenjo-Daro and Harappa, excavations uncovered large buildings that have been interpreted as granaries. At Harappa, the "granary" is a building measuring 40 × 50 meters, constructed on a mud-brick foundation. It consists of a series of two rows of six rooms built along a central passage. At Mohenjo-Daro, the "granary" is a building measuring 50 × 27 meters. The foundation is divided into 27 square blocks (Kenoyer 1998). There is no evidence to decisively support the identification of these structures as granaries. However, the edifices are clearly the remains of large public buildings of some kind.

The most impressive structure found on a Harappan site is the **Great Bath** of Mohenjo-Daro (see Figure 12.6). At the center of the Great Bath is a 12 × 7 meter brick-lined basin; it is 3 meters deep, sealed with gypsum mortar and asphalt, and surrounded by an impressive pillared gallery. A flight of stairs at each end leads to the bottom of the basin. A large well found in an adjoining room was the source of water for filling the Great Bath. Archaeologists have developed a wide array of interpretations of this structure, ranging from a site of sacred rituals of cleanliness to a nice place to cool off on a hot summer day.

Excavations at the site of **Dholavira**, located in the Gujarat region of India, have exposed a town covering an area of approximately 50 hectares surrounded by fortification walls. The town is divided into a Lower, Middle, and Upper area, each of which is surrounded by its own wall. The Upper Town is subdivided into two sectors, and access to these areas is controlled by massive gates. The practice of dividing space found at Dholavira is characteristic of Harappan settlements. The division of space within Harappan settlements is linked to civic control, and it is interesting to consider whether the movements of people living in towns like Dholavira would have been restricted based on status (Wright 2010). The excavations at Dholavira have also uncovered large open areas that might have been the setting for large public gatherings, similar perhaps to the courtyards at the center of Minoan palaces. The most spectacular discoveries at Dholavira have been large wells and six massive water tanks, one of which is shown in Figure 12.7. The largest of these measures 73 × 30 meters and extended to a depth of 10 meters through alluvium and into the bedrock. Flights of 30 steps were found in three corners of this water tank.

FIGURE 12.6 The Great Bath at Mohenjo-Daro, Pakistan

■ Writing

The **Harappan script** is known mostly from small carved stone sealings used to mark vessels and bundles (Kenoyer 1998). Other inscribed objects include flat pieces of copper, a gold

FIGURE 12.7 Massive water tank at Dholavira

pendant, a bronze axe, and small incised tablets. The writing is limited to a small number of characters per inscription. Although over 400 different signs have been identified, the longest known inscription has a series of 26 signs. Given the large number of symbols, it appears likely that the writing system was either logographic (signs representing words) or ideographic (signs representing concepts). To date, the Harappan script has not been deciphered (see Figure 12.8).

The unreadable inscriptions on the Harappan seals leave many unanswered questions. Are the inscriptions the names of the owners of the seals? Or perhaps the names of deities with whom the owners were identified? The questions increase when we consider the depictions on the seals. The most common scene is of a bull, an elephant, or a rhinoceros, often shown standing in front of what appears to be an incense burner. But more fantastic creatures, including unicorns, three-headed animals, and what appears to be a horned tiger, are also found. The most enigmatic seals show what appear to be deities. One type of deity appears as a three-headed horned person sitting in a lotus position. In a more complex scene, a figure wearing a crescent-shaped headdress faces a kneeling person and a bull. Below this scene is a procession of what appears to be people wearing bangles and headdresses.

The seals afford evidence of a complex administrative system. Carefully standardized stone weights offer further evidence for control over the flow of goods. These weights are usually plain cubes of rock carefully carved to adhere to a strict standard.

FIGURE 12.8 The script on these seals from the Indus Valley has not been deciphered, and the significance of the scenes shown remains an enigma

▪ Government

The people of the Harappan civilization lived in highly organized cities with a bureaucracy that used a writing system, seals, and weights. The influence of this bureaucracy was so pervasive that even bricks were made to a standard size. The power of the Harappan state is vividly expressed by its construction and maintenance of an urban sewage system unparalleled among other early state societies. Although the vitality of the Harappan state is evident, the structure of the state remains obscure. The identity of the elite, the basis of their claim to power, and their relation to other sectors of society remain largely unknown.

The Harappan elite appear not to have lived very differently from other members of society or to have expressed their power by constructing monuments or burying their dead with pomp and splendor. Clay figurines of women are often adorned by elaborate floral headdresses, bead necklaces, and belts. Beads are ubiquitous on Harappan sites and include translucent tubular carnelian beads. Drilling holes the length of these beads required tremendous skill, and perhaps it is not surprising that Harappan carnelian beads are prominent among the items of wealth found in the Royal Tombs of Ur in Mesopotamia.

Only a handful of sculptures that can be considered depictions of royalty have been found on Harappan sites. The most impressive is a small steatite sculpture known as the "priest king" (see Figure 12.9). This sculpture depicts a bearded man wearing a headband with a circular ornament at the center of his forehead and a similar ornament on a bracelet around his right forearm. He is dressed in a cloth adorned with a geometric pattern. In 1999, excavators working at Harappa noticed a fragment of thread preserved in the hollow area of a copper bangle (Good, Kenoyer, and Meadow 2009). Detailed analysis showed that this thread was silk from a native species of silkworm. This discovery was replicated on a thread fragment recovered from a copper wire ornament. The use of silk by the Harappans is surprising, as it was thought that silk was not developed until 2,000 years later in China. This discovery points to the likelihood that Harappan displays of status used elaborate textiles that do not survive in the archaeological record.

FIGURE 12.9 Sculpture of the "priest king" found at Mohenjo-Daro. Notice the diadems on his head and arm and the elaborate pattern on his cloak. These might be indicative of his high status in Harappan society. The height is 17.5 centimeters.

▪ Summing Up the Evidence

The cities of the Harappan civilization remain deeply puzzling. These large population centers were exquisitely organized down to the minute details of their sewage channels and standardized building materials. This degree of planning is unparalleled in the ancient world. Yet the leaders remain almost invisible. There are elite areas in the large cities of Mohenjo-Daro and Harappa, but impressive burials and palaces are noticeably absent. The only monumental architecture of note is, of all things, a bath! Were the Harappan cities based on an egalitarian form of social organization different from that of any other known early state societies? If not, was it perhaps an ethos of equality that in fact cloaked a very real social inequality? Ultimately, we are left to wonder about the identity of the person sculpted so powerfully into the figure of the "priest king." Was this the ruler of the city? If so, what was his power, and on what was it based?

12.2 China

Chinese archaeologists stress the continuity of Chinese culture going as far back in time as the Neolithic. As a result, the culture history of China is highly developed, as is the study of particular types of artifacts. Until recently, the ideological demands of the modern Chinese state have often limited the ability of Chinese archaeologists to think freely about the processes of state formation. Political tensions, as well as the difficulty of mastering the Chinese language and culture history, have often stood in the way of interaction between Chinese archaeologists and their international colleagues. In recent years, there has been a gradual shift, and a new generation of Chinese archaeologists shows a real interest in developments in archaeological method and theory. At the same time, a number of international teams have been working in China to explore the process of state formation, often through archaeological survey. As a result, the picture of state formation in China is in flux, with new questions emerging and archaeologists struggling to keep pace with the flow of new data.

■ The Three Dynasties

According to Chinese historical texts, the **Three Dynasties**—Xia, Shang, and Zhou—emerged in northern China during the period between 2000 B.C. and 500 B.C. The Three Dynasties mark the transition to urban state societies in China (see Figure 12.10). The **Yi-Luo Valley** in the central plains of northern China has been identified as the political center of the Xia and Early Shang Dynasties (Lee 2004). **Erlitou**, a very large site in the Yi-Luo Valley, might have been the capital of the Xia Dynasty. This site, which covers 400 hectares, was inhabited between 1800 B.C. and 1600 B.C. Two large palace enclosures built on a rammed-earth terrace have been identified at Erlitou. The artifacts recovered there include a wide range of elite goods such as bronze—including the earliest bronze ritual vessels—and jade. Although the area excavated is an impressive 20,000 square meters, this is still only 0.5% of the total site area.

Yanshi is a similarly impressive site located 10 kilometers northeast of Erlitou. The construction of massive palace enclosures at Yanshi appears to correlate with the downfall of Erlitou. Thus, the fate of these neighboring settlements appears to be tightly linked and may be connected to the Shang conquest of the Xia that is recorded in historical documents.

The Yi-Luo River Valley Archaeological Project was launched in 1998 to explore the broader regional context for the emergence of the urban centers at Erlitou and Yanshi (see Figure 12.11). The survey area is immediately to the east of Yanshi and incorporates three tributaries of the Yi-Luo River (Liu et al. 2004). The survey found that the Early Longshan period (3000 B.C.– 2000 B.C.), which precedes the emergence of Erlitou, included two large village sites of 13 to 20 hectares. The rise of the Erlitou site is correlated with the emergence of a 60-hectare regional center at Shaochia, an 18-hectare secondary center, and more than 40 village sites of less than 5 hectares. Combining these results with information from excavations at Erlitou, the survey team identified a four-tier settlement hierarchy with a major urban center, two levels of secondary centers, and widely dispersed villages. These results suggest that Erlitou stood at the apex of a complex regional settlement organization.

Anyang was discovered when inscribed bones began to appear on the antiquities market and their source was tracked to a small village in northern China. Intensive

Three Dynasties The Xia, the Shang, and the Zhou Dynasties, which emerged in northern China during the period between 2000 B.C. and 500 B.C.

Yi-Luo Valley A region where surveys have documented the complex settlement hierarchy associated with the cities of Erlitou and Yanshi, which are earlier than Anyang.

Erlitou A city in the Yi-Luo Valley that predates Anyang.

Yanshi A large settlement in the Yi-Luo Valley that appears to be slightly later than Erlitou.

Anyang A site in northern China and the capital of the Late Shang Dynasty.

FIGURE 12.10 Map of China showing the location of sites and survey areas related to early state societies

FIGURE 12.11 Map showing the location of the Yi-Luo Valley survey area, delineated by dashed lines, relative to the sites of Erlitou and Yanshi

Shang Dynasty The second of three powerful dynasties that emerged in northern China during the period between 2000 B.C. and 500 B.C.

oracle bones Bones that were used in divination rituals. Inscriptions on oracle bones are a major source of written evidence about the Shang Dynasty.

FIGURE 12.12 Oracle bone from Anyang, China. The inscription records the prediction made, as well as the actual course of events.

excavations at the site recovered the remains of an immense city that was the capital of the Late **Shang Dynasty** (1200 B.C.–1045 B.C.). The palace-temple area at Anyang consists of large structures built on platforms of stamped earth, arranged in clusters that reflect their functions as residences, temples, and ceremonial areas. The buildings themselves were made of very simple materials. In contrast to the elite, who lived in houses built on platforms, most of the people outside this zone lived in small houses dug into the ground.

The excavations at Anyang have uncovered a massive burial ground with over 1,000 simple burials and 11 deep burial pits reached by ramps. Large numbers of sacrificial victims, some with their heads buried separately from their bodies, are found in the pits. The tomb of Fu Hao, the wife or consort of one of the kings, was discovered intact in the palace-temple area across the river from the burial ground. The tomb of Fu Hao included an enormous quantity of burial goods, including 440 bronzes and almost 600 jades.

Analysis of skeletal remains from non-elite burials, both from formal burial areas and refuse pits, has produced new insight into the health of the general population in Anyang (Zhang et al. 2016). Linear enamel hypoplasia, horizontal grooves or pits that form on the front teeth as a result of stress during childhood, is one of the features recorded in this study. Roughly 80% of the skeletons had linear enamel hypoplasia, and this high frequency was consistent across age and sex. Indicators of stress during adulthood were also identified, with frequencies highest among females found buried in refuse pits.

The inscribed bones that first led archaeologists to Anyang are **oracle bones**, used by the Shang kings to predict the outcomes of events ranging from battles to the weather (see Figure 12.12). The king posed a question to his ancestors in a special ceremony. This involved applying a heat source to specially prepared hollows on the back of the bone to produce cracks on the front. These cracks were then interpreted by the king to determine the course of future events. Beginning in the Late Shang period, the question posed, the divination, and the eventual outcome were carefully inscribed on the bone. In total, over 150,000 inscribed oracle bones have been recovered, providing a unique perspective on the lives of the rulers of the Shang Dynasty and the earliest record of systematic writing from China (Keightley 2000). In later periods, historical records and economic transactions were recorded on silk and bamboo slips; however, none of these documents have survived from the Shang period. The other source of inscriptions from Anyang is elaborate bronze vessels (see Figure 12.13).

In 1986, two pits filled with spectacular artifacts were found at the site of **Sanxingdui**, located in Sichuan Province over 1,000 kilometers southeast of Anyang, dating to the same time period as Anyang (Ge and Linduff 1990). Some of the bronzes were similar to pieces from Anyang, but others, such as the gilded bronze head shown in Figure 12.14, were of a unique style that stunned experts in Chinese art. The wealth of the finds from these pits made it clear that Sanxingdui was a major center, and subsequent research has shown that it was the location of a large urban settlement. Critical questions revolve around the relationship of Sanxingdui and Anyang.

FIGURE 12.13 Shang bronze vessel from Anyang, China

Survey projects in other regions of China have also uncovered evidence of the shift to increased social complexity. A survey in the **Rizhao** area of Shandong Province, on the coast of the Yellow Sea, far from the Shang and Xia capitals, found a significant increase in population and a four-tier settlement system several centuries before the founding of Erlitou (Underhill et al. 2008). In the Rizhao area survey, two very large sites covering between 250 and 375 hectares were identified. Although these sites are slightly smaller than Erlitou, the survey results show that they were also urban centers at the apex of a complex settlement hierarchy. The Rizhao area survey found a significant decrease in settlement size and number of sites in the Shang period.

Located in Inner Mongolia, the **Chifeng region** is at the interface between the agricultural area of the Yellow River Basin and the areas to the north and east that were occupied by societies of pastoral nomads. A survey project in the Chifeng region did not find the kind of massive settlement found in the Yi-Luo Valley or in Shandong, but even here there was a clear shift to larger settlement size and increased population around 2000 B.C. The largest single site is 23 hectares. An interesting point is that several sites also have defensive walls.

▲▲ **Sanxingdui** A site in Sichuan Province where excavations uncovered a spectacular trove of artifacts that are unique in style and contemporary with Anyang.

▲▲ **Rizhao** A region in Shandong Province where a survey has found evidence of a complex settlement hierarchy that is earlier than the Yi-Luo Valley cities.

▲▲ **Chifeng region** An area in Inner Mongolia where a survey has found an increase in population around 2000 B.C.

■ The Basis of Authority in Early China

Although military strength was critical to the power of the Shang rulers, their legitimacy rested on the unique role they fulfilled by performing rituals (Chang 1994). The power of divination was reserved for the ruler, who possessed the vessels necessary for performing rituals. The richly decorated bronze vessels of the Shang Dynasty have been described as "the politically all-important ritual symbols" (Chang 1994, 68). The significance of these vessels went beyond the considerable effort involved in acquiring tin and copper and the skill needed to cast such elaborate forms. The bronze vessels were used in rituals that were the exclusive domain of royalty and nobility as essential tools of political authority, tying together ritual, warfare, and political power. The power of the rulers flowed not from their identification with a god, but from their essential role in connecting the human world with the divine. Archaeologists are able to trace the outlines of elaborate rituals of feasting and sacrifice used by Shang rulers to harness the power of their ancestors and of divine forces.

FIGURE 12.14 Gilded bronze head from Sanxingdui

Archaeology in China's Three Gorges

ROWAN FLAD, HARVARD UNIVERSITY

I have had the great fortune of being involved in archaeology in China during a period of growth and vibrancy. Only since the beginning of the 1990s has it been possible for foreign archaeologists to engage in collaborative fieldwork within the People's Republic of China, and I was lucky to be a graduate student when some of the first collaborations were getting off the ground.

The fieldwork I was involved with included archaeologists from the Sichuan Provincial Institute of Archaeology, Peking University, and UCLA, where I received my PhD in 2004. We were focused on investigating Zhongba, one of the largest known sites in the area to be flooded by a reservoir behind the Three Gorges Dam, a massive hydroelectric project on the Yangtze River. The construction of this dam, the world's largest, was something that had been considered and explored by successive governments since the early years of the twentieth century, but only in the 1990s did work begin in earnest. This project required an intense effort by all of the archaeological institutions across China to try to salvage as much as possible of the cultural heritage in the reservoir zone prior to flooding.

Most counties in the reservoir zone had one or more archaeological units responsible for the management of archaeological resources. One of these units was Peking University, which was given the responsibility over a county called Zhong Xian. In the university's initial assessment of the area to be flooded, one site in particular stood out as being clearly of extreme importance—the site of Zhongba.

Zhongba was a mound located 6 kilometers up a tributary to the Yangtze called the Ganjing River. This mound rose over 15 meters from the surrounding river channel and was covered with pottery sherds and other archaeological debris. In order to accomplish the monumental task of excavating the majority of this site before the dam waters arrived, the Peking University group teamed up with the Provincial Institute in Sichuan Province and several archaeologists from UCLA, one of whom was me.

I first visited Zhongba in early 1999 on a research trip that focused on examining archaeological sites related to early salt production around the Sichuan Basin. Sichuan, located in central China, was an inland sea that evaporated throughout the Mesozoic era. During this evaporation process, thick salt deposits crystallized and were subsequently buried. During historical periods, this salt was accessed through deep wells and served as an important resource for state finance. Salt was a resource monopolized by many successive Chinese imperial governments, and its production and distribution were vital to healthy economies.

Our project involved digging relatively large excavation units (10 × 10 meters) across the entire expanse of the Zhongba site mound. The seasons were long—about six months of the year were spent in the field. This was necessary because the deposits were very deep (nearly 15 meters in some places) and the excavations needed to be completed before the reservoir waters began to rise. We would have worked even longer seasons, but the main part of the site was surrounded by water of the Ganjing River during the high-water period in the summer months.

At Zhongba, salt was made from brine that was accessible near the

On Shang sites, elite burials exhibit a significant focus on feasting (Nelson 2003). This is a break from earlier periods, when evidence for feasting was found in burials of people from all levels of society. The emphasis on feasting at elite burials appears to indicate that during the Shang Dynasty the world of the ancestors was socially stratified. As Sarah Nelson (2003) writes, "By this point, social stratification is so marked that only royalty are feasted and only the royal dead can apparently become spirits" (87). The evidence for feasting consists mostly of the vessels recovered from excavation. Most of these are designed for drinking wine, but others are shaped for preparing and eating meat and grains. These vessels were cleaned after use and carefully stacked in the tombs.

Most large sites have produced extensive evidence for sacrifice. Sacrifice appears distinct from feasting, since in many cases complete animals are interred (Jing and Flad 2005). Animals found in sacrificial pits include dogs, pigs, cattle, horses, and elephants. The numbers can be quite large. For example, at Anyang there are over 200 site. Our excavations and analyses documented the prehistoric salt production (from about 2500 B.C. to 200 B.C.) using chemical analyses of ceramics as well as comparisons with other known salt-production sites around the world. We were able to examine the organization of production through a careful analysis of the pottery vessels that were used to evaporate brine and through a study of the archaeological features and their spatial distribution across the production area at the site. The vessels included several types that were used primarily for salt production, such as *huandiguan* (rounded-bottom jarlets) that were probably used for brine evaporation and the creation of salt cakes. We also documented extensive processing of animals—including pigs, deer, dogs, cattle, bears, monkeys, rhinos, and many types of fish—in the salt-production area. It is possible that some of these animals had their meat preserved with salt for transportation to other communities far away from Zhongba. The work at Zhongba has led to further collaboration on the archaeology of Sichuan, a region that was extremely important to

the mosaic of cultural development in China during the Neolithic and Bronze Ages. For the past several years, since I began teaching at Harvard University, I have been helping lead a team of archaeologists conducting an archaeological survey in the Chengdu Plain, northwest of the capital of Sichuan Province. This project seeks to

document and understand the changes that took place in settlements over the last several millennia B.C. as complex polities developed and thrived in this region. It is one of many collaborative projects begun during the last decade as Chinese archaeology continues to develop and become increasingly international. ▲

FIGURE 12.15 The Zhongba mound in the middle of the course of the Ganjing River, about 6 kilometers upstream from its confluence with the Yangtze

horses buried in 66 pits and over 220 dogs in 34 pits. Humans were also sacrificed in large numbers. There are also pits with a combination of different animals, as well as pits with both human and animal sacrifices. The discoveries at Sanxingdui suggest that objects were also linked to sacrifice. In the two large pits discovered in 1986, the objects had all been burnt and broken. The scale of the offerings in these pits is remarkable. One of them included 735 bronzes, 61 gold objects, 486 worked pieces of jade, 67 elephant tusks, and 4,600 seashells. These had been arranged in layers according to the types of artifacts and had clearly not been thrown into the pit haphazardly.

■ Conflict and Consolidation

The emerging state societies of the Three Dynasties covered a massive region stretching from Sichuan in the west to the Yellow Sea in the east and affecting societies living as far north as Mongolia. However, during these periods, China cannot be regarded as a single unified political entity, and in fact the hallmark of the latter part of the Zhou Dynasty (1100 B.C.–256 B.C.) is the conflict among polities. Cities dating to the Zhou Dynasty are often very large settlements fortified by massive walls of rammed earth. For example, the city of Xiadu, a capital of the Yan state dating to the later periods of the Zhou Dynasty, measures 4.5 kilometers from east to west and between 4 and 6 kilometers from north to south. The entire city is enclosed by a rammed-earth city wall with foundations 50 meters thick. Palaces, residential neighborhoods, cemeteries, and workshops are all located in discrete areas within the city walls.

Warfare during the Zhou Dynasty drew on new tools, including iron weapons and horses. The military power of local states during the later part of the Zhou Dynasty is made palpable by the discovery made at the royal cemetery of the state of Qi at Linzi, where a pit was excavated with the remains of more than 600 sacrificial horses. In 2008, a major new site from the early Zhou Dynasty was discovered at Chenzhuang in Shandong Province. Among the finds made at Chenzhuang are a city wall, an altar, and incised bronze vessels, as well as burials of horses and chariots (Jin 2012). Analysis of plant remains recovered by flotation shows that there is a high frequency of clover and other plants that served as fodder, indicating that Chenzhuang was likely a military base for an army equipped with horses.

The unification of China in 221 B.C. under Ying Zheng, the First Emperor of Qin, whose tomb was described in the opening to this chapter, marks a turning point in the history of the Chinese state. One of the most spectacular acts undertaken by the First Emperor was linking together preexisting fortifications to create the Great Wall that marks out the northern border of his empire (see Figure 12.16).

FIGURE 12.16 The Great Wall built by the First Emperor marked the northern border of his empire

■ Summing Up the Evidence

It is a fair bet that the coming decade will see significant developments in our understanding of state formation in China. The pace of fieldwork is impressive, and there is an increasingly lively discussion of issues related to archaeological method and theory. A distinctive element of early Chinese states is the importance of ritual for establishing the power of the rulers. Archaeological research on feasting and sacrifice is providing important insight into how these rituals actually played out. Excavations and surveys across China are beginning to undermine an approach to state formation in China that focuses exclusively on Anyang. It is now clear that state formation was a complex process that took place across a wide geographical region, stretching at the very least from Sichuan in the south to Inner Mongolia in the north. State formation also stretches back to the pre–Shan Dynasty urban sites found in the Yi-Luo Valley and Shandong. During the Zhou Dynasty, there was increasing conflict among polities that resulted in the building of large fortifications around many cities. China was unified under the First Emperor in 221 B.C. and soon turned to defending its borders and extending trade routes and diplomatic connections.

Archaeology and Development

The Three Gorges Dam in China is only the latest and largest dam construction to cause substantial destruction of archaeological sites. Building of the massive dam across the Yangtze River was completed in 2006 and is creating a narrow reservoir that will extend over 600 kilometers. The goal of this huge project is to generate power and control flooding in the area downriver from the dam. The impact of the dam includes the displacement of over 1 million people. Environmentalists have raised concerns about the potential effects of this project. Moreover, the dam has led to the flooding of hundreds of archaeological sites.

Although the scale of the Three Gorges Dam is unprecedented, the flooding of archaeological sites by artificial reservoirs is a recurrent threat. The building of the Aswan Dam in Egypt (completed in 1971) led to an international mobilization organized by the United Nations Educational, Scientific and Cultural Organization to rescue archaeological sites located along the portion of the Nile Valley that would be flooded (Hassan 2007). The transport of the Abu Simbel monumental sculptures to dry ground received particular notice and demonstrated that at least some mitigation of the effects of dam construction is possible. The experience gained from the Aswan project set some guidelines for archaeological responses to dam construction. Because the scale of the threat to archaeological resources from these projects is so vast, the response requires coordinated international efforts. Initial archaeological research must also include systematic surveys and detailed planning so that there is a sound basis for prioritizing which sites should be excavated.

Today, dam construction threatens archaeological sites around the world. Projects in Turkey and the Sudan have caused international concern, but there are many other works that receive only local attention. Rarely are archaeologists able to stop dam construction or even alter the design of a dam. A notable exception is the Côa Valley in Portugal, where intense lobbying by archaeologists saved the Upper Paleolithic open-air art sites in the valley just before they were to be flooded.

Archaeologists have often gained important knowledge from the opportunities afforded by dam construction. For example, the sites of Abu Hureyra and Habuba Kebira in Syria are among the sites excavated in advance of Syrian damming of the Euphrates River. Yet archaeologists are painfully aware that there is no mitigation that will truly redress the damage caused by dams. Even where sites are transported or fully excavated, which happens in only a small percentage of cases, what is lost is the original context of the site and the potential for future research. These sites are a nonrenewable resource, and every loss is irreversible. Archaeologists are left to act as advocates for the preservation of the archaeological record, but they are also forced to make pragmatic choices to respond to destruction that they cannot prevent. The experience with the Aswan Dam highlights the importance of strong international organizations that can mobilize an effective archaeological response to large-scale development. ●

FIGURE 12.17 Satellite photo of the Three Gorges Dam, showing the reservoir flooding the valley behind the dam for a distance of more than 600 kilometers

FIGURE 12.18 The relocation of Abu Simbel, Egypt

12.3 Beyond the Chinese Boundary: Japan, Central Asia, and Cambodia

The unification of China by the First Emperor affected areas far beyond the territories under direct control of the emperor. In some areas, expansion took place by military action and the garrisoning of troops. A notable example is the establishment of the Lelang commandery near Pyongyang, North Korea, in 180 B.C. But a broader consideration of the influence of China on its neighbors shows that military domination was only one aspect of a far more complex network of interactions. Archaeologists explore such relationships between empires and their neighbors as interactions between a core and its periphery. However, it is important to think about the influence of China on its neighbors as part of the dynamics of the development of local communities rather than only as China's influence emanating outward from the center to the periphery (Yao 2012). Here, we will briefly explore the effect of interaction with China on state formation in Japan; the culture of the people who lived along the Silk Route across central Asia; and the emergence of the spectacular city of Angkor, Cambodia.

■ Mirrors and Keyhole-Shaped Tombs: The Origins of the State in Japan

Chinese histories report that in A.D. 238, the court received a visit from representatives of **Himiko**, Queen of Wa, bringing gifts of cloth and slaves (Kidder 2007). In A.D. 240 envoys from China visited Wa and presented Himiko with gifts, including 100 bronze mirrors. Himiko is described as coming from Yamatai and was involved with sorcery. It is clear that Wa refers to Japan but controversy has raged over the identification of Yamatai (Edwards 1996). It now appears that Himiko was Princess Yamatototohi-momoso-hime, who lived in the Kinai region east of Osaka Bay. This princess is also associated with sorcery, and she was part of a male/female ruling pair.

FIGURE 12.19 The Hashihaka keyhole burial mound

Around A.D. 200 a new form of burial monument appears in Japan. These are **keyhole-shaped tombs** that consist of a circular mound paired with a trapezoidal platform. The prevalence of massive keyhole-shaped tombs marks the **Kofun period** (A.D. 250–710) and the onset of state formation in Japan. One of the largest and earliest of these tombs is the Hashihaka, shown in Figure 12.19, which might be the burial of Princess Yamato. A striking component of the burial goods found in the keyhole-shaped tombs is the presence of **triangular-rimmed bronze mirrors** from China, shown in Figure 12.20. Mirrors are known from earlier burials in Japan, but the appearance of this particular type of mirror is correlated with the beginning of the Kofun period. The iconography of some of the mirrors shows a powerful figure in Chinese mythology, the **Queen Mother of the West**, who symbolizes power and longevity (Barnes 2007). It is intriguing that characteristics of the Queen Mother of the West are shared with the Japanese descriptions of Princess Yamato.

When the Emperor of China gave Himiko the mirrors, he was creating a relationship of allegiance between the land of Wa (Japan) and China. Kobayashi Yukio has argued that the mirrors might have played a crucial role in developing relationships between elites in Kofun societies (Kobayashi 2006). Kobayashi suggests that once these mirrors were brought over to Japan, the exchange among Japanese elites would have created relationships of alliance and thus fueled the transition toward social complexity. The presence of these mirrors in burials likely had powerful religious significance. According to Chinese beliefs, the mirrors "light the soul's way to the next world" (Cahill 1993 quoted in Barnes 2007, 181).

Certainly more than the exchange of mirrors was behind the development of social complexity in Kofun-period Japan. Notably, the objects placed in tombs include armor, and the Japanese chronicles speak of conflict. Nonetheless, the influence of the Chinese state on Japanese societies seems to have operated on many levels beyond a simple transfer of power from the Chinese core to the Japanese periphery. The gifts from China to the emerging rulers of Japan brought with them religious associations that underpinned the emerging status of the elites. The exchange of

keyhole-shaped tombs Monumental burial mounds characteristic of the Kofun period.

Kofun period A period of initial stages of state formation in Japan.

triangular rimmed bronze mirrors Ornate bronze mirrors manufactured in China that are found in Kofun-period tombs.

Queen Mother of the West A Chinese deity represented on triangular-rimmed bronze mirrors.

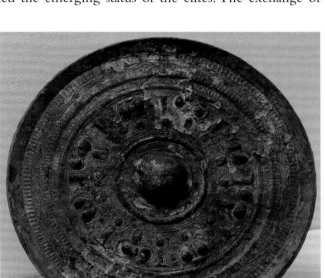

FIGURE 12.20 Triangular-rimmed mirror dating to the Kofun Period

these objects was also an important component in the formation of alliances among the powerful members of Kofun society.

■ Mummies of the Tarim Basin

The spectacular preservation of burials in the desert of the **Tarim Basin** has brought public attention to the archaeology of central Asia (Mallory and Mair 2000). The Tarim Basin lies along the **Silk Route** that linked East to West and was home to both settled societies and groups of nomadic pastoralists. Much of the public presentation of the Tarim Basin has focused on the Caucasian appearance of the people who lived in this far-western province of China. However, efforts to pigeonhole the people of the Tarim Basin into any kind of category is an excellent example of the futility of using race as a framework for understanding human variation. The Tarim Basin is an area of contact and exchange, and the populations reflect this dynamic. Recent genetic analyses of the mummies from the Xiaohe cemetery come to the conclusion that even 4,000 years ago the maternal lineages of the people, as indicated by mitochondrial DNA, came from both East and West (Li et al. 2010). It is interesting that this study indicates that the paternal lineage derives completely from western Eurasia.

As the Chinese Empire consolidated its power, the pastoral societies of central Asia, united under the **Xiongu Empire**, represented a constant threat (Barfield 2001). Central Asia was also of interest as a source of horses and as an opening for trade routes reaching to the West. Beginning in the first century B.C., the Han Dynasty successfully brought the Tarim Basin under imperial rule, opening a period of enhanced trade of commodities and ideas across the Silk Route.

The spectacular preservation of textiles on the Tarim mummies provides a unique window into the local response to the trade along the Silk Route. The Yingpan site is located at the eastern end of the Tarim Basin. Excavations in 1995 uncovered a series of burials dating to the period between 206 B.C. and A.D. 420. **Tomb 15 at Yingpan** contained the remains of a tall (1.8 meters) 30-year-old man. This burial, shown in Figure 12.21, was found wrapped in rich garments, including a red woolen robe and silk trousers. His head rested on a satin pillow, and his face was covered by a hemp mask with a band of gold adorning his forehead. Burial goods included a necklace, bows and arrows, a cup made of glass, and a comb. The clothing of the man in Tomb 15 shows a mixture of techniques, materials, and motifs drawn from China, the Middle East, and Hellenistic Europe. The main material used is silk from China, but the dyes, particularly those used for the color yellow, are from the West (Liu et al.

FIGURE 12.21 The burial in Tomb 15 at Yingpan

2011). The silk lining of the man's caftan is particularly remarkable. This precious garment is embroidered with nude figures with upraised weapons, ornate pomegranate trees, and dancing goats (Jones 2009). The style of the naked figures is drawn from Hellenistic Greek art, and the pomegranate trees may be derived from Persian motifs. This remarkable garment brings our attention to the Silk Route not only as a conduit between East and West, but also as the setting for the dynamic creation of local identities drawing on influences that are almost global in scale.

■ The Archaeology of Angkor

The great city of **Angkor**, shown in Figure 12.22, located on the southern Mekong Plain in Cambodia between the Tonle Sap Lake and the Kulen Hills, is a landscape reconfigured by human action. The establishment of Angkor dates to the reign of Jayavarman II (A.D. 802–A.D. 835), and the city was abandoned around A.D. 1431. The entire complex of roadways, canals, artificial lakes, and habitations surrounds the spectacular temple enclosure of Angkor Wat.

The power of Angkor was based on intensive rice agriculture, taxation, military force, and the ritual position of the rulers. Many questions remain about the power of the rulers of Angkor and over the degree to which they controlled the massive irrigation system that was essential to rice cultivation. The scale of the artificial basins constructed at Angkor is staggering. The largest, the **Western Baray**, built by Suryavarman (A.D. 1006–A.D. 1050), is 8 × 2.1 kilometers and can store as much as 70 million cubic meters of water (Higham 2002, 312). Beyond their agricultural function, these basins might have been symbolic oceans that served as a complement to the temples, which represented sacred mountains. The elaborate temples of Angkor Wat clearly indicate that the ritual position of the rulers of Angkor was essential to their power as rulers. The king was associated with the god Shiva, and royal power depended on adherence to dharma or moral law. Charles Higham (2002) writes that Angkor is "the outstanding example of building in the name of majesty and sacred power" (348).

Angkor A massive city on the southern Mekong Plain founded in A.D. 802.

Western Baray The largest artificial basin at Angkor, measuring 8 × 2.1 kilometers.

FIGURE 12.22 View of Angkor

Extensive mapping using airborne LIDAR is adding to our understanding of Angkor and other urban sites in Cambodia (Evans et al. 2013; Evans 2016). The capacity of LIDAR to see features hidden by vegetation is ideal for this landscape. At Angkor it is now clear how far the structured urban center extends beyond Angkor Wat itself. Based on the LIDAR survey the size of the city was 35 square kilometers, most of which is laid out on a grid of streets and canals. Most of the city consists of mounds and associated ponds, but the LIDAR survey has also identified several enigmatic features, such as spirals known as coiled embankments at the southern edge of Angkor Wat, shown in Figure 12.23.

The spread of ideas across the **Southern Silk Route**, which stretched along the southern coast of Asia, included the Hindu and Buddhist religions at the core of the ideology of Angkor. But archaeological research is showing that the development of the urban center of Angkor was also built on local developments toward social complexity in Southeast Asia.

By A.D. 245, Chinese histories mention two early southeastern Asian states, Funan and Zehnla. Archaeological research in Southeast Asia has traced out a history of emerging social hierarchy stretching from the Neolithic to the Iron Age. **Noen U-Loke**, Thailand, dated between 300 B.C. and A.D. 200, is a particularly large Iron Age settlement that covers an area of 12 hectares (Higham 2002). Burial goods include necklaces of agate, gold beads, and a range of bronze and iron ornaments. The site is protected by a series of five circular moats, and there is a range of bronze and iron weaponry. One of the skeletons, of a young man, was found with an iron arrowhead embedded in his spine, leaving little doubt that violent conflict was a threat in Iron Age Thailand.

Between A.D. 100 and A.D. 550, cities emerge in the Mekong Delta. **Oc Eo**, Vietnam, is a particularly well-documented site, measuring 3 kilometers by 1.5 kilometers. Oc Eo is protected by five walls and four moats and is crisscrossed by a canal system. The excavations at Oc Eo provide evidence of a prosperous trading center with large temples and a wide range of materials for the manufacture of jewelry,

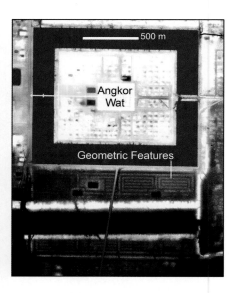

FIGURE 12.23 The use of LIDAR has fundamentally changed our understanding of Angkor Wat and contemporary sites. On the bottom left the LIDAR image shows mounds regularly spaced across a field that is currently under cultivation. These mounds are not visible in the satellite image of the same field shown in the upper left. The LIDAR image on the right reveals previously unknown geometric structures south of Angkor Wat.

including diamonds, amber, rubies, garnets, and carnelian. A particularly striking find made at Oc Eo is an a gold coin of the Roman emperor Antoninus Pius, a clear indication of the extent of the trading systems that linked East to West in the period preceding the founding of Angkor.

Angkor Borei, Cambodia, is located 70 kilometers northeast of Oc Eo, and the two sites appear to have been linked by canals. A rich body of both Hindu and Buddhist sculpture, as shown in Figure 12.24, has been found at Angkor Borei, as well as the earliest known inscription in Khmer, the native language of Cambodia. An archaeological research survey in the area surrounding Angkor Borei has begun to document the broader settlement system connected to this large city of approximately 300 hectares (Stark 2003). Radiocarbon dating of excavations on the site suggests that Angkor Borei was already a large settlement in the Iron Age. An innovative program of direct dating of brick architecture at Angkor Borei indicates that the earliest large-scale architecture dates to early in the first millennium A.D., contemporary with Oc Eo. The initial data indicate that the first monumental construction on the site was dedicated to civic projects such as the city wall and that the monumental religious architecture developed 200 or 300 years later as part of the adoption of Indian religious practice by the elite of an existing urban center (Stark et al. 2006).

▲▲ **Angkor Borei** A city in the Mekong Delta contemporary with Oc Eo with monumental shrines and fortifications.

■ Summing Up the Evidence

The impact of the Chinese Empire on surrounding regions was profound, but the nature of this influence varied considerably. The gift of bronze mirrors to Japan appears to have been intended to form a relationship of allegiance; within Japan, the redistribution of these mirrors appears to have served to form alliances among elites. The Silk Route placed the nomadic people who inhabited the Tarim Basin at the crossroads of a trade network that stretched from Europe to East Asia. The clothing of the man buried in Tomb 15 at Yingpan shows the local response to the dynamic exchanges between East and West. In Cambodia and Vietnam, the emergence of large cities was stimulated by the trade along the Southern Silk Route; however, the development of social complexity in this region has deep roots stretching back to the Bronze Age. It is striking that the Southern Silk Route was not only an economic network, but also a conduit for ideas, beliefs, and ideologies.

FIGURE 12.24 Sculpture from Angkor Borei, Cambodia

TOOLBOX

Underwater Archaeology

The most important thing about underwater archaeology is that it is archaeology. Much of the motivation that leads people to underwater sites is the search for treasure, often gold bullion that went down with ships lost at sea. The distinction between treasure hunting and archaeology is the respect archaeologists have for the careful recording of the context of discoveries. Underwater archaeologists use many of the same techniques as archaeologists working on land, including survey, mapping, and stratigraphic excavation, although the tools used often differ. On underwater sites, lighting and photography are a challenge, as are seemingly simple procedures like maintaining a grid. Artifacts recovered from underwater sites must also often undergo a complex process of conservation when they are transferred to dry conditions. On the other hand, underwater archaeologists can use tools not available to other archaeologists, including sonar for detecting site location and an airlift or dredge to pull away deposits. An additional advantage of underwater archaeology is that, due to the anaerobic environment, wood and other perishable materials are often preserved. The range of underwater archaeological sites includes harbors and submerged settlements, but it is shipwrecks that have pushed the development of the field. Shipwrecks provide essential information about seafaring technology and maritime trade. Because shipwrecks are a powerful draw to treasure and adventure seekers, underwater archaeologists often have to battle to preserve this unique archaeological legacy. Shipwreck archaeology has also pushed the application of new technologies, from three-dimensional imaging of the ocean floor to submersibles and underwater vehicles used to gain access to wrecks at depths beyond the reach of conventionally equipped divers (Ballard 2008).

Underwater archaeology has had a major impact on the archaeology of the Mediterranean world. One of the greatest discoveries made by underwater archaeologists is the wreck of a ship dated to the Egyptian New Kingdom at the site of Ulu Burun, off the southern coast of Turkey (Bass 1986). Excavations at Ulu Burun have recovered a rich assemblage of trade items, including copper, tin, and glass ingots; storage jars containing traces of organic products; and more exotic items such as gold and ivory. More recently, the remains of two ships, given the names *Tanit* and *Elissa*, dating to the eighth century B.C. were identified on the seabed 33 nautical miles off the coast of Israel at a depth of 400 meters (Ballard et al. 2002). Using a remotely operated vehicle, it was possible not only to document the shipwrecks, but also to retrieve representative artifacts. It is important to emphasize that the archaeological team took extreme care not to damage the shipwrecks and that the provenience of all artifacts was carefully recorded. The results show that both vessels sailed from the coast of Lebanon to either Egypt or Carthage in North Africa carrying a cargo of roughly 10 tons of wine each. The wine was transported in highly standardized storage vessels known as amphora that had been sealed against leakage with resin. Traces of tartaric acid, an organic acid found in grapes, were found by chemical analysis of the interior of these vessels.

In Asia, underwater archaeology remains in its early stages. Few governments or research organizations have been able to commit the resources for projects independent of

---

SUMMARY

- The Harappan civilization developed along the Indus River Valley. The material culture of the Harappan civilization is essentially uniform across the entire region.
- The two largest Harappan cities are Harappa and Mohenjo-Daro. These cities are characterized by a regular grid of roadways and an impressive sewage system. Excavations at Dholavira have uncovered a Harappan city with large water tanks and neighborhoods separated by walls.
- There is little evidence of monumental architecture on Harappan sites. One exception is the Great Bath at Mohenjo-Daro. There is little evidence for the concentration of wealth in the hands of the elites of Harappan cities.
- The Harappan script is found on a range of artifacts, including seals. The script has not yet been deciphered.
- The Three Dynasties—the Xia, the Shang, and the Zhou—emerged in northern China during the period between 2000 B.C. and 500 B.C.
- Survey in the Yi-Luo Valley has revealed that the cities of Erlitou and Yanshi, which date to the Xia and Early Shang Dynasties, were at the top of a complex settlement hierarchy.

salvage companies. Some of the most interesting underwater archaeology has been carried out by archaeologists working with salvage companies that use the sale of artifacts to make a profit. The collaboration between archaeologists and companies working to sell artifacts for profit raises complex ethical questions that are particularly acute in the underwater archaeology of Southeast Asia, where the cost of research is high and the potential payoff from the recovery of treasure ships is very high. The excavation of a ninth century A.D. shipwreck off the Indonesian island of Belitung that produced vivid evidence of the Southern Silk Route was the result of a partnership between an underwater archaeologist and a salvage company working under permit from the Indonesian government (Flecker 2001). The cargo of this ship consisted of 10 tons of lead ingots and a large quantity of Chinese ceramics, along with the spice star anise that also comes from China.

The methods used to construct the ship point to India or the Middle East as the port of origin, while the cargo dominated by Chinese ceramics popular in the Middle East suggests that this ship sank while plying a trade route connecting China to the Middle East. ●

ADDITIONAL READING: Amanda Bowens, ed. 2009. Underwater Archaeology: The NAS Guide to Principles and Practice. Malden, MA: Blackwell.

FIGURE 12.25 Excavation of the shipwreck at the site of Ulu Burun, Turkey. Notice how the divers are carefully mapping the site—in this case, a cargo of copper ingots.

- Anyang was the capital of the Late Shang Dynasty between 1200 B.C. and 500 B.C. Excavations at Anyang have recovered large quantities of oracle bones, a massive burial ground, and the remains of a large city.
- Excavations at Sanxingdui in Sichuan Province have uncovered great hoards of remarkable artifacts contemporary with Anyang.
- Survey in the Rizhao area of Shandong Province has uncovered evidence of a complex settlement hierarchy that is earlier than the Yi-Luo Valley sites. Survey in the Chifeng region of Inner Mongolia has demonstrated an increase in settlement size around 2000 B.C.

- The legitimacy of Shang rulers rested on the role they played in performing rituals.
- Feasting associated with elite burials and sacrificial deposits are important features of Shang Dynasty sites.
- The initial stages of state formation in Japan date to the Kofun period (A.D. 250–A.D. 710). Keyhole-shaped tombs are characteristic of the Kofun period, and triangular-rimmed bronze mirrors are among the objects found with burials.
- Mummies found in the Tarim Basin on the Silk Route linking West to East show evidence of the creation of local identities that draw on influences from a wide geographic range.

- Angkor is a large city on the southern Mekong Plain, Cambodia, founded in A.D. 802. Monumental architecture at Angkor includes lavishly sculpted temples and massive basins such as the Western Baray.
- The Hindu and Buddhist religions reached Southeast Asia along the maritime Southern Silk Route.
- By the Iron Age, there are large settlements in Southeast Asia, such as the fortified site of Noen U-Loke, Thailand. Oc Eo, Vietnam, and Angkor Borei, Cambodia, are large cities that developed in the Mekong Delta before the founding of Angkor.

KEY TERMS

REVIEW QUESTIONS

1. Why do archaeologists find the absence of monumental architecture and elaborate burials in the Harappan cities surprising?
2. Is the association of the Shang ruler with the performance of rituals unique, or are there parallels to the role of rulers in Mesopotamia, Egypt, the Aegean, or the Indus?
3. How has survey been used to understand the development of social complexity in China?
4. How did interaction with China shape the development of social complexity in Japan?

FROM CITY TO EMPIRE

SOCIAL COMPLEXITY IN MESOAMERICA

The complex societies of Mesoamerica expand our understanding of urbanism and the institutions that underlie both cities and empires. After reading this chapter, you should understand:

- The archaeological evidence for the nature of social organization in the city of Teotihuacán.
- The structure of Maya cities and the historical record recovered from Maya hieroglyphic texts.
- The history and organization of the Aztec Empire.

Recording Maya glyphs

13 TIMELINE

SITES		La Venta	Monte Albán	San Bartolo

EVENTS

PERIODS

OLMEC

| 1500 BC | 1000 BC | 500 BC | 0 |

SITES DISCUSSED IN CHAPTER 13

Gulf of
Mexico

Teotihuacán
Tenochtitlán
Capilco • Otumba
Cuexcomate
La Venta •
Yaxchilán • Tikal
Monte Albán • Bonampak • Dos Pilas
Aguateca
Copán •

PACIFIC
OCEAN

Copán, Tikal,
Teotihuacán

Tenochtitlán

SPANISH CONQUEST OF TENOCHTITLÁN

POSTCLASSIC MAYA

CLASSIC MAYA

AZTEC EMPIRE

TOLTEC

500 AD   1000 AD   1500 AD   2000 AD

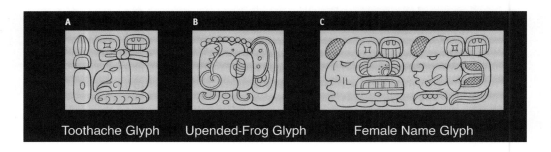

FIGURE 13.1 A: The toothache glyph, indicating that the date that follows is the date when a ruler took to the throne. B: The upended-frog glyph, indicating that the date that follows is a birth date. C: The name glyph of the woman on Stela 3. The profile with a cross-hatched oval over the forehead indicates that the person named was a woman.

Toothache Glyph   Upended-Frog Glyph   Female Name Glyph

I n 1961, Tatiana Proskouriakoff noticed that a series of inscriptions from the Maya site of Piedras Negras featured one sign, known as the "toothache sign," along with another sign, the "upended-frog," with each placed next to the sign for a date (see Figure 13.1). The Maya calendar had already been deciphered, so Proskouriakoff was able to determine that the date associated with the upended-frog sign was 20 to 30 years earlier than the date associated with the toothache sign. On the basis of this observation, she came to the conclusion that the toothache sign indicated the date a ruler ascended to the throne and that the upended-frog sign indicated the ruler's birth date. This modest hypothesis had major implications for the study of the ancient Maya. If Proskouriakoff was correct, then the Maya had recorded the history of their rulers and this history could be deciphered.

Proskouriakoff then turned to three stelae, numbered 1 through 3 (see Figure 13.2). On the front of these large stones, the inscription is badly eroded, but on the back, the well-preserved carving of a woman wearing a robe is clearly seen. Proskouriakoff found that Stelae 1 and 2 showed the upended-frog glyph (indicating the date of birth), followed by a name. The name was prefixed by a profile with a cross-hatched oval or lock of hair on the forehead, a prefix indicating that the person was a woman. The date and the name on both stelae were the same.

On the third stela, a girl kneels next to the woman. The upended-frog glyph date for the girl is 33 years later than the birth date of the main figure. Proskouriakoff concluded, "How can one reasonably doubt that [the] robed figures are portraits of the same person, that the person is a woman, and that her little daughter, not yet born when Stela 1 was erected, is shown on Stela 3?" (Proskouriakoff 1961, 16). Proskouriakoff had succeeded in reading a small piece of Maya history. Subsequent advances in deciphering Maya hieroglyphs came at a steady pace, and today much of the history recorded by the Maya that survives can be read.

Mesoamerica is not a geographically defined region, but rather a region whose indigenous inhabitants share a number of cultural traits, including a complex calendar, an emphasis on bloodletting, and a ball game played on a special court (Coe 1993). In this chapter, we begin by briefly exploring the evidence for the emergence of social complexity and urbanism in Mesoamerica. We then take a more in-depth look at both the urban center of Teotihuacán and the Maya cities. The last part of this chapter examines the emergence of the Aztec Empire. A number of authors have argued that there are aspects of the development of state societies in Mesoamerica that do not fit well with general models for state formation. Richard Blanton and colleagues have posited that while some Mesoamerican states were hierarchical, in others a different power strategy was dominant (Blanton et al. 1996). In a hierarchical state, there are clear patterns of dominance, with a single ruler at the apex of society holding a monopoly on power. Blanton refers to the political strategy underlying hierarchical states as *exclusionary*. Other societies developed a *corporate* political strategy in which power is shared across different sectors. In a corporate setting, social

FIGURE 13.2 The back of Stela 3 from Piedras Negras, showing a woman sitting on a throne with a child beside her

Figure 11.8 from Expedition 4 (1), Figure 5, p. 17 (1961). Reprinted by permission of University of Pennsylvania Museum.

forces actually inhibit the centralization of power in a single individual. Old King-dom Egypt presents perhaps the ultimate example of a hierarchical state, with the construction of monumental funerary complexes built around the body of the king. Yet even in Old Kingdom Egypt, there were countervailing forces, most likely from the social structure organized around lineages and households. In Mesopotamia, the ruler was clearly politically dominant, but the power of the palace was balanced by that of the temple. Perhaps the best examples of an urban society with a corporate power strategy are the cities of the Indus Valley. The layout of Mohenjo-Daro and Harappa show evidence of planning and a central authority, yet there is an almost complete absence of indications of the concentration of power in the hands of a sin-gle ruler. In Mesoamerica, the city of Teotihuacán, although very different from the cities of the Indus Valley, might also be best understood in the context of corporate strategy, or even as the emergence of a corporate strategy in response to the excesses of hierarchical rulers. The rulers of Maya cities were clearly powerful individuals. But even with the Maya, there are indications of tension between the ruling lineages and a political body that was more broadly representative of the elite of the city.

Olmec The earliest complex society in Mesoamerica. Olmec sites are located along the Gulf Coast of Mexico.

▲▲ **Monte Albán** The site of the oldest city in Mesoamerica, located in the Oaxaca Valley.

13.1 The Origins of Urbanism and Social Complexity

The earliest evidence of emerging political complexity in Mesoamerica is found on **Olmec** sites along the Gulf Coast of Mexico (Benson et al. 1996). Between 1200 B.C. and 300 B.C., the Olmec constructed a series of major ceremonial centers in towns with populations numbering in the thousands. The Olmec developed a highly sophisticated artistic tradition that included monumen-tal sculptures of human heads carved out of volcanic rock, such as the sculpture from the site of La Venta, shown in Fig-ure 13.3. These sculptures give a vivid sense of the prestige of Olmec society's leaders. Particularly significant is the head-gear depicted on the sculptures, which is possibly related to competition in a ball game. Hollow clay sculptures of infants with what appear to be adult heads are often found on Olmec sites. These delicate figures stand in sharp contrast to the raw power expressed in the monumental stone sculptures, raising the question of whether the latter depict leaders or divinities. The Olmec also produced spectacular sculptures from jade and other hard stones. At the site of La Venta, a cache of 16 male figures carved from jade and serpentine was found, standing in front of a series of polished stone axes (Lauck 1996). It is possible that this scene represents a town council, a balance to the power of the rulers depicted through the monumental sculptures.

The first city in Mesoamerica was located at the site of **Monte Albán**, in the Oaxaca Valley in the Mexican high-lands. Between 500 B.C. and 350 B.C., the population of Monte Albán grew first to 5,000 and then to 17,000 in neighbor-hoods built around a central plaza (Blanton et al. 1993). In the period between 350 B.C. and 250 B.C., Monte Albán was surrounded by a defensive wall. The central plaza became the focus of monumental construction that included temples, a possible palace, and a ball court.

FIGURE 13.3 La Venta colossal Olmec head

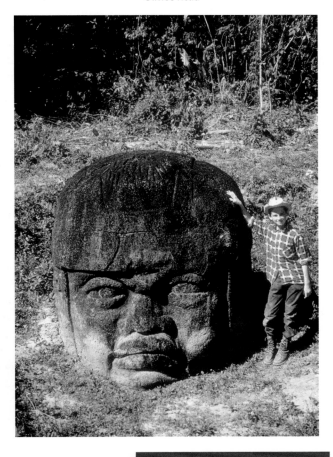

▲▲ **Teotihuacán** An enormous city with a population of over 80,000 located in the Valley of Mexico and established around 2,000 years ago.

Avenue of the Dead A road that stretches for 5 kilometers through the center of Teotihuacán.

Pyramid of the Sun The largest monument at Teotihuacán, rising to 64 meters.

Ciudadela A very large compound in Teotihuacán that includes a large courtyard where the Temple of the Feathered Serpent is located.

Temple of the Feathered Serpent A structure at the back of the Ciudadela adorned with the sculpted heads of the feathered serpent deity.

13.2 Teotihuacán

Beginning 2,000 years ago (A.D. 1–A.D. 200), **Teotihuacán** grew into an enormous city covering an area of 20 square kilometers, with a population of more than 80,000 (Sugiyama 2004). Teotihuacán, shown in Figure 13.4, is located 7,000 meters above sea level in the highland Valley of Mexico, a rich agricultural area dotted by lakes. The Teotihuacán Mapping Project surveyed the entire area of the city and carried out systematic collections of artifacts (Millon 1970; Millon, Drewitt, and Cowgill 1973). This project, which produced the site map shown in Figure 13.5, is perhaps the largest-scale urban survey ever undertaken.

Teotihuacán was laid out along a road, known as the **Avenue of the Dead**, that stretches for 5 kilometers and enters the city from the south. Surveys indicate that the growth of Teotihuacán was fueled by the depopulation of the surrounding countryside. During the period of the initial growth of Teotihuacán, between A.D. 1 and A.D. 200, the great monuments that line the Avenue of the Dead—the Pyramid of the Sun, the Ciudadela, the Temple of the Feathered Serpent, and the Pyramid of the Moon—were built. While this program of monumental construction was under way, little effort was put into elaborating the residential areas of the city. The **Pyramid of the Sun** is the largest monument at Teotihuacán, rising to 64 meters and encompassing over 9 million cubic meters. A cave runs below the pyramid for about 100 meters. This natural feature was clearly of great importance, but excavations found that most of the contents of the cave had been looted in antiquity.

The **Ciudadela** is a very large compound that some archaeologists think might have housed a palace. At the back of the main courtyard in the compound is the **Temple of the Feathered Serpent** (also known as the Feathered Serpent Pyramid), so named for the carved heads of the deity that adorn the monument's surface (see Figure 13.6 on p. 360). Excavations in the 1980s revealed burials of sacrificial victims distributed symmetrically along the four sides of the temple. The grave goods found with these male victims suggest they held high-status positions related to the military. A series of skeletons was found with necklaces consisting of

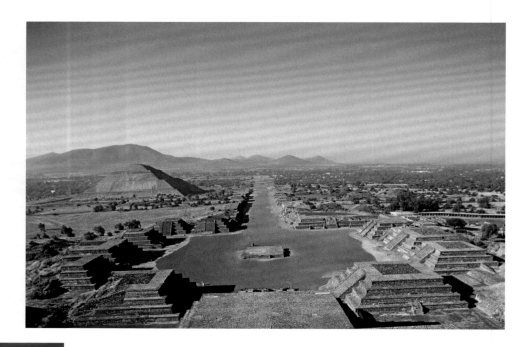

FIGURE 13.4 View down the Avenue of the Dead in Teotihuacán. The Pyramid of the Sun is on the left.

FIGURE 13.5 Map of the central area of Teotihuacán from the Teotihuacán Mapping Project

Temple of the Feathered Serpent

Ciudadela

Avenue of the Dead

Pyramid of the Sun

N

0   1300 ft

400 m

Pyramid of the Moon

shell replicas of human upper jaws (maxillae). In one case, the necklace is made of actual human jaws (see Figure 13.7 on p. 360). The burials in the temple make it clear that there was a relationship between military power and prestige in Teotihuacán. They also vividly demonstrate the role of human sacrifice in Teotihuacán ritual.

Around A.D. 400, a remarkable event took place. The facade of the Temple of the Feathered Serpent was smashed and burnt and then re-covered with a new layer of construction. This destruction of the facade of the temple had been preceded by a shift away from monumental construction. Beginning around A.D. 200, the residential areas of the city were reconfigured into apartment complexes, multifamily dwellings enclosed within massive walls. There is a great deal of variation between the apartment compounds, but all of the apartments were built along the same orientation as the Avenue of the Dead. It is estimated that 50 to 100 people

FIGURE 13.6 Facade of the Temple of the Feathered Serpent, Teotihuacán

Pyramid of the Moon A pyramid complex used for both symbolic functions and the production of military supplies, located at the north end of the Avenue of the Dead in Teotihuacán.

FIGURE 13.7 A human skull with maxillae and tooth-shaped beads from Teotihuacán

lived in a complex. Some of the compounds have been identified as residences of groups coming from outside the Valley of Mexico. The construction of the apartments, along with the destruction of the facade of the Temple of the Feathered Serpent, might have been the result of a gradual increase in the power of kin groups at the expense of the centralized ruler. The presence of burials near sacrificial altars in the main apartment complexes might indicate the development of ritual built around the ancestors of kin groups. These ancestral lineages would have rivaled the military cult found in the Temple of the Feathered Serpent.

The tension between lineages and the military as sources of power may have been central to the dynamics of the political life of Teotihuacán (Headrick 2007). But who would have stood at the apex of political authority? To address this question, we must turn to the art from Teotihuacán. There are a number of monumental sculptures from the center of the city, but it is unclear whether these represent individuals or gods. The paintings found on the walls of buildings provide a rich body of data. Powerful military leaders, clearly identifiable by their costume, which includes an elaborate headdress, goggles, earspools, and a mirror worn behind the neck, are often depicted in these paintings. Most of the warriors grasp a spear thrower, or atlatl, in one hand and a bunch of darts in the other. The ruler, or the member of the elite, is rarely shown in isolation, but is often part of a pattern in which the same image is repeated many times. The impression is that the art is an effort to at once recognize the power of the ruling elite while also stripping them of their individual identity, suggesting that (at least at the level of artistic representation) the political office was more important than the person filling it.

Recent excavations at the **Pyramid of the Moon**, at the northern end of the Avenue of the Dead, have provided new insight into the relationship between military power and the rulers of Teotihuacán. A series of pits found within the Pyramid of the Moon complex has yielded debris from obsidian workshops (see Figure 13.8). This volcanic glass was a critical component of the Teotihuacán military prowess; the atlatl darts fired by Teotihuacán warriors were made of obsidian. The excavators at the Pyramid of the Moon found that the workshops within the compound were producing thousands of atlatl dart points (Carballo 2007). This discovery makes it clear that the function of the pyramid complex went beyond the symbolic to include the production of military supplies. But the distinction between military and ritual might have been artificial for the

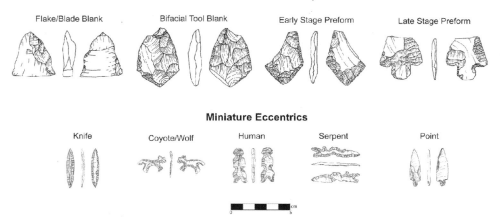

Dart Point Production Sequence

Flake/Blade Blank   Bifacial Tool Blank   Early Stage Preform   Late Stage Preform

Miniature Eccentrics

Knife   Coyote/Wolf   Human   Serpent   Point

FIGURE 13.8 Drawings of obsidian artifacts recovered from pits outside the Pyramid of the Moon. The top row includes pieces discarded in the process of manufacturing dart points, while the lower row contains miniatures chipped into the form of tools or figures.

inhabitants of Teotihuacán. In other pits, the debris from the production of sacrificial knives in the shape of animals and bound prisoners was found. Obsidian was not only an essential weapons component, but also a material with powerful symbolic resonance.

Excavations within the pyramid itself raise further questions about the military and its role in the political and ritual structure of the city. Along the main north–south axis of the pyramid, a series of burial deposits of sacrificial victims was found. Evidently, these were put in place each time the pyramid structure was expanded. These burial deposits included a careful arrangement of human and animal sacrificial victims and a range of burial goods. These are very complex deposits that resist generalization. Brief consideration of Burial 2 gives a sense of the nature of the discoveries. One adult male aged 40 to 50 was buried in a seated position near the eastern edge of the chamber. His hands were crossed behind his back and probably bound. He was wearing beads, earspools, and a pendant, all of which indicate elite status. Isotopic analysis of the skeletal remains indicates that he was not from the Valley of Mexico. Spread around the tomb were objects, including obsidian blades in the shape of people, shell pendants, greenstone figurines, and jars in the shape of the storm god, Tlaloc. Finally, there were bones of a range of animals, including an eagle, a falcon, and a horned owl. Two pumas and a wolf appear to have been buried alive in cages. There are compelling reasons to interpret the animals found in the burial as representative of military units or of warriors who transform into animals in the heat of battle. The sole human skeleton appears to be a foreign warrior captured in battle and sacrificed for the consecration of the pyramid.

■ Summing Up the Evidence

The scale of Teotihuacán, along with its extensive urban planning and monumental construction, indicates a strongly centralized state. It is likely that the great monuments, including the Temple of the Feathered Serpent, Pyramid of the Sun, and Pyramid of the Moon, were built by rulers seeking to advance their power. If this is the case, the destruction of the Temple of the Feathered Serpent and the shift to building apartment complexes speaks clearly of a strong reaction against centralizing

TOOLBOX

Human Osteoarchaeology

Forensic scientists have become unlikely pop culture heroes. Their uncanny abilities to make deductions from the most minute (and gruesome) details appeal to our taste for the macabre and our desire for definitive answers. Human osteoarchaeologists are responsible for developing many of the methods used by forensic scientists, but their goal is not to solve a crime, but rather to contribute to an archaeological understanding of the past. In the late nineteenth and early twentieth centuries, the field of human osteoarchaeology—the analysis of human skeletons recovered on archaeological sites—was an extension of physical anthropology, and the major goal of analysis was often to describe the physical attributes of populations. Today, human osteoarchaeologists use tools from the biological and medical sciences and integrate their research into broad archaeological frameworks. Among the key areas of research are quality of life (including diet and nutrition, disease, and growth and development), behavior and lifestyle, and population history (Larsen 2006). Human osteoarchaeologists often work in close collaboration with archaeologists who study artifacts to combine evidence from the physical and cultural remains found in burials. The analyses of the complex mortuary deposits uncovered in the Pyramid of the Moon at Teotihuacán offer an excellent example of this kind of collaborative research (Spence and Pereira 2007; Sugiyama and López Lujan 2007).

As in all areas of archaeological analysis, it is critical that human osteoarchaeologists be aware of the challenges posed by the nature of the type of material they study. One particular problem facing human osteoarchaeologists is *selective mortality*. As stated by James Wood and colleagues (1992), "There is one, and perhaps only one, irrefutable fact about the cases making up a skeletal series: they are dead. We never have a sample of all the individuals who were at risk of disease or death at a given age, but only of those who did in fact die at that age" (344). Essentially, we are missing that part of the population that did not succumb to disease.

In recent years, the development of laws in the United States restricting excavation of human remains and requiring repatriation of skeletal material under the terms of the Native American Graves Protection and Repatriation Act has had a major impact on human osteoarchaeology. The current climate in many regions creates significant challenges for research on human skeletal remains. In this context, it is crucial to foster discussion of the significance of human osteoarchaeology for an integrated analysis of the archaeological record. ●

FIGURE 13.9 Excavation of a Neolithic skeleton in northern Italy

power in favor of a corporate political structure. Is it possible that a hierarchical leader pursuing an exclusionary political strategy was not the linchpin of this society? According to George Cowgill (1997), "pride and a sense of citizenship, and not just submission to overawing deities and overpowering rulers, may explain much about [Teotihuacán's] stability and why there was no abundance of self-glorifying rulers" (153). Certainly, the forces that came together to create an urban society on an unprecedented scale for the Americas will continue to challenge archaeologists well into the future.

13.3 The Maya

The modern Maya live in an area stretching from southern Mexico through Guatemala and Belize, as well as in parts of Honduras and El Salvador. Beginning around 2,000 years ago, the Maya developed a state society with a complex writing system and large urban centers. Much of their written history was lost under Spanish rule, which brought with it devastating disease and the systematic imposition of European culture, including the burning of most Maya books (Coe 1999). However, archaeology has made major strides in reconstructing the Maya past. The decipherment of Maya hieroglyphics has afforded spectacular insight into the detailed history of the early cities. The study of modern Maya oral traditions and cultural practices also plays a significant role in understanding the remains of the Maya past.

■ The Setting and Chronology

The Maya cities developed in the lowland zones that run from the foothills of the Sierra Madre in the south to the Caribbean Sea in the north. The Maya lowlands are divided into the tropical rain forests of the southern zone and the flat scrublands of the Yucatán in the northern zone. Most of the early cities developed along rivers and swamps in the southern zone. The northern zone became the dominant focus of Maya settlement in later periods. Maya sites in the northern zone are located near *cenotes*—sinkholes that were a critical source of water.

The main agricultural method used in the Maya region is slash-and-burn cultivation, in which the forest is cleared by burning. After a number of growing seasons, the field is abandoned, and the forest is allowed to regenerate. Slash-and-burn cultivation is a shifting system of agriculture in which field systems move over time as areas are cleared, exploited, and then left fallow. The Maya also developed methods for growing crops on extensive raised fields in swamps. The use of raised fields was a critical component of the intensified agriculture needed to support large population centers. There is little evidence that Maya agriculture depended on large-scale irrigation projects. However, there is some evidence for large-scale projects; for example, canal systems that are poorly understood have been found around some cities (Demarest 2004).

The Maya cities developed during the Classic period, which dates to between A.D. 250 and A.D. 900 (Houston and Inomata 2009). The preceding period is referred to as the Preclassic. Excavations at the site of Ceibal have found that already at the beginning of the Middle Preclassic (950 B.C.), settlement had begun to coalesce around a ceremonial complex (Inomata et al. 2015). Around A.D. 900, many of the large cities were abandoned in what is known as the Maya collapse. During the subsequent Postclassic period, which lasted from A.D. 900 to the arrival of the Spanish in A.D. 1519, most large Maya settlements were located in the northern Yucatán Peninsula.

■ The City

The ruins of Classic-period Maya cities are covered by dense forest undergrowth. On many excavations, machetes are as important as trowels. Steep pyramids, their

FIGURE 13.10 The central area of the Maya city of Copán in a reconstruction by Tatiana Proskouriakoff. This drawing places the monuments within an empty jungle setting. Today, we know that the city of Copán covered a wide area beyond the pyramids and palaces.

▲▲ **Copán** A large Maya city with two large pyramids and an elaborate ball court at its center.

FIGURE 13.11 The hieroglyphic stairway at Copán

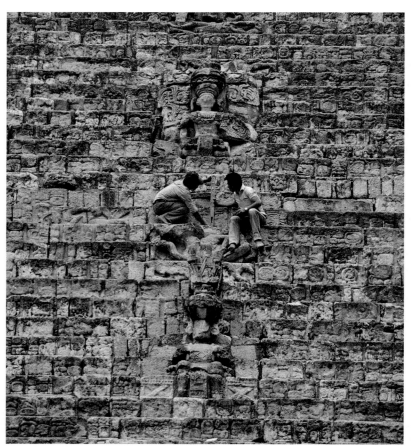

apexes often visible above the forest canopy, are the defining feature of the cities. These pyramids sit in the central area of the city together with royal residences, ball courts, and open plazas. Extensive survey work and excavation on Maya sites has demonstrated that these cities stretched far beyond the central area to include large residential areas with populations of up to 20,000 living on small house mounds.

The central area of **Copán**, Honduras, has been the focus of intensive research. The center of Copán includes two large pyramids and an elaborate ball court (see Figure 13.10). An inscription recounting the dynastic history of Copán covers the entire face of the northern pyramid in what is known as the hieroglyphic stairway (shown in Figure 13.11). This feature led from an altar at the base of the pyramid to a temple structure at the top. The inscription of the history of Copán in such a powerful setting has been interpreted as an effort to connect the troubled rulers of the late periods with the glorious achievements of the great ancestral kings (Fash 1991).

The Maya pyramids were built up over centuries as new rulers tore down and built over the temples of their predecessors (Figure 13.12). The tops of the pyramids served as temple platforms, while the rulers and their families were buried within the expanding structures. Research on the Maya pyramids

FIGURE 13.12 Cutaway view of the southern pyramid at Copán showing the elaborately decorated buried structure of Rosalila. This illustration shows how the Maya pyramids were built up over time as early constructions were encased by later building phases.

involves not only mapping their surface, but also tunneling into them to find the earlier structures that were encased as the pyramids were expanded and rebuilt. At Ceibal the structure known as A-20 began in the Middle Preclassic (950 B.C.) as a natural rise in the limestone bedrock that was sculpted and covered with clay. A-20 continued to develop into a pyramid through multiple construction phases over hundreds of years (Inomata 2013). At the southern pyramid of Copán, the archaeological tunneling has resulted in the discovery of a completely intact temple from the early stages of the city's history. Unlike other structures that were destroyed before being built over, this one, known as Rosalila, appears to have been so revered that it was encased in pristine condition. Rosalila was a rectangular edifice elaborately decorated with painted stucco figures. These sculptures present fantastic depictions of gods, birds, and snakes. In the floor of one of the rooms in Rosalila, a cache of spectacular flint artifacts in the shape of a deity were found (see Figure 13.13). These objects, known as eccentric flints, are among the finest objects of chipped stone ever made.

At the site of Caracol, Belize, airborne LIDAR been used to map the entire settlement (Chase et al. 2011). The results of the LIDAR survey at Caracol confirmed that this was a large city of roughly 170 square kilometers (see Figure 13.14). The survey also showed the degree to which the Maya modified their landscape by building causeways, walls, and extensive agricultural terraces.

Tikal One of the major Maya urban centers.

FIGURE 13.13 Eccentric flint from Rosalila, Copán

■ Government

Maya cities were ruled by dynasties of powerful kings. The exact timing of the emergence of kingship among the Maya is the subject of debate. The earliest king documented at the site of **Tikal** is Yax Ehb' Xook, who appears to have lived around A.D. 100 (Martin 2003). However, it

FIGURE 13.14 Details of Altar Q from Copán that shows the succession of the kings of the ruling dynasty

is not clear that Yax Ehb' Xook was the ruler of a city. It appears that the year 378 marked a major change in the history of Tikal. The glyphs speak of the arrival of a new ruler coming from outside and ending the dynastic line. This new ruler either came from the highland Mexican city of Teotihuacán or was in some way heavily influenced by it.

The foundation of the royal dynasty at the city of Copán dates to A.D. 426. The first king of Copán, named Yax K'uk' Mo', came from outside of the city and possibly had links to Teotihuacán. One of the burials at Copán appears to be the remains of Yax K'uk' Mo'. Skeletal analysis has shown that this individual suffered several traumas during his life, perhaps as the result of warfare or participating in ball games (Buikstra et al. 2004).

On the basis of the evidence from Tikal and Copán, it appears that the founding of the Maya cities was linked in some cases with the arrival of a ruler connected to Teotihuacán. Once established, the ruling dynasties maintained their power for generations, often hundreds of years. Monuments were frequently used to connect the ruler with the prestige of the dynasty. The hieroglyphic staircase at Copán is the most spectacular example of such monuments, and the monument known as Altar Q, shown in Figure 13.14, also displays the dynastic succession. The rulers of the Maya cities rarely claimed to be gods themselves; however, they were viewed as uniquely sacred individuals (Houston 2000). There is no sense of a strong distinction between the palace and the temple. The dynasty was closely identified with the temple complexes at the core of the Maya city.

Although the rulers of Maya cities were able to draw on the prestige of their dynastic lineage and the sacred aspect of their office, their power was not absolute or unchallenged. There is evidence that, particularly during the later part of the Classic period, a broader aristocracy came to challenge the power of the ruler. A particularly intriguing discovery made at Copán was a building known as Popol Na—literally, a *mat house*—which appears to have been the locale for meetings of a council of aristocrats. The tension between the power of the aristocracy and that of the royal lineage seems to have been a critical dynamic in the history of Maya cities.

TOOLBOX

Geophysical Methods

Geophysical methods are used to gain an idea of what lies below a surface without excavation. In effect, geophysical methods allow archaeologists to detect invisible features. The two main geophysical methods used by archaeologists are magnetometry and ground-penetrating radar.

Magnetometry works by detecting magnetic anomalies in the soil. These anomalies are often evidence of buried features such as tombs, pit houses, channels, and roadways (Pasquinucci and Trément 2000). In practice, a magnetometry survey involves walking along a landscape with an instrument that records magnetic readings. The data obtained are collated by computer to present a picture of subsurface anomalies that are interpreted by the archaeologist and used to guide further research.

Ground-penetrating radar (GPR) involves transmitting an electromagnetic pulse into the ground (Conyers and Goodman 1997). Depending on what the pulse encounters as it travels, it is either reflected back to the surface or continues to travel until it is completely dissipated. The analyst uses GPR instruments to build up a reflection profile that provides a picture of any variation in the sediments below the ground. The reflection profile can provide information about the depth and extent of anomalies that might indicate buried archaeological features.

At the Maya site of Kaminaljuyu, Guatemala, GPR was used as a response to the pressures of excavating under salvage conditions (Valdes and Kaplan 2000). The site today is in a modern urban setting that has been heavily affected by development. Plans to build a shopping complex and a hotel in the area led to urgent salvage excavations. The GPR survey allowed archaeologists to rapidly survey areas that they would not have had time to test by excavation. The survey succeeded in locating a series of buried objects, ranging from a car muffler to significant archaeological features, including the floor of a house and two ritual caches. ●

FIGURE 13.15 Ground-penetrating radar reflection profile from a site in northern Australia. The arcs (known as hyperbolic reflections) indicate the location of burials.

■ Inequality

The burials of Maya royalty do not contain large quantities of elaborate goods. The tomb of Yax K'uk Mo', the founder of the Copán dynasty, included jade and shell ornaments, the remains of a headdress made of shells, a number of pottery vessels, and a cache of eccentric flints. These are clearly high-status objects, but they are not an overwhelming display of wealth. It is possible that much greater wealth, including textiles and feathers that have not survived, were originally buried with Yax K'uk Mo'.

The development of household archaeology has begun to make an important contribution to understanding the structure of Maya society. By moving away from the monuments of the center, household archaeologists cast light on the lives of ordinary people and study diversity among households (Robin 2003). Excavations of Maya houses have found that not all people had equal access to high-status

FIGURE 13.16 Excavating domestic architecture at Aguateca

objects. Particularly as one moves out to small agricultural hamlets, the range of artifacts becomes limited mostly to locally produced objects used in daily life. However, household archaeologists have also found evidence that high-status trade items were not restricted to elite residences.

At the site of **Aguateca**, Guatemala, archaeologists have discovered a unique window into the lives of the Maya at the very end of the Classic period (Inomata and Stiver 1998). The town of Aguateca was burnt and abandoned, most probably the result of a military attack. The people were forced to flee their homes, leaving behind much of what they owned. After the houses burnt, their walls collapsed, sealing the floors under rubble (see Figure 13.16). In one of the houses, the tools of a scribe were discovered, providing a vivid picture of the position of scribes in Maya society (see Figure 13.17). The scribe's rooms, in the north and center of the building, included a large number of high-status artifacts, indicating that scribes were members of the Maya elite. It is interesting that the scribe's room contrasts with the southern part of the building, where cooking vessels and tools used in weaving were found. The excavators suggest that this was the home of a nuclear family in which the male was a scribe and the female, probably his wife, carried out tasks related to food preparation and weaving in the southern part of the building. The excavation of the house at Aguateca points to the many levels of differentiation found in state societies. On a broad scale, there are significant differences between groups within society; however, on a smaller scale, there is also differentiation within households.

▲▲ **Aguateca** A site that was abandoned and burnt, probably in a military attack, leaving archaeologists with a unique record of the daily life of the Maya.

FIGURE 13.17 Plan of the scribe's house at Aguateca. The symbols show where different types of artifacts were found.

➤ Halved-Shell Ink Pots
● Mortars for Pigment Preparation
◗ Pestles for Pigment Preparation

▯ Bone Needles
⌒ Spindle Whorls

One aspect of wealth that is largely invisible archaeologically is richly woven cloth and other elaborate items of clothing. The contemporary Maya are renowned for their colorful clothing, which features many design elements that can be found on Classic Maya sculptures and paintings. Depictions of the Maya rulers show that, in addition to wearing beautifully woven garments, they donned highly elaborate head-dresses made of flowers and feathers (see the Yaxchilán lintel, Figure 13.22 on p. 372).

Painted murals from the site of Calakmul, Mexico, provide rare illustrations of daily life during the Classic Maya period. In the Calakmul paintings shown in Figure 13.18, we see people going about daily chores of preparing food and carrying vessels. They are clothed simply in colorful textiles, providing a view of life away from the elaborate rituals of the palace (Vargas et al. 2009).

Maya hieroglyphs A complex combination of pictographic and syllabic script that initially developed to record major events in the lives of rulers.

■ Maya Hieroglyphics

Like the cuneiform writing system of Mesopotamia, the **Maya hieroglyphic** writing system developed from pictographic signs representing concepts to a system that uses these same signs to represent syllables. However, Maya scribes never discarded the pictographic meaning of signs, resulting in a highly complex writing system in which the same sign could represent either a concept or a syllable. The development of Maya script was not purely the outgrowth of economic functions. The major reason for the development of written script was to record the timing of ritual events in the lives of rulers. Whereas cuneiform writing developed out of the economic needs of the ruling elite of the cities of Mesopotamia, the Maya hieroglyphic writing developed out of the connection between rulers and ritual.

Maya script emerged fully during the Classic period through the coalescence of traditions dating back to the end of the Olmec period (Houston 2000). The first tradition was the use of a segment of an image to represent the whole. An example found in Olmec art is the use of the eye of a jaguar to represent the animal. The progressive abstraction of these forms lies behind many of the Maya hieroglyphs.

The second tradition was the recording of a complex calendar (Fash 1991). The earliest-recorded calendar date comes from Stela C from the Olmec site of Tres Zapotes, dated to 300 B.C. The Maya calendar was an extraordinarily complex system of multiple overlapping systems. The Long Count records time from a zero date (August 13, 3114 B.C., according to our calendar). The Maya used a series of four units for measuring time:

1 ki . . . day
20 kin . . . uinal = 20 days
18 uinal . . . tun = 360 days
20 tun . . . katun = 7,200 days
20 katun . . . baktun = 144,000 days

The Maya also used a 260-day ritual calendar with 23 numbers and 20 named days, a 365-day solar calendar, and at least two other systems. The complexity of the Maya calendar reflects the centrality and significance the people attached to measuring time, matched by an intense interest in recording astronomical events.

There is very slight evidence that Maya script might also have drawn on a tradition of using written records in economic transactions. If such records existed, they must have been

FIGURE 13.18 Calakmul mural showing *ul*, a gruel made of maize, being served and consumed. The hieroglyphic reads *aj ul*, which means "maize gruel person." How does this scene compare to the rolled-out view of the vessel shown in Figure 13.20?

Gender and Sexuality in the Field

CHELSEA BLACKMORE, UNIVERSITY OF CALIFORNIA, SANTA CRUZ, USA

Prior to August 11, 2016, Section 53 of the Belize Criminal Code read: "Every person who has carnal intercourse against the order of nature with any person or animal shall be liable to imprisonment for 10 years." Beginning in 2010, Caleb Orozco and the United Belize Advocacy Movement (UNIBAM) argued that the section infringed on the constitutional protections of human dignity, personal privacy, equity, and protection from discrimination. On August 11, 2016, the Belize Supreme Court ruled that Section 53 was unconstitutional. Having this law overturned in Belize was a major victory for LGBTIQ activists worldwide, particularly in the Caribbean, where homosexuality continues to be largely criminalized. So what does this have to do with archaeology? Simply put, archaeologists don't live in a fieldwork bubble (hopefully we don't!). We work with, even become friends with, people in our field communities. And as such, how we act is impacted by the laws, moralities, and ideologies of these same places.

When I started dissertation fieldwork in 2003, I was barely out to myself, let alone to my family, or friends. I kept my sexuality to myself for a long time, unsure of how people would react and how those reactions might affect my ability to finish my dissertation research. Fortunately for me, I was going to school in California, and I had a supportive family and faculty supervisors who would help me in any way. But my fear of being out had as much, if not more, to do with the sexist and homophobic undertones I had experienced during previous archaeological projects in the United States. It was hard to ignore when strong women, regardless of their sexuality, were called dykes or the countless times that well-meaning friends suggested I was going through a phase.

In Belize, it was hard to ignore the conservatism of some people (much as it was when I went back to Florida

to visit family), and it was hard not to worry about what would happen if I opened up to those closest to me. All in all, when I did open up, people were overwhelmingly supportive; many even encouraged me to bring my partner down to visit. At the same time, I was quite guarded in who I told and how I talked about my partner. Outside of circles of people I trusted, I lied when working overseas (as I often do traveling to other socially conservative places, including within the United States). It was easier to use male pronouns when I talked about my partner. I even occasionally wore a band on my ring finger to warn off interested parties. And this had as much to do with my gender as my sexuality. I am hardly the first woman, queer or not, to invoke a

mythical husband or boyfriend while traveling alone. As a white woman working in Belize, I hold a place of relative privilege—something I did not quite recognize at the time. While I worried about what my "field family" would think, it was a different world for queer Belizeans living there full time. What was the worst that could happen to me—having to change field topics or sites and losing some cherished friendships? Sure. But others faced losing family, friends, employment, and more. At the time, I did not have much of a queer community and knew few queer archaeologists. I found my voice eventually by throwing myself deep into feminist and queer theory. I made my own community, starting with the ideas and politics of those who inspired me. ▲

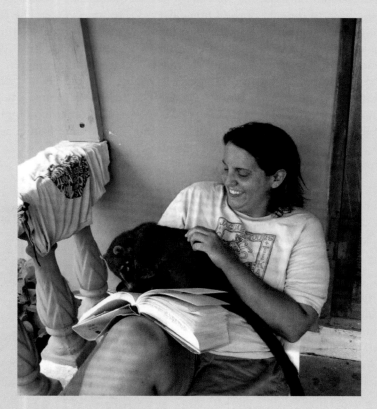

FIGURE 13.19 After a day of fieldwork, Chelsea Blackmore plays with the neighborhood coatimundi

written on perishable materials that have not survived. One of the main sources of evidence for the use of writing to record transactions comes from drawings of a deity writing numbers on leaves.

The Maya documents that survive deal largely with the recording of events in the lives of the rulers of cities, particularly the dates when the rulers performed significant rituals. Most of the surviving texts are monuments carved in stone or inscriptions on clay vessels (see Figure 13.20). More complex religious and historical documents were probably written in books known as codices, only a small number of which have survived. Depictions of daily life are rare, although the recently discovered murals from the site of Calakmul (Vargas et al. 2009) are a striking exception. A unique expression of the wealth of Maya mythology is found in the **Popol Vuh**, which was transcribed following the Spanish conquest (Coe 1993). The Popol Vuh tells the epic tale of the hero twins Hunahpu and Xbalnque and their battle with the lords of the underworld, known as Xibalbá. The tale hinges on the skill and trickery of the twins, which allow them to vanquish the lords of the underworld before rising up through the surface of the earth and into the sky, where they become the sun and the moon. A ball game played to the death is central to the story.

Discoveries at the site of **San Bartolo**, Guatemala, have uncovered evidence of the Maya mythology and script predating the Classic period (Saturno et al. 2005). When archaeologists arrived at San Bartolo in 2002 the site had already been trenched by looters. One of the trenches ran through a building that has come to be known as Las Pinturas Pyramid. While seeking shade, Bill Saturno, who was leading the expedition, noticed painted murals. Subsequent excavation uncovered complex and intricate mythological scenes dated between 100 B.C. and A.D. 100. These paintings have parallels in Classic Maya iconography and the mythology of the Popol Vuh. On the left side of the mural on the north wall five babies are shown emerging from a gourd. Facing them is a large figure with feathers and a serpent's face. To the right of this figure there is an elaborate flowered mountain at the top of which a jaguar and snake stalk small birds. A woman crouches in a cave in the right side of the flowered mountain, holding a plate of tamales out to a procession of figures, several clearly representing gods, who stride along the back of a snake apparently bearing water and maize out of the mountain. The west wall shows a series of deities

A

B

FIGURE 13.20 Painted Maya pot. A: Photograph of the vessel. B: Rolled-out view showing the presentation of tribute to a seated lord.

(top): © The Trustees of the British Museum/Art Resource, NY. (bottom): © The Trustees of the British Museum/Art Resource, NY.

FIGURE 13.21 Deity in royal garb from the west wall of Las Pinturas at San Bartolo

FIGURE 13.22 Limestone carved lintel from Yaxchilán, Mexico. Lady Wak Tuun is shown during a bloodletting ritual. She holds a stingray spine, a rope used in bloodletting, and bloodied paper. In front of her, a vision serpent emerges from a bowl containing strips of paper.

depicted as royal hunters, one of which is shown in Figure 13.21, presenting offerings to trees representing the four corners of the earth.

As archaeologists excavated deeply into Las Pinturas, they came on a block from an earlier construction phase with hieroglyphic inscriptions dated between 200 B.C. and 300 B.C. (Saturno 2006). These hieroglyphics are difficult to decipher but one appears to be the sign for Ajaw, or ruler.

■ Ritual, Violence, and Warfare

Bloodletting and sacrifice were important elements of Maya ritual (Schele and Miller 1986). Some of the most vivid scenes of bloodletting are found on a series of carvings from the site of Yaxchilán. In these scenes, the ruler and his wife are seen drawing blood from their tongues and collecting the drops on special paper (see Figure 13.22). The bloodletting brings on spectacular visions of enormous snakes with the heads of gods.

The ball game also played a major role in Maya society. The epic battle between the hero twins of the Popol Vuh and the lords of the underworld appears to be at the heart of much of Maya ritual practice. Echoing the centrality of the ball game to Maya ritual is the position of the ball court at the core of the city. The ball court consists of a bare patch of ground, flanked on either side by a banked structure. The game was played with a heavy rubber ball that, apparently, had to be shot through a ring without the use of the hands. Some archaeologists have argued that, as it was in the myth of the Popol Vuh, in real life the ball game was played to the death.

However, violence in the Maya world went beyond ritual and sport. From sites such as Aguateca, there is clear evidence that cities were conquered and burnt. Inscriptions record the capture of cities and the death of their rulers, and a vivid series of murals from the site of Bonampak shows scenes of prisoners being tortured and killed. It is not clear how the Maya carried out their warfare. There is no evidence of standing armies, and Maya weaponry appears to have been limited to flint- and obsidian-tipped spears and armor made from skins.

■ The Maya Collapse

In the period around A.D. 870, the cities of the southern Maya lowlands collapsed. New construction ended, and the cities were gradually deserted. This collapse was the result of factors internal to Maya society, as well as factors related to the external environment. One factor that played a role in weakening the power of the Maya rulers was the ratcheting up of cycles of violence and warfare. By the end of the Classic period, warfare was widespread and its consequences often catastrophic, as demonstrated by the burnt town at Aguateca. Excavations at the large urban center of Dos Pilas have uncovered a radical transformation of the site beginning in A.D. 761, when a defensive palisade was built around the central area with stones ripped from the temples and pyramids. The residents built a tightly packed siege village in the open plazas and began living in the area once reserved for ritual and ceremony (Demarest 2004). A number of archaeologists argue that the increasing power of the nobility led to a further weakening of the power of the rulers or even resulted in a "nobles revolt" (Fash 1991).

External environmental factors also contributed to the Maya collapse. A series of severe droughts occurred during the period of the Maya collapse (Haug et al. 2003). It is likely that these intense short-term climatic events played a role in the abandonment of the Classic Maya cities. One likely scenario is that the Maya intensified agriculture to support the growing population of their urban centers and as a result lacked the resilience to adapt when faced with reduced rainfall (Douglas et al. 2015; Lentz et al. 2014). Evidence for agricultural intensification in the periods leading up to the Maya collapse includes terrace systems and basins used for irrigation.

■ Summing Up the Evidence

Maya kings ruled over large urban centers. The emergence of both cities and state society among the Maya is closely linked with external influences, particularly from the highland city of Teotihuacán. The power of the Maya kings was based on the prestige of the royal lineage and reinforced by the king's critical ceremonial role. The prestige of the royal lineage was literally built into the city in the form of monumental inscriptions and pyramids that encased the burials of the kings. The hieroglyphic writing system was developed as a tool for recording the timing of ritual events in the lives of rulers. The eventual collapse of the Maya cities appears to have been the result of a number of factors, including warfare, ecological degradation, and external climatic events. Of these factors, the intensified warfare between cities seems to have played a decisive role.

13.4 The Aztec Empire

In 1519, Spanish soldiers arrived at the city of **Tenochtitlán**, the capital of the **Aztec Empire**. Tenochtitlán was at that time one of the largest cities in the world

▲▲ **Tenochtitlán** The capital of the Aztec Empire and the largest indigenous city ever built in the Americas; located in the Valley of Mexico.

Aztec Empire A large Mesoamerican empire based in Tenochtitlán.

Archaeology and Tourism

Copán is a critical site for the archaeology of the Maya. It is also a major tourist destination. The rapid growth of cultural tourism has obvious implications for archaeological site development and protection. But there are also more subtle issues raised by the intersection of archaeology and tourism. For example, in Honduras, the prominence of Copán and the Maya history has led to the eclipse of other aspects of the heritage of Honduras, with a resulting impact on national identity and politics (Mortensen 2007). The demands of the tourist industry can also lead to the "packaging" of archaeological sites. At the fourteenth-century site of Bagan in Burma (now known as Myanmar), reconstruction of the archaeological remains has led to widespread criticism, including a comment by one UN official that "a Disney-style fantasy version of one of the world's great religious and historical sites is being created by (the military) government" (quoted in Hudson 2008, 553). In the case of Bagan, the reconstruction is fueled by a combination of politics, development, and religious reverence.

The threats posed by tourist development are balanced by positive economic and cultural potential. Visiting archaeological sites gives tourists direct access to the remains of our shared cultural heritage. For local communities, particularly in areas of the world with few employment opportunities, the economic potential of archaeological tourism can be very important. The International Council on Monuments and Sites (ICOMOS) has recognized that it is critical to develop tools to enhance understanding and cooperation between the archaeological community and the tourism industry. In its 1999 International Cultural Tourism Charter, the organization lays out the following principles for cultural tourism:

- Conservation should provide responsible and well-managed opportunities for members of the host community and visitors to experience and understand that community's heritage and culture at first hand.

- The relationship between heritage places and tourism is dynamic and may involve conflicting values that require careful management.

- Conservation and tourism planning for heritage places should ensure that the visitor experience will be worthwhile, satisfying, and enjoyable.

- Host communities and indigenous peoples should be involved in planning for conservation and tourism.

- Tourism and conservation activities should benefit the host community.

- Tourism promotion should protect and enhance cultural heritage.

This is a strong set of principles, but noticeably absent is any mention of the interests of researchers, which include archaeologists. However, in most cases, research is an essential element of sustained tourist development of archaeological sites. Visitors come with questions, and they expect that, if a site is worth visiting, it must also be worth exploring scientifically.

The strength of the ICOMOS principles is their emphasis on finding management solutions to bridge different worldviews.

There is a clear sense of need for a new kind of expertise, one that combines the skills of planning and management with an understanding of the issues involved in research, conservation, heritage, and tourism. In her study of Copán, Lena Mortensen (2007) states that recent developments "straddle borders that explode the once hermeneutic circles that have traditionally controlled the production of scholarly knowledge" (133). The task facing archaeologists responding to the economic and political interests inherent in the rapidly growing cultural tourism industry offers a fundamental challenge to archaeological theory (for discussion of hermeneutics, see Chapter 2, p. 49). ●

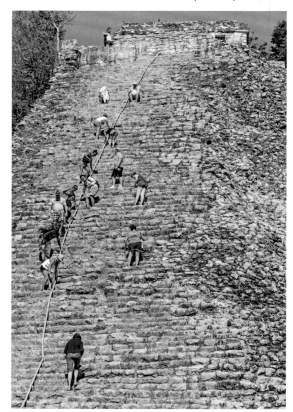

FIGURE 13.23 Tourists climbing the pyramid at the Maya site of Coba, Mexico

and the largest city ever built in Mesoamerica. The Spanish conquistador Bernal Diaz del Castillo wrote that "so high, majestic, and splendid did the temples, towers, and houses of the town, all built of massive stone and lime, rise up out of the midst of the lake . . . many of our men believed what they saw was a mere dream" (Bernal Diaz del Castillo 1568 [1844], 219). Tenochtitlán was built on an island in Lake Texcoco in the Valley of Mexico and was connected to the mainland by a series of causeways (Figure 13.24). At the center of the city rose the great twin pyramids of the **Templo Mayor**, the spiritual center of the Aztec universe.

Two years of bloody and treacherous warfare led to the final conquest of Tenochtitlán (Townsend 2000). The end of the Aztec Empire came on August 13, 1521, when, at the close of a 93-day siege, the last Aztec king, Cuauhtemoc, was captured as he tried to escape the city by canoe. In a powerful symbolic act, the Spanish built their cathedral near the ruins of the Templo Mayor in the heart of what has become Mexico City.

Some of the priests who arrived on missions to convert indigenous people to Christianity carefully documented Aztec history, religion, and society. Among the most important historical source is a series of books known as the **Florentine Codex**, compiled by the Spanish friar **Bernardo de Sahagún** (Brumfiel 2001). The Florentine Codex consists of the interviews Sahagún carried out with Aztec informants, both in the Aztec language, Nahuatl, and in Spanish translation. This text is accompanied by extensive illustrations drawn by indigenous artists. Illustrated books were also kept by the Aztecs themselves; however, few have survived. Archaeological research has confirmed many of the descriptions in the Florentine Codex with spectacular discoveries at the site of the Templo Mayor in Mexico City. Archaeology has also extended our understanding of the Aztec Empire by uncovering evidence of the lives of the people living in areas beyond Tenochtitlán.

■ The History of the Aztecs

The Aztecs were aware of both the Olmec and Teotihuacán and drew explicit connections to those societies. Among the precious objects found in ritual caches in the

Templo Mayor A double pyramid at the center of Tenochtitlán that was the core of the Aztec world.

Florentine Codex A document that is a major source of information on Aztec history and culture, compiled soon after the Spanish conquest of the Aztecs.

Bernardo de Sahagún The Spanish friar who compiled the Florentine Codex.

FIGURE 13.24 Spanish map of the city of Tenochtitlán, built on an island and reached by causeways. The sacred precinct of the Templo Mayor is located in the center of the city.

Templo Mayor was an Olmec stone mask (Matos Moctezuma 1988). A number of objects from Teotihuacán were also found in excavations at the Templo Mayor, and Aztec architecture makes frequent reference to styles that originated in Teotihuacán. The name *Teotihuacán* is not the original name of the city, but rather the name used by the Aztecs, which, in the Aztec language, Nahuatl, means "the place where gods (or rulers) are made."

Aztec kings traced their genealogy back to the rulers of the **Toltec Empire**, which developed between A.D. 950 and A.D. 1150 after the fall of Teotihuacán (Smith 2003). The Aztec kings depict the Toltec Empire as great and powerful; however, archaeology paints a rather more modest picture. The Toltec capital, **Tula**, was the largest city of its time, but its population of 50,000 was far smaller than that of either Teotihuacán or the Aztec capital of Tenochtitlán. It is also far from clear that Tula did actually control a large empire; there is little archaeological evidence for Toltec control of regions beyond Tula.

While the Aztec rulers traced their genealogy back to the Toltec, they also traced their origins to people who migrated from afar. The location of the Aztec homeland of **Aztlán** remains unknown and is perhaps mythical (Smith 2003). There was a series of migrations from Aztlán into the Valley of Mexico during the period between A.D. 1200 and A.D. 1250. All of these migrants are known as Aztecs, after the homeland of Aztlán. The first group of Aztec migrants settled in the Valley of Mexico, while the second wave settled in the surrounding valleys. The final group to arrive was the Mexica, who had to settle for a desolate area known as "grasshopper hill." Even in this setting, the Mexica faced attack by a coalition of Tepanecs (an earlier group of settlers from Aztlán) and their allies from the town of Culhuacán (Townsend 2000). The Mexica were roundly defeated and forced to resettle in an even more desolate setting under the protection of Culhuacán. An alliance then developed between the two groups.

The Mexica approached one of the leaders of Culhuacán and asked for his daughter as a bride for the main Mexica deity, Huitzilopochtli. The Culhuacán leader complied, thus paving the way for a further strengthening of the alliance between the two groups. But when the Culhuacán chieftain was invited to festivities with the Mexica, he recognized in horror the flayed skin of his daughter on the body of the Mexica priest. The outraged people of Culhuacán chased the Mexica to uninhabited islands in Lake Texcoco. As the Mexica fled, one of their priests had a vision that they should settle at a sacred spot marked by an eagle perched on a cactus. When the Mexica found an eagle on a cactus the next day, they immediately built a crude temple, which developed over time into the Templo Mayor at the core of the great city of Tenochtitlán. Today, the Mexican flag pictures an eagle perched on a cactus, in recognition of this significant turning point in the history of Mesoamerica.

How did the Mexica go from being despised outcasts to the rulers of a great empire? One must recognize that the origins of empires are often highly mythologized; this is clearly the case for the Mexica origin stories. Nonetheless, the Mexica's rapid rise to power is remarkable. This increase in power rested on a series of conflicts and alliances with neighboring groups, as well as on the consistent growth of Tenochtitlán as an urban center. In 1428, an alliance among the cities of Tenochtitlán, **Texcoco**, and **Tlapocán** was established (Figure 13.25). This **Triple Alliance** allowed the rapid expansion of the area dominated by the Aztecs to regions far beyond the limits of the Valley of Mexico. Within the Triple Alliance, the Mexica rulers of Tenochtitlán were dominant, and their power grew along with the empire. Among the Aztec groups that migrated to the Valley of Mexico from Aztlán, it was the outcast Mexica, the last to arrive, who came to rule over the entire Valley of Mexico and far beyond.

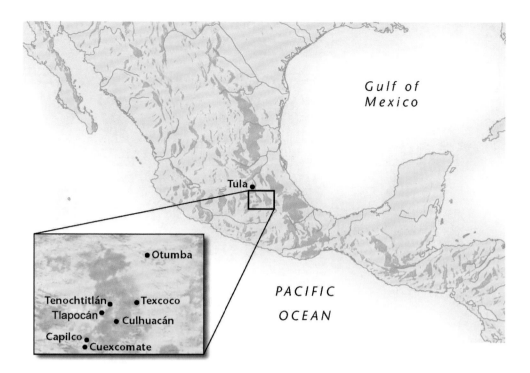

FIGURE 13.25 Map of the Aztec Empire

Gulf of Mexico

Tula

PACIFIC OCEAN

Otumba

Tenochtitlán
Tlapocán
Culhuacán
Texcoco
Capilco
Cuexcomate

▪ Aztec Economy

The rise of Tenochtitlán and the expansion of the Aztec Empire resulted in a dramatic increase in population in the Basin of Mexico. Archaeological surveys have shown that 40% of the sites in the Basin of Mexico date to the period of the expansion of the Aztec Empire (Nichols 2004). Population estimates for the Basin of Mexico during this period range between 800,000 and 9.25 million, a fourfold increase over preceding periods. The large populations of the Basin of Mexico relied on an intensification of agriculture and a system for exacting tribute from conquered territories.

Tenochtitlán relied heavily on the expansion of raised agricultural fields, known as **chinampas**, within the swamps of the lakes of the Basin of Mexico (Smith 2003). The chinampa plots are artificial islands built up between long, straight drainage canals. By periodically scraping the muck out of the canals to use as fertilizer, the productivity of the plots was maintained. Archaeological surveys on the outskirts of Mexico City have uncovered the gridlike system of Aztec chinampa drainage canals and fields. In addition to farming chinampa plots, the Aztecs constructed extensive terrace walls to farm hillsides and dug large irrigation canals to open valleys to farming.

Tributes from the conquered territories flowed into Tenochtitlán, supporting the growing population of the city and enriching the Aztec elite. An early colonial document known as the Codex Mendoza reproduces an Aztec list of tribute by province (see Figure 13.26; Smith 2003). Historical documents emphasize the significance of markets in the Aztec economy, as well as the role played by professional merchants known as pochteca (Hirth 1998; Nichols et al. 2002). All provinces provided textiles of cotton and maguey, as well as warrior costumes and shields. A variety of other goods, including tropical feathers, rubber balls, wooden beams, and incense, were also major tribute items. Notably, the only foods that were major

chinampas Raised agricultural beds built in swamps; critical for Aztec agriculture.

FIGURE 13.26 Aztec tribute list from the Codex Mendoza. How would you describe the objects shown in this illustration?

tribute items were salt, honey, chili, and cacao beans. The Aztecs lacked draft animals for transporting tribute, so all items had to be carried to Tenochtitlán by porters.

Archaeological excavations on sites outside the Basin of Mexico provide insight into the impact that the Aztec expansion had on what became the periphery of the empire. At the site of **Otumba** in the Teotihuacán Valley, an intensive survey, along with limited excavation, has provided evidence about the organization of craft production under the Aztecs (Charlton, Nichols, and Charlton 1991). On the basis of the artifacts recovered, craft workshops for production of obsidian blades, ceramic figurines, basalt grinding stone, and maguey fiber textile were identified at Otumba. One of the most spectacular discoveries provided evidence of specialized craft workshops for the production of ground stone artifacts from obsidian, including delicate earspools and lip plugs known as labrets. Because obsidian is volcanic glass, the production of ground objects requires considerable skill. It is not surprising that a large number of the ground obsidian objects that were found had been broken and discarded in the process of manufacture. There is also evidence at Otumba that cotton textiles and censers (a special type of pottery vessel used in religious practices) were

▲▲ **Otumba** A site in the Teotihuacán Valley where excavations have produced evidence about the nature of the Aztec organization of craft production.

made in households rather than in specialized workshops. The research at Otumba shows that the Aztec demand for tribute placed a high pressure on the peripheral territories to increase their production of specialized crafts.

Excavations at the rural sites of **Cuexcomate** and **Capilco** in Morelos, to the south of the Basin of Mexico, have uncovered evidence of how people living in rural provincial settlements experienced the Aztec expansion (Smith 2003). Capilco is the smaller of the two sites, with a total of 21 houses; Cuexcomate has over 150 houses, as well as temples and storehouses. Both these sites grew significantly during the period of Aztec expansion. Capilco expanded from an estimated population of 72 to 116 and Cuexcomate from an estimated population of 237 to 803. All of the houses excavated at these rural sites yielded artifacts used in preparing food: blades, grinding stones, and large quantities of pottery. Spindle whorls and spinning bowls used in making cotton textiles were also found in every house, along with ritual artifacts, including figurines and incense burners. Surprisingly, all of the houses contained a large number of items that were traded over a distance, such as elaborately painted pottery vessels. There was no difference in the amount of trade goods per house between Capilco and the larger town of Cuexcomate. It is interesting to note that, during the period of Aztec expansion, the amount of trade goods found in the houses at both sites actually decreased, while the number of artifacts used in making cloth found in each house increased.

The archaeological evidence from Otumba, Capilco, and Cuexcomate demonstrates the impact of the Aztec expansion on the people living beyond the Valley of Mexico. In many ways, the expansion acted as a stimulus, spurring the intensity of craft production at Otumba and leading to an increase in population at Capilco and Cuexcomate. However, the rise of power of Tenochtitlán fundamentally rerouted the exchange of trade goods within the areas under Aztec rule. The need to provide tribute required increased specialization; evidence of this was found not only at Otumba, but also in the peasant houses at Capilco and Cuexcomate, in the form of increased textile manufacture. At the same time that craft production increased, the access to trade goods of those living at sites like Capilco and Cuexcomate actually decreased. The expansion of the Aztec Empire saw increased centralization of both wealth and power in the core of the empire in the city of Tenochtitlán.

■ Ritual and Human Sacrifice

In 1978, workers were digging a trench for electrical cables near the cathedral in Mexico City when they hit a monumental stone sculpture. This fortuitous discovery led archaeologists to the core of the Aztec spiritual world: the Templo Mayor that once rose above the center of Tenochtitlán. The sculpture (shown in Figure 13.27) uncovered by the electric company workers is a spectacular rendition of the dismembered body of **Coyolxauhqui**, a goddess killed by the Aztec patron deity **Huitzilopochtli** in a central event in Aztec mythology (Matos Moctezuma 1992). In this myth, a woman named Coatlicue living on the mountain of Coatepec was impregnated by a ball of feathers. When Coatlicue's 400 children learned of her pregnancy, they were enraged. One of these children, Coyolxauhqui, urged her siblings to kill their mother. At the very moment the siblings approached the Coatepec mountain to carry out the murder, Huitzilopochtli was born, fully grown, and immediately dressed for war. With a magical snake, Huitzilopochtli wounded Coyolxauhqui and cut off her head. As her body fell down the mountain, it broke into pieces, as is depicted on the sculpture discovered in Mexico City. Huitzilopochtli then chased down and killed the 400 siblings.

▲▲ Cuexcomate The larger of two rural sites in Morelos, to the south of the Basin of Mexico, that have produced insight into rural life under the Aztecs.

▲▲ Capilco The smaller of two rural sites in Morelos, to the south of the Basin of Mexico, that have produced insight into rural life under the Aztecs.

Coyolxauhqui A goddess killed by the Aztec patron god Huitzilopochtli in a central event in Aztec mythology.

Huitzilopochtli The Aztec patron god.

FIGURE 13.27 Excavation of the Coyolxauhqui stone. Notice how the body has broken into pieces.

Excavations following the discovery of the Coyolxauhqui sculpture expanded rapidly until much of the sacred precinct was uncovered. The sculpture lay at the base of a double pyramid; on the top of these were the two temples of the gods Tlaloc and Huitzilopochtli. The pyramid represents the hill of Coatepec in the architectural retelling of the defeat of Coyolxauhqui and the victory of the Aztec patron Huitzilopochtli.

The excavation of the pyramid at Templo Mayor showed that, like other Meso-american pyramids, it had been built in stages, with each new pyramid encapsulating its predecessor. Within the body of the pyramid, more than 100 ceremonial caches (such as the one shown in Figure 13.28) of artifacts were found (Matos Mocte-zuma 1988). These caches often bring together artifacts from across the domains

FIGURE 13.28 Ceremonial cache found in the Templo Mayor excavations. Notice the flint knife inserted in the nasal cavity of the skull.

controlled by the Aztec Empire. The symbolic meaning of the caches is often difficult to understand; however, many appear to express the placement of the Templo Mayor at the center of the Aztec spiritual world. Two of the caches (Caches 7 and 61) are particularly intriguing in that they are nearly identical. Both were placed in small stone-walled chambers and consist of three levels. The lowest level features strombus shells oriented from north to south. Above this is a layer of crocodile remains, and above these remains are the figures of a seated god. On the right side of these seated gods, some coral was placed, and on the left, a clay vessel was found depicting the god Tlaloc. The meaning of this arrangement is enigmatic, but it might represent levels of creation, from the sea (the shells), to the land (the crocodiles), to the heavens (the seated god).

Other caches in the Templo Mayor provide evidence of the important role human sacrifice played in Aztec ritual. Worked human skulls, known as "skull masks," have been found in a number of the caches. The masks are made up of the front part of the skull. The eye sockets are filled with white shell discs, and round pieces at the center of the shell discs represent the irises. In some cases, carefully flaked flint knives have been found inserted horizontally between the teeth of the skull or vertically into its nasal cavity.

Human sacrifice played a critical role in Aztec ritual, and the sacrifice of war captives or slaves was an important part of the ritual cycle. Historical descriptions of the Templo Mayor mention racks with large numbers of human skulls. No such large concentration of skulls has ever been found at the site; however, the excavations did uncover a large platform decorated with sculptures depicting 240 skulls.

A detailed description of a variety of human sacrificial rituals is found in the Florentine Codex. For example, sacrifices staged at the Templo Mayor commonly involved four men stretching out the victim on the sacrificial stone. His breast was then cut open by the priest, and his heart was seized and dedicated to the sun. The victim's corpse was then sent toppling down the side of the pyramid. Finally, a priest removed the head and placed it on the skull rack (Smith 2003). For the Aztecs, the act of sacrifice transformed the victim into a deity. However, as the Aztec Empire expanded, ritual sacrifice also came to play a role in projecting the empire's power and terrifying its opponents. In one case, during the reign of Ahuizotl (1486–1502), a massive slaughter took place on the occasion of the rededication of the Templo Mayor. It appears that Ahuizotl was using ritual slaughter as a particularly brutal form of propaganda.

Archaeological research on sites outside the Basin of Mexico shows that the violent ritual found in the core of the empire did not have wide currency in the peripheral regions (Brumfiel 2001). Ceramic figurines are found on most Aztec-period sites, and it is likely that they were used in household rituals (Figure 13.29). During the period of Aztec dominance, the female figurines outnumber the male figurines three to one. Few of the male figurines represent warriors. The women shown in Aztec formal art are usually depicted in a subservient, kneeling position. However, when shown in figurines, the women are usually standing and are often holding two children. The low number of figurines depicting warriors suggests that the ritual practices of rural people differed significantly from those of the people of Tenochtitlán. The question then is, who was the audience for the rituals enacted at the Templo Mayor? It is likely that the goal of these rituals was at least as much to inspire a spirit of warfare in the men of fighting age within the city of Tenochtitlán as to terrify the Aztecs' subjects. Clearly, people's experience of these rituals would vary, depending on their place in society. The elite and the warriors were active participants in the rituals. For the city masses, the events taking place at the Templo Mayor must have been difficult to avoid. For people in the provinces, by contrast,

FIGURE 13.29 An Aztec household figurine

the rituals practiced at the temple would have been a terrifying rumor few would have experienced in person.

■ Summing Up the Evidence

Since empires are characterized by social heterogeneity, different members of society have vastly differing experiences and worldviews. For this reason, it is important to take great care before making blanket generalizations about an empire such as that of the Aztecs. Archaeological excavations on rural sites have shown that, although the impact of the Aztec Empire varied, it was significant. Surveys demonstrate that the advent of the Aztecs saw a significant rise in population in the Valley of Mexico. The Aztecs ruled through a Triple Alliance, but the city of Tenochtitlán was clearly the dominant party. Excavations in the Templo Mayor in the middle of modern Mexico City have brought archaeologists to the heart of the Aztec Empire. The evidence from these excavations vividly illustrates the ideology of warfare and human sacrifice, which were essential to the empire. But there was more to Aztec ideology than violence: The discoveries at the Templo Mayor also uncover the paths the Aztecs took to connect themselves to an illustrious past. The symbolism of the sculptures connects the Aztecs to the mythological time of Huitzilopochtli. On a semimythological plane, the Templo Mayor was built on the actual spot where the Mexica refugees from Aztlán decided to make their last stand. But at the same time that the descendants of the Mexica rooted themselves in a uniquely Aztec mythical past, they also found connections with their Mesoamerican predecessors. The inclusion of Olmec and Teotihuacán objects speaks to a reverence for antiquity that is strongly reminiscent of the interest of the Aztecs' European contemporaries in the antiquities of Greece and Rome.

SUMMARY

- In a hierarchical state, an exclusionary political strategy leads to a single individual holding a monopoly on power. In societies with a corporate political strategy, power is shared across different sectors.
- The Olmec sites of 1200 B.C. to 300 B.C. on the Gulf Coast of Mexico are the earliest evidence of political complexity in Mesoamerica.
- By 500 B.C., the site of Monte Albán in the Oaxaca Valley had grown into a large city with a population of 5,000.
- Beginning around 2,000 years ago, Teotihuacán, in the Valley of Mexico, had grown into a city with a population of more than 80,000 people.
- The major monuments of Teotihuacán, including the Pyramid of the Sun, Ciudadela and the Temple of the Feathered Serpent, and the Pyramid of the Moon, were built along the Avenue of the Dead.
- Excavations of the Temple of the Feathered Serpent and the Pyramid of the Moon uncovered elaborate burials of sacrificial victims.
- Beginning around A.D. 200, the residential areas of Teotihuacán were reconfigured into apartment complexes.

- In the fourth century, the facade of the Temple of the Feathered Serpent was destroyed before being covered over.
- The absence of individualized depictions of rulers in the art of Teotihuacán is one line of evidence suggesting that this might have been a society with a corporate political strategy.
- The Maya hieroglyphic writing system developed out of the connection between rulers and rituals.
- The core of the Maya city included royal residences, open plazas, pyramids, and ball courts.
- Maya cities were ruled by powerful dynasties. The power of the king derived from the prestige of the dynasty and the sacred aspect of kingship.
- Violence and warfare in Maya society were closely linked to rituals of bloodletting. There is clear evidence of warfare between Maya cities.
- Around A.D. 870, cities in the southern Maya lowlands collapsed.
- The Aztec capital of Tenochtitlán was built on an island in Lake Texcoco in the Valley of Mexico and had a very large population.

- Tenochtitlán fell to the Spanish in 1521. Texts such as the Florentine Codex provide extensive documentation of Aztec history, religion, and society.
- The Aztec traced their genealogy back to the Toltec Empire, which developed after the fall of Teotihuacán.
- The Aztec migrated to the Valley of Mexico from a region to the north known as Aztlán.
- The formation of a Triple Alliance among Tenochtitlán, Texcoco, and Tlapocán was a critical event in the formation of the Aztec Empire. Within this alliance, Tenochtitlán was the dominant force.

- The economy of Tenochtitlán relied on intensified agriculture, including the farming of raised fields known as chinampas.
- Excavations at the provincial sites of Otumba, Capilco, and Cuexcomate shed light on the effect of the Aztec expansion at the periphery of the empire.
- A chance discovery led archaeologists to the Templo Mayor, the massive pyramid temple that stood at the center of Tenochtitlán. The Templo Mayor was the site of rituals involving human sacrifice.

KEY TERMS

Aguateca, 368
Avenue of the Dead, 358
Aztec Empire, 373
Aztlán, 376
Bernardo de Sahagún, 375
Capilco, 379
chinampas, 377
Ciudadela, 358
Copán, 364
Coyolxauhqui, 379
Cuexcomate, 379
Florentine Codex, 375
Huitzilopochtli, 379
Maya hieroglyphs, 369
Monte Albán, 357
Olmec, 357

Otumba, 378
Popol Vuh, 371
Pyramid of the Moon, 360
Pyramid of the Sun, 358
San Bartolo, 371
Temple of the Feathered Serpent, 358
Templo Mayor, 375
Tenochtitlán, 373
Teotihuacán, 358
Texcoco, 376
Tikal, 365
Tlapocán, 376
Toltec Empire, 376
Triple Alliance, 376
Tula, 376

REVIEW QUESTIONS

1. How did the elite of Teotihuacán and the Maya cities use architecture to establish their position of power?
2. How did the Maya script develop and what was the role of writing in Maya society?
3. What insight does archaeology yield about the impact of Aztec expansion on people living at the periphery of the empire?

BRINGING THE FOUR PARTS TOGETHER

STATES AND EMPIRE IN THE ANDES

The Inca Empire developed out of a long history of social complexity in the Andes. After reading this chapter, you should understand:

- The major characteristics and the archaeological interpretation of the site of Chavín de Huántar.

- The emerging understanding of social complexity in the Moche and Nasca societies, including the roles of violence and feasting.

- The basic characteristics of the political and economic organization of the Inca Empire.

Machu Picchu, Peru. This spectacular site appears to meld into the mountain landscape.

14 TIMELINE

SITES

Chavín de Huántar

EVENTS

PERIODS

CHAVÍN HORIZON

1000 BC   **500** BC   0

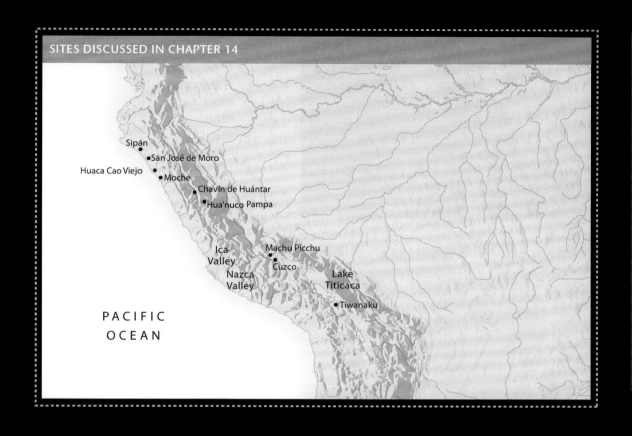

SITES DISCUSSED IN CHAPTER 14

Sipán
San José de Moro
Huaca Cao Viejo
Moche
Chavín de Huántar
Hua'nuco Pampa
Ica Valley
Nazca Valley
Machu Picchu
Cuzco
Lake Titicaca
Tiwanaku

PACIFIC OCEAN

Tiwanaku

Sipan

Machu Picchu

Cuzco

MURDER OF ATAWALLPA

MOCHE

NASCA

INCA EMPIRE

500 AD   1000 AD   1500 AD   2000 AD

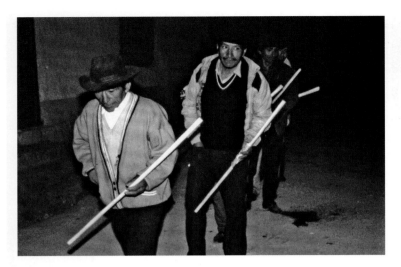

FIGURE 14.1 Outgoing staff-holders walk through the village of Tupicocha on New Year's Eve

Just before midnight on New Year's Eve, men from around the village of Tupicocha in the highlands of Peru slowly congregate in the center of town (see Figure 14.1). These are the *varayuq*, or staff-holders. By the end of the night, the 10 *varayuq* will have ended their one-year term in office and turned their responsibilities over to a new set of staff-holders. The staffs are sticks of wood that have been carefully incised by the current staff-holder or his assistant. At the end of each year, the staff, which serves much like a policeman's badge, is retired and replaced with a new one. Checking to make sure that the new staffs have been properly marked is a serious business, undertaken in near silence while a crowd watches the procedure. The exchange of staffs and the annual reassignment of public offices in Tupicocha are examples of the small-scale interactions that underlie the structures of today's societies and those of the past. The use of staffs as markers of office continues an Andean tradition that goes back at least 3,000 years. Depictions of the deities from some of the earliest complex societies in the Andes include a figure holding a staff.

The environment of the Andes varies considerably (see Figure 9.8 on p. 245). The Pacific coast is a dry desert with rich marine resources and narrow zones of arable land along river valleys. Moving east from the coast, one ascends the high peaks of the Andes and the intermountain valley. Continuing east, one descends into the tropical lowlands of the Amazon Basin. The Amazon Basin has become the focus of intense archaeological interest with the discovery of large numbers of earthworks in areas that are now rain forest. Current research is grappling with the question of the size of past populations in the Amazon and the ecological impact of these societies (Carson et al. 2014; Heckenberger and Góes Neves 2009). The hallmark of Andean prehistory is the knitting together of these different environmental and cultural landscapes, culminating in the **Tawantinsuyu**, "the four parts together," of the Inca Empire. In this chapter, we begin at the highland site of **Chavín de Huántar**, which provides evidence for interregional connections based on the spread of a religious cult rather than on the bureaucratic organization of a state. We then move on to consider the **Nasca** and **Moche** societies, which emerged along the river valleys of the southern and northern coast of Peru, respectively. The Nasca and Moche raise further questions regarding the relationship between ritual and social structure. Finally, we will consider the history and structure of the Inca Empire.

Tawantinsuyu The Inca name for their empire; the name means "the four parts together."

Chavín de Huántar A major ceremonial center in the Andean highlands constructed around 800 B.C.

Nasca A culture that developed along the southern Pacific coast of Peru and that flourished beginning 2,000 years ago.

Moche A culture that developed along the Pacific coast of Peru at the same time as the Nasca.

14.1 Chavín de Huántar

The origins of social complexity in the Andean region can be traced back to the Cotton Preceramic (see Chapter 9). Cotton Preceramic sites such as Caral, Aspero, and El Paraiso reached a size of over 50 hectares close to 6,000 years ago. But many archaeologists stress the significance of the site of Chavín de Huántar as a major turning point in the development of Andean social complexity. The initial construction of the temple at Chavín is dated to 900 B.C. The temple structure was expanded around 500 B.C. before being abandoned at some point between 390 B.C. and 200 B.C. Recent reanalysis of the temple structure has produced an earlier chronology for the site, according to which construction ceased around 500 B.C. (Kembel 2008). Further excavation and radiocarbon dating are needed to resolve these chronological questions.

FIGURE 14.2 Aerial view of Chavín de Huántar

■ The Setting and the Temple

Chavín de Huántar is located in a narrow valley in the highlands of Peru, at the confluence of the Huachesca and Mosna Rivers (see Figure 14.2). The site is at an elevation of 3,150 meters above sea level, and the mountains rise steeply from the valley floor. Although the soils of the valley support a range of agriculture and the slopes above the valley floor are used for grazing llamas and alpacas, the valley itself is too narrow to have ever supported a large population.

The rivers that flow past Chavín cannot be navigated, so visitors would have arrived on foot, descending from the mountains on paths along one of the rivers. Arriving at the valley floor, travelers were met by a wall of dressed stones rising 11 meters above ground level. A row of busts of humans and animals, many

FIGURE 14.3 One of the colossal stone heads that adorned the west wall of the temple at Chavín de Huántar

FIGURE 14.4 Plan of the Chavín Old Temple. Note that the entrance to the temple structure went through the Circular Plaza, which is enclosed within the two wings of the building.

Lanzón An engraved monolith at the core of the temple at Chavín de Huántar.

FIGURE 14.5 View of the Lanzón through the corridors of Chavín

of which have fangs and wear a contorted expression, projected out from this massive wall (see Figure 14.3). These heads appear to represent the transformation of a shaman into an animal form during a drug-induced trance. Working their way around this edifice, visitors reached an open area on the eastern side of the monumental complex (see Figure 14.4). At the center of this open area was a circular courtyard sunken into the ground. Those descending into the courtyard would find themselves enclosed within the wings of the temple structure. Staring straight ahead, their eyes would be drawn to the western staircase, which rose to an opening in the temple. On either side of the staircase were carved images of jaguars and mythical figures that appeared to be moving toward the temple. We do not know if visitors would have been allowed past this point or if the interior of the temple was reserved for priests. The temple interior consists of a warren of narrow passageways, known as galleries, embedded in earth and rubble fill. The galleries create a complex maze lit only by natural light filtering in through ventilation shafts. The overall impression is that the layout of the galleries was intentionally designed to create a sense of confusion. Walking directly from the staircase leading up from the circular courtyard, the visitor reaches the intersection of two galleries (see Figure 14.5). In the center of the intersection stands a 4-meter-high granite shaft known as the **Lanzón**, carved in the form of a fanged human deity (see Figure 14.6). The play of light on the sculpted surface of the irregularly shaped rock of the Lanzón would have had a powerful effect on visitors.

The actual function of the temple at Chavín remains unclear. One intriguing proposal is that Chavín was an oracular site where people would come for prophecies or cures at the hands of the priests. There was a chamber situated directly above the Lanzón that might have served for ceremonies drawing on the power of this object. Or perhaps libations would have been poured over the Lanzón from this chamber. Surprisingly, there is only limited evidence of feasting at Chavín. This is in clear contrast to other ritual centers we have considered, such as Pueblo Bonito and Cahokia. Excavations in one of the galleries did produce a large collection of pottery vessels that are likely associated with drinking maize beer. However, even the size of the circular courtyard is inconsistent with the use of the temple as a setting for massive public gatherings.

Rather than creating a setting for bringing together large numbers of people, the design of Chavín is structured to affect the perceptions of individuals. Chavín was not a theater where one sat back to watch; it was a construct where the visitor was immersed in sensory experience. Moving down into the circular courtyard would create a feeling of enclosure that would be accentuated by penetrating the temple's narrow galleries. The galleries' layout creates dislocation, while the sheer size of the Lanzón gives a sense of awe. Some archaeologists have proposed that it was also possible to create powerful sound effects by controlling the flow of water through drainage channels running through the temple. In one case, it was observed that pouring water down the drainage canal below the staircase leading to the temple creates a very loud noise, more like applause (or the roar of a jaguar) than running water. The iconography of the figures at the site also makes it clear that those entering the temple were often in a drug-induced trance state. A range of psychoactive plants were available in the area around Chavín, and these plants are clearly represented in the art at the site.

■ The Chavín Horizon

The occupation site of Chavín in itself is unremarkable. The site was neither an urban center nor the core of a state. The population of the valley during the initial stage of temple construction is estimated at 500, a number that would rise to a maximum of 1,000 at the time of the expansion of the temple, around 500 B.C. However, it is the widespread influence of Chavín that has made this site central to the study of the emergence of social complexity in the Andes. Chavín connections span the entire range of Andean environments, from the Amazon Basin to the east to the coastal regions to the west. However, Chavín was not an empire, and it was not strictly political power that led to the widespread network of connections radiating out from this site. The term *Chavín Horizon* recognizes the extent of linkages to Chavín, but it leaves open the question of what underlies these connections.

A number of the animals represented in Chavín art, including snakes, jaguars, crested eagles, and caymans, are native to the Amazon tropical lowlands and are not found in the highlands. The crops depicted in the Chavín sculptures, including manioc, bottle gourd, and hot peppers, are also native to the lowlands and cannot be grown in the highlands around Chavín. The people of Chavín drew heavily on the imagery of Amazonia in creating their religious center, but it does not appear that the settlement was constructed by migrants from the east. It is possible that the movement of individual charismatic or shamanistic leaders played a role in the transfer of religious beliefs from Amazonia to Chavín.

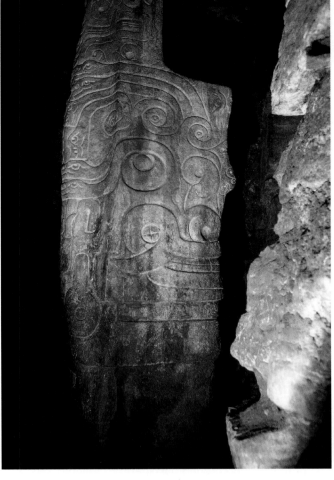

FIGURE 14.6 Detail view of the Lanzón

FIGURE 14.7 Textile from the coast of Peru in the Chavín style. A figure with clawed hands and feet that is related to the staff god is faintly visible at the center of the image.

Textile Fragment. Peru; Chavín. Precolumbian, 4th–3rd B.C. Cotton, refined iron earth pigments, H. 5¾ × W. 12¼ in. (14.6 × 31.1 cm). Bequest of Jane Costello Goldberg, from the Collection of Arnold I. Goldberg, 1986 (1987.394.704). The Metropolitan Museum of Art, New York, NY/© The Metropolitan Museum of Art/Art Resource, NY.

Chavín de Huántar: The Beginnings of Social Complexity in the Andes

DR. JOHN W. RICK, STANFORD UNIVERSITY

I fell in love with archaeology at the age of six, while accompanying my parents on a year-long plant-collecting trip to Peru. Staring into the face of a 1,500-year-old mummy we happened upon on the dry desert coast fired my imagination, and now, 50 years later, I am an archaeologist in the Department of Anthropological Sciences at Stanford University. I began my Peruvian work by excavating 14,000-foot-altitude cave sites for 15 years, but since 1995, I have been working at the World Heritage site of Chavín de Huántar, a complex of monumental structures—the ruins of some of the world's most fascinating temples.

Chavín de Huántar consists of roughly 3,000-year-old major temple platforms, decorated with strange rock sculptures, and contains many labyrinth-like underground passages. The site is nestled in a very narrow valley in the north-central Andes Mountains of Peru, close to some of the highest snowcapped peaks of South America. Chavín is intriguing

to me because it comes early in the process of the development of Andean political authority, which culminates 2,500 years later in the incredibly powerful Inca state. Not long before Chavín's time, most Andean people were living in independent, egalitarian groups, so how did the strong patterns of leadership develop, and how did people come to accept the idea of priest-leaders who could impose their will, demanding resources and undertaking massive temple projects? My project at Chavín attempts to connect the unusual features of the site with the rituals and other activities that early cult leaders used to convince converts that their emerging authority was not only legitimate, but also inevitable. Ceremonies involving the reflection of sunlight onto idol-like sculptures deep in the temples, the use of psychoactive drugs, and the extensive manipulation of loud, imposing sounds in closed architectural space argue that the temples created a new world for inductees in which the priests'

connection to strong natural powers would have been clear.

Nearly every year since 1995 our research team has converged on Chavín, now growing to more than 100 students, professional archaeologists, and specialists of many nationalities, along with numerous local workers and trained site conservators. The small town of Chavín at times seems overrun by our personnel, and we add a major economic input for the local economy. We take over one or more local hotels and lead a modest, but comfortable existence, sharing rooms, but enjoying frequent hot water and electricity most of the time. My team shares my feeling of awe as every day we work in the shadow of ancient monumental mounds, finding evidence of the complex engineering and the religious activity that made Chavín so successful in converting the very idea of what human social organization was. The strategies that the priests of Chavín implanted in their architecture are still effective, and we are constantly impressed by the remaining evidence of the grandeur that

Artifacts in the Chavín style are found across the highlands and along the coastal lowlands to the west. Some of the most vivid examples of Chavín iconography come from painted textiles found on coastal sites, where dry conditions allow for the preservation of these fragile materials (see Figure 14.7). Unfortunately, many of the textiles come from looted tombs, so little can be said about their context. One group of looted textiles comes from a tomb at the coastal site of Karwa. These textiles were decorated with scenes that follow the conventions of Chavín art. However, there are significant differences between the deities depicted on the Karwa textiles and those that appear on the sculptures at Chavín. Notably, the staff god at Karwa is depicted as a female, whereas the same figure at Chavín is of indeterminate gender. The textiles found at Karwa suggest that aspects of the Chavín cult were practiced on the coast at a distance of over 500 kilometers from Chavín. However, it is less clear how and why this belief system spread so widely. It is important to emphasize the skill involved in the painting of intricate Chavín-inspired designs on the Karwa textiles. When considering the spread of the Chavín cult, one must keep in mind fueled ancient conversion. But another feeling we have is gratefulness for the privilege of working in such an important site, an opportunity generously given to us by modern Peruvian cultural authorities. We experience, as well, the life of a traditional little Andean town and are usually in Chavín for their patron saint fiesta—a weeklong blowout of music and celebration, dancing, and sporting events. Some years we are even asked to put on a show in the town's plaza, ranging from break-dancing to folk singing and even bagpipe-playing on one of the fiesta evenings.

But the most overwhelming experiences are the discoveries and realizations we have in our excavations and later analyses, as we find major clues to the very different world of ritual and belief that Chavín represents. A special moment came in 2001, when we excavated in one of the underground passages of Chavín, hoping against hope that the contents of this gallery might still be intact. In late July, we revealed the first of 20 perfectly intact conch shell trumpets resting on the gallery floor, instruments still capable of emitting the same deafening, but haunting bellow that ancient ears heard eons ago. These massive shells had been brought at least 1,000 kilometers from the ocean waters of Ecuador, far to the north.

Unbeknownst to us, on the same days we were recovering these beautifully engraved trumpets, Dr. Alejandro Toledo, president-elect of Peru, was being inaugurated in Machu Picchu to the sound of identical conch shells. When we heard of this coincidence, we were amazed at the continuity of the role these instruments played and still play in establishing and reinforcing authorities of South America. ▲

FIGURE 14.8
Moche vessel showing a man blowing a conch shell, reflecting a cultural practice that connects back to the conch shell cache discovered at Chavín

that the religious system encompassed more than just a collection of mythological beliefs; the system also employed highly developed skills in making artifacts and, one presumes, in enacting rituals.

■ Summing Up the Evidence

The temple at Chavín was designed to create a powerful sensory impression on individuals or small groups visiting the site. The sacred core of the temple was the Lanzón, which stood in a strategically located gallery. Rituals at the temple involved the use of psychoactive drugs that would have further heightened the experience of this built environment. The cult of Chavín drew on mythology from the tropical lowlands to the east, and its influence extended across the highlands and down to sites along the coast. Chavín was not a city, and there is no evidence for a Chavín state. The influence of Chavín appears to have flowed from the ritual prestige or oracular powers of the temple and the associated cult. Chavín forces us to look beyond aspects of social hierarchy and technology and seriously examine the significance of religious systems in creating the conditions for the emergence of social complexity.

14.2 Nasca and Moche

The Nasca societies of the southern coast of Peru and the Moche societies of the northern coast have challenged archaeologists and intrigued the general public. The Nasca and the Moche both developed around 2,000 years ago and persisted for close to 1,000 years. While some archaeologists see indications of Nasca and Moche urbanism and state bureaucracy, others are more cautious. Helaine Silverman has emphasized the importance of kinship in Andean social organization, particularly the significance of **ayllus**, or kin-based farming communities (Silverman and Proulx 2002). Lineages within the ayllus are ranked, providing for a degree of social complexity within a kinship system. Thus, there is reason to be cautious about ascribing all evidence of social complexity (such as large monumental architecture) to a state society in which kinship has been eclipsed by bureaucracy.

■ Nasca

The Nasca culture developed in the narrow Nasca and Ica Valleys of the southern coast of Peru. This culture is best known for **Nasca Lines**, the large patterns they created on the desert floor. These "drawings" include depictions of humans and animals, as well as a large number of straight lines that stretch for miles along the desert (Aveni 2000). In most cases, the figures created by the lines are visible only in aerial photographs. To create the lines, the Nasca cleared black desert rocks and stacked them along the edge of a trail, leaving the lighter colored desert surface exposed (see Figures 14.9 and 14.10). The purpose of this undertaking is a mystery that has intrigued archaeologists as well as UFO enthusiasts. Survey and aerial photography have shown that the lines are not randomly distributed across the desert floor; instead, they radiate out from a series of central points. Although some archaeologists argue

FIGURE 14.9 Aerial photograph of Nasca Lines depicting a hummingbird

FIGURE 14.10 View along one of the paths creating the hummingbird

FIGURE 14.11 An elaborately decorated Nasca polychrome vessel from the village site of Marcaya

that the lines served as astronomical observatories, it seems more likely that they were paths walked along in ritual processions, perhaps related to rain ceremonies. Although the ancient Nasca were unable to view their creations, they were able to experience the figures and lines sketched onto the desert floor with their bodies as they walked.

The site of **Cahuachi**, a ceremonial center that stretches along an area 2 kilometers long, is the largest known Nasca site. Cahuachi consists of 40 mounds interspersed with large enclosures. Excavations have uncovered mostly ceremonial objects, including caches of panpipes, engraved gourds, elaborately decorated textiles, and llama burials. There is little evidence to date of extensive habitation. Kevin Vaughn has proposed that Cahuachi was a pilgrimage site that, along with secondary ceremonial sites, served to integrate villages dispersed across the foothills of the Andes (Vaughn and Linares Grados 2006). To support this argument, Vaughn points to the prevalence of elaborately decorated polychrome pottery vessels in Nasca villages (see Figure 14.11). In excavations at the village site of Marcaya, Vaughn found polychrome pottery in all houses, although some vessel shapes were found only in elite houses. Neutron activation analysis (see the Tracking Trade Routes Toolbox in Chapter 11, pp. 310–311) of polychrome vessels from Marcaya and other Nasca village sites has identified the source for the clay used in making these vessels as a place near Cahuachi (Vaughn et al. 2006). This evidence indicates that polychrome pottery was produced at Cahuachi and then widely distributed to villages in the surrounding area, perhaps by pilgrims returning from ceremonial feasts.

Research in the Chincha Valley has identified lines on the desert floor oriented toward platform mounds dating to the period that precedes the Nasca, known as the Late Paracas Period (Stanish et al. 2014). These are all straight lines oriented toward the setting of the June solstice sun.

■ Moche

The Moche societies of the northern coast of Peru built impressive mounds, including a massive structure known as the **Huaca del Sol**, made of more than 140 million mud bricks, located at the site of Moche. Unfortunately, the looting of Moche sites has also been large in scale. In the most extreme case, during the colonial period, the Spanish diverted the Moche River to remove the mud bricks and get to the gold buried inside the Huaca del Sol. The first completely intact burials were discovered in the 1980s at the site of **Sipán** in the Lambyeque Valley (see Figure 14.12). Similar discoveries were subsequently made at the site of **San José de Moro** in the Jequetepeque Valley. The wealth of burial goods found with the elite of Sipán and San José de Moro is simply amazing. Most of the objects, including worked gold, adorn the body of the main burial. Many of the specific items found in the Sipán burials can be identified in the paintings of warriors found on pottery vessels (see Figure 14.13). Before the discoveries at Sipán, these paintings were often interpreted as depictions of deities. Now they are recognized as representations of warrior elites. It is now clear that military power was essential to the social hierarchy of the Moche and that a major goal of military conflict was the provision of victims for ritual sacrifice. The paintings on the pottery vessels show manacled prisoners being led up to

FIGURE 14.12 Gold anthropomorphic crab from Sipán. Note that the figure wears the helmet and skull necklace of a warrior. Why do you think that the choice was made to represent a warrior as a crab?

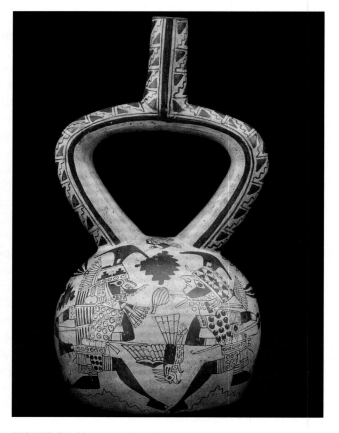

FIGURE 14.13 Moche fine-line pottery vessel showing warriors

a figure seated on a platform and then being killed and dismembered. The discovery of a series of murals at the site of **Huaca Cao Viejo** in the Chicama Valley showing a line of prisoners and sacrificial scenes provides further support for viewing conflict and sacrifice as a key activity of the Moche elite (see Figure 14.14). Near the **Huaca de la Luna** at the site of Moche, the actual remains of sacrificial victims in various states of dismemberment were uncovered, providing visceral evidence that these rituals actually did take place.

There remains little question that violence and human sacrifice were an integral aspect of Moche ritual and society. But the scope of military action and the social context of violence remain unclear. The wealth of the Moche burials and the scale of monumental construction might point to a state society. A number of Moche sites have produced evidence of large, dense occupation, with populations estimated at a minimum of 5,000 people, leading some archaeologists to consider these sites to be the urban centers of states (Chapdelaine, Pimentel, and Bernier 2000). Recent research at the Gallinazo group site in the Viru Valley has identified evidence of a large urban occupation, with preliminary population estimates between 14,000 and 21,000 people (Millaire 2010). However, it is also possible that Moche society was essentially kinship based, with an ayllu system that allowed for hierarchy to emerge within kin groups, generating the wealth of displays found in elite burials without the bureaucracy characteristic of state societies. One essential question is whether Moche violence was political or ritual. Were these wars of conquest leading to political domination or ritual combat limited to capturing victims for sacrifice? Jeffrey Quilter has argued that politics and ritual may not be mutually exclusive domains. He recognizes the effect of the emergence of a violent ritual cult and questions "the emotional power of participating in or watching fellow human beings transformed into chunks of rotting flesh, flayed skins, and dismembered carcasses" (Quilter 2002, 172). Quilter implies that the violence inherent in Moche ritual would inevitably have had an effect on Moche politics.

Ultimately, resolving the question of whether the Moche were state societies requires moving beyond the centers to look at the settlements where people lived. Surveys and excavations have indicated a range of site sizes within each of the valleys, consistent with the hierarchical settlement system characteristic of a state

Huaca Cao Viejo A Moche site where a mural showing a line of prisoners was found.

Huaca de la Luna A massive mud-brick mound at the site of Moche where actual remains of sacrificial victims were uncovered and found in various states of dismemberment.

FIGURE 14.14 Cleaning one of the murals from Huaca Cao Viejo that shows scenes of battle

TOOLBOX

Metallurgy

In rare instances, metals are found in such a pure state that they can be hammered into tools or ornaments without any processing. Artifacts made of pure, or native, copper are found on prehistoric sites in eastern North America. But most metals must first be smelted by heating ores to a high temperature. Once smelted, metals can be shaped by hammering or casting.

Copper can be smelted at relatively low temperatures, but early metalworkers rapidly realized that the material could be strengthened by mixing it with other metals to create alloys. Bronze is a copper alloy produced by mixing copper and tin or arsenic. Both copper and tin are found in limited deposits, so bronze metal production often involved extensive trade. The Ulu Burun shipwreck found off the coast of Turkey provides vivid evidence of this trade. Both tin and bronze were recovered from the hull of the ship as stacks of "oxhide"-shaped ingots (Bass 1986).

Although iron offers the advantage of being more widely available than copper or tin, the metal also needs to be heated to very high temperatures in order to be smelted. Iron metallurgy did not develop indigenously in the Americas. In Africa, archaeologists have uncovered a fascinating record of the indigenous development of iron smelting (Schmidt 1997).

Copper, bronze, and iron provided new and effective raw materials for the manufacture of both tools and weapons. However, archaeological metallurgists also stress the symbolic aspects of metal production. Dorothy Hosler (1995) has studied metal production in western Mexico under the Tarascan Empire. She found that western Mexican artisans placed an emphasis on producing objects worn by elites and used in rituals rather than utilitarian tools. These artisans were most interested in two physical properties of the copper alloys they worked: sound and color. One of the most important types of artifacts produced was bells that were shaped by means of an elaborate technique known as the lost-wax method. High-status or ritual objects were made using copper alloys that had high levels of arsenic or tin. Laboratory experiments have shown that the amount of tin or arsenic found in artifacts is far higher than needed to enhance the mechanical properties of the resulting alloy. Moreover, utilitarian items did not have these high levels of arsenic or tin. Although the high levels of these metals do not alter the mechanical quality of the alloys, they do

FIGURE 14.15 Experimental copper smelting. The tubes are tuyeres used to blow air into the fire to increase the temperature.

society. However, more research is needed to understand the function of these various types of sites.

■ Summing Up the Evidence

Nasca Lines and Moche human sacrifice are both evidence of societies with highly developed religious systems. The challenge for archaeologists is to understand the relationship between ritual practice and political structure in these societies. Currently, alter the color, creating increasingly golden or silvery hues.

Historical texts about the Tarascans indicate that they saw sound and color as connected. For example, they believed metallic sounds can create metallic color. As Hosler (1995) reconstructs the process, "Smelting, that is, winning metal from its ore through heat, gives birth to sound (and song), and it also gives birth to the golden metallic colors" (113). Looking at Tarascan metallurgy demonstrates that it is important not to reduce the study of technology to simply an examination of the utilitarian functions of tools: Often, even the most elaborate technologies are shot through with symbolic elements.

Metallurgical analysis of Moche artifacts has demonstrated that a number of techniques were used to enhance the surface qualities of objects to give them a metallic or golden sheen. The Moche occasionally used casting to form their metal artifacts, but their main technique was hammering out thin sheets of metal and using a range of methods, including soldering and welding, to join the sheets together to form complex objects. The key trick employed by Moche artisans to produce a surface that was rich in gold or silver was to use alloys in which these metals were mixed with copper. The Moche mastered two sophisticated methods to enrich the surface of their artifacts. The first method was

to actually coat an artifact with a thin layer of gold, using a method known today as electrochemical replacement plating (Lechtman, Erliz, and Barry 1982). In an experimental study, Heather Lechtman was able to demonstrate that the Moche dissolved gold in a solution of corrosive materials such as salt and potassium nitrate. Copper sheets could then be dipped in the boiling solution for five minutes, resulting in an even, thin coating of gold. Further heating was required to bond the gold layer to the underlying matrix. Analysis of an ornamental plate

from the Sipán tombs has shown clear evidence for the use of this method (Hörz and Kallfass 2000). The second method used to enrich an artifact was to deplete the amount of copper at the surface of the object. This was achieved by repeatedly heating and cooling a metal sheet. In the process, copper oxides formed at the surface. These copper oxides could then be removed by soaking the sheet in a solution of acid plant juice or stale urine (ammonia), resulting in a surface that was depleted in copper relative to the underlying matrix. ●

FIGURE 14.16 Cleaned and reconstructed banner from Sipán

there is debate whether the Nasca and the Moche should be considered state societies. A social structure based on ayllus, or hierarchically organized kinship groups, provides an alternative basis for the kinds of elaborate practices found among these peoples.

14.3 The Inca Empire

The **Inca Empire**—known as Tawantinsuyu, "the four parts together"—thrived for over a century, tying together a vast realm under the royal Inca in the capital

Inca Empire An empire that thrived for over a century and at its peak ruled over 12 million people from northern Chile to Ecuador.

Ancient Agriculture and Modern Development

In the Bolivian highlands, archaeologists working at the ancient city of Tiwanaku are faced with a puzzle. One thousand years ago, Tiwanaku had a large population. A massive pyramid and sunken courtyard at the center of the city provide a vivid indication of Tiwanaku's power. Today, the area surrounding this ancient city is relatively underpopulated and faces many economic challenges. A team of archaeologists and agricultural scientists led by Alan Kolata has been working to understand the agricultural system that sustained the urban center of Tiwanaku. Through a combination of survey and test excavation, the team has learned that an extensive area around Tiwanaku was farmed using a system of raised fields. Ditches were excavated and the dirt piled onto the patches of ground between the ditches. Water was diverted from rivers into the complex network of artificial ditches. The result was an effective combination of irrigation and drainage. The raised fields would also provide some insulation from cold, and the stagnant water in the ditches would fill with plants that could be heaped up onto the fields as fertilizer.

Kolata and his colleagues began to wonder whether the poverty of the villagers who live in the area today is in part due to the abandonment of raised-field agriculture. To explore this possibility, the team worked with a number of villages, developing plots of raised fields to grow potatoes and other crops. The results were promising, although several archaeologists have raised critiques of Kolata's ideas about Tiwanaku agriculture (Kolata 1996). The raised fields were productive and in many cases yielded more produce with less commercial fertilizer than the methods the villagers had been using. But the yield was dependent on the motivation of the particular group of farmers. Moreover, there is nothing in the study that suggests that raised fields are an instant cure for the economic problems of the region. However, Kolata's study has brought historical depth and ecological insight to the agricultural issues facing contemporary Bolivia. The research of Kolata's team has shown that archaeologists can provide insight into the historical component of ecological issues facing rural populations. ●

FIGURE 14.17 Rehabilitated raised fields near Lakaya

city, Cuzco (D'Altroy 2002). At the peak of the empire, the Inca ruled more than 12 million people in a region that stretched across 3,000 kilometers from Ecuador to northern Chile. Not only was the Inca Empire massive, but also it covered a highly heterogeneous region, ranging from the river valleys of the Pacific coast to the high-altitude valleys of the Andean altiplano.

In 1533, the immense and powerful kingdom of Tawantinsuyu fell to a group of 168 Spanish soldiers under the command of Francisco Pizarro. Facing an army of 80,000 Inca soldiers, Pizarro was nevertheless able to capture the Inca ruler Atawallpa and hold him for a ransom that today would amount to $50 million in jewels and melted gold. Even though the Inca paid the ransom, Pizarro executed Atawallpa on July 26, 1533. The ruler's murder set off the rapid disintegration of the Inca Empire.

The early history of the Inca is shrouded in myth. The Inca believed that the god Wiraqocha created their ancestors, who then journeyed until they reached Cuzco, where they founded their capital. The initial expansion of the Inca realm appears to have taken place during the reign of the eighth ruler, Wiraqoch Inka. The history of the remaining rulers in the Inca dynasty is a succession of wars of conquest punctuated by conflicts over succession to the throne. The most violent war of succession took place immediately before the arrival of Pizarro. Waskhar and his half-brother, Atawallpa, engaged in a long battle across much of the empire before Waskhar was captured and his family slaughtered.

■ Inca Society

One of the most intriguing aspects of Inca society was the power exerted by deceased rulers. After death, the emperor was mummified as part of an elaborate collective ritual. The mummified ruler continued to play an active role in the ceremonial and political life of Cuzco. Food was burnt in front of mummies, and through mediums, the rulers were able to communicate their wishes. The role of the deceased emperor was not limited to ceremonial functions. The property amassed by the emperor during his life passed to his kin-group descendants, known as **panaqa**. But the new ruler did not belong to the panaqa of the deceased king. He therefore had to go out and build his own fortune. This dynamic played an important role in the expansion of the Inca Empire, since each ruler was forced to carve out his own wealth.

The panaqa controlled considerable resources, including the royal estates of the former rulers. These estates, which included agricultural fields, pastures, forests, and mines, provided physical support for the emperor and his descendants (Niles 2004). In some cases, the estates served important ritual functions. The most famous of the royal estates is **Machu Picchu**. Located on a high mountain peak at the western end of the **Urubamba Valley**, Machu Picchu was built by Pachacuti Inca Yupanqui between 1450 and 1470 (Burger and Salazar 2004). Machu Picchu is a small walled settlement that includes royal and aristocratic complexes built in the classic Inca masonry style in which stone blocks are carefully fit together. There are also subsidiary buildings that appear to have housed the people who served the members of Pachacuti's panaqa. There are a large number of shrines, some of which are built around striking natural rock outcroppings.

Analysis of burials recovered at Machu Picchu indicates that the people who served Pachacuti's panaqa were drawn from across the empire (Burger and Salazar 2004). One of the most unusual lines of evidence comes from deformed skulls that were found at the site. In the highlands, the normal practice was to bind an infant's head with cloth strips, while on the coast it was more common to flatten the skull by tying the child's head to a cradleboard. Skeletons from Machu Picchu show both types of cranial deformation, indicating that the people buried at the site came from the coast and the highlands. The range of pottery vessels found with the burials at Machu Picchu offers further evidence of the ethnic diversity of the people buried there.

Feasting and the exchanging of gifts played a central role in Inca society. At state centers, the elite spent much time hosting feasts of corn beer, coca leaves, meat, and music for their subjects (Burger and Salazar 2004). Large feasting halls often adjoined open plazas. The large feasting hall at Machu Picchu is located outside the walls and was probably used to fête local farmers. At the large Inca center of **Hua'nuco Pampa**, over 600 kilometers north of Cuzco, two enormous halls

panaqa The collective descendants of the Inca emperor.

▲▲ **Machu Picchu** An Inca royal estate on a high mountain peak at the western end of the Urubamba Valley.

▲▲ **Urubamba Valley** The location of Machu Picchu, the most famous of the Inca royal estates.

▲▲ **Hua'nuco Pampa** An Inca center 600 kilometers north of Cuzco.

FIGURE 14.18 Inca storage vessel

khipu A system of knotted strings used by the Inca to record information.

and a series of subsidiary buildings were constructed alongside the main plaza (Morris and Thompson 1985). The substantial quantities of pottery recovered from the buildings around the plaza consist mainly of large jars, like the vessel shown in Figure 14.18, and plates, evidence that the plaza and the adjoining buildings were the site of large-scale feasting. Providing large-scale feasts is one of the most distinctive aspects of the Inca political economy. This apparent demonstration of generosity challenges us to carefully consider the sources of legitimacy for the Inca Empire.

■ Building Empire

The Inca engaged in constant military campaigns to maintain and expand their empire. Integrating and controlling heterogeneous conquered territories required effective mechanisms of administration. The Inca developed an impressive and extensive system of roads. These were critical for the movement of goods, people, and information. The Inca did not have a formal writing system; however, they did employ an elaborate method for recording information using knotted ropes known as **khipu**. In bringing together the four corners of Tawantinsuyu, the Inca showed a great deal of flexibility. In some areas, they ruled through local elites with a minimum of interference; in others, they installed distinctive administrative centers to allow for direct rule.

WARFARE. The Inca were able to field very large military forces consisting of tens of thousands of troops (D'Altroy 2002). These armies were drawn from the diverse ethnic groups belonging to Tawantinsuyu. The emperor often rode with the army, carried aloft on a litter. Weapons included arrows, sling stones, and javelins. The tactics of warfare were essentially massed frontal assaults followed by hand-to-hand combat

FIGURE 14.19 Ruins of Saqsawaman

using maces, clubs, and spears. Feigned retreats and similar tricks were often used to draw out an enemy, who could then be routed in a surprise counterattack. Forts and garrisons were built in strategic locations. In Cuzco, the massive structure known as Saqsawaman (see Figure 14.19) appears to have served both as a temple to the sun and as a fortress. An early Spanish traveler described Saqsawaman as being built of "such big stones . . . as big as pieces of mountains or crags" (Hyslop 1990, 53). The outer walls of the fortress were constructed on three terraces in a zigzag pattern designed to deter a frontal assault.

ROADS. Tawantinsuyu stretched over a vast and varied landscape. Control of the Inca Empire demanded the rapid movement of information, military force, and tribute. The Inca built a network linking together approximately 40,000 kilometers of roads (Hyslop 1984). Many of these were preexisting roads that the Inca brought into their system. The scale of the roadways and their method of construction varied with the local topography and the importance of the road. The width of the roads varied from 1 to 4 meters, and the construction ranged from a simple line of stones leading through the desert to elaborate stone-built roads with drains to control the flow of water. Bridges were erected in many places to allow the roads to cross bodies of water. In some cases, the bridges were simple floating barges built of reeds; however, where the road needed to cross deep chasms, impressive suspension bridges were built out of reed cables woven together. The bridge built over the Apurimac River spanned 45 meters (see Figure 14.20). The floor of the bridge was 1.5 meters wide and could support a line of people and animals. The Spanish would even ride their horses over the bridge at a gallop. In some cases where a suspension bridge was not built, a cable was connected to the two sides of a chasm, and a large basket was suspended from the cable. People or animals were then pulled from one bank to another by people hauling ropes attached to the basket.

One of the primary functions of the road system was as a conduit for rapid communication across Tawantinsuyu. Relay messengers were stationed every 6 to 9 kilometers. It is estimated that, as a group, these messengers could cover 240 kilometers a day. Approximately 1,000 roadside lodging and storage areas, known

FIGURE 14.20 Grass rope bridge spanning the Apurimac River, Peru

as *tampu*, were also built along the roads. These installations served as Inca administrative centers.

KHIPU. It would have taken many transfers of information to get a message from the northern end of Tawantinsuyu to the capital in Cuzco. Because the messengers were drawn from the diverse cultures of the Inca Empire, they might well have not spoken the same language. Furthermore, since the Inca lacked written documents, one would think that their road system would be more likely to resemble a game of broken telephone than an effective means for administering an empire. There are many situations in which a system for recording information would have been crucial for the Inca. However, they did not develop a classic writing system. In place of signs impressed in clay or written on paper, they used a system of knotted strings known as khipu.

A khipu consists of a series of colored pendant strings tied onto a main cord. Groups of knots are tied along the pendant strings. Sometimes top cords were also tied to the main cords and subsidiary cords were attached to the pendant strings (see Figure 14.21). There are three basic types of khipu knots: a long knot with four turns, a single knot, and a figure eight knot (see Figure 14.22).

Khipus are a highly complex system in which the number and placement of cords and knots can be manipulated into an endless set of configurations. When one considers that the color of the cords and even the way they were spun could also be controlled, the potential of khipus to code information seems almost limitless. Unfortunately, historical sources provide no glossary for translating or reading khipus. The system could code information, but the nature of the code remains the subject of debate. At one extreme is the theory that khipus were personal memory devices used to help jog the memory of individuals, known as *khipu kamayuq*, charged with keeping communal memory (see Figure 14.23). One khipu kamayuq could not read another's khipu. A second theory holds that khipus were a form of writing or at least a coding system for language (Urton 2003). According to this position, khipus were records—administrative texts and even histories—that could be read by Inca administrators. A third theory argues that khipus were indeed recording devices, but that they were used mostly for accounting and economic purposes (Ascher and Ascher 1981). There is support for this position, as khipus are well designed to record numerical values by means of knots neatly arranged to represent numbers in decimal position. It is curious that the Inca responded to the need to manage information through the development of a code of knots rather than a script. One intriguing possibility is that the use of strings and knots to record information reflects the centrality of textiles in Andean society.

FIGURE 14.21 Inca khipu with knotted strings hanging from a main cord

■ Summing Up the Evidence

The Inca tied together an impressively large and heterogeneous geographic region through the use of military power, an extensive road system, and an administrative apparatus that made use of khipus to keep records. It is important to

FIGURE 14.22 Diagram showing how khipu knots can be used to record numbers

Single knot:
All numbers greater than 9. Multiplied by a power of 10 based on position on the pendant string.

Long knot:
Numbers 2-9. Number of turns indicates the number.

Figure eight knot:
Number 1.

FIGURE 14.23 Khipu kamayuq with a khipu. Illustration from a sixteenth-century Spanish manuscript.

emphasize that the Inca realms were not only geographically varied, but also culturally and linguistically diverse. The expansionist dynamic of the Inca was driven in large part by a system of inheritance that passed the emperor's wealth on to his descendants, known as his panaqa, rather than to his successor. As a result, each new ruler had to accumulate his own wealth, often accomplished through military conquest. The Inca system of inheritance also resulted in frequent internal battles. The final battle of succession between Atawallpa and his half-brother, Waskhar, fatally weakened the Inca Empire on the eve of the arrival of Pizarro.

The fall of the Inca Empire is part of a global transformation that is still under way. The spread of Europeans, along with their culture and institutions, that began in the fifteenth century has had a dramatic impact on societies around the world, creating what anthropologists often refer to as a world system. The European expansion is richly documented in a wide range of written sources. Yet even here, archaeology can play a critical role through the branch of the discipline known as historical archaeology (Deetz 1996; Orser 2004). The written record was composed largely by Europeans, leaving many indigenous societies to be mistakenly perceived as "people without history" (Wolf 1982). Archaeologists can contribute to giving a voice to these people and recovering a history that is otherwise lost. Examples of such research efforts include the archaeology of indigenous people who lived during the process of European contact, as well as the archaeology of slave communities. Historical archaeologists also work in urban industrial centers, examining the changing technologies and social relations that powered European expansion. Here again, archaeologists can contribute to our understanding of aspects of society that are poorly represented in historical documents.

TOOLBOX

Tracking Ancient Diseases

Because many diseases leave no evidence on the skeleton, detecting the traces of illness in ancient populations is often extremely challenging. Even in cases where diseases do leave a clear trace on the skeleton, the interpretation of these pathologies can be ambiguous. Tuberculosis in the prehistoric Americas is a good example. In severe cases, the disease can lead to spinal deformities that can be identified on archaeological skeletons. But these same spinal deformities can be caused by infections other than tuberculosis. As a result, many researchers have been reluctant to accept skeletal evidence of tuberculosis in the Americas before European contact. It has long been thought that tuberculosis was a European disease brought to the Americas by European settlers.

Another way to trace diseases in archaeological remains is to extract tissue and identify infectious agents directly. Unfortunately, this is rarely possible. However, in a pioneering study, DNA was extracted from mummified human remains that showed lesions consistent with a diagnosis of tuberculosis (Salo et al. 1994). This study has demonstrated that tuberculosis was present in the Americas before European contact.

The Chiribaya were an agricultural group that lived on the southern Peruvian coast between A.D. 1000 and A.D. 1300. The aforementioned DNA analysis was carried out on the spontaneously mummified body of a Chiribaya woman dated to A.D. 1040. DNA was extracted from a lesion on the right lung and was then amplified with the use of polymerase chain reaction. The results showed a clear match between the DNA recovered from the mummy's lung and the DNA of modern tuberculosis.

The genetic analysis of the lineage of Tutankhamun discussed in the Archaeology and Genetics Toolbox in Chapter 11, p. 318, also succeeded in isolating the DNA of malaria from four mummies, including Tutankhamun's (Hawass et al. 2010). This evidence is leading to a reappraisal of the history of malaria in human populations. ●

FIGURE 14.24 Scanning electron microscope image of *Mycobacterium tuberculosis*, the bacteria that causes most cases of tuberculosis. Archaeologists are able to identify tuberculosis based on skeletal deformities or by extracting samples of ancient DNA.

SUMMARY

- Construction of the temple complex at Chavín de Huántar began around 900 B.C. The temple structure consists of a series of narrow passageways known as galleries.
- The Lanzón is a carved stone that stands in a strategic location in one of the central galleries at Chavín de Huántar.
- The temple complex at Chavín de Huántar was designed to create a complex sensory experience for a limited number of people.
- The Chavín Horizon spans extensive areas of the Andean highlands and coast. This phenomenon appears to reflect the spread of religious practices rather than the expansion of a political power.
- Hierarchically organized kinship groups, known as ayllus, play an important role in the social complexity of Andean societies.
- Beginning 2,000 years ago, the Nasca societies of the southern coast of Peru created the Nasca Lines, enormous patterns on the desert floor.
- The Moche societies on the northern coast of Peru were contemporary with the Nasca. The Moche built very large burial mounds, including the Huaca del Sol.
- The discovery of intact Moche burials at Sipán and San José de Moro uncovered a wealth of burial goods.
- There is considerable evidence indicating the centrality of violence and warfare to Moche society, including paintings on ceramics showing captives and sacrificial victims, murals showing captives at the site of Huaca Cao Viejo, and the remains of dismembered sacrificial victims at the Huaca de la Luna.
- The Inca Empire Tawantinsuyu covered an area that stretched over 3,000 kilometers and had a population of 12 million.
- In 1533, the Inca Empire fell to a small group of Spanish soldiers under the command of Pizarro.
- The property of the Inca emperor was passed on to his descendants, collectively known as his panaqa. The site of Machu Picchu was an estate belonging to the panaqa of Pachacuti.
- Feasting and the exchanging of gifts played an important role in Inca society. At the Inca center of Hua'nuco Pampa, two enormous halls used for feasting have been excavated.
- The Inca built an extensive network of roads to facilitate communication across the empire. The Inca used a system of knotted strings known as khipu to record information.

KEY TERMS

ayllus, 392
Cahuachi, 392
Chavín de Huántar, 386
Huaca Cao Viejo, 395
Huaca de la Luna, 395
Huaca del Sol, 394
Hua'nuco Pampa, 399
Inca Empire, 397
khipu, 400
Lanzón, 388

Machu Picchu, 399
Moche, 386
Nasca, 386
Nasca Lines, 392
panaqa, 399
San José de Moro, 394
Sipán, 394
Tawantinsuyu, 386
Urubamba Valley, 399

REVIEW QUESTIONS

1. What are ayllus, and how do they affect our view of the Moche and the Nasca?
2. What is the evidence for warfare and violence in Moche society?
3. How were the Inca able to maintain their dominion over the large territories that made up Tawantinsuyu?

BRINGING IT BACK HOME
ARCHAEOLOGY OF AND IN THE MODERN WORLD

As we arrive at the end of this book, a journey in a sense, we are filled with images from far away, both in place and in time. However, in closing, it is important to recall that archaeology is not only about exploring the unknown, but also about recognizing the traces of the past in our familiar world. Increased awareness of the past that surrounds us in our daily lives can also profoundly alter our sense of the world in which we live.

EPILOGUE

Excavation of the remains of a boat in Boston

The small hill of Canteen Kopje, shown in Figure E.1, just outside the town of Barkley West, South Africa, was the location of the first major diamond mine in the interior of Africa (Roberts 1976). In 1870, as reports spread of miners striking it lucky, people headed north to this remote location and set up a massive tent camp. The mining at Canteen Kopje pulled Europeans from the coastal settlements around Cape Town deeply into the interior. A number of years ago I decided to spend some of my research season in South Africa excavating at the edge of the hill at Canteen Kopje, which is also an important Paleolithic site. We set up our grid, and as we began excavating, artifacts started popping up almost immediately. However, instead of the remains of human occupation dating back hundreds of thousands of years, we found a metal can, shards of glass that had been chipped into tools, and small stone tools made on multicolored translucent pebbles. These simple artifacts were left behind during the nineteenth-century mining on this hill and bear witness to the interactions between the miners and the groups of hunter-gatherers and pastoralists who already lived along the Vaal.

Our unexpected discoveries at Canteen Kopje provide an example of the way archaeologists can study the emergence of the modern world, an important part of historical archaeology (Orser 1996). Studying the recent past archaeologically may seem odd. After all, why dig when we can read documents? In fact, most historical archaeology projects include research in the archives, but survey and excavation bring a unique perspective. A brief consideration of the archaeology of the slave trade and the archaeology of industrialization provides a sense of the contributions made by historical archaeologists.

The archaeology of the slave trade charts a network that stretched from Africa across the Atlantic. Archaeologists have been remarkably successful in unearthing the experience of individuals caught up in the slave trade and their struggle to maintain tradition and identity in the most difficult circumstances. On the island of Gorée, Senegal, the site of the port where African slaves departed to the Americas

(Figure E.2), excavations in the Bambarra Quarter trace the impact of the intensification of the slave trade (Croff 2009). In one of the houses dating to the early to mid-eighteenth century, a group of four bottles was found standing upright buried below a dirt floor. A Senegalese student working on the excavation suggested that these bottles might be evidence of a practice still followed in Senegal today, the ritual burial of open vessels to protect against spirits in the land. It is intriguing that this tradition might have been brought by slaves to the Americas, where it was transformed into the bottle trees found among the African diaspora living in the southern United States (Thompson and Cornet 1981).

Working at the other end of the slave trade, Matthew Cochran, a graduate student excavating in Annapolis, Maryland, made a discovery that shows how historical archaeology can bring to light aspects of the past not recorded in written history. As Cochran excavated 4 feet below the modern surface in levels dating to the early eighteenth century, he saw what appeared to be a flat stone surrounded by small pieces of lead shot (see Figure E.3). Recognizing that this was something unusual, he freed the rock, which turned out to be a clay bundle. A crack in the clay showed a pile of pins and nails, raising the possibility that this object might be from hoodoo rituals, African customs brought to Maryland by slaves. The bundle was then x-rayed, revealing 300 pieces of metal and a stone axe poking out through the clay (see Figure E.4 on p. 410). This unassuming assemblage of artifacts is, on close examination, precious evidence of the ephemeral realm of African beliefs, the spiritual world of eighteenth-century slaves. Bundles of metal objects are a well-known element of West African ritual, and stone blades are associated with the god of thunder and lightning. Mark Leone of the University of Maryland, the director of the excavation at Annapolis, states that "the bundle is African in design. . . . The people who made this used local materials. But their knowledge of the charms and the spirit world probably came with them directly from Africa" (Wilford 2008).

The study of the rise of industrial society is another important branch of historical archaeology. Industrial archaeologists explore the remains of installations such as mines, factories, and canals, but they also investigate the human dimension of industrialization. For example, archaeological research in Lowell, Massachusetts,

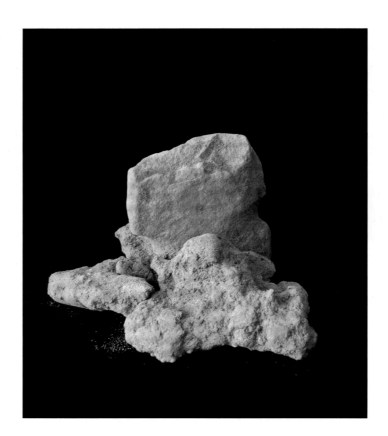

FIGURE E.3 Clay bundle found in excavations in Annapolis, Maryland

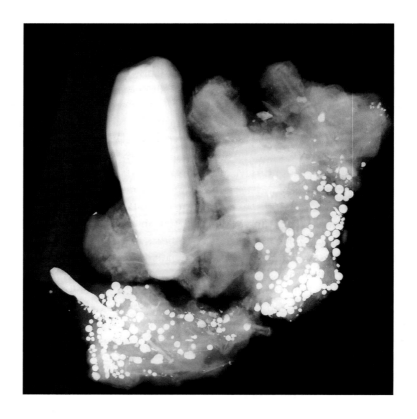

FIGURE E.4 X-ray photograph of the bundle revealing the metal objects and stone axe packed inside

brings out how the lines between working class and middle class were blurred as Lowell grew during the nineteenth century into a center for industrialized textile manufacture (Mrozowski 2005). Comparison of the artifacts from worker and managerial neighborhoods shows that all members of this community shared a common repertoire of material culture. They also shared access to alcohol and narcotics, as indicated by the high proportion of liquor and medicine bottles found in all contexts. But archaeological research also found evidence of stark contrasts in the lives of the workers and managers. Fragments of glass chimney fragments used for both oil and gas lamps were only found in the houses of members of the managerial class, showing a difference in access to lighting. There is also clear evidence that efforts to improve the sanitary facilities in managerial houses were not extended to the homes of workers.

Excavations in Ludlow, Colorado, where in 1914 Colorado National Guard troops fought a vicious battle with striking miners, have produced an archaeological record of modern labor conflict (McGuire and Reckner 2005). Archaeologists have uncovered the remains of a tent camp burnt to the ground after the fighting in which 20 of the people living in the miners' camp were killed. The goal of this project is to gain insight into the everyday experience of mining families living in Colorado and how this lived experience shaped the emerging class-consciousness that crossed ethnic lines. This project has also drawn interest and support of contemporary labor unions and has been active in developing educational and commemorative programs.

The archaeology of Ludlow points to the potential of the archaeological record to serve not only as the basis for research, but also as the means of bringing a consciousness of the past into our lives. Pierre Nora used the evocative term "Places of Memory" for locations or objects that become saturated with historical meaning (Nora 1996–1998). The discovery of an African slave cemetery in Lower Manhattan in 1991 offers a vivid illustration of the emotional effect of the actual physical remains of the past (Mack and Blakey 2004). Although historians have known that slavery was widespread in early Manhattan, the discovery of the cemetery grounded this historical knowledge in a concrete physical presence. After a protracted political debate, the skeletons from the African Burial Ground were moved to Howard University, where an emphasis was placed on connecting the researchers with the descendant community. Perhaps the most compelling aspects of the research relate to the quality of life of enslaved New Yorkers as preserved in the details about the experience of individuals. The skeleton of a 35- to 40-year-old woman was found buried with a newborn infant. The woman's skeleton showed evidence of heavy labor, including a fractured vertebra that never fully healed. Her teeth were badly decayed, indicating that eating would have been painful. Her bones were also riddled with signs of infection. It is likely that her poor health was a factor in the baby's early death. The skeletal remains recovered from the African Burial Ground paint a grim picture of childhood experience. The skeleton of a six-year-old shows evidence of poor health at birth, malnutrition, infection, and hard labor. These discoveries powerfully bring home the realities of enslaved life in early Manhattan. In 2003 the skeletons were ceremonially reinterred at the Burial Ground (Figure E.5). Developments in digital technology open new ways for archaeologists to share the results of their research. The final reports of the excavation and analysis of the African Burial Ground are now available online with both technical reports and syntheses written for the general public (www.gsa.gov/portal/content/249941). The Digital Archaeological Archive of Comparative Slavery is an exciting initiative that brings together comprehensive data from excavations in the United States and the Caribbean (www.daacs.org/).

Places of Memory create an authentic tie between present and past. In a particularly visceral example, the events of September 11, 2001, transformed Ground Zero (shown in Figure E.6) into one of the most profound Places of Memory of our time, a place whose physical presence raises deep emotions. Looking at sites like Ground Zero, Alfredo González-Ruibal (2008) calls for an archaeology of the "super-modern," the unprecedented conflicts, development, and destruction of the twentieth century.

FIGURE E.6 Ground Zero, New York

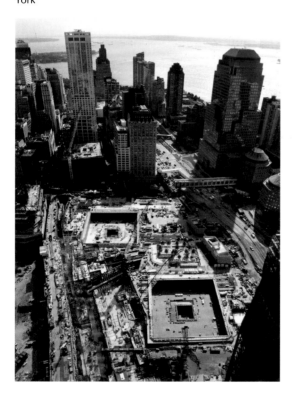

The social theorist Walter Benjamin developed a beautiful and harrowing image of the "angel of history" that might apply to the archaeological record. Benjamin writes of a painting by Paul Klee that shows an angel contemplating something he is about to move away from. For Benjamin, this is an image of the angel of history: "His face is turned toward the past. Where we perceive a chain of events, he sees one single catastrophe which keeps piling wreckage upon wreckage and hurls it in front of his feet" (Benjamin 1968, 257). Benjamin's angel would like to stay and heal the wreck before his eyes, but a "storm irresistibly propels him into the future to which his back is turned, while the pile of debris before him grows skyward. This storm is called progress" (Benjamin 1968, 258). Certainly, the events of recent years, from New Orleans to Port au Prince, have left scenes of overwhelming devastation seared on our minds. The lethal collapse of buildings, our shelter from the elements and the constructs that shape our lives, seems to mock our faith in human achievement. Benjamin's vision is a horrifying idea of progress that cautions us not to assume that it implies improvement.

Yet, as an archaeologist, I find something lacking from Benjamin's vision. As we look back on the "wreckage of progress" that archaeologists have uncovered and continue to uncover, what do we see? There are many answers to this question, and it is largely a matter of personal perspective. What I find lacking from Benjamin's vision is

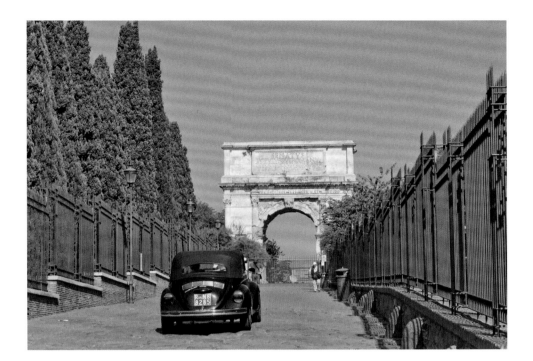

FIGURE E.7 In Rome, the modern city flows around and through the remains of the ancient capital. In this photo a Volkswagen Beetle, a relic of the recent past, makes its way slowly up the road to the Roman Forum.

a sense of the humanity of the past. The archaeological record is profoundly human. A handaxe is not only a shaped stone, but also a stone that bears the traces of every blow used to sculpt the tool, as well as the microtraces left after the tool was used. A pot bears the imprints of the hands of the person who made it and the paint strokes or incisions applied as decoration. Walls are not simply architectural spaces, but the remnants of structures in which people spent their lives.

Benjamin's vision can be balanced by the words of the late Israeli poet Yehuda Amichai. In one of his poems, Amichai writes of sitting by David's Tower in Jerusalem after going shopping. He becomes the point of reference for a tour guide who says, "You see that man with the baskets? Just to the right of his head there's an arch from the Roman period." In the poem, Amichai looks to the day when the guide says, "You see that arch from the Roman period? It's not important: but next to it, left and down a bit, there sits a man who's bought fruit and vegetables for his family" (Amichai 1996, 137–138). So that is where we leave our journey, not with the gold of kings or the bones of early hominins, but with a person alive in a world saturated with the past (Figure E.7). Wherever we live, some part of us is that person.

APPENDICES

APPENDIX A

Political Map of the World, 2012

AFGH. = Afghanistan
ALB. = Albania
ARM. = Armenia
AUS. = Austria
AZER. = Azerbaijan
BANG. = Bangladesh
BEL. = Belgium
BELA. = Belarus
B & H. = Bosnia and Herzegovina
BUL. = Bulgaria
C. AFR. REP. = Central African Republic
CAM. = Cameroon
CRO. = Croatia
C. V. = Cape Verde
CYP. = Cyprus
CZE. = Czech Republic
DEN. = Denmark
EQ. GUINEA = Equatorial Guinea
EST. = Estonia
GAM. = Gambia
G.-B. = Guinea-Bissau
GER. = Germany
GUI. = Guinea
HOND. = Honduras
HUN. = Hungary
ISR. = Israel
KAMP. = Kampuchea
KYRG. = Kyrgyzstan
LAT. = Latvia
LEB. = Lebanon
LIECH. = Liechtenstein
LITH. = Lithuania
LUX. = Luxembourg
MAC. = Macedonia
MOL. = Moldova
MON. = Montenegro
MYAN. = Myanmar
NETH. = Netherlands
POL. = Poland
ROM. = Romania
RUS. = Russia
SER. = Serbia
SLO. = Slovakia
SLOV. = Slovenia
SWITZ. = Switzerland
SYR. = Syria
TAJIK. = Tajikistan
THAI. = Thailand
TURK. = Turkmenistan
UZBEK. = Uzbekistan
U.A.E. = United Arab Emirates

APPENDIX B
COMMONLY USED METRIC SYSTEM UNITS AND SYMBOLS

QUANTITY MEASURED	UNIT	SYMBOL	RELATIONSHIP
Length, width,	millimeter	mm	10 mm = 1 cm
distance, thickness,	centimeter	cm	100 cm = 1 m
girth, etc.	meter	m	
	kilometer	km	1 km = 1,000 m
Mass (weight)	milligram	mg	1,000 mg = 1 g
	gram	g	
	kilogram	kg	1 kg = 1,000 g
	metric ton	t	1 t = 1,000 kg
Time	second	s	
Temperature	degree Celsius	°C	
Area	square meter	m2	
	hectare	ha	1 ha = 10,000 m^2
	square kilometer	km^2	1 km^2 = 100 ha
Volume	milliliter	mL	1,000 mL = 1 L
	cubic centimeter	cm^3 or cc	1 cm^3 = 1 mL
	liter	L	1,000 L = 1 m^3

Conversion Table

TO CONVERT FROM	TO	MULTIPLY BY*
acres (ac)	hectares (ha)	0.4
feet (ft)	meters (m)	0.3
inches (in.)	centimeters (cm)	2.54
miles (mi)	kilometers (km)	1.6
ounces (oz)	grams (g)	28
pounds (lb)	kilograms (kg)	0.45 or divide by 2.2
yards (yd)	meters (m)	0.9

*approximate, except for the inches-to-centimeter multiplier, which is exact.

APPENDIX C
THE HOMININ WHO'S WHO

National Museums of Kenya, Nairobi.
©1985 David L. Brill.

Australopithecus

- **3.5–2.5 million years ago**
- **Brain size: 450–475 cc**
- **Found in East Africa, South Africa, and Chad**
- **Species include *Australopithecus bahrelghazali*, *Australopithecus afarensis*, and *Australopithecus africanus***
- **Bipedal with small canines**

Kenyanthropus

- **3.5 million years ago**
- **Brain size: 450–475 cc**
- **Only one species known, *Kenyanthropus platyops***
- **Similar to *Australopithecus***

Paranthropus

- **2.5–1.4 million years ago**
- **Brain size: 450–475 cc**
- **Found in East Africa and South Africa**
- **Also known as robust *Australopithecus*; species include *Paranthropus robustus* and *Paranthropus boisei***
- **Massive molars and muscles for chewing**

Homo habilis

- **2.5–1.6 million years ago**
- **Brain size: 500–800 cc**
- **Found in East Africa and South Africa**
- **First member of genus *Homo***
- **Increased brain size**

Hominoids are members of the biological superfamily that includes humans, great apes, and gibbons.

Homo erectus

- 1.9 million–45,000? years ago
- Brain size: 750–1,250 cc
- Found in Africa, Asia, and Europe
- Early *Homo erectus* is often referred to as *Homo ergaster*
- First hominin found outside of Africa, increased brain size

Homo neanderthalensis

- 175,000–30,000 years ago
- Brain size: 1,200–1,700 cc
- Found in Europe and the Middle East
- Some anthropologists prefer to label this group of fossils *Homo sapiens neanderthalensis*
- Large brain size, muscular, and adapted to the cold

Homo Sapiens Sapiens

- 160,000 years ago until today
- Brain size: 1,200–1,700 cc
- Found throughout the globe
- All living humans belong to this species, which is often referred to as "modern humans"
- Globular braincase, vertical forehead, decreased body mass

Homo floresiensis

- 38,000–18,000 years ago
- Brain size: 380 cc
- Found only on the island of Flores
- Some anthropologists question whether this is in fact a distinct species
- Small brain and body size

Hominins are members of the human lineage after it split with the chimpanzee lineage.

APPENDIX D
DATING METHODS

Radiocarbon Dating

TOOLBOX ON P. 29

- Time range: Beginning 40,000 years ago.
- Material dated: Organic remains including charcoal, bone, wood, and shell.
- The death of an organism removes it from the carbon-exchange reservoir, and radioactive carbon-14 begins to decay at a steady rate. The concentration of carbon-14 relative to other isotopes of carbon is the basis for calculating the time since the death of the organism.
- Because of fluctuations in the concentration of carbon-14 in the global reservoir, carbon-14 dates have to be calibrated to arrive at a calendar date (see p. 162).
- Accelerator Mass Spectrometry (AMS) allows for the dating of very small samples (see p. 162).

Argon Dating

TOOLBOX ON P. 80

- Effective for dating all periods of hominin evolution.
- Materials dated: Volcanic rock and ash, as well as meteoric glass (tektites).
- Measures the accumulation of argon-40 from the decay of potassium-40. The decay of potassium-40 takes place at a constant rate. The accumulation clock is zeroed at the time of a volcanic eruption because argon diffuses out of a material at high temperatures. Consequently, after an eruption there is no argon in lava and ash. Argon then begins to accumulate as a result of the decay of potassium.
- Can be used only in areas with volcanic deposits.

Paleomagnetic Dating

TOOLBOX ON P. 80

- Effective for dating all periods of hominin evolution.
- Material dated: Sediments.
- Determines whether sediments were deposited in periods of normal or reversed polarity. Can be used to situate a stratigraphic context in the paleomagnetic time scale.

Luminescence Dating

TOOLBOX ON P. 129

- Most effective for the more recent periods of hominin evolution (since 200,000 years ago).
- Materials dated: Sediments (optically stimulated resonance, or OSL), burnt flint and pottery (thermoluminescence or TL), and teeth (electron spin resonance, or ESR).
- Measures the accumulation of electrons in crystal lattices. The clock is zeroed when the material is heated (TL), when it is exposed to sunlight (OSL), or upon the initial growth of the crystal (ESR).
- The background radiation at the find must be measured with a dosimeter.

Dendrochronology

TOOLBOX ON P. 281

- Most useful for the last 10,000 years.
- Material dated: Wood.
- The ring pattern found in a piece of wood is matched to the fluctuations in a long-term chronology.

REFERENCES

Abu El-Haj, N. *Facts on the Ground: Archaeological Practice and Territorial Self-Fashioning in Israeli Society*. Chicago: University of Chicago Press, 2001.

Adams, R. M., and H. Nissen. *The Uruk Countryside: The Natural Setting of Urban Societies*. Chicago: University of Chicago Press, 1972.

Adcock, G. J., et al. "Mitochondrial DNA Sequences in Ancient Australians: Implications for Modern Human Origins." *Proceedings of the National Academy of Sciences* 98.2 (2001): 537–42.

Adovasio, J. M., et al. "Meadowcroft Rockshelter 1977: An Overview." *American Antiquity* 43 (1978): 632–51.

Agrawal, D. P. *The Archaeology of India*. Scandinavian Institute of Asian Studies Monograph Series. Malmö, Sweden: Curzon Press, 1985.

Ahler, S. A., and P. R. Geib. "Why Flute? Folsom Point Design and Adaptation." *Journal of Archaeological Science* 27 (2000): 799–820.

Aiello, L. C., and P. Wheeler. "The Expensive-Tissue Hypothesis." *Current Anthropology* 36.2 (1995): 199–221.

Aimers, J., and D. M. Rutecki. "Brave New World: Interpreting Sex, Gender, and Sexuality in the Past." *SAA Archaeological Record* 16.1 (2016): 9–11.

Aitken, M. J. *Science-Based Dating in Archaeology*. London: Longman, 1990.

Aitken, M. J., Chris Stringer, and Paul Mellars. *The Origin of Modern Humans and the Impact of Chronometric Dating*. Princeton, NJ: Princeton University Press, 1993.

Akins, N. J. "The Burials of Pueblo Bonito." In *Pueblo Bonito: Center of the Chacoan World*, edited by J. E. Neitzel, 94–106. Washington, DC: Smithsonian Press, 2003.

Alcock, S., et al., eds. *Empires*. Cambridge: Cambridge University Press, 2001.

Alemseged, Z. "A Juvenile Early Hominin Skeleton from Dikika, Ethiopia." *Nature* 443 (2006): 296–301.

Algaze, G. *The Uruk World System: The Dynamics of Expansion of Early Mesopotamian Civilization*. Chicago: University of Chicago Press, 1993.

Allan, S. *The Formation of Chinese Civilization: An Archaeological Perspective*. New Haven, CT: Yale University Press, 2005.

Allchin, F. R., and B. Allchin. *The Rise of Civilization in India and Pakistan*. Cambridge World Archaeology Series. Cambridge, UK: Cambridge University Press, 1982.

Amichai, Y. *Selected Poetry of Yehuda Amichai*, translated by Chana Bloch and Stephen Mitchell. Berkeley, CA: University of California Press, 1996.

Andah, B. W. "Identifying Early Farming Traditions of West Africa." In *The Archaeology of Africa: Food, Metals, and Towns*, edited by T. Shaw, 240–53. London: Routledge, 1993.

Anderson, M. K. "From Tillage to Table: The Indigenous Cultivation of Geophytes for Food in California." *Journal of Ethnobiology* 17.2 (1997): 149–69.

Anderson, M. K. "The Fire, Pruning, and Coppice Management of Temperate Ecosystems for Basketry Material by California Indian Tribes." *Human Ecology* 27.1 (1999): 79–113.

Antón, S. C., R. Potts, and L. C. Aiello. "Evolution of Early Homo: An Integrated Biological Perspective." *Science* 345.6192 (2014): 1236828.

Arensburg, B. "A Middle Paleolithic Human Hyoid Bone." *Nature* 338 (1989): 758–60.

Arnold, B. "The Past as Propaganda: Totalitarian Archaeology in Nazi Germany." *Antiquity* 64 (1990): 464–78.

Arsuaga, J. L. de, A. Klatt, and J. C. Sastre. *The Neanderthal's Necklace: In Search of the First Thinkers*. New York: Four Walls Eight Windows, 2002.

Ascher, M., and R. Ascher. *Code of the Quipu: A Study in Media, Mathematics, and Culture*. Ann Arbor, MI: University of Michigan Press, 1981.

Asfaw, B., et al. "Australopithecus Garhi: A New Species of Early Hominid from Ethiopia." *Science* 284 (1999): 629–35.

Aveni, A. F. *Nasca: Eighth Wonder of the World?* London: British Museum Press, 2000.

Axelsson, E., et al. "The Genomic Signature of Dog Domestication Reveals Adaptation to a Starch-Rich Diet." *Nature* 495.7441 (2013): 360–64.

Baadsgaard, A., et al. "Human Sacrifice and Intentional Corpse Preservation in the Royal Cemetery of Ur." *Antiquity* 85.327 (2011): 27–42.

Bafna, S. "Space Syntax: A Brief Introduction to Its Logic and Analytical Techniques." *Environment and Behavior* 35 (2003): 17–28.

Bahn, P. G. "The 'Unacceptable Face' of the West European Upper Paleolithic." *Antiquity* 52 (1978): 183–92.

Bahn, P. G. *Written in Bones: How Human Remains Unlock the Secrets of the Dead*. Newton Abbot, Devon, UK: David & Charles, 2002.

Baillie, M. G. L. *A Slice through Time: Dendrochronology and Precision Dating*. London: Batsford, 1995.

Ballard, C. "Writing (Pre)History: Narrative and Archaeological Explanation in the New Guinea Highlands." *Archaeology of Oceania* 38 (2003): 135–48.

Ballard, R. D., ed. *Archaeological Oceanography*. Princeton, NJ: Princeton University Press, 2008.

Ballard, R. D., et al. "Iron-Age Shipwrecks in Deep Water off Ashkelon, Israel." *American Journal of Archaeology* 106 (2002): 151–68.

Balter, V., et al. "Les Néandertaliens Étaient-Ils Essentiellement Carnivores? Résultats Préliminaires sur les Teneurs en Sr et en Ba de la Paléobiocénose Mammalienne de Saint-Césaire." *Comptes Rendus de l'Académie des Sciences: Earth and Planetary Sciences* 332 (2001): 59–65. Balter, Vincent, et al. "Ecological and Physiological Variability of Sr/Ca and Ba/Ca in Mammals of West Europe Mid-Wurmian Food Webs." *Palaeogeography, Palaeoclimatology, Palaeoecology* 186 (2002): 127–43.

Banning, E. B. *The Archaeologist's Laboratory: The Analysis of Archaeological Data: Interdisciplinary Contributions to Archaeology*. New York: Kluwer Academic/Plenum, 2000.

Banning, E. B. *Archaeological Survey: Manuals in Archaeological Method, Theory, and Technique*. New York: Kluwer Academic/Plenum, 2002.

Barfield, T. J. "The Shadow Empires: Imperial State Formation along the Chinese-Nomad Frontier." In *Empires*, edited by S. Alcock, T. D'Altroy, K. Morrison, and C. Sinopoli, 10–41. Cambridge, UK: Cambridge University Press, 2001.

Barker, P. "The Process Made Me Do It: Or, Would a Reasonably Intelligent Person Agree That CRM Is Reasonably Intelligent." In *Archaeology and Cultural Resource Management: Visions for the Future*, edited by L. Sebastian and W. D. Lipe, 65–90. Santa Fe, NM: School for Advanced Research, 2009.

Barlow, K. R. "Predicting Maize Agriculture among the Fremont: An Economic Comparison of Farming and Foraging in the American Southwest." *American Antiquity* 67.1 (2002): 65–88.

Barnes, G. *State Formation in Japan: Emergence of a 4th-Century Ruling Elite*. New York: Routledge, 2007.

Barrett, J. C. *Fragments from Antiquity: An Archaeology of Social Life in Britain, 2900–1200 B.C.* Social Archaeology Series. Oxford, UK: Blackwell, 1993.

Bartstra, G.-J. "Homo erectus: The Search for His Artifacts." *Current Anthropology* 23.3 (1982): 318–20.Bar-Yosef, Ofer. *A Cave in the Desert: Nahal Hemar.* Jerusalem, Israel: Israel Museum, 1985.

Bar-Yosef, O. "The Walls of Jericho: An Alternative Interpretation." *Current Anthropology* 27.2 (1986): 157–62.

Bar-Yosef, O., et al. "Netiv Hagdud: An Early Neolithic Village Site in the Jordan Valley." *Journal of Field Archaeology* 18 (1991): 405–23.

Bar-Yosef, O., et al. "The Excavations at Kebara Cave, Mt Carmel." *Current Anthropology* 33.5 (1992): 497–550.

Bar-Yosef, O., and F. R. Valla. *The Natufian Culture in the Levant.* Ann Arbor, MI: International Monographs in Prehistory, 1991.

Bass, G. "A Bronze Age Shipwreck at Ulu Burun: 1984 Campaign." *American Journal of Archaeology* 90 (1986): 269–96.

Bawden, G. *The Moche.* Malden, MA: Blackwell, 1999.

Bednarik, R. G. "Direct Dating Results from Australian Cave Petroglyphs." *Geoarchaeology: An International Journal* 13.4 (1998): 411–18.

Bednarik, R. G. "The Dating of Rock Art: A Critique." *Journal of Archaeological Science* 29 (2002): 1213–33.

Bell, E. E., M. A. Canuto, and R. J. Sharer, eds. *Understanding Early Classic Copan.* Philadelphia, PA: University of Pennsylvania Museum of Archaeology and Anthropology, 2004.

Bellwood, P. S. *First Farmers: The Origins of Agricultural Societies.* Malden, MA: Blackwell, 2005.

Bellwood, P. S., and C. Renfrew, eds. *Examining the Farming/Language Dispersal Hypothesis.* McDonald Institute Monographs. Cambridge, UK: McDonald Institute for Archaeological Research, 2002.

Bender, B. *Farming in Prehistory: From Hunter-Gatherer to Food-Producer.* London: J. Baker, 1975.

Bender, B. "Theorizing Landscapes, and the Prehistoric Landscapes of Stonehenge." *Man* 27.4 (1992): 735–55.

Benjamin, Walter. *Illuminations: Essays and Reflections,* translated by Harry Zohn. New York: Schocken, 1968.

Benson, E. P., et al. *Olmec Art of Ancient Mexico.* Washington, DC: National Gallery of Art, 1996.

Benson, L. V., et al. "Ancient Maize from Chacoan Great Houses: Where Was It Grown?" *Proceedings of the National Academy of Sciences* 100.22 (2003): 13111–15.

Benson, L. V., and M. S. Berry. "Climate Change and Cultural Response in the Prehistoric American Southwest." *Kiva* 75.1 (2009): 87–117.

Berger, L. R., et al. "Australopithecus Sediba: A New Species of Homo-Like Australopith from South Africa." *Science* 328.5975 (2010): 195–204.

Berger, L. R., et al. "Homo Naledi, a New Species of the Genus Homo from the Dinaledi Chamber, South Africa." *Elife* 4 (2015): e09560.

Berger, T. D., and E. Trinkaus. "Patterns of Trauma among the Neanderthals." *Journal of Archaeological Science* 22.6 (1995): 841–52.

Berna, F., et al. "Microstratigraphic Evidence of In Situ Fire in the Acheulean Strata of Wonderwerk Cave, Northern Cape Province, South Africa." *Proceedings of the National Academy of Sciences* 109 (2012): E1215–20.

Berrin, K., and E. Pasztory, eds. *Teotihuacán: Art from the City of the Gods.* New York: Thames and Hudson, 1993.

Binford, L. R. "Archaeological Systematics and the Study of Cultural Process." *American Antiquity* 31 (1965): 203–10.

Binford, L. "Archaeological Perspectives." In *New Perspectives in Archaeology,* edited by S. Binford and L. Binford, 5–32. Chicago: Aldine, 1968.

Binford, L. *In Pursuit of the Past: Decoding the Archaeological Record.* New York: Thames and Hudson, 1983.

Binford, S., and L. Binford, eds. *New Perspectives in Archaeology.* Chicago: Aldine, 1968.

Bird, M. I., et al. "Radiocarbon Analysis of the Early Archaeological Site of Nauwalabila I, Arnhem Land, Australia: Implications for Sample Suitability and Stratigraphic Integrity." *Quaternary Science Reviews* 21 (2002): 1061–75.

Blanton, R. E. *Ancient Mesoamerica: A Comparison of Change in Three Regions.* New York: Cambridge University Press, 1987.

Blanton, R. E., et al. *Ancient Mesoamerica: A Comparison of Change in Three Regions,* 2nd ed. Cambridge, UK: Cambridge University Press, 1993.

Blanton, R. E., et al. "A Dual-Processual Theory for the Evolution of Mesoamerican Civilization." *Current Anthropology* 31 (1996): 1–14.

Blench, R. "Ethnographic and Linguistic Evidence for the Prehistory of African Ruminant Livestock, Horses, and Ponies." In *The Archaeology of Africa: Food, Metals, and Towns,* edited by T. Shaw. London: Routledge, 1993.

Blumenschine, R. J., et al. "Late Pliocene Homo and Hominid Land Use from Western Olduvai Gorge, Tanzania." *Science* 299 (2003): 1217–21.

Bobe, R., and A. K. Behrensmeyer. "The Expansion of Grassland Ecosystems in Africa in Relation to Mammalian Evolution and the Origin of the Genus Homo." *Palaeogeography, Palaeoclimatology, Palaeoecology* 207.3 (2004): 399–420.

Bocherens, H., et al. "New Isotopic Evidence for Dietary Habits of Neanderthals from Belgium." *Journal of Human Evolution* 40 (2001): 497–505.

Boëda, E. "Levallois: A Volumetric Construction, Methods, and Technique." In *Definition and Interpretation of Levallois Technology,* edited by H. Dibble and O. Bar-Yosef, 41–68. Madison, WI: Prehistory Press, 1995.

Boëda, E., et al. "A Levallois Point Embedded in the Vertebra of a Wild Ass (*Equus africanus*): Hafting, Projectiles and Mousterian Hunting Weapons." *Antiquity* 73.280 (1999): 394–402.

Boesch, C. "Animal Behaviour: The Question of Culture." *Nature* 379 (1996): 207–8.

Boesch, C., and H. Boesch-Achermann. *The Chimpanzees of the Taï Forest: Behavioural Ecology and Evolution.* Oxford, UK: Oxford University Press, 2000.

Boivin, N. "Rock Art and Rock Music: Petroglyphs of the South Indian Neolithic." *Antiquity* 78 (2004): 38–53.

Boone, E. H. "Glorious Imperium: Understanding Land and Community in Moctezuma's Mexico." In *Moctezuma's Mexico: Visions of the Aztec World,* edited by E. M. Moctezuma and D. Carrasco, 159–74. Boulder, CO: University of Colorado, 1992.

Bordes, F. *A Tale of Two Caves.* New York: Harper & Row, 1972.

Boric, D. "Body Metamorphosis and Animality: Volatile Bodies and Boulder Artworks from Lepenski Vir." *Cambridge Archaeological Journal* 15.1 (2005): 35–69.

Boserup, E. *The Conditions of Agricultural Growth.* London: George Allen and Unwin, 1965.

Bourget, S., and K. L. Jones. *The Art and Archaeology of the Moche: An Ancient Andean Society of the Peruvian North Coast.* Austin, TX: University of Texas Press, 2008.

Bousman, C. B., et al. "The Paleoindian-Archaic Transition in North America: New Evidence from Texas." *Antiquity* 76 (2002): 980–90.

Bowens, A., ed. *Underwater Archaeology: The NAS Guide to Principles and Practice*. Malden, MA: Blackwell, 2009.

Bowler, J. M., et al. "New Ages for Human Occupation and Climatic Change at Lake Mungo, Australia." *Nature* 421 (2003): 837–40.

Bowler, P. J. *Theories of Human Evolution: A Century of Debate, 1844–1944*. Baltimore, MD: Johns Hopkins University Press, 1986.

Brackenridge, H. M. *Views of Louisiana Together with a Journal of a Voyage up the Missouri River, in 1811*. 1814. Reprint, Chicago: Quadrangle Books, 1962.

Braje, T. J. "A mid-twentieth-century Anthropocene makes the Holocene more important than ever." *Antiquity* 90 (2106): 517–18.

Branch, N., et al. *Environmental Archaeology: Theoretical and Practical Approaches*. Key Issues in Environmental Change Series. London: Hodder Arnold, 2005.

Braswell, G. E. *The Maya and Teotihuacán: Reinterpreting Early Classic Interaction*. Austin, TX: University of Texas Press, 2003.

Brooks, A. S., et al. "Dating and Context of Three Middle Stone Age Sites with Bone Points in the Upper Semliki Valley, Zaire." *Science* 268 (1995): 548–53.

Brose, D. S., J. A. Brown, and D. W. Penney, eds. *Ancient Art of the American Woodland Indians*. New York: Abrams, 1985.

Brose, D. S., and N. Greber, eds. *Hopewell Archaeology: The Chillicothe Conference*. Kent, OH: Kent State University Press, 1979.

Brown, A. D. "Wetlands and Drylands in Prehistory: Mesolithic to Bronze Age Human Activity and Impact in the Severn Estuary, Southwest Britain." PhD thesis, University of Reading, 2005.

Brown, J. A. "Charnel Houses and Mortuary Crypts: Disposal of the Dead in the Middle Woodland Period." In *Hopewell Archaeology: The Chillicothe Conference*, edited by D. S. Brose and N. Greber. Kent, OH: Kent State University Press, 1979.

Brown, P., et al. "A New Small-Bodied Hominin from the Late Pleistocene of Flores, Indonesia." *Nature* 431 (2004): 1055–61.

Bruins, H. J., et al. "Geoarchaeological Tsunami Deposits at Palaikastro (Crete) and the Late Minoan IA Eruption of Santorini." *Journal of Archaeological Science* 35 (2008): 191–212.

Brumfiel, E. "Aztec Hearts and Minds: Religion and the State in the Aztec Empire." In *Empires*, edited by S. Alcock et al., 283–310. Cambridge, UK: Cambridge University Press, 2001.

Brumm, A., et al. "Early Stone Technology on Flores and Its Implications for *Homo floresiensis*." *Nature* 441 (2006): 624–28.

Brunet, M., et al. "The First Australopithecine 2,500 Kilometers West of the Rift Valley (Chad)." *Nature* 378 (1995): 273–75.

Brunet, M., et al. "New Material of the Earliest Hominid from the Upper Miocene of Chad." *Nature* 434 (2005): 752–55.

Bryan, F. "A Review of the Geology of the Clovis Finds Reported by Howard and Cotter." *American Antiquity* 2 (1938, 1939): 113–30, 43–51.

Buchanan, B., M. Collard, and K. Edinborough. "Paleoindian Demography and the Extraterrestrial Impact Hypothesis." *Proceedings of the National Academy of Sciences* 105 (2008): 11651–54.

Buikstra, J., et al. "Tombs from the Copan Acropolis: A Life History Approach." In *Understanding Early Classic Copan*, edited by E. E. Bell, M. A. Canuto, and R. J. Sharer, 191–214. Philadelphia, PA: University Museum, 2004.

Buikstra, J., and L. Beck, eds. *Bioarchaeology: The Contextual Analysis of Human Remains*. Amsterdam: Academic Press, 2006.

Bulmer, S. *The Prehistory of the New Guinea Highlands*. Auckland, New Zealand: University of Auckland, 1976.

Bunn, H. T. "A Taphonomic Perspective on the Archaeology of Human Origins." *Annual Review of Anthropology* 20 (1991): 433–67.

Burger, R. L. "An Overview of Peruvian Archaeology." *Annual Review of Anthropology* 18 (1989): 37–69.

Burger, R. L. *Chavín and the Origins of Andean Civilization*. London: Thames and Hudson, 1992.

Burger, R. L., and L. C. Salazar. *Machu Picchu: Unveiling the Mystery of the Incas*. New Haven, CT: Yale University Press, 2004.

Butzer, K. W. "Ecology in the Long View: Settlement Histories, Agrosystemic Strategies, and Ecological Performance." *Journal of Field Archaeology* 23 (1996): 141–80.

Cadogan, G., E. Hatzaki, and A. Vasilakis, eds. *Knossos: Palace, City, State. Proceedings of the Conference in Herakleion Organised by the British School at Athens and the 23rd Ephoreia of Prehistoric and Classical Antiquities of Herakleion, in November 2000, for the Centenary of Sir Arthur Evans's Excavations at Knossos*. London: British School at Athens, 2004.

Cain, C. R. "Notched, Flaked and Ground Bone Artefacts from Middle Stone Age and Iron Age Layers of Sibudu Cave, KwaZulu-Natal, South Africa." *South African Journal of Science* 100 (2004): 195–97.

Cameron, C. "Sacred Earthen Architecture in the Northern Southwest: The Bluff Great House Berm." *American Antiquity* 67.4 (2002): 677–96.

Cann, R. L. "Tangled Genetic Routes." *Nature* 416 (2002): 32–51.

Carballo, D. "Implements of State Power: Weaponry and Martially Themed Obsidian Production near the Moon Pyramid, Teotihuacán." *Ancient Mesoamerica* 18 (2007): 173–90.

Carbonell, E. "Out of Africa: The Dispersal of the Earliest Technical Systems Reconsidered." *Journal of Anthropological Archaeology* 18.2 (1999): 119–36.

Carbonell, E., et al. "The Pleistocene Site of Gran Dolina, Sierra de Atapuerca, Spain: A History of the Archaeological Investigations." *Journal of Human Evolution* 37.3–4 (1999): 313–24.

Carbonell, E., et al. "Les Premiers Comportements Funéraires Auraient-Ils Pris Place; Atapuerca, il y a 350,000 Ans?" *L'Anthropologie* 107.1 (2003): 1–14.

Carneiro, R. L. "A Theory of the Origin of the State." *Science* 169 (1970): 733–38.

Carr, C., and D. T. Case, eds. *Gathering Hopewell: Society, Ritual, and Ritual Interaction*. New York: Springer, 2006.

Carrasco, D. "Toward the Splendid City: Knowing the Worlds of Moctezuma." In *Moctezuma's Mexico: Visions of the Aztec World*, edited by E. M. Moctezuma and D. Carrasco, 99–148. Boulder, CO: University of Colorado, 1992.

Carson, J. F., et al. "Environmental Impact of Geometric Earthwork Construction in Pre-Columbian Amazonia." *Proceedings of the National Academy of Sciences* 111.29 (2014): 10497–502.

Casana, J. "Satellite Imagery-Based Analysis of Archaeological Looting in Syria." *Near Eastern Archaeology* 78.3 (2015): 142–52.

Castelletti, L., M. Cottini, and M. Rottoli. "Early Holocene Plant Remains from Uan Afuda Cave, Tadrart Acacus (Libyan Sahara)." In *Before Food Production in North Africa*, edited by S. di Lernia and G. Manzi, 91–102. Forli, Italy: A.B.A.C.O. Edizioni, 1998.

Castleden, R. *The Making of Stonehenge*. London: Routledge, 1993.

Cauvin, J., and T. Watkins. *The Birth of the Gods and the Origins of Agriculture*. New Studies in Archaeology. Cambridge, UK: Cambridge University Press, 2000.

Cessford, C. "A New Dating Sequence for Çatalhöyük." *Antiquity* 75 (2001): 717–25.

Chaloupka, G. *Journey in Time: The World's Longest Continuing Art Tradition: The 50,000 Year Story of the Australian Aboriginal Rock Art of Arnhem Land*. Chatswood, NSW: Reed, 1993.

Chandler, S. M. "Innovative Approaches to Mitigation." In *Archaeology and Cultural Resource Management: Visions for the Future*, edited by L. Sebastian and W. D. Lipe, 115–41. Santa Fe, NM: School for Advanced Research, 2009.

Chang, K. *Shang Civilization*. New Haven, CT: Yale University Press, 1980.

Chang, K. *Art, Myth, and Ritual: The Path to Political Authority in Ancient China*. Cambridge, MA: Harvard University Press, 1983.

Chang, K. *The Archaeology of Ancient China*, 4th ed. New Haven, CT: Yale University Press, 1986.

Chang, K. "Ritual and Power." In *China: Ancient Culture, Modern Land*, edited by R. E. Murowchick, 60–69. Norman, OK: University of Oklahoma Press, 1994.

Chapdelaine, C., V. Pimentel, and H. Bernier. "A Glimpse at Moche Phase III Occupation at the Huacas of Moche Site, Northern Peru." *Antiquity* 75 (2000): 361–72.

Charlton, T. H., D. L. Nichols, and C. O. Charlton. "Aztec Craft Production and Specialization: Archaeological Evidence from the City-State of Otumba, Mexico." *World Archaeology* 23.1 (1991): 98–114.

Chase, A. F., et al. "Airborne LiDAR, Archaeology, and the Ancient Maya Landscape at Caracol, Belize." *Journal of Archaeological Science* 388 (2011): 387–98.

Chase, P. G. "Relationships between Mousterian Lithic and Faunal Assemblages at Combe Grenal." *Current Anthropology* 27 (1986): 69–71.

Chatters, J. C., et al. "Late Pleistocene Human Skeleton and mtDNA Link Paleoamericans and Modern Native Americans." *Science* 344.6185 (2014): 750–54.

Chauvet, J.-M., E. B. Deschamps, and C. Hillaire. *Dawn of Art: The Chauvet Cave: The Oldest Known Paintings in the World*. New York: Abrams, 1996.

Chen, T.-M., et al. "ESR Dating of Tooth Enamel from Yunxian *Homo erectus* Site, China." *Quaternary Science Reviews* 16 (1997): 455–58.

Cherry, J. "Polities and Palaces: Some Problems in Minoan State Formation." In *Peer Polity Interaction and Socio-Political Change*, edited by C. Renfrew and J. Cherry, 19–46. Cambridge, UK: Cambridge University Press, 1986.

Childe, V. G. *What Happened in History*. Harmondsworth, UK: Penguin, 1942.

Chilton, E. "Mobile Farmers of Pre-Contact Southern New England: The Archaeological and Ethnohistorical Evidence." *New York State Museum Bulletin* 494 (1999): 157–76.

Chilton, E. "'Towns They Have None': Diverse Subsistence and Settlement Strategies in Native New England." *New York State Museum Bulletin* 496 (2002): 265–88.

Chilton, E., T. B. Largy, and K. Curran. "Evidence for Prehistoric Maize Horticulture at the Pine Hill Site, Deerfield, Massachusetts." *Northeast Anthropology* 59 (2000): 23–46.

Chippindale, C., et al. *Who Owns Stonehenge?* London: Batsford, 1990.

Chirikure, S., and G. Pwiti. "Community Involvement in Archaeology and Cultural Heritage Management: An Assessment from Case Studies in Southern Africa and Elsewhere." *Current Anthropology* 49 (2008): 467–85.

Clark, D. *Analytical Archaeology*. New York: Columbia University Press, 1978.

Clark, J. D., and S. A. Brandt, eds. *From Hunters to Farmers: The Causes and Consequences of Food Production in Africa*. Berkeley, CA: University of California Press, 1984.

Clark, J. E., and M. E. Pye. *Olmec Art and Archaeology in Mesoamerica*. Washington, DC: National Gallery of Art, 2000.

Clark, R. M., et al. "Pattern of Diversity in the Genomic Region near the Maize Domestication Gene Tb1." *Proceedings of the National Academy of Sciences* 101.3 (2004): 700–707.

Clarke, R. J. "First Ever Discovery of a Well-Preserved Skull and Associated Skeleton of an Australopithecus." *South African Journal of Science* 94.10 (1998): 1–6.

Cleal, R., K. E. Walker, and R. Montague. *Stonehenge in Its Landscape: 20th Century Excavations*. English Heritage Archaeological Report, vol. 10. London: English Heritage, 1995.

Clottes, J., P. G. Bahn, and M. Arnold. *Chauvet Cave: The Art of Earliest Times*. Salt Lake City, UT: University of Utah Press, 2003.

Clutton-Brock, J. "The Spread of Domestic Animals in Africa." In *The Archaeology of Africa: Food, Metals, and Towns*, edited by T. Shaw, 61–70. London: Routledge, 1993.

Coe, M. D. *The Maya: Ancient Peoples and Places*, 5th ed. New York: Thames and Hudson, 1993.

Coe, M. D. *The Olmec World: Ritual and Rulership*. Princeton, NJ: The Art Museum, Princeton University, 1995.

Coe, M. D. *Breaking the Maya Code*. New York: Thames and Hudson, 1999.

Coe, M. D. *Angkor and the Khmer Civilization*. New York: Thames and Hudson, 2003.

Cohen, C., and J.-J. Hublin. *Boucher de Perthes, 1788–1868: Les Origines Romantiques de la Préhistoire. Un Savant, une Époque*. Paris: Belin, 1989.

Cohen, M. N. *The Food Crisis in Prehistory: Overpopulation and the Origins of Agriculture*. New Haven, CT: Yale University Press, 1977.

Coles, J. M. *Experimental Archaeology*. New York: Academic Press, 1979.

Conard, N. "Laminar Lithic Assemblages from the Last Interglacial Complex in Northwestern Europe." *Journal of Anthropological Research* 46.3 (1990): 243–62.

Conard, N. "Palaeolithic Ivory Sculptures from Southwestern Germany and the Origins of Figurative Art." *Nature* 426 (2003): 830–32.

Conard, N. "A Female Figurine from the Basal Aurignacian of Hohle Fels Cave in Southwestern Germany." *Nature* 459 (2009): 248–52.

Conard, N., M. Malina, and S. Munzel. "New Flutes Document the Earliest Musical Tradition in Southwestern Germany." *Nature* 460 (2009): 737–40.

Conkey, M. "The Identification of Prehistoric Hunter-Gatherer Aggregation Sites: The Case of Altamira." *Current Anthropology* 21.5 (1980): 609–30.

Conklin, W. J., and J. Quilter. *Chavín: Art, Architecture, and Culture*. Los Angeles, CA: Cotsen Institute of Archaeology, University of California, Los Angeles, 2008.

Connah, G. *African Civilization: Precolonial Cities and States in Tropical Africa: An Archaeological Perspective*. Cambridge, UK: Cambridge University Press, 1987.

Conyers, L. B., and D. Goodman. *Ground-Penetrating Radar: An Introduction for Archaeologists*. Walnut Creek, CA: AltaMira Press, 1997.

Copley, M. S., et al. "Direct Chemical Evidence for Widespread Dairying in Prehistoric Britain." *Proceedings of the National Academy of Sciences* 100 (2003): 1524–29.

Cordell, L. *Archaeology of the Southwest*, 2nd ed. New York: Academic Press, 1997.

Coughlin, S., and M. F. Seeman. "Hopewellian Settlements at the Liberty Earthworks, Ross County, Ohio." In *Ohio Hopewell*

Community Organization, edited by W. S. Dancey and P. J. Pacheco, 231–50. Kent, OH: Ohio University Press, 1997.

Cowan, C. W., and P. J. Watson, eds. The Origins of Agriculture: An International Perspective. Washington, DC: Smithsonian Institution Press, 1992.

Cowgill, G. "State and Society at Teotihuacán, Mexico." Annual Review of Anthropology 26 (1997): 129–63.

Craig, O. E., et al. "Feeding Stonehenge: Cuisine and Consumption at the Late Neolithic Site of Durrington Walls." Antiquity 89.347 (2015): 1096–109.

Craig, O. E., Thompson, et al. "Earliest Evidence for the Use of Pottery." Nature 496.7445 (2013): 351–54.

Crawford, G. W., and C. Shen. "The Origins of Rice Agriculture: Recent Progress in East Asia." Antiquity 72 (1998): 858–66.

Crawford, G. W., and D. G. Smith. "Paleoethnobotany in the Northeast." In People and Plants in Ancient Eastern North America, edited by P. E. Minnis, 172–257. Washington, DC: Smithsonian Books, 2003.

Crawford, G. W., D. G. Smith, and V. E. Bowyer. "Dating the Entry of Corn (Zea Mays) into the Lower Great Lakes Region." American Antiquity 62.1 (1997): 112–19.

Crawford, H. E. W. Sumer and the Sumerians. Cambridge, UK: Cambridge University Press, 1991.

Croff, R. L. "Village des Bambaras: An Archaeology of Domestic Slavery and Urban Transformation on Goree Island, Senegal, A.D. 17th–19th Centuries." PhD diss., Yale University, 2009.

Crown, P. L., et al. "Ritual Drinks in the Pre-Hispanic US Southwest and Mexican Northwest." Proceedings of the National Academy of Sciences 112.37 (2015): 11436–42.

Crown, P. L., and W. J. Judge, eds. Chaco & Hohokam: Prehistoric Regional Systems in the American Southwest. School of American Research Advanced Seminar Series. Santa Fe, NM: School of American Research Press, 1991.

Crumley, C. "Heterarchy and the Analysis of Complex Societies." Archaeological Papers of the American Anthropological Association 18 (1995): 1–5.

Cullen, B. "Testimony from the Iceman." Smithsonian 33.11 (2003): 42–45.

Cutting, M. "The Use of Spatial Analysis to Study Prehistoric Settlement Architecture." Oxford Journal of Archaeology 22 (2003): 1–21.

D'Altroy, T. N. The Incas. Peoples of America Series. Oxford, UK: Blackwell, 2002.

D'Andrea, A. C., et al. "Late Jomon Cultigens in Northeastern Japan." Antiquity 69 (1995): 146–52.

D'Andrea, D. E., et al. "Ethnoarchaeological Approaches to the Study of Prehistoric Agriculture in the Ethiopian Highlands". In The Exploitation of Plant Resources in Ancient Africa, edited by M. Van der Veen, 101–22. New York: Plenum, 1999.

d'Errico, F. "New Model and Its Implications for the Origin of Writing: The La Marche Antler Revisited." Cambridge Archaeological Journal 5.2 (1995): 163–206.

d'Errico, F., et al. "Archaeological Evidence for the Emergence of Language, Symbolism, and Music: An Alternative Multidisciplinary Perspective." Journal of World Prehistory 17 (2003): 1–70.

d'Errico, F., and A. Nowell. "A New Look at the Berekhat Ram Figurine: Implications for the Origins of Symbolism." Cambridge Archaeological Journal 10.1 (2000): 123–67.

d'Errico, F., P. Villa, et al. "A Middle Palaeolithic Origin of Music? Using Cave-Bear Bone Accumulation to Assess the Divje Babe I Bone Flute." Antiquity 72 (1998): 65–80.

d'Errico, F., J. Zilhao, et al. "Neanderthal Acculturation in Western Europe?" Supplement, Current Anthropology 39 (1998): S1–43.

Dalan, R. A. Envisioning Cahokia: A Landscape Perspective. DeKalb, IL: Northern Illinois University Press, 2003.

Dancey, W. S., and P. J. Pacheco, eds. Ohio Hopewell Community Organization. Kent, OH: Kent State University Press, 1997.

Dart, R. A. "The Predatory Transition from Ape to Man." International Anthropological Linguistics Review 1.4 (1953): 201–18.

Darwin, C. On the Origin of Species. London: John Murray, 1859.

David, B., et al. "New Optical and Radiocarbon Dates from Ngarrabullgan Cave, a Pleistocene Archaeological Site in Australia: Implications for the Comparability of Time Clocks and for the Human Colonization of Australia." Antiquity 71.271 (1997): 183–88.

David, N., and C. Kramer. Ethnoarchaeology in Action. Cambridge World Archaeology Series. Cambridge, UK: Cambridge University Press, 2001.

Davis, H. A. "Archaeologists Looked to the Future in the Past." In Archaeology and Cultural Resource Management: Visions for the Future, edited by L. Sebastian and W. D. Lipe, 19–40. Santa Fe, NM: School for Advanced Research, 2009.

Davis, S. J. M. The Archaeology of Animals. New Haven, CT: Yale University Press, 1987.

Day, M. H. Guide to Fossil Man, 4th ed. Chicago: University of Chicago Press, 1986.

Dayan, T. "Early Domesticated Dogs of the near East." Journal of Archaeological Science 21 (1994): 633–40.

De Heinzelin, J., et al. "Environment and Behavior of 2.5-Million-Year-Old Bouri Hominids." Science 284 (1999): 625–29.

De Lumley, H., et al. "Les Industries Lithiques Préoldowayennes du Debut du Pleistocene Inferieur du Site de Dmanissi en Georgie." L'Anthropologie 109.1 (2005): 1–182.

Deacon, H. J., and J. Deacon. Human Beginnings in South Africa: Uncovering the Secrets of the Stone Age. Walnut Creek, CA: AltaMira Press, 1999.

Deacon, T. W. The Symbolic Species: The Co-Evolution of Language and the Brain. New York: W. W. Norton, 1997.

Debaine-Francfort, C. The Search for Ancient China. London: Thames and Hudson, 1999.

Deetz, J. J. F. In Small Things Forgotten: The Archaeology of Early American Life. Garden City, NY: Anchor Press/Doubleday, 1996.

Defleur, A., et al. "Neanderthal Cannibalism at Moula-Guercy, Ardèche, France." Science 286 (1999): 128–31.

Demarest, A. A. Ancient Maya: The Rise and Fall of a Rainforest Civilisation. Case Studies in Early Societies, 3. Cambridge, UK: Cambridge University Press, 2004.

deMenocal, P. "Cultural Responses to Climate Change during the Late Holocene." Science 292 (2001): 667–73.

Denham, T. "Archaeological Evidence for Mid-Holocene Agriculture in the Interior of Papua New Guinea: A Critical Review." Archaeology of Oceania 38 (2003): 159–76.

Denham, T., and C. Ballard. "Jack Golsen and the Investigation of Prehistoric Agriculture in Highland New Guinea: Recent Work and Future Prospects." Archaeology of Oceania 38 (2003): 129–34.

Denham, T. P., et al. "Origins of Agriculture at Kuk Swamp in the Highlands of New Guinea." Science 301 (2003): 189–93.

Desmond, A. J., and J. R. Moore. Darwin. New York: Warner Books, 1992.

Desmond, A. J., and J. R. Moore. Darwin's Sacred Cause: How a Hatred of Slavery Shaped Darwin's Views on Human Evolution. Boston, MA: Houghton Mifflin Harcourt, 2009.

Devries, T. J., et al. "Determining the Early History of El Niño." Science 276 (1997): 965–67.

Dhillon, N. P. S., and K. Ishiki. "Genomic Variation and Genetic Relationships in *Ipomoea* spp." *Plant Breeding* 118 (1999): 161–65.

Di Lernia, S. "Cultural Control over Wild Animals during the Early Holocene: The Case of Barbary Sheep in Central Sahara." In *Before Food Production in North Africa*, edited by S. di Lernia and G. Manzi, 113–26. Forli, Italy: A.B.A.C.O. Edizioni, 1998.

Di Lernia, S., and G. Manzi, eds. *Before Food Production in North Africa*. Forli, Italy: A.B.A.C.O. Edizioni, 1998.

Diamond, J. *Collapse: How Societies Choose to Fail or Succeed.* New York: Viking, 2005.

Diaz el Calillo, B. *Memoirs, of the Conquistador Bernal Diaz del Castillo Written by Himself Containing a True and Full Account of the Discovery and Conquest of Mexico and New Spain.* London (1568 [1844]): J. Hatchard.

Dibble, H. "The Interpretation of Middle Paleolithic Scraper Morphology." *American Antiquity* 52 (1987): 109–17.

Dillehay, Tom D. *Monte Verde: A Late Pleistocene Settlement in Chile.* Washington, DC: Smithsonian Institution Press, 1989.

Dillehay, T. D. *The Settlement of the Americas: A New Prehistory.* New York: Basic Books, 2000.

Dincauze, D. F. *Environmental Archaeology: Principles and Practices.* Cambridge, UK: Cambridge University Press, 2000.

Dirks, P. H. G. M., et al. "Geological and Taphonomic Context for the New Hominin Species Homo Naledi from the Dinaledi Chamber, South Africa." *eLife* 4 (2015): e09561.

Dixon, E. J. *Bones, Boats, and Bison: Archaeology and the First Colonization of Western North America.* Albuquerque, NM: University of New Mexico Press, 1999.

Dixon, E. J. "Human Colonization of the Americas: Timing, Technology and Process." *Quaternary Science Reviews* 20 (2001): 277–99.

Dobres, M.-A. *Technology and Social Agency: Outlining a Practice Framework for Archaeology.* Oxford, UK: Blackwell, 2000.

Dobres, M.-A., and J. E. Robb. *Agency in Archaeology.* London: Routledge, 2000.

Dolukhanov, P., et al. "The Chronology of Neolithic Dispersal in Central and Eastern Europe." *Journal of Archaeological Science* 32 (2005): 1441–58.

Dominguez-Rodrigo, M. "Hunting and Scavenging by Early Humans: The State of the Debate." *Journal of World Prehistory* 16.1 (2002): 1–54.

Dominguez-Rodrigo, M., et al. "Woodworking Activities by Early Humans: A Plant Residue Analysis on Acheulian Stone Tools from Peninj (Tanzania)." *Journal of Human Evolution* 40 (2001): 289–99.

Dominguez-Rodrigo, M., R. B. Egido, and C. P. Egeland. *Deconstructing Olduvai.* Dordrecht, The Netherlands: Springer, 2007.

Douglas, P. M. J., et al. "Drought, Agricultural Adaptation, and Sociopolitical Collapse in the Maya Lowlands." *Proceedings of the National Academy of Sciences* 112.18 (2015): 5607–12.

Driessen, J., and C. F. Macdonald. *The Troubled Island: Minoan Crete before and after the Santorini Eruption.* Liege: Universite de Liege, 1997.

Duarte, C., et al. "The Early Upper Paleolithic Human Skeleton from the Abrigo do Lagar Velho (Portugal) and Modern Human Emergence in Iberia." *Proceedings of the National Academy of Sciences* 96 (1999): 7604–9.

Duller, G. A. T. "Dating Methods: The Role of Geochronology in Studies of Human Evolution and Migration in Southeast Asia and Australasia." *Progress in Physical Geography* 25.2 (2001): 267–76.

Edwards, P. "Wadi Hammeh 27: An Early Natufian Site at Pella, Jordan." In *The Natufian Culture in the Levant*, edited by O. Bar-Yosef and F. Valla, 123–48. Ann Arbor, MI: International Monographs in Prehistory, 1991.

Edwards, W. "In Pursuit of Himiko. Postwar Archaeology and the Location of Yamatai." *Monumenta Nipponica* 51 (1996): 53–79.

Ekserdjian, D. *Bronze.* London: Royal Academy of Arts, 2012.

Elton, S., L. C. Bishop, and B. Wood. "Comparative Context of Plio-Pleistocene Hominin Brain Evolution." *Journal of Human Evolution* 41 (2000): 1–27.

Enloe, J. G. "Food Sharing in the Paleolithic: Carcass Refitting at Pincevent." In *Piecing Together the Past: Applications of Refitting Studies in Archaeology*, edited by J.L. Hofman and J.G. Enloe, 296–315. BAR International Series, vol. 578. Oxford, UK: British Archaeological Reports, 1992.

Enloe, J. G. "Food Sharing Past and Present: Archaeological Evidence for Economic and Social Interactions." *Before Farming* 1 (2003): 1–23.

Erickson, D. L. "An Asian Origin for a 10,000-Year-Old Domesticated Plant in the Americas." *Proceedings of the National Academy of Sciences* 102 (2005): 18315–20.

Estalrrich, A., and A. Rosas. "Handedness in Neandertals from the El Sidrón (Asturias, Spain): Evidence from Instrumental Striations with Ontogenetic Inferences." *PloS one* 8.5 (2013): e62797.

Eubanks, M. "An Interdisciplinary Perspective on the Origin of Maize." *Latin American Antiquity* 12.1 (2001): 91–98.

Evans, D. H. "Airborne Laser Scanning as a Method for Exploring Long-Term Socio-Ecological Dynamics in Cambodia." *Journal of Archaeological Science* 74 (2016): 164–75.

Evans, D. H., et al. "Uncovering Archaeological Landscapes at Angkor Using LIDAR." *Proceedings of the National Academy of Sciences* 110.31 (2013): 12595–600.

Evans, J. G., and T. P. O'Connor. *Environmental Archaeology: Principles and Methods*, 2nd ed. Stroud, UK: Sutton, 2005.

Eyre-Walker, A., et al. "Investigation of the Bottleneck Leading to the Domestication of Maize." *Proceedings of the National Academy of Sciences* 95 (1998): 4441–46.

Fagan, B. M. *Eyewitness to Discovery: First-Person Accounts of More than Fifty of the World's Greatest Archaeological Discoveries.* Oxford, UK: Oxford University Press, 1996.

Fajardo, D. S., D. R. La Bonte, and R. L. Jarret. "Identifying and Selecting for Genetic Diversity in Papua New Guinea Sweet Potato *Ipomoea batatas* (L.) Lam. Germplasm Collected as Botanical Seed." *Genetic Resources and Crop Evolution* 49 (2002): 463–70.

Fash, W. L. *Scribes, Warriors, and Kings: The City of Copán and the Ancient Maya.* New Aspects of Antiquity Series. London: Thames and Hudson, 1991.

Faupl, P., W. Richter, and C. Urbanek. "Dating of the Herto Hominin Fossils." *Nature* 426 (2003): 621–22.

Ferring, R., et al. "Earliest Human Occupations at Dmanisi (Georgian Caucasus) Dated to 1.85–1.78 Ma." *Proceedings of the National Academy of Sciences* 108 (2011): 10432–36.

Fforde, C., J. Hubert, and P. Turnbull, eds. *The Dead and Their Possessions: Repatriation in Principle, Policy, and Practice.* One World Archaeology, vol. 43. London: Routledge, 2002.

Fiedel, S. "Artifact Provenience at Monte Verde: Confusion and Contradictions." *Scientific American Discovery Archaeology* 1.6 (1999): 1–14.

Fiedel, S., and G. Haynes. "A Premature Burial: Comments on Grayson and Meltzer's 'Requiem for Overkill.'" *Journal of Archaeological Science* 31 (2004): 121–31.

Field, J., et al. "Archaeology and Australian Megafauna." *Science* 294 (2001): 696–702.

Field, J., Richard Fullagar, and Garry Lord. "A Large Area Archaeological Excavation at Cuddie Springs." *Antiquity* 75.290 (2001): 696–702.

Finney, B. "Myth, Experiment, and the Reinvention of Polynesian Voyaging." *American Anthropologist* 93 (1991): 383–404.

Firestone, R. B., et al. "Evidence for an Extraterrestrial Impact 12,900 Years Ago that Contributed to the Megafaunal Extinctions and the Younger Dryas Cooling." *Proceedings of the National Academy of Sciences* 104 (2007): 16016–21.

Fitton, J. L. *Minoans.* London: British Museum Press, 2002.

Fladmark, K. R. "Routes: Alternate Migration Corridors for Early Man in North America." *American Antiquity* 44.1 (1979): 55–69.

Flannery, K. "Culture History v. Culture Process: A Debate in American Archaeology." *Scientific American* 217 (1967): 119–22.

Flannery, K. "The Origins of Agriculture." *Annual Review of Anthropology* 2 (1973): 271–310.

Flannery, K., ed. *Guila Naquitz: Archaic Foraging and Early Agriculture in Oaxaca, Mexico.* New York: Academic Press, 1986.

Flecker, M. "A Ninth-Century A.D. Arab or Indian Shipwreck in Indonesia: First Evidence for Direct Trade with China." *World Archaeology* 32 (2001): 335–54.

Flecker, M. *The Archaeological Excavation of the 10th Century Intan Shipwreck.* BAR International Series, vol. 1047. Oxford, UK: Archaeopress, 2002.

Flenley, J., and P. G. Bahn. *The Enigmas of Easter Island: Island on the Edge,* 2nd ed. Oxford, UK: Oxford University Press, 2003.

Ford, R. I. "Corn Is Our Mother." In *Corn and Culture in the Prehistoric New World,* edited by S. Johannessen and C. A. Hastorf, 513–26. Boulder, CO: Westview Press, 1994.

Formicola, V., and A. Buzhilova. "Double Child Burial from Sunghir (Russia): Pathology and Inferences for Upper Paleolithic Funerary Practices." *American Journal of Physical Anthropology* 124.3 (2004): 189–98.

Frayer, D. W., and M. D. Russell. "Artificial Grooves on the Krapina Neanderthal Teeth." *American Journal of Physical Anthropology* 74.3 (1987): 393–405.

Freedman, A. H., et al. "Genome Sequencing Highlights the Dynamic Early History of Dogs." *PLoS Genet* 10.1 (2014): e1004016.

French, E. B. *Mycenae: Agamemnon's Capital.* Stroud, UK: Tempus, 2002.

Fried, M. H. *The Evolution of Political Society: An Essay in Political Anthropology.* New York: Random House, 1967.

Frison, G. C. "Paleoindian Large Mammal Hunters on the Plains of North America." *Proceedings of the National Academy of Sciences* 95 (1998): 14576–83.

Frison, G. C. *Survival by Hunting: Prehistoric Human Predators and Animal Prey.* Berkeley, CA: University of California Press, 2004.

Frison, G. C., R. L. Andrews, J. M. Avovasio, R. C. Carlisle, and R. Edgar. "A Late Paleoindian Animal Trapping Net from Northern Wyoming." *American Antiquity* 51 (1986): 352–61.

Fritz, G. J. "Gender and the Early Cultivation of Gourds in Eastern North America." *American Antiquity* 64.3 (1999): 417–29.

Fu, Q., et al. "Complete Mitochondrial Genomes Reveal Neolithic Expansion into Europe." *PLoS One* 7.3 (2012): e32473.

Fu, Q., Pavao Rudan, Svante Pääbo, and Johannes Krause. "Complete Mitochondrial Genomes Reveal Neolithic Expansion into Europe." *PLoS One* 7.3 (2012): e32473.

Galaty, M. L., and William A. Parkinson. *Rethinking Mycenaean Palaces II.* Los Angeles, CA: Cotsen Institute of Archaeology at UCLA, 2007.

Gamble, C. *Timewalkers: The Prehistory of Global Colonization.* Stroud, UK: Sutton, 1993.

Gargett, R. "Grave Shortcomings: The Evidence for Neanderthal Burial." *Current Anthropology* 30.2 (1989): 157–90.

Garlake, P. S. *Great Zimbabwe.* London: Thames and Hudson, 1973.

Gaudzinski, S. "On Bovid Assemblages and Their Consequences for the Knowledge of Subsistence Patterns in the Middle Palaeolithic." *Proceedings of the Prehistoric Society* 62 (1996): 19–39.

Ge, Y., and K. Linduff. "Sanxingdui: A New Bronze Age Site in Southwest China." *Antiquity* 64 (1990): 505–13.

Gebel, H. G., et al. "Ba'ja Hidden in the Petra Mountains: Preliminary Results of the 1997 Investigations." In *The Prehistory of Jordan II: Perspectives from 1997,* edited by H. G. Gebel, Z. Kafafi, and G. O. Rollefson, 221–62. Berlin: Ex Oriente, 1997.

Geller, P. L. "Bodyscapes, Biology, and Heteronormativity." *American Anthropologist* 111.4 (2009): 504–16.

Geneste, J.-M., and H. Plisson. "Hunting Technologies and Human Behavior: Lithic Analysis of Solutrean Shouldered Points." In *Before Lascaux: The Complex Record of the Early Upper Paleolithic,* edited by H. Knecht, A. Pike-Tay, and R. White, 117–35. Boca Raton, FL: CRC Press, 1993.

Gero, J. M., and M. W. Conkey. *Engendering Archaeology: Women and Prehistory.* Social Archaeology Series. Oxford, UK: Blackwell, 1991.

Gibbons, A. "Ancient Island Tools Suggest *Homo erectus* Was a Seafarer." *Science* 279 (1998): 1635–37.

Gibson, J. L. *The Ancient Mounds of Poverty Point: Place of Rings.* Gainesville, FL: University of Florida Press, 2000.

Gichuki, S. T., et al. "Genetic Diversity in Sweet Potato (*Ipomoea batatas*)." *Genetic Resources and Crop Evolution* 50 (2003): 429–37.

Gifford-Gonzalez, D. "Early Pastoralists in East Africa: Ecological and Social Dimensions." *Journal of Anthropological Archaeology* 17 (1998): 166–200.

Glazko, G. V., and M. Nei. "Estimation of Divergence Times for Major Lineages of Primate Species." *Molecular Biological Evolution* 20.3 (2003): 424–34.

Goebel, T., M. R. Waters, and M. Dikova. "The Archaeology of Ushki Lake, Kamchatka, and the Pleistocene Peopling of the Americas." *Science* 301 (2003): 501–5.

Goldberg, P., et al. "Site Formation Processes at Zhoukoudian, China." *Journal of Human Evolution* 41.5 (2001): 483–530.

Goldberg, P., and R. Macphail. *Practical and Theoretical Geoarchaeology.* Malden, MA: Blackwell, 2006.

Golsen, J., and D. S. Gardner. "Agriculture and Sociopolitical Organization in New Guinea Highlands Prehistory." *Annual Review of Anthropology* 19 (1990): 395–417.

González-Ruibal, A. "Time to Destroy: An Archaeology of Supermodernity." *Current Anthropology* 49 (2008): 247–79.

Good, I. L., J. M. Kenoyer, and R. H. Meadow. "New Evidence for Early Silk in the Indus Civilization." *Archaeometry* 51 (2009): 457–66.

Goodall, J. *The Chimpanzees of Gombe: Patterns of Behavior.* Cambridge, MA: Harvard University Press, 1986.

Gordon, A. L., C. F. Giulivi, and A. G. Ilahude. "Deep Topographic Barriers within the Indonesian Seas." *Deep-Sea Research Part II* 50 (2003): 2205–28.

Goren, Y., et al. *Inscribed in Clay: Provenance Study of the Amarna Tablets and Other Ancient Near Eastern Texts.* Tel Aviv: Emery and Claire Yass Publications in Archaeology, 2004.

Goren, Y., A. N. Goring-Morris, and I. Segal. "The Technology of Skull Modelling in the Pre-Pottery Neolithic B (PPNB): Regional Variability, the Relation of Technology and Iconography and Their Archaeological Implications." *Journal of Archaeological Science* 28 (2001): 671–90.

Goren-Inbar, N., et al. "Pleistocene Milestones on the Out-of-Africa Corridor at Gesher Benot Ya'aqov, Israel." *Science* 289 (2000): 944–47.

Goring-Morris, A. N., and A. Belfer-Cohen. "The Articulation of Cultural Processes and Late Quaternary Environmental Changes in Cisjordan." *Paleorient* 23.2 (1998): 71–93.

Gould, S. J. "On Replacing the Idea of Progress with an Operational Notion of Directionality." In *Evolutionary Progress?* edited by M. H. Nitecki, 319–38. Chicago: University of Chicago Press, 1988.

Gould, S. J., and R. C. Lewontin. "The Spandrels of San Marco and the Panglossian Paradigm: A Critique of the Adaptationist Programme." *Proceedings of the Royal Society of London B* 205 (1979): 581–98.

Gowlett, J., et al. "Early Archaeological Sites, Hominid Remains and Traces of Fire from Chesowanja, Kenya." *Nature* 294 (1981): 125–29.

Granger, D. E., and P. F. Muzikar. "Dating Sediment Burial with In-Situ-Produced Cosmogenic Nuclides: Theory, Techniques, and Limitations." *Earth and Planetary Science Letters* 188 (2001): 269–81.

Grayson, D. K. *The Establishment of Human Antiquity*. New York: Academic Press, 1983.

Grayson, D. K., and D. J. Meltzer. "Clovis Hunting and Large Mammal Extinction: A Critical Review of the Evidence." *Journal of World Prehistory* 16.4 (2002): 313–59.

Grayson, D. K., and D. J. Meltzer. "North American Overkill Continued?" *Journal of Archaeological Science* 31 (2004): 133–36.

Green, E. L. *Ethics and Values in Archaeology*. New York: Free Press, 1984.

Green, R., et al. "Analysis of One Million Base Pairs of Neanderthal DNA." *Nature* 440 (2006): 330–36.

Green, R., et al. "A Complete Neanderthal Mitochondrial Genome Sequence Determined by High-Throughput Sequencing." *Cell* 134 (2008): 416–26.

Gremillion, K. J. "Early Agricultural Diet in Eastern North America: Evidence from Two Kentucky Rockshelters." *American Antiquity* 61.3 (1996): 520–36.

Gremillion, K. J. "Eastern Woodlands Overview." In *People and Plants in Ancient Eastern North America*, edited by P. E. Minnis, 17–50. Washington, DC: Smithsonian Books, 2003.

Griffin, J. B. "Eastern North American Archaeology: A Summary." *Science* 156 (1967): 175–91.

Groube, L., et al. "A 40,000 Year-Old Human Occupation Site at Huon Peninsula, Papua New Guinea." *Nature* 324 (1986): 453–55.

Guidon, N., et al. "Nature and Age of the Deposits in Pedra Furada, Brazil: Reply to Meltzer, Adovasio & Dillehay." *Antiquity* 70 (1996): 408–21.

Guilaine, J. *Premiers Paysans du Monde: Naissances des Agricultures*. Collection des Hespérides. Paris: Errance, 2000.

Guthrie, R. D. "Rapid Body Size Decline in Alaskan Pleistocene Horses Before Extinction." *Nature* 426 (2003): 169–71.

Gutierrez, M., et al. "Exploitation d'un Grand Cétacé au Paléolithique Ancien: Le Site de Dungo V a Baia Farta (Benguela, Angola)." *Comptes Rendus de l'Academie des Sciences: Earth and Planetary Sciences* 332 (2001): 357–62.

Haaland, R. "Sedentism, Cultivation, and Plant Domestication in the Holocene Middle Nile Region." *Journal of Field Archaeology* 22 (1995): 157–74.

Haberle, S. G. "The Emergence of an Agricultural Landscape in the Highlands of New Guinea." *Archaeology of Oceania* 38 (2003): 149–58.

Halligan, J. J., et al. "Pre-Clovis Occupation 14,550 Years Ago at the Page-Ladson Site, Florida, and the Peopling of the Americas." *Science Advances* 2.5 (2016): e1600375.

Hallo, W. W., and W. K. Simpson. *The Ancient Near East: A History*. New York: Harcourt Brace Jovanovich, 1971.

Hard, R., and J. R. Roney. "A Massive Terraced Village Complex in Chihuahua, Mexico, 3,000 Years Before Present." *Science* 279 (1998): 1661–64.

Hard, R., and J. R. Roney. "The Transition to Farming on the Rio Casas Grandes and in the Southern Jornada Mogollon Region." In *The Late Archaic: Across the Borderlands*, edited by B. J. Vierra, 141–86. Austin, TX: University of Texas, 2005.

Hardy, D. A. *Thera and the Aegean World III: Proceedings of the Third International Congress, Santorini, Greece*. London: Thera Foundation, 1990.

Hardy, K., et al. "Neanderthal Medics? Evidence for Food, Cooking, and Medicinal Plants Entrapped in Dental Calculus." *Naturwissenschaften* 99.8 (2012): 617–26.

Harlan, J. R. "The Tropical African Cereals." In *The Archaeology of Africa: Food, Metals, and Towns*, edited by T. Shaw, 53–59. London: Routledge, 1993.

Harlan, J. R. *The Living Fields: Our Agricultural Heritage*. Cambridge: Cambridge University Press, 1995.

Harmand, S., et al. "3.3-Million-Year-Old Stone Tools from Lomekwi 3, West Turkana, Kenya." *Nature* 521.7552 (2015): 310–15.

Harris, D. R., ed. *The Archaeology of V. Gordon Childe: Contemporary Perspectives*. London: UCL Press, 1994.

Harris, E. C. *Principles of Archaeological Stratigraphy*. London: Academic Press, 1989.

Harrison, P. D. *The Lords of Tikal: Rulers of an Ancient Maya City*. New Aspects of Antiquity Series. London: Thames and Hudson, 1999.

Hassan, F. "The Aswan High Dam and the International Rescue Nubia Campaign." *African Archaeological Review* 24 (2007): 73–94.

Hastorf, C. A. "The Cultural Life of Early Domestic Plant Use." *Antiquity* 72 (1998): 773–888.

Hastorf, C. A. "Recent Research in Paleoethnobotany." *Journal of Archaeological Research* 7.1 (1999): 55–103.

Hastorf, C. A., and V. Popper, eds. *Current Paleoethnobotany: Analytical Methods and Cultural Interpretations of Archaeological Plant Remains*. Chicago: University of Chicago Press, 1988.

Haug, G. H., et al. "Climate and the Collapse of Maya Civilization." *Science* 299 (2003): 1731.

Hawass, Z., et al. "Ancestry and Pathology in King Tutankhamun's Family." *Journal of the American Medical Association* 303.7 (2010): 638–47.

Hayashida, F. "Archaeology, Ecological History, and Conservation." *Annual Review of Anthropology* 34 (2005): 43–65.

Hayden, B. "Nimrods, Piscators, Pluckers, and Planters: The Emergence of Food Production." *Journal of Anthropological Archaeology* 9 (1990): 31–69.

Haynes, C. V. "Younger Dryas 'Black Mats' and the Rancholabrean Termination in North America." *Proceedings of the National Academy of Sciences* 105 (2008): 6520–25.

Haynes, C. V., et al. "A Clovis Well at the Type Site 11,500 B.C.: The Oldest Prehistoric Well in America." *Geoarchaeology: An International Journal* 14.5 (1999): 455–70.

Haynes, C. V., R. E. Reanier, and W. P. Barse. "Dating a Paleoindian Site in the Amazon in Comparison with Clovis Culture." *Science* 275 (1997): 1948–52.

Haynes, G. *The Early Settlement of North America: The Clovis Era*. Cambridge, UK: Cambridge University Press, 2002.

Headrick, A. *The Teotihuacán Trinity: The Sociopolitical Structure of an Ancient Mesoamerican City*. Austin, TX: University of Texas Press, 2007.

Heckenberger, M., and E. G. Neves. "Amazonian Archaeology." *Annual Review of Anthropology* 38 (2009): 251–66.

Hedges, S. B. "A Start for Population Genomics." *Nature* 408 (2000): 652–53.

Hegmon, M., and S. Kulow. "Painting as Agency, Style as Structure: Innovations in Mimbres Pottery Designs from Southwest New Mexico." *Journal of Archaeological Method and Theory* 12 (2005): 313–34.

Heizer, R. F. *Man's Discovery of His Past; Literary Landmarks in Archaeology.* Englewood Cliffs, NJ: Prentice-Hall, 1962.

Hendon, J. A., and R. A. Joyce. *Mesoamerican Archaeology: Theory and Practice.* Blackwell Studies in Global Archaeology, vol. 1. Malden, MA: Blackwell, 2004.

Henshilwood, C. S., F. d'Errico, and I. Watts. "Engraved Ochres from the Middle Stone Age Levels at Blombos Cave, South Africa." *Journal of Human Evolution* 57.1 (2009): 27–47.

Henshilwood, C. S., et al. "Emergence of Modern Human Behavior: Middle Stone Age Engravings from South Africa." *Science* 295 (2002): 1278–80.

Henshilwood, C. S., et al. "A 100,000-Year-Old Ochre-Processing Workshop at Blombos Cave, South Africa." *Science* 334 (2011): 219–22.

Henshilwood, C. S., et al. "Klipdrift Shelter, Southern Cape, South Africa: Preliminary Report on the Howiesons Poort Layers." *Journal of Archaeological Science* 45 (2014): 284–303.

Henshilwood, C. S., and J. Sealy. "Bone Artifacts from the Middle Stone Age at Blombos Cave, Southern Cape, South Africa." *Current Anthropology* 38 (1997): 890–95.

Hide, R. *Pig Husbandry in New Guinea: A Literature Review and Bibliography.* Canberra, Australia: Australian Centre for International Agriculture Research, 2003.

Higgs, E. S., ed. *Papers in Economic Prehistory.* Cambridge, UK: Cambridge University Press, 1972.

Higham, C. *Early Cultures of Mainland Southeast Asia.* Chicago: Arts Media, 2002.

Higham, C., and T. L.-D. Lu. "The Origins and Dispersal of Rice Cultivation." *Antiquity* 72.278 (1998): 867–77.

Higham, T., C. B. Ramsey, and C. Owen, eds. *Radiocarbon and Archaeology.* Oxford, UK: Oxford University School of Archaeology, 2004.

Higham, T., et al. "The Timing and Spatiotemporal Patterning of Neanderthal Disappearance." *Nature* 512.7514 (2014): 306–9.

Hill, J. "Broken K Pueblo: Patterns of Form and Function." In *New Perspectives in Archaeology*, edited by S. Binford and L. Binford, 103–42. Chicago: Aldine, 1968.

Hirth, K. "The Distributional Approach: A New Way to Identify Marketplace Exchange in the Archaeological Record." *Current Anthropology* 39 (1998): 451–76.

Hodder, I. *Reading the Past.* Cambridge, UK: Cambridge University Press, 1986.

Hodder, I. *The Domestication of Europe: Structure and Contingency in Neolithic Societies.* Social Archaeology Series. Oxford, UK: Blackwell, 1990.

Hodder, I. *The Archaeological Process: An Introduction.* Oxford, UK: Blackwell, 1999.

Hodder, R. P., and I. Hodder, eds. *Contemporary Archaeology in Theory.* Oxford, UK: Blackwell, 1996.

Holl, A. F. C. "The Dawn of African Pastoralisms: An Introductory Note." *Journal of Anthropological Archaeology* 17.2 (1998a): 81–96.

Holl, A. F. C. "Livestock Husbandry, Pastoralisms, and Territoriality: The West African Record." *Journal of Anthropological Archaeology* 17.2 (1998b): 143–65.

Hooton, E. A. *Apes, Men, and Morons.* New York: Putnam, 1937.

Hörz, G., and M. Kallfass. "The Treasure of Gold and Silver Artifacts from the Royal Tombs of Sipan, Peru: A Study on the Moche Metalworking Techniques." *Materials Characterization* 45 (2000): 391–420.

Hosler, D. "Sound, Color, and Meaning in the Metallurgy of Ancient West Mexico." *World Archaeology* 27.1 (1995): 100–15.

Houston, S. D. "Into the Minds of Ancients: Advances in Maya Glyph Studies." *Journal of World Prehistory* 14.2 (2000): 121–201.

Houston, S. D., and T. Inomata. *The Classic Maya.* Cambridge, UK: Cambridge University Press, 2009.

Houston, S., and K. Taube. "An Archaeology of the Senses: Perception and Cultural Expression in Ancient Mesoamerica." *Cambridge Archaeological Journal* 10.2 (2000): 261–94.

Hovers, E., W. H. Kimbel, and Y. Rak. "The Amud 7 Skeleton—Still a Burial. Response to Gargett." *Journal of Human Evolution* 39 (2000): 253–60.

Howard, E. B. "An Outline of the Problem of Man's Antiquity in North America." *American Anthropologist* 38 (1936): 394–413.

Hublin, J. J., et al. "The Mousterian Site of Zafarraya (Andalucía, Spain): Dating and Implications on the Paleolithic Peopling Processes of Western Europe." *Comptes Rendus de l'Académie des Sciences*, Serie IIa 321.10 (1995): 931–37.

Huckell, B. B., and J. D. Kilby, eds. *Readings in Late Pleistocene North America and Early Paleoindians: Selections from American Antiquity.* Washington, DC: Society for American Archaeology, 2004.

Hudson, B. "Restoration and Reconstruction of Monuments at Bagan (Pagan), Myanmar (Burma), 1995–2008." *World Archaeology* 40 (2008): 553–71.

Huffman, O. F. "Geologic Context and Age of the Perning/Mojokerto *Homo erectus*, East Java." *Journal of Human Evolution* 40 (2001): 353–62.

Huffman, T. "Mapungubwe and Great Zimbabwe: The Origin and Spread of Social Complexity in Southern Africa." *Journal of Anthropological Archaeology* 28 (2009): 37–54.

Humle, T., and T. Matsuzawa. "Ant-Dipping among the Chimpanzees of Bossou, Guinea, and Some Comparisons with Other Sites." *American Journal of Primatology* 58 (2002): 133–48.

Hunt, G.n R. "Manufacture and Use of Hook-Tools by New Caledonian Crows." *Nature* 379.6562 (1996): 249–51.

Hunt, G. R., and R. D. Gray. "Diversification and Cumulative Evolution in New Caledonian Crow Tool Manufacture." *The Royal Society* 270 (2003): 867–74.

Hunter, J., and I. Ralston. *The Archaeology of Britain: An Introduction from the Upper Palaeolithic to the Industrial Revolution.* London: Routledge, 1999.

Hyodo, M., et al. "Paleomagnetic Dates of Hominid Remains from Yuanmou, China, and Other Asian Sites." *Journal of Human Evolution* 43 (2002): 27–41.

Hyslop, J. *The Inka Road System.* Studies in Archaeology Series. Orlando, FL: Academic Press, 1984.

Hyslop, J., and American Council of Learned Societies. *Inka Settlement Planning.* Austin, TX: University of Texas Press, 1990.

Imamura, K. *Prehistoric Japan: New Perspectives on Insular East Asia.* Honolulu, HI: University of Hawaii Press, 1996.

Ingman, M., et al. "Mitochondrial Genome Variation and the Origin of Modern Humans." *Nature* 408 (2000): 708–13.

Ingold, T. *Hunters, Pastoralists, and Ranchers: Reindeer Economics and Their Transformations.* Cambridge, UK: Cambridge University Press, 1980.

Ingold, T. *The Perception of the Environment: Essays on Livelihood, Dwelling and Skill.* London: Routledge, 2000.

Inomata, T. "Early Ceremonial Constructions at Ceibal, Guatemala, and the Origins of Lowland Maya Civilization." *Science* 340.6131 (2013): 467–71.

Inomata, T., et al. "Development of Sedentary Communities in the Maya Lowlands: Coexisting Mobile Groups and Public Ceremonies at Ceibal, Guatemala." *Proceedings of the National Academy of Sciences* 112.14 (2015): 4268–73.

Inomata, T., and L. R. Stiver. "Floor Assemblages from Burned Structures at Aguateca, Guatemala: A Study of Classic Maya Households." *Journal of Field Archaeology* 25.4 (1998): 431–52.

Isaac, B. "Implementation of NAGPRA: The Peabody Museum of Archaeology and Ethnology, Harvard." In *The Dead and Their Possessions: Repatriation in Principle, Policy, and Practice*, edited by C. Fforde, J. Hubert, and P. Turnbull, 160–70. London: Routledge, 2002.

Isaac, G. L. "The Foodsharing Behavior of Protohuman Hominids." *Scientific American* 238 (1978): 90–108.

Jablonski, D. "Extinction: Past and Present." *Nature* 427 (2004): 589.

Janes, R. R. *Archaeological Ethnography among Mackenzie Basin Dene, Canada*. Calgary, AB: Arctic Institute of North America, University of Calgary, 1983.

Jansen, M. "Water Supply and Sewage Disposal at Mohenjo-Daro." *World Archaeology* 21.2 (1989): 177–92.

Jantz, R. L., and D. W. Owsley. "Variation among Early North American Crania." *American Journal of Physical Anthropology* 114 (2001): 146–55.

Jarrige, J. F. *Les Cités Oubliées de L'indus*. Paris: Musée National des Arts Asiatiques Guimet, 1989.

Jaubert, J., et al. "Early Neanderthal Constructions Deep in Bruniquel Cave in Southwestern France." *Nature* 534.7605 (2016): 111–14.

Jin, G. Y. "An Important Military City of the Early Western Zhou Dynasty: Archaeobotanical Evidence from the Chenzhuang Site, Gaoqing, Shandong Province." *Chinese Science Bulletin* 57 (2012): 253–60.

Jing, Y., and R. Flad. "New Zooarchaeological Evidence for Changes in Shang Dynasty Animal Sacrifice." *Journal of Anthropological Archaeology* 24 (2005): 252–70.

Jing, Z., G. Rapp, Jr., and T. Gao. "Geoarchaeological Aids in the Investigation of Early Shang Civilization on the Floodplain of the Lower Yellow River, China." *World Archaeology* 29 (1997): 36–50.

Jones, R., and J. Allen. *Archaeological Research in Kakadu National Park*. Canberra, Australia: Australian National Parks and Wildlife Service, 1985.

Jones, R. A. "Centaurs on the Silk Road: Recent Discoveries of Hellenistic Textiles in Western China." *The Silk Route* 6 (2009): 23–32.

Joordens, J., et al. "*Homo erectus* at Trinil on Java Used Shells for Tool Production and Engraving." *Nature* 518.7538 (2015): 228–31.

Joyce, R. A. "Academic Freedom, Stewardship and Cultural Heritage: Weighing the Interests of Stakeholders in Crafting Repatriation Approaches." In *The Dead and Their Possessions: Repatriation in Principle, Policy, and Practice*, edited by C. Fforde, J. Hubert, and P. Turnbull, 99–107. London: Routledge, 2002.

Joyce, R., and J. Lopiparo. "PostScript: Doing Agency in Archaeology." *Journal of Archaeological Method and Theory* 12 (2005): 365–74.

Juzhong, Z., and W. Xiangkun. "Notes on the Recent Discovery of Ancient Cultivated Rice at Jiahu, Henan Province: A New Theory Concerning the Origin of *Oryza japonica* in China." *Antiquity* 72 (1998): 897–901.

Kaessmann, H., and S. Paabo. "The Genetical History of Humans and the Great Apes." *Journal of Internal Medicine* 251 (2002): 1–18.

Kansa, E. "Openness and Archaeology's Information Ecosystem." *World Archaeology* 44.4 (2012): 498–520.

Kaplan, L., and T. F. Lynch. "Phaseolus (Fabaceae) in Archaeology: AMS Radiocarbon Dates and Their Significance for Pre-Columbian Agriculture." *Economic Botany* 53.3 (1999): 261–72.

Kappelman, J. "The Evolution of Body Mass and Relative Brain Size in Fossil Hominids." *Journal of Human Evolution* 30 (1996): 243–76.

Karkanas, P., et al. "Evidence for Habitual Use of Fire at the End of the Lower Paleolithic: Site-Formation Processes at Qesem Cave, Israel." *Journal of Human Evolution* 53 (2007): 197–212.

Katzenberg, A. M., et al. "Stable Isotope Evidence for Maize Horticulture and Paleodiet in Southern Ontario." *American Antiquity* 60 (1995): 335–50.

Keatinge, R. W., ed. *Peruvian Prehistory*. Cambridge, UK: Cambridge University Press, 1988.

Keefer, D. K., et al. "Early Maritime Economy and El Niño Events at Quebrada Tacahuay, Peru." *Science* 281 (1998): 1833–35.

Keeley, L. "Technique and Methodology in Microwear Studies: A Critical Review." *World Archaeology* 5 (2001): 323–36.

Keightley, D. N. "Sacred Characters." In *China: Ancient Culture, Modern Land*, edited by R. E. Murowchick, 70–79. Norman, OK: Oklahoma University Press, 1994.

Keightley, D. N. *The Ancestral Landscape: Time, Space, and Community in Late Shang China, ca. 1200–1045 B.C.* Berkeley, CA: University of California Center for Chinese Studies, 2000.

Keller, A., et al. "New Insights into the Tyrolean Iceman's Origin and Phenotype as Inferred by Whole-Genome Sequencing." *Nature Communications* 3 (2012): Article 698.

Kelly, R. "The Three Sides of a Biface." *American Antiquity* 53 (1988): 717–34.

Kembel, S. R., 2008. The Architecture at the Monumental Center of Chavín de Huántar: Sequence, Transformations, and Chronology. In *Chavín: Art, Architecture, and Culture*, edited by W. J. Conklin and J. Quilter, 35–84. Los Angeles, CA: Cotsen Institute.

Kemp, B. J. *Ancient Egypt: Anatomy of a Civilization*, 2nd ed. London: Routledge, 2006.

Kenoyer, J. M. *Ancient Cities of the Indus Valley Civilization*. Karachi, Pakistan: Oxford University Press and American Institute of Pakistan Studies, 1998.

Kenyon, K. *Excavations at Jericho*. Vol. 3, The Architecture and Stratigraphy of the Tell. London: British School of Archaeology in Jerusalem, 1981.

Kidder, A. V., and S. J. Guernsey. *Archeological Explorations in Northeastern Arizona*. Washington, DC: Government Printing Office, 1919.

Kidder, J. E. *Himiko and Japan's Elusive Chiefdom of Yamatai*. Honolulu: University of Hawaii Press, 2007.

Killen, J. T. "Critique: A View from the Tablets." In *Rethinking Mycenaean Palaces II*, edited by M. Galaty and W. Parkinson. Los Angeles, CA: Cotsen Institute, 2007.

Kimbel, W. H., et al. "Late Pliocene *Homo* and Oldowan Tools from Hadar Formation (Kada Hadar Member), Ethiopia." *Journal of Human Evolution* 289 (1996): 550–61.

Kinahan, J. "The Rise and Fall of Nomadic Pastoralism in the Central Namib Desert." In *The Archaeology of Africa: Food, Metals, and Towns*, edited by T. Shaw, 373–85. London: Routledge, 1993.

King, M. L., and S. B. Slobodin. "A Fluted Point from the Uptar Site, Northeastern Siberia." *Science* 273 (1996): 634–36.

Kirch, P. *The Lapita Peoples: Ancestors of the Oceanic World*. Oxford, UK: Blackwell, 1997.

Kirch, P. *On the Road of the Winds: An Archaeological History of the Pacific Islands before European Contact*. Berkeley, CA: University of California Press, 2000.

Kislev, M., A. Hartmann, and O. Bar-Yosef. "Early Domesticated Fig in the Jordan Valley." *Science* 312 (2006): 1372–74.

Kistler, L., et al. "Transoceanic Drift and the Domestication of African Bottle Gourds in the Americas." *Proceedings of the National Academy of Sciences* 111.8 (2014): 2937–41.

Kittler, R., M. Kayser, and M. Stoneking. "Molecular Evolution of *Pediculus humanus* and the Origin of Clothing." *Current Biology* 13 (2003): 1414–17.

Klein, R. G., and Blake Edgar. *The Dawn of Human Culture*. New York: Wiley, 2002.

Klein, R. G. "Whither the Neanderthals?" *Science* 299 (2003): 1525–26.

Knecht, H., A. Pike-Tay, and Randall Keith White. *Before Lascaux: The Complex Record of the Early Upper Paleolithic*. Boca Raton, FL: CRC Press, 1993.

Kobayashi, Y. "Treatise on Duplicate Mirrors." (Introduced and interpreted by W. Edwards. In *"Capital and Countryside" in Japan, 300–1180: Japanese Historians Interpreted in English*, edited by J.R. Piggott, 54–76. Ithaca, NY: Cornell University Press, 2006.

Kolata, A. L. *The Tiwanaku: Portrait of an Andean Civilization*. Cambridge, MA: Blackwell, 1993.

Kolata, A. L. *Tiwanaku and Its Hinterland: Archaeology and Paleoecology of an Andean Civilization*. Smithsonian Series in Archaeological Inquiry. Washington, DC: Smithsonian Institution Press, 1996.

Kraft, K. H., et al. "Multiple Lines of Evidence for the Origin of Domesticated Chili Pepper, *Capsicum annuum*, in Mexico." *Proceedings of the National Academy of Sciences* 111.17 (2014): 6165–70.

Kramer, C. *Village Ethnoarchaeology: Rural Iran in Archaeological Perspective*. New York: Academic Press, 1982.

Krings, M., et al. "DNA Sequence of the Mitochrondrial Hyper-Variable Region II from the Neanderthal Type Specimen." *Proceedings of the National Academy of Sciences* 96 (1999): 5581–85.

Laland, K. N., and M. J. O'Brien. "Niche Construction Theory and Archaeology." *Journal of Archaeological Method and Theory* 17.4 (2010): 303–22.

Lambers, K., et al. "Combining Photogrammetry and Laser Scanning for the Recording and Modelling of the Late Intermediate Period Site of Pinchango Alto, Palpa, Peru." *Journal of Archaeological Science* 34 (2007): 1702–12.

Lang, C., et al. "Gazelle Behaviour and Human Presence at Early Neolithic Göbekli Tepe, South-East Anatolia." *World Archaeology* 45.3 (2013): 410–29.

Langbroek, M., and W. Roebroeks. "Extraterrestrial Evidence on the Age of the Hominids from Java." *Journal of Human Evolution* 38 (2000): 595–600.

Langergraber, K. E., et al. "Generation Times in Wild Chimpanzees and Gorillas Suggest Earlier Divergence Times in Great Ape and Human Evolution." *Proceedings of the National Academy of Sciences* 109.39 (2012): 15716–21.

Larsen, C. S. "The Changing Face of Bioarchaeology: An Interdisciplinary Science." In *Bioarchaeology: The Contextual Analysis of Human Remains*, edited by J. Buikstra and L. Beck, 359–74. Amsterdam: Academic Press, 2006.

Larson, E. J. *Summer for the Gods: The Scopes Trial and America's Continuing Debate over Science and Religion*. New York: Basic Books, 1997.

Lauck, R. G. "La Venta: An Olmec Capital." In *Olmec Art of Ancient Mexico*, edited by E. P. Benson and B. de la Fuente, 73–82. Washington, DC: National Gallery of Art, 1996.

Lavallée, D. *The First South Americans: The Peopling of a Continent from the Earliest Evidence to High Culture*. Salt Lake City, UT: University of Utah Press, 2000.

Laville, H., J. P. Rigaud, and James Sackett. *Rock Shelters of the Perigord: Geological Stratigraphy and Archaeological Succession*. Studies in Archaeology Series. New York: Academic Press, 1980.

Leakey, M. D. *Olduvai Gorge. Vol. 3, Excavations in Beds I and II, 1960–1963*. Cambridge, UK: Cambridge University Press, 1971.

Leakey, M. D., et al. "New Four Million Year Old Hominid Species from Kanpoi and Allia Bay, Kenya." *Nature* 393 (1995): 62–66.

Leakey, M. D., and John Michael Harris, eds. *Laetoli, a Pliocene Site in Northern Tanzania*. Oxford, UK: Clarendon Press and Oxford University Press, 1987.

Leakey, M. G., et al. "New Hominid Genus from Eastern Africa Shows Diverse Middle Pliocene Lineages." *Nature* 410 (2001): 433–40.

Leakey, R. E., and A. Walker. *The Nariokotome Homo erectus Skeleton*. Cambridge, MA: Harvard University Press, 1993.

Lebot, V. "Biomolecular Evidence for Plant Domestication in Sahul." *Genetic Resources and Crop Evolution* 46 (1999): 619–28.

Lechtman, H., A. Erliz, and E. Barry. "New Perspectives on Moche Metallurgy: Techniques of Gilding Copper at Loma Negra, Northern Peru." *American Antiquity* 47 (1982): 3–30.

Lee, R. B. *The Dobe Ju/'Hoansi*, 3rd ed. Case Studies in Cultural Anthropology. South Melbourne, Australia: Wadsworth Thomson Learning, 2003.

Lee, Y. K. "Control Strategies and Polity Competition in the Lower Yi-Luo Valley, North China." *Journal of Anthropological Archaeology* 23 (2004): 172–195.

Lehner, M. *The Complete Pyramids*. New York: Thames and Hudson, 1997.

Lentz, D. L., et al. "Forests, Fields, and the Edge of Sustainability at the Ancient Maya City of Tikal." *Proceedings of the National Academy of Sciences* 111.52 (2014): 18513–18.

Leone, M., P. Potter, and P. Shackel. "Toward a Critical Archaeology." *Current Anthropology* 28.3 (1987): 283–302.

Lepper, B. T., and R. W. Yerkes. "Hopewellian Occupations at the Northern Periphery of the Newark Earthworks: The Newark Expressway Sites Revisited." In *Ohio Hopewell Community Organization*, edited by W. S. Dancey and P. J. Pacheco, 175–206. Kent, OH: Ohio University Press, 1997.

Leroi-Gourhan, A. *Pincevent: Campement Magdalénien de Chasseurs de Rennes*. Guides Archéologiques de la France, 3. Paris: Ministère de la Culture, Direction du Patrimoine, 1984.

Leroi-Gourhan, A. "The Flowers Found with Shanidar IV, a Neanderthal Burial in Iraq." *Science* 190.4214 (1975): 562–64.

Levison, M., Ward, R. G., and Webb, J. W. *The Settlement of Polynesia: A Computer Simulation*. Minneapolis, MN: University of Minnesota Press, 1973.

Lewontin, R. C. *Human Diversity*. New York: Scientific American Library, 1982.

Li, C., et al. "Evidence That a West-East Admixed Population Lived in the Tarim Basin as Early as the Early Bronze Age." *BMC Biology* 8 (2010): 15.

Li, X., et al. "The Earliest Writing? Sign Use in the Seventh Millennium B.C. at Jiahu, Henan Province, China." *Antiquity* 77.295 (2002): 31–44.

Lieberman, D. E. "Another Face in Our Family Tree." *Nature* 410 (2001): 419–20.

Lieberman, L., and F. L. C. Jackson. "Race and Three Models of Human Origin." *American Anthropologist* 97 (1995): 231–42.

Lillios, K. "Objects of Memory: The Ethnography and Archaeology of Heirlooms." *Journal of Archaeological Method and Theory* 6.2 (1999): 235–62.

Linares, O. "African Rice (*Oryza glaberrima*): History and Future Potential." *Proceedings of the National Academy of Sciences* 99.25 (2002): 16360–65.

Linduff, K., R. Drennan, and G. Shelach. "Early Complex Societies in NE China: The Chifeng International Collaborative Archaeological Research Project." *Journal of Field Archaeology* 29 (2004): 45–73.

Linseele, V., et al. "New Archaeozoological Data from the Fayum 'Neolithic' with a Critical Assessment of the Evidence for Early Stock Keeping in Egypt." *PloS one* 9.10 (2014): e108517.

Lipe, W. D., et al. "Cultural and Genetic Contexts for Early Turkey Domestication in the Northern Southwest." *American Antiquity* 81.1 (2016): 97–113.

Liu, J., et al. "Identification of Ancient Textiles from Yingpan, Xinjiang, by Multiple Analytical Techniques." *Journal of Archaeological Science* 38 (2011): 1763–70.

Liu, L., and X. Chen. *State Formation in Early China*. London: Duckworth, 2003.

Liu, L., et al. "Settlement Patterns and Development of Social Complexity in the Yiluo Region, North China." *Journal of Field Archaeology* 29 (2004): 75–100.

Liu, L., et al. "Evidence for the Early Beginning (c. 9000 cal. BP) of Rice Domestication in China: A Response." *The Holocene* 17.8 (2007): 1059–68.

Llamas, B., et al. "Ancient Mitochondrial DNA Provides High-Resolution Time Scale of the Peopling of the Americas." *Science Advances* 2.4 (2016): e1501385.

Lloyd, S. *The Archaeology of Mesopotamia: From the Old Stone Age to the Persian Conquest.* London: Thames and Hudson, 1978.

Londo, J., et al. "Phylogeography of Asian Wild Rice, *Oryza rufipogen*, Reveals Multiple Independent Domestications of Cultivated Rice, *Oryza sativa.*" *Proceedings of the National Academy of Sciences* 103.25 (2006): 9578–83.

Lordkipanidze, D., et al. "The Earliest Toothless Hominin Skull." *Nature* 434 (2005): 717–18.

Lordkipanidze, D., et al. "A Complete Skull From Dmanisi, Georgia, and the Evolutionary Biology of Early Homo." *Science* 342.6156 (2013): 326–31.

Loring Brace, C., et al. "Old World Sources of the First New World Human Inhabitants: A Comparative Craniofacial View." *Proceedings of the National Academy of Sciences* 98.17 (2001): 10017–22.

Lourandos, H. *Continent of Hunter-Gatherers: New Perspectives in Australian Prehistory.* Cambridge, UK: Cambridge University Press, 1997.

Lu, H., et al. "Earliest Domestication of Common Millet (*Panicum miliaceum*) in East Asia Extended to 10,000 Years Ago." *Proceedings of the National Academy of Sciences* 106 (2009): 7367–72.

Lu, T. L. D. "Some Botanical Characteristics of Green Foxtail (*Setaria viridis*) and Harvesting Experiments on the Grass." *Antiquity* 72.278 (1998): 902–7.

Lu, T. L. D. *The Transition from Foraging to Farming and the Origin of Agriculture in China.* BAR International Series, vol. 774. Oxford, UK: British Archaeological Reports, 1999.

Lucquin, A., et al. "Ancient Lipids Document Continuity in the Use of Early Hunter-Gatherer Pottery through 9,000 Years of Japanese Prehistory." *Proceedings of the National Academy of Sciences* (2016): 201522908.

Lynch, T. F., ed. *Guitarrero Cave: Early Man in the Andes.* New York: Academic Press, 1980.

Maag, C. "Ohio Indian Mounds: Hallowed Ground and a Nice Par 3." *New York Times*, 2005.

Mabry, J. B. "Changing Knowledge About the First Farmers in Southeastern Arizona." In *The Late Archaic: Across the Borderlands*, edited by B. J. Vierra, 41–83. Austin, TX: University of Texas Press, 2005.

MacGillivray, J. A. *Minotaur: Sir Arthur Evans and the Archaeology of the Minoan Myth.* New York: Hill and Wang, 2000.

Mack, M. E., and M. L. Blakey. "The New York African Burial Ground Project: Past Biases, Current Dilemmas, and Future Research Opportunities." *Historical Archaeology* 38.1 (2004): 10–17.

Mackay, A. and Welz, A. "Engraved ochre from a Middle Stone Age context at Klein Kliphuis in the Western Cape of South Africa." *Journal of Archaeological Science* 35, (2008): 1521–32.

Magid, A. A., and I. Caneva. "Economic Strategy Based on Food-Plants in the Early Holocene Central Sudan: A Reconsideration." In *Before Food Production in North Africa*, edited by S. di Lernia and G. Manzi, 79–90. Forli, Italy: A.B.A.C.O. Edizioni, 1998.

Mallory, J. P., and V. Mair. *The Tarim Mummies.* New York: Thames and Hudson, 2000.

Mandryk, C. A. S., et al. "Late Quaternary Paleoenvironments of Northwestern North America: Implications for Inland Versus Coastal Migration Routes." *Quaternary Science Reviews* 20 (2001): 301–14.

Mann, J., et al. "Social Networks Reveal Cultural Behavior in Tool-Using Dolphins." *Nature Communications* 3 (2012): Art 980.

Manning, S. W., et al. "Chronology for the Aegean Late Bronze Age 1700–1400 B.C." *Science* 312 (2006): 565–69.

Marean, C., et al. "Early Human Use of Marine Resources and Pigment in South Africa during the Middle Pleistocene." *Nature* 449 (2007): 905–8.

Marshack, A. "Upper Paleolithic Notation and Symbol." *Science* 178 (1972): 817–28.

Marshall, F., and E. Hildebrand. "Cattle Before Crops: The Beginnings of Food Production in Africa." *Journal of World Prehistory* 16.2 (2002): 99–143.

Marshall, J. "A New Chapter in Archaeology: The Prehistoric Civilisation of the Indus." *Illustrated London News*, January 7, 1928.

Marshall, Y. *Community Archaeology.* London: Routledge, 2002.

Martin, R. D., et al. "Comment on 'The Brain of Lb1, *Homo floresiensis.*'" *Science* 312 (2006): 999.

Martin, S. "In Line of the Founder: A View of Dynastic Politics at Tikal." In *Tikal: Dynasties, Foreigners, and Affairs of State*, edited by J. Sabloff. Santa Fe, NM: SAR Press, 2003.

Mathieu, J. *Experimental Archaeology: Replicating Past Objects, Behaviors, and Processes.* Oxford, UK: Archaeopress, 2002.

Matos Moctezuma, E. *The Great Temple of the Aztecs: Treasures of Tenochtitlán.* New Aspects of Antiquity Series. London: Thames and Hudson, 1988.

Matos Moctezuma, E. "Aztec History and Cosmovision." In *Moctezuma's Mexico: Visions of the Aztec World*, edited by D. Carrasco and E. M. Moctezuma, 3–99. Boulder, CO: University of Colorado, 1992.

Matos Moctezuma, E., and M. Zabé. *Treasures of the Great Temple*, English language ed. La Jolla, CA: ALTI Publishing, 1990.

Matson, R. G. "The Spread of Maize Agriculture in the U.S. Southwest." In *Examining the Farming/Language Dispersal Hypothesis*, edited by P. Bellwood and C. Renfrew, 341–56. McDonald Institute Monographs. Cambridge, UK: McDonald Institute for Archaeological Research, 2003.

Matsuoka, Y., et al. "A Single Domestication for Maize Shown by Multilocus Microsatellite Genotyping." *Proceedings of the National Academy of Sciences* 99.9 (2002): 6080–84.

Matthews, R. *The Archaeology of Mesopotamia: Theories and Approaches.* Approaching the Ancient World Series. London: Routledge, 2003.

Mazza, P. P. A., et al. "A New Palaeolithic Discovery: Tar-Hafted Stone Tools in a European Mid-Pleistocene Bone-Bearing Bed." *Journal of Archaeological Science* 33.9 (2006): 1310–18.

McBrearty, S., and A. Brooks. "The Revolution that Wasn't: A New Interpretation of the Origin of Modern Human Behavior." *Journal of Human Evolution* 39.5 (2000): 453–563.

McCauley, J. F., et al. "Subsurface Valleys and Geoarchaeology of the Eastern Sahara." *Science* 218 (1982): 1004–20.

McDonald, M. M. A. "Early African Pastoralism: View from Dakhleh Oasis (South Central Egypt)." *Journal of Anthropological Archaeology* 17 (1998): 124–42.

McElhinny, M. W., and P. McFadden. *Paleomagnetism: Continents and Oceans.* International Geophysics Series, vol. 73: New York: Academic Press, 2000.

McGovern, P. "Fermented Beverages of Pre- and Proto-Historic China." *Proceedings of the National Academy of Sciences* 101 (2004): 17593–98.

McGovern, P., et al. "The Archaeological Origin and Significance of the Dolphin Vase as Determined by Neutron Activation Analysis." *Bulletin of the American Schools of Oriental Research* 296 (1994): 31–43.

McGuire, B. *The Archaeology of Geological Catastrophes.* London: Geological Society, 2000.

McGuire, R. H. *Archaeology as Political Action.* Berkeley, CA: University of California Press, 2008.

McGuire, R. H., and P. Reckner. "Building a Working Class Archaeology: The Colorado Coal Field War Project." In *Industrial Archaeology: Future Directions,* edited by E.C. Casella, 217–41. New York: Springer, 2005.

McIntosh, R. J. *The Peoples of the Middle Niger: The Island of Gold.* Peoples of Africa Series. Malden, MA: Blackwell, 1998.

McIntosh, S., and R. J. McIntosh. "Cities without Citadels: Understanding Urban Origins along the Middle Niger." In *The Archaeology of Africa: Food, Metals, and Towns,* edited by T. Shaw, 622–41. London: Routledge, 1993.

Mackay, A., and A. Welz. "Engraved ochre from a Middle Stone Age context at Klein Kliphuis in the Western Cape of South Africa." *Journal of Archaeological Science* 35.6 (2008): 1521–32.

McKeown, F. P. "Implementing a 'True Compromise': The Native American Graves Protection and Repatriation Act after Ten Years." In *The Dead and Their Possessions: Repatriation in Principle, Policy, and Practice,* edited by C. Fforde, J. Hubert, and P. Turnbull, 108–32. London: Routledge, 2002.

McNeil, C. L., et al. "Evidence Disputing Deforestation as the Cause for the Collapse of the Ancient Maya Polity of Copan, Honduras." *Proceedings of the National Academy of Sciences* 107 (2010): 1017–22.

Mellaart, J. *Çatal Hüyük: A Neolithic Town in Anatolia.* London: Thames and Hudson, 1967.

Mellars, P. *The Neanderthal Legacy: An Archaeological Perspective from Western Europe.* Princeton, NJ: Princeton University Press, 1996.

Mellars, P., and C. Stringer. *The Human Revolution: Behavioural and Biological Perspectives on the Origins of Modern Humans.* Princeton, NJ: Princeton University Press, 1989.

Meltzer, D. J. *First Peoples in a New World: Colonizing Ice Age America.* Berkeley, CA: University of California Press, 2009.

Meltzer, D. J., J.M. Adovasio, and T. D. Dillehay. "On a Pleistocene Human Occupation at Pedra Furada, Brazil." *Antiquity* 68 (1994): 695–714.

Meltzer, D. J., et al. "On the Pleistocene Antiquity of Monte Verde, Southern Chile." *American Antiquity* 62.4 (1997): 659–63.

Mercader, J., M. Panger, and C. Boesch. "Excavation of a Chimpanzee Stone Tool Site in the African Rainforest." *Science* 296 (2002): 1452–55.

Meskell, L., and P. Pels. *Embedding Ethics.* Oxford, UK: Berg, 2005.

Metcalf, M. "Construction and Labor at Pueblo Bonito: Center of the Chacoan World." In *Pueblo Bonito: Center of the Chacoan World,* edited by J. E. Neitzel. Washington, DC: Smithsonian Institution Press, 2003.

Meyer, C., et al. "The Massacre Mass Grave of Schöneck-Kilianstädten Reveals New Insights into Collective Violence in Early Neolithic Central Europe." *Proceedings of the National Academy of Sciences* 112.36 (2015): 11217–22.

Michab, M., et al. "Luminescence Dates for the Paleoindian Site of Pedra Pintada, Brazil." *Quaternary Geochronology* 17 (1998): 1041–46.

Miles, J., et al. "New Applications of Photogrammetry and Reflectance Transformation Imaging to an Easter Island Statue." *Antiquity* 88.340 (2014): 596–605.

Millaire, J. F. "Primary State Formation in the Virú Valley, North Coast of Peru." *Proceedings of the National Academy of Sciences* 107 (2010): 6186–91.

Miller, D. S., V. T. Holliday, and J. Bright. "Clovis across the Continent." In *Paleoamerican Odyssey,* edited by K. E. Graf, C.V. Ketron, and M. R. Waters, 207–20. Texas A&M University Press, 2014.

Miller, G. H., et al. "Pleistocene Extinction of *Genyornis newtoni:* Human Impact on Australian Megafauna." *Science* 283 (1999): 205–8.

Millon, R. "Teotihuacán: Completion of Map of Giant Ancient City in the Valley of Mexico." *Science* 170 (1970): 1077–82.

Millon, R., R. Drewitt, and G. Cowgill. *Urbanization at Teotihuacán, Mexico.* Austin, TX: University of Texas Press, 1973.

Milner, G. R. *The Cahokia Chiefdom: The Archaeology of a Mississippian Society.* Smithsonian Series in Archaeological Inquiry. Washington, DC: Smithsonian Institution Press, 1998.

Milo, R. G. "Evidence for Hominid Predation at Klasies River Mouth, South Africa, and Its Implications for the Behaviour of Early Modern Humans." *Journal of Archaeological Science* 25 (1998): 99–133.

Minnegal, M., and P. D. Dwyer. "Intensification and Social Complexity in the Interior Lowlands of Papua New Guinea: A Comparison of Bedamuni and Kubo." *Journal of Anthropological Archaeology* 17 (1998): 375–400.

Minnis, P. E., ed. *People and Plants in Ancient Eastern North America.* Washington, DC: Smithsonian Books, 2003.

Miracle, P. "Through the Clovis Barrier." *Antiquity* 73 (1999): 944–47.

Mitchell, P. "Practicing Archaeology at a Time of Climatic Catastrophe." *Antiquity* 82 (2008): 1093–103.

Mithen, S. "Technology and Society during the Middle Pleistocene: Hominid Group Size, Social Learning, and Industrial Variability." *Cambridge Archaeological Journal* 4.1 (1994): 3–32.

Mocella, V., et al. "Revealing Letters in Rolled *Herculaneum* papyri by X-ray Phase-Contrast Imaging." *Nature Communications* 6 (2015): 1–6.

Molloy, B. *The Cutting Edge: Studies in Ancient and Medieval Combat.* Stroud, UK: Tempus, 2007.

Molloy, B. "Martial Arts and Materiality: A Combat Archaeology Perspective on Aegean Swords of the Fifteenth and Fourteenth Centuries B.C." *World Archaeology* 40 (2008): 116–34.

Montgomery, J. *Tikal: An Illustrated History: The Ancient Maya Capital.* New York: Hippocrene Books, 2001.

Moore, A. M. T., G. C. Hillman, and A. J. Legge. *Village on the Euphrates: From Foraging to Farming at Abu Hureyra.* Oxford, UK: Oxford University Press, 2000.

Moore, M. W., et al. "Continuities in Stone Flaking Technology at Liang Bua, Flores, Indonesia." *Journal of Human Evolution* 57 (2009): 503–26.

Morgan, L. H. *Ancient Society: Or, Researches in the Lines of Human Progress from Savagery, through Barbarism to Civilization.* Chicago: C.H. Kerr, 1877.

Morlan, R. E. "Current Perspectives on the Pleistocene Archaeology of Eastern Beringia." *Quaternary Research* 60 (2003): 123–32.

Morris, C., and D. E. Thompson. *Huánuco Pampa: An Inca City and Its Hinterland.* London: Thames and Hudson, 1985.

Morris, C., and A. Von Hagen. *The Inka Empire and Its Andean Origins.* New York: Abbeville, 1993.

Mortensen, L. "Working Borders: The Contexts of Copan Archaeology." *Archaeologies: Journal of the World Archaeological Congress* 3 (2007): 132–52.

Morwood, M., et al. "Archaeology and Age of a New Hominin from Flores in Eastern Indonesia." *Nature* 431 (2004): 1087–91.

Moser, S., et al. "Transforming Archaeology through Practice: Strategies for Collaborative Archaeology and the Community Archaeology Project at Quseir." *World Archaeology* 34 (2002): 220–48.

Mrozowski, S. A. "Cultural Identity and the Consumption of Industry." In *Industrial Archaeology: Future Directions*, edited by E.C. Casella, 243–60. New York: Springer, 2005.

Muke, J., and H. Mandui. "In the Shadows of Kuk: Evidence for Prehistoric Agriculture at Kana, Wahgi Valley, Papua New Guinea." *Archaeology of Oceania* 38 (2003): 177–85.

Murowchick, R. E. *China: Ancient Culture, Modern Land.* Cradles of Civilization Series. North Sydney, Australia: Weldon Russell, 1994.

Murray, T. *Archaeology of Aboriginal Australia: A Reader.* St. Leonards, Australia: Allen & Unwin, 1998.

Muzzolini, A. "The Emergence of a Food-Producing Economy in the Sahara." In *The Archaeology of Africa: Food, Metals, and Towns*, edited by T. Shaw, 227–39. London: Routledge, 1993.

Nadel, D., ed. *Ohalo Ii-II: A 23,000 Year-Old Fisher-Hunter-Gatherers' Camp on the Shore of the Sea of Galilee.* Haifa, Israel: Hecht Museum, 2002.

Naveh, D. "PPNA Jericho: A Socio-Political Perspective." *Cambridge Archaeological Journal* 13.1 (2003): 83–96.

Neitzel, J. E. *Pueblo Bonito: Center of the Chacoan World.* Washington, DC: Smithsonian Institution Press, 2003.

Nelson, D. E., et al. "New Dates on Northern Yukon Artifacts: Holocene Not Upper Pleistocene." *Science* 232 (1986): 749–50.

Nelson, S. M. "Feasting the Ancestors in Early China." In *The Archaeology and Politics of Food and Feasting in Early States and Empires*, edited by T.L. Bray, 65–89. New York: Kluwer, 2003.

Nerlich, A. G., et al. "Ötzi Had a Wound on His Right Hand." *The Lancet* 362 (2003): 334.

Nettle, D. "Linguistic Diversity of the Americas Can Be Reconciled with a Recent Colonization." *Proceedings of the National Academy of Sciences* 96 (1999): 3325–29.

Neumann, K. "New Guinea: A Cradle of Agriculture." *Science* 301 (2003): 180–81.

Neumann, T. W., R. M. Sanford, and K. G. Harry. *Cultural Resources Archaeology: An Introduction*, 2nd ed. Lanham, MD: AltaMira, 2010.

Nichols, D. L. "Rural and Urban Landscapes of the Aztec State." In *Mesoamerican Archaeology: Theory and Practice*, edited by R. A. Joyce and J. A. Hendon, 265–95. Oxford, UK: Blackwell, 2004.

Nichols, D. L., and T. H. Charlton. *The Archaeology of City-States: Cross-Cultural Approaches.* Smithsonian Series in Archaeological Inquiry. Washington, DC: Smithsonian Institution Press, 1997.

Nichols, D. L., et al. "Neutrons, Markets, Cities, and Empires: A 1,000-Year Perspective on Ceramic Production and Distribution in the Postclassic Basin of Mexico." *Journal of Anthropological Archaeology* 21 (2002): 25–82.

Niles, S. A. "The Nature of Inca Royal Estates." In *Machu Picchu: Unveiling the Mystery of the Incas*, edited by R. L. Burger and L. C. Salazar. New Haven, CT: Yale University Press, 2004.

Nissen, H. "Uruk: Key Site of the Period and Key Site of the Problem." In *Artefacts of Complexity: Tracking the Uruk in the near East*, edited by J.N. Postgate, 1–17. London: British School of Archaeology in Iraq, 2002.

Nitecki, M. H. *Evolutionary Progress.* Chicago: University of Chicago Press, 1988.

Noonan, J. P., et al. "Sequencing and Analysis of Neanderthal Genomic DNA." *Science* 314 (2006): 1113–18.

Nora, P. *Realms of Memory: Rethinking the French Past.* New York: Columbia University Press, 1996–1998.

O'Brien, M., and R. L. Lyman. "Evolutionary Archeology: Current Status and Future Prospects." *Evolutionary Anthropology* 11 (2002): 26–36.

O'Connell, J., and J. Allen. "When Did Humans First Arrive in Greater Australia and Why Is It Important to Know?" *Evolutionary Anthropology* 6.4 (1998): 132–46.

O'Connor, D. *Abydos: Egypt's First Pharaohs and the Cult of Osiris.* New York: Thames and Hudson, 2009.

O'Sullivan, P. B., et al. "Archaeological Implications of the Geology and Chronology of the Soa Basin, Flores, Indonesia." *Geology* 29.7 (2001): 607–10.

Odell, G. "Stone Tool Research at the End of the Millennium: Classification, Function, and Behavior." *Journal of Archaeological Research* 9.1 (2001): 45–100.

Opitz, R., and W. F. Limp. "Recent Developments in High-Density Survey and Measurement (HDSM) for Archaeology: Implications for Practice and Theory." *Annual Review of Anthropology* 44 (2015): 347–64.

Oppenheim, A. L., and E. Reiner. *Ancient Mesopotamia: Portrait of a Dead Civilization*, rev. ed. Chicago: University of Chicago Press, 1977.

Orser, C. E. *A Historical Archaeology of the Modern World.* New York: Plenum, 1996.

Orser, C. E. *Historical Archaeology.* Upper Saddle River, NJ: Prentice Hall, 2004.

Ovchinnikov, I. V., et al. "Molecular Analysis of Neanderthal DNA from the Northern Caucasus." *Nature* 404 (2000): 490–93.

Owsley, D. W., and R. L. Jantz. "Archaeological Politics and Public Interest in Paleoamerican Studies: Lessons from Gordon Creek Woman and Kennewick Man." *American Antiquity* 66.4 (2001): 565–75.

Panagiotaki, M. "Contacts between Knossos and the Pediada Region in Central Crete." In *Knossos: Palace, City, State*, edited by E. Cadogan, E. Hatzaki, and A. Vasilakis, 177–86. London: British School at Athens, 2004.

Panger, M. A., et al. "Older than the Oldowan? Rethinking the Emergence of Hominin Tool Use." *Evolutionary Anthropology* 11 (2002): 235–45.

Parker Pearson, M., et al. "The Age of Stonehenge." *Antiquity* 81 (2007): 617–39.

Parker Pearson, M., et al. "Who Was Buried at Stonehenge?" *Antiquity* 83 (2009): 23–29.

Parker Pearson, M., et al. "Craig Rhos-y-felin: A Welsh Bluestone Megalith Quarry for Stonehenge." *Antiquity* 89.348 (2015): 1331–52.

Parker Pearson, M., et al. "The Stonehenge Riverside Project Summary Interim Report 2005." Available at www.shef.ac.uk/content/1/c6/02/21/27/PDF-Interim-Report-2005-summary.pdf.

Parker Pearson, M., and Ramilisonina. "Stonehenge for the Ancestors: The Stones Pass on the Message." *Antiquity* 72 (1998): 308–26.

Parkington, J., D. Morris, and N. Rusch. *Karoo Rock Engravings*. Cape Town, South Africa: Creda, 2008.

Partridge, T. C., et al. "Lower Pliocene Hominid Remains from Sterkfontein." *Science* 300 (2003): 607–12.

Pasquinucci, M., F. Trément, and POPULUS Project. *Non-Destructive Techniques Applied to Landscape Archaeology*. Archaeology of Mediterranean Landscapes, vol. 4. Oxford, UK: Oxbow Books, 2000.

Pauketat, T. R. "Resettled Farmers and the Making of a Mississippian Polity." *American Antiquity* 68.1 (2003): 39–66.

Pauketat, T. R. *Ancient Cahokia and the Mississippians*. Case Studies in Early Societies, vol. 6. Cambridge, UK: Cambridge University Press, 2004.

Pauketat, T. R., et al. "The Residues of Feasting and Public Ritual at Early Cahokia." *American Antiquity* 67.2 (2002): 257–79.

Pavlov, P., J. I. Svendsen, and S. Indrelid. "Human Presence in the European Arctic Nearly 40,000 Years Ago." *Nature* 413 (2001): 64–67.

Pearson, R. "Social Complexity in Chinese: Coastal Neolithic Sites." *Science* 213 (1981): 1078–86.

Pearson, R., and A. Underhill. "The Chinese Neolithic: Recent Trends in Research." *American Anthropologist* 89 (1987): 807–22.

Pei, A. "Notes on New Advancements and Revelations in the Agricultural Archaeology of Early Rice Domestication in the Dongting Lake Region." *Antiquity* 72 (1998): 878–85.

Peretto, C. "The First Peopling of Southern Europe: The Italian Case." *Comptes Rendus Palevol* 5.1–2 (2006): 283–90.

Perlés, C. *The Early Neolithic in Greece: The First Farming Communities in Europe*. Cambridge World Archaeology Series. Cambridge, UK: Cambridge University Press, 2001.

Perry, L. "Starch Granule Size and the Domestication of Manioc (*Manihot esculenta*) and Sweet Potato (*Ipomoea batatas*)." *Economic Botany* 56.4 (2001): 335–49.

Phillipson, D. W. "The Antiquity of Cultivation and Herding in Ethiopia." In *The Archaeology of Africa: Food, Metals, and Towns*, edited by T. Shaw, 344–57. London: Routledge, 1993.

Pigeot, N. *Magdaléniens d'Étiolles: Économie de Débitage et Organisation Sociale (l'Unité d'Habitation U5)*. Paris: Editions du Centre National de la Recherche Scientifique, 1987.

Pikirayi, I. *The Zimbabwe Culture: Origins and Decline in Southern Zambezian States*. Walnut Creek, CA: AltaMira Press, 2001.

Pineda, R. F. "The Late Preceramic and Initial Period." In *Peruvian Prehistory*, edited by R. W. Keatinge, 67–98. Cambridge, UK: Cambridge University Press, 1988.

Pinter, N., and S. Ishman. "Impacts, Mega-Tsunami, and Other Extraordinary Claims." *GSA Today* 18 (2008): 37–38.

Piperno, D. R., and K. V. Flannery. "The Earliest Archaeological Maize (*Zea mays* L.) from Highland Mexico: New Accelerator Mass Spectrometry Dates and Their Implications." *Proceedings of the National Academy of Sciences* 98.4 (2001): 2101–3.

Pitulko, V. V., et al. "The Yana RHS Site: Humans in the Arctic Before the Last Glacial Maximum." *Science* 303 (2004): 52–56.

Pitulko, V. V., et al. "Early Human Presence in the Arctic: Evidence from 45,000-Year-Old Mammoth Remains." *Science* 351.6270 (2016): 260–63.

Plog, S. *Ancient Peoples of the American Southwest*. London: Thames and Hudson, 1997.

Plug, I. "Resource Exploitation: Animal Use during the Middle Stone Age at Sibudu Cave, KwaZulu-Natal, South Africa." *South African Journal of Science* 100 (2004): 151–58.

Pollock, S. *Ancient Mesopotamia: The Eden that Never Was*. Case Studies in Early Societies. Cambridge, UK: Cambridge University Press, 1999.

Pope, G. "Bamboo and Human Evolution." *Natural History* 98.10 (1989): 48–57.

Portal, J. *The Terracotta Warriors*. London: British Museum, 2007.

Postgate, J. N. *Early Mesopotamia: Society and Economy at the Dawn of History*, rev. ed. London: Routledge, 1994.

Postgate, J. N., ed. *Artefacts of Complexity: Tracking the Uruk in the Near East*. Iraq Archaeological Reports, no. 5. London: British School of Archaeology in Iraq, 2002.

Potter, B. A., et al. "New Insights into Eastern Beringian Mortuary Behavior: A Terminal Pleistocene Double Infant Burial at Upward Sun River." *Proceedings of the National Academy of Sciences* 111.48 (2014): 17060–65.

Potts, R. *Early Hominid Activities at Olduvai*. Foundations of Human Behavior Series. New York: A. de Gruyter, 1988.

Potts, R. "Hominin Evolution in Settings of Strong Environmental Variability." *Quaternary Science Reviews* 73 (2013): 1–13.

Prado-Martinez, J., et al. "Great Ape Genetic Diversity and Population History." *Nature* 499.7459 (2013): 471–75.

Preece, R. C., et al. "Humans in the Hoxnian: Habitat, Context and Fire Use at Beeches Pit, West Stow, Suffolk, UK." *Journal of Quaternary Science* 21 (2006): 485–96.

Prentice, G. "Origins of Plant Domestication in the Eastern United States: Promoting the Individual in Archaeological Theory." *Southeastern Archaeology* 5 (1986): 103–19.

Preston, D. "Fossils and the Folsom Cowboy." *Natural History* 106.1 (1997): 16–21.

Proctor, R. "From Anthropologie to Rassenkunde: Concepts of Race in German Physical Anthropology." In *Bones, Bodies, Behavior: Essays on Biological Anthropology*, edited by G. Stocking, 138–79. Madison, WI: University of Wisconsin, 1988.

Proskouriakoff, T. "The Lords of the Maya Realm." *Expedition* 4.1 (1961): 14–21.

Proskouriakoff, T. *An Album of Maya Architecture*, new ed. Norman, OK: University of Oklahoma Press, 1963.

Prüfer, K., et al. "The Complete Genome Sequence of a Neanderthal from the Altai Mountains." *Nature* 505.7481 (2014): 43–49.

Quiles, A., et al. "A High-Precision Chronological Model for the Decorated Upper Paleolithic Cave of Chauvet-Pont d'Arc, Ardèche, France." *Proceedings of the National Academy of Sciences* 113.17 (2016): 4670–75.

Quilter, J. "Architecture and Chronology at El Paraíso, Peru." *Journal of Field Archaeology* 12 (1985): 279–97.

Quilter, J. *Life and Death at Paloma: Society and Mortuary Practices in a Preceramic Peruvian Village*. Iowa City, IA: University of Iowa Press, 1989.

Quilter, J. "Moche Politics, Religion, and Warfare." *Journal of World Prehistory* 16 (2002): 145–95.

Quilter, J., et al. "Subsistence Economy of El Paraíso, an Early Peruvian Site." *Science* 251 (1991): 277–83.

Radini, A., et al. "Neanderthals, Trees and Dental Calculus: New Evidence from El Sidron." *Antiquity* 90.350 (2016): 290–301.

Radovanovic, I. "Houses and Burials at Lepenski Vir." *European Journal of Archaeology* 3.3 (2000): 330–49.

Rasmussen, M., et al. "Ancient Human Genome Sequence of an Extinct Palaeo-Eskimo." *Nature* 463 (2010): 757–62.

Rasmussen, M., et al. "The Ancestry and Affiliations of Kennewick Man." *Nature* 523 (2015): 455–58.

Rawson, J. "The First Emperor's Tomb: The Afterlife Universe." In *The First Emperor: China's Terracotta Army*, edited by J. Portal, 114–52. London: British Museum, 2007.

Raymond, J. S. "A View from the Tropical Forest." In *Peruvian Prehistory*, edited by R. W. Keatinge, 279–302. Cambridge, UK: Cambridge University Press, 1988.

Reich, D., et al. "Genetic history of an archaic hominin group from Denisova Cave in Siberia." *Nature* 468 (2010): 1053–60.

Reitz, E. J. "Faunal Remains from Paloma, an Archaic Site in Peru." *American Anthropology* 90 (1988): 310–22.

Reitz, E. J., and E. S. Wing. *Zooarchaeology*, 2nd ed. Cambridge, UK: Cambridge University Press, 2008.

Renfrew, C. *Social Archaeology*. Edinburgh, UK: Edinburgh University Press, 1984.

Renfrew, C. "Introduction: Peer Polity Interaction and Sociopolitical Change." In *Peer Polity Interaction and Socio-Political Change*, edited by C. Renfrew and J. Cherry, 1–18. Cambridge, UK: Cambridge University Press, 1986.

Renfrew, C. *Archaeology and Language: The Puzzle of Indo-European Origins*. New York: Cambridge University Press, 1990.

Renfrew, C, and J. F. Cherry, eds. *Peer Polity Interaction and Sociopolitical Change*. Cambridge, UK: Cambridge University Press, 1986.

Renfrew, C., P. Forster, and M. Hurles. "The Past within Us." *Nature Genetics* 26 (2000): 253–54.

Richards, M. P., et al. "Neanderthal Diet at Vindija and Neanderthal Predation: The Evidence From Stable Isotopes." *Proceedings of the National Academy of Sciences* 97.13 (2000): 7663–66.

Richards, M. P., et al. "Stable Isotope Evidence of Diet at Neolithic Çatalhöyük, Turkey." *Journal of Archaeological Science* 30 (2003): 67–76.

Richter D, Grün R, Joannes-Boyau R, Steele TE, Amani F, Rué M, Fernandes P, Raynal JP, Geraads D, Ben-Ncer A, Hublin JJ. The age of the hominin fossils from Jebel Irhoud, Morocco, and the origins of the Middle Stone Age. 2017. *Nature* 546: 293–6.

Rightmire, G. P. "Human Evolution in the Middle Pleistocene: The Role of *Homo heidelbergensis*." *Evolutionary Anthropology* 6.6 (1998): 218–27.

Rindos, D. *The Origins of Agriculture: An Evolutionary Perspective*. San Diego, CA: Academic Press, 1984.

Roach, N. T., et al. "Elastic Energy Storage in the Shoulder and the Evolution of High-Speed Throwing in *Homo*." *Nature* 498.7455 (2013): 483–86.

Roberts, B. *Kimberley: Turbulent City*. Cape Town, South Africa: D. Phillip, 1976.

Roberts, M., and S. Parfitt. *Boxgrove: A Middle Pleistocene Hominid Site at Eartham Quarry, Boxgrove, West Sussex*. London: English Heritage, 1999.

Roberts, R. G., et al. "The Human Colonisation of Australia: Optical Dates of 53,000 and 60,000 Years Bracket Human Arrival at Deaf Adder Gorge, Northern Territory." *Quaternary Science Reviews* 13 (1994): 575–83.

Roberts, R. G., et al. "Luminescence Dating of Rock Art and Past Environments Using Mud-Wasp Nests in Northern Australia." *Nature* 387 (1997): 696–99.

Roberts, R. G., et al. "New Ages for the Last Australian Mega-Fauna: Continent-Wide Extinction about 46,000 Years Ago." *Science* 292 (2001): 1888–90.

Robertshaw, P. "The Beginnings of Food Production in Southwestern Kenya." In *The Archaeology of Africa: Food, Metals, and Towns*, edited by T. Shaw, 358–71. London: Routledge, 1998.

Robin, C. "New Directions in Classic Maya Household Archaeology." *Journal of Archaeological Research* 11.4 (2003): 307–56.

Roche, H., et al. "Early Hominid Stone Tool Production and Technical Skill 2.34 Myr Ago in West Turkana, Kenya." *Nature* 399 (1999): 57–60.

Rodríguez-Vidal, J., et al. "A Rock Engraving Made by Neanderthals in Gibraltar." *Proceedings of the National Academy of Sciences* 111.37 (2014): 13301–6.

Rohling, E. J., et al. "Magnitudes of Sea-Level Lowstands of the Past 500,000 Years." *Nature* 394 (1998): 162–65.

Roksandic, M., et al. "Interpersonal Violence at Lepenski Vir Mesolithic/Neolithic Complex of the Iron Gates Gorge (Serbia-Romania)." *American Journal of Physical Anthropology* 129.3 (2006): 339–48.

Rollefson, G. O. "Ain Ghazan (Jordan): Ritual and Ceremony III." *Paleorient* 24 (1998): 43–58.

Rollefson, G. O. "Ritual and Social Structure at Neolithic 'Ain Ghazal." In *Life in Neolithic Farming Communities*, edited by I. Kuijt, 163–90. New York: Plenum, 2000.

Roosevelt, A. C., et al. "Paleoindian Cave Dwellers in the Amazon: The Peopling of the Americas." *Science* 272 (1996): 373–84.

Rosen, S. "Paradigms and Politics in the Terminal Pleistocene Archaeology of the Levant." In *Perspectives on the Past: Theoretical Biases in Mediterranean Hunter-Gatherer Research*, edited by G. Clark. Philadelphia, PA: University of Pennsylvania Press, 1991.

Roth, A. M. *Egyptian Phyles in the Old Kingdom: The Evolution of a System of Social Organization*. Studies in Ancient Oriental Civilization, vol. 48. Chicago: Oriental Institute of the University of Chicago, 1991.

Rothman, Mitchell S. *Uruk Mesopotamia and Its Neighbors: Cross-Cultural Interactions in the Era of State Formation*. School of American Research Advanced Seminar Series. Santa Fe, NM: School of American Research Press, 2001.

Rothman, M. S. "Studying the Development of Complex Society: Mesopotamia in the Late Fifth and Fourth Millennia B.C." *Journal of Archaeological Research* 12.1 (2004): 75–119.

Ruvolo, M. "Genetic Diversity in Hominid Primates." *Annual Review of Anthropology* 26 (1997a): 515–40.

Ruvolo, M. "Molecular Phylogeny of the Hominoids: Inferences from Multiple Independent DNA Sequence Data Sets." *Molecular Biological Evolution* 14.3 (1997b): 248–65.

Sabloff, J., and G. Willery. *A History of American Archaeology*. San Francisco, CA: Freeman, 1980.

Sahlins, M. D. *Stone Age Economics*. Chicago: Aldine-Atherton, 1972.

Sala, N., et al. "Lethal Interpersonal Violence in the Middle Pleistocene." *PloS one* 10.5 (2015): e0126589.

Salo, W. L., A. C. Aufderheide, J. Buikstra, and T. A. Holcomb. "Identification of Mycobacterium Tuberculosis DNA in a Pre-Columbian Peruvian Mummy." *Proceedings of the National Academy of Sciences of the United States of America* 91 (1994): 2091–94.

Salomon, F. "How an Andean 'Writing Without Words' Works." *Current Anthropology* 42 (2001): 2–27.

Sanchez, G., et al. "Human (Clovis)—gomphothere (*Cuvieronius* sp.) Association~ 13,390 Calibrated yBP in Sonora, Mexico." *Proceedings of the National Academy of Sciences* 111.30 (2014): 10972–77.

Sandgathe, D. M., and B. Hayden. "Did Neanderthals Eat Inner Bark?" *Antiquity* 77.298 (2003): 709–18.

Sandweiss, D. H., et al. "Geoarchaeological Evidence from Peru for a 5000 Years B.P. Onset of El Niño." *Science* 273 (1996): 1531–32.

Sandweiss, D. H., et al. "Quebrada Jaguay: Early South American Maritime Adaptations." *Science* 281 (1998): 1830–32.

Sandweiss, D. H., et al. "Variation in Holocene El Niño Frequencies: Climate Records and Cultural Consequences in Ancient Peru." *Geology* 29.7 (2001): 603–6.

Sankararaman, S., et al. "The Date of Interbreeding Between Neandertals and Modern Humans." *PLoS Genetics* 8.10 (2012): e1002947.

Santos, G. M., et al. "A Revised Chronology of the Lowest Occupation Layer of Pedra Furada Rock Shelter, Brazil: The Pleistocene Peopling of the Americas." *Quaternary Science Reviews* 22 (2003): 2303–10.

Saraydar, S. C. *Replicating the Past: The Art and Science of the Archaeological Experiment.* Long Grove, IL: Waveland Press, 2008.

Sassaman, K. "Structure and Practice in the Archaic Southeast." In *North American Archaeology*, edited by T. Pauketat and D. D. Loren, 79–107. Malden, MA: Blackwell, 2005.

Saturno, W. A. "Early Maya Writing at San Bartolo, Guatemala." *Science* 311 (2006): 1281–83.

Saturno, W. A., et al. *The Murals of San Bartolo, El Petén, Guatemala. Part 1: The North Wall.* Ancient America, no. 7. Barnardsville, NC: Center for Ancient American Studies, 2005.

Saunders, J. W., et al. "A Mound Complex in Louisiana at 5,400–5,000 Years Before Present." *Science* 277 (1997): 1796–99.

Sawyer, S., et al. "Nuclear and Mitochondrial DNA Sequences from Two Denisovan Individuals." *Proceedings of the National Academy of Sciences* 112.51 (2015): 15696–700.

Scarre, C. *The Seventy Wonders of the Ancient World: The Great Monuments and How They Were Built.* New York: Thames & Hudson, 1999.

Scarre, C., and G. Lawson, eds. *Archaeoacoustics.* McDonald Institute Monographs. Cambridge, UK: Cambridge University Press, 2006.

Scarre, C., and G. Scarre. *The Ethics of Archaeology: Philosophical Perspectives on Archaeological Practice.* Cambridge, UK: Cambridge University Press, 2006.

Scham, S., and A. Yahya. "Heritage and Reconciliation." *Journal of Social Archaeology* 3 (2003): 399–416.

Schele, L., and M. E. Miller. *The Blood of Kings: Dynasty and Ritual in Maya Art.* New York and Fort Worth, TX: G. Braziller and Kimbell Art Museum, 1986.

Schick, K. D., et al. "Continuing Investigations into the Stone Tool-Making and Tool-Using Capabilities of a Bonobo (*Pan Paniscus*)." *Journal of Archaeological Science* 26 (1999): 821–32.

Schick, K. D., and N. Toth. *Making Silent Stones Speak: Human Evolution and the Dawn of Technology.* New York: Simon & Schuster, 1993.

Schiffer, M. B. *Formation Processes of the Archaeological Record.* Albuquerque, NM: University of New Mexico Press, 1987.

Schirmer, W. "Some Aspects of Building at the 'Aceramic-Neolithic' Settlement of Cayonu Tepesi." *World Archaeology* 21.3 (1990): 365–87.

Schmidt, K. "Gobekli Tepe and the Early Neolithic Sites of the Urfa Region: A Synopsis of New Results and Current Views." *Neolithics* 10.1 (2001): 9–11.

Schmidt, P. R. *Iron Technology in East Africa: Symbolism, Science, and Archaeology.* Bloomington, IN: Indiana University Press, 1997.

Schmidt, P. R., and R. J. McIntosh, eds. *Plundering Africa's Past.* Bloomington, IN: Indiana University Press, 1996.

Schmitz, R. W., et al. "The Neanderthal Type Site Revisited: Interdisciplinary Investigations of Skeletal Remains from the Neander Valley, Germany." *Proceedings of the National Academy of Sciences* 99.20 (2002): 13342–47.

Schnapp, A. *The Discovery of the Past.* New York: Abrams, 1996.

Schreiber, K. "The Wari Empire of Middle Horizon Peru: The Epistemological Challenge of Documenting an Empire without Documentary Evidence." In *Empires*, edited by S. Alcock et al. Cambridge, UK: Cambridge University Press, 2001.

Schwartz, J. H., and I. Tattersall. "Whose Teeth?" *Nature* 381 (1996): 201–2.

Scott, B., et al. "A New View from la cotte de st brelade, Jersey." *Antiquity* 88.339 (2014): 13–29.

Scott, K. "The Large Mammal Fauna." In *La Cotte de St. Brelade 1961–1978*, edited by P. Callow and J.M. Cornford, 109–38. Norwich, UK: Geo Books, 1986.

Sebastian, L. *The Chaco Anasazi: Sociopolitical Evolution in the Prehistoric Southwest. New Studies in Archaeology.* Cambridge, UK: Cambridge University Press, 1992.

Sebastian, L., and W. D. Lipe, eds. *Archaeology and Cultural Resource Management: Visions for the Future.* Santa Fe, NM: School for Advanced Research, 2009.

Semah, F., et al. "Did Early Man Reach Java during the Late Pliocene?" *Journal of Archaeological Science* 27 (2000): 763–69.

Semaw, S. "The World's Oldest Stone Artefacts from Gona, Ethiopia: Their Implications for Understanding Stone Technology and Patterns of Human Evolution Between 2.6–1.5 Million Years Ago." *Journal of Archaeological Science* 27 (2000): 1197–214.

Semaw, S., et al. "2.5-Million-Year-Old Stone Tools from Gona, Ethiopia." *Nature* 385 (1997): 333–34.

Sereno, P., et al. "Lakeside Cemeteries in the Sahara: 5,000 Years of Holocene Population and Environmental Change." *PLOS One* 3 (2008): 1–22.

Service, E. R. *Primitive Social Organization: An Evolutionary Perspective*, 2nd ed. New York: Random House, 1971.

Service, E. R. *Origins of the State and Civilization.* New York: Norton, 1975.

Shanks, M., and C.Y. Tilley. *Re-Constructing Archaeology: Theory and Practice. New Studies in Archaeology.* Cambridge, UK: Cambridge University Press, 1987a.

Shanks, M., and C.Y. Tilley. *Social Theory and Archaeology.* Cambridge, UK: Polity Press, 1987b.

Shannon, L. M., et al. "Genetic Structure in Village Dogs Reveals a Central Asian Domestication Origin." *Proceedings of the National Academy of Sciences* 112.44 (2015): 13639–13644.

Shea, J., Z. Davis, and K. Brown. "Experimental Tests of Middle Paleolithic Spear Points Using a Calibrated Crossbow." *Journal of Archaeological Science* 28.8 (2001): 807–16.

Shen, G., et al. "Age of Zhoukoudian *Homo erectus* Determined with 26Al/10Be Burial Dating." *Nature* 458 (2009): 198–200.

Sherratt, A. "The Secondary Exploitation of Animals in the Old World." *World Archaeology* 15 (1983): 90–104.

Silverberg, R. *Mound Builders of Ancient America: The Archaeology of a Myth.* Athens, OH: Ohio University Press, 1968, 1986.

Silverman, H., and D. A. Proulx. *The Nasca.* Malden, MA: Blackwell, 2002.

Sklenar, K. *Archaeology in Central Europe: The First 500 Years.* Leicester, UK: Leicester University Press, 1983.

Slater, P. A., K. M. Hedman, and T. E. Emerson. "Immigrants at the Mississippian Polity of Cahokia: Strontium Isotope Evidence for Population Movement." *Journal of Archaeological Science* 44 (2014): 117–27.

Smith, A. B. "Keeping People on the Periphery: The Ideology of Social Hierarchies Between Hunters and Herders." *Journal of Anthropological Archaeology* 17 (1998): 201–15.

Smith, B. D. *The Emergence of Agriculture*. New York: Scientific American Library, 1995.

Smith, B. D. "The Initial Domestication of *Cucurbita pepo* in the Americas 10,000 Years Ago." *Science* 276 (1997): 932–34.

Smith, B. D. "Low-Level Food Production." *Journal of Archaeological Research* 9.1 (2001): 1–43.

Smith, B. D. "Niche Construction and the Behavioral Context of Plant and Animal Domestication." *Evolutionary Anthropology: Issues, News, and Reviews* 16.5 (2007): 188–99.

Smith, B. D. "The Cultural Context of Plant Domestication in Eastern North America." *Current Anthropology* 52.S4 (2011): S471–84.

Smith, B. D., and C. Wesley Cowan. "Domesticated Crop Plants and the Evolution of Food Production Economies in Eastern North America." In *People and Plants in Ancient Eastern North America*, edited by P. E. Minnis, 105–25. Washington, DC: Smithsonian Books, 2003.

Smith, C. E. "Plant Remains from Guitarrero Cave." In *Guitarrero Cave: Early Man in the Andes*, edited by T. F. Lynch, 87–119. New York: Academic Press, 1980.

Smith, C. E., and H. M. Wobst, eds. *Indigenous Archaeologies: Decolonizing Theory and Practice*. London: Routledge, 2005.

Smith, C., et al. "Not Just Old But Old and Cold?" *Nature* 410 (2001): 771–72.

Smith, F. H., et al. "Direct Radiocarbon Dates for Vindija G1 and Velika Pecina Late Pleistocene Hominid Remains." *Proceedings of the National Academy of Sciences* 96.22 (1999): 12281–86.

Smith, M. E. *The Aztecs*, 2nd ed. Peoples of America Series. Malden, MA: Blackwell, 2003.

Society for American Archaeology. "Principles of Archaeological Ethics," adopted 1996. Available at www.saa.org/publicftp/PUBLIC/resources/ethics.html.

Soffer, O., J. M. Adovasio, and D. C. Hyland. "The 'Venus' Figurines: Textiles, Basketry, Gender, and Status in the Upper Paleolithic." *Current Anthropology* 41.4 (2000): 511–37.

Solis, R. S., J. Haas, and W. Creamer. "Dating Caral, a Preceramic Site in the Supe Valley on the Central Coast of Peru." *Science* 292 (2001): 723–26.

Sonett, C. P. "The Present Status of Understanding of the Long-Period Spectrum of Radiocarbon." In *Radiocarbon after Four Decades*, edited by R. E. Taylor, A. Long, and R. S. Kra, 50–61. New York: Springer Verlag, 1992.

Souden, D. *Stonehenge Revealed*. London: Collins & Brown, in Association with English Heritage, 1997.

Spector, J. "What This Awl Means: Toward a Feminist Archaeology." In *Engendering Archaeology: Women and Prehistory*, edited by J. Gero and M. Conkey, 388–406. Oxford, UK: Blackwell, 1991.

Spence, M. W., and G. Pereira. "The Human Skeletal Remains of the Moon Pyramid, Teotihuacán." *Ancient Mesoamerica* 18 (2007): 147–57.

Spencer, F. *Piltdown: A Scientific Forgery*. London: Oxford University Press, 1990.

Speth, J. D., et al. "Early Paleoindian Big-Game Hunting in North America: Provisioning or Politics?" *Quaternary International* 285 (2013): 111–39.

Spindler, K. *The Man in the Ice: The Discovery of a 5,000-Year-Old Body Reveals the Secrets of the Stone Age*. Toronto, ON: Doubleday Canada, 1994.

Spooner, N. A. "Human Occupation at Jinmium, Northern Australia: 116,000 Years Ago or Much Less?" *Antiquity* 72.275 (1998): 173–78.

Squier, E. G., and Edwin Davis. *Ancient Monuments of the Mississippi Valley*. Smithsonian Classics of Anthropology. Washington, DC: Smithsonian Institution, 1848.

Srejovic, D. *Europe's First Monumental Sculpture: New Discoveries at Lepinski Vir*. New York: Stein and Day, 1972.

Stafford, C. R., and S. D. Creasman. "The Hidden Record: Late Holocene Landscapes and Settlement Archaeology in the Lower Ohio River Valley." *Geoarchaeology: An International Journal* 17.2 (2002): 117–40.

Stafford, M. D., et al. "Digging for the Color of Life: Paleoindian Red Ochre Mining at the Powars II Site, Platte County, Wyoming, USA." *Geoarchaeology: An International Journal* 18.1 (2003): 71–90.

Stanford, C. *The Hunting Ape: Meat Eating and the Origins of Human Behavior*. Princeton, NJ: Princeton University Press, 1999.

Stanford, D., and B. Bradley. "The Solutrean Solution: Did Some Ancient Americans Come from Europe?" *Discovering Archaeology* 2.1 (2000): 54–55.

Stanish, C., et al. "A 2,300-Year-Old Architectural and Astronomical Complex in the Chincha Valley, Peru." *Proceedings of the National Academy of Sciences* 111.20 (2014): 7218–23.

Stark, M. "Angkor Borei and the Archaeology of Cambodia's Mekong Delta." In *Art and Archaeology of Fu Nan: Pre-Khmer Kingdom of the Lower Mekong Valley*, edited by J. Khoo, 87–106. Bangkok, Thailand: Orchid Books, 2003.

Stark, M., et al. "Monumentality in the Mekong Delta: Luminescence Dating and Implications." *Bulletin of the Indo-Pacific Prehistory Association* 26 (2006): 110–20.

Steadman, S. "Recent Research in the Archaeology of Architecture: Beyond the Foundations." *Journal of Archaeological Research* 4 (1996): 51–93.

Stearns, S. C. "Evolutionary Medicine: Its Scope, Interest and Potential." *Proceedings of the Royal Society of London B: Biological Sciences* 279.1746 (2012): 4305–21.

Steele, J. "Stone Legacy of Skilled Hands." *Nature* 399 (1999): 24–25.

Stein, G. *Rethinking World-Systems: Diasporas, Colonies, and Interaction in Uruk Mesopotamia*. Tucson, AZ: University of Arizona Press, 1999.

Stiner, M. C., et al. "Paleolithic Population Growth Pulses Evidenced by Small Animal Exploitation." *Science* 283 (1999): 190–93.

Stock, J. T., et al. "F-81 Skeleton for Wadi Mataha, Jordan and Its Bearing on Human Variability in the Epipaleolithic of the Levant." *American Journal of Physical Anthropology* 128.2 (2005): 453–65.

Storck, P. L. *Journey to the Ice Age: Discovering an Ancient World*. Vancouver, BC: UBC Press, in Association with the Royal Ontario Museum, 2004.

Storck, P. L., and A. Spiess. "The Significance of New Faunal Identifications Attributed to an Early Paleoindian (Gainey Complex) Occupation at the Udora Site, Ontario, Canada." *American Antiquity* 59 (1994): 121–42.

Stordeur, D. "Organisation de l'espace construit et organisation sociale dans le Néolithique de Jerf el Ahmar (Syrie, Xe-IXe millénaire av. J.-C.)." In *Habitat et société. XIXe Rencontres Internationales d'Archéologie et d'Histoire d'Antibes*, edited by F. Braemer, S. Cleuziou, and A. Coudart, 131–49. Juan-les-Pins: Éditions APDCA, 1999.

Stordeur, D., et al. "Les Bâtiments Communautaires de Jerf el Ahmar et Mureybet Horizon PPNA (Syrie)." *Paléorient* 26.1 (2000): 29–44.

Storm, P. "The Evolution of Humans in Australasia from an Environmental Perspective." *Palaeogeography, Palaeoclimatology, Palaeoecology* 171 (2001): 363–83.

Straus, L. G. "Solutrean Settlement of North America? A Review of Reality." *American Antiquity* 65.2 (2000): 219–26.

Stringer, C. B. "The Status of Homo heidelbergensis (Schoetensack 1908)." *Evolutionary Anthropology* 21 (2012): 101–107.

Stringer, C. B., and P. Andrews. "Genetic and Fossil Evidence for the Origin of Modern Humans." *Science* 239 (1988): 1263–68.

Stringer, C. B., et al. "Neanderthal Exploitation of Marine Mammals in Gibraltar." *Proceedings of the National Academy of Sciences* 105 (2008): 14319–24.

Stringer, C., and R. McKie. *African Exodus: The Origins of Modern Humanity.* New York: Henry Holt, 1998.

Sugiyama, S. "Governance and Polity at Classic Teotihuacán." In *Mesoamerican Archaeology: Theory and Practice,* edited by J. A. Hendon and R. A. Joyce, 97–123. Oxford, UK: Blackwell, 2004.

Sugiyama, S., and R. C. Castro. "The Moon Pyramid Project and the Teotihuacán State Polity." *Ancient Mesoamerica* 18 (2007): 109–25.

Sugiyama, S., and L. L. Lujan. "Dedictory Burial/Offering Complexes at the Moon Pyramid, Teotihuacán." *Ancient Mesoamerica* 18 (2007): 127–46.

Surovell, T. A., et al. "On the Dating of the Folsom Complex and Its Correlation with the Younger Dryas, the End of Clovis, and Megafaunal Extinction." *PaleoAmerica* 2 (2016): 1–9.

Sutikna, T., et al. "Revised Stratigraphy and Chronology for *Homo floresiensis* at Liang Bua in Indonesia." *Nature* 532 (2016): 366–69.

Sutton, M. Q., B. S. Arkush, and Joan S. Schneider. *Archaeological Laboratory Methods: An Introduction,* 2nd ed. Dubuque, IA: Kendall/Hunt, 1998.

Suwa, G., et al. "The First Skull of *Australopithecus boisei*." *Nature* 389 (1997): 489–92.

Swedlund, A., and D. Anderson. "Gordon Creek Woman Meets Kennewick Man: New Interpretations and Protocols Regarding the Peopling of the Americas." *American Antiquity* 64.4 (1999): 569–76.

Swedlund, A., and D. Anderson. "Gordon Creek Woman Meets Spirit Cave Man: A Response to Comment by Owsley and Jantz." *American Antiquity* 68.1 (2003): 161–67.

Swisher, C. C., et al. "Age of the Earliest Known Hominids in Java, Indonesia." *Science* 263.5150 (1994): 1118–21.

Swisher, C. C., et al. "Latest *Homo erectus* of Java: Potential Contemporaneity with *Homo sapiens* in Southeast Asia." *Science* 274 (1996): 1870–74.

Taché, K., and O. E. Craig. "Cooperative Harvesting of Aquatic Resources and the Beginning of Pottery Production in North-Eastern North America." *Antiquity* 89.343 (2015): 177–90.

Tackney, J. C., et al. "Two Contemporaneous Mitogenomes from Terminal Pleistocene Burials in Eastern Beringia." *Proceedings of the National Academy of Sciences* 112.45 (2015): 13833–38.

Tankersley, K. B. "Sheriden: A Clovis Cave Site in Eastern North America." *Geoarchaeology: An International Journal* 12.6 (1997): 713–24.

Tattersall, I., and J. H. Schwartz. "Hominids and Hybrids: The Place of Neanderthals in Human Evolution." *Proceedings of the National Academy of Sciences* 96 (1999): 7117–19.

Tattersall, I., and J. H. Schwartz. *Extinct Humans.* Boulder, CO: Westview Press, 2000.

Taylor, R. E., et al. "Radiocarbon Analyses of Modern Organics at Monte Verde, Chile: No Evidence for a Local Reservoir Effect." *American Antiquity* 64.3 (1999): 455–60.

Taylor, R. E., and M. J. Aitken, eds. *Chronometric Dating in Archaeology.* New York: Plenum, 1997.

Taylor, R. E., A. Long, and R. S. Kra, eds. *Radiocarbon after Four Decades: An Interdisciplinary Perspective.* New York: Springer Verlag, 1992.

Taylor, W. W. *A Study of Archaeology.* Carbondale, IL: Southern Illinois University Press, 1948.

Tchernov, E., and F. Valla. "Two New Dogs, and Other Natufian Dogs, from the Southern Levant." *Journal of Archaeological Science* 24 (1997): 65–95.

Tegel, W., et al. "Early Neolithic Water Wells Reveal the World's Oldest Wood Architecture." *PloS one* 7.12 (2012): e51374.

Templeton, A. R. "Out of Africa Again and Again." *Nature* 416 (2002): 45–47.

Texier, P.-J., et al. "A Howiesons Poort Tradition of Engraving Ostrich Eggshell Containers Dated to 60,000 Years Ago at Diepkloof Rock Shelter, South Africa." *Proceedings of the National Academy of Sciences* 107 (2010): 6180–85.

Thieme, H. "Lower Paleolithic Hunting Spears from Germany." *Nature* 385 (1997): 807–10.

Thomas, D. H. *Skull Wars: Kennewick Man, Archaeology, and the Battle for Native American Identity.* New York: Basic Books, 2000.

Thomas, J. *Rethinking the Neolithic.* Cambridge, UK: Cambridge University Press, 1991.

Thomas, J. *Time, Culture, and Identity: An Interpretive Archaeology.* London: Routledge, 1996.

Thomas, J. *Understanding the Neolithic,* rev. 2nd ed. London: Routledge, 1999.

Thomas, J. *Archaeology and Modernity.* London: Routledge, 2004.

Thomas, J., et al. "The Date of the Greater Stonehenge Cursus." *Antiquity* 83 (2009): 40–53.

Thompson, R. F., and J. Cornet. *The Four Moments of the Sun: Kongo Art in Two Worlds.* Washington, DC: National Gallery of Art, 1981.

Thornton, R. "Repatriation as Healing the Wounds of the Trauma of History: Cases of Native Americans in the United States of America." In *The Dead and Their Possessions: Repatriation in Principle, Policy, and Practice,* edited by C. Fforde, J. Hubert, and P. Turnbull, 17–24. London: Routledge, 2002.

Tieme, C., et al. "The Problems in ESR Dating of Tooth Enamel of Early Pleistocene and the Age of Longgupo Hominid, Wushan, China." *Quaternary Science Reviews* 20 (2001): 1041–45.

Tilley, C., and M. Shanks. *Social Theory and Archaeology.* Albuquerque, NM: University of New Mexico Press, 1987.

Tobias, P. V. "Encore Olduvai." *Science* 299 (2003): 1193–94.

Tomasello, M. *The Cultural Origins of Human Cognition.* Cambridge, MA: Harvard University Press, 1999.

Toro Moyano, I. *Les industries lithiques archaïques de Barranco Leon et de Fuente Nueva 3 Orce, bassin de Guadix-Baza, Andalousie.* Paris: Editions CNRS, 2010.

Toth, N., et al. "Pan the Tool-Maker: Investigations into the Stone Tool-Making and Tool-Using Capabilities of a Bonobo (*Pan paniscus*)." *Journal of Archaeological Science* 20 (1993): 81–91.

Townsend, R. F. *The Aztecs.* London: Thames and Hudson, 2000.

Tozzer, A. M., et al. *Landa's Relación de las Cosas de Yucatán: A Translation.* Papers of the Peabody Museum of American Archaeology and Ethnology, Harvard University, vol. 18. Cambridge, MA: Peabody Museum, 1941.

Trigger, B. G. *A History of Archaeological Thought.* Cambridge, UK: Cambridge University Press, 1989.

Trigger, B. G. *Understanding Early Civilizations: A Comparative Study.* Cambridge, UK: Cambridge University Press, 2003.

Trinkaus, E., et al. "An Early Modern Human from the Pestera Cu Oase, Romania." *Proceedings of the National Academy of Sciences* 100 (2003): 11231–36.

Trinkaus, E., and Pat Shipman. *The Neanderthals: Changing the Image of Mankind.* New York: Knopf, 1993.

Underhill, A., et al. "Changes in Regional Settlement Patterns and the Development of Complex Societies in Southeastern Shandong, China." *Journal of Anthropological Archaeology* 27 (2008): 1–29.

Underhill, P. A., et al. "Y Chromosome Sequence Variation and the History of Human Populations." *Nature Genetics* 26 (2000): 358–61.

Urton, G. *Signs of the Inka Khipu: Binary Coding in the Andean Knotted-String Records.* The Linda Schele Series in Maya and Pre-Columbian Studies. Austin, TX: University of Texas Press, 2003.

Valdes, J. A., and J. Kaplan. "Ground-Penetrating Radar at the Maya Site of Kaminaljuyu, Guatemala." *Journal of Field Archaeology* 27.3 (2000): 329–42.

Valdez, L. M., and J. E. Valdez. "Reconsidering the Archaeological Rarity of Guinea Pig Bones in the Central Andes." *Current Anthropology* 38.5 (1997): 896–97.

Valladas, H., et al. "Thermoluminescence Dating of Mousterian Proto-Cro-Magnon Remains from Israel and the Origin of Modern Man." *Science* 331 (1988): 614–16.

Van den Bergh, G. D., J. de Vos, and P. Y. Sondaar. "The Late Quaternary Paleogeography of Mammal Evolution in the Indonesian Archipelago." *Palaeogeography, Palaeoclimatology, Palaeoecology* 171 (2001): 385–408.

Van den Bergh, G. D., et al. "The Liang Bua Faunal Remains: A 95 K.yr. Sequence from Flores, East Indonesia." *Journal of Human Evolution* 57 (2009): 527–37.

Van Schaik, C. P., et al. "Orangutan Cultures and the Evolution of Material Culture." *Science* 299 (2003): 102–5.

Van Tilburg, J. *Easter Island: Archaeology, Ecology, and Culture.* Washington, DC: Smithsonian Institution Press, 1994.

Van den Bergh, G. D. et al. "Earliest hominin occupation of Sulawesi, Indonesia." *Nature* 529 (2016): 208–11.

Vandermeersch, B. *Les Hommes Fossiles de Qafzeh, Israël. Cahiers de Paléontologie.* Paris: Editions du Centre National de la Recherche Scientifique, 1981.

Vargas, R. C., et al. "Daily Life of the Ancient Maya Recorded on Murals at Calakmul, Mexico." *Proceedings of the National Academy of Sciences* 106 (2009): 19245–49.

Vaughn, K. J. "Households, Crafts, and Feasting in the Ancient Andes: The Village Context of Early Nasca Craft Consumption." *Latin American Antiquity* 15 (2004): 61–88.

Vaughn, K. J., et al. "Ceramic Production in Ancient Nasca: Provenance Analysis of Pottery from the Early Nasca and Tiza Cultures through INAA." *Journal of Archaeological Science* 33 (2006): 681–89.

Vaughn, K. J., and M. L. Grados. "Three Thousand Years of Occupation in Upper Valley Nasca: Excavations at Upanca." *Latin American Antiquity* 17 (2006): 595–612.

Verhoeven, M. "Ritual and Ideology in the Pre-Pottery Neolithic B of the Levant and Southeast Anatolia." *Cambridge Archaeological Journal* 12.2 (2002): 233–58.

Vitelli, K. D., and C. Colwell-Chanthaphonh. *Archaeological Ethics*, 2nd ed. Lanham, MD: AltaMira Press, 2006.

Vos, J. de. "Dating Hominid Sites in Indonesia." *Science* 266 (1994): 1726.

Wadley, L. "Vegetation Changes between 61,500 and 26,000 Years Ago: The Evidence from Seeds in Sibudu Cave, KwaZulu-Natal." *South African Journal of Science* 100 (2004): 167–73.

Walker, C. B. F. *Cuneiform.* Reading the Past, vol. 3. Berkeley, CA: University of California Press, 1987.

Waller, S. "Intentionality of Rock-Art Placement Deduced from Acoustical Measurements and Echo Myths." In *Archaeoacoustics*, edited by C. Scarre and G. Lawson, 31–40. McDonald Institute Monographs. Cambridge, UK: Cambridge University Press, 2006.

Walter, R. C., et al. "Early Human Occupation of the Red Sea Coast of Eritrea During the Last Interglacial." *Nature* 405 (2000): 65–69.

Wang, J., et al. "Research on Digitizing Processing of the Terracotta Warriors and Horses of the Qin Dynasty." In *Proceedings of the 2003 International Conference on Geometric Modeling and Graphics*, 2003.

Wanpo, H., et al. "Early *Homo* and Associated Artefacts from Asia." *Nature* 378 (1995): 275–78.

Wanpo, H., et al. "Whose Teeth?" *Nature* 381 (1996): 201–2.

Wasylikowa, K., et al. "Examination of Botanical Remains from Early Neolithic Houses at Nabta Playa, Western Desert, Egypt, with Special Reference to Sorghum Grains." In *The Archaeology of Africa: Food, Metals, and Towns*, edited by T. Shaw, 154–63. London: Routledge, 1993.

Watchman, A. L., et al. "Micro-Archaeology of Engraved and Painted Rock Surface Crusts at Yiwarlarlay (the Lightning Brothers Site), Northern Territory, Australia." *Journal of Archaeological Science* 27 (2000): 315–25.

Watchman, A. L., and R. Jones. "An Independent Confirmation of the 4 Ka Antiquity of a Beeswax Figure in Western Arnhem Land, Northern Australia." *Archaeometry* 44.1 (2002): 145–53.

Waters, C. N., et al. "The Anthropocene Is Functionally and Stratigraphically Distinct from the Holocene." *Science* 351 (2016): aad2622.

Waters, M. R., et al. "Pre-Clovis Mastodon Hunting 13,800 Years Ago at the Manis Site, Washington." *Science* 334 (2011): 351–53.

Waters, M. R., S. L. Forman, and J. M. Pierson. "Diring Yuriakh: A Lower Paleolithic Site in Central Siberia." *Science* 275 (1997): 1281–84.

Waters, M. R., and T. W. Stafford. "Redefining the Age of Clovis: Implications for the Peopling of the Americas." *Science* 315.5815 (2007): 1122–26.

Watkins, J. "The Politics of American Archaeology: Cultural Resources, Cultural Affiliation, and Kennewick." In *Indigenous Archaeologies: Decolonizing Theory and Practice*, edited by C. Smith and H. M. Wobst, 189–206. London: Routledge, 2005.

Watkins, T. "The Origins of House and Home?" *World Archaeology* 21.3 (1990): 336–47.

Watson, P. J., and M. Kennedy. "The Development of Horticulture in the Eastern Woodlands of North America: Women's Role." In *Engendering Archaeology: Women and Prehistory*, edited by J. Gero and M. Conkey, 255–75. Oxford, UK: Blackwell, 1991.

Watson, P. J., S. A. LeBlanc, and C. L. Redman. *Archaeological Explanation: The Scientific Method in Archaeology.* New York: Columbia University Press, 1984.

Weiner, S. *Microarchaeology: Beyond the Visible Archaeological Record.* Cambridge University Press, 2010.

Wells, H. G. *The Time Machine.* 1895. Reprinted in *The Time Machine and The Invisible Man.* New York: New American Library, 1984.

Wendorf, F., et al. "The Use of Plants during the Early Holocene in the Egyptian Sahara: Early Neolithic Food Economies." In *Before Food Production in North Africa*, edited by S. di Lernia and G. Manzi, 71–78. Forli, Italy: A.B.A.C.O. Edizioni, 1998.

Wendorf, F., and R. Schild. "Nabta Playa and Its Role in Northeastern African Prehistory." *Journal of Anthropological Archaeology* 17 (1998): 97–123.

Wetterstrom, W. "Foraging and Farming in Egypt: The Transition from Hunting and Gathering to Horticulture in the Nile Valley." In *The Archaeology of Africa: Food, Metals, and Towns*, edited by T. Shaw, 162–225. London: Routledge, 1993.

Wheatley, D., and M. Gillings. *Spatial Technology and Archaeology: The Archaeological Applications of GIS.* London: Taylor & Francis, 2002.

Wheeler, M. *Archaeology from the Earth.* Harmondsworth, UK: Penguin Books, 1954.

Wheeler, R. J., et al. "Archaic Period Canoes from Newnans Lake, Florida." *American Antiquity* 68 (2003): 533–51.

White, R. "Husbandry and Herd Control in the Upper Paleolithic." *Current Anthropology* 30.5 (1989): 609–32.

White, R. "Beyond Art: Toward an Understanding of the Origins of Material Representation in Europe." *Annual Review of Anthropology* 21 (1992): 537–64.

White, T. D., et al. "Pleistocene *Homo sapiens* from Middle Awash, Ethiopia." *Nature* 423 (2003): 742–52.

White, T. D., et al. "*Ardipithecus ramidus* and the Paleobiology of Early Hominids." *Science* 326.64 (2009): 75–86.

White, T. D., G. Suwa, and B. Asfaw. "*Australopithecus ramidus*, a New Species of Early Hominid from Aramis, Ethiopia." *Nature* 371 (1994): 306–12.

White, T. D., G. Suwa, and B. Asfaw. "Corrigenda: *Australopithecus ramidus*, a New Species of Early Hominid from Aramis, Ethiopia." *Nature* 375 (1995): 88.

White, C. D., M. W. Spence, H. Le Q. Stuart-Williams, and Henry P. Schwarcz. "Oxygen Isotopes and the Identification of Geographical Origins: The Valley of Oaxaca Versus the Valley of Mexico." *Journal of Archaeological Science* 25.7 (1998): 643–55.

Whiten, A., et al. "Cultures in Chimpanzees." *Nature* 399 (1999): 682–85.

Whittle, A. *Europe in the Neolithic: The Creation of New Worlds*. Cambridge, UK: Cambridge University Press, 1996.

Wiessner, P. W. "Embers of Society: Firelight Talk among the Ju/'hoansi Bushmen." *Proceedings of the National Academy of Sciences* 111.39 (2014): 14027–35.

Wilford, J. N. "Under Maryland Street, Ties to African Past." *New York Times*, October 20, 2008.

Wilkins, J., B. J. Schoville, K. S. Brown, and M. Chazan. "Evidence for Early Hafted Hunting Technology." *Science* 338.6109 (2012): 942–46.

Willcox, G. "Measuring Grain Size and Identifying near Eastern Cereal Domestication: Evidence from the Euphrates Valley." *Journal of Archaeological Science* 31 (2004): 145–50.

Willey, G. R., and P. Phillips. *Method and Theory in American Archaeology*. Chicago: University of Chicago Press, 1958.

Williamson, B. S. "Middle Stone Age Tool Function from Residue Analysis at Sibudu Cave." *South African Journal of Science* 100 (2004): 174–78.

Wills, W. H., and T. C. Windes. "Evidence for Aggregation and Dispersal during the Basketmaker III Period in Chaco Canyon, New Mexico." *American Antiquity* 54 (1989): 347–69.

Windes, T. C. "This Old House: Construction and Abandonment at Pueblo Bonito." In *Pueblo Bonito: Center of the Chacoan World*, edited by J. E. Neitzel, 14–32. Washington, DC: Smithsonian Press, 2003.

Wittfogel, K. *Oriental Despotism: A Comparative Study of Total Power*. New Haven, CT: Yale University Press, 1957.

Wobst, H. M. "The Archaeo-Ethnology of Hunter-Gatherers or the Tyranny of the Ethnographic Record in Archaeology." *American Antiquity* 43.2 (1978): 303–9.

Wolf, E. R. *Europe and the People without History*. Berkeley, CA: University of California Press, 1982.

Wolpoff, M. H., and R. Caspari. *Race and Human Evolution*. New York: Simon & Schuster, 1997.

Wood, B. "The Oldest Whodunnit in the World." *Nature* 385 (1997): 292–93.

Wood, B., and M. C. Collard. "The Human Genus." *Science* 284 (1999): 65–71.

Wood, B., and B. G. Richmond. "Human Evolution: Taxonomy and Paleobiology." *Journal of Anatomy* 196 (2000): 19–60.

Wood, B., and A. Turner. "Out of Africa and Into Asia." *Nature* 378.6554 (1995): 239–40.

Wood, J., et al. "The Osteological Paradox: Problems of Inferring Prehistoric Health from Skeletal Samples." *Current Anthropology* 33 (1992): 343–70.

Wrangham, R. W. *Catching Fire: How Cooking Made Us Human*. New York: Basic Books, 2009.

Wrangham, R. W., et al. "The Raw and the Stolen: Cooking and the Ecology of Human Origins." *Current Anthropology* 40.5 (1999): 567–94.

Wright, H. T., and G. A. Johnson. "Population, Exchange, and Early State Formation in Southwestern Iran." *American Anthropologist* 77 (1975): 267–89.

Wright, R. P. *The Ancient Indus: Urbanism, Economy and Society*. New York: Cambridge University Press, 2010.

Wu, X. "Early Pottery at 20,000 Years Ago in Xianrendong Cave, China." *Science* 336 (2012): 1696–700.

Wylie, A. "Archaeological Cables and Tacking: The Implications of Practice for Bernstein's 'Options beyond Objectivism and Relativism.'" *Philosophy of the Social Sciences* 19.1 (1989): 1–18.

Yamei, H., et al. "Mid-Pleistocene Acheulean-Like Stone Technology of the Bose Basin, South China." *Science* 287.5458 (2000): 1622–26.

Yao, A. "Sarmatian Mirrors and Han Ingots (100 B.C.–A.D. 100): How the Foreign Became Local and Vice Versa." *Cambridge Archaeological Journal* 22 (2012): 57–70.

Yellen, J. E., et al. "A Middle Stone Age Worked Bone Industry from Katanda, Upper Semliki Valley, Zaire." *Science* 268 (1995): 553–56.

Yesner, D. R. "Human Dispersal into Interior Alaska: Antecedent Conditions, Mode of Colonization, and Adaptations." *Quaternary Science Reviews* 20 (2001): 315–27.

Yi, S., D. L. Ellsworth, and Wen-Hsiung Li. "Slow Molecular Clocks in Old World Monkeys, Apes, and Humans." *Molecular Biological Evolution* 19.12 (2002): 2191–98.

Yoffee, N. *Myths of the Archaic State: Evolution of the Earliest Cities, States, and Civilizations*. Cambridge, UK: Cambridge University Press, 2005.

Young, B. W., and M. L. Fowler. *Cahokia, the Great Native American Metropolis*. Urbana, IL: University of Illinois Press, 2000.

Zazula, G. D., et al. "Ice-Age Steppe Vegetation in East Beringia." *Nature* 423 (2003): 603.

Zerubavel, Y. *Recovered Roots: Collective Memory and the Making of Israeli National Tradition*. Chicago: University of Chicago Press, 1995.

Zettler, R. L., L. Horne, and D. P. Hansen. *Treasures from the Royal Tombs of Ur*. Philadelphia, PA: University of Pennsylvania Museum of Archaeology and Anthropology, 1998.

Zhang, H., et al. "Osteoarchaeological Studies of Human Systemic Stress of Early Urbanization in Late Shang at Anyang, China." *PLoS ONE* 11.4 (2016): e0151854.

Zhang, J., et al. "Oldest Playable Musical Instruments Found at Jiahu Early Neolithic Site in China." *Nature* 401 (1999): 366–68.

Zhijun, Z. "The Middle Yangtze Region in China Is One Place Where Rice Was Domesticated: Phytolith Evidence from the Diaotonghuan Cave, Northern Jiangxi." *Antiquity* 72.278 (1998): 885–97.

Zhu, R., et al. "Magnetostratigraphic Dating of Early Humans in China." *Earth-Science Reviews* 61 (2002): 341–59.

Zhu, R. X., et al. "New Evidence on the Earliest Human Presence at High Northern Latitudes in Northeast Asia." *Nature* 431 (2004): 559–62.

Zilhao, J. "The Rock Art of the Côa Valley, Portugal: Significance, Conservation, and Management." *Conservation and Management of Archaeological Sites* 2.4 (1998): 193–206.

Zollikofer, C. P. E., et al. "Virtual Cranial Reconstruction of *Sahelanthropus tchadensis*." *Nature* 434.7034 (2005): 755–59.

Zrubavel, Y. *Recovered Roots: Collective Memory and the Making of Israeli National Tradition*. Chicago: University of Chicago Press, 1995.

Zuk, M. *Paleofantasy: What Evolution Really Tells Us about Sex, Diet, and How We Live*. New York: W.W. Norton & Company, 2013.

Zvelebil, M. "Demography and Dispersal of Early Farming Populations at the Mesolithic-Neolithic Transition: Linguistic and Genetic Implications." In *Examining the Farming/Language Dispersal Hypothesis*, edited by P. Bellwood and C. Renfrew. McDonald Institute Monographs. Cambridge, UK: McDonald Institute for Archaeological Research, 2002.

CREDITS

TEXT CREDITS

Part 1 Wells, H.G. 1895. *The Time Machine.*
Chapter 3 From the Field: Courtesy of Andrew Du
Chapter 4 From the Field: Courtesy of Lynne Schepartz
Chapter 5 From the Field: Courtesy of Laura Kaagan
Chapter 6 From the Field: Courtesy of Susan Blair
Chapter 8 From the Field: Courtesy of Elizabeth Chilton
Chapter 9 From the Field: Courtesy of Catherine D'Andrea
Chapter 10 From the Field: Courtesy of Sarah Herr
Chapter 12 From the Field: Courtesy of Rowan Flad
Chapter 13 From the Field: Courtesy of Chelsea Blackmore
Chapter 14 From the Field: Courtesy of John W. Rick

PHOTO CREDITS

PART 1 i.1 Jon Arnold Images Ltd/Alamy Stock Photo; i.2 Matthew Thayer/The Maui News via AP; i.3 ANNIE GRIFFITHS BELT/National Geographic Creative

Chapter 1 opener Kenneth Garrett; 1.1 Michael Chazan; 1.2 Reuters/Mariana Bazo; 1.3 Pasquale Sorrentino/Science Photo Library; 1.4 Bettmann/Getty Images; 1.5 Copyright © This Land Archaeology, Inc.; 1.6 www.BibleLandPictures.com/Alamy Stock Photo; 1.7 Michael Chazan; 1.8 Michael Chazan; 1.11 Georg Gerster Air Photography; 1.12 Village on the Euphrates by AMT Moore, GC Hillman, and AJ Legge, Copyright © 2002. Oxford University Press, Inc.; 1.13 Michael Chazan; 1.15 New applications of photogrammetry and reflectance transformation imaging to an Easter Island statue by James Milesa, Mike Pittsa, Hembo Pagia1 and Graeme Earla. Antiquity. Figures 2 and 5; 1.16 Robin Weaver/Alamy Stock Photo; 1.17 Michael Chazan; 1.19 Richard Lee; 1.20 Michael Chazan; 1.22 Ira Block/National Geographic/Getty Images; 1.23 The Washington Times/ZUMAPRESS/Newscom

Chapter 2 opener Hulton Archive/Getty Images; 2.1 Bibliotheque des Arts Decoratifs, Paris, France/Archives Charmet/Bridgeman Images; 2.2 Michael Chazan; 2.3 De Agostini/SuperStock; 2.4 Copyright ©The Huntington Library, Art Collections & Botanical Gardens/Bridgeman Images; 2.5 PAUL D STEWART/SCIENCE PHOTO LIBRARY; 2.6 PAUL D STEWART/SCIENCE PHOTO LIBRARY; 2.7 Time Life Pictures/Mansell/The LIFE Picture Collection/Getty Images; 2.8 Fox Photos/Hulton Archive/Getty Images; 2.9 National Portrait Gallery, London; 2.10 MOLA/Getty Images; 2.11 Pasquale Sorrentino/Look at Sciences; 2.12 Hodder, Ian. The Archaeological Process: An Introduction. Oxford, U.K.: Blackwell, 1999; 2.13 Florian Kopp/ImageBroker/Glow Images; 2.14 SCIENCE PHOTO LIBRARY; 2.15 Stockfolio/Alamy Stock Photo

PART 2 ii.2 British Library, London, U.K./Copyright © British Library Board. All Rights Reserved/Bridgeman Images; ii.4 Jackie Curtis/Science Source; ii.5 Hero Images/Getty Images

Chapter 3 opener JOHN READER/SCIENCE PHOTO LIBRARY; 3.1 Zollikofer; 3.2 Jay Matternes; 3.3 JOHN READER/SCIENCE PHOTO LIBRARY; 3.4 Hulton Archive/Getty Images; 3.5 Sabena Jane Blackbird/Alamy Stock Photo; 3.6 Geological Society, London, U.K./Bridgeman Images; 3.7 Kenneth Garrett Photography; 3.8 MAURICIO ANTON/SCIENCE PHOTO LIBRARY; 3.9 Michael Chazan; 3.10 Michael Chazan; 3.11 Michael Chazan; 3.12 Hubert Yann/Alamy Stock Photo; 3.13 Dr Clive Bromhall/Oxford Scientific/Getty Images; 3.14 Kappelman, John. "The Evolution of Body Mass and Relative Brain Size in Fossil Hominids", Journal of Human Evolution 30 (1996): 243–76; 3.15 Look at Sciences; 3.16 Philippe Plailly/Look at Sciences; 3.18 World History Archive/Alamy Stock Photo; 3.20 Michael Chazan; 3.21 Michael Chazan; 3.22 Jorge Fernandez/Alamy Stock Photo

Chapter 4 opener Volker Steger/Science Source; 4.1 Chris Hellier/Corbis via Getty Images; 4.3 Harold L. Dibble; 4.4 The Boxgrove Project, UCL Institute of Archaeology; 4.5 Philippe Plailly/Eurelios/Look at Sciences; 4.6 John Gowlett; 4.7 Gordon Donovan/Alamy Stock Photo; 4.8 Kenneth Garrett Photography; 4.9 Francesco d'Errico; 4.10 John Reader/Science Photo Library; 4.13 Bence Viola, University of Toronto; 4.14 Dmitri Kessel/The LIFE Picture Collection/Getty Images; 4.15 Harold L. Dibble; 4.16 Bordes, Francois. Mousterian Cultures in France, Science magazine, v. 134, no. 3482, 1961, American Association for the Advancement of Science; 4.17 Dibble, Harold, "The Interpretation of Middle Paleolithic Scraper Morpholog", American Antiquity 52 (1987): 109–17, Figure 04-19: Boëda, Eric, et al. "A Levallois Point Embedded in the Vertebra of a Wild Ass (Equus Afri-canusafricanus): Hafting, Projectiles and Mousterian Hunting Weapons", Antiquity 73.280 (1999): 394–402; 4.18 Michael Chazan/Alexandra Sumner; 4.19 Tracey Saxby, Integration and Application Network, University of Maryland Center for Environmental Science; 4.20 Paul Goldberg; 4.21 Dr. Yoel Rak; 4.22 Michael Chazan; 4.23 Kenneth Garrett Photography

Chapter 5 opener Philippe Plailly/Look at Sciences; 5.1 SISSE BRIMBERG/National Geographic Creative; 5.2 M&G Therin-Weise/age footstock; 5.3 Image first published in Lombard, M. & Pargeter, J. 2008, Journal of Archaeological Science 35: 2523–2531; 5.4 The Granger Collection, NYC; 5.5 Chris Henshilwood & Francesco d'Errico; 5.6 John Reader/Science Photo Library; 5.9 Tomas Abad/Alamy Stock Photo; 5.10 Randall White/New York University; 5.11 Musee des Antiquites Nationales, St. Germain-en-Laye, France/Bridgeman Images; 5.12 Gianni Dagli Orti/De Agostini Picture Library/Getty Images; 5.13 Danielle MacDonald; 5.14 Lion Man, Aurignacian Culture, Paleolithic/Museum der Stadt, Ulm, Germany/Bridgeman Images; 5.15 H. Jenson/Tuebingen University, INSTITUT FÜR UR- UND FRÜHGESCHICHTE, ABTEILUNG ÄLTERE URGESCHICHTE UND QUARTÄRÖKOLOGIE; 5.16 IRA BLOCK/National Geographic Creative; 5.17 H. Jenson/Tuebingen University, INSTITUT FÜR UR- UND FRÜHGESCHICHTE, ABTEILUNG ÄLTERE URGESCHICHTE UND QUARTÄRÖKOLOGIE; 5.18 The Natural History Museum/Alamy Stock Photo; 5.19 Mithen, Steven, "Technology and Society during the Middle Pleistocene: Hominid Group Size, Social Learning, and Industrial Variability", Cambridge Archaeological Journal 4.1 (1994): 3-32; 5.20 AKG Images; 5.21 From "Husbandry and Herd Control in the Upper Paleolityic", by Randall White, Paul G. Bahn, Jean Clottes, et al., in Current Anthropology 30(5), 609–632. Copyright © 1989, Copyright © 1989 The Wenner-Gren Foundation for Anthropological Research; 5.22 Michael Chazan

Chapter 6 opener Tony Heald/Nature Picture Library; 6.1 Denver Museum of Nature & Science; 6.3 Courtesy of Dr. Mark Moore/University of New England, Australia; 6.4 Courtesy Gert van den Bergh/University of Wollongong; 6.5 Cary Wolinsky/Aurora Photos; 6.6 Steven David Miller/Nature Picture Library; 6.8 Stephen Alvarez/National Geographic/Getty Images; 6.9 Lynn Johnson/National Geographic/Getty Images; 6.10 Carolina Biological Supply Co/Visuals Unlimited, Inc./Science Photo Library; 6.11 Kenneth Garrett Photography; 6.14 Pennsylvania Historical and Museum Commission 1999; 6.15 Roosevelt, A.C., et al. "Paleoindian; Cave Dwellers in the Amazon: The Peopling of the Americas", Science 272 (1996): 373–84; 6.16 akg-images/De Agostini Picture Library; 6.17 Roosevelt, A.C., et al. "Paleoindian Cave Dwellers in the Amazon: The Peopling of the Americas", Science 272 (1996): 373–84; 6.18 Stacey Espenlaub, University of Pennsylvania, Museum of Archaeology and Anthropology; 6.19 Courtesy of Susan Blair/The University New Brunswick; 6.20 Chase Studio/Science Source; 6.21 University of Colorado Museum/Joe Ben Wheat Photo; 6.23 Bousman, C.B., et al., "The Paleoindian-Archaic transition in North America: new evidence from Texas", Antiquity 76 (2002):980–990, Copyright © Antiquity Publications Ltd 2002; 6.24 Figure 3 reprinted from Bousman et al. 2002 Antiquity 76: 80-990; 6.25 Dr. Ryan J. Wheeler

PART 3 iii.1 MARIA STENZEL/National Geographic Creative; iii.2 Nico Smit/Alamy Stock Photo iii.3 Hillel S. Burger/Peabody Museum of Archaeology and Ethnology/Harvard University; iii.4 H.Obermaier and P.Wenert (1919) Public domain; iii.5 Dave Hamman/Getty Images; iii.7 STEPHEN SHARNOFF/National Geographic Stock

Chapter 7 opener Photo courtesy of Gary Rollefson; 7.1 Bettman/Getty Images; 7.2 PikiWiki - Israel free image collection project; 7.3 Michael Chazan; 7.4 Michael Chazan; 7.5 Michael Chazan; 7.6 Courtesy of Brigham Young University and Joel C. Janetski; 7.7 Michael Chazan; 7.8 Richard Olsenius/National Geographic; 7.9 akg-images/Bible Land Pictures/Jerusalem Photo by: Z.Radovan; 7.10 Copyright © Bernadette Arnaud/Look at Sciences; 7.11 AMT Moore, GC Hillman, and AJ Legge Copyright © 2002/Oxford University Press; 7.13 Kfar Hhoresh Archives; 7.14 Erich Lessing/Art Resource, NY; 7.15 VINCENT J. MUSI/National Geographic Creative; 7.17 Look at Sciences; 7.18 Courtesy Dr. Joy McCorriston; 7.19 Courtesy Avi Gopher; 7.20 DEA/M. SEEMULLER/De Agostini Picture Library/Getty Images; 7.21 Erich Lessing/Art Resource, NY; 7.22 Dr Harald Stäuble, Archaeological Heritage Office Saxony, Germany; 7.21 Gilles Tosello; 7.23 South Tyrol Museum of Archaeology, Bolzano, Italy/Wolfgang Neeb/Bridgeman Images

Chapter 8 opener The Village of Secoton, from 'Admiranda Narratio.', published by Theodore de Bry (coloured engraving), Bry, Theodore de (1528-98), after White, John (d.1593)/Service Historique de la Marine, Vincennes, France/Bridgeman Images; 8.1 MPI/Stringer Ohio; 8.2 Courtesy of Hugh Iltis/Doebly Lab/University of Wisconsin, Madison; 8.3 Wendy Connett/Alamy Stock Photo; 8.4 Science-based Dating in Archaeology by M. J. Aitken. Copyright © 1990. Reprinted by permission of Pearson Education; 8.5 Courtesy of Desert Archaeology, Inc; 8.6 Courtesy of Desert Archaeology, Inc; 8.7 David Dove; 8.8 Copyright © President and Fellows of Harvard College 1995, All rights reserved Copyright © 2006 Harvard University Peabody Museum Harvard University, 26-7-10/95879 T85, Photograph by Hillel Burger; 8.9 Maria Montoya and Julian Martinez (San Ildefonso Pueblo, Native American, ca. 1887-1980; 1879-1943). "Jar"c. 1939. Blackware. 11? × 13 in. (dia.) The National Museum of Women in the Arts, Washington, DC. Gift of Wallace and Wilhelmina Holladay; Palace of the Governors Photo Archive, New Mexico History Museum, Santa Fe; 8.11 Richard A. Cooke/Corbis; 8.12 Courtesy of the Louisiana Division of Archaeology; 8.13 Werner Forman/Art Resource, NY; 8.14 The Ohio Historical Society; 8.15 Dario Pignatelli/Reuters; 8.16 Matthew Traucht via Flickr; 8.17 Dr Elizabeth Chilton

Chapter 9 opener Neil Palmer/Alamy Stock Photo; 9.1 Elena A.A. Garcea; 9.2 Catherine D'Andrea, Ph. D; 9.3 Jean-Loic Le Quellec/Look at Sciences; 9.4 Reinhard Dirscherl/Alamy Stock Photo; 9.5 Denham, T.P., et al., "Origins of Agriculture at Kuk Swamp in the Highlands of New Guinea", Science 301 (2003): 189–93; 9.6 CAMR/A. Barry Dowsett/Science Source; 9.7 POWER AND SYRED/SCIENCE PHOTO LIBRARY; 9.8 Universal Images Group North American LLC/Alamy Stock Photo 9.9 The Granger Collection, NYC; 9.10 Novastock/Stock Connection/Glow Images, Inc; 9.11 From Life and Death at Paloma by Jeffrey Quilter Copyright © 1989, theUniversity of Iowa Press, used by permission of Jeffrey Quilter; 9.12 Mark Green/Alamy Stock Photo; 9.13 Copyright © RMN-Grand Palais/Art Resource, NY; 9.14 Peter Horree/Alamy Stock Photo; 9.15 Data from Clark, R.M., et al. "Pattern of Diversity in the Genomic Region near the Maize Domestication Gene Tb1", Proceedings of the National Academy of Sciences 101.3 (2004): 700–07; 9.16 Lowell Georgia/Corbis Documentary/Getty Images; 9.17 akg-images/Catherine Bibollet

PART 4 iv.1 SARAH LEEN/National Geographic Creative; iv.2 Hi-Story/Alamy Stock Photo; iv.3 imageBROKER/Alamy Stock Photo; iv.4 Bettmann/Getty Images; iv.5 Copyright © Ancient Art & Architecture/DanitaDelimont.com; iv.6 PA Images/Alamy Stock Photo

Chapter 10 opener Robert Harding/Alamy Stock Photo; 10.1 JAMES P. BLAIR/National Geographic Creative; 10.2 Victoria & Albert Museum, London, U.K./Bridgeman Images; 10.3 Private Collection/Copyright © Historic England/Bridgeman Images; 10.4 Arcaid Image/Alamy Stock Photo; 10.5 KAZUHIKO SANO/National Geographic Creative; 10.6 Kenneth Geiger/National Geographic Stock; 10.7 Adam Stanford/Aerial Cam; 10.8 Copyright © T.J. Ferguson; 10.9 NASA (Public domain); 10.10 Manfred Gottschalk/Alamy Stock Photo; 10.11 Manuscript Acc 80-33a, National Anthropological Archives, Smithsonian Institution; 10.12 Image 412138, American Museum of Natural History Library; 10.13 NASA (Public domain); 10.14 Georg Gerster/Science Source; 10.15 Blickwinkel/Alamy Stock Photo; 10.16 OTIS IM-BODEN/National Geographic Stock; 10.17 Photo by Terraserver, composition by Michael Chazan; 10.18 National Geographic Creative/Alamy Stock Photo; 10.19 IRA BLOCK/National Geographic Creative; 10.20 Ariadne Van Zandbergen/Alamy Stock Photo; 10.21 Nat Farbman/The LIFE Picture Collection/Getty Images; 10.22 Ariadne Van Zandbergen/Alamy Stock Photo; 10.23 Roderick J. McIntosh; 10.24 akg-images/Africa Media Online/Roger de la Harpe/africanpictures.net

Chapter 11 opener KENNETH GARRETT/National Geographic Creative; 11.1 The Trustees of the British Museum; 11.3 Copyright © Ancient Art & Architecture/DanitaDelimont.com; 11.4 REUTERS/Gleb Garanich; 11.5 Janzig/MiddleEast/Alamy

INDEX

Childe, V. Gordon 42–3, 180, 261
Chilton, Elizabeth S. 231
chimpanzees: human evolution and 57–61, 67; as hunters 81–2, 84; Kanzi 77, 79; sharing of meat 84; species of 59; Taï Forest 76–7, 79; tools used by 76–7, 79
China 336–43; authority in 339, 340, 341; Chifeng region 339; conflict in 341–2; consolidation in 341–2; map of 337; Sanxingdui 339; summing up the evidence 342; Three Dynasties 337–9, 340, 342; Three Gorges Dam 340, 341, 343; timeline 328–9; Yi-Luo Valley 337–8, 339, 342
chinampas 377
chronology, creating 27–8, 30
Cishan 251
Ciudadela 358–60
Clactonian 98
Clark, Graham 43
Clarke, David 45
climate: of Chaco Canyon 280, 281–2; Fertile Crescent 190; of Gobero 237, 238; human osteoarchaeology and 362; impact of change on ancient civilizations 254; in Iraq 190; Neanderthals' adaptation to 102, 103, 106; plant remains preserved by 204; Pleistocene climate change 94–6; pollen for reconstructing past conditions 243; postdepositional processes caused by 22; settlements in eastern North America and 230, 232; shift to agriculture caused by 183–4, 186; Younger Dryas and 195, 197
Clovis: adaptations 171–2; culture and chronology 159–60; points 159; pre-Clovis model 159, 163
Clovis culture 159–60
Clovis first model 159
coastal migration 165–6
coastal villages in Andes, agriculture and 247–8
Côa Valley 144, 343
Codex Mendoza 377–8
Cody Complex 173
Combe Grenal 107
commercialization 4–5
community archaeology 31
community in agriculture, defined 179
comparison 30
Conkey, Margaret 145
conservation 30, 31–2
Copán 364–75, 374
cores 75
Cotton Preceramic 248
Coyolxauhqui 379–80
Crawford Lake 12
Cuddie Springs 155
Cuexcomate 379
cultural resource management (CRM) 3–4, 18, 31, 45–6, 47, 275
cultural tourism 374
culture: Clovis 159–60; history 41–4, 48, 169, 336–7; human evolution and 60–2; Minoan, in Aegean 319–20; Neanderthal 106–18; Yangshao 252
cuneiform 302–3, 310
cylinder seals 302

D

D'Andrea, Catherine 239
Dart, Raymond 79, 80

Darwin, Charles 40, 57, 59, 105, 132
dating methods 27–8, 422–3; see also individual dating methods
datum point 15
Dawson, Charles 70
death pits 300, 301
de Chardin, Teilhard 70
Dederiyeh Cave 128
deduction 44
Deetz, James 44
de Jussieu, Antoine 39
dendrochronology 28, 162, 277, 281, 423
Denisova Cave 103–4
Denisovans 103–4
depositional unit 14
d'Errico, Francesco 141
de Sahagún, Bernardo 375
development and archaeology 343
D5000 66
dhaka 286
Dholavira 334
Dibble, Harold 108–9
Diepkloof 126
diet of Neanderthals 112–13
Digital Archaeological Archive of Comparative Slavery 411
Digital Archaeological Record 32
Dikka 68, 71
Dillehay, Tom 163–4, 168
direct percussion 75
diseases, tracking ancient 404
dispersal 87
display 30, 31–2
Djoser complex 312
DK, stone circle at 84–5
Dmanisi 88
DNA; see also genetic evidence: aDNA (ancient DNA) 23, 54; in inheritance 105; mitochondrial 58–9, 103–4, 132–3, 135, 163, 346; of mummies of Tarim Basin 346; nuclear 58–9, 104; of Ötzi the Iceman 210; in tracking ancient diseases 404
dogs, skeletons of 196
Dolní Věstonice 137, 144
domestication: in Andean highlands 244–7; of animals 203, 245; defined 179; indigenous, of plants 224–6; map of major centers of 184; of plants in Africa 236–7; of plants in East Asia 249–50; of plants in Mesoamerica 215–17; of sheep 203
Downtown Cahokia 283, 284
dried figs 203
drones 10
Du, Andrew 72, 73
Dubois, Eugene 88
Dufour bladelets 135
Dunnell, Robert 53
Durrington Walls 272
dynasties of China 337–9

E

early arrival model 159, 166, 168
Early Dynastic period 297, 298–9, 300, 302, 303, 307, 309
Early Neolithic 197–203; domestication and 202–3; ritual and 200–2; settlements and 197–8, 200; technology and 197

government: in Egypt 307–9; in Indus Valley 336; Maya 365–6; in Mesopotamia 298–9
Graham Clark 43, 44
grains, harvesting of 203
Gran Dolina 96
Grand Plaza 283–4
Gravettian 136, 139, 144
Great Bath 334
Great Houses 276, 277–8, 280, 281
Great Serpent Mound 214
Great Sphinx 37, 312, 314
Great Zimbabwe 286–7, 289; defined 286; Hill Complex 286–7; layout of 286–7; Mapungubwe 287, 289; society, organization of 287, 289; summing up the evidence 289
ground-penetrating radar (GPR) 9, 367
Ground Zero 412
Guilá Naquitz 216, 217
Guitarrero Cave 244–5
Gunbilngmurrung 156

H

Habuba Kebira 303–4, 343
Hadar 68, 77–8
Hammath Tiberius 14
Hamoukar 304
Haplogroups 208–9, 221
Harappa 334
Harappan period 332–6
Harappan script 331, 334–5
hard-hammer direct percussion 75
Harris matrix 15, 199
Hashihaka 344, 345
Hayonim Cave 118
Hempel, Carl 44
Hemudu 252–3
hermeneutics 48–9
Herr, Sarah 275
Herto 123
heterarchy 321
Hierakonpolis 307
hieroglyphics 309, 364, 369, 371–3
Higgs, Eric 43
Hill Complex 286–7
Himiko 344
Hodder, Ian 48, 49, 273–4
Hohle Fels 139–40
Hohlenstein 138–9
home-base/food-sharing model 84
hominins: Acheulian 74, 75–6, 96–8; brain size of 66, 67, 69; dating early sites of 80, 81; defined 66; Dmanisi 88; early 64–90; in East African Rift Valley 69, 71; East Asian 88–9, 250; expansion of 87–9; fire used by 86–7; fossil record of 67–9; as hunter-gatherers 79, 80, 81–4, 85–7; living floors and base camps of 84–6; in Lower Paleolithic 71, 72, 98–101; occupation of Western Europe, initial 96; Oldowan 72, 73–4; Perning 88–9; radiation of, early 66, 67–9; Sangiran 88–9; sharing 84; skeletons of 67, 68, 69; stone circle at DK 84–5; summing up the evidence 89; symbolic behavior and 86–7; timeline 64–5; tool use, origin of 76–9; Ubeidiya 87–8

hominoids 57
Homo antecessor 96, 103
Homo erectus 66, 67–9, 421; *see also* hominins
Homo floresiensis 151–3, 421
Homo habilis 67, 68–9, 73, 74, 78, 420
Homo heidelbergensis 99, 102
Homo neanderthalensis 102, 421; *see also* Neanderthals
Homo sapiens 57, 101, 122, 123, 150, 170; *see also* modern humans
Homo sapiens idaltu 123
Homo sapiens neanderthalensis 101–2, 421; *see also* Neanderthals
Homo sapiens sapiens 122, 421
Hopewell 226–8
horizontal excavation 11–12, 15–16; controlling horizontal space 15–16; defined 12; vertical excavation compared to 11
Hosler, Dorothy 396
House of Slaves 409
Howiesons Poort 124, 126
Hoyo Negro skeleton 170
Huaca Cao Viejo 395
Huaca de la Luna 395
Huaca del Sol 394
Hua'nuco Pampa 399–400
Huitzilopochtli 379–80
human antiquity 36, 39–40
human evolution 56–176; biological classification of humans 57; culture and 60–2; early hominins 64–90; fossil record of 59–60; genetic evidence 58–9; introduction 57–62; phylogeny 57–8, 59; of religion 105
humanity in shift to agriculture 180–2
human osteoarchaeology 20, 362
human sacrifice in Aztec Empire 379–82
Humboldt Current 244
Hunt, Gavin 76
hunter-gatherers: African, villages of 237; Andean, coastal villages of 247; animals' relationship with 181; Australian 156, 208; Canteen Kopje miners and 408; complex 184, 185; domestication of plants and 196, 215–16, 238; East Asian, pottery produced by 250; generalized 184, 185; hominins 79, 80, 81–4, 85–7; Late Archaic 217, 232; Mesolithic 208–9; Neanderthals 109, 112–13, 114, 116, 117, 118; in New World 163; shift from hunting to agriculture 181–5, 190–2, 196, 208
hunting magic 143
Huxley, Thomas 58, 59
hybridization hypothesis 131

I

Iberian Peninsula 134
Ice Age 89, 94–6, 116, 154, 271
ice-free corridor 160
ice sheets 94–5
imperial archaeology 40–1
Inca Empire 397–403; building 400–2; defined 397; fall of 403; Inca society 399–400; khipu and 400, 402; roads 401–2; Saqsawaman 401; summing up the evidence 402–3; tampu and 401–2; timeline 385; warfare 400–1
Inca society 399–400
indigenous burial remains, repatriation of 167

Sed festival 312
selective mortality 362
seriation 27, 28
Service, Elman 260–1
settlements, agriculture and: in Early Neolithic 197–8, 200; in Geometric Kebaran period 192, 193–4; in Kebaran period 192, 193–4; in Late Neolithic 205–6; in Natufian 195–6
sexuality, gender and 370
Shabik'eschee Village 220–1
shamans and trances 143–4
Shang Dynasty 337–9, 340
Shanidar Cave 115, 128
shell middens 224–5
shell mounds 175
Silk Route 346
Sima de los Huesos 101
Sipán 394
skeletons: from Abrigo Lagar Velho 131; from African Burial Ground 411; from Anyang 338; *Ardipithecus ramidus* 67; *Australopithecus afarensis* 68; Bruniquel horse engraving discovery and 141; burial rituals and 115, 116, 118; comparison, in faunal analysis 30, 47; counting bones, in quantification 24; disease and 404; of dogs 196; from Dolní Věstonice 137; of extinct elephant 82–3; of first modern humans 137, 146, 150, 154, 155, 167, 170, 192–4, 198, 200; from Folsom 150; of foraminifera 95; form Noen U-Loke 348; genetic evidence and 170; Haplogroup U and 208–9; of hominins 67, 68, 69; Hoyo Negro skeleton 170; human osteoarchaeology and 362; from Jerf el Ahmar 198; from Jericho tower 198; of juvenile adolescent *Homo erectus* 69; from Kebara Cave 113, 115; from Kebaran and Geometric Kebaran sites 192; from Kefar Hahoresh 200, 201; of Kennewick Man 167, 170; La Chapelle fossil 94; from Lake Mungo 154; from Linear Band Keramik 209; of macaws in Room 38 279; from Machu Picchu 399; megafauna extinction and 155; from Mohenjo-Daro 332, 334; from Mound 72 284; of Neanderthals 94, 103, 111, 113, 115, 116, 128, 131; from Ohalo 192, 194; from Paloma 247–8; plastered skulls 200–1; from Qafzeh Cave 128; repatriation of 167; from Royal Tombs at Ur 300–2; from Saint Césaire 131; from Skhul Cave 128; from Teotihuacán 111, 358–61; from Wadi Mataha 192–4
Skhul Cave 128
slave trade 408–9
smelting 20, 26, 319, 396, 397
Smith, B. D. 230
social complexity: in Andes 390, 391; in Cahokia 282–6; in Chaco Canyon 276–82, 289; in Chavín de Huántar 390, 391; cities, defining 261; comparative perspectives 289; defining 259–64; ecology and society 263–4; Great Zimbabwe and 286–7, 289; in Mesoamerica 354–83; political complexity, categorizing 259–61; in Pueblo Bonito 277–86; state formation, comparative approach to 261–3; Stonehenge and 268–76; timeline 266–7; urbanism and 357; without the state 266–90
society; *see also* state societies: ecology and 263–4; empires in 262–3; Great Zimbabwe 287, 289; Inca 399–400; industrial 409, 411; inequality in 261–2; Moche 395; Neanderthals 117–18; types of 260–1; urban 261

Society for American Archaeology 4
soft-hammer direct percussion 75
soil micromorphology 15, 114
Solutrean 136, 138
Solutrean hypothesis 168, 170
Southern Silk Route 348
space syntax 333
spandrels 185
Spaulding, A. C. 43, 44
specialization in Mesopotamia 299
species, defined 57
squash 216–17
Stanford, Craig 84
Stanford, Dennis 170
starch grains 243
state formation 261–3; comparative approach to 261–3; models of 263
State Historical Protection Offices (SHPOs) 46
state societies 260–3; *see also* state formation; cities in 261; defined 260; irrigation systems in 263; power in 263–4
steatite 300
Stela 3 356
stelae 319, 356
stewardship 4
Stiner, Mary 118
stone circle at DK 84–5
Stonehenge 268–76; Amesbury Archer and 273; bluestones and 270–1; burials and timber structure and 269–70; comparative perspectives 289; constructed landscape of 271; context of 271–3; defined 268–9; development of 269–71; digging holes and 271; Durrington Walls and 272; earthwork circle and 269, 270; map of 272; meaning of 273–4, 276; Sarsen Circle and 270, 271; sketch of 269; stone monument and 270–1; summing up the evidence 276; trilithons and 271
stone tools 75; Binford, Lewis and 108; Binford-Bordes debate and 108; Boëda, Eric and 109–10; Bordes, François and 106–9; Chase, Philip and 108; Dibble, Harold and 108–9; Frison effect and 108–9; Levallois method and 109–10; Mellars, Paul and 108; in Middle Paleolithic 106–10, 124; Neanderthal ethnicity and 106–10; study of 20, 75, 109; in Upper Paleolithic 136; used by Neanderthals 106–10
strata 13
stratified society 260
stratigraphic analysis: archaeological 13, 14–15, 17; culture history and 41–2; of dating plant remains 216; geological 8, 13, 16, 17; Harris matrix 15, 199; soil micromorphology 15, 114; taphonomic analysis 15, 158
stratigraphic beds 71, 77, 82, 84
stratigraphic feature 14
stratigraphic section or profile 14, 17
stratigraphic sequence 13, 16, 27, 95, 107, 128, 163, 164, 165, 174, 190, 216, 244
stratigraphy 14
Study of Archaeology, A (Taylor) 43–4
subsistence: Archaic 172–4; defined 43
Sunda 151, 152